Python Programming

An Object-Oriented Approach

Python Programming

An Object-Oriented Approach

Anita Goel
Professor
Department of Computer Science
Dyal Singh College
University of Delhi

Universities Press

PYTHON PROGRAMMING: AN OBJECT-ORIENTED APPROACH

UNIVERSITIES PRESS (INDIA) PRIVATE LIMITED

Registered Office
3-6-747/1/A & 3-6-754/1, Himayatnagar, Hyderabad 500 029, Telangana, India
info@universitiespress.com; www.universitiespress.com

Distributed by
Orient Blackswan Private Limited

Registered Office
3-6-752 Himayatnagar, Hyderabad 500 029 Telangana, India

Other Offices
Bengaluru / Chennai / Guwahati / Hyderabad
Kolkata / Mumbai / New Delhi / Noida / Patna

First published 2025

502158

ISBN 978-93-93330-39-0

Typeset in Adobe Garamond Pro 11 points *by*
Cameo Corporate Services Limited, Coimbatore

Printed in India by
B.B. Press, Tronica City, Ghaziabad 201 102

Published by
Universities Press (India) Private Limited
3-6-747/1/A & 3-6-754/1, Himayatnagar, Hyderabad 500 029, Telangana, India

To

My Parents – *Urmila and Amar Chand*

and

My Parents-in-law – *Pushpa and Gopal Krishan*

Preface

Python is a new language used for programming purposes. Python language is like a stepping stone to the field of programming. In universities and colleges, Python programming is being taught as a first course in programming, followed by other programming courses. Over the years since it was first released in 1991, Python has spread its wings and is currently a primary language for use in web development, data analysis and visualization, machine learning, data science, artificial intelligence and many more. It is simple to use and is user-friendly.

About the Book

This book is written with the aim to introduce the Python language to the reader in a systematic way that is easy to understand. Much attention has been paid to include chapters that are required by the students studying different courses. The book deals with both theoretical concepts and the practical aspects of programming in Python. The defining elements of this book are as follows:

Style of Writing

- Each chapter of this book is followed by a unique set of **assessment questions based on Bloom's Taxonomy**. Bloom's taxonomy is a hierarchical model for the cognitive domain framed in 1956 and revisited in 2001 by a team of cognitive psychologists. Bloom's taxonomy has been applied to the field of education in computer science for course design and evaluation and structuring assessments.
- The *language used* is easy to understand, and facilitates easy grasping of concepts.
- The chapters are *logically arranged* in sequence.
- The book is written in a *reader-friendly* manner, both for the students and the teachers. It is devoid of complex explanations. During my thirty-five years of teaching, I have realized that students prefer to read a book written in lucid format.
- The content is generally presented in the form of bullets, organized sequentially. This makes it easy to understand and remember points.
- Wherever required, the explanation is *supported by diagrams, pictures, and images.*
- *Solved examples* and *Programming examples* are provided for key ideas and concepts.
- Generally, the method to solve a problem is explained first and then the problem is solved.
- The topics are clearly demarcated to include the complete content in it.

- *Exercises* are included for practice, in addition to the *solved examples*.
- The *Summary* of each chapter captures essence of discussion to enable easy recapitulation.
- The *Keywords* provided at the end of each chapter serve two purposes:
    - It provides the list of key words that have occurred in the chapter.
    - It serves as a memory-aid for students to revise the chapter.

Content of Book

Basic Python (Chapters 1–12)

The chapters included in the book are:

- Two chapters on Basics of Computer.
    - Introduction to Computers
    - Programming Fundamentals
- Four chapters on Basics of Python.
    - Python Environment Setting
    - Basic Data Types, Literals and Variables
    - Operators and Expressions
    - Control Flow
- One chapter on Function and Module.
- Five chapters on Sequence, Set and Mapping Type.
    - String
    - List and Tuple
    - Set and Dictionary
    - Files
    - Error and Exception Handling

Advanced Python (Chapters 13–18) and Case Studies

- The chapters included in Advanced Python are:
    - Classes and Objects
    - Inheritance and Polymorphism
    - GUI Programming – Tkinter
    - Python Libraries
    - Using Python to Access Web Data
    - Using Databases with Python
    - Case Studies

Appendices

- Useful appendices provided for further reference are:
    - The Python Standard Library
    - `os.path` – Common Pathname Manipulations
    - `pathlib` – Object-Oriented File System Paths

Target Audience

This book has been written keeping in mind that a reader is doing a course in programming language. Several chapters have been included that cover the syllabi of different universities in India. The book is well-suited for the target audience in different universities:

- B.Tech. (IT, Computer Science and other streams), B.E.
- DCA, BCA, B.Sc. (Prog), B.Sc. (Hons), B.Sc. (IT), MCA, M.Sc. (IT), DOEACC level courses
- B.Sc. in Computer Science, Physics, Chemistry, Botany, Zoology and Mathematics
- B.Com (P), B.com (Hons), BA(P), BDP, BBA, MBA, BBE
- Skill universities, Polytechnics, Training institutes, Technical institutes
- *Any learner* interested in programming.

Pedagogical Features

Pedagogy is the art and science of how knowledge and skill is imparted to the learner. It deals with the way teaching occurs, teaching and learning approach, the way content is delivered, and the student learning. The pedagogical features in this book are:

- **Start-of-chapter Aids**
  - Introduction – Provides a need for including the chapter.
  - Learning Outcomes of Chapter – An overall view of the takeaway from the chapter for a learner is provided, at the start of each chapter.
- **In-between Chapter Aids**
  - Visualization – Supports the concepts with figures, diagrams, and images.
  - Bulleted Text – Follows a bulleted approach of writing the text in contrast to long paragraphs. The bulleted text approach is easier to read, understand and grasp.
  - Program Code – Executed code with output provided, wherever required.
- **End-of-chapter Aids**
  - Summary – It reviews the major concepts discussed in the chapter.
  - Keywords – A list of keywords used, provided at the end of each chapter helps in locating topics effortlessly.
  - Programming Language Keywords – A list of keywords from programming language used in the chapter are provided.
  - Questions – The questions at the end of each chapter are given based on Bloom's Taxonomy. The assessment is divided into six parts:
    - A1: Bloom Level: Knowledge/Remember
    - A2: Bloom Level: Comprehend/Understand
    - A3: Bloom Level: Application/Apply
    - A4: Bloom Level: Analyze
    - A5: Bloom Level: Evaluate
    - A6: Bloom Level: Create/Synthesize
  - Objective questions – Questions in the form of True/False, MCQ and Fill in the Blanks are provided in each chapter. Additionally, abbreviations, differences and short notes are also given.

Feedback

For interacting with the author, or for suggestions and comments about this book, please send an email at goel.anita@gmail.com.

Acknowledgement

My writing of this book has been a long journey on a roller-coaster road. The book has been revised several times for improving the writing style, adding more content, and for many more such reasons. My family was my strong support during this journey. I am grateful to my family members for their backing.

My loving husband, Ajay, stood by me during the difficult times I faced at the time of writing this book. His way of taking regular updates from me about the completion of the book and his offer of help and support, whenever needed, has been my strong motivation. I feel blessed to be with him. My special thanks to my son Anirudh, and my daughter Ashima, who are my greatest source of inspiration. The times they would smile at my struggle and help me in their own special ways to make me comfortable while writing the book are some cherished moments that I keep from my journey of book-writing. The sweet gesture of my loving daughter-in-law Manya, who would peep into my room to check how much the book has progressed, needs special mention.

I express my deep gratitude and respect to my mother Urmila and my father Amar Chand. Their blessings and direction have served as a guiding light for me. My mother's way of checking on the book's progress, seeking updates from me and my children, is a beautiful memory. I feel blessed that I am carrying forward the legacy of book-writing from my maternal grandfather Late Mr C S Jain. I express my deep love for my in-laws, Pushpa and Gopal Krishan. I have always felt that God has been beautifully partial to me by connecting me to my in-laws.

I am obliged to my support staff at home, who take care of the house affairs efficiently, so that I could devote my time on writing of the book. Special thanks to Julie.

I am grateful to Dr S C Gupta, Prof. S K Wasan and Dr Mukul Sinha, who have inculcated the habit of writing in me. I thank them for their valuable motivation and encouragement.

I thank Thomas Mathew Rajesh, Kallol Das, Ramesh and the team of Universities Press (India) Private Limited for their support. The long discussions with them have led the book to its present form. I am grateful to Kallol Das for his ideas and suggestions and for the support he provided me during the writing of this book.

This is not the first book on this topic. I thank the authors of the books on similar topic, whose books have been a source of ideas for me.

During my journey of book-writing, I have been helped by my family, friends, and colleagues. I express my gratitude to them, one and all, for their support has been invaluable.

I indebted to the Almighty for the blessings showered on me, without which it would not have been possible to accomplish this humungous task.

Anita Goel

About the Author

Anita Goel is Professor of Computer Science in Dyal Singh College, University of Delhi, India. She has also held the post of Principal of the college, for some time. She is an academician, administrator, researcher, and author with over 35 years of work experience. She has taught undergraduate, post-graduate and pre-Ph.D. students in several universities in India. She was a Fellow in Computer Science and Academic Secretary at Institute of Lifelong Learning, University of Delhi, India, where she was responsible for e-content creation in Computer Science.

With over 75 research paper publications in reputed international journals and conferences to her credit, Dr Goel has guided several students to their Ph.D. degrees. Her primary focus areas are Cloud Computing, Microservices, Serverless Computing, Software Engineering, Web Applications, Technology Enhanced Education (MOOC Platforms), and Applications of Machine Learning. She is a reviewer and member of editorial board for several international journals. She has also delivered invited talks and presented papers in international conferences.

Dr Goel has authored more than 20 books with international publishers. Her book titled *Computer Fundamentals* has been an Amazon best-seller.

Brief Contents

Contents

UNIT I Basics of Computer

CHAPTER 1 Introduction to Computer

CONTENTS

1.1 Introduction

Computer is an electronic device based on the concept of input–process–output. It accepts data as input, processes the data and generates output. The *computing devices* have evolved from simple mechanical machines, such as ABACUS, Pascal's Adding and Subtraction Machine, Leibniz's Multiplication and Division Machine, Jacquard's punched-card system, Babbage's Analytical Engine and Hollerith's tabulating machine, to the first electronic computer. Charles Babbage is also called the *father of computer.*

Digital computers are electronic computers that process the input data in the form of 0 and 1. The computers we use are digital computers. The *characteristics of computer* are – speed, accuracy, diligence, storage capability and versatility. The computer processes data at a very high speed, at the rate of Millions of Instructions Per Second (MIPS). It maintains a high degree of precision and provides output accurately. It is diligent because it does not get tired. All calculations are done with high accuracy and speed. Computers can store large amount of data that can be retrieved when required. They are versatile as they can perform different tasks with ease. However, they can perform only those tasks for which they have been programmed. They cannot do any work for which instructions have not been provided.

In this chapter, we discuss the basics of the computer system.

Learning Outcomes of this chapter

After completion of the chapter, the learner will be able to:

- Describe the evolution of computers – generations and types
- Define the concept of input–process–output
- Identify the different components of a computer
- Distinguish among the different components of a computer
- Describe functionality of components of a computer
- Assess the features required during the purchase of a computer.

1.2 Generations of Computer

The evolution of computers is defined in terms of the *generations* of computer. Currently, there are five generations of computer. The generations of computer differ from each other in terms of hardware technology, software, physical appearance and their computing characteristics. A next generation computer is more powerful, fast and efficient, and, also cheaper and smaller, than its predecessors. Table 1.1 presents the hardware, software and the key characteristics, physical appearance and the applications for each generation of computer.

Table 1.1 Generations of computer

Generation	Hardware	Software	Physical appearance / Characteristics/Applications
1	Vacuum tubes	Machine language	Large in size. Computation time is in milliseconds. Expensive to operate
2	Transistors	Assembly language. Languages like, FORTRAN, COBOL	Smaller in size, less expensive, low maintenance than first generation. Based on stored program concept. Computation time is in microseconds.
3	Integrated Chip (IC)	High level languages, like, Pascal, BASIC	Lesser power consumption and lower maintenance than second generation. Produced commercially. Computation time is in nanoseconds
4	Large-Scale Integration (LSI), Very-Large-Scale Integration (VLSI) chips, Microprocessors	High Level languages like, C, C++. Graphical User Interface (GUI)	Small, portable, reliable and cheap. Computation time is in picoseconds. Available to home user and also for commercial use.
5	Super-Large-Scale Integration (SLSI) chips	Based on artificial intelligence	Capable of learning and self-organization. Uses parallel processing. Large memory requirement. They are still being developed.

1.3 Types of Computer

The computers are broadly classified into four categories based on their size and type – (1) Microcomputer, (2) Minicomputer, (3) Mainframe computer, and (4) Supercomputer.

- *Microcomputers* are small single-user computer. Desktop computer, laptop, netbook, tablet computer, handheld computer and smart phone are microcomputers.
- *Minicomputers* are multi-user computers that can support 4–200 users simultaneously. They have high processing speed and more storage capacity than the microcomputers. The users access minicomputers from their microcomputer.
- *Mainframe computers* are multi-user, multi-programming and high-performance computers. They can handle large workloads. They are used in centralized databases. The users access mainframe computers from their terminals.
- *Supercomputers* can perform trillions of calculations per second. The processing speed of supercomputer is measured in FLOPS. They are used in compute-intensive tasks.

In addition to these, computers are embedded in appliances and devices such as washing machines and microwave ovens. Computers are also available for use in the cloud. A simple device is needed for connecting to the Internet and accessing online cloud infrastructure.

1.4 The Computer System

The computer system (Figure 1.1) consists of four parts – (1) Hardware, (2) Software, (3) Data, and (4) Users.

Hardware is the mechanical components of the computer. It includes devices like keyboard, monitor, hard disk drive, floppy disk drive, microprocessor chips, video card, sound card, battery and motherboard.

Software is a set of instructions that instruct the computer about how a task is to be performed. The instructions are written in a language understood by the computer. It is also called program. Software is a set of programs. The instructions to perform a task are written in the software. The hardware performs the task. A computer can have multiple software on the same hardware. For example, the instruction to add two numbers is software, and the addition is carried out by thc hardware.

Data are the raw facts. For example, *15, August*, and *1947* are just data representing values. The data is input to a computer. The computer processes the data to generate information. For example, the above data is processed as 15 August 1947. It provides us with the date when India got independence.

Users are people who interact with the computer. The users can be programmers, data entry operators, and computer hardware engineers.

Figure 1.1 Parts of a computer system

1.4.1 The Input–Process–Output Concept

A computer is an electronic device based on input–process–output concept. The data is accepted as input, then processed and the output is generated.

- The *input* data is accepted by the computer from different input devices like, keyboard, mouse and video camera. The data can be in the form of text, sound, images, and video.
- The input data is processed by the computer. The *processing* to be done is defined in the program. The program is executed on the hardware. The hardware performs processing according to the

instructions of the software. The processing can be simple or complex, like, addition, modification or generating weather report.

- The output is the result generated after processing of data. Like input, the processed data or output may be in the form of text, sound, image, video or document. The output is provided to the user by output devices like, monitor, printer, plotter and speaker.
- During input–process–output cycle, the main memory of the computer is used for storing data and instructions, temporarily. Also, secondary storage devices like hard disk and optical disk are used for storing data, permanently.

1.5 The Components of a Computer

A computer consists of three main components:

1) Input–Output (I/O) Unit,
2) Central Processing Unit (CPU), and
3) Memory Unit.

1.5.1 Input–Output Unit

A user interacts with the computer via input–output unit. The purpose of the input unit is to accept data from the user while the output unit provides processed data to the user. The input–output units are accessible to the user via devices that are connected externally to the computer cabinet.

Input devices are used for providing input data to a computer. The data can be in the form of text, video, audio and image. The data can be input to a computer in different ways – typing, pointing and clicking, pointing and picking, from audio and video devices and optical devices. The different types of input devices are shown in Figure 1.2.

- ***Keyboard*** and ***mouse*** are common input devices.
- ***Trackball*** looks like an upside-down mouse, but has functionality of mouse.
- ***Joystick*** is commonly used for playing video games.
- ***Digitizing Tablet*** is used in Computer Aided Design (CAD) to input drawings and sketches. It consists of a flat-bed electronic tablet on which a pen with electronic head is moved to make drawings.
- ***Light Pen*** is a light-sensitive pen-like device that is used for selecting objects and making drawings on the computer screen.
- ***Touch Screen*** requires the user to place a fingertip on the computer screen. It is used in Automated Teller Machines (ATM) and supermarkets.
- ***Microphone*** is an audio input device. It is used to input a person's voice.
- ***Video camera*** and ***webcam*** capture video and is a video input device.
- ***Digital camera*** captures still images.
- ***Scanner*** looks like a photocopy machine on which a paper, picture or text is placed and content is input directly to the computer, without copying or typing. Utility software that come with scanners allow the stored documents to be manipulated.
- ***Optical Character Reader*** (OCR) recognizes characters in a scanned document and generates text files that can be stored in the computer.

- ***Magnetic Ink Character Reader (MICR)*** recognizes magnetic encoding numbers printed at the bottom of bank cheques.
- ***Optical Mark Reader (OMR)*** detects marks made on a paper based on their shade intensity. It is used in objective type tests, where the student is required to darken the circle of the chosen option.
- ***Bar code reader*** reads machine readable bar codes that are adjacent vertical lines of different width. Bar codes are used in books and different products available in the market.

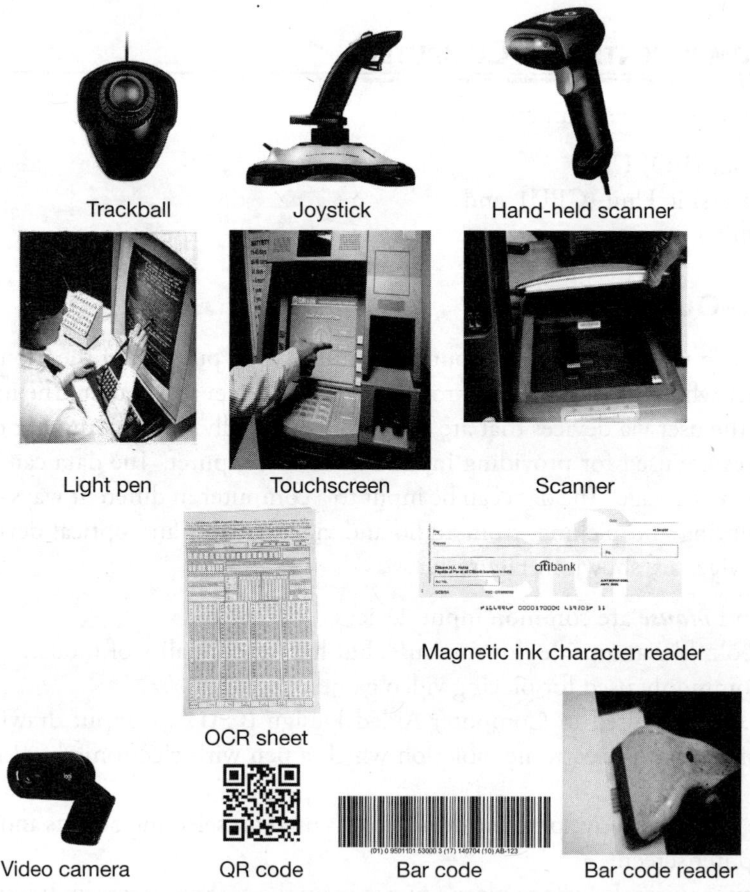

Figure 1.2 Input devices

Output devices provide output from computer to the user. The output can be text, graphics, audio or video. The output can be presented from a computer in different ways – on paper using printers and plotters, or on devices like monitor, data projector, speakers and headphone. The different types of output devices are shown in Figure 1.3.

- ***Printer*** is a common output device for printing text, images and graphics.
  - o ***Dot matrix printer*** is an impact printer. The printing happens when the typeface strikes the paper and inked ribbon. It is generally used in accounting applications.

- o *Ink-jet printer* and *Laser printer* are non-impact printers. They provide high-quality text and graphics printing. Nowadays, generally inkjet and laser printers are used.
- *Plotter* is used for drawing graphs and maps. Since plotters can draw accurate and colorful lines, they are used for drawings in AUTOCAD, CAD and CAM applications.
- *Monitor* is a common output device.
- *Data projector* displays output on a large white screen. It is used for presenting output to a large gathering in conferences and meetings.
- *Speakers and Headphones* provide audio output from the computer. They are commonly used for customer service, like in airlines and banks.

Figure 1.3 Output devices

Courtesy: Freepick.com

1.5.2 Central Processing Unit

The CPU processes the data. It controls, coordinates and supervises the operations of the computer. It consists of three main parts – Arithmetic and Logic Unit (ALU), Control Unit (CU) and Registers.

- **ALU** performs arithmetic and logic operations on the input data. It consists of two units – arithmetic unit and logic unit. Arithmetic unit performs arithmetic operations like, addition, subtraction, multiplication and division on the data. Logic operations like testing for greater than, less than or equal to condition on the data, are performed by the logic unit.
- **CU** controls and coordinates activity of the other units of the computer. It does not do any actual processing on its own. It directs the computer for tasks like when to fetch data and instructions, where to store result, and sequencing of events during processing. The instruction set of the CPU is held by the CU.
- **Registers** are high-speed storage areas within the CPU, with very less storage capacity. Registers are directly manipulated by the CPU. Registers hold the data currently being processed in the

CPU, temporarily. The purpose of each register is different. For example, Accumulator (ACC) and Program Counter (PC) registers store the result of arithmetic and logic operations, and address of the next instruction to be processed, respectively.

1.5.3 Memory Unit

The computers are based on *Von Neumann architecture*. It is a stored program architecture where all data and instructions to be processed are first required to be stored in memory.

Memory unit is for temporary storage of data and instructions, output and intermediate results, during processing. The CPU fetches data and instructions from memory, processes it, and stores the result back into memory. Figure 1.4 shows interaction among the components of a computer. The memory unit comprises of primary memory or main memory and cache memory.

- ***Primary memory*** is of two kinds – Random Access Memory (RAM) and Read Only Memory (ROM). The computer uses RAM to store data and instructions temporarily, during processing. RAM affects the speed and power of a computer. ROM is a non-volatile primary memory. It stores data needed for start-up of the computer, and instructions for initializing the different devices attached to the computer.
- ***Cache memory*** is high-speed memory placed in between RAM and CPU, to increase the speed of processing. Cache memory is available at three levels – L1, L2 and L3. The fastest cache is L1.
- The main memory is volatile; thus, data and instructions will get destroyed when the computer is switched off. For permanent storage of data and programs, computers have ***secondary memory***. For processing by CPU, the data or program stored in secondary memory is brought into RAM. Magnetic disks and optical disks are examples of secondary memory.

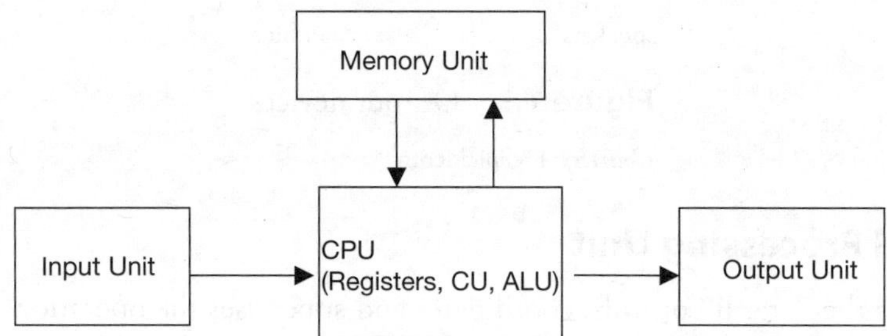

Figure 1.4 Components of computer

Internal Memory and External Memory

In an alternative terminology, CPU registers, cache memory and primary memory are also referred to as ***internal memory***. The characteristics of internal memory are – limited storage capacity, temporary storage (volatile), fast access, and high cost. Secondary memory is also called ***external memory***. The characteristics of secondary memory devices are – very high storage capacity, permanent storage (non-volatile) unless erased by user, relatively slower access, and low cost.

The memory is characterized on the basis of capacity (amount of data that a memory can store), access time (time interval between read/write request), and availability of data. Computer memory is organized hierarchically to provide the fastest speed and largest capacity. Figure 1.5 shows the hierarchy of memory. Memory with low access time *(fastest speed)* and largest capacity is required. With respect to CPU, the memory is organized as – Registers (nearest to CPU), Cache, Primary memory, Secondary memory (farthest from CPU).

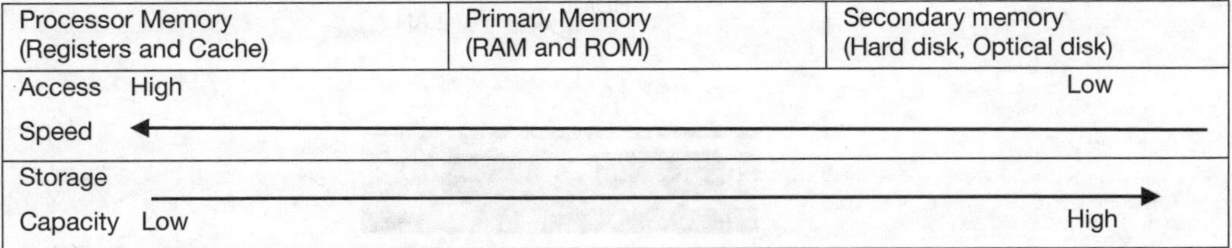

Figure 1.5 Memory hierarchy

Binary digit** or **bit is the basic unit of memory. A *bit* is 0 or 1. ***Byte*** is a group of 8 bits. One byte is smallest unit of data handled by the computer. One byte can store 2^8, i.e., 256 different combinations of bits to represent 256 symbols. Also, 1 KB is 1024 bytes. 1 MB is 1024 KB and this hierarchy goes on – Gigabyte (GB), Terabyte (TB), Petabyte (PB), Exabyte (EB), Zettabyte (ZB), Yottabyte (YB).

1.6 Inside a Computer and Interconnections

The main components inside the computer cabinet are motherboard, memory chips, expansion slots, ports and interface, power supply, processor, cables and storage devices.

- **Motherboard** is an important component of computer. The computer is built around the motherboard. It is a Printed Circuit Board (PCB) having several chips and connectors mounted on it. It has the processor, memory chips, interfaces and sockets. The hard disk drive, optical drive and RAM are plugged into interfaces on the motherboard.
- **Complementary Metal-Oxide Semiconductor (CMOS) chip** saves system information, such as time, system date, and essential system settings. A button battery on motherboard provides power to the CMOS chip.
- **Ports and sockets** on the rear side of the computer are connected to the motherboard (Figure 1.6). The input–output devices connect to the computer via ports and sockets that are physically different in shape, size and number of pins. The ports available on a computer cabinet are as follows:
  - **Universal Serial Bus (USB) port** to connect the mouse, keyboard, monitor, camera and printer
  - **RJ45 connector (LAN or Ethernet port)** to connect to a network
  - **Audio plugs (Line-In, Line-Out, Microphone)** to connect speakers and microphone
  - **High-Definition Multimedia Interface (HDMI)** port to connect audio-video devices, and projector
  - **SCSI Port** to connect hard disk drives and network connectors
  - **Firewire (IEEE 1394)** to connect multimedia devices like video camera. It is an expensive technology. Hard disk drive and new DVD drives connect via firewire.

There are some ports that were popular earlier but are not found in computers nowadays. These ports are – *Parallel port* to connect old printers; *Serial port* to connect old peripherals. *PS/2 port* to connect mouse and keyboard and *VGA connector* to connect monitor.

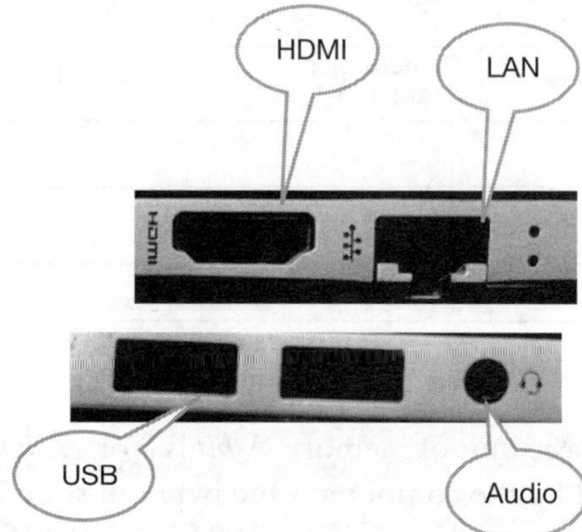

Figure 1.6 Ports and sockets on the rear side of a computer

- **Expansion Slots** are on motherboard. The expansion cards that provide new features or increased performance are inserted into slots. The different slots are –
    - **Industry Standard Architecture (ISA)** slot to connect modem and input devices.
    - **Accelerated Graphic Port (AGP)** slot to connect graphics card.
    - **Peripheral Component InterConnect (PCI)** slot to connect audio, video and graphics. It is faster than ISA card.
    - **PCI Express Slot** is faster than AGP and PCI card, up to 16x speed.

A computer generally has 2 PCI and 2 PCI Express slots.

- **Ribbon cables** carry data to different components on the motherboard. They are flat, insulated and narrow.
- **Power supply** is a metal box attached to the computer chassis and to the system board. It converts AC power to DC power. Power supply has a fan for cooling.
- **RAM** chips are on the motherboard.
- **Storage disk drives** such as hard disk drive, CD drive and DVD drive are inside the computer. The storage devices like CD are inserted externally into the CD drive. The drives can also be plugged externally, using USB port.
- **Processor** is the main component on the motherboard. Some commonly available processers are – Intel core i3, i5 and i7.
- **Ethernet card** allows connecting to LAN, cable or DSL modem. Ethernet adapters are built into a motherboard or inserted in a PCI slot.

Bus is a set of wires that allows information and signals to travel between components inside or outside a computer. A wire can carry one bit at a time. The width of the bus is determined by the number of wires in the bus. The components of computer, i.e., CPU, I/O unit and memory unit are connected with each other by bus. System Bus and Expansion Bus are two types of buses.

System bus connects components inside the motherboard like, CPU and system memory.
Expansion bus allows external devices, expansion slots, I/O ports and drive connections to interact with the CPU.

System bus and expansion bus comprise of three kinds of buses:

Control bus to carry commands,
Address bus to carry address of devices, and
Data bus to carry data.

The performance of a computer is affected by some parameters (bigger the better) as follows:

- Size of Registers – E.g., 32-bit CPU, 64-bit CPU
- Capacity of RAM - E.g., 1 GB, 4 GB, 8 GB RAM
- Speed of Clock – E.g., Clock speed of more than 1 GHz
- Width of Bus – E.g., 36-bit address bus addresses 64 GB memory. Data bus speed 100 MHz and 400 MHz
- Cache memory – E.g., 64KB to 32MB, L1, L2, L3.
- Number of CPU cores – E.g., Dual core, Quad core.

Summary

- Digital computers process the data in the form of 0 and 1.
- Speed, accuracy, diligence, storage capability and versatility are the key characteristics of a computer.
- The classification of computers on the basis of their size and type is – microcomputer, minicomputer, mainframe and supercomputer.
- Hardware, software, data and users are the four parts of a computer system. Hardware refers to the mechanical components; software is the set of instructions; data is raw facts and; users are the people who interact with the computer.
- A computer works on the concept of input–process–output.
- Input–Output unit, Central Processing Unit, and Memory Unit are the three main components of a computer.
- Keyboard, mouse trackball joystick, digitizing tablet, light pen, touch screen, microphone, video camera, webcam, digital camera, scanner, OCR, MICR, OMR are input devices.
- Dot matrix printer, ink-jet printer, laser printer, plotter, monitor, data projector, speakers and headphone are output devices.
- The CPU consists of Arithmetic and Logic Unit, Control Unit and Registers. The ALU performs arithmetic and logic operations; CU controls and coordinates activity of other units of computer, and registers are high-speed storage areas in CPU.

- Computers use stored program architecture (Von Neumann architecture) that requires all data and instructions to be first stored in memory and then processed.
- RAM and ROM are the two kinds of primary memory. RAM is volatile and ROM is non-volatile.
- Cache memory is placed in between RAM and CPU.
- Secondary memory is used for permanent storage of data and programs.
- Computer memory is organized hierarchically to provide the fastest speed and the largest capacity.
- Byte is the smallest unit of data handled by the computer.
- The main components inside the computer cabinet are – motherboard, memory chips, expansion slots, ports and interface, power supply, processor, cables and storage devices.
- USB port, RJ45 connector, LAN or Ethernet port, Line-In, Line-Out, Microphone, HDMI, SCSI Port and Firewire (IEEE 1394) are the ports available on a computer cabinet.
- ISA, AGP, PCI and PCI Express slot are expansion slots on the motherboard.
- The bus allows information and signals to travel among components, inside or outside of a computer.
- The system bus connects components inside a motherboard like, CPU and system memory.
- The expansion bus connects external devices, expansion slots, I/O ports and drive connections to the computer.
- The parameters that affect performance of a computer are – register size, RAM capacity, clock speed, bus width, cache memory and number of CPU cores.

Keywords

Accelerated Graphic Port (AGP)
Arithmetic and Logic Unit (ALU)
Audio plugs
Bar code reader
Binary digit or bit
Bus
Byte
Cache memory
CMOS chip
Computer
Control Unit (CU)
CPU
Data
Data projector
Digital camera
Digital computers
Digitizing tablet
Dot matrix printer
Ethernet port
Expansion bus
Expansion slots
External memory
Firewire (IEEE 1394)
Generations of computer
Hardware
HDMI
Headphone
Industry Standard Architecture (ISA)
Ink-jet printer
Input devices
Input–Output (I–O) Unit,
Input–process–output
Internal memory
Joystick
Keyboard
Laser printer
Light Pen
Magnetic Ink Character Reader (MICR)
Mainframe
Memory unit
Microcomputers
Microphone
Minicomputers
Monitor
Motherboard
Mouse
Optical Character Reader (OCR)
Optical Mark Reader (OMR)
Output devices
Parallel port
PCI Express slot
PCI slot

Plotter
Ports and sockets
Power supply
Primary memory
Printer
Processor
PS/2 port
Random Access Memory (RAM)
Read Only Memory (ROM)
Registers
Ribbon cables
Scanner
SCSI Port
Secondary memory
Serial port
Software
Speakers
Supercomputer
System bus
Touch screen
Trackball
USB port
Users
VGA connector
Video camera
Von Neumann architecture
Webcam

ASSESSMENT

A.1 Bloom Level: Knowledge/Remember

Review Questions

1. List the key characteristics of the computer.
2. Who is known as the father of computer?
3. Define a computer.
4. Name three computing devices that existed before the first electronic computer.
5. What does Von Neumann architecture state?
6. List the four parts of a computer system.
7. List the three main components of a computer.
8. Name the components of a CPU
9. 1 Kilobyte (KB) = _____ bytes
10. 1 Megabyte (MB) = _____ KB
11. 1 Gigabyte (GB) = _____ MB = _____ KB
12. 1 Terabyte (TB) = _____ GB = _____ KB
13. How many levels are there for the cache memory?
14. State the key features of (1) Internal memory, and (2) External memory.
15. List the memory hierarchy.
16. Name 5 input devices.
17. List two applications of the bar code reader.
18. List the ports in a computer.
19. List the expansion slots in a computer.
20. List the factors affecting the performance of a computer.
21. Give full form of the following abbreviations:

(a) CPU
(b) ALU
(c) CU
(d) CAD
(e) ATM
(f). MICR
(g) OMR
(h). OCR
(i) USB
(i) RAM
(k) ROM
(l) PCB
(m) CMOS
(n) LSI
(o) MIPS
(p) VLSI
(q) SLSI
(r) HDMI
(s) PCI
(t) ISA
(u) AGP
(v) EB
(w) ZB
(x) YB

22. Match the task with the device:

Column A	Column B
1 Playing video games	a Printer
2 Scan a paper	b Video camera
3 Type input text	c Scanner
4 Visual display on screen	d Joystick
5 Full motion video	e Plotter
6 Printouts	f Keyboard
7 Drawing maps	g Projector
8 Visual display to large audience	h Microphone
9 Input a song you are singing	i Monitor

23. Match the generation of computer with the hardware:

Column A	Column B
1 First generation computers	a VLSI
2 Second generation computers	b SLSI
3 Third generation computers	c Vacuum Tubes
4 Fourth generation computers	d IC
5 Fifth generation computers	e Transistor

Fill in the Blanks

Secondary	zero	five	CPU
ALU CU	ROM	1024	largest
Expansion	Registers		ROM
register Bit	256	OCR	address
width	fastest	Data	fourth	Control
RAM	one	register	USB

1. Digital computer uses ________ and ________ to represent data.
2. There are ________ generations of computer.
3. The generation of computer that started supporting GUI interfaces is________.
4. CPU consists of________, ________ and ________.
5. ________ and ________ are the two kinds of primary memory.
6. ________ is the basic unit of memory.
7. ____________ memory is nearest to CPU.
8. 8 bits can store ________ symbols.
9. I TB = ________ GB.
10. Memory with ________ speed and ________capacity is required.
11. If capacity is 1 TB, it is ________ memory.
12. ________ is small capacity, highest cost, very high-speed memory in CPU.

13. ________ memory comes programmed by the manufacturer.

14. ________ technique is for recognizing printed page.

15. Bus ________ is number of wires in the bus.

16. ________, ________ and ________ bus are the three kinds of system bus.

17. ________ bus connects external devices to the computer.

18. ________ port is used for connecting the mouse.

State True/False

1. Computers get bored after a long and complex calculation.
2. BASIC and Pascal languages started with the second generation of computers.
3. Laptop is a mainframe computer.
4. Register is a high-speed memory outside the CPU.
5. Registers have very less storage capacity.
6. ROM is volatile memory.
7. Bit is the smallest unit of data representation in computer.
8. Cache memory is both inside and outside the CPU.
9. OMR detects marks on a paper by their darkness.
10. System bus connects components inside the motherboard, like CPU and system memory.

Multiple Choice Questions (MCQ)

1. Which of the following is not an internal memory?
   (a) CD (b) Register
   (c) Cache (d) ROM
2. 1 PB is
   (a) 1024 TB
   (b) 1024 GB
   (c) 1024 * 1024 KB
   (d) 1024 * 1024 * 1024 KB

A.2 Bloom Level: Comprehend/Understand

Review Questions

1. Describe the features of microcomputer, minicomputer, mainframe and supercomputer.
2. Explain the task of the different parts of a computer system.
3. Explain the concept of input–process–output.
4. What is the task of CPU?
5. What is the task of ALU?
6. What is the task of control unit?
7. What is the function of the registers in CPU?
8. What is the task of primary memory?
9. What is the purpose of cache memory?
10. What is the purpose of ROM?
11. What is the need for secondary memory?
12. What is the purpose of CMOS chip?

13. "Memory is characterized by two key factors – Capacity and access time". Explain.

14. Write a short note on input devices.

15. Write a short note on output devices.

16. Describe the different components inside a computer cabinet.

Multiple Choice Questions (MCQ)

1. Identify the odd one.
   (a) Microcomputer (b) Minicomputer
   (c) Maxicomputer (d) Supercomputer

2. Identify the odd one.
   (a) RAM (b) ROM
   (c) Cache (d) Hard disk

3. Identify the odd one.
   (a) Netbook (b) Desktop
   (c) Laptop (d) Supercomputer

A.3 Bloom Level: Application/Apply

1. Arrange in increasing order of capacity – PB, ZB, TB, EB.
   (a) TB, PB, EB, ZB (b) TB, EB, PB, ZB
   (c) TB, PB, ZB, EB (d) TB, EB, ZB, PB

Answer Questions 2 and 3 using the following data:
A – Register, B – Cache, C – RAM, D – Disk.

2. Memory hierarchy according to high-to-low access speed is ______.
   (a) ABCD (b) DCBA
   (c) ACBD (d) DBCA

3. Memory hierarchy according to high-to-low storage capacity is ______.
   (a) ABCD (b) DCBA
   (c) ACBD (d) DBCA

4. From the computer that you are working on, demonstrate how you can view the system configuration.

5. Open the CPU box of the computer you are working on, and identify the different components inside the box.

A.4 Bloom Level: Analyze

1. How does the system time and date remain correct even after you switch off the computer?

2. Organize the events, at least six, that occur, if computer has to read a file from the disk.

3. Give differences between the following:
   a) System bus and expansion bus
   b) Primary memory and secondary memory
   c) Registers and cache memory
   d) Cache memory and RAM
   e) First-generation computers and second-generation computers
   f) Second-generation computers and third-generation computers
   g) Third-generation computers and fourth-generation computers
   h) Fourth-generation computers and fifth-generation computers

A.5 Bloom Level: Evaluate

1) What do you mean by – "Computer is accurate, diligent and versatile"?
2) Evaluate the expansion ports in terms of its usefulness to the user.
3) Justify the use of cache memory in a computer.

A.6 Bloom Level: Create/Synthesize

1) Formulate the specification of a modern laptop or desktop.
2) On the computer that you are working on, formulate the configuration of the peripheral devices attached to your computer.
3) On the computer that you are working on, formulate the specifications of your computer, including the ports and sockets.

ANSWERS

A.1 Bloom Level: Knowledge/Remember

Review Questions

22. (1) d (2) c (3) f (4) i (5) b (6) a (7) e (8) g (9) h
23. (1) c (2) e (3) d (4) a (5) b

Fill in the Blanks

1. Zero, one **2.** five **3.** fourth **4.** ALU, CU, registers
5. RAM, ROM **6.** Bit **7.** Register **8.** 256
9. 1024 **10.** Fastest, largest **11.** secondary **12.** register
13. ROM **14.** OCR **15.** width **16.** data, address, control
17. expansion **18.** USB

True/False

1. False **2.** False **3.** False **4.** False **5.** False **6.** False **7.** True **8.** True
9. True **10.** True

Multiple Choice Questions (MCQ)

1. a **2.** a

A.2 Bloom Level: Comprehend/Understand

Multiple Choice Questions (MCQ)

1. c **2.** d **3.** d

A.3 Bloom Level: Application/Apply

Multiple Choice Questions (MCQ)

1. a **2.** a **3.** b

CHAPTER 2

Programming Fundamentals

CONTENTS

2.1 Introduction

A computer system consists of hardware and software. The computer hardware cannot perform any task on its own. It needs to be instructed about the tasks to be performed. A *program* is a set of instructions that instruct the computer about the way a task is to be performed. A program is required for getting any task done by the computer. Software consists of a set of interrelated programs. Software is required for the working of the computer itself, and some software are required by the programmer or user.

For writing the programs, the programmer needs to follow the steps of analyzing the problem, design a solution for the problem, code the solution in a programming language, and finally execute the program. There are different paradigms that the programmer can follow during programming.

In this chapter, the fundamentals of programming are discussed. The focus is on understanding the different types of software and the strategies for problem solving. Also, the programming paradigm for Python is discussed.

Learning Outcomes of this chapter

After completion of the chapter, the learner will be able to:

- List the different types of software in a computer
- Identify the system software and application software
- List problem solving strategies
- Differentiate between the different ways of program design
- Demonstrate the use of program design in problem-solving
- Justify the use of a particular program design for a problem
- Distinguish between the programming paradigms.

2.2 Evolution of Languages

Programming languages are used for writing a program. Each language has a unique set of keywords and its own syntax. The programming language must be understood, both by programmer and computer. A computer understands the language of 0's and 1's, while the programmer is more comfortable with English-like language. Therefore, some programming languages are easier for the programmer to use and write the programs, while some other languages are easier for the computer to understand but difficult for the programmer.

Programming languages fall into three categories:

- *High-level language* – The program is written in English-like language.
- *Assembly language* – It uses symbolic representation of machine code.
- *Machine language* – The program is a collection of bits.

A program written in any of the programming languages must be converted into machine language for the computer to understand it. For this, translator software is used (discussed later in chapter).

The programming languages are also categorized into generations of languages. This is based on how they have evolved over a period. Table 2.1 shows generations of programming languages.

Table 2.1 Generations of programming language

Generation	Language *(Some examples)*
I	Machine language
II	Assembly language
III	C, COBOL, Visual Basic, Pascal, C++, Java, Javascript
IV	Python, Ruby, Perl
V	LISP, Prolog, Mercury

2.2.1 Machine Language

A program written in machine language is nearer to the machine than to the programmer. The programmer is required to write the code using binary digits. The combination of the digits (0's and 1's) is symbolic of the characters or symbols used in the program. The key features of a machine language program are –

- Binary code is a combination of bits that are used for writing a machine language program. In addition to other fields, the program instruction comprises of the type of instruction, like arithmetic or logical, and the operation to be performed within it, such as subtract and compare.
- A machine language code is directly understood by the computer; hence, there is no need to use a translator software.
- The code is closer to the computer than it is to the programmer and does not require translation, so a machine language program executes fast.
- Machine language is hardware-dependent. As a result, a program written for a kind of computer processor such as Intel, may not work on a computer having a different processor. Thus, the programs are not portable.
- Machine language programs also depend on the software used on a computer machine, like the operating system and devices. A machine language program written for a particular machine may not execute on another machine even if it has same kind of processor.
- It is difficult to write a machine language program as they are both hardware and software dependent and use binary code for writing the program. Thus, programs are generally not written in machine language.

2.2.2 Assembly Language

A program written in machine language is nearer to the machine than to the programmer. The programmer is required to write the code using binary digits. The combination of the digits (0's and 1's) is symbolic of the characters or symbols used in the program.

The assembly language is symbolic and has English-like illustration of the machine code. Therefore, it is easier for the programmer to write an assembly language program than the machine code.

The key features of assembly language program are:

- The symbolic representation of the instructions is hardware-dependent. They are not portable.
- It uses registers for manipulation.
- The program in assembly language (source code) must be translated into machine language for the machine to understand it. The translator software used for this purpose is the assembler (discussed later in the chapter). The translated code is called the **object code**.
- Though Assembly language is symbolic in nature, it is still difficult to write programs in Assembly language.
- Assembly language is generally used for writing the programs that require high speed and good efficiency.
- A view of the assembly language source code is:

```
MOV    D, C
MVI    A, 02H
ADD    P
INR    D
INX    A
```

2.2.3 High-level Language

A program written in machine language is nearer to the machine than to the programmer. The programmer is required to write the code using binary digits. The combination of the digits (0's and 1's) is symbolic of the characters or symbols used in the program.

A high-level language program is written in an English-like language. Some examples of high-level languages are C, C++, Java, Lisp, and Prolog. The key features of a machine language program are –

- Programs in high-level languages are easy to write and understand than the machine language or assembly language programs.
- The program in high-level languages (source code) must be translated into machine language for the machine to understand it. The translator software used for this purpose is the interpreter or the compiler (discussed later in the chapter). The translated code is called the **object code.**
- The programs are not dependent on the hardware or the computer software. Thus, they are portable programs.
- The size of a program written in a high-level language may be more because a line of machine code or assembly code may correspond to multiple lines in a high-level language.
- A view of the high-level language program in C language is –

```
int main()
{
   printf("Hello World");
   return 0;   }
```

2.3 SOFTWARE FOR PROGRAMMING

Software consists of a set of instructions that tells the computer how the tasks are to be performed. The hardware carries out the task. Software can be broadly classified in two categories:

1. *System software:* It provides basic functions that are performed by the computer. It is necessary for the functioning of a computer. The system software interacts with hardware and application software for its working, and
2. *Application software*: It is used by the users for performing a specific task. The application software interacts with system software and computer users.

2.4 SYSTEM SOFTWARE

System software is required for the working of the computer system. The user of the computer, generally does not directly interact with the system software. System software is mainly required for two purposes –

(1) *To manage computer resources among the different software.* Operating system, device drivers and system utilities are some system software for managing computer resources. System software manages operations of components of the computer, such as processor and memory, and operations of the devices like input-output devices attached to the computer. System software provides support for various services requested by the application software.

(2) *To provide environment for development and execution of application software.* Programming language software, translator, linker and loader are system software. They provide services to application software required during their development and execution. Tools are also provided by the system software required for development of the application software.

Some system software are discussed in the following subsections.

2.4.1 Operating System

Operating System (OS) is a main system software required for managing the computer resources among different software and users. Computer users require resources, like CPU, I/O devices and memory; OS intermediates between the user and system hardware, such as allocation of memory, processor time, access to I/O devices and many more. OS controls and manages the usage of hardware among the application software and the different users. The key functions of OS are:

- It provides an interface to the user that is convenient to use.
- It facilitates efficient operations of the computer system resources.
- It manages resources of the computer.
- The main tasks performed by the operating system are –
    - *Process Management* – Handles activities, like access to shared resources like memory, I/O and CPU; execution of applications; manage a process; schedule a process; and synchronization, and deadlock handling for processes.
    - *Memory Management* – Handles allocation, de-allocation, reallocation of memory; free memory; and track of memory usage.

- *File Management* – Handles creation and deletion of files and directories; allocation of space to files; and back-up of files.
- *Device Management* – Handles opening and closing of device drivers; and control and monitoring the device driver.
- *Protection and Security* – Handles protecting of system resources. It uses user authentication, encryption and back-up of data to provide basic protection.
- *User Interface or Command Interpreter* – Handles user interface either as a command line or a graphical user interface.

- Some available OS are – Microsoft Disk Operating System (MS-DOS), Windows 8, Windows 10, Linux, UNIX and macOS Mojave (Figure 2.1).

Figure 2.1 Different operating systems

2.4.2 Device Driver

Device Driver software are required for devices attached to the computer, like keyboard, mouse, hard disk, printer, microphone, scanner, digital camera, and monitor. A user uses a device by giving commands, which are different from how the device interprets them. For example, a user gives a command to print a page. But how the command is translated to a form that the printer understands and executes it, is handled by the device driver. Each device has its own driver, supplied by the device manufacturer.

During writing of the programs, the programmers are not concerned with the hardware device they must use, because the device driver takes care of interfacing with the device. Sometimes, you may find an update version of the device driver for a particular device.

The computer comes pre-loaded with device drivers of common devices attached to a computer, like keyboard, mouse, and monitor. Such devices are named as plug-and-play devices. In case a device driver of a device is not installed on your computer, then the same can be downloaded online. For example, you may purchase a new printer. The device driver for the printer can be downloaded online from the website of the provider. It is to be noted that each device has its own unique device driver.

2.4.3 System Utility

System utility software are required for maintenance of computer and also for providing system details to the user. Some examples of system utilities are –

- *Anti-virus* utility scans the computer for virus (Figure 2.2). For example, McAfee, Symantec and Windows Defender.
- *File Management utility* manages files and folders. For example, Windows Explorer.
- *Data Compression* and *Disk Compression* compresses files, and disk contents, respectively.

- *Disk Defragmenter* consolidates file fragments into contiguous storage location.
- *Disk CleanUp* removes unnecessary files, like, temporary files from hard disk.
- *Backup Utility* creates duplicate copy of files in another disk or CD.
- *Disk Partitioning* divides a drive into multiple logical drives.
- *System Profiling Utility* provides information about the computer's hardware and software.
- *Network Managers* check the computer network.

Figure 2.2 Antivirus utility

2.4.4 Translator Software

Translator software converts a program written in high-level language and assembly language to a machine-level language program. Assembler, Compiler and Interpreter are translator software.

- **Assembler** converts a program written in assembly language into machine code. The machine language is dependent on architecture of the processor; therefore, the corresponding assembly language program shall also differ for different computer architecture.
- **Compiler** translates a program written in high-level language to machine language. The high-level language program is referred as *source code* and the compiled program is called *object code.* A compiler converts source code into object code. The object code is executable and runs as a stand-alone code. During execution, the executable does not require availability of the compiler. Compilers are unique to a programming language. Programming languages, like C++ and COBOL use a compiler. During compilation, source code is broken into small pieces, an intermediate representation is created, and object code for intermediate representation is constructed. If there are errors in the program during compilation, the syntax errors are reported by the compiler.
- **Interpreter** is used to convert the high-level language program into machine language, like compiler, but it works differently. It performs line-by-line execution of source code. Interpreter reads the source code line-by-line, converts it into machine-understandable form, executes the line, and then proceeds to next line. A programming language has its own interpreter. Programming languages, like, BASIC and Python use an interpreter.

2.4.5 Linker

Linker is a software that links object modules and libraries referenced in a program into a single executable program. A source code may include reference to libraries. Also, a program may have many independent modules that may not be stored in a single object file. Before execution, these modules and libraries are required to be linked together. This task is performed by the linker software. The linking happens before execution of the program. *Executable code* is a compiled and linked program.

2.4.6 Loader

Loader software loads and re-locates executable program in the main memory. It assigns storage space to the program in the main memory for execution. For a program that has to be executed, the loader works in the background, performing the task of loading the program into memory.

2.4.7 Programming Languages

Programming languages are used for writing a program. Each language has a unique set of keywords and its own syntax. The programming language must be understood, both by the programmer and the computer. A computer understands the language of 0's and 1's, while the programmer is more comfortable with English-like language. Programming languages fall into three categories:

- *High-level language* – The program is written in English-like language.
- *Assembly language* – It uses symbolic representation of machine code.
- *Machine language* – The program is a collection of bits.

A program written in high-level language and assembly language is converted into machine language.

2.5 Application Software

A software used by a user for accomplishing a specific task is an application software. A single program, or a set of programs written for a specific purpose, both are application software. Application software are written for different kinds of applications, like graphics, word processors, media players, database applications, telecommunication and accounting. Some examples of application software (Figure 2.3) are – MS-Word, Adobe Photoshop, Tally software, MS-EXCEL, PowerPoint, AutoCAD, Open Office, Google Docs and Internet Explorer.

- *Word processing software:* To write letter, reports, documents. For example, MS-WORD, OpenOffice Writer.
- *Spreadsheet software:* Used for creating budget and tables. For example, MS-EXCEL, OpenOffice Calc.
- *Presentation software:* To make presentations, slide shows. For example, MS-PowerPoint, OpenOffice Impress.
- *Text Editor software:* To write source code. For example, Notepad++, Sublime Text, Visual Studio code.
- *Image processing software:* To assist in drawing and graphics. For example, Adobe Photoshop.
- *Accounting software*: To assist in accounting like, salary, tax returns. For example, Tally.
- *Software packages:* Contain multiple software. For example, MS-Office, Google Docs, Sun OpenOffice.
- *CAD/CAM software:* To assist in architectural design. For example, AutoCAD, Autodesk.
- *Geographic Information Systems:* To capture, manage, and present data, images and maps. For example, ArcGIS.
- *Web browser software:* To access the World Wide Web. For example, Internet Explorer, Mozilla Firefox, Google Chrome.

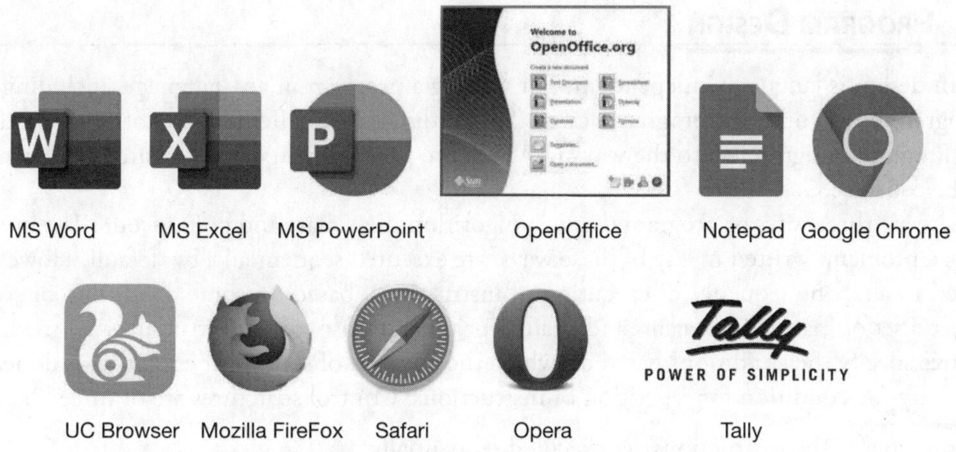

Figure 2.3 Application software

2.6 Problem Solving

For solving any problem using computer, a program is written that instructs the computer about the steps to be performed while solving the problem. For writing a program, a series of steps are followed – Problem analysis, Program design, Program development and Program testing.

***Problem analysis*:** It requires the programmer to understand the problem, analyze it, identify different solutions to the problem, and then choose a solution that suits the best.

Program design: It involves representing the chosen solution in a form that can be coded. It includes defining of the logic to solve the problem. There are several ways for representing the program design:

- Write an *algorithm.* It is an explanation of the solution using English-like words.
- Draw a *flowchart.* It is diagrammatic representation of the solution.
- Write a *pseudocode.* It is written using structured programming constructs.

***Program development*:** It involves writing the code and executing the program. There are several steps to be followed:

- Select a programming language, like Python, C++ or Java.
- Convert flowchart/algorithm/pseudocode into a program, in the selected programming language.
- Compile/interpret the program and remove the syntax errors. Execute the program.

***Program testing*:** It involves testing the written program and checking that the desired results are generated. If the results are incorrect then the errors are rectified. After the program has been successfully tested, install the tested program onto the user computer. It is essential that proper documentation of the program is done so that any update or error correction is easier to do during the maintenance of the program.

2.7 Program Design

Program design is language-independent. For writing a program in any language, including Python, the program has to undergo program design. So, we discuss the different ways of program design, in detail. Program design refers to the ways in which the problem can be represented in a form so that it can be coded.

There are three ways of program design – algorithm, flowchart and pseudocode. The instructions to solve a problem, written in any of these ways, are executed sequentially, by default. However, there is a need to alter the sequence of execution of instructions, based on some condition, or sometimes to repeat a set of instructions again and again. For this purpose, control structures are used. Control structures specify the conditions based on which the decision of statement execution is done, or, they may specify the condition for repetition of instructions. Control structures are of three kinds:

- Sequential – The instructions are executed sequentially.
- Selection – A condition is checked. Based on the outcome of the condition, the decision is made about the next statement to be executed.
- Iterative – A set of statements are executed repeatedly, a defined number of times.

The control structures are used in the preparation of flowchart and pseudocode.

We examine the three ways of program design in the following subsections.

2.7.1 Algorithm

Algorithm is an ordered sequence of English-like representation of the solution of the problem. The steps in an algorithm are ordered, well defined, finite and unambiguous. Here, we show some algorithms.

Algorithm 1: Add three numbers.
D = A + B + C
Step 1. Start
Step 2. Read the three numbers A, B, C
Step 3. Compute the sum of A, B and C and store the result in D
Step 4. Print D
Step 5. Stop

Algorithm 2: Find the area of a circle.
Area = (22/7) * Radius^2
Step 1. Start
Step 2. Read radius of the circle in R.
Step 3. Multiply R with R and 22. Then divide by 7. Store the result in A.
Step 4. Print A.
Step 5. Stop

Algorithm 3: Find sum of squares of N natural numbers.
$1^2 + 2^2 + 3^2 + 4^2 + \ldots + (N-1)^2 + N^2$
Step 1. Start
Step 2. Read N.

Step 3. Store 0 in SUM.
Step 4. Multiply N with N and add to SUM. Update SUM.
Step 5. Decrement N by 1. Update N.
Step 6. Repeat Step 4 and Step 5 until N is 0.
Step 7. Print SUM.
Step 8. Stop

Algorithm 4: Find factorial of a number N.
N! = 1 * 2 * 3 * 4 * … * (N – 1) * N
Step 1. Start
Step 2. Read N.
Step 3. Store 1 in FACT.
Step 4. Multiply FACT with N. Update FACT.
Step 5. Decrement N by 1. Update N.
Step 6. Repeat Step 4 and Step 5 until N is 1.
Step 7. Print FACT.
Step 8. Stop

2.7.2 Flowchart

Flowchart is a diagrammatic representation of the solution to the problem. Since a flowchart is a diagrammatic representation, it moves across language barriers and facilitates easy communication among the programmers. For drawing a flowchart, symbols are defined for depicting different tasks. The symbols vary in their shapes. Also, lines are drawn for connecting the symbols. Table 2.2 shows the key symbols used in a flowchart, along with their description.

Table 2.2 Key flowchart symbols and their description

Tasks	Description	Symbol
Process	Statements or operation	
Decision	Branch for a decision	
Input/Output	Input and Output	
Connector	Join of flow	
Terminator	End the flowchart	
Flow Lines	Direction of flow	

The flowcharts can be drawn on the computer easily and the flowchart symbols are available in most of the word processing software. For example, in MS-Word, the symbols are available in <Insert><Illustrations ><Shapes>.

While drawing a flowchart, some rules need to be followed:

- A flowchart has a Start and End
- The direction of flow must be from top to bottom or from left to right
- The relevant symbols must be used.

Figure 2.4 shows flowcharts for some problems defined in the algorithms. We see that in the first and second flowchart, the statements will be executed in a sequential order. But, in the third flowchart, both condition and repetition are used. A condition is checked, and based on the result of the condition (True or False), the next statement to be executed is decided. Also, a set of statements execute repetitively (loop), until the condition to exit the repetition is fulfilled.

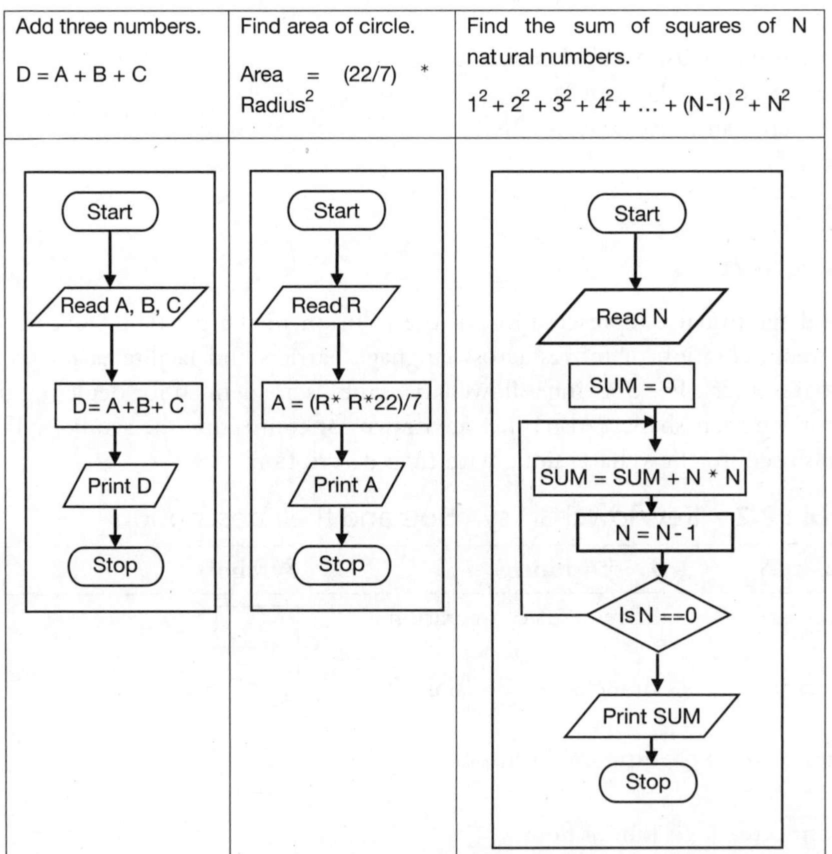

Figure 2.4 Examples of flowchart

Flowcharts have some limitations too. The solution of a complex and long problem may result in a flowchart running across several pages. As a result, it might become difficult to understand the flowchart. Also, changing a flowchart with an update in the problem definition is a difficult task.

2.7.3 Pseudocode

Pseudocode uses the structured constructs of programming language to define an ordered sequence of English-like instructions. The structured constructs are generic and do not bind to a particular programming language. Some of the common terms used for representing different actions in a pseudocode are – INPUT, GET, READ for input of data, OUTPUT, PRINT, DISPLAY for output of data, COMPUTE, CALCULATE for performing calculations, and INCREMENT for incrementing. It also uses ADD, SUBTRACT, INITIALIZE for addition, subtraction and initialization, respectively. The control structures are also written using specific terms, like, IF-THEN-ELSE and CASE statement for condition, WHILE and WHILE-DO for repetitive execution.

Figure 2.5 shows some examples of pseudocode.

```
READ values of A, B and C
COMPUTE D = A + B + C
PRINT D
STOP
```

(i) Find the sum of three numbers

```
READ values of radius in R
COMPUTE AREA = (22/7) * R * R
PRINT AREA
STOP
```

(ii) Find the area of a square

```
READ N
INITIALIZE SUM to zero
DO WHILE (N greater than 0)
COMPUTE SUM = SUM _ N * N
DECREMENT N
PRINT SUM
STOP
STOP
```

(iii) Find the sum of squares of N natural numbers.

```
READ N
INITIALIZE FACT to 1
DO WHILE (N greater than 1)
COMPUTE FACT = FACT * N
DECREMENT N
PRINT FACT
STOP
```

(iv) Find the factorial of N.

```
READ values of A, B, C
IF A > B THEN
ASSIGN A to MAX
ELSE
ASSIGN B to MAX
IF MAX > C THEN
PRINT MAX is greatest
ELSE
PRINT C is greatest
STOP
```

(v) Find the greatest of three numbers.

Figure 2.5 Examples of pseudocode

From among the three ways to represent program design, the programmers generally prefer to write pseudocode. This is because it is easy to translate a pseudocode into a program, as it uses programming constructs.

A point to be noted here is that algorithm, flowchart and pseudocode are independent of the programming language used for writing a program. Having written the program design, the next step is to identify a programming language and write the program.

2.8 PROGRAMMING PARADIGM

Programming paradigm is a model for writing of a program. There are several programming paradigms, but here we focus on only two paradigms – structured programming and object-oriented programming.

Structured programming involves building of programs using small modules that are easy to read and write. A problem is divided into different independent but related tasks. Each independent task is defined as module. A module may further consist of small functions and procedures. A key point to be noted here is that in structured programming, the approach to develop the program is process-centric. The functionality of the complete program is divided into modules. As a result, the modules are tightly bound to each other and are cohesive. Any change performed on a single module may require changing other related modules too. C, COBOL and Pascal are a few structured programming languages.

Object-Oriented Programming (OOP) involves building of programs using entities called objects. A problem is divided into different components or parts, which interact with each other to provide the functionality of the program. An object consists of data and methods that operate on the data. The objects are complete by themselves and are re-usable. We shall discuss OOP in more detail in the next section.

2.9 OBJECT-ORIENTED PROGRAMMING

Object-oriented programming is different from structured programming. In object-oriented approach, the focus is on viewing the system as consisting of objects and we look at the interaction between them. In structured approach, the focus is on the processes in the system. Modules are created on the basis of their functionality and they are tightly woven.

The terms commonly associated with object-oriented programming are as follows:

- **Object** is an entity that is characterized by state, behavior and unique identity. The data attribute represents the object's state; and methods represent the object behavior.
- **Class** consists of a set of objects that share a common structure and behavior. Object is a runtime instance of the class.
- Interaction between the objects is via message passing.
- Object-oriented software has four unique features – Abstraction, Encapsulation, Inheritance and Polymorphism.
- **Abstraction** focuses on relevant attributes of an object and ignores the irrelevant ones. Encapsulation is a way of implementing abstraction.
- **Encapsulation** means information hiding. Encapsulation is the process that hides the non-essential information and shows only the essential information. It hides the data defined in the class; interaction with the class is via the method interface.

- **Inheritance** allows a new class (derived class or subclass) to be derived from an already existing class (base class or superclass). The subclass inherits all data and method of the superclass. It may override some or all of the data and methods of the base class or add its own new data and methods.
- **Polymorphism** means many forms. It refers to an entity changing its form depending on the circumstances. It is a phenomenon where the same message sent to two different objects produces two different sets of actions. This feature increases the flexibility of the program.
- *C++* and *Java* are object-oriented programming languages.

After having selected a suitable programming language, the code for the problem is written, executed and tested for correct results. After successful completion, the program is ready for use.

A program written in any programming language has certain characteristics that make it a good program. Some key characteristics of a good program are that it should be (1) readable, (2) well-documented, (3) generic, and (4) portable.

Python is an object-oriented language.

Summary

- Program is a set of instructions that is written to perform a specific task.
- High-level language, assembly language and machine language are the three categories of programming languages.
- Machine language is hardware-dependent.
- A program written in machine language executes fast but is difficult to write.
- Assembly language is symbolic and has English-like representation of the machine code.
- An assembly language program is also machine-dependent though easier to write than a machine language program.
- A program written in a high-level language is English-like. The programs are portable.
- System software and Application software are the two categories of software.
- System software manages the computer resources and provides suitable environment to the application software for development.
- Operating system is system software that manages resources of the computer among different users and the software.
- Device driver is system software that is required to handle devices attached to the computer.
- System utilities are system software required for maintenance of the computer.
- Assembler converts an assembly language program to machine code.
- Compiler translates a source code written in high-level language to an object code.
- Interpreter interprets, line-by-line, a program written in high-level language.
- The libraries and models referred in a program are linked by the linker.
- For execution, the loader assigns memory space to the program for execution.
- Application software is used by the user for different purposes, like for document preparation, performing calculations, and accessing Internet.
- Problem analysis, program design, program development and program testing are the different steps that are required to be followed when writing a program.

- Program design can be represented using three ways – algorithm, flowchart and pseudocode.
- Algorithm uses simple English-like language; flowchart is a diagrammatic representation and pseudocode uses structured constructs for representing the program design.
- Sequence, selection and iteration are the three kinds of control structures.
- Structured programming paradigm focuses on dividing a problem based on processes in the system.
- Object-oriented programming divides a problem based on objects in the system.
- Programs written using structured programming are highly cohesive. In contrast, object-oriented approach uses message passing to interact with different objects. As a result, object-oriented programs are less cohesive. It is easy to make changes to a program written using object-oriented approach.
- Object and class are terms used with object-oriented programming.
- Abstraction, encapsulation, inheritance and polymorphism are unique features of object-oriented programming.
- A good program is readable; it does not have hard-coded values and is well documented.

Keywords

Program
Software
System software
Application software
Operating system
Device drivers
System utility
Machine language
High-level language
Assembly language
Translator software
Assembler
Compiler
Interpreter
Source code
Object code
Linker
Loader
Problem analysis
Program design
Program development
Program testing
Algorithm
Control structures
Sequential structure
Selection construct
Iteration
Flowchart
Flowchart symbols
Pseudocode
If–Then statement
DO–WHILE statement
WHILE statement
Programming paradigm
Structured Programming
Object-Oriented Programming (OOP)
Class
Object
Abstraction
Encapsulation
Inheritance
Polymorphism

Assessment

A.1 Bloom Level: Knowledge/Remember

Review Questions

1. Define: (1) Program, (2) Object, (3) Class.
2. List the two main categories of software.
3. List any three system software.
4. Name three operating systems.

5. Name any five system utilities.
6. List two antivirus utilities.
7. List a file management utility.
8. List the three categories of programming languages.
9. List any four application software.
10. List the steps of problem-solving that are followed for the development of a program.
11. Name two high-level languages that use compiler for translation.
12. Name two high-level languages that use interpreter for translation.
13. List the four unique features of object-oriented software.
14. Give an example of a plug and play device.
15. List the key characteristics of a good program.
16. Give an example of object-oriented language.
17. Give full form of the following abbreviations:
    (i) OS (ii) MS-DOS (iii) OOP
18. Match the following:

Column A	*Column B*
(i) Windows defender	a Operating system
(ii) MS-DOS	b Anti-virus
(iii) MS-Excel	c Application software
(iv) Internet Explorer	
(v) Opera	
(vi) Safari	
(vii) Unix	
(viii) Symantec	

Fill in the blanks

Assembly	Sequence	Machine
Loader	Decision	Flowchart
Assembler	Pseudocode	Selection
Iteration	Windows Explorer	
Polymorphism	Object System	
Application	Operating System	
Assembly	Compiler	Interpreter
High-level	Machine	

1. Software can be broadly classified into two categories: __________ software and __________ software.
2. __________ software is required for managing computer resources among the users.
3. __________ is an example of file management utility.
4. __________ language uses symbolic representation of the machine code.
5. __________, __________ and __________ are translator software.
6. Assembler converts a program written in __________ language into __________ language.
7. Compiler converts a program written in __________ language into __________ language.
8. A compiled program is called __________ code.
9. __________ software loads and relocates executable program in main memory.

10. __________ is used to represent the solution diagrammatically, during program design.

11. __________ is used to represent the solution using structured programming constructs, during program design.

12. __________, __________, and __________ are the three kinds of control structures.

13. ◇ is the symbol of __________ in a flowchart.

14. In object-oriented approach, __________ means an entity changing its form depending upon the circumstances.

State True/False

1. MS-DOS is an operating system.
2. A device driver is not needed for a keyboard attached to a computer.
3. Machine language is an English-like language.
4. Executable code is a compiled and linked program.
5. The aim of problem analysis is to represent the solution as a flowchart.
6. The errors from a program are removed during program design.
7. Program design is independent of the programming language.
8. In object-oriented approach, interaction between the objects is via message passing.

Multiple Choice Questions (MCQ)

1. Which of the following is not anti-virus software?
   (a) Avira (b) AVG
   (c) Symantec (d) Bluestone
2. Identify the language that uses an interpreter for translation.
   (a) C++ (b) C
   (c) BASIC (d) COBOL
3. Identify the object-oriented programming language.
   (a) COBOL (b) Pascal
   (c) Java (d) C

A.2 Bloom Level: Comprehend/Understand

Review Questions

1. What is the purpose of system software?
2. What is the need of operating system?
3. Describe the need for device driver software.
4. What is the purpose of system utility?
5. What is the purpose of the utilities – (a) Disk defragmenter, (b) Disk partitioning, (c) Disk compression, and (d) File management?
6. Explain the purpose of the following application software in one line – (a) Word processing software, (b) Image processing software, (c) Accounting software, (d) Spreadsheet software, (e) Presentation software, (f) Web browser software, (g)

Geographical Information Systems (h) Text Editor software (i) CAD/CAM software

7. What is the purpose of assembler?
8. What is the purpose of compiler?
9. What is the purpose of interpreter?
10. What are plug-and-play devices?
11. What is the purpose of linker?
12. What is the purpose of loader?
13. Explain the structured programming paradigm.
14. Explain the object-oriented programming paradigm.
15. Write short notes on:
    a) System software
    b) Programming language
    c) Translator software
    d) Program design
    e) Application software
    f) Control structures
    g) Object-oriented programming

Multiple Choice Questions (MCQ)

1. Identify the odd one.
   (a) MS-DOS (b) Linux
   (c) Avira (d) Solaris
2. Identify the odd one.
   (a) Operating System
   (b) Device driver
   (c) Anti-virus
   (d) Compiler
3. Identify the odd one.
   (a) C (b) Pascal
   (c) COBOL (d) Python

A.3 Bloom Level: Application/Apply

Review Questions

1. Arrange following statements in a sequence from start to end of the task.
   a) Select a way of program design.
   b) Choose a programming language.
   c) Identify solution to the program.
   d) Do proper documentation of the program.
2. Given the following statements.
   i. System profiling utility removes unnecessary files such as temporary files from hard disk.
   ii. Disk Defragmenter divides a drive into multiple logical drives.
   iii. Disk CleanUp removes unnecessary files such as temporary files from hard disk.
   iv. Network managers manage files and folders.

   Examine and choose an option below that shows all TRUE statements.
   a) (i) and (iii) only.
   b) (i) and (ii) only.
   c) (ii) and (iii) only.
   d) (iii) only.
3. Give an example each of the following application software - (a) Word processing software, (b) Image processing software, (c) Accounting software, (d) Spreadsheet software, (e) Presentation software, (f) Web browser software.

Programming Assignment

1. Write the algorithm, draw a flowchart, and write pseudocode for the following:
   a) To find the sum of square root of first N integers.
   b) To find the sum of first N integers.
   c) To find the sum of all even numbers and odd numbers till 100.
   d) To find the first n numbers in a Fibonacci series. A Fibonacci series is $f(0) = 0$, $f(1) = 1$. $f(2) = f(0) + f(1)$ or $f(n) = f(n - 1) + f(n - 2)$.
   e) To find the sum of digits of a number. (For example, in number 321, find 3 + 2 + 1)
   f) To check whether a number is prime.
   g) To convert the temperature from Celsius to Fahrenheit. *Hint: F= (C * (5/9)) + 32*
   h) To find Least Common Divisor (LCD) of two numbers. *Hint: LCM of two integers is the smallest positive integer that is perfectly divisible by both the numbers.*
   i) To check whether a number is Armstrong or not. *Hint: A positive number is Armstrong if it is equal to the sum of the cubes of its digits. For example, 0, 1, 153 =* $(1^3 + 5^3 + 3^3)$*, 370, 371 and 407.*

A.4 Bloom Level: Analyze

1. A program for computing factorial is written using structured programming and object-oriented programming. Compare and contrast the similarities and differences between the two programs.
2. Though a flowchart is not much recommended for use as it may run across several pages, examine situations where flowchart is better suited for program design.
3. Give differences between the following:
   a) Compiler and Interpreter
   b) Source code and Object code
   c) Selection and Iteration
   d) Abstraction and Encapsulation
   e) Machine language and Assembly language
   f) Assembly language and High-level Language
   g) Algorithm and Flowchart
   h) Flowchart and Pseudocode
   i) System Software and Application Software
   j) Assembler and Compiler
   k) Compiler and Interpreter
   l) Linker and Loader

A.5 Bloom Level: Evaluate

1) Defend the argument that a program written using object-oriented programming is easy to be changed in comparison to a program written using structure programming.
2) "It is better to use pseudocode instead of algorithms." Justify the statement.
3) "Selecting a well-suited programming language is crucial." Justify the statement.
4) "In object-oriented software, already-created methods can be used for writing new methods". Justify the statement.

5) "In object-oriented software, non-essential detail can be hidden". Defend the statement.

A.6 Bloom Level: Create/Synthesize

1) Some characteristics of good program are discussed in this chapter. Formulate more points that you think make a good program. (*Hint: Proper indentation*)
2) Given a problem to be solved, formulate a checklist for the user that facilitates selection from one of the program-design ways – algorithm, flowchart and pseudocode.
3) Check your system, and create a list of system utilities provided by your system.

Answers

A.1 Bloom Level: Knowledge/Remember

Review Questions

16. (1) b (2) a (3) c (4) c (5) c (6) c (7) a (8) b

Fill in the Blanks

1. System, Application **2.** Operating System **3.** Windows explorer **4.** Assembly
5. Compiler, Assembler, Interpreter **6.** Assembly, Machine
7. High-level, Machine **8.** Object **9.** Loader **10.** Flowchart
11. Pseudocode **12.** Sequence, Selection, Iteration **13.** Decision
14. Polymorphism

True/False

1. True **2.** False **3.** False **4.** True **5.** False **6.** False **7.** True **8.** True

Multiple Choice Questions (MCQ)

1. d **2.** c **3.** c

A.2 Bloom Level: Comprehend/Understand

Multiple Choice Questions (MCQ)

1. c **2.** d **3.** d

A.3 Bloom Level: Application/Apply

Review Questions

1. (c) (a) (b) (d) **2.** (c)

UNIT II Basics of Python

CHAPTER 3

Python Environment Setting

Contents

3.1 Introduction

Python is a high-level programming language. It was developed by Guido Van Rossum of the Netherlands in 1991. The language was named "Python" by the creator from the title of his favorite series "Monty Python's Flying Circus". Python is available under the GNU General Public License (GPL).

To start using the Python programming language for writing programs, there is a need to install Python software on the machine. Also, there is a need to get familiar with the programming interface. Here, we discuss Python programming using version Python 3.7 and above. The Python version gets updated from time to time.

In this chapter, we discuss features of the Python programming language. The steps to be followed to install the Python software and other related packages are discussed in detail. Python can be programmed in two modes – interactive mode and script mode. The differences between the two programming modes are also discussed.

Learning Outcomes of this chapter

After completion of the chapter, the learner will be able to:

- List the features of Python programming language
- Install Python software on the machine
- Install other Python-related packages
- Describe features of the Python shell
- Use the Python shell
- Differentiate between interactive mode and script mode.

3.2 Features of Python

Python is a high-level interpreted language. Python is a general-purpose, interactive and object-oriented programming language. It is a user-friendly and English-like language. Some of the key features of Python language are described here:

- ***Python is a general-purpose language.*** It is used for both scientific and non-scientific programming.
- ***Python is an interpreted language.*** A program written in high-level language has to be either compiled or interpreted. Python is an interpretive language. Python performs line-by-line execution of the code.
    - o Python code is interpreted every time the code is run. As a result, the execution is relatively slow in comparison to a program written in a compiled programming language, like C. This is because in compilation, the compiled code is executed directly, without the need to re-compile the code each time the program is run.
    - o Python code is interpreted line by line; if a portion of code is written, it can be checked for errors immediately. This is an advantage over a compiled language code, where errors are displayed only when a complete program is compiled.

- ***Python is an interactive language.*** For beginners, it is easy to learn. The programmer can start writing a simple code at the Python prompt, and execute them to see the result immediately.
- ***Python is an object-oriented language***. This means it has all features of object-oriented language, like, encapsulation, abstraction, inheritance and polymorphism. Since Python is easy to learn, it is easier to shift to any other object-oriented language by learning only the syntax of the language.
- ***Python is open-source***. It is easily available and is free of cost. Small and big organizations readily use Python for programming.
- ***Python is easy to learn and understand.*** Programs written in Python are simple and readable. Python uses more English keywords frequently. Python has fewer syntax constructions than other languages. Python programs are easy to learn and understand. This is because it has beginner-friendly features, such as simple syntax.

Python programming language supports simple text programs, and programming for World Wide Web and games. It has widespread use in industry applications too. Google search engine, YouTube, Dropbox, IBM, Cisco and HP are some organizations that use Python programming language.

3.3 Installation of Python Software

The steps for installation of Python software on a Windows 10 machine are described as follows:

1. Open the site for download of software. https://www.python.org/downloads/. A web page appears (Figure 3.1).

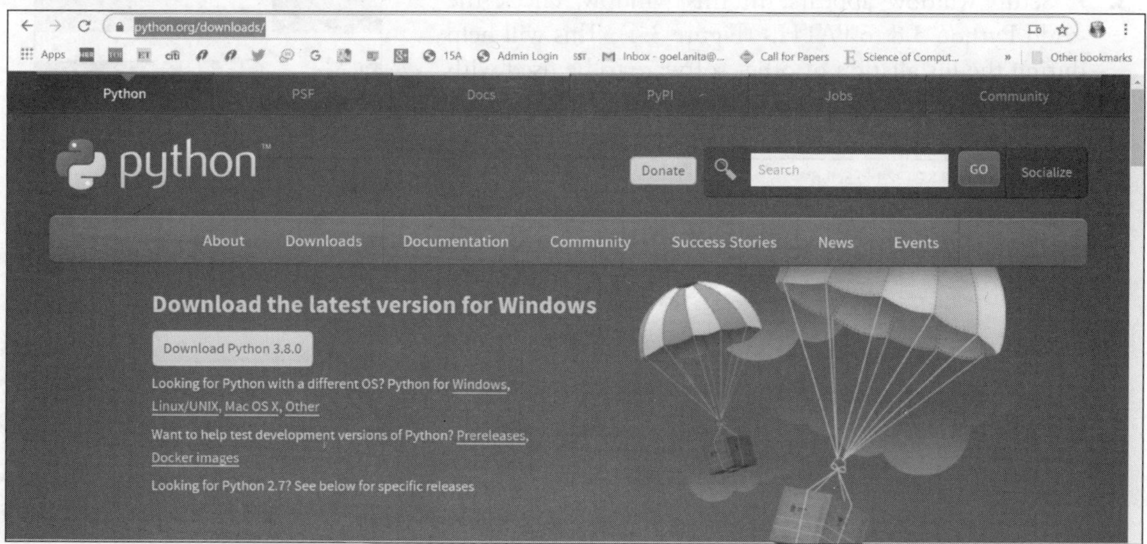

Figure 3.1 Python dowlaod site

2. Click on <Download Python 3.8.0>
3. A <Save As> window appears. Select the location where you want to save the Python software (Figure 3.2).

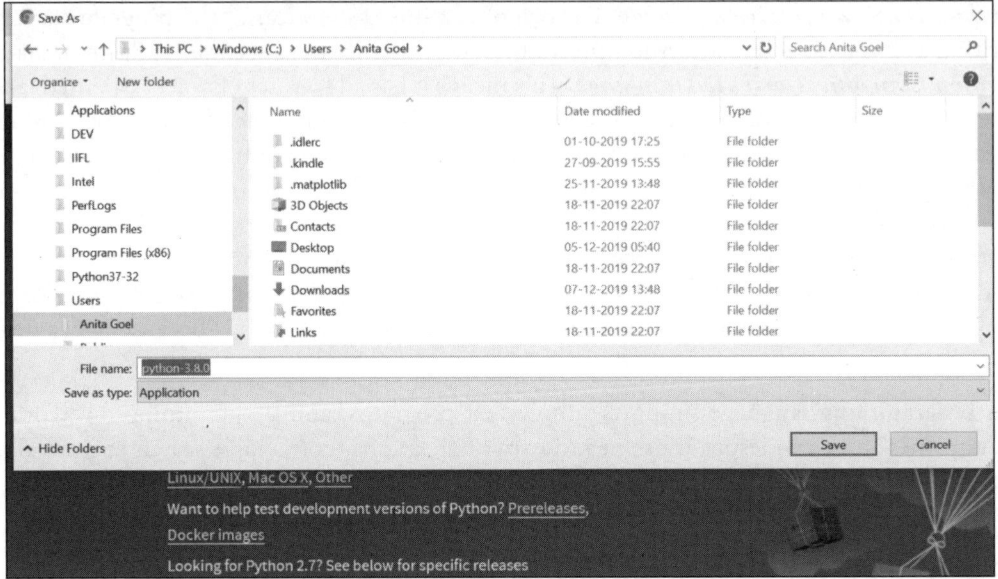

Figure 3.2 Save Python software

4. After the software is saved, Run the software. For this, click on <Open> in <Python- 3.8.0.exe> (Figure 3.3).
5. A Setup window appears. In this window, check the <Add Python 3.8 to PATH> (Figure 3.4). This will help during the installation of other software to be used with Python, like matplotlib.

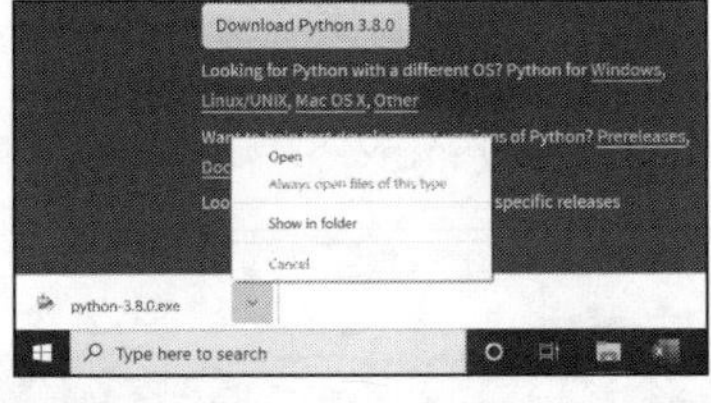

Figure 3.3 Run Python software

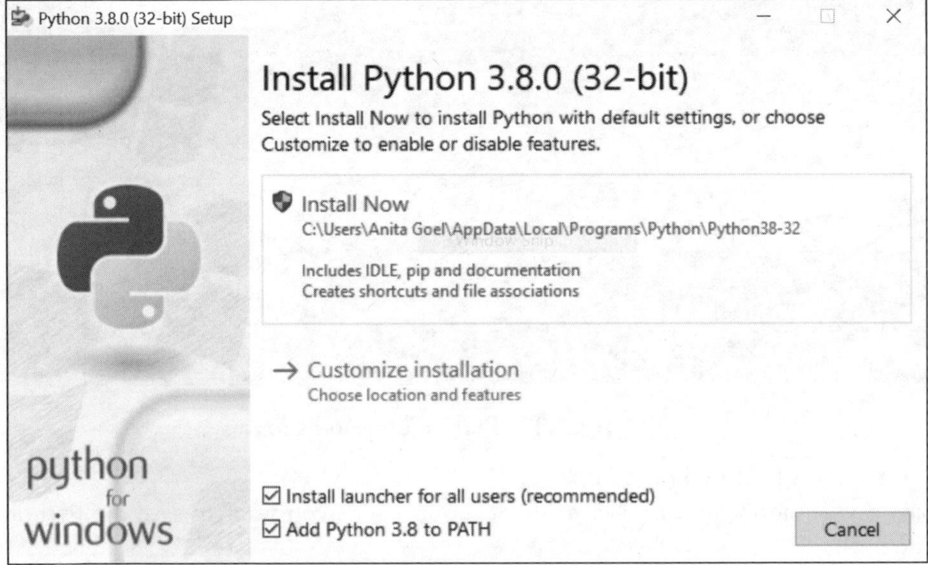

Figure 3.4 Python Install setup

6. Click <Install Now>. A Setup Progress bar appears (Figure 3.5). After the installation is successful, <Setup was successful> appears on the window (Figure 3.6).

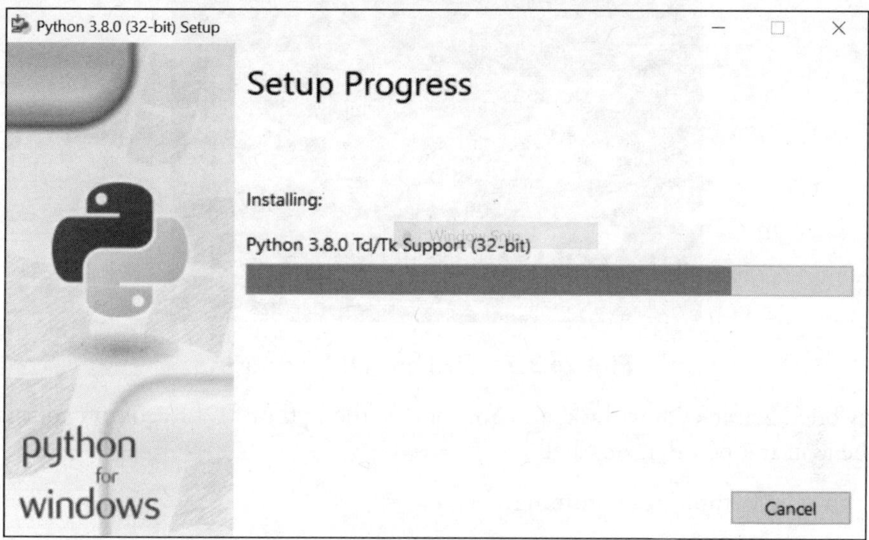

Figure 3.5 Python Install setup progress bar

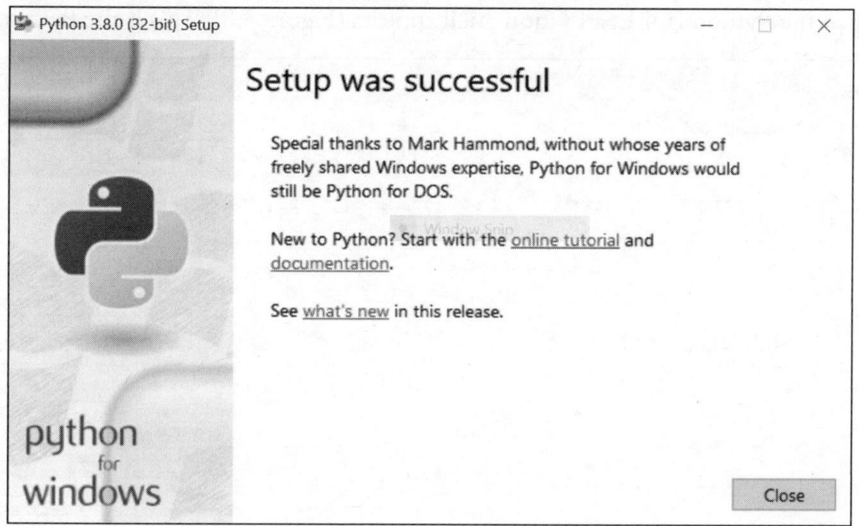

Figure 3.6 Python Install Setup successful

7. Python software has been successfully installed.
8. Click on Windows logo. Right click on Python IDLE (Figure 3.7).

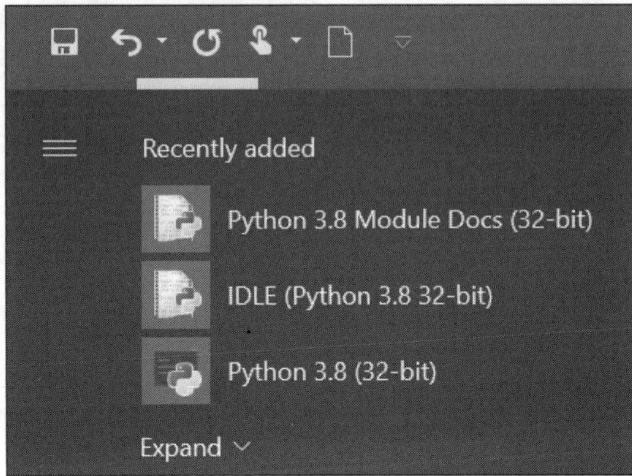

Figure 3.7 Python IDLE listing

9. Click <More>. Select <Pin to Taskbar>. You can see the Python IDLE icon on your taskbar.
10. Click the icon to open Python Shell.

Yippee! You can start Python programming.

3.4 Understanding the Python Window

When you open the Python IDLE, a Python Shell appears (Figure 3.8). This is the Python Interpreter.

```
Python 3.8.0 Shell
File  Edit  Shell  Debug  Options  Window  Help
Python 3.8.0 (tags/v3.8.0:fa919fd, Oct 14 2019, 19:21:23) [MSC v.1916 32 bit (In
tel)] on win32
Type "help", "copyright", "credits" or "license()" for more information.
>>> |
```

Figure 3.8 Python shell

On the Python Interpreter, we see the following:

- There are seven tabs – File, Edit, Shell, Debug, Options, Window and Help. The options provided by the different tabs are shown in Figure 3.9, (i)–(vii).

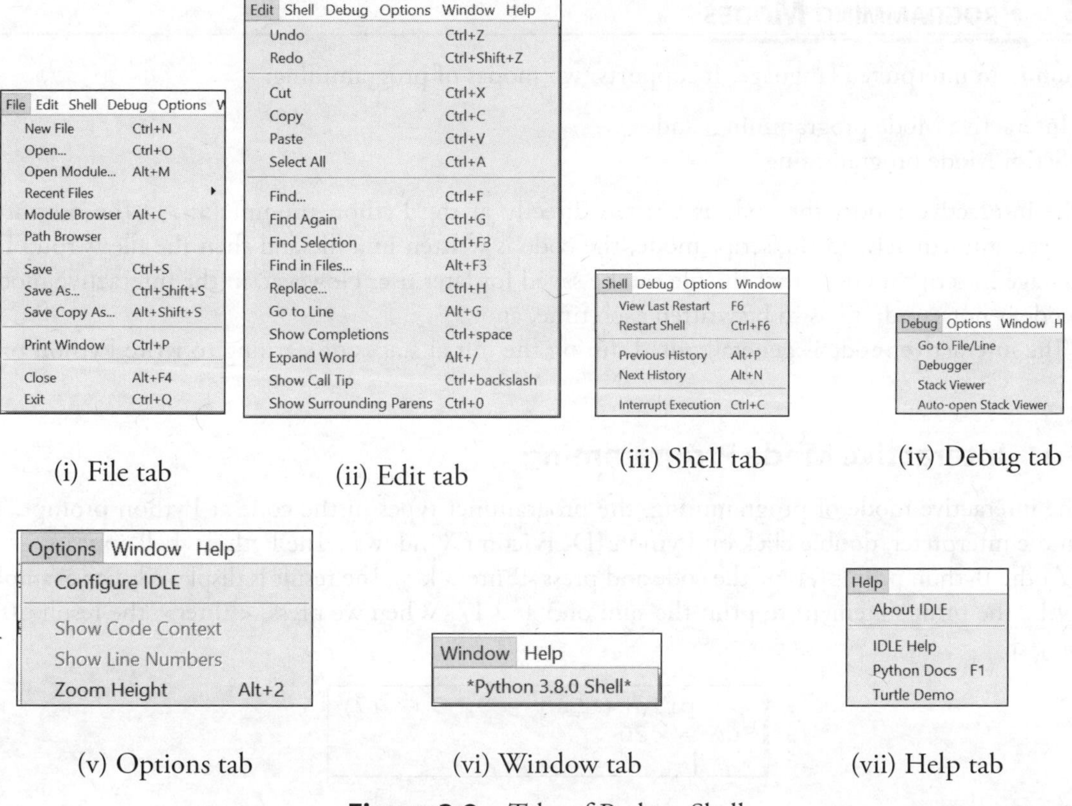

(i) File tab (ii) Edit tab (iii) Shell tab (iv) Debug tab

(v) Options tab (vi) Window tab (vii) Help tab

Figure 3.9 Tabs of Python Shell

- The version of Python Interpreter is also shown (Python 3.8.0).
- There is a Python prompt >>>. This is where programming in interactive mode can be done. For example, if we write a code to print "Hello", then "Hello" is displayed.

```
>>> print("Hello")
Hello
>>> |
```

The tabs in the shell can be used to make the interface more comfortable. For example,

- To view line numbers in the code, use
  <Options> <Show Line numbers>
- To change the font face or font size, use
  <Options> <Configure IDLE>

3.5 Programming Modes

Python is an interpreted language. It supports two modes of programming:

- Interactive Mode programming, and
- Script Mode programming.

In the interactive mode, the code is written directly at the Python prompt (>>>). The output is displayed immediately. In the script mode, the code is written in a file and then the file is run. The advantage in script mode is that the file can be saved for later use. However, in the interactive mode, the code is not saved; it has to be written each time, anew.

The interactive mode is generally used during the initial stages of learning to write Python programs.

3.5.1 Interactive Mode Programming

In the interactive mode of programming, the programmer types in the code at Python prompt. To open the interpreter, double click on Python IDLE icon (Windows). The Python shell appears.

At the Python prompt, type the code and press <Enter> key. The result is displayed. For example, we write the print statement to print the sum of 3 and 17. When we press, <Enter>, the result 20 is displayed.

```
>>> print("Sum = ", 3 + 17)
Sum =  20
>>> |
```

We also see that when we write the command incorrectly, for example, if the quotes in print statement are not matching, the interpreter displays syntax error.

```
>>> print(Sum = ", 3 + 17)

SyntaxError: EOL while scanning string literal
>>> |
```

In interactive mode, to repeat already written commands,

- Use upward (^) navigation key to scroll history of commands and downward key (v) to scroll forward commands.
- Press <Enter> key on the command you want to select.
- The command will be displayed again.
- You can edit the command or run it again.
- To close the interpreter, use the key combination <CTRL + D > or type quit().

The interactive mode of programming is preferred for experimentation purposes. In the interactive mode, the code executed by the interpreter goes away, i.e., it does not get stored in a file. When the programmer wants the same code the next time, he/she will have to type the code again. For storing the code in a file, the script mode of programming is used.

3.5.2 Script Mode Programing

In script mode programming, the Python code is saved in a file. The file is also known as a module or program. The modules are simple text files having Python statements. The script mode programming makes it possible to modify the code, save and run the code. It allows repeated re-running of the code.

To create a script and run it in ***Windows***, use the following steps:

1. Double click on Python IDLE icon. Python shell is displayed.
2. Click <File> <New File>. A new "untitled" shell window opens.
3. Write your Python code.
4. Save the file in <File> <Save As>. Select the correct folder. Enter a name of the file. The Python program is stored with .py extension.
5. Click <Run> <Run Module>. Python shell will open and the output is displayed.

To create a script and run it in **Linux**, use the following steps:

1. Create a file `filename.py` in the directory with an editor (like vi editor)
2. Write your Python code.
3. Save the file.
4. Make the file executable, by:
   ```
   $ chmod +x filename.py
   ```
5. Run the file using the following command:
   ```
   $./filename.py
   ```

3.6 Installation of Software Packages

Several software like, Tkinter, Matplotlib, Numpy Panda need to be installed.

In Python 3 and above, Tkinter is pre-installed. To check whether Tkinter is already installed, write the following on Python prompt:

```
>>> import Tkinter
```

For installing any software package, do the following:

1. Check for `pip` installation. In Python 3 versions, `pip` will be already installed. `pip` is the package installer for Python.
2. From menu, open command prompt <cmd>
3. Go to C directory. (Use command cd..)
4. When you are in C:\> folder. You can check whether pip is installed by writing
   ```
   $ pip --version
   ```
5. If pip is installed, the above command will display the version number.
6. Install Matplotlib package (Figure 3.10) using the following command:
   ```
   $ pip install matplotlib
   ```
7. The Matplotlib package gets successfully installed (Figure 3.11). A sample program and its output using matplotlib are shown in Figure 3.12.

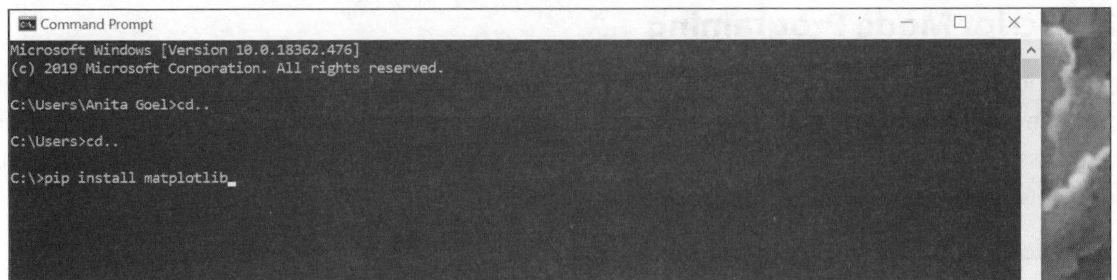

Figure 3.10 Install matplotlib

```
Command Prompt
/pyparsing-2.4.5-py2.py3-none-any.whl (67kB)
    100% |████████████████████████████████| 71kB 3.1MB/s
Collecting python-dateutil>=2.1 (from matplotlib)
  Downloading https://files.pythonhosted.org/packages/d4/70/d60450c3dd48ef87586924207ae8907090de0b306af2bce5d134d78615cb
/python_dateutil-2.8.1-py2.py3-none-any.whl (227kB)
    100% |████████████████████████████████| 235kB 3.5MB/s
Collecting cycler>=0.10 (from matplotlib)
  Using cached https://files.pythonhosted.org/packages/f7/d2/e07d3ebb2bd7af696440ce7e754c59dd546ffe1bbe732c8ab68b9c834e6
1/cycler-0.10.0-py2.py3-none-any.whl
Collecting numpy>=1.11 (from matplotlib)
  Downloading https://files.pythonhosted.org/packages/ce/ad/2e88f36b56f64f70c081b32fa5512dacedf12005ccb0c2d300d44dcc1215
/numpy-1.17.4-cp37-cp37m-win32.whl (10.7MB)
    100% |████████████████████████████████| 10.7MB 1.3MB/s
Requirement already satisfied: setuptools in c:\python37-32\lib\site-packages (from kiwisolver>=1.0.1->matplotlib) (40.8
.0)
Collecting six>=1.5 (from python-dateutil>=2.1->matplotlib)
  Downloading https://files.pythonhosted.org/packages/65/26/32b8464df2a97e6dd1b656ed26b2c194606c16fe163c695a992b36c11cdf
/six-1.13.0-py2.py3-none-any.whl
Installing collected packages: kiwisolver, pyparsing, six, python-dateutil, cycler, numpy, matplotlib
Successfully installed cycler-0.10.0 kiwisolver-1.1.0 matplotlib-3.1.2 numpy-1.17.4 pyparsing-2.4.5 python-dateutil-2.8.
1 six-1.13.0
You are using pip version 19.0.3, however version 19.3.1 is available.
You should consider upgrading via the 'python -m pip install --upgrade pip' command.

C:\>
```

Figure 3.11 Matplotlib installation complete

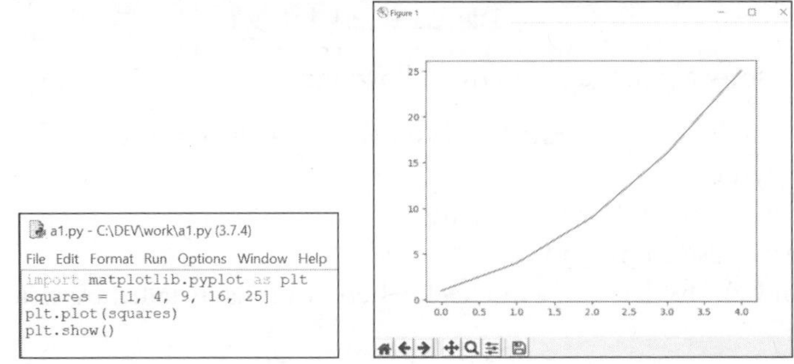

Figure 3.12 A sample program and output on matplotlib

Likewise, any software can be installed.

a. pip install numpy – to install Numpy
b. pip install panda – to install Panda.

Let us get started with Python programming!

CHAPTER 4 Basic Data Types, Literals and Variables

CONTENTS

4.1 INTRODUCTION

Python programming language has a defined set of fundamental elements and rules that are to be used for writing the programs. There is a need to understand the basic building blocks of the language, to start writing programs in Python language. The ways to describe the data, supported data types, rules for defining identifiers, literals, variables and assigning values to variables are some of the basics that need to be understood. Also, Python has a defined structure along with rules for the structure that have to be followed while writing a program.

In this chapter, we shall discuss the key terminologies like, identifier, literal, variables, assignment statement and objects. Next, we shall analyze the basic data types in Python and describe some of the simple input and code with the basic elements.

Learning Outcomes of this chapter

After completion of the chapter, the learner will be able to:

- List the rules of naming an identifier
- Identify the literals of different data types
- Differentiate between scalar and non-scalar objects
- Use input and output statements
- List the features of basic data types
- Recognize errors in Python code
- Critically evaluate a Python code for the provided functionality
- Develop simple programs based on the concepts discussed
- Distinguish between correct and incorrect program based on the concepts discussed.

4.2 IDENTIFIER

In Python, identifier is the name of an object. The object can be a variable, function, module, class or another object. Python follows some rules to define an identifier. The rules are stated as follows:

- Identifier is a combination of letters A–Z, a–z, underscore (_), and digits (0–9).
- Other characters like,), @, and % are not allowed for defining the identifier.
- The first character of identifier must be a letter or an underscore. The first character of an identifier cannot be a digit.
- Python is a case-sensitive language. Thus, identifiers are case-sensitive. SUM_TOTAL, sum_total, Sum_Total are three different identifiers.

The following identifiers are valid:

_sum, sum_total number1, n01, add_first_number

The following identifiers are invalid:

3Street, @45, root-node root node

4.2.1 Naming Convention for Identifiers

The Python language provides guidelines for the naming convention of identifiers. Some key points are stated as follows:

- Names should be easy to read. For example, sum_total is better read than sumtotal.
- Names may be chosen according to their use. For example, sum, fact, fib and marks are names than can identify with sum, factorial, Fibonacci, and marks, respectively.
- Descriptive names are useful instead of short ones. For example, last_name, first_name, insertValue are better than ln, fn and iV.
- Class names start with an uppercase letter. All other identifiers start with a lowercase letter.
- An identifier that starts with a single leading underscore indicates a private identifier.
- An identifier that starts with two leading underscores indicates a strongly private identifier.
- An identifier that starts with two leading and two trailing underscores indicates that the identifier is a language-defined special name.
- An identifier cannot be a reserved word (discussed in next section).

According to Google Python Style Guide (https://google.github.io/styleguide/pyguide.html), the naming convention for identifiers, some ways of naming identifiers are as follows:

- module_name, package_name, method_name, function_name, global_var_name, instance_var_name, function_parameter_name, local_var_name. For example, student_info, car_details.
- ClassName, ExceptionName. For example, TempEmployee, BankAccount.
- GLOBAL_CONSTANT_NAME. For example, STUD_COUNT, TOTAL_EMP.

4.3 KEYWORDS OR RESERVED WORDS

Keywords are reserved words of the Python language. The reserved words have a predefined meaning in Python and cannot be used as identifiers. There are 33 keywords in Python 3. However, this number may vary in course of time. Keywords are case sensitive. Table 4.1 shows the list of keywords.

Table 4.1 Keywords in Python

False	class	finally	is	return
None	continue	for	lambda	try
True	def	from	nonlocal	while
and	del	global	not	with
as	elif	if	or	yield
assert	else	import	pass	
break	except	in	raise	

Kindly note that all keywords except `True`, `False`, and `None` are in lowercase letters. `None` represents absence of value. The truth value represented by `None` is False

4.4 Built-in Data Type

A program, as we know, is a set of instructions for the computer to perform certain tasks or operations. While writing a program, we may need to use data on which certain operations can be performed. For example, a program may process numbers like, 2, 4, 2.3 or strings like "Good Morning" and many more. To understand the data, we must know an important concept of 'data type'.

Data type is defined as a set of values and a set of allowed operations on the values. A data type defines –

(1) values that the type of a data hold, and
(2) the operations that can be performed on the data of that type.

Python supports several built-in data types.

The data type in Python are of two types – Simple and Compound (Figure 4.1).

- **Simple Type** are the ones whose elements cannot be broken down further. The numeric type and Boolean data type are simple type. The numeric type consists of three data types – integer (`int`), float (`float`) and complex number (`complex`).
- **Compound Type** are the ones whose elements can be broken down further. It consists of the sequence type, set and dictionary. The sequence type consists of the three data types – string, list and tuple.

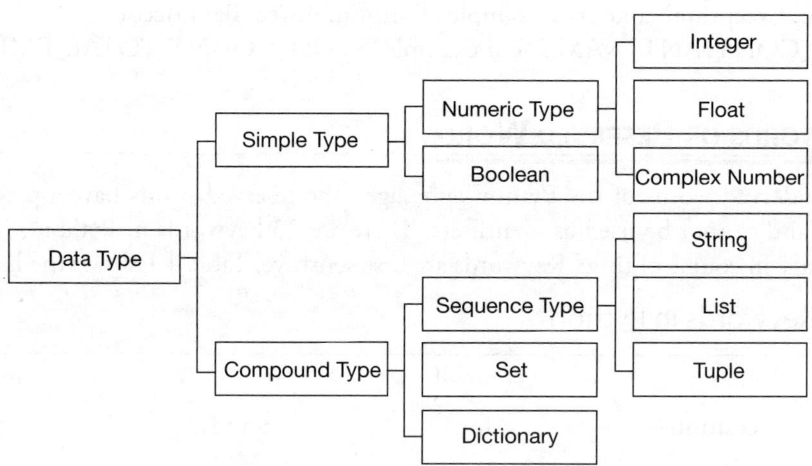

Figure 4.1 Common data types in Python.

Here, we discuss the simple type and introduce the string data type.

- **`int`** data type represents integers (e.g., 23, 45, 23242434).
- **`float`** data type represents floating-point numbers (e.g., 11.3, 6.02, 2e3).
- **`complex`** data type represents complex numbers (e.g., 3+1j, 6j).
- **`str`** data type represents string. A string may consist of a sequence of characters (e.g., "Hello", "12", "Good Morning").
- **`bool`** data type represents Boolean vales – `True` and `False`.

The data type provides a meaning to the data and defines operations by which the value of a data type can be stored and manipulated. Let us take the number 5; it is an integer and belongs to data type `int` in Python; whereas, string "Good" is of data type `str`. When we perform addition operation, the addition of integers returns an integer, 5 + 6 = 11; but, addition of two strings "Good" and "Morning" concatenates the two strings to give the output "Good Morning".

Python provides the above-defined basic built-in data type as part of the language. Thus, when you write a program, use the data type and perform operations on them, the Python language handles the operations; you, as a user, need not worry about how the operations are performed. Python also provides additional data types that are discussed in later chapters.

In Python, everything is an object. The built-in types like, int, float, bool, string, and complex are objects.

In addition to the built-in data types, Python also allows users to create their own data type. These are called user-defined data types. A user-defined data type is created by defining classes. They are used to create objects, which is an instance of the class. Chapter 13 of the book discusses the classes and objects in detail.

4.5 Literal or Constant

In Python, literal is a value. A value is a fundamental entity that a program manipulates. A literal is called so because its value is used literally. The value 8 is an integer and 1.1 is float and they represent themselves and nothing else, i.e., its value cannot be changed. So, they are referred to as literal or constant. The literals of different data types are – integer, float, complex, boolean and string.

4.5.1 Integer Literal

- `int` literal is a sequence of digits 0 to 9. It may also have a positive (+) or negative (–) sign. A literal without any sign is considered positive.
- Some examples of `int` literals are: 3, 89, 29999999, –45, –1.
- In Python, the range of values of type `int` is limited by the amount of memory on the computer system.

4.5.2 Float Literal

- Float literal is a sequence of digits with a decimal point.
- It may have a positive (+) or negative (–) sign with it. A literal without any sign is considered positive.
- Some examples of `float` literals are: 3.14, 89.0, 2.002, 45.34215.
- A `float` literal can also be represented in scientific notation. For example, 2.3e12 is the scientific notation of the number 2.3×10^{12}.

4.5.3 Complex Literal

- Complex numbers are written with a "j" as the imaginary part.
- Some examples of `complex` literals are: 3 + 4j, 2 + 5j, 5j.

4.5.4 Boolean Literal

- A *bool* literal is two values – `True` and `False`.
- True and False are both reserved words.
- A non-zero value is considered as True.
- A zero value is considered as False.

4.5.5 String Literal

- `str` literal is a sequence of characters enclosed in quotes.
- The quotes can be single quotes ('), double quotes (") or triple quotes ('''). However, the same type of quote must start and end a string.
- The triple quotes are used to span the string across multiple lines.
- The characters in a string can be digits, alphabets, symbols and whitespace characters. Some examples of whitespace characters are: newline ('\n') and, tab ('\t') including null.
- Two operations can be performed on strings:
  - **Concatenation:** The operator (+) is used to concatenate two or more strings. It appends one string at the end of another string. For example, "Good" + "Morning" will result in output "GoodMorning".
  - **Repetition:** The operator (*) is used for repetition. It repeats a string for a number of times. For example, "Good" * 4 will give "GoodGoodGoodGood".

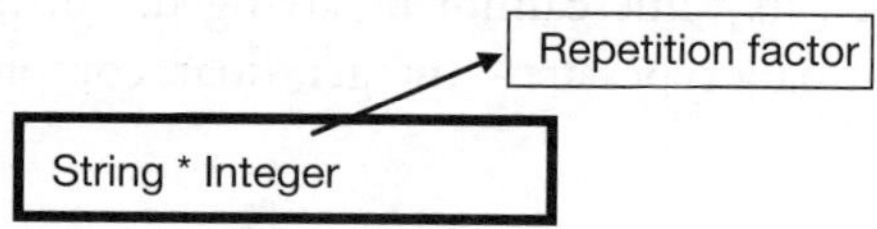

4.6 Variable, Operator, Expression

In Python, a **variable** is a name or identifier associated with a value. A variable is like a name tag that gets attached to a value. The value of a variable can change during computation. For example, a variable *x* can be assigned value 5, and then the same variable *x* can be assigned value 6. Programmers can choose the variable name. It is suggested to follow the Python Style Guide naming convention for variable names. Some examples of variables are: x, y, sum_total, subj_grade.

In Python, the **operator** defines an operation on a data type. For example, the operator + is used for addition. The data type *int* defines the addition operation to add integers, and data type `float` defines the addition operation to add float numbers. Likewise, for performing different operations, different operators are defined for different data types. The operators are discussed in detail in Chapter 5.

The literals, variables and operators combine to form an **expression**. For example, z = x – y is an expression. The expression is evaluated to get a value. The evaluation of the expression is done in accordance with the operator precedence rules. The expressions are discussed in detail in Chapter 5.

4.7 Assignment Statement

In Python, assignment statement is used for assigning value to a variable. An assignment statement defines an identifier as a variable and a value of a data type is associated to the variable. The syntax of simple assignment statement is:

variable = expression

The sign "equal to" (=) is an assignment operator. This is not equality but assignment operator. To the left of = sign is the variable and to the right of = sign is the value stored in the variable.

An example of assignment statement is as follows:

x = 5

In the above statement,

- 5 is a value of `int` data type
- = is the assignment operator
- x is a variable assigned a value 5

Some key properties of assignment statement are:

- An assignment *creates a reference to value* instead of copying the value. So, variables are like pointers.

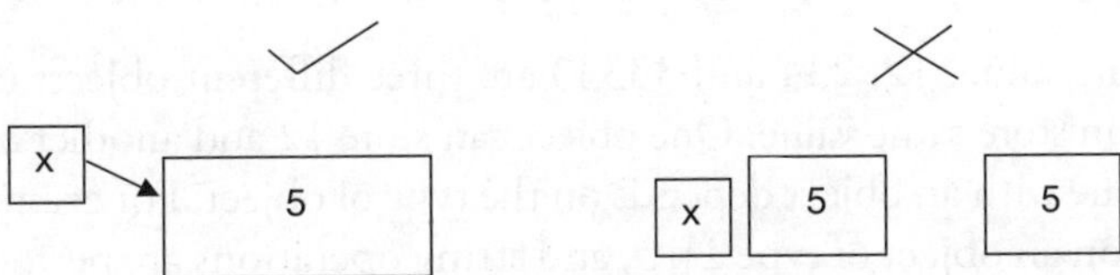

- In Python, variables do not have to be declared explicitly. The declaration happens automatically during assignment. During the assignment, Python creates the variable name. There is no need to pre-define the variable.

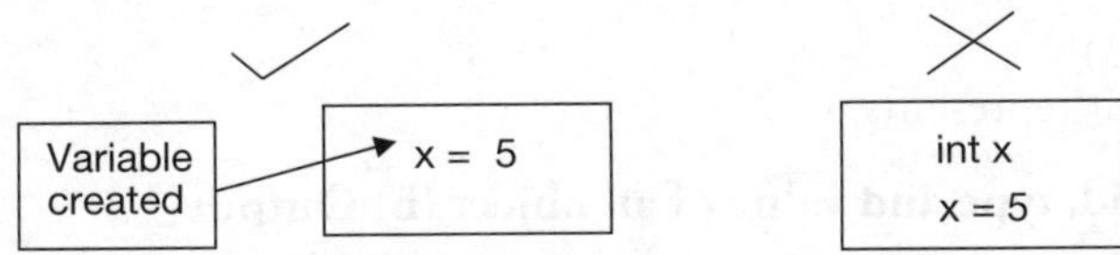

- The variable names must be assigned a value before they are used. Otherwise, an exception is raised. For example, $y = x + 5$ will result in an exception since x does not have a value.
- In an assignment statement, the left side must be a single variable. The right side is an expression (discussed in Chapter 5). The expression on the right side is first evaluated and the value generated is associated to the left-side variable.

  Examples of correct assignment statement are:
  $a = 12$
  $x = y + 5$
  Examples of incorrect assignment statement are:
  $12 = a$
  $x + y = 5$

- Python allows assigning single value to multiple variables in a single statement. For example, $x = y = z = 5$.
  Here, value 5 is assigned to variables x, y and z.
- Python allows assigning multiple values to multiple variables in a single statement. For example, x, y, a = 5, 10.2, "Hello".
  Here, values 5 and 10.2 are assigned to variables x and y, respectively, and string "Hello" is assigned to variable a.

4.8 Object

Python is an object-oriented programming language. Object is the basic building block in object-oriented language. An object has an identity, type and value.

- ***Identity*** is unique for an object. It is the memory address where the object is stored.
- ***Type*** defines behavior of the object. It defines values that an object of a type represents and the set of operations that can be performed on the object.
- ***Value*** of an object is the value it represents.

In Python programs, all data values are represented by objects. Since value is of a data type, an object is representation of value from a data type. Some properties of objects are as follows:

- An object stores one value. 12, 234 and 33333 are three different objects of type `int`.
- Different objects can store same value. One object can store 12 and another object can also store 12.
- What all can be done with an object depends on the type of object. For example, integer operations can be performed on an object of type `int`, and string operations are performed on object of type `str`.

In Python, we can find the identity, type and value of an object as follows:

- `id` (object) for Identity
- `type` (object) for Type
- `Value` is the value it represents.

Example 4.1: (a) Print id, type and value of an object (b) Output

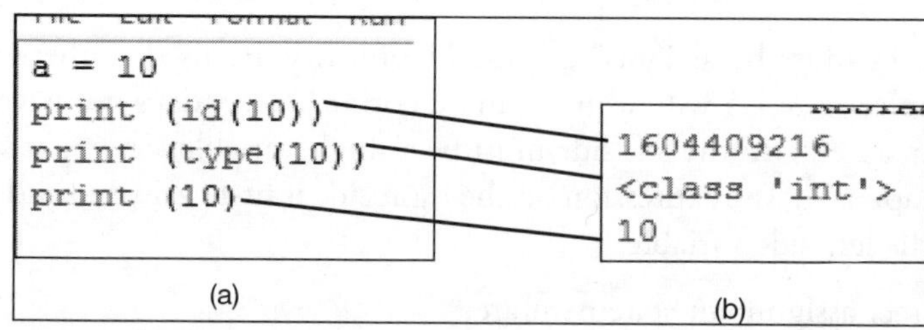

In Python, a variable refers to an object. The steps taken by Python language when we write a statement

$a = 10$

are as follows:

- An object is created with literal or value 10.
- The object with value 10 has a unique identifier (unique storage location in memory).
- The variable named '*a*' refers to the object 10. The variable gets bound to the object by the assignment statement. (The left side of assignment gets bound to the value on right side.)
- The type of object is *int*, because object 10 is an integer.
- Operations of type integer can be performed on the object, like, add, subtract.

Figure 4.2 is a diagrammatic representation of object and its reference variable.

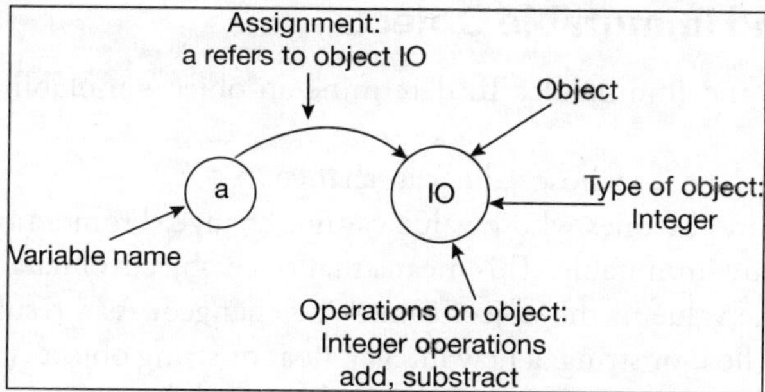

Figure 4.2 Object and reference variable

In Python, the size in bytes occupied by the different data types is much higher than the size of a data type in C or C++. This is because in Python, everything is an object. So, it has its overheads of maintaining an object. We can use the function *getsizeof()* (discussed in later chapters) to get the size of any data type. In Python, the data types themselves are considered as objects. Thus, data type *int* is also an object.

In Example 4.2 (do not worry about the code, see output values), we see that for the assigned data, *int* occupies 12 bytes, *float* 16 bytes and *string* 26 bytes, in a 64-bit machine on which Python 3.6 is installed.

Example 4.2: (a) Size of data types (b) Output

```
import sys
d = {
      "int": 0,
      "float": 0.0,
      "str": "a",
      "object": object(),
 }
for k, v in sorted(d.items()):
      print (k, sys.getsizeof(v))
```

(a)

```
float 16
int 12
object 8
str 26
```

(b)

4.8.1 Scalar and Non-scalar Objects

Objects can be scalar and non-scalar.

- ***Scalar object*** cannot be divided further. Objects of built-in data types – int, float, bool and None are scalar objects. Some examples of scalar objects are:
  - o −3, 5, 2001 (objects of type int)

- o 3.0, 67.4, −33.4, 8.2E−3 3.4E−5 (objects of type float).
- o True, False (objects of type bool)
- o None is a single value

- ***Non-scalar objects*** can be decomposed further. Objects of built-in data type `str` are non-scalar objects. Some examples are: "good", "Hello Students" and "Beautiful". The strings can be further decomposed like, "go", "o", "d", "Hello", "Students", "Beauti", "ful".

4.8.2 Mutable and Immutable Objects

Objects can be mutable and immutable. To determine an object's mutability, we have to check its data type.

Mutable objects are the ones whose value can change.

Immutable objects are the ones whose value cannot change. From among the basic data types, `int`, `float` and `str` are immutable. This means that once objects of data types `int`, `float` and `str` type are created, the value of the object cannot be changed. As a result, when an operation is performed using integer, float or string, a new integer, float or string object is created. Example 4.3 (a) shows the code. We see that integer value 10 is assigned to *x* and then integer value 30 is assigned to *x*. In Example 4.3 (b) we see that the id of *x* is different for both assignments. So, when a value assigned to a variable is changed, it results in a new variable, and the value of existing variable does not change. Thus, we see that data type `int` is immutable.

Example 4.3: (a) Show immutable objects (b) Output

```
x = 10
print("id(x)= ", id(x))
y = 20
print("id(y)= ", id(y))
x = 30
print("id(x)= ", id(x))
```

(a)

```
id(x)=  1753900352
id(y)=  1753900512
id(x)=  1753900672
```

(b)

4.9 Simple Input Output

When writing a Python program, there is a need to show the result of the program to the user. Also, there may be a need to get input from the user. Python has built-in functions to support the input and output functionality (Functions are discussed in detail in later chapters).

We discuss two functions here:

- Print function – shows output on the screen, and
- Input function – accepts input from the user keyboard.

4.9.1 Output Statement

For output, print function is used. A simple print statement has name of the function "print", followed by parameters to be printed in parenthesis. The syntax of `print()` function is as follows:

```
print ("objects, sep='', end='\n', file=sys.stdout, flush=False)
```

where,
`objects` are values to be printed.
`sep` is separator between objects. By default, it is space character ‘’.
`'\n'` is newline. After printing all values, end the statement. By default, it is newline.
`sys.stdout` is default standard output device, i.e., screen.
(Flush will be explained in later chapters)

The `print()` statement prints an empty line in the output. It is used for showing blank lines in the output. Example 4.4 shows Python code with print statement: (1) Print with string object, (2) Print with string and variable, (3) Print with string, variable and string, (4) Print a blank line, and (5) Print integer objects, string and separator. Figure 4.6 (b) shows output after execution of the code.

Example 4.4: (a) Show using the Print statement (b) Output

```
print('This is my brief introduction')
name = 'Ashima'
print('My name is ', name)
print('I am beautiful')
a = 18
print('I am ', a, 'years old')
print()      #prints a blank line in output
print(2,4, 'are my lucky numbers',sep=' and ')
```


(a)

```
This is my brief introduction
My name is  Ashima
I am beautiful
I am  18 years old

2 and 4 and are my lucky numbers
>>> |
```

(b)

4.9.2 Input Statement

For taking input from the user, input function is used. A simple input statement has the name of the function “input”, followed by parenthesis. The syntax of `input()` function is as follows:

```
input([prompt])
```

where, `prompt` is a string to be displayed on the screen. It is optional to specify a prompt.

When input statement is executed, the prompt is displayed on the screen, and it waits for the user action. For example, an input statement a= input (‘Enter your age’), when executed, will display the prompt ‘Enter your age’ and wait for the user to enter the data. Example 4.5 (a) shows a Python code with input statement and (b) shows the output after execution of the code.

Example 4.5: (a) Using input statement (b) Output

```
print('This is my brief introduction')
name = input('=====Enter your name')
print('My name is ', name)
print('I am beautiful')
a = input('======Enter your age')
print('I am ', a, 'years old')
print()      #prints a blank line in output
print(2,4, 'are my lucky numbers',sep=' and ')
```

(a)

```
This is my brief introduction
=====Enter your nameAnita
My name is  Anita
I am beautiful
======Enter your age18
I am  18 years old

2 and 4 and are my lucky numbers
>>>
```

(b)

It must be noted that Python accepts all inputs as strings. To get the integer value or float value, the user must convert the string into `int` or `float`. For example, to convert the input to integer, the type conversion `int` is used, i.e., int(input("Enter ")). So, whenever you input a number as a string, int converts the string into an integer.

Example 4.6. (a) Input Integer conversion (b) Output

```
a = input("enter")
print(type(a))

a = int(input("enter"))
print(type(a))
```

(a)

```
enter2
<class 'str'>
enter2
<class 'int'>
```

(b)

4.10 Writing a Program (Python Syntax)

A program written in Python is easy to read. When writing a program, a set of rules defined for the programming language, also called the syntax, have to be followed. The syntax of Python language is discussed in the following subsections.

4.10.1 Python Lines – Logical, Physical, Blank

On Python IDLE, each new line is a physical line. Physical line is a sequence of characters that is terminated by an end-of-line sequence. The end-of-line can be carriage return (CR), line feed (LF) or return/enter. Implicitly, Python assumes that a physical line corresponds to a logical line.

- **One Physical line, One Logical line:** One statement of Python (logical) is written in one physical line. Python code (1) in Example 4.7 shows that each physical line has one logical statement.
- **Multiline – One Logical line, Many Physical lines – Use backslash (\):** When writing a program, a single Python statement may be spread across multiple physical lines. The complete statement in different physical lines forms a logical line of Python. A logical line is created from one or more physical lines. Every logical line terminates with a newline character. The Python code (2) shown in Example 4.7 shows one logical statement spread across multiple physical lines by using the backslash at the end of the physical line.
- **One Physical line, Many Logical lines – Use semicolon (;):** When writing a program, more than one Python statement (logical line) may be on one physical line. To specify more than one logical statement on a single physical line, use semicolon (;) at the end of a logical statement. The Python code (3) in Example 4.7 shows that in one physical line there are two logical statements separated by semicolon.

Implicitly, it is suggested to use a single statement per line, as it makes the codes more readable.

Example 4.7: (a) Logical and Physical Lines (b) Output

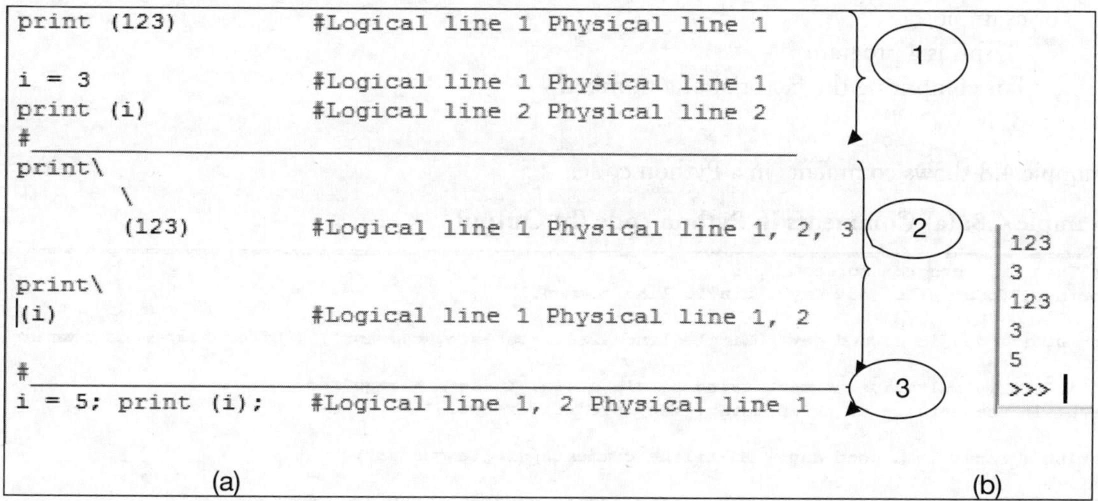

Blank line is a line having only whitespaces, tabs, form feeds, or a comment. Python interpreter ignores the blank line. When writing a Python code, if you press <Enter> key without writing on the line, a blank line is inserted in the code.

4.10.2 Comment

Comment is a text written in English with a purpose of describing the task that the code will perform. Comments are important while writing a program. The comments in a code make it easy for other programmers to understand the code. The comments help the author to understand the code months later, when they might forget the details of the program.

During execution of Python program, the interpreter ignores the comments. The comments do not affect working of the program. A comment can also be after a statement. There can be multiple comments in a single program.

In Python, there are two ways to write a comment:

1. Single-line comment
2. Multi-line comment

Single-line comment

- Single-line comment starts with hash (#) symbol.
- It is used for writing short comments.
- Everything after the hash is considered as a comment up to end of the physical line or the newline character.
- For example,
  # This is a factorial program.

Multi-line comment

- Multi-line comment starts with three single quotes (‘‘‘) and ends with three single quotes (’’’), or, start with three double quotes (“““) and end with three double quotes (”””).
- It is used for writing detailed description in the code, spread across multiple lines.
- For example,
  ‘‘‘ This is a program
  For computing the factorial of a number.
  3! Is 3*2*1’’’

Example 4.8 shows comments in a Python code.

Example 4.8: (a) Comments in Python code (b) Output

```
# This is a program for comments
print ("Today is a good day - Single line comment")

print ("Today is a good day - Single line after statement comment") # after statement comment

''' This is multiline comment using single quote. These are required to
explain the details of the program. They are not executed'''

print ("Today is a good day - Multiline comments single quotes")

""" This is for multiline comments using double quotes. These are required to
explain the details of the program. They are not executed"""

print ("Today is a good day - Multiline comments double quotes")
```

(a)

```
Today is a good day - Single line comment
Today is a good day - Single line after statement comment
Today is a good day - Multiline comments single quotes
Today is a good day - Multiline comments double quotes
>>>
```

(b)

4.10.3 Indentation

Most programming languages like C, C++, Java use braces { } to define a block of code for class, function definitions and control flow statements. Python does not use braces for defining a block of code. Python uses indentation. Indentation is enforced rigidly.

- A block of code starts with indentation and ends with the first un-indented statement.
- The number of spaces in indentation is not fixed. The programmer can choose the number of spaces.
- Statements that are together must have same indentation.
- Within a block, all statements must be indented to the same extent. Alternatively, all statements on consecutive lines indented with the same number of spaces form a block.
- Generally, four whitespaces are used for indentation and is preferred over tab.

Let us see some examples of indentation.

Example 4.9 shows that a program with wrong indentation, when run, gives syntax error. From this error, it is noted that in the program, a block cannot be started arbitrarily. Blocks should follow some rules, which will be discussed in later chapters.

Example 4.9: Incorrect indentation and syntax error

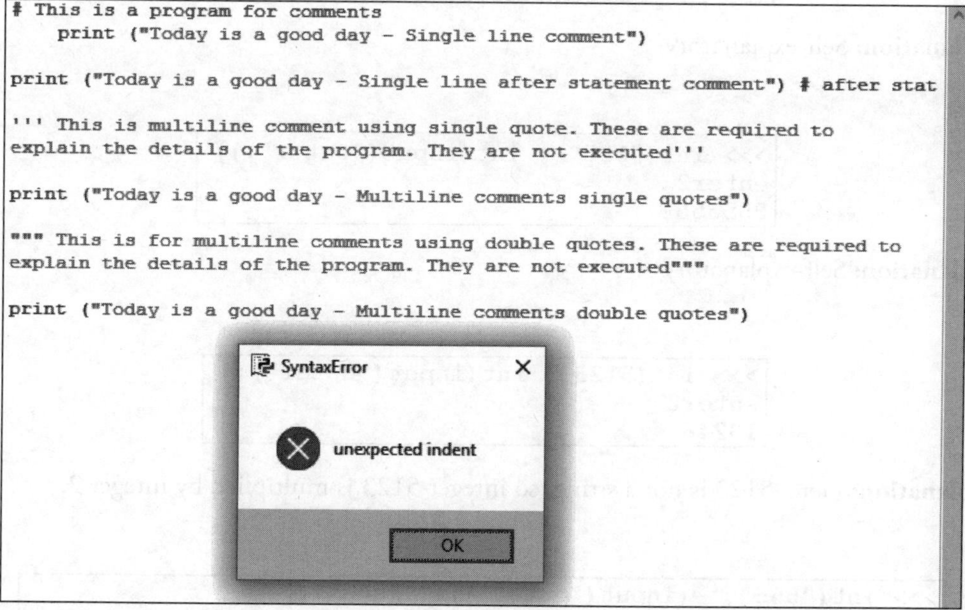

4.11 Solved Questions with Explanation

1) Find the output:

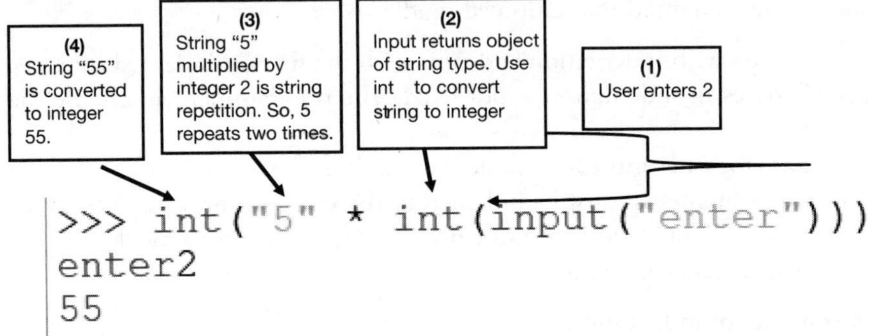

2)

```
>>> int("55" * int(input("enter")))
enter2
5555
```

Explanation: Self-explanatory

3)

```
>>> int("555" * int(input("enter")))
enter2
555555
```

Explanation: Self-explanatory

4)

```
>>> int(5123 * int(input("enter")))
enter2
10246
```

Explanation: Here, 5123 is not a string, so integer 5123 is multiplied by integer 2.

5)

```
>>> int("555" * (input("enter")))
enter2
Traceback (most recent call last):
  File "<pyshell#21>", line 1, in <module>
    int("555" * (input("enter")))
TypeError: can't multiply sequence by non-int of type 'str'
```

Explanation: Here, the input is not converted into type `int`. So, the input is of type string. A string cannot be replicated by a string. So it shows error.

6)

```
IO
>>> float("456" * int(input("enter")))
enter4
456456456456.0
```

Explanation: Here, string 456 is replicated 4 times. Then it is represented as `float`.

7)

```
>>> str("456" * int(input("enter")))
enter4
'456456456456'
```

Explanation: Here, string 456 is replicated 4 times. Then it is represented as `string`.

8)

```
>>> int("456" * int(input("enter")))
entera
Traceback (most recent call last):
  File "<pyshell#30>", line 1, in <module>
    int("456" * int(input("enter")))
ValueError: invalid literal for int() with base 10: 'a'
>>> |
```

Explanation: Here, the user has entered a string "a". A string cannot be replicated by a string. So it shows error. The error is in the input value.

9)

```
>>> int(2 * input("enter"))
enter4
44
```

Explanation: Here, the input is a string 4. It is not converted into `int`. So, the string 4 is replicated 2 times.

10)

```
>>> int(456 * input("enter"))
enter2
22222222222222222222222222222222222222222222222222222222222222222222222222222222
22222222222222222222222222222222222222222222222222222222222222222222222222222222
22222222222222222222222222222222222222222222222222222222222222222222222222222222
22222222222222222222222222222222222222222222222222222222222222222222222222222222
22222222222222222222222222222222222222222222222222222222222222222222222222222222
22222222222222222222222222222222222222222222222222222222
```

Explanation: Here, the input is a string 2. It is not converted into `int`. So, the string 2 is replicated 456 times.

11)

```
a = "Hello"
b = "learner"
c = (a + b *4)
print(c)
```

```
Hellolearnerlearnerlearnerlearner
```

Explanation: Here, only b is reapeated 4 times and a only once.

12)

```
a = "Hello"
b = "learner"
d = ((a + b) * 4)
print(d)
```

```
HellolearnerHellolearnerHellolearnerHellolearner
```

Explanation: Here, both a and b are concatenated and then repeated 4 times.

13) Find the output (for the codes in the left column).

Code	Output and explanation
>>> "3" + 9	Error. Cannot add string and integer
>>> "23" * 2	2323
>>> "78" + "56"	7856
>>> "23" * "2"	Error. Cannot replicate a string with a non-int
>>> "23" + "abc"	23abc
>>> "23" * "abc"	Error. Cannot replicate a string with a non-int
>>> 3 + 4.5	7.5
>>> 4.3 * "abc"	Error. Cannot replicate a string with a non-int of type float
>>> 4.3 + 4e1	44.3
>>> 22 * 2.0	44.0

14) Identify the type of literals.

Literal	Type
>>> 33	<int>
>>> 23.1	<float>
>>> True	<bool>
>>> 2e3	<float>
>>> "Good"	<str>
>>> 'Good'	<str>
>>> Good	Not a literal
>>> 234.123	<float>

4.12 PROGRAMMING EXAMPLES

In this section, a few sample programs are given with their output.

Program 4.1: Program to print "Hello!" on the screen.

```
# Program to print "Hello!" on the screen
print ("Hello!")
```

Output

```
Hello!
```

Program 4.2: Accept the name of the user and print "Hello" with the user name.

```
# Accept name of the user and print Hello with the user name
print("\n====================================")
name = input("Enter your name ")
print("Hello", name)
print("\n====================================")
```

Output

```
====================================
Enter your name Anirudh
Hello Anirudh

====================================
```

Program 4.3: Accept the name of the user, and print 5 sentences for the user.

```
#Accept name of the user, and print 5 sentences for the user
name = input("\nEnter your name ")
print("\n===================================")
print("Hello", name)
print(name, "you are beautiful")
print(name, "you are intelligent")
print(name, "you are a good programmer")
print(name, "it seems you love Python")
print("\n===================================")
```

Output

```
Enter your name Ashima

===================================
Hello Ashima
Ashima you are beautiful
Ashima you are intelligent
Ashima you are a good programmer
Ashima it seems you love Python

===================================
```

Program 4.4: Accept the details of the user and print his/her details.

```
# Accept the details of the user and print their details
name = input("\nEnter your name ")
age = input("Enter your age ")
qual = input("Enter your qualification ")
course = input("Enter your course ")
print("\n===================================")
print("Name:            ", name)
print("Age:             ", age)
print("Qualification: ", qual)
print("Course:          ", course)
print("===================================")
```

Output

```
Enter your name Ashima
Enter your age 20
Enter your qualification B.Tech (Computer Science)
Enter your course Bachelor in Computer Science

===================================
Name:            Ashima
Age:             20
Qualification:   B.Tech (Computer Science)
Course:          Bachelor in Computer Science
===================================
```

Program 4.5: Print all vowels in the output.

```
# Print all vowels in the output
print("Vowels in English are - a, e, i, o, u")
```

Output

```
Vowels in English are - a, e, i, o, u
```

Program 4.6: Accept four integers from the user. Print them in separate lines using (1) 4-print statements (2) single-print statement.

```
# Accept 4 integers from the user. Print them in separate lines using
#(1) 4 print statements (2) single print statement

int1 = input("Enter first integer")
int2 = input("Enter second integer")
int3 = input("Enter third integer")
int4 = input("Enter fourth integer")
print("\n===================================")
print(int1)
print(int2)
print(int3)
print(int4)
print("The integers are:\n", int1,"\n", int2, "\n", int3, "\n", int4)
print("\n===================================")
```

Output

```
Enter first integer5
Enter second integer6
Enter third integer7
Enter fourth integer8

===================================
5
6
7
8
The integers are:
 5
 6
 7
 8

===================================
```

Program 4.7: Accept two strings from the user and print it as a single string with a space.

```
# Accept two strings from the user and print it as a single string with a space.

str1 = input("Enter your first name ")
str2 = input("Enter your last name ")
print("Your name is", str1, str2)
print("\n===================================")
```

Output

```
Enter your first name Ashima
Enter your last name Goel
Your name is Ashima Goel

================================
```

Program 4.8: Accept an integer from the user. Print its id, type and value.

```
# Accept an integer from user. Print its id, type and value
int1 = input("Enter an integer number ")
print("\n================================")
print("Id=", id(int1))
print("Type=", type(int1))
print("Please note that input() accepts input as a string")
print("Value=", int1)
print("\n================================")
```

Output

```
Enter an integer number 34

================================
Id= 63736928
Type= <class 'str'>
Please note that input() accepts input as a string
Value= 34

================================
```

Program 4.9: Accept a string from the user. Print its id, type and value.

```
# Accept a string from user. Print its id, type and value
s1 = input("Enter a String ")
print("\n================================")
print("Id=", id(s1))
print("Type=", type(s1))
print("Value=", s1)
print("\n================================")
```

Output

```
Enter a String Hello Students

================================
Id= 63812016
Type= <class 'str'>
Value= Hello Students

================================
```

Program 4.10: Accept a float value from the user. Print its id, type and value.

```
# Accept a Float value from user. Print its id, type and value
f1 = input("Enter Float value ")
print("\n=================================")
print("Id=", id(f1))
print("Type=", type(f1))
print("Value=", f1)
print("\n=================================")
```

Output

```
Enter Float value 3.23

=================================
Id= 63736992
Type= <class 'str'>
Value= 3.23

=================================
```

Program 4.11: Accept two strings from the user. Concatenate the two strings.

```
# Accept two strings from the user. Concatenate the two strings
s1 = input("Enter a String ")
s2 = input("Enter second string")
print("\n=================================")
print(s1 + s2)
print("\n=================================")
```

Output

```
Enter a String Environment
Enter second stringDay

=================================
EnvironmentDay

=================================
```

Program 4.12: Accept a string from the user and repeat it five times.

```
# Accept a string from the user and repeat it five times

s1 = input("Enter a String ")
print("\n=================================")
print("The user string repeated five times is as follows-")
print(s1 * 5)
print("\n=================================")
```

Output

```
Enter a String Happy

================================
The user string repeated five times is as follows-
HappyHappyHappyHappyHappy

================================
```

Program 4.13: Accept words from the user that describe him/her positively. Take the words from the user and print it with "I AM" followed by the word. (E.g., I AM strong.)

```
#Accept words from the user that describe them positively.
#Take the words from the user and print it with "I AM" followed by the word.
#(E.g. I AM strong)

s1 = input("Enter First word that describes you positively ")
s2 = input("Enter Second word that describes you positively ")
s3 = input("Enter Third word that describes you positively ")
s4 = input("Enter Fourth word that describes you positively ")
s5 = input("Enter Fifth word that describes you positively ")

print("\n================================")
print("I AM", s1)
print("I AM", s2)
print("I AM", s3)
print("I AM", s4)
print("I AM", s5)
print("\n================================")
```

Output

```
Enter First word that describes you positively Strong
Enter Second word that describes you positively Beautiful
Enter Third word that describes you positively Happy
Enter Fourth word that describes you positively Honest
Enter Fifth word that describes you positively Success

================================
I AM Strong
I AM Beautiful
I AM Happy
I AM Honest
I AM Success

================================
```

Program 4.14: Accept the name of the user. Accept five things that they like to eat. Display output in five lines as- "XYZ likes to eat PQR".

```
#Accept the name of the user.
#Accept five things they like eating the most.
#Display a sentence"user name  likes eating ___momos"

n1 = input("Enter your name ")
s1 = input("Enter First thing you like to eat ")
s2 = input("Enter Second thing you like to eat ")
s3 = input("Enter Third thing you like to eat ")
s4 = input("Enter Fourth thing you like to eat ")
s5 = input("Enter Fifth thing you like to eat ")

print("\n==================================")
print(n1, "likes to eat", s1)
print(n1, "likes to eat", s2)
print(n1, "likes to eat", s3)
print(n1, "likes to eat", s4)
print(n1, "likes to eat", s5)
print("\n==================================")
```

Output

```
Enter your name Prachi
Enter First thing you like to eat momos
Enter Second thing you like to eat noodles
Enter Third thing you like to eat rajma-chawal
Enter Fourth thing you like to eat chat-papri
Enter Fifth thing you like to eat gulab jamun

==================================
Prachi likes to eat momos
Prachi likes to eat noodles
Prachi likes to eat rajma-chawal
Prachi likes to eat chat-papri
Prachi likes to eat gulab jamun

==================================
```

Program 4.15: Show a menu that allows a user to select the operations performed using calculator.

```
#Show a menu that allows a user to select the operations
#performed using calculator.

print("\n==================================")
print("The operation perfored using calculator are as follows-")
print("1. Addition\n2. Subtraction\n3. Multiplication\n4. Division")
s1 = input("\nEnter your choice (1-4)")
print("\nYou selected ", s1)
print("Goodbye")
print("\n==================================")
```

Output

```
====================================
The operation perfored using calculator are as follows-
1. Addition
2. Subtraction
3. Multiplication
4. Division

Enter your choice (1-4)3

You selected  3
Goodbye

====================================
```

Program 4.16: Define values of different data types and assign variables to them.

```
a = p = q = 10
s1, s2, s3 = "Rahul's roll number", 2, "is lucky number"
b = 2.5
c = "Good Morning"
d = "Student"
e = "Hello! you are so smart"

print ("a=", a)
print ("p=", p)
print ("q=", q)
print ("s1, s2, s3=", s1, s2, s3)
print ("b=", b)
print ("c=", c)
print ("d=", d)
print ("e=", e)
```

Output

```
a= 10
p= 10
q= 10
s1, s2, s3= Rahul's roll number 2 is lucky number
b= 2.5
c= Good Morning
d= Student
e= Hello! you are so smart
>>> |
```

Program 17: Define string literals and perform operations on them.

```
a = "Hello"
b = 'Students'
c = a + b
d = (a + b) * 3
print ("a (Double quotes)=", a, "\nb (single quotes)=", b,
        "\nc (Concatenation)=", c , "\nd (Repetition)=", d)
e = """The quotes in string can be of the following types
    1. Single quotes
    2. Double quotes
    3. Triple quotes   """
print (e)
```

Output

```
a (Double quotes)= Hello
b (single quotes)= Students
c (Concatenation)= HelloStudents
d (Repetition)= HelloStudentsHelloStudentsHelloStudents
The quotes in string can be of the following types
        1. Single quotes
        2. Double quotes
        3. Triple quotes
>>> |
```

SUMMARY

- A data type defines the set of values, and the operations that can be performed on the values.
- `int`, `float`, `str`, `bool` and `None` are basic built-in data types in Python.
- The value of a data type is a literal.
- Operators are used for performing operations on a data type.
- An identifier defines a name. There are rules and naming conventions for defining identifiers.
- Python has 33 keywords.
- Variable is a name associated with a value. It is not predefined or declared explicitly.
- Expression is a combination of literals, variables and operators.
- Assignment statement assigns value to a variable.
- Object is the basic building block in Python. Object has identity, type and value.
- A variable refers to an object.
- Objects can be scalar or non-scalar objects.
- Objects whose value can change are mutable objects; others are immutable objects.
- The `int` data type represents integers, `float` represents floating-point numbers and `str` represents string.
- String concatenation can be performed using (+) operator.
- String repetition can be performed using (*) operator.
- A bool literal is True and False.

- None is an object that represents absence of value.
- Print function is used for showing output on the screen.
- Input function is used for taking input from the user.
- Python syntax defines rules that have to be followed while writing a program.
- Python defines a new line as a physical line.
- A Python statement spread across different physical lines forms a logical line.
- Python allows writing multiple logical lines in a single physical line using semicolon (;) and one logical line in multiple physical lines using backslash (\).
- Blank line is ignored by the Python interpreter.
- Comments in Python program describe the program. They are ignored by the interpreter.
- Comments can be in a single line or in multiple lines.
- Python uses indentation for defining a block of code.

Keywords

Reserved word
Naming convention
Variable
Expression
Assignment statement
Object
Scalar objects
Non-scalar objects
Mutable objects
Immutable objects
Integers
String
Boolean
Python syntax
Physical line
Logical line
Multiline
Blank line
Comments
Single-line comment
Multi-line comment
Indentation
Data type
Literal
Value
Operator
Identifier

Programming Language Keywords

```
int
float
str
bool
None
True
False
id (object)
print()
input()
type (object)
String concatenation (+)
String repetition (*)
```

ASSESSMENT

A.1 Bloom Level: Knowledge/Remember

Review Questions

1. Define the following:

a) Data type b) Literal
c) Identifier d) Variable
e) Expression f) Assignment
g) Object h) Physical line
i) Logical line j) Comment

2. Name the basic built-in data types in Python.

3. Give three examples each, of valid values of data type `int`, `float`, `string`.

4. What is the value of type `None`?

5. What is the value of type `bool`?

6. What is the value of 2.3e6?

7. State the rules for defining identifiers.

8. What is the meaning of Python syntax?

9. Match the operator with their use:

	Operator		**Used for**
1	=	a	String concatenation
2	singe quote (')	b	Multi-line comment
3	Triple quote (''')	c	Assignment
4	+	d	Multiple logical lines in single physical line
5	*	e	one logical line in multiple physical lines
6	Semicolon (;)	f	String literal
7	#	g	String repetition
8	\	h	Single-line comment

Fill in the blanks

1. ________ and __________ are the two values of bool data type.

2. There are _______ keywords in Python.

3. _______, _________ and _________ combine to form an expression.

4. The set of operations that can be performed on an object is defined using _______ of object.

5. <class 'int'> is ______ of object.

6. Based on decomposition, objects are identified as _______ objects and _______ objects.

7. _____ objects are the ones whose value can change.

8. The ______ data type represents integers.

9. The ______ data type represents floating-point numbers.

10. The ______ data type represents strings.

11. The __________ quotes are used to span string across multiple lines.

12. ________ is the newline character.

13. The truth value of None is ________.

14. _______ function is used for showing output to the user.

15. ________ function is used to accept input from the user.

16. ________ is the default separator between objects in a print function.

17. _______ character is used to display one logical line in many physical lines.

18. _____ symbol is used for writing one Python statement in many logical lines.

19. ____ line and ______ line are the two ways of writing comments.

20. ____ symbol is used for writing single-line comment.

21. _______ single quotes or double quotes are used for writing multi-line comment.

22. _____________ is used for defining a block of code.

State True/False

1. Bool data type is for a sequence of characters called strings.
2. 45 is a floating-point number.
3. 2, 2.0 and –2 are valid integers.
4. The value of a literal cannot be changed.
5. Reserved words are case-sensitive
6. 3sum is a valid identifier.
7. A variable is a name tag attached to a value.
8. An assignment statement creates a copy of the value instead of referencing to the value.
9. In Python, variables are pre-defined.
10. Different objects can store the same value.
11. None is a scalar object.
12. Objects of `int`, `float` and `str` are immutable.
13. "*" is a string concatenation operator.
14. A zero means True.
15. None represents absence of value.
16. A single Python statement cannot be written on multiple physical lines.
17. i=5; y=3 is a valid Python syntax.
18. Comments affect the working of a Python program.
19. The number of spaces in indentation is fixed.

A.2 Bloom Level: Comprehend/Understand

Review Questions

1. Describe the naming convention for identifiers.
2. Describe syntax of: (a) Print function (b) Input function.
3. Explain how a literal is different from a variable.
4. What is the difference between 5 and x=5?
5. Identify the identifier names that are correct:
   a) A1 b) a1
   c) _a d) @a1
   e) %a1 f))a1
   g) A1@ h) A1%
   i) A1) j) Aa11
   k) _aaa
6. Segregate reserved words from the keywords:
   a) def b) defn
   c) for d) formula
   e) lambda f) lamb
   g) while h) wiley
   i) None j) none
   k) Def l) fore
7. Identify the scalar and non-scalar objects:
   a) 10.2 b) 10
   c) "10.2" d) '10'

Multiple Choice Questions (MCQ)

1. Identify the odd one out:
   (i) 2.0 (ii) −3.14
   (iii) 2 (iv) 13e3

2. End of line cannot be ______.
   (i) CR (Carriage return)
   (ii) LF (Line Feed)
   (iii) Return/Enter
   (iv) Tab

A.3 Bloom Level: Application/Apply

Review Questions

1. Identify the literals, type of literals and variables used in the following statements. Name the type of expression used in the third statement, the operators used in each statement and binding of objects in the following statements.

```
x = 55
y = 2
z = x – y
```

2. For the statement: S = "Good Morning", identify the object and type of object. Also identify some operations that can be performed on object, variable name and operator name

3. If a = 10.6, what is the (1) type of object, and (2) value it represents?

4. What will be the output when the following assignment statements are executed?
   a) x = 5
   b) 5 = x
   c) x = "this is green"
   d) x, y = 2
   e) x, y = 2, 4
   f) x, y = "2", 2
   g) x = a + 5
   h) x = y = z = 5
   i) x, y, a, b = 2, 4
   j) x=2=y=2

Multiple Choice Questions (MCQ)

1. Select the character not allowed in an identifier:
   (i) a (ii) 9
   (iii) @ (iv) _ (underscore)

2. Find the incorrect identifier:
   (i) SUM (ii) Sum
   (iii) sum2 (iv) 2sum

3. Identify the correct assignment:
   (i) 6 = a (ii) a + b =5
   (iii) 6 – x = a (iv) x = y + 5

4. Find the non-scalar object:
   (i) −10 (ii) 5.67
   (iii) "Hello" (iv) True

5. Find the invalid integer:
   (i) 5 (ii) −5
   (iii) +5 (iv) 5.0

6. Find the invalid float:
   (i) 5.0 (ii) −5.0
   (iii) −5e3 (iv) 5

7. The output of "Bless You" * 2 is:
   (i) Bless YouBless You
   (ii) BlessBless YouYou
   (iii) Bless You*2
   (iv) Error

A.4 Bloom Level: Analyze

1. Consider the following statements:
   a) x = 5 ------(1)
      y = 10
      x = 2 -------(2)
   b) y = "Apple"
      x = "Banana" ------(1)
      x = "Carrot" -------(2)
   Is the variable x in statement (1) and (2) the same variable? Justify your answer.
2. What is the similarity or difference between the three variables – Add, ADD and add?
3. What is the difference between the following variables:
   a) _sum b) _ _sum c) _ _sum_ _
4. Differentiate between the following:
   (a) Scalar objects and non-scalar objects
   (b) Mutable objects and non-mutable objects

A.5 Bloom Level: Evaluate

1. Evaluate the following code critically in terms of Python syntax.

a)
```
a = input("enter")
  print(type(a))
```

b)
```
3s = input("Enter a String ")
print(3s * 5)
print("\n===============================")
```

c)
```
# This is a program for comments

''' This is multiline comment using single quote. These are required to
explain the details of the program. They are not executed'''
```

d)
```
word = 'word'
sentence = "This is a\
sentence."
paragraph = """This is a paragraph. It is
made up of multiple lines and sentences."""
print (word, sentence, paragraph)
```

2. Determine whether the code satisfies the requirements. If not, state the reason and correct it.
   a) Print the following:

      1

      1 2

      1 2 3

      Code
      Print("1")
      Print("1", "2")
      Print("1", "2", "3")

   b) Print the following statement in a single line using multi-line print statement.
      "Mother Earth supports life.We must take care of it;otherwise we will suffer"

      Code
      print("Mother Earth supports life.\
      We must take care of it;\
      otherwise we will suffer")

c) Print the following statement as follows:

I am very beautiful.
        Beauty lies within.
I am a pure soul.
        Pure souls are always happy.
-----My strength is my inner beauty-----

Code

```
print("I am very beautiful.")
print(\t"Beauty lies within.")
print("I am a pure soul.")
print(\t"Pure souls are always happy.")
print("-----My strength is my inner beauty----- ")
```

A.6 Bloom Level: Create/Synthesize

Programming Assignment

1. The value 70 is to be assigned to variables p, q, r. Write an assignment statement to assign a single value to multiple variables
2. The value 10 is to be assigned to variable x, and "Good Morning" to variable s. Assign these values in a single assignment statement.
3. Write a Python statement to print the id, type and value of object 100.
4. Write a Python statement to:
   a. Concatenate "You", "are", "beautiful" in a single string.
   b. Repeat string "Beautiful World" three times.
5. Write the command for printing a blank line.
6. Write a Python statement for printing "Hello World".
7. Assign "Beautiful Sun" to a variable and print the value of the variable.
8. Accept your name as input in a variable x. Print the output as follows – "Your name" is a lovable person. (Here, "Your name" should show your name).
9. Accept your name and age as input. Display output as "Name" is "age" years old (Here, name and age should show the input you have taken)
10. WAP to create the following pattern

a.

```
    1
  1   2
1   2   3
```

b.

```
1 2 3 4
  2 3
   1
```

c.

```
1
    2
3
    4
```

Answers

A.1 Bloom Level: Knowledge/Remember

Review Questions

9. (1) c (2) f (3) b (4) a (5) g (6) d (7) h (8) e

Fill in the Blanks

1. True, False
2. 33
3. Literals, Variables, Operators
4. Type
5. Type
6. Scalar. Non-scalar
7. Mutable
8. Int
9. Float
10. Str
11. Triple
12. \n
13. False
14. Print
15. Input
16. Space (" ")
17. \
18. ;
19. Single, Multi
20. #
21. Three
22. Indentation

True/False

1. False
2. False
3. False
4. True
5. True
6. False
7. True
8. False
9. False
10. True
11. True
12. True
13. False
14. False
15. True
16. False
17. True
18. False
19. False

A.2. Bloom Level: Comprehend/Understand

Review Questions

5. Correct – (a), (b), (c), (j), (k)
6. Reserved – (a), (c), (e), (g), (i)
7. Scalar (a), (b)

Multiple Choice Questions (MCQ)

1. iii
2. iv

A.3. Bloom Level: Application/Apply

Review Questions

1.
   - Literals – 55, 2
   - Type of literals – int
   - Variables – x, y, z
   - Type of expression in third statement – Integer (Because both x and y are integers)
   - Operators used – Assignment operator ("=")
   - Binding of objects - binds RHS to LHS
     - Object 55 is bind to x
     - Object 2 is bind to y
     - Object x-y is bind to z

2.
   - Object "Good Morning"
   - Type of object – string
   - Some operation on object – String concatenation, string repetition
   - Variable name – S
   - Operator name – Assignment

3. Type is <float>
   Value is 10.6

4.
   (a) x is assigned value 5.
   (b) Error. A literal cannot be assigned a value.
   (c) x is assigned the string, "this is green".
   (d) Error. Cannot assign same integer value to two literals.
   (e) Assign 2 to x and 4 to y.
   (f) Assign "2" to x and 2 to y.
   (g) Error. Variable *a* does not have a value.
   (h) x, y, z are assigned value 5.
   (i) Error. Cannot assign same integer value to two literals.
   (j) Error. Cannot assign value to literal.

Multiple Choice Questions (MCQ)

1. iii **2.** iv **3.** iv **4.** iii **5.** iv **6.** iv **7.** i

A.5. Bloom Level: Evaluate

1. (a) Indentation error
   (b) Invalid Identifier
   (c) Correct. Uses single line and multiline comments.
   (d) Correct. Continues a sentence on multiple lines.

2. (a) Required spacing will not be generated. A tab should be used in print statement.
   (b) Correct
   (c) In statements 2 and 4, the "\t" should be within quotes. There is error in the code.

CHAPTER 5 Operators and Expressions

Contents

5.1 Introduction

The variables and constants, as stand-alone entities, serve little purpose. The variables need to be assigned values, and combined with constants to perform a specific task. Operators are used for combining operands – variables and constants. Operators have a specific symbol and they perform a particular task. They allow different kind of actions, such as addition subtraction, and comparison to be performed on the operands. The combination of operands and operators form an expression. The evaluation of the expression is based on certain rules.

In this chapter, the different categories of operators in Python, their algebraic functions and meaning are discussed. A description of the expressions is presented along with the rules of evaluation of expressions. The hierarchy of precedence of operators is also listed. It is used during evaluation of expressions when there are two or more operators in an expression.

Learning Outcomes of this chapter

After completion of the chapter, the learner will be able to:

- Identify different kind of operators
- List the operations that can be performed using the operators
- Classify the operators
- Describe functionality of the operators
- Use operators in expressions
- Recognize errors in expressions
- Evaluate expressions
- Formulate expressions
- Develop simple programs based on the concepts discussed.

5.2 Operator and Operand

An **operator** is a symbol that is a representation for a specific action to be performed. For example, + is an operator that represents the addition operation.

An **operand** is an object on which the operator operates. An operand can be a constant or a variable name. For example, in 2 + 3 there is an operator + and two operands – constants 2 and 3.

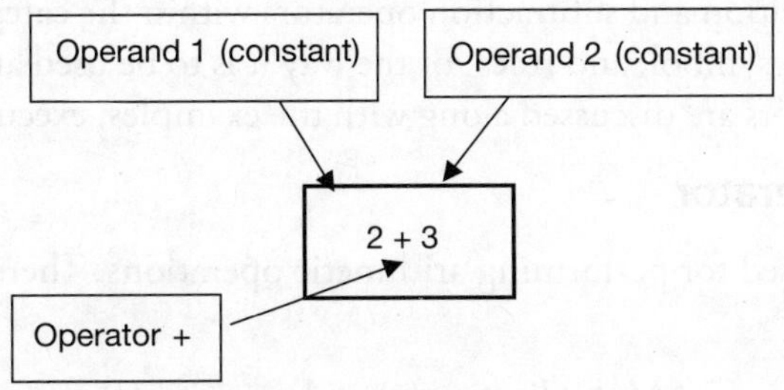

5.3 Classification of Operators

The operators are classified based on the following criteria:

1. Number of operands on which the operator operates
2. Role of the operator.

The first classification takes into account the number of operands that are required for using an operator. The second classification considers the task that the operators perform. The task could be arithmetic calculation or any other logical operation.

Number of Operands

The operators are divided into two types based on number of operands on which they operate:

1. **Unary operators** work on a single operand. For example, in –5, "–" is a unary operator as it operates on one operand 5. The operator denotes that 5 is a negative number. The operator is on the left of the operand. Some other unary operators are + (plus) and ~ (not).
2. **Binary operators** require two operands for performing the operation. For example, in 23 – 12, "–" is a binary operator as it operates on two operands 23 and 12. The operator denotes that 12 will be subtracted from 23. The operator is in between the two operands. Some other binary operators are + (addition), and * (multiplication).

Role of Operator

Based on the ***task performed*** by the operator, the operators are categorized as follows:

1. Arithmetic operators
2. Relational operators
3. Logical operators
4. Bitwise operators
5. Augmented assignment operators
6. Identity operators

The different categories of operators focus on specific tasks, such as arithmetic operators for arithmetic operations, and logical operators for logic operations. Further, within each category, there are several operators; for example, addition and subtraction operators within the category arithmetic. Each operator within a category has a symbol, and rules for the way it is to be used and evaluated. In the following subsections, the operators are discussed along with the examples, executed code and their outputs.

5.3.1 Arithmetic Operator

Arithmetic operators are used for performing arithmetic operations. There are seven arithmetic operators: +, –, *, /, %, //, **.

- *Addition* (+), *Subtraction* (–), *Multiplication* (*) and *Division* (/) are self-explanatory.
- *Modulus* (%) divides two numbers and gives the remainder of the division as the answer.
- *Floor division* (//) divides two numbers; the answer is an integer less than or equal to the result of the division. If the result is positive, the fraction part is discarded. If the answer is negative, the result is rounded to the next smallest integer (Floor of –2.5 is –3 because –3 is less than –2). For example,

- o 7//2 is 3 (7 divided by 2 is 3.5. Integer less than 3.5 is 3)
- o –7//2 is –4 (–7 divided by 2 is –3.5. Integer less than –3.5 is –4)

- *Exponentiation* (**) is one number raised to the power of another number. For example, 5**2 means 5 raised to power 2, i.e., five multiplied two times; the answer is 25.

The operands in arithmetic operation are numeric values – integer or float – with or without sign. A number without sign is assumed as a positive number. The result of an arithmetic operation is a numeric value.

Table 5.1 shows arithmetic operators, operations that can be performed with them and some examples.

Table 5.1 Arithmetic operators

Name	Algebraic Function	Meaning	Examples	
Addition	A + B	Add A and B	89 + 3 = 92 89 + 3.0 = 92.0	89.0 + 3 = 92.0 89.0 + 3.0 = 92.0
Subtraction	A – B	Subtract B from A	99 – 5 = 94 99.0 – 5 = 94.0	99 – 5.0 = 94.0 5 – 99.0 = -94.0
Multiplication	A * B	Multiply A and B	5 * 4 = 20 5.0 * 4 = 20.0	5.0 * 4.0 = 20.0 –5 * 4.0 = –20.0
Division	A / B	Divide A by B	8/2 = 4.0 8.0/2 = 4.0	8/2.0 = 4.0 9/2 = 4.5
Modulus or Mod	A % B	Remainder of A divided by B	8 % 2 = 0 9 % 2 = 1	8.5 % 2 = 0.5 9.0 % 2 = 1.0
Floor division	A // B	Greatest integer less than or equal to the result of A divided by B	9//2 = 4 11//2 = 5	–11//2 = –6 –11.0//2 = –6.0
Exponentiation	A ** B	Raised to power. A is multiplied B times	2 ** 3 = 8 2 ** –3 = 0.125	2.0 ** 3 = 8.0 –2 ** 3 = –8

Example 5.1. (a) Using the arithmetic operators (b) Output

```
#=======Assignment Operator====
a = 29
b = 11
print ( a, "+", b, " = ", a + b)
print ( a, "-", b, " = ", a - b)
print ( a, "*", b, " = ", a * b)
print ( a, "/", b, " = ", a / b)
print ( a, "%", b, " = ", a % b)
print ( a, "//", b, " = ", a//b)
print ( a, "//", -b, " = ", a//-b)
b = 2
print ( a, "**", b, " = ", a**b)
```

(a)

```
29 + 11  =  40
29 - 11  =  18
29 * 11  =  319
29 / 11  =  2.6363636363636362
29 % 11  =  7
29 // 11  =  2
29 // -11  =  -3
29 ** 2  =  841
>>>
```

(b)

5.3.2 Relational Operator

Relational operators are used for comparison. There are six relational operators: ==, <, >, <=, >=, !=. The operations that can be performed using relational operators are: equal to (==), greater than (>), less than (<), greater than or equal to (>=), less than or equal to (<=), and not equal to (!=). The operands in relational operation are values that can be compared. The values can be integer, float or string. The result of relational operation is a Boolean value – True or False.

Comparison of strings: String comparison is: (1) from left to right, and (2) character by character. Every character has an ASCII value –

- ASCII value of a to z is 97 to 122,
- ASCII value of A to Z is 65 to 90, and
- ASCII value of 0 to 9 is 48 to 57

When strings are compared, the ASCII value of each character is compared from left to right. For example, "ABC" < "abc"; "10" < "11".

Table 5.2 shows the relational operators, operations that can be performed with them and a few examples.

Table 5.2 Relational operators

Name	Algebraic Function	Meaning	Examples	
Equal to	A = = B	If A and B are equal Return True; else False	2 = = 3 ⇒False 1.0 = = 1 ⇒True	'ABC' = = 'abc' ⇒ False
Greater than	A > B	If A is greater than B Return True; else False	2 > 3 ⇒ False 1.0 > 1 ⇒ False	'ABC' > 'abc' ⇒ False
Less than	A < B	If A is less than B Return True; else False	2 < 3 ⇒ True 1.0 < 1 ⇒ False	'ABC' < 'abc' ⇒ True
Greater than or equal to	A >= B	If A is greater or equal to B, Return True; else False	2 >= 3 ⇒ False 1.0 >= 1 ⇒ True	'ABC' >= 'abc' ⇒ False
Less than or equal to	A <= B	If A is less or equal to B, Return True; else False	2 <= 3 ⇒ True 1.0 <= 1 ⇒ True	'ABC' <= 'abc' ⇒ True
Not equal to	A != B	If A and B are not equal, Return True; else False	2 !=3 ⇒True 1.0 ! = 1 ⇒ False	'ABC' != 'abc' ⇒ True

Example 5.2 (a) shows the Python code for relational operators and Example 5.2 (b) shows the output after execution of the code. We see that "BookABC" < "book" is True, though the number of characters in "BookABC" is more than in "book". It is because ASCII code of "B" is 66 and that of "b" is 98.

Example 5.2. (a) Using the relational operators (b) Output

```
#=========Relational Operator====
a = 29
b = 11
print ( a, "==", b, " = ", a == b)
print ( a, ">", b, " = ", a > b)
print ( a, "<", b, " = ", a < b)
print ( a, ">=", b, " = ", a >= b)
print ( a, "<=", b, " = ", a <= b)
print ( a, "!=", b, " = ", a!= b)
b = 29
print ( a, "==", b, " = ", a==b, "\n")
a="Book"; b="book"
print ( a, "==", b, " = ", a == b)
print ( a, "<", b, " = ", a < b)
a="Book"; b="ABook"
print ( a, ">", b, " = ", a > b)
a="Book"; b="BookA"
print ( a, "<", b, " = ", a < b)
a="BookABC"; b="book"
print ( a, "<", b, " = ", a < b)
```

(a)

```
29 == 11  =  False
29 > 11  =  True
29 < 11  =  False
29 >= 11  =  True
29 <= 11  =  False
29 != 11  =  True
29 == 29  =  True

Book == book  =  False
Book < book  =  True
Book > ABook  =  True
Book < BookA  =  True
BookABC < book  =  True
>>>
```

(b)

5.3.3 Logical Operator

Logical operators are used for combining multiple values required for decision making. There are three logical operators – `and`, `or`, `not`. The operators `and` and `or` are binary operators. `not` is a unary operator. In Python, the values interpreted as "false" are as follows:

- False (reserved word)
- None (reserved word)
- Numeric zero in all formats
- Empty strings and containers (containers will be discussed later).

All other values are interpreted as "true".

The operands in a logical operation are values that can be evaluated to be true or false. However, the output of logical operator is the value of last evaluated operand and not *True* or *False*. The last evaluated operand is determined as follows:

- `and` operation – The first operand is evaluated. If it is false, its value is returned; if it is true, the second operand is evaluated and its value is returned.
- `or` operation – The first operand is evaluated. If it is true, its value is returned; if it is false, the second operand is evaluated and its value is returned.
- `not` operation returns true if the operand is false, and false if the operand is true.

Table 5.3 shows the truth table for the logical operators. Table 5.4 shows logical operators, operations that can be performed with them and some examples.

Table 5.3 Truth table of logical operators in Python

op 1	op 2	op1 and op2
False	False	op1
False	True	op1
True	False	op2
True	True	op2

op1	op2	op1 or op2
False	False	op2
False	True	op2
True	False	op1
True	True	op1

op1	Not op1
False	True
True	False

Table 5.4 Logical operators

Name	Algebraic function	Meaning	Examples		
and	A and B	If false, return A else B	1 and 2 = 2	0 and 2 = 0	‘’ and ‘a’ = ‘’
or	A or B	If true, return A else B	1 or 2 = 1	0 or 2 = 2	‘’ or ‘a’ = ‘a’
not	not A	If false, return true If true return false	Not 1 = false	Not 0 = True	Not ‘’ = True

Example 5.3. (a) Using the logical operators (b) Output

```
#========Logical Operator====
a = 29
b = 11
print ( a, "and", b, " = ", a and b)
print ( a, "or", b, " = ", a or b)
print ( "not", a, " = ", not a)
a=0
print ( a, "and", b, " = ", a and b)
print ( a, "or", b, " = ", a or b)
a="Book"; b= None
print ( a, "and", b, " = ", a and b)
a=""; b= None
print ( a, "and", b, " = ", a and b)
print ( a, "or", b, " = ", a or b)
print ( "not", a, " = ", not a)
```

(a)

```
29 and 11  =  11
29 or 11  =  29
not 29  =  False
0 and 11  =  0
0 or 11  =  11
Book and None  =  None
 and None  =
 or None  =  None
not  =  True
>>> |
```

(b)

5.3.4 Bitwise Operator

Bit is the smallest unit in the computer. A bit has a single binary value: 0 or 1. A numeric data is a combination of bits – 8 bits, 16 bits or 32 bits. Bitwise operators manipulate individual bits of the numeric data. The numeric data is of type integer. To perform bitwise operation on two numbers A and B, do the following:

- Convert both A and B into binary. Represent any negative number in 2’s complement form (2’s complement is computed by adding 1 to 1’s complement of the binary number).

- Perform bitwise operation according to the rules defined below, on the corresponding bit of each number.

An example

Step 1: A = 12 B = 3

Step 2: A = 0000 1100 B = 0000 0011

Step 3: Apply any operation on the corresponding bits, vertically.

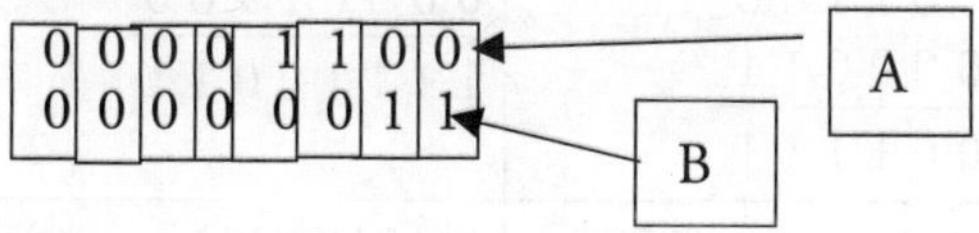

The result of bitwise operation is a sequence of bits.
There are six bitwise operators: &, |, ~, ^, <<, >>.

- *Bitwise and* (&) returns 1 if bits of both the operands are 1, otherwise 0.
- *Bitwise or* (|) returns 1 if any one or both bits of the operands is 1, otherwise 0
- Bitwise *not* (~) is a unary operator. It returns 1 if the bit is 0, and 0 if the bit is 1.
- Bitwise XOR (^) returns 1 if bits of both operands are different, otherwise 0. Table 5.5 shows the truth tables of the bitwise operators &, |, ~ and ^.

Table 5.5 Truth Table of bitwise operators in Python

op 1	op 2	op1 & op2
0	0	0
0	1	0
1	0	0
1	1	1

op1	op2	op1 | op2
0	0	0
0	1	1
1	0	1
1	1	1

op1	~ op1
0	1
1	0

op 1	op 2	op1 ^ op2
0	0	0
0	1	1
1	0	1
1	1	0

- Left shift (<<) shifts bits of the first operand to the left, by the numeric value of the second operand. The second operand is always a positive integer. A left shift by *n* bits is also defined as multiplication by 2 ** *n*. The space created on the right side after shifting is filled with 0. During shifting, the shifted bits fall out.

- Right shift (>>) shifts bits of the first operand to the right, by the numeric value of the second operand. The second operand is always a positive integer. A right shift by *n* bits is also defined as division by 2 ** *n*. The space created on the left side after shifting is filled with 0. During shifting, the shifted bits fall out.

Let us see a few examples:

Bitwise and (&)	**Bitwise or (|)**	**Bitwise not (~)**	**Bitwise XOR (^)**
12 & 3 0 0 0 0 1 1 0 0 0 0 0 0 0 0 1 1 0 0 0 0 0 0 0 0	12 | 3 0 0 0 0 1 1 0 0 0 0 0 0 0 0 1 1 0 0 0 0 1 1 1 1	~12 0 0 0 0 1 1 0 0 1 1 1 1 0 0 1 1	12 ^ 3 0 0 0 0 1 1 0 0 0 0 0 0 0 0 1 1 0 0 0 0 1 1 1 1
$(0000\ 0000)_2 = (0)_{10}$	$(0000\ 1111)_2 = (15)_{10}$	$(1111\ 0011)_2 = (-13)_{10}$	$(0000\ 1111)_2 = (15)_{10}$

Left shift (<<)		**Right shift (>>)**		
12<<3		12>>3		
0 0 0 0 1 1 0 0	A	0 0 0 0 1 1 0 0		A
0 0 0 1 1 0 0 0	shift 1	0 0 0 0 0 1 1 0		shift 1
0 0 1 1 0 0 0 0	shift 2	0 0 0 0 0 0 1 1		shift 2
0 1 1 0 0 0 0 0	shift 3	0 0 0 0 0 0 0 1	1 Fall-out	shift 3
$(0110\ 0000)_2 = (96)_{10}$		$(0000\ 0001)_2 = (1)_{10}$		
This is equivalent to $12 * 2^3 = 96$		This is equivalent to 12 divided by $2^3 = 1$		

Let us see bitwise operation on negative numbers: –6 and –2.

Find 2's complement of –6:
6 in binary: 0000 0110
1's complement: 1111 1001
Add 1: 1111 1010

Find 2's complement of –2:
2 in binary: 0000 0010
1's complement: 1111 1101
Add 1: 1111 1110

Perform bitwise and operation.

```
1 1 1 1 1 0 0 0
1 1 1 1 1 1 1 0
---------------
1 1 1 1 1 0 1 0
```

To see the result, convert the answer 1111 1010 into 2's complement form and add negative sign.
1's complement: 0000 0101
Add 1: 0000 0110
The result is –6.

Table 5.6 shows bitwise operators, operations that can be performed with them and some examples.

Table 5.6 Bitwise operators

Name	Algebraic function	Meaning	Examples	
Bitwise and	A & B	Compare each bit of A and B. If corresponding bits are 1, return 1; else 0	6 & 2 = 2	–4 & –2 = –4
Bitwise or	A | B	Compare each bit of A and B. If corresponding bits are 0, return 0; else 1	6 | 2 = 6	–6 | –2 = –2
Bitwise Invert	~ A	Reverse bits of A: 0 to 1 and 1 to 0	~6 = –7	~ –6 = 5
Bitwise XOR	A ^ B	Compare each bit of A and B. If corresponding bits are same, return 0; else 1	6 ^ 2 = 4	–6 ^ –2 = 4
Left shift	A << B	Shift left, bits of A by B number of bits	6 << 2 = 24	–6 << –2 gives Error. Negative shift count
Right shift	A >> B	Shift right, bits of A by B number of bits	6 >> 2 = 1	–6 >> –2 gives Error. Negative shift count

Example 5.4.(a) Using bitwise operators (b) Output

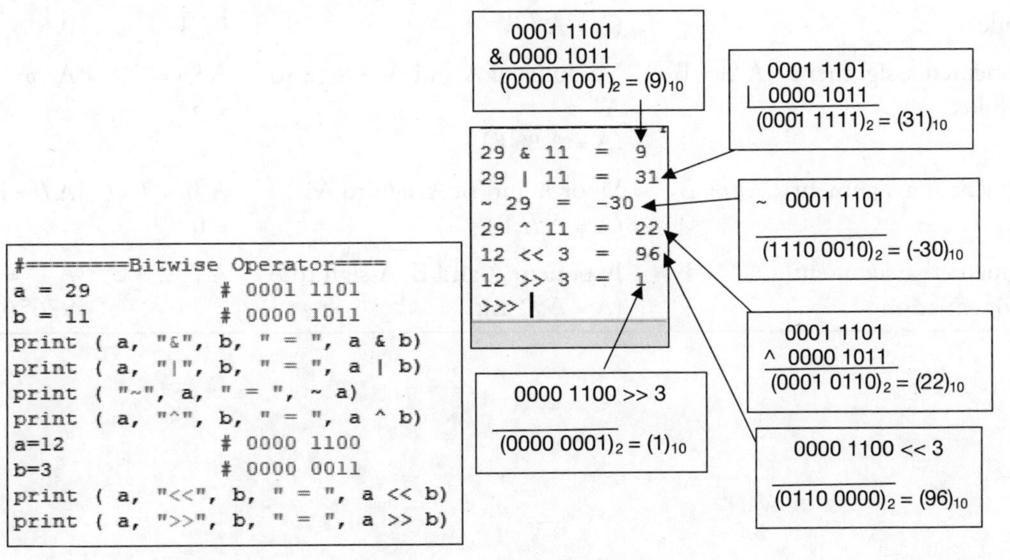

5.3.5 Augmented Assignment Operator

The assignment operator has already been discussed in Chapter 4. The assignment operator is combined with binary operator for shorthand notation, also called as **augmented assignment**. The syntax of augmented assignment is:

x *operator* = expression (**Note**: Expression is discussed later in this chapter)

It is evaluated as: x = x *operator* expression

For example, a += 5 means a = a + 5

A statement using an augmented assignment operator is called augmented assignment statement.

Table 5.7 shows assignment operators, operations that can be performed with them and some examples.

Table 5.7 Assignment and augmented assignment operators

Name	Algebraic function	Meaning	Examples Let A = 5, B = 10	
Augmented assignment Add	A += B	Add A and B. Assign to A (A = A + B)	A += 6 = 11	A += B = 15
Augmented assignment Subtract	A −= B	Subtract A and B. Assign to A (A = A - B)	A−= 7 = −2	A−=B = −5
Augmented assignment Multiply	A *= B	Multiply A and B. Assign to A (A = A * B)	A*= 7 = 35	A*= B = 50
Augmented assignment Divide	A /= B	Divide A and B. Assign to A (A = A / B)	A /= 7 = 0.71	A /= B = 0.5
Augmented assignment Modulus	A %= B	Modulus of A and B. Assign to A (A = A % B)	A % = 7 = 5	A %= B = 5
Augmented assignment Floor	A //= B	Floor A and B. Assign to A (A = A // B)	A // = 7 = 0	A //= B = 0
Augmented assignment Exponentiation	A **= B	Exponent A and B. Assign to A (A = A ** B)	A ** 2 = 25	A ** = B = 9765625

Example 5.5. (a) Using augmented assignment operators (b) Output

```
a = 29
b = 11
print (a,end=" ")
a += b
print ( "+=", b, " = ", a)

a = 29
print (a,end=" ")
a -= b
print ( "-=", b, " = ", a )

a = 29
print (a,end=" ")
a *= b
print ( "*=", b, " = ", a )

a = 29
print (a,end=" ")
a /= b
print ( "/=", b, " = ", a )

a = 29
print (a,end=" ")
a %= b
print ( "%=", b, " = ", a )

a = 29
print (a,end=" ")
a //= b
print ( "//=", b, " = ", a )

a = 12
print (a,end=" ")
a **= 2
print ( "**=", 2, " = ", a )
```

(a)

```
29 += 11  =  40
29 -= 11  =  18
29 *= 11  =  319
29 /= 11  =  2.6363636363636362
29 %= 11  =  7
29 //= 11  =  2
12 **= 2  =  144
>>> |
```

(b)

Note: print (a, "+=", b, " = ", a+=b) will give syntax error. This is because a += b is an augmented assignment statement. In `print()`, you cannot use statement; you can only use expression.

5.3.6 Identity Operator

Identity operators compare the memory locations of two objects. There are two identity operators: (1) *is*, and (2) *is not*. The operations using identity operators check if the variables point to the same object or not. The operands are two variables. The identity operators check if the first variable and the second variable point to the same object. The result of identity operation is True or False. The id of object can be checked using `id()` function.

Let us understand why A = "a" and B = "a" gives A is B as True. In Python, A = "a" creates an object "a" and variable A that point to object "a". B = "a" creates another variable B that points to same object "a". Thus, both A and B point to the same object, i.e., the same memory location. Hence, they have same identity.

Table 5.8 shows identity operators, operations that can be performed with them and some examples.

Table 5.8 Identity operators

Name	Algebraic Function	Meaning	Examples	
Identity same	A is B	If identity of A is same as identity of B return True; else False	A = 2; B = 3 A is B = False	A = "a"; B = "a" A is B = True
Identity not same	A is not B	If identity of A is not same as identity of B return True; else False	A = 2; B = 2 A is not B = False	A = "Book" B = "book" A is not B = True

Example 5.6. (a) Using identity operators (b) Output

```
# Identity Operators
a = 10; b = 10
print ( a, "is", b, " = ", a is b)
print ( "id(", a, ") ==", "id(", b, ")", " = ", id(a) == id(b))
b = 20
print ( a, "is", b, " = ", a is b)
print ( a, "is not", b, " = ", a is not b, "\n")
a = "ABC"
b = "ABc"
print ( a, "is", b, " = ", a is b)
print ( "id(", a, ") ==", "id(", b, ")", " = ", id(a) == id(b))
b = "ABC"
print ( a, "is", b, " = ", a is b)
print ( a, "is not", b, " = ", a is not b)
```

(a)

```
10 is 10  =  True
id( 10 ) == id( 10 )  =  True
10 is 20  =  False
10 is not 20  =  True

ABC is ABc  =  False
id( ABC ) == id( ABc )  =  False
ABC is ABC  =  True
ABC is not ABC  =  False
>>>
```

(b)

5.4 Expression

An expression is a combination of one or more constants, variable and operator. A constant alone is an expression. A variable alone is also an expression. Some examples of expressions are:

$x = y$ # single variable
$x = 5$ # single constant
$x = y + 3$ # variable, operator and constant
$x = y + 9 - z$ # variables, operators and constant

The expressions are evaluated according to certain rules. The right-hand side of expression is evaluated to get the value of the expression or result. The result is an object of a particular type and is assigned to the left-hand side.

When an expression is typed at the Python prompt, it can also be written without assignment operator, as:

```
>>> 5
>>> 7 + 3
>>> x + 9 – y
```

The answer is evaluated and displayed on the prompt.

5.4.1 Precedence Rules

For evaluating an expression, certain rules have to be followed, which are defined as follows:

- The portion of expression within parenthesis is evaluated first.
- The operator with higher precedence is evaluated first. The *precedence of operator* is defined on the basis of the type of operator, and its priority among operators of the same type. Table 5.9 shows the precedence of operators. Level 1 has the highest precedence and Level 12 has the lowest precedence.

  For example, in an expression x = 3 + 4 / 2, firstly, division is done as it has higher precedence than addition. Thus, x will be assigned value (3 + 2), i.e., 5.

  We see that if expressions are not evaluated correctly, we get a different result (3 + 4 = 7 and 7 / 2 is 3.5)

- When two operators have same precedence, associativity determines the order of operation. *Associativity of operator* is the direction of evaluation of operator in an expression having more than one operator of same precedence – left to right or right to left. Table 5.9 shows the associativity of operators.

  For example, x = 2 * 5 / 2 has both operators having same precedence. From left to right associativity, first 2 * 5 = 10 is evaluated and then 10 / 2 will give 5.0 as the result.

Table 5.9 Precedence of operators

Operator	Type of operator	Precedence	Associativity
**	Arithmetic	Level 1	R → L
Unary + Unary –	Arithmetic	Level 2	R → L
~	Bitwise		
* / // %	Arithmetic	Level 3	L → R
+ –	Arithmetic	Level 4	L → R
<< >>	Bitwise	Level 5	L → R
&	Bitwise	Level 6	L → R
^	Bitwise	Level 7	L → R
|	Bitwise	Level 8	L → R
is is not	Identity	Level 9	L → R
< <= > >= != = =	Relational		
not	Logical	Level 10	L → R
and	Logical	Level 11	L → R
or	Logical	Level 12	L → R

Let us see the difference in express evaluation with an example:

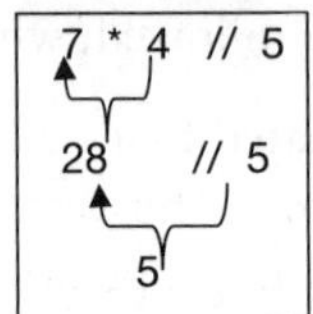

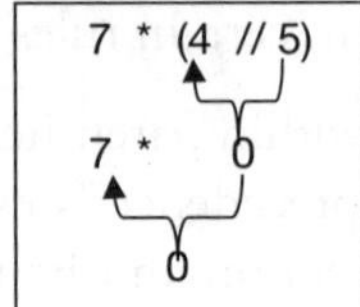

Example 5.7. (a) An expression evaluation (b) Output

```
#====Expression Evaluation====
print("7 * 4 // 5 = ", 7 * 4 // 5)
print("7 * (4 // 5) = ", 7 * (4 // 5))
print("3 ** 2 ** 3 = ", 3 ** 2 ** 3)
print("(3 ** 2) ** 3 = ", (3 ** 2) ** 3)
print ("(12 - 6) * 2 = ", (12 - 6) * 2)
print ("12 - 6 * 2 = ", 12 - 6 * 2)
a = 10
b = 5
c = 3
d = 2
print("(a + b) * (c + d)=", (a + b) * (c + d))
print("(a + b) * c / d=", (a + b) * c / d)
print ("a or b=", a or b)
print ("( a or b) * c=", ( a or b) * c)
```

(a)

```
7 * 4 // 5 =  5
7 * (4 // 5) =  0
3 ** 2 ** 3 =  6561
(3 ** 2) ** 3 =  729
(12 - 6) * 2 =  12
12 - 6 * 2 =  0
(a + b) * (c + d)= 75
(a + b) * c / d= 22.5
a or b= 10
( a or b) * c= 30
>>>
```

(b)

5.5 Solved Questions with Explanation

1) Find the output:

```
a = 10
b = 20
print(a++2)
```

Output

```
12
```

Explanation: It will add 2 to the value of a and print 12.

2)

```
a = 10
b = 20
print(a++2)
print(a)
```

Output

```
12
10
```

Explanation: It will add 2 to the value of a and print 12. But the value of a is not changed.

3)

```
a=22
a=+10
print(a)
```

Output

```
10
```

Explanation: a=+10 is not augmented operator. This simply assign 10 to a.

4)

```
a=22
a+=6
print(a)
```

Output

```
28
```

Explanation: a+=10 is an augmented assignment operator. It increments a and assigns the incremented value to a.

5)

```
a = 10
a+= 22 * 5-5
print(a)
```

Output

```
115
```

Explanation: 22 * 5 = 110. Subtract 5 from 110 = 105. Add 10 (augment a). So 115.

6)

```
a = 10
b = 90
c = a * b/30
print(c)
d = a * (b/30)
print(d)
```

Output

```
30.0
30.0
```

Explanation: Both operators have the same precedence.

7)

```
a = 10
b = 90
c = 30
avg = a + b + c/3
print(avg)
avg = (a + b + c)/3
print(avg)
```

Output

```
110.0
43.333333333333336
```

Explanation: This is to find average of three numbers. The first avg line only divides c by 3 and not a and b. The next avg line with brackets finds the actual average.

8)

```
a=25
a=a<<3
print(a)
12<<3
```

Output

```
200
```

Explanation: First, 25 is converted into binary 00011001. Then, left shift three times will make a as 11001000. This is 200.

5.6 Programming Examples

In this section, a few sample programs are given, with their output.

Program 5.1: Program to multiply a number by 2^n without using the multiplication operator.

```
#Multiply by power of 2 without using multiplication operator
a=25
a=a<<3
print(a)
```

Output

```
200
```

Program 5.2: Program to divide a number by 2^n without using the division operator.

```
#Divide by power of 2 without using division operator
a=24
a=a>>2
print(a)
```

Output

```
6
```

Program 5.3: Program to print the number of days, minutes and seconds in a day and year.

```
#WAP to print number of days, hours, minutes and second in a day and year
year = 365
day=24
hour = 60
min = 60
print("No. of hours in a day = ", day)
print("No. of minutes in a day = ", day*hour)
print("No. of seconds in a day = ", min * day * hour)
print("==============================================")
print("No. of days in a year = ", year)
print("No. of hours in a year = ", year * day)
print("No. of minutes in a year = ", year* day *hour)
print("No. of seconds in a year = ", year * min * day * hour)
```

Output

```
No. of hours in a day =  24
No. of minutes in a day =  1440
No. of seconds in a day =  86400
==============================================
No. of days in a year =  365
No. of hours in a year =  8760
No. of minutes in a year =  525600
No. of seconds in a year =  31536000
```

Program 5.4: WAP to convert a Celsius temperature into Fahrenheit.

```
#WAP to convert celsius into fahrenheit
C = 100
F = (C * 9/5 ) + 32
print("The celsius temperature", C, "into Fahrenheit is= ", F)
```

Output

```
The celsius temperature 100 into Fahrenheit is=  212.0
```

Program 5.5: WAP to convert a Fahrenheit temperature into Celsius.

```
#WAP to convert fahrenheit into celsius
F = 212
C = (F - 32) * (5/9)
print("The Fahrenheit temperature", F, "into Celsius is= ", C)
```

Output

```
The Fahrenheit temperature 212 into Celsius is=  100.0
```

SUMMARY

- An operator is a symbol that performs a particular operation on an operand.
- Unary operator and binary operators are classified on the basis of the number of operands on which they operate.
- Unary and binary operators work on one and two operands, respectively.
- Based on the role of operators, they are classified as arithmetic operator, relational operator, logical operator, bitwise operator, augmented assignment operator, membership operator and identity operator.
- There are seven arithmetic operators – addition (+), subtraction (–), multiplication (*), division (/), modulus (%), floor (//) and exponentiation (**).
- There are six relational operators – equal to (==), greater than (>), less than (<), greater than or equal to (>=), less than or equal to (<=), and not equal to (!=).
- The three logical operators are – `and`, `or`, `not`.
- There are six bitwise operators – bitwise `and` (&), bitwise `or` (|), bitwise `not` (~), bitwise XOR (^), left shift (<<) and right shift (>>)
- The sign "equal to" (=) is the assignment operator.
- Augmented assignment is the assignment operator combined with a binary operator.
- There are two identity operators – `is` and `is not`.
- An expression is a combination of constants, variables and operators.
- The different operators have a precedence of evaluation relative to each other.
- There are rules of expression evaluation – parenthesis, precedence and associativity.

KEYWORDS

Operator
Operand
Unary operator
Binary operator
Arithmetic operator
Relational operator
Logical operator
Bitwise operator
Assignment operator
Membership operator
Identity operator
Augmented assignment
Operator precedence
Operator priority
Operator associativity
Expression
Parenthesis
Precedence order
Associativity

Programming Language Keywords

Addition (+)
Subtraction (–)
Multiplication (*)
Division (/)
Modulus (%)
Floor division (//)
Exponentiation (**)
Equal to (==)
Greater than (>)
Less than (<)
Greater than equal to (>=)
Less than equal to (<=)
Not equal to (!=)
Logical and
Logical or
Logical not
Bit
Bitwise and (&)
Bitwise or (|)
Bitwise not (~)
Bitwise XOR (^)
Left shift (<<)
Right shift (>>)
Assignment operator (=)
Identity (is)
Identity (is not)

Assessment

A.1 Bloom Level: Knowledge/Remember

Review Questions

1. Define: operator, operand and expression.
2. Name the operators classified on the basis of the number of operands.
3. Name the operators classified on the basis of the role of the operators.
4. Name the seven arithmetic operators.
5. Name the six relational operators.
6. Name the three logical operators.
7. Name the six bitwise operators.
8. Identify the operators: (+), (–), (*), (/), (%), (//), (**), (==), (>), (<), (>=), (<=), (&), (|), (~), (^), (<<) (>>), (=).
9. Name the two identity operators.
10. List the rules for expression evaluation.

Fill in the blanks

1. "+" is an example of ____________.
2. An _______ is an object on which the operator operates.
3. The operators are classified on the basis of ____________ and ____________.
4. ____________ and ____________ are the two kind of operators classified based on the number of operands.
5. Unary operators work on _______ operand.
6. Binary operators work on ________ operands.
7. Mod operator provides ________ of the division.
8. ** is an operator for ________.
9. The types of operators used for comparison are ________.
10. != is the symbol for ________ comparison.
11. The ASCII value of "A" is ____.
12. The ASCII value of "a" is ______.
13. The ASCII value of "0" is ______.
14. If op1 is true and op2 is true, then "op1 or op2" is _______.
15. If op1 is true and op2 is true, then "op1 and op2" is _______.
16. If op1 is true, then "not op1" is ______.

17. Bitwise operators manipulate individual _________ of the data.

18. The bitwise and (&) operation returns 1 if both bits are _______.

19. _______ is the assignment operator.

20. The assignment operator combined with binary operator is called __________ assignment in shorthand notation.

21. A is B returns True if identity of A is __________as identity of B.

22. The associativity of unary operators is _______ to _______.

State True/False

1. An operator is an object on which the operand operates.
2. In expression 2 + 3, 2 is a variable.
3. In expression 2 + 3, "+" is an operator.
4. Unary operator works on two operands.
5. Binary operators work on two operands.
6. Floor divides two numbers and gives the greatest integer less than or equal to the quotient.
7. // is the symbol of mod operator.
8. == is an assignment operator.
9. The string comparison is done from right to left.
10. The string comparison is done character by character.
11. Logical operators combine multiple values for decision making.
12. "not" is a unary operator.
13. "None" is interpreted as false in Python.
14. Bitwise XOR (^) returns 1 if bits of both operands are same.
15. A<<B shifts B to the right by A bits.
16. An assignment creates a reference to the object instead of copying the object.
17. There is no need to pre-define variables in Python.
18. 5 is an expression.
19. A variable alone is an expression.

Multiple Choice Questions (MCQ)

1. If first operand is True, the output of logical operator "and" is _____.
   (i) True
   (ii) False
   (iii) the first evaluated value
   (iv) the last evaluated value

2. If first operand is True, the output of logical operator "or" is _____.
   (i) True
   (ii) False
   (iii) the first evaluated value
   (iv) the last evaluated value

3. The output of left shift by n is ______.
   (i) multiplication by n
   (ii) multiplication by 2^n
   (iii) division by n
   (iv) division by 2^n

4. The output of right shift by n is ______.
   (i) multiplication by n
   (ii) multiplication by 2^n
   (iii) division by n
   (iv) division by 2^n

A.2 Bloom Level: Comprehend/Understand

Review Questions

1. What is the basis of operator classification?
2. Explain the relation between operator and operand, with examples.
3. Describe the function of floor and modulus arithmetic operators.
4. What rules are followed for string comparison?
5. Describe the rules for evaluation of logical operators.
6. Explain the working of "A & B", if A = 7 and B = 8.
7. What is augmented assignment? Give examples.
8. Explain how A*= B works.
9. Segregate the operators into arithmetic, logical, bitwise and relational operators
   - o **
   - o >>
   - o %
   - o >
   - o and
   - o <=
   - o ~
   - o //
   - o &
   - o !=
   - o not
   - o = =

A.3 Bloom Level: Application/Apply

Review Questions

1. Evaluate the following expressions:
   i. 2 + 8 / 2 – 3
   ii. (20 / 10) – 89 // 2
   iii. 9 * 2 ** 3 /2
   iv. 25 / 5 and 0
   v. 9 and 8 / 2
2. Find 2's complement of the following
   i. –5 ii –10
3. Evaluate the following:
   i. 5//2
   ii. 5.0//2
   iii. –5.0//2
   iv. 5**2
   v. 5*2
   vi. 5%3
   vii. 5%3.0
   viii. 5**2.0
   ix. 5/3
   x. 5+5.0
   xi. 15.0/2
   xii. 5**–2
4. Evaluate the following:
   i. 10 < 3
   ii. 10 < 10.0
   iii. 2 != 5
   iv. 3 >= 2
   v. 1 and 2
   vi. 0 and 2
   vii. 2 and 2
   viii. 1 or 2
   ix. 0 or 2
   x. 2 or 2
   xi. "" and "Pen"
   xii. "Pen" and "Pencil"
   xiii. not "pen"
5. Fill in the blanks to get the correct result:
   i. (_ + 5 * 7) + 10 = 60
   ii. (2 + __) ** 3 = 125

iii. 35 and 78 = 78
iv. ___ and 9 = 0
v. __ or 89 = 67
vi. 0 or ____ = 77
vii. (17% 4 + __) = 6
viii. 8<< _ = 16
ix. (8>> _) & 2 = 0

6. Represent the following operations using operands and operators in Python:
   i. $a + 2–3/2$
   ii. $(b + \sqrt{b^2 - 4ac})/2a$
   iii. $2a + 7//2$
   iv. $a^2 + b^2 >= 2$

Multiple Choice Questions (MCQ)

1. Which is a unary operation?
   (i) 1 + 2 (ii) -3
   (iii) 4 – 3 (iv) 2 * 3

2. 8//3 is ______.
   (i) 2.66 (ii) 2
   (iii) 3 (iv) 2.6

3. -20//3 is ______.
   (i) -6.66 (ii) -6
   (iii) -7 (iv) -6.6

4. 5**2 is ______.
   (i) 10 (ii) 25
   (iii) 10 (iv) 52

5. 5 <= 2 is ______.
   (i) True (ii) False
   (iii) Equal (iv) Error

6. 1.0 == 1
   (i) True (ii) False
   (iii) Not defined (iv) Error

7. "Asia" < "asia"
   (i) True (ii) False
   (iii) Not defined (iv) Error

8. "Africa" < "Africasouth"
   (i) True (ii) False
   (iii) Not defined (iv) Error

9. In logical operation "5 and 2" the output is ______.
   (i) True (ii) False
   (iii) 5 (iv) 2

10. In logical operation "5 or 2" the output is ______.
   (i) True (ii) False
   (iii) 5 (iv) 2

11. In logical operation "0 and 12" the output is ______.
   (i) True (ii) False
   (iii) 0 (iv) 12

12. In logical operation "0 or 12" the output is ______.
   (i) True (ii) False
   (iii) 0 (iv) 12

13. 5 << –1 is ______.
   (i) 10 (ii) 2
   (iii) incorrect (iv) 0

14. 5 >> 2 is ______.
   (i) 1 (ii) 3
   (iii) 4 (iv) 0

15. 5 << 1 is ______.
   (i) 10 (ii) 6
   (iii) 12 (iv) 0

16. 1 ^ 2 is ______.
   (i) 1 (ii) 2
   (iii) 3 (iv) 0

17. After execution of A = 6; A += 6; the value of A is ______.
   (i) 6 (ii) 7
   (iii) 12 (iv) 36

18. After execution of A = 6; B = 7; A += B; the value of A and B is ______.
   (i) 6, 13 (ii) 13, 7
   (iii) 13, 13 (iv) 6, 7

19. A = "Apple"; B = "apple"; "A is not B" is ______.
(i) True (ii) False
(iii) Not defined (iv) None

20. 3 + 4 * 6 is ______.
(i) 24 (ii) 27
(iii) 42 (iv) 7

21. (3 + 4) * 6 is ______.
(i) 24 (ii) 27
(iii) 42 (iv) 7

A.4 Bloom Level: Analyze

1. Differentiate between 5/3 and 5//3 and 5%3.
2. Differentiate between unary and binary operators with examples.
3. Organize the arithmetic operators in decreasing order of precedence in an expression.
4. Will the evaluation of the following pairs of expressions give the same result? Justify your answer.

i.	2 + 4 / 9 >3	4 / 9 + 2 > 3
ii.	2 * 4 / 2 +5	4 /2 * 2 + 5
iii.	1 and 2	1 or 2
iv.	2 * (3 **3 +2)	(2 * 3**3) + 2
v.	8<<2 +7	8>>2 + 7

A.5 Bloom Level: Evaluate

1. Evaluate the following code critically in terms of Python syntax. If correct, evaluate the result.

i.
```
>>> print((-8<<2) and 5)
```
ii.
```
>>> print((-8<<2) or 5)
```
iii.
```
>>> print(3/(2 + -2) + 4)
```
iv.
```
>>> print("ab" is "AB")
```
v.
```
>>> print(2+=2)
```

2. Determine whether the code satisfies the requirements. If not, state the reason and correct it.

Let a = 10, b = 20, c = 5.

i. Print the following expressions:

$$\frac{a}{b} - \frac{c}{d} = \frac{ad - bc}{bd}$$

Code
```
x = ((a/b) - c/d)
y = (a*d - b* c)/b * d
print(x == y)
```

ii. $$\frac{a}{b} \times \frac{c}{d} = \frac{ac}{bd}$$

Code
```
x = ((a/b) * c/d)
y = (a*c / b*d)
print(x == y)
```

iii. $(a + b)(a - b) = a^2 - b^2$

Code
```
x = (a+b) * (a-b)
y = (a*a - b*b)
print(x == y)
```

iv. $(a + b)^2 = a^2 + 2ab + b^2$

Code
```
x= (a+b) * (a+b)
y = (a*a +2a*b + b*b)
print(x == y)
```

v. $a^m \times a^n$

Code
```
Print(a**m * a**n)
```

vi. a^m / a^n

Code
```
Print(a**m / a**n)
```

vii. $ax^2 + bx + c$

Code
```
Print(ax**2 + b * x + c)
```

A.6 Bloom Level: Create/Synthesize

Programming Assignment

1. Multiply 5 by 4 using logical operator.
2. Divide 16 by 8 using logical operator.
3. Write an expression to add 2 and 10 and then multiply the result with 10.
4. Write an expression to evaluate the comparison of 10 left shift by 2 then multiplied by 2 with 20 right shift by 2 and then multiplied by 2.
5. Write an expression to find the value of 220 added to 6 and then divided by 3.
6. Write an expression for quadratic equation in Python. Accept values of a, b and c from user. Print the output of the quadratic equation.
7. Write formula for evaluating the areas of circle, triangle, square, rectangle, trapezoid, polygon, cone and sphere. Accept parameters from user and display the output.
8. Write formula for evaluating the volumes of cone, sphere, cylinder and cube. Accept parameters from user and display the output.
9. WAP to find the sum of the first n terms of arithmetic progression.
   (**Hint**: $S_n = n/2(2a + (n - 1)d)$)
10. WAP to find sum of first n terms of geometric progression.
    (**Hint**: $S_n = a(1 - r^n)/(1 - r)$)

Answers

A1. Bloom Level: Knowledge/Remember

Fill in the Blanks

1. operator
2. operand
3. number of operands, role of operator
4. unary, binary
5. one
6. two
7. remainder
8. exponentiation
9. relational
10. not equal to
11. 65
12. 97
13. 48
14. opl
15. op2
16. false
17. bits
18. 1
19. =
20. augmented
21. same
22. right, left

True/False

1. False
2. False
3. True
4. False
5. True
6. True
7. False
8. False
9. False
10. True
11. True
12. True
13. True
14. False
15. False
16. True
17. True
18. True
19. True

Multiple Choice Questions (MCQ)

1. iv
2. iii
3. ii
4. iv

A3. Bloom Level: Application/Apply

Review Questions

1. (i) 3.0 (ii) -42.0 (iii) 36.0 (iv) 0 (v) 4.0
2. (i) 1111 1011 (ii) 1111 0110
3. (i) 2 (ii) 2.0 (iii) -3.0 (iv) 25 (v) 10 (vi) 2 (vii) 2.0 (viii) 25.0 (ix) 1.666667 (x) 10.0 (xi) 7.5 (xii) 0.04
4. (i) False (ii) False (iii) True (iv) True (v) 2 (vi) 0 (vii) 2 (viii) 1 (ix) 2 (x) 2 (xi) ‘’ (xii) ‘Pencil’ (xiii) False
5. (i) 15 (ii) 3 (iii) 78 (iv) 0 (v) 67 (vi) 77 (vii) 5 (viii) 1 (ix) 1
6. (i) a + 2 – 3 / 2 (ii) (b + (((b * b) – (4*a*c))**0.5))/(2*a) (iii) 2*a + 7//2 (iv) a**2 + b**2 >=2

Multiple Choice Questions (MCQ)

1. ii	**2.** ii	**3.** iii	**4.** ii	**5.** ii	**6.** i	**7.** i	**8.** i
9. iv	**10.** iii	**11.** iii	**12.** iv	**13.** iii	**14.** i	**15.** i	**16.** iii
17. iii	**18.** ii	**19.** i	**20.** ii	**21.** iii			

A5. Bloom Level: Evaluate

1.

i. Correct. 5
ii. Correct, –32
iii. Error. Division by zero.
iv. Correct. False
v. Error. Invalid syntax

2.

i. (c/d), (b * d)
ii. (b) (c/d), ((a*c), (b *d)
iii. Correct
iv. (2 * a * b)
v. Correct
vi. Correct
vii. (a*x**2)

CHAPTER

6 Control Flow

Contents

6.1 Introduction

Until now, we have written simple Python programs where we note that the statements are executed sequentially, in order. By default, execution starts from the first statement and flows sequentially from the first statement to the next and so on. However, while writing Python programs, situations may arise where there is a need for decision making based on some values. Also, when writing programs, situations may arise where there is a need to repeat a certain set of tasks. So, there is a need that provisions are made in the Python programs to handle the decision-making and the repetitive tasks.

In this chapter, we discuss the tools that control the program execution sequence, also known as **Control Flow.** The different kinds of control flow statements are discussed.

Learning Outcomes of this chapter

After completion of the chapter, the learner will be able to:

- Identify the control flow tools
- List the conditional statements
- List the iterative statements
- Use control flow tools in a program
- List the statements for controlling the loop
- Describe functionality of the different control statements
- Recognize errors in conditional and iterative statements
- Formulate a control flow statement
- Develop programs based on the concepts discussed.

6.2 Understanding Control Flow

Control flow is described in terms of Control and Flow. The first word "Control" means controlling the sequence of execution. In simple terms, it means that controlling behavior of the program results in a shift from the default behavior to a different one. Next, "Flow" relates to the sequence of execution of program statements. In a Python program, by default, the execution starts from the first statement and flows sequentially from the first statement to the next and so on. So, the task of control flow is to control the flow of program execution to get the desired behavior or result. This means that the sequential execution of statements in a Python program is controlled and execution flow of the statements is defined.

For example, in a library management system, we may want the program to allow issue of a book only if currently, total books issued to a student is less than three. For this, we first have to check the number of books issued to a student. Depending on the outcome, it is decided whether another book can be issued or not. Thus, the issue of book is now controlled by checking the number of books already issued to a student. The flow will depend on the result of control; if three books have already been issued, then another book will not be issued, else if less than three books have been issued, another book can be issued to the student.

Control flow allows us to control the order in which the statements in the program are executed. The program execution is controlled by the use of **control flow tools.**

There are three main types of control flow tools in Python:

- Conditional statements
- Iterative statements or Loop statements
- Function calls

This chapter covers the conditional and iterative statements. Functions are covered in later chapters.

6.3 Conditional Statement

The conditional statement works by first evaluating the condition, and then selecting from alternative actions based on outcome of the condition evaluation. The selection of an action transfers control from one point to the other. Python has the following conditional statements:

1. `if` statement
2. `if-else` statement
3. `if-elif-else` statement
4. Nested `if-else` statement

The conditional statements are discussed in the following subsections.

6.3.1 `if` Statement

The problems, for which the program is written, often require a set of actions to happen if the condition is true and no special action if the condition is false. For this kind of decision-making, `if` statement is provided in Python. The format of `if` statement in Python is as follows:

```
if Boolean expression:
    statement(s)
```

`if` statement is a compound statement; a compound statement has a header and a body. In the `if` statement,

Header is `if Boolean expression:`
Body is `statement(s)`

The important points to note about `if` statement is shown diagrammatically as follows:

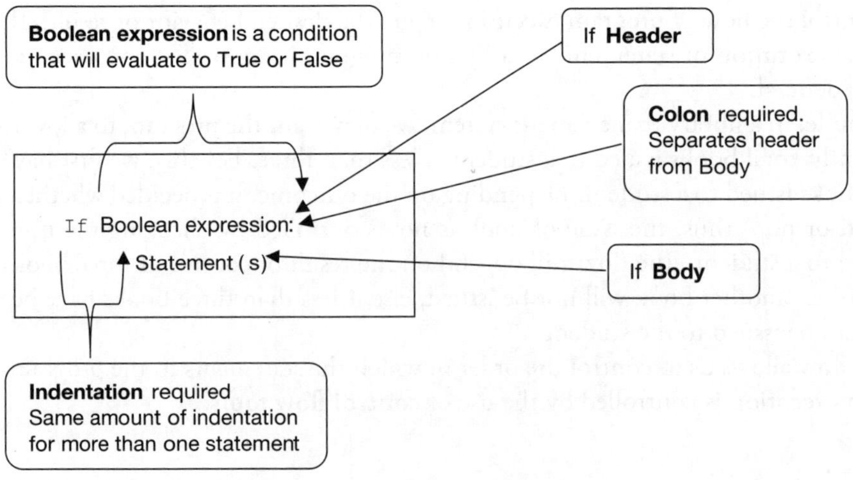

The `if` statement is executed as follows:

- The Boolean expression in `if` statement is the condition that is evaluated first. The result of evaluation is either True or False.
- If result is True, the body of `if` statement is executed.
- If result is False, the body is skipped. The execution control comes to the next statement following `if` statement.

Figure 6.1 shows the flowchart of `if` statement.

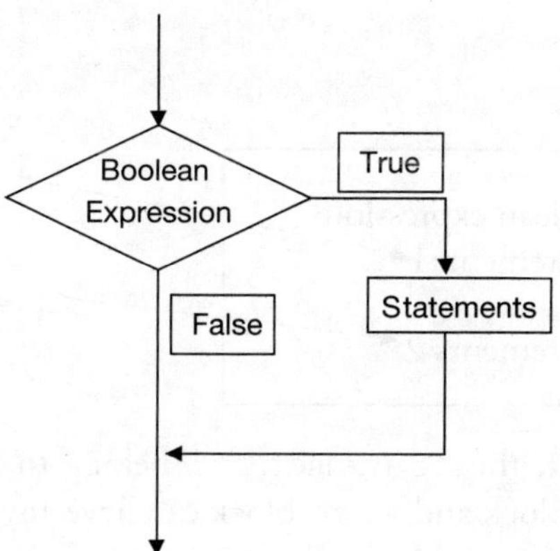

Figure 6.1 (a) Flowchart of `if` statement

> **Programming Tip**:
> Correct way if x:
> Incorrect way if x is True:
> If x == True:
> If bool(x):

For example, let us accept a number from the user. Then we check whether the number is positive. If the number is positive, display a message to the user; otherwise do nothing.

Example 6.1 (a) Python code to check if a number is positive (b) Output

```
# Print a message if number is positive

a = int(input("Enter the number "))
if a > 0:
    print("The number", a, "is positive")
```

(a)

```
Enter the number 3
The number 3 is positive
```

(b)

6.3.2 `if-else` Statement

Python programs that are written for common problems, often require a set of actions to happen if the condition is true and another set of actions to happen if the condition is false. To implement this kind of decision, the `if-else` statement is provided in Python. The format of `if-else` statement in Python is as follows:

```
if Boolean expression:
      statements1
else:
      statements2
```

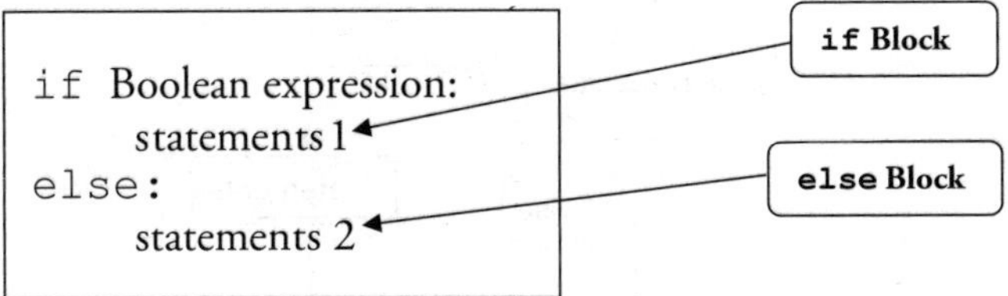

In the `if-else` statement, the `statements1` belong to `if` block, and `statements2` belong to `else` block. The `if` block and `else` block can have any number of statements. But there has to be at least one statement in each block. The `if-else` statement is executed as follows:

- The Boolean expression in `if-else` statement is the condition that is evaluated first. The result of evaluation is either True or False.
- If result is True, `if` block is executed.
- If result is False, `else` block is executed.
- After execution of `if` block or `else` block, the execution control comes to the next statement following the `if-else` statement.

Figure 6.2 shows the flowchart of `if-else` statement.

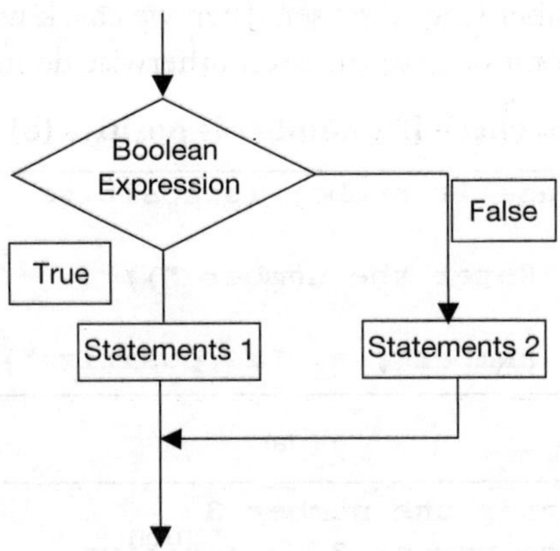

Figure 6.2 Flowchart of `if-else` statement

For example, let us accept a number from the user and check if the number is odd or not. Depending on whether the number is odd or not, a message is displayed, accordingly.

Example 6.2 (a) Python code to check if number is odd or not (b) Output

```
# Print a message if number is odd or not

a = int(input("Enter the number "))
if a%2 != 0:
    print("The number", a, "is odd")
else:
    print("The number", a, "is not odd")
```

(a)

```
Enter the number 4
The number 4 is not odd
```

(b)

6.3.3 `if-elif-else` Statement

The problems for which Python programs are written often require a set of actions to happen, after checking for multiple conditions that are mutually exclusive. It means that the program checks if a given condition is true or false, then it checks for another condition, and so on. These are also referred to as conditions that are chained together. To enable this kind of decision-making, `if-elif-else` statement is provided in Python. The format of `if-elif-else` statement in Python is as follows:

```
if Boolean expression1:
     statements1
elif Boolean expression2:
     statements2
elif Boolean expression3:
     statements3
elif Boolean expression4:
     statements4
     :
     :
else:
     statements5
```

`elif` is an abbreviation of `else if`. Any number of `elif` is allowed but only one (optional) `else` statement is allowed. The `elif` and `else` are also called branches of the `if-elif-else` statement. The `else` must be last branch in the statement.

The `if-elif-else` statement is executed as follows:

- Only one branch will be executed.

- The conditions are checked in a sequence.
- `expression1` is the condition that is evaluated first. The result of evaluation is either True or False.
- If result is True, `if` block is executed (`statements1`).
- If result is False, `expression2` is evaluated. The result of evaluation is either True or False.
- If result is True, `statements2` is executed.
- If result is False, `expression3` is evaluated and so on.
- `Else` block is executed when none of `elif` has been executed. `Else` is a final catch-all situation.
- After execution of `if` block, `elif` block or `else` block, the execution control comes to the next statement following the `if-elif-else` statement.

Figure 6.3 shows the flowchart of `if-elif` statement.

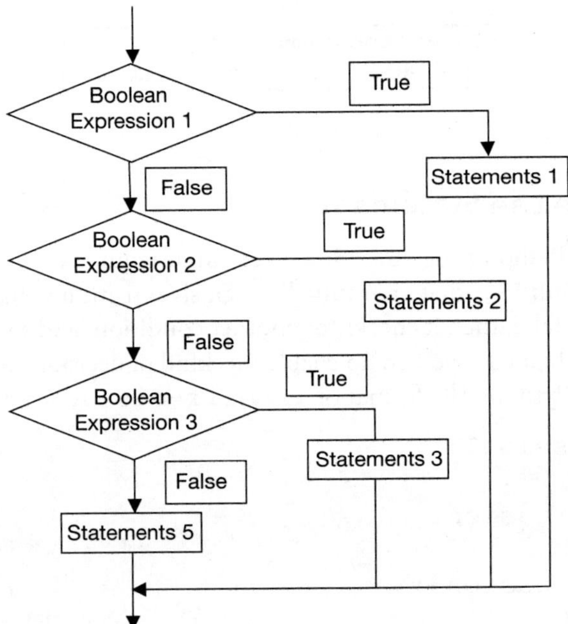

Figure 6.3 Flowchart of `if-elif` statement

So, the syntax of complete `if` statement can be written as:

```
if expression:  statements
{elif expression: statements}
{else: statements}
```

For example, let us accept an integer from the user and check if it is positive, negative or zero, and accordingly, a message is displayed.

Example 6.3 (a) Python code to check if integer is positive, negative or zero (b) Output

```
# Find whether an integer is positive, negative or zero

a = int(input("Enter the number "))
if a == 0:
    print("The number", a, "is zero")
elif a<0:
    print("The number", a, "is negative")
else:
    print("The number", a, "is positive")
```

(a)

```
Enter the number 5
The number 5 is positive
>>>
```

```
Enter the number -3
The number -3 is negative
>>>
```

```
Enter the number 0
The number 0 is zero
```

(b)

6.3.4 Nested `if-else` Statement

In a nested `if-else` statement, the `if` body or `if-else` body contains another `if` statement or `if-else` statement. One conditional is nested within another. There can be any number of nested `if` statements inside one another. The statements need to be indented properly for identifying the nesting.

Some ways in which nesting can happen are as follows:

```
if Boolean
expression1:
Statements1
else:
if Boolean
expression2:
      Statements2
else:
      Statements3
```

```
if Boolean
expression1:
Statements1
else:
if Boolean
expression2:
      Statements2
```

```
if Boolean expres-
sion1:
if Boolean
expression2:
      Statements1
else:
      Statements2
```

Also, several options exist for representing multiple conditions, like

- Nested `if` statement
- Using logical operators
- Using short form for Boolean expression

For example, to check whether an integer is a positive two-digit number, the `if` condition can be written in the following ways:

Nested `if` statement

```
if x > 9:
   if x<100:
      print(x, "is a positive two-digit number")
```

Using Logical operator

```
if x > 9 and x <100:
   print(x, "is a positive two-digit number")
```

Using short form of Boolean expression

```
if 9 < x < 100:
   print(x, "is a positive two-digit number")
```

For example, let us write a program to find the greatest of three numbers. Example 6.4 (a) shows the Python code and 6.4 (b) shows the output after execution of the code. To show the use of different options for writing multiple conditions, the first `if` statement is nested, the second `if` statement uses the short form of Boolean expression and the third `if` statement uses logical operator.

Example 6.4 (a) Python code to find maximum of three numbers (b) Output

```
#Find maximum of three numbers

a = int(input("Enter the number 1 "))
b = int(input("Enter the number 2 "))
c = int(input("Enter the number 3 "))

if a > b:
    if a> c:
        print("The number", a, "is greatest")
    else:
        print("The number", c, "is greatest")
if a < b > c:
    print("The number", b, "is greatest")
if a < b and b < c:
    print("The number", c, "is greatest")
```

(a)

```
Enter the number 1 45
Enter the number 2 34
Enter the number 3 67
The number 67 is greatest
>>>
```

(b)

6.4 Iterative Statements

Iteration, as a word, means repetition. Python provides iterative statements so that a statement or a set of statements in the code can be executed again and again. In Python, the statement(s) are iterated while the condition is true. The iteration stops and exits when the condition becomes false. Python has the following iterative statements:

1. `while` statement
2. `for` statement
3. Nested loops

In addition to the `for` and `while` statements, there are other loop operations and concepts in Python, which will be discussed in the later chapters. The iterative statements are discussed in the following subsections.

6.4.1 `while` Statement

The `while` statement is a common way to code the loops. The loop executes repeatedly while the condition is true. The syntax of the `while` statement is as follows:

```
while expression:
      statement(s)
```

The `while` statement is a compound statement. A compound statement has a header and a body.

Header is `while expression:`
Body is `Statement(s)`

The important points to note about `while` statement is shown diagrammatically as follows:

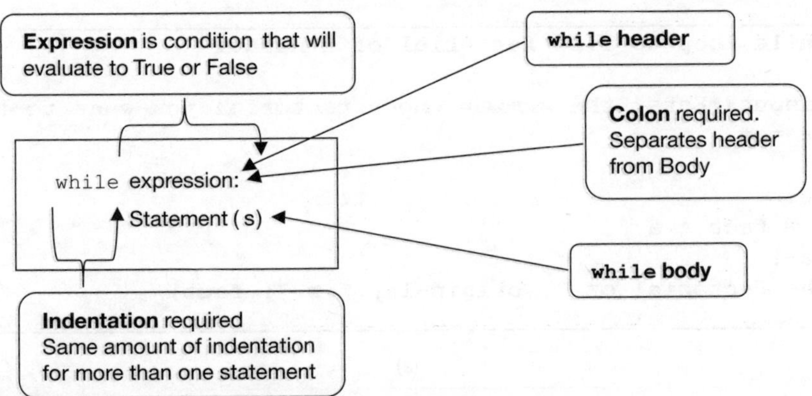

The `while` statement is executed as follows:

- The expression in `while` statement is evaluated first. The result of evaluation is either True or False.
- If the result is True, the body of `while` statement is executed; then, the execution control goes to the start of the `while` statement, for the next iteration. Again, the expression in the `while`

statement is evaluated. If the result of evaluation is True, then the body of `while` statement is executed, again. This sequence is repeated until the result of evaluation is False.

- If result is False, the body is skipped and `while` loop is exited. The execution control comes to the next statement following the `while` statement.

It is to be noted that loop counter in the expression of `while` statement must be initialized before the `while` loop and must be manipulated inside the `while` loop. If loop counter does not change for the next iteration, then it might lead to an infinite loop.

Also, since `while` loops are based on condition, you may not know in advance, the number of times the loop will iterate.

Figure 6.4 shows the flowchart of `while` statement.

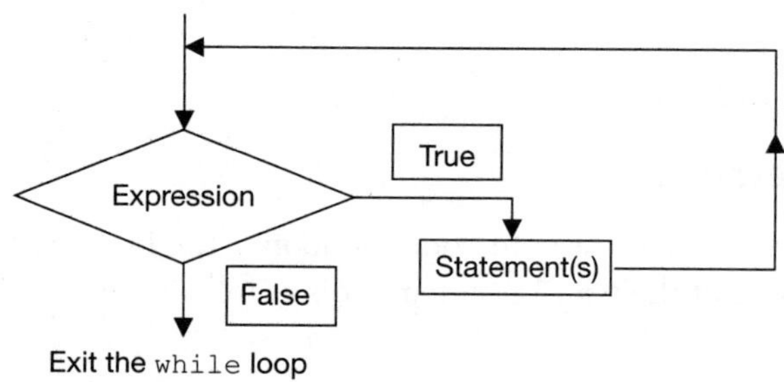

Figure 6.4 Flowchart of **`while`** statement

For example, let us write a program to find the factorial of a number using the `while` loop. For this, we accept the number from the user, find the factorial using the `while` loop and display the result to the user.

Example 6.5 (a) Python code to find factorial of a number (b) Output.

```
#Using while loop to find factorial of a number

a = int(input("Enter the number whose factorial you want to find "))
originala = a
fact = 1
while a>0:
    fact = fact * a
    a = a-1
print("The factorial of ", originala, "is ", fact)
```

(a)

```
Enter the number whose factorial you want to find 5
The factorial of  5 is  120
```

(b)

6.4.2 for Statement

Python has for statement for repeated execution of a statement or a block of statements. A for statement has a loop counter, loop variable or target whose value forms basis of the repeated execution. Since the for statement is based on a counter, most often the number of iterations is known before entering the for statement. The format of the for statement in Python is as follows:

```
for target in iterable:
    statement(s)
```

where,

iterable is a sequence that has a beginning and an end, and a way to go through all the items in it.
target is the control variable of the for statement that is assigned value from the iterable, during each iteration.

It may be noted that the "in" keyword is not related to the membership operator.

The important points to note about for statement are shown diagrammatically as follows:

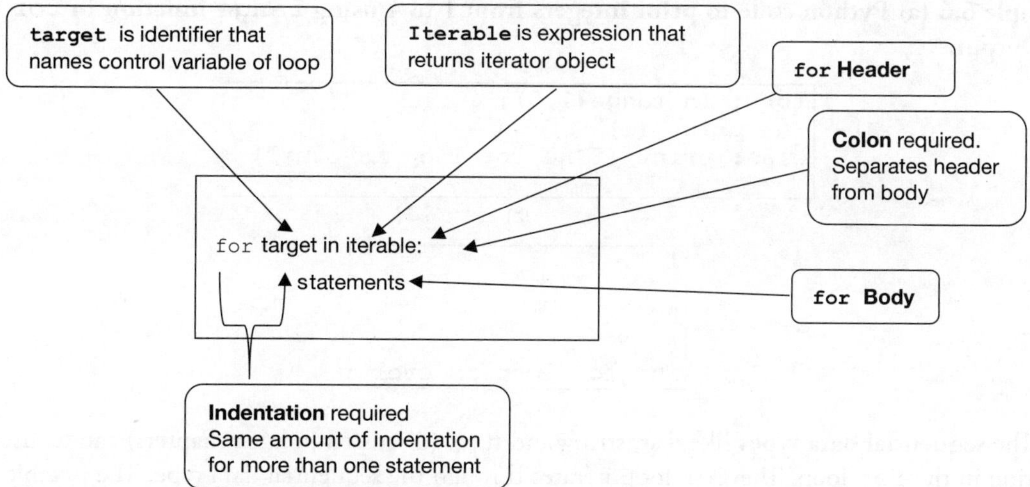

The for statement/loop is executed as follows:

- The iterable provides the items of iterator.
- The target steps through the items of iterator (from iterable), in order.
- The statement(s) in for loop execute once for each item of iterator.
- The loop ends when either (1) items are exhausted, or (2) exception is raised, or (3) break or return statement is executed.
- The loop body does not execute at all if the iterator yields no items.
- When the for loop terminates, the target remains bound to the last value to which the loop statement has bound it.
- In cases where the iterator is a mutable object, value of the object must not be altered within the for statement.

The `for` loop is generally executed using two ways:

1. `range()` function, and
2. Sequential data types

The **`range()`** function in Python is used when iteration is to be done over a sequence of integers. There are three syntax of `range` function.

1. **`range(n)`** – It returns a list having consecutive integers from 0 to n – 1
2. **`range(start, end)`** – It returns a list having consecutive integers from start to end – 1. If start is greater than end, then empty list is returned.
3. **`range(start, end, increment)`** – It returns a list having integers from start to end – 1, where each adjacent item has a difference of the increment.

For example, let us write a program to print the integers 1 to 4 using the `range()` function in the `for` loop. For this, we use range (start, end). Since the integers have to be printed till 4, the end is taken as 5.

Example 6.6 (a) Python code to print integers from 1 to 4 using `range` function in `for` loop (b) Output.

```
for i in range(1,5):
    print (i)
else: print ("The for loop is over")
```

(a)

```
1
2
3
4
The for loop is over
```

(b)

The **sequential data types** like, list, string and tuple (discussed in later chapters) can be used for iteration in the `for` loop. The `for` loop iterates through the sequential data type. The iterable is an object that can be a list, tuple, string, dict, set etc. The `for` loop can iterate over any iterable.

For example, let us write a program to print the integers 1 and 4 using the `iterable` in the `for` loop. For this, we define iterable as a list.

Example 6.7 (a) Python code to print integers from 1 and 4 using iterable in `for` loop (b) Output.

```
iterable = [1, 4]
for target in iterable:
    print(target)
```

(a)

```
1
4
```

(b)

When using sequential data types, the internal implementation of the `for` statement is as follows:

1. An iterable is an object. For example, iterable is a list `x = [5, 20]`.
2. Get iterator from iterable. For this, `iter()` function gets created. For example, `y = iter(x)`.
3. Get each item of iterator using `next()` function. For example, `next(y)`.

For example,

```
iterable = [1, 4]          #define the list
iterator = iter(iterable)  #get iterator using iter() from list
print (next(iterator))     #get each item of iterator using next()
```

6.4.3 Nested Loops

The defining of one loop within another is called nested loop. Python allows nested loops. In a nested loop, another `for` loop can be defined within a `for` loop, or, a `while` loop within a `while` loop can be defined. Also, any type of loop can be defined inside of any other type of loop. So, `for` loop can be defined within `while` loop, and vice-versa.

The syntax of nested `for` loop is as follows:

```
for target1 in iterable:
        for target2 in iterable:
                statement2(s)
        statement1(s)
```

The syntax of nested `while` loop is as follows:

```
while expression1:
        while expression2:
                statement2(s)

        statement1(s)
```

The syntax of `while` loop inside `for` loop is:

```
for target1 in iterable:
        while expression:
                statement(s)

        statement1(s)
```

The *nested loops* are executed as follows:

- The nested loop may be `for-for`, `while-for`, `for-while` or `while-while`.
- For the first value of the outer loop, the whole inner loop executes.
- For the next value of the outer loop, the whole inner loop executes
- This continues, until the outer loop stops. When the outer loop stops, the inner loop does not execute further.

For example, let us write a program to create a triangular pattern of stars.

Example 6.8 (a) Python code to print triangular pattern from stars (b) Output

```
#WAP to print stars 1-7-1

n = 7
for i in range(n):
    for j in range(i):
        print("*", end="")
    print("")

while n>=0:
    j=n
    while j>0:
        print("*", end="")
        j = j-1
    n = n-1
    print("")
```

(a)

```
*
**
***
****
*****
******
*******
******
*****
****
***
**
*
```

(b)

6.5 Loop Control Statements

The loop statements – `for` loop and `while` loop – allow repeated execution of a set of statements, easily and in an efficient manner. The iteration in `while` loop is while the test expression is true; and in `for` loop, till the loop counter iterates over the sequence. However, sometimes there is a need to change the execution sequence of the loop or terminate the loop without checking the expression or loop counter. This may be due to some condition arising within the body of the loop. Loop control statements are used for this purpose. They are used to handle iterations based on some conditions defined within the body of the loop.

There are three loop control statements in Python: (1) Break, (2) Continue, and (3)Pass.

Break statement is used to terminate the loop and exit it. The control is transferred to the statement immediately following the loop statement.

Continue statement causes the remainder part of loop's current iteration to be skipped. The control comes to header of the loop for next iteration.
Pass statement is a null statement and does nothing. It is required in the loop for syntax purposes.
The loop control statements are discussed in detail in the following subsections.

6.5.1 Break

The `break` statement is used to exit from the loop when an external condition is true. It is included in the body of the loop, usually in a conditional statement. When a condition becomes true in a conditional statement, and you do not want to iterate over the loop again, use the `break` statement.

The `break` statement can be used in both `while` and `for` loops. In the program, `break` statement results in a break out of a loop.

In a loop, when `break` statement is executed, execution of the loop terminates. The program control comes to next statement after the loop.

In a nested loop, when `break` statement is executed, execution of the current loop terminates and program control comes to the enclosing loop.

The working of `break` statement in `for` loop, `while` loop and nested loop is shown below:

Loops	Nested Loops

for var in sequence
    # code inside for loop
    if condition:
        break
    # code inside for loop ----- (1)
→# code outside for loop
	for var in sequence 1
	    for var1 in sequence 2
	        # code inside for loop 2
	        if condition:
	            break
	        # code inside for loop 2
	    → # code inside for loop 1
	# code outside nested loop

while test expression
    # code inside while loop
    if condition:
        break
    # code inside while loop---- (2)
→# code outside while loop
	while test expression 1
	    while test expression 2
	        # code inside while loop 2
	        if condition:
	            break
	        # code inside while loop 2
	    → # code in while loop 1
	# code outside nested loop

For example, let us write a program to print the letters of a word until a vowel is found in the word. For this, we iterate over each character in the word, check whether it is a vowel. If no, we print the character and continue with the next iteration; if yes, then we print the vowel and stop.

Example 6.9 (a) Python code to print characters of word until a vowel is found (b) Output

```
# WAP to print letters of the word until a vowel is found

word = input("Enter a word ")
for letter in word:
   if letter in "aeiou":
      print ("The first vowel in", word, "is :", letter)
      break
   print("The letter is ", letter)
print("The rest of the characters of", word, "will not print")
```

(a)

```
Enter a word Python
The letter is  P
The letter is  y
The letter is  t
The letter is  h
The first vowel in Python is : o
The rest of the characters of Python will not print
>>>
```

```
Enter a word Banana
The letter is  B
The first vowel in Banana is : a
The rest of the characters of Banana will not print
```

(b)

Let us understand this program.

- A string is taken as input in word.
- The `for` loop is run over each letter of the word.
- The `if` statement checks if a letter is a vowel.
- If yes, then it prints the letter. The `break` statement is used to exit `for` loop once a vowel is found in a word.
  - o The `break` statement will take the control out of the loop.
  - o The control comes to the last `print` statement.
- If no, then the letter is printed and the next iteration of `for` loop is executed.

6.5.2 Continue

The `continue` statement is used in loops to skip code inside a loop for the current iteration, when a condition is true. The loop does not terminate, but the current iteration is terminated, and execution continues with the next iteration of the loop. It is included in the body of the loop, usually in a conditional statement. Use `continue` with conditional statement for a condition when you do not want to execute rest of the statements, if a particular condition becomes true.

In the program, `continue` statement results in continuation of the next iteration. `Continue` statement means that the program continues with the loop, but in the next iteration. So, when `continue` is executed, control comes to the top of the loop. The `continue` statement can be used in both `while` and `for` loops. In a `while` loop, the exit condition is evaluated again and executed. In case of `for` loop, the iteration will move to the next item.

In a loop, when `continue` statement is executed, it terminates execution of current iteration of the loop and program control comes to next iteration of the loop.

In a nested loop, when `continue` statement is executed, it terminates execution of current loop and program control comes to the enclosing loop.

The working of `continue` statement in `for` loop, `while` loop and `nested` loop is shown below.

Loop	Nested Loop

for var in sequence
  # code inside *for* loop
  if condition:
    continue
  # code inside *for* loop ------ (1)
# code outside *for* loop 	
	for var in sequence 1
	  for var1 in sequence 2
	    # code inside *for* loop 2
	    if condition:
	      continue
	    # code inside *for* loop 2
	  # code inside *for* loop 1
	# code outside nested loop

while test expression
  # code inside *while* loop
  if condition:
    continue
  # code inside *while* loop---- (2)
# code outside while loop 	
	while test expression1
	  while test expression2
	    # code inside *while* loop2
	    if condition:
	      continue
	    # code inside *while* loop2
	  # code inside *while* loop1
	# code outside nested loop

For example, let us write a program to print all characters of a word and also mention when a character is a vowel. For this, we iterate over each character in the word, check whether it is a vowel. If yes, we print that the character is a vowel and continue with the next iteration. If no, we print the character.

Example 6.10 (a) Python code to print all characters of word and also identify vowels (b) Output

```
# WAP to print all vowels of the in a word

word = input("Enter a word ")
for letter in word:
    if letter in "aeiou":
        print ("The letter is ", letter, "- a vowel")
        continue
    if letter != " ":
        print("The letter is ", letter)
|
```

(a)

```
Enter a word Python
The letter is  P
The letter is  y
The letter is  t
The letter is  h
The letter is  o – a vowel
The letter is  n
>>>
```

```
Enter a word This is a beautiful world
The letter is  T
The letter is  h
The letter is  i – a vowel
The letter is  s
The letter is  i – a vowel
The letter is  s
The letter is  a – a vowel
The letter is  b
The letter is  e – a vowel
The letter is  a – a vowel
The letter is  u – a vowel
The letter is  t
The letter is  i – a vowel
The letter is  f
The letter is  u – a vowel
The letter is  l
The letter is  w
The letter is  o – a vowel
The letter is  r
The letter is  l
The letter is  d
>>>
```

(b)

Let us understand this program.

- A string is taken as input in word
- The `for` loop is run over each letter of the word.
- The `if` statement checks if a letter is a vowel.
- If yes, then it prints the letter. The `continue` statement is used to skip the rest of the statements in `for` loop and go for the next iteration when a vowel is found in a word.
- If no, then the letter is printed if it is not a blank.
- The next iteration of `for` loop is executed.

6.5.3 Pass

The `pass` statement, on execution, does nothing. It is a null statement. It is used in loops where a statement is required syntactically, but no action is to be performed, because when `pass` statement is executed, nothing happens. It is usually used in `if` statement and is the only statement. Using it as a placeholder, the program compiles successfully.

The `pass` statement can be used in both `while` and `for` loops.

For example, let us write a program to print all characters of a word and use pass when a vowel is present. For this, we iterate over each character in the word, check whether it is a vowel. If yes, we pass. The character is printed.

Example 6.11 (a) Python code to print all characters of word and use pass when a vowel is present (b) Output

```
# WAP to print all characters of a word
#Version 1: Using pass as placeholder

word = input("Enter a word ")
for letter in word:
   if letter in "aeiou":
         pass
         print("This is pass", letter)
   if letter != "":
         print("The letter is ", letter)

#Version 2: Replacing code for pass

word = input("Enter a word ")
for letter in word:
   if letter in "aeiou":
         print ("The letter is ", letter, "- a vowel")
         continue
   if letter != " ":
         print("The letter is ", letter)
```

(a)

```
Enter a word Python
The letter is  P
The letter is  y
The letter is  t
The letter is  h
This is pass o
The letter is  o
The letter is  n
```

```
Enter a word Python
The letter is  P
The letter is  y
The letter is  t
The letter is  h
The letter is  o - a vowel
The letter is  n
>>>
```

(b)

Let us understand this program.

- In the first version, we see that when a letter is a vowel, we use pass as a placeholder.
- In the second version we put the code that will execute when a letter is a vowel.
- The output of the program is also shown for the two versions.

So, we see that pass can be used as a placeholder

- when nothing is to be done
- when in future, we want to replace the code; otherwise an empty body will report an error.

6.6 Else Statement with Loops

In Python, `for` loop and `while` loop support the `else` statement with it. The `else` part is optional. For both `for` and `while` loops, the `else` part is executed only if during the iteration, neither `break` nor `continue` statement is executed.

The format of the `for` statement with `else` is as follows:

```
for target in iterable:
      statement(s)
else:
      statement(s)
```

The format of the `while` statement with `else` is as follows:

```
while expression:
      statement(s)
else:
      statement(s)
```

The `else` statement is executed in the following cases:

- In `for` loop, `else` statement is executed after the loop has iterated completely over the iterable.
- In `while` loop, `else` statement is executed when the `while` expression becomes false.

For example, let us write a program to find all prime numbers between any two numbers.

Example 6.12 (a) Python code to print all prime numbers between any two numbers (b) Output

```
# WAP to find all prime numbers between any two numbers

num1 = int(input("Enter low range "))
num2 = int(input("Enter high range "))

for num in range( num1, num2+1):
  #  if num>1:
        for i in range( 2, num//2 ):
            if num % i == 0:
              break
        else:
            print(num, "is a prime number between", num1,"and", num2)
```

(a)

```
Enter low range 22
Enter high range 44
23 is a prime number between 22 and 44
29 is a prime number between 22 and 44
31 is a prime number between 22 and 44
37 is a prime number between 22 and 44
41 is a prime number between 22 and 44
43 is a prime number between 22 and 44
>>> |
```

(b)

6.7 Accumulation Pattern

Accumulation Pattern is a programming pattern where a sequence is traversed and while iterating the sequence, it keeps updating a variable. The variable is called the accumulator. When the traversal is complete, the variable has an accumulated single value. For example, sum of all elements.

To create an accumulation pattern, there is a need for the following:

- Initialize a variable (accumulator)
- Iterate over a sequence
- Update accumulator on each iteration.

Let us take an example of finding the sum of numbers in a list.

Example 6.13 (a) Python code to find the sum of n numbers using accumulation pattern (b) Output

```
1 # accumulator pattern
2 x = 0
3 for i in range(11):
4     x = x + i
5 print(x)
```

(a)

```
55
```

(b)

We note the following:

- Line 2: The variable (accumulator) is initialized to 0
- Line 4: The `for` loop iterates 10 times
- Line 5: The accumulator is updated each time during the iteration
- Line 6: The sum of elements gets accumulated in `x` and is printed.

Some examples of programs that use accumulator are:

- Find the product of first n numbers.
- Find the square of a number using addition.

The accumulator pattern shall be discussed in the chapters corresponding to sequence data types.

6.8 Solved Questions with Explanation

1) Find the output:

```
letter = input("Enter a character: ")
if ('a'<letter<='z'):
    print("Letter is in lowercase")
elif ('A'<letter<='Z'):
    print("Letter is in uppercase")
```

Output

```
Enter a character: w
Letter is in lowercase
>>>
```

```
Enter a character: G
Letter is in uppercase
```

Explanation: It checks whether the input character is in uppercase or lowercase.

2) Find the output:

```
age = int(input("Enter your age: "))
if (age>=18):
    print("Eligible for Voting")
else:
    print("Not eligible for Voting")
```

Output

```
Enter your age: 45
Eligible for Voting
>>>
```

```
Enter your age: 11
Not eligible for Voting
>>>
```

Explanation: It checks whether a person is eligible for voting or not. It checks if the age is equal to or greater than 18.

3) Find the output:

```
a = int(input("Enter a number: "))
if (a > 5 and a <10):
    print("Hello")
else:
    print("Good Bye")
```

Output

```
Enter a number: 5
Good Bye
>>>
```

```
Enter a number: 66
Good Bye
>>>
```

```
Enter a number: 3
Good Bye
>>>
```

```
Enter a number: 7
Hello
>>>
```

Explanation: It checks whether the given number is between 5 and 10. If yes, it prints Hello; otherwise Goodbye

4) Find the output:

```
i = 2; j = 4; k = 6; print(i, j, k)      # (1)
if i<j:
    if j<k:
        i = k  #  (2)
    else:
        i = j  #  (3)
else:
    if j> k:
        j = k  #  (4)
    else:
        k = j  #  (5)
print(i, j, k) #  (6)
```

Output

```
2 4 6
6 4 6
>>> |
```

If (1) is replaced by the following what will be the output at (1) and (6)

```
i = -2; j = -4; k = 6; print(i, j, k)
i = 2; j = 6; k = 4; print(i, j, k)
i = 2; j = 6; k = 2; print(i, j, k)
i = 6; j = 2; k = 4; print(i, j, k)
i = 6; j = 4; k = 2; print(i, j, k)
```

```
-2 -4 6
-2 -4 -4
>>>
```

```
2 6 4
6 6 4
>>>
```

```
2 6 2
6 6 2
>>>
```

```
6 2 4
6 2 2
>>>
```

```
6 4 2
6 2 2
>>> |
```

Explanation: Identify the if-statement that executes with change in the values of i, j, k.

5) Find the output:

```
# Accept a word. Print all letters except "a". Count number of "a" in word
word = input("Enter a word: ")
count=0
for letter in word:
    if letter == 'a':
        count+=1
        continue
    print('Current Letter :', letter)
print("Letter a occurred", count, "times")
```

Output

```
Enter a word: abracadabra
Current Letter : b
Current Letter : r
Current Letter : c
Current Letter : d
Current Letter : b
Current Letter : r
Letter a occurred 5 times
>>>
```

```
Enter a word: Python
Current Letter : P
Current Letter : y
Current Letter : t
Current Letter : h
Current Letter : o
Current Letter : n
Letter a occurred 0 times
```

Explanation: When letter a appears, count is incremented and `continue` gets executed. `Continue` skips the current loop, and goes for the next iteration. The `print` statement gets skipped.

6) Find the output for following and justify the answer:

```
for x in range(1,5):
     print(x)
     continue
     print(x, "again")
```

```
for x in range(1,5):
     print(x)
     break
     print(x, "again")
```

Output

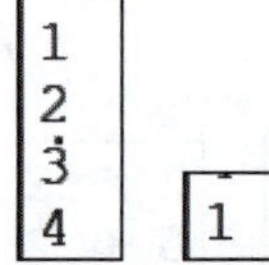

Explanation: In `continue`, the statements following it get skipped and control goes to the next iteration. But in `break`, it exits the loop. So in the first case, 1 to 4 is printed but in the second case only 1 is printed. The `print` statement with `again`, does not get printed in both cases, as the control does not come to that statement in both cases.

7) Find the output for following and justify the answer:

```
n = n1 = int(input("Enter first number"))
n2 = int(input("Enter second number"))
m = int(input("Enter the multiple"))
while n<=n2:
    if n%m == 0:
        print("The number", n, "is multiple of", m,
                "between", n1, "and", n2)
    n=n+1
```

Output

```
Enter first number3
Enter second number12
Enter the multiple3
The number 3 is multiple of 3 between 3 and 12
The number 6 is multiple of 3 between 3 and 12
The number 9 is multiple of 3 between 3 and 12
The number 12 is multiple of 3 between 3 and 12
>>>
```

```
Enter first number4
Enter second number15
Enter the multiple3
The number 6 is multiple of 3 between 4 and 15
The number 9 is multiple of 3 between 4 and 15
The number 12 is multiple of 3 between 4 and 15
The number 15 is multiple of 3 between 4 and 15
>>> |
```

Explanation: The program finds all multiples of m between n1 and n2.

6.9 Programming Examples

In this section, few sample programs are given with their output.

Program 6.1: WAP to (1) accept two numbers from the user; (2) check whether they are equal or not and (3) print message if the numbers are equal.

```
# Print a message if two numbers are equal

a = int(input("Enter the first number "))
b = int(input("Enter the second number "))

if a == b:
    print("The number", a, "and", b, "are equal")
```

Output

```
Enter the first number 1
Enter the second number 1
The number 1 and 1 are equal
```

Program 6.2: WAP to (1) accept a number from the user; (2) check whether the number is positive or not and (3) print the message accordingly.

```
# Print a message if number is positive or not

a = int(input("Enter the number "))
if a > 0:
    print("The number", a, "is positive")
else:
    print("The number", a, "is not positive")
```

Output

```
Enter the number -2
The number -2 is not positive
```

Program 6.3: WAP to (1) accept two numbers from the user; (2) check whether they are equal or not and (3) print the message accordingly.

```
# Print a message if two numbers are equal or not

a = int(input("Enter the first number "))
b = int(input("Enter the second number "))
if a == b:
    print("The number", a, "and", b, "are equal")
else:
    print("The number", a, "and", b, "are not equal")
```

Output

```
Enter the first number 2
Enter the second number 3
The number 2 and 3 are not equal
```

Program 6.4: WAP to (1) accept a number from the user; (2) check whether the number is even or not and (3) print message accordingly.

```
# Print a message if number is even or not

a = int(input("Enter the number "))
if a%2 == 0:
    print("The number", a, "is even")
else:
    print("The number", a, "is not even")
```

Output

```
Enter the number 3
The number 3 is not even
>>>
```

Program 6.5: WAP to (1) accept a year from the user; (2) check whether year is leap year or not and (3) print message accordingly.

```
#WAP to check whether a year is leap year or not

year = int(input("Enter the year to check for leap year "))
if (year%4 == 0 and year%100 != 0 or year %400 ==0):
    print (year , "is a leap year")
else:
    print(year , "is not a leap year")
```

Output

```
Enter the year to check for leap year 1994
1994 is not a leap year
```

Program 6.6: WAP to find sum of the first 100 natural numbers, using (1) `while` loop and (2) `for` loop.

```
#Use while loop to find sum of first 100 numbers

num = 1; sum = 0
while num<=100:
    sum = sum + num
    num = num + 1
print("The sum of first", num-1, "numbers is ", sum)
```

Output

```
The sum of first 100 numbers is  5050
```

```
#Use for loop to find sum of first 100 numbers
sum=0
for num in range(1,101,1):
    sum = sum + num
print("The sum of first", num, "numbers is ", sum)
```

Output

```
The sum of first 100 numbers is  5050
```

Program 6.7: WAP to find the factorial of n, using `for` loop.

```
#Using for loop to find factorial of a number

a = int(input("Enter the number whose factorial you want to find "))
fact = 1
for i in range(1,a+1,1):
    fact = fact * i
print("The factorial of ", a, "is ", fact)
```

Output

```
Enter the number whose factorial you want to find 6
The factorial of  6 is  720
```

Program 6.8: Find sum of series 1 + (1 + 2) + (1 + 2 + 3) …. n terms.

```
# Find sum of series 1 + (1+2)+ (1+2+3) + ... + (1+2+3..+n)
# The sum is given by (n(n+1)(n+2))/6

n = int(input("Enter the number till where you want to find the sum "))
sum = (n * (n + 1)* (n + 2))/6
print("Sum =", sum)
```

Output

```
Enter the number till where you want to find the sum 5
Sum = 35.0
```

Program 6.9: Find sum of the series 1 + 2 + 3 + … + n.

```
# Find sum of series 1 + 2 + 3 + … + n

a = int(input("Enter the number till where you want to find the sum "))
num = 1; sum = 0
while num<=a:
    sum+=num
    num+=1
print("The sum of first", a, "numbers is ", sum)
```

Output

```
Enter the number till where you want to find the sum 5
The sum of first 5 numbers is  15
```

```
Enter the number till where you want to find the sum 10
The sum of first 10 numbers is  55
```

Program 6.10: WAP to find the Least Common Multiple (LCM) of two numbers.

```
# Python Program to find the L.C.M. of two input number

print("============================")
print("Find LCM of Two Numbers")
print("============================")
x = int(input("Enter the First number: "))
y = int(input("Enter the Second number: "))

# find the greater number
if x > y:
   big = x
else:
   big = y

while(True):
   if((big % x == 0) and (big % y == 0)):
         lcm = big
         break
   big += 1
print("The L.C.M. of",x, "and", y, "is= ", lcm)
```

Output

```
==========================
Find LCM of Two Numbers
==========================
Enter the First number: 23
Enter the Second number: 12
The L.C.M. of 23 and 12 is=  276
>>>
```

```
==========================
Find LCM of Two Numbers
==========================
Enter the First number: 12
Enter the Second number: 45
The L.C.M. of 12 and 45 is=  180
>>> |
```

Program 6.11: WAP to find the factors of a number.

```
# WAP to find factors of a given number

print("=========================")
print("Find Factors of a Number")
print("=========================")
x = int(input("Enter the Number: "))
print("The factors of",x,"are as follows-")
for i in range(1, x + 1):
    if x % i == 0:
        print(i)
```

Output

```
==========================
Find Factors of a Number
==========================
Enter the Number: 8
The factors of 8 are:
1
2
4
8
```

```
==========================
Find Factors of a Number
==========================
Enter the Number: 10
The factors of 10 are as follows-
1
2
5
10
```

```
==========================
Find Factors of a Number
==========================
Enter the Number: 36
The factors of 36 are as follows-
1
2
3
4
6
9
12
18
36
```

Program 6.12: WAP to find whether a given number is Armstrong number or not.
Armstrong number is a number in which the sum of the digits raised to the power of the number of digits in the number is the number itself.

For a 3-digit number xyz, it is $x^3 + y^3 + z^3$
For a 4-digit number abcd, it is $a^4 + b^4 + c^4 + d^4$
E.g. 0, 1, 153, 370, 371.407, 1634, 8208, and 9474.

```
# WAP to check if the number is an Armstrong number or not

print("==========================")
print("Check Armstrong Number")
print("==========================")
n = int(input("Enter a number: "))
sumcube = 0
temp = ntemp = n              # number stored in temp, ntemp
numdigit=0
while(temp>0):               #numdigit counts number of digits
    numdigit=numdigit + 1
    temp=temp//10
# find sum of cube of each digit
while ntemp > 0:
   digit = ntemp % 10          # separate a digit from ntemp(rightmost)
   sumtemp = digit ** numdigit
   print(digit, "**", numdigit, "= ", sumtemp)
   sumcube += sumtemp          # add cube of digit to the sum

   ntemp //= 10                # remove digit from ntemp(rightmost)

if n == sumcube:
   print(n,"is an Armstrong number")
else:
   print(n,"is not an Armstrong number")
```

Output

```
==========================
Check Armstrong Number
==========================
Enter a number: 153
3 ** 3 =  27
5 ** 3 =  125
1 ** 3 =  1
153 is an Armstrong number
>>>
```

```
==========================
Check Armstrong Number
==========================
Enter a number: 1634
4 ** 4 =  256
3 ** 4 =  81
6 ** 4 =  1296
1 ** 4 =  1
1634 is an Armstrong number
>>>
```

```
==========================
Check Armstrong Number
==========================
Enter a number: 9474
4 ** 4 =  256
7 ** 4 =  2401
4 ** 4 =  256
9 ** 4 =  6561
9474 is an Armstrong number
```

```
==========================
Check Armstrong Number
==========================
Enter a number: 145
5 ** 3 =  125
4 ** 3 =  64
1 ** 3 =  1
145 is not an Armstrong number
```

Program 6.13: WAP to find whether a given number is a prime number or not.

```
# WAP to check if a number is prime or not

#check number is divisible by any number between 2 and number/2.
#If no, it is prime
print("==============================")
print("Check Prime Number")
print("==============================")

n = int(input("Enter a number: "))
if n > 1:
    for i in range(2, int(n/2)+1):
        if (n % i) == 0:
            print(n, "is not a prime number")
            break
    else:
        print(n, "is a prime number")
else:
    print(n, "is not a prime number")
```

Output

```
==============================
Check Prime Number
==============================
Enter a number: 23
23 is a prime number
```

```
==============================
Check Prime Number
==============================
Enter a number: 24
24 is not a prime number
```

```
==============================
Check Prime Number
==============================
Enter a number: 0
0 is not a prime number
```

Program 6.14: WAP to find the reverse of a given number.

```
# WAP to reverse a number

print("==============================")
print("Reverse a Number")
print("==============================")
n = int(input("Enter a number: "))
nrev = 0
while(n > 0):
    lastDigit = n % 10
    nrev = nrev * 10 + lastDigit
    n = n // 10
print(nrev)
```

Output

```
==========================
Reverse a Number
==========================
Enter a number: 2345
5432
```

```
================================
Reverse a Number
================================
Enter a number: 275397578
875793572
```

Program 6.15: WAP to print the multiplication table of `n`.

```
num = int(input("Multiplication Table of n-Enter n:"))
for i in range(1, 11):
    print(num, 'x', i, '=', num*i)
```

Output

```
Multiplication Table of n-Enter n:6
6 x 1 = 6
6 x 2 = 12
6 x 3 = 18
6 x 4 = 24
6 x 5 = 30
6 x 6 = 36
6 x 7 = 42
6 x 8 = 48
6 x 9 = 54
6 x 10 = 60
>>>
```

Summary

- There is a need to control the execution of statements for decision-making and performing repetitive tasks.
- Control means controlling the sequence of execution.
- Flow is the sequence of execution of program statements.
- Control flow tools control the program execution sequence.
- There are three types of control flow tools – conditional statements, iterative statements and function calls.
- `if`, `if-else`, `if-elif-else`, and nested `if-else` statements are conditional statements.
- `if` statement is used for decision-making when the given condition is true. No action is done if the condition is false.
- `if-else` statement is used when a set of actions happen if the given condition is true and another set of action happen if condition is false.
- `if-else-if` statement is used for checking of multiple conditions that are mutually exclusive.
- Nested `if-else` statement has one condition statement nested within another.
- Nested `if` statement can also be written using logical operators and Boolean expression.

- while, for and nested loops are the iterative statements.
- When using while loop, the number of times the loop will iterate may not be known in advance.
- When using for loop, most often the number of iterations are known before entering the loop.
- Range() is used to iterate over a sequence of integers in for loop.
- Sequential data types like list, string and tuple are used to iterate in for loop.
- Iterable is anything that can be iterated. Iter() on iterables returns iterator object. Next() on iterator object allows each item of the iterable to be accessed.
- Nested loops are those that define one loop within another.
- Break, Continue and Pass are loop control statements.
- Break is used to terminate the loop and exit it when an external condition is true.
- Continue is used to skip the rest of the code for current iteration when an external condition is true.
- Pass statement is a null statement and does nothing. It is generally used as a placeholder.
- In for-else and while-else, the else part is executed only when neither break nor continue is executed during the iteration.

KEYWORDS

Body	for statement	Nested if
Break statement	Function calls	Nested if-else
Conditional statement	Header	Nested loops
continue statement	If statement	Pass statement
Control	Iterable	Sequential data type
Control flow	Iterative statement	Target
Control flow tools	Loop control statement	while statement
Flow	Loop statement	

PROGRAMMING LANGUAGE KEYWORDS

break	range(n)
continue	range(start, end)
elif	range(start,end,increment)
else	while
for	For-else
if	If-elif-else
iter()	If-else
iterator.next()	while-else
pass	

Assessment

A.1 Bloom Level: Knowledge/Remember

Review Questions

1. What is the need for control flow statements?
2. What do you mean by control flow?
3. Name the control flow tools.
4. What is the default flow of execution of programs?
5. Name three conditional statements.
6. Name two iterative statements.
7. Draw a flowchart to show the working of (a) `if` (b) `if-else` (c) `if-elif-else`, and (d) nested `if` statements.
8. List the three statements to control execution of a loop.
9. Can a `while` loop be defined inside a `for` loop?
10. Can `else` statement be used with `for` statement?
11. List the three statements that may be used to end a `for` loop.
12. List the three different ways using which the nesting of `for` statement can happen.
13. State the Boolean condition for a `while` loop to execute.

Fill in the blanks

1. The Boolean expression in `if` statement is in ____________.
2. _______statement is used to skip an iteration.
3. _______ statement is used to exit the loop.
4. ________ is a placeholder statement.
5. _________ statement repeats a set of statements again and again while the condition is true.
6. Anything that can be iterated is __________.
7. The __________ variable successively rebinds to each item of the iterator.
8. The value of the iterator object must not be altered in `for` loop if it is ________.
9. `for` loop is executed using ________ function and ________ data type.
10. __________ is the start value in range(10).
11. __________ is the end value in range(10).
12. If x=[2,4], `print(x.next())` will show _______.
13. __________, __________ and __________ are loop control statements.

State True/False

1. Flow relates to controlling the sequence of execution.
2. Colon separates the header from the body in `if-else` statement.
3. The `else` part is executed when Boolean expression of `if` statement is evaluated to True.

4. When a loop terminates, the loop control variable has value zero.
5. The value of mutable iterator object must not be altered in `for` loop.
6. In range (5,6), 6 is the increment value.
7. `continue` statement is used to terminate the loop and exit it.
8. `pass` is a null statement.
9. `break` statement causes the current iteration to be skipped.
10. In `for-else` statement, if `break` statement gets executed, `else` part is not executed.

Multiple Choice Questions (MCQ)

1. Identify the loop that is not available in Python:
   (i) `for` loop
   (ii) `while` loop
   (iii) `do-while` loop
   (iv) Nested `for` loop
2. Which of the following is TRUE for break statement?
   (i) Exits all nested loops
   (ii) Exits current loop
   (iii) Exits iteration and goes to next iteration of loop
   (iv) Stops the program
3. Which of the following is TRUE for `continue` statement?
   (i) Exits all nested loops
   (ii) Exits current loop
   (iii) Exits iteration and goes to next iteration of loop
   (iv) Stops the program
4. Which of the following is the correct `if` statement?
   (i) `if y:`
   (ii) `if y is True:`
   (iii) `if y==True:`
   (iv) `if (bool(y):`

A.2 Bloom Level: Comprehend/Understand

Review Questions

1. Describe the syntax of the `if` statement.
2. Explain the working of `if`, `if-else` and `if-elif-else` statements.
3. Describe the difference between `break` and `continue` statements, with examples.
4. What is the use of `pass` statement?
5. What is the significance of indentation in the body of `while` loop?
6. Explain the use of `range()` function in `for` loop.
7. Explain the working of `for` loop (using examples) for sequential data type.
8. Explain the difference between `break` and `continue` statement, with examples.
9. Explain the working of `break` in `for` statement and `while` statement.
10. What is the value of the target identifier after the `for` loop is exited, i.e., the last value the `for` loop is bound?
11. Describe, with examples, the different ways in which multiple conditions can be represented using (1) nested `if` (2) logical operator, and (3) short form of Boolean expression.

A.3 Bloom Level: Application/Apply

1) Under what circumstances can a `while` statement enter an infinite loop?

2) How many times statements (1) and (2) will be executed in the following code?

```
ct = 0
while ct < 2:
    print("Inside while")       #(1)
    ct = ct + 1
else:
    print("Inside else")        #(2)
```

3) In a `for` statement, identify the values that will be assigned to the target, in order.
`iterator = [1, 2, 5]`
`target = ?`

4) Show the output of the following expressions:
   a) `range(1,5,2)`
   b) `range(5)`
   c) `range(1,5)`
   d) `range(1,10,-3)`

5) Write the following using (1) logical operator, and (2) short form of Boolean expression:

```
if x > 5:
    if color == 'blue':
        x = x + 10;
```

6) Find the errors:
   a)
```
input(n)
if n> 0:
    print("n is positive")
```

7) Let iterator = [5, 10, 20]. After the `for` loop exits, the target has value:
   (i) 20 (ii) 0
   (iii) undefined (iv) error

8) If you have to check whether x is equal to y, identify the correct statement.
   (i) `if x=y` (ii) `if x=y:`
   (iii) `if x==y` (iv) `if x==y:`

9) Identify the correct output for the following statement:

```
'A' + 'M' if '11'.isdigit() else 'P' + 'M'
```

   (i) AM (ii) PM
   (iii) APM (iv) AP

A.4 Bloom Level: Analyze

1. Differentiate between `if` statement and `if-else` statement.

2. State the difference in output:
`range(1, 4)` and `iterable[1, 4]`

3. Is the following code correct?

```
a=5
i = 9 if a > 6 else 0
print(i)
```

If no, why? If yes, what is the output?

4. Identify the difference between (a) and (b). Will they give the same result?
   a) `If x > 2 and x > 10:`
   b) `If 2 < x < 10:`

5. Differentiiate and analyze the output with justification.

a)
```
for x in 'Smart':
    if x =='o':
        pass
    print(x, end=' ')
```

```
for x in 'Smart':
    print(x, end=' ')
```

b)

```
x='abcd'
for i in range(len(x)):
    x='a'
    print(x)
```

```
x='abcd'
for i in range(len(x)):
    x='a'
    print(x, end=' ')
```

c)

```
x='365'
for i in x:
    print(i)
```

```
x=365
for i in x:
    print(i)
```

d)

```
x=12
if x > 2 and x > 10:
    print(x)
```

```
x=12
if 2 < x < 10 :
    print(x)
```

e)

```
lst= [5, 2, 6, 10, 0 , 9, 20]
s1 = 0
s2 = 0
for i in lst:
    if (i % 2 == 0):
        s1 = s1 + i
        continue
    if (i % 5 == 0):
        s2 = s2 + i
print(s1 , end=" ")
print(s2)
```

```
lst= [5, 2, 6, 10, 0 , 9, 20]
s1 = 0
s2 = 0
for i in lst:
    if (i % 2 == 0):
        s1 = s1 + i
    if (i % 5 == 0):
        s2 = s2 + i
print(s1 , end=" ")
print(s2)
```

f)

```
a=10
i = 5 if a > 7 else 0
print(i)
```

```
a=10
if a > 7:
    i = 5
else:
    i = 0
print(i)
```

A.5 Bloom Level: Evaluate

1. For the following code, answer the following questions: (i) What is the output? (ii) How many times will the loop run?

```
i=2
while(i>0):
        i = i-1
        print(i)
```

2. Evaluate the following codes: (i) What is the purpose of the code? (ii) What is the output? (iii) Justify your answer.

a)

```
a, b = 0, 1
while b<13:
    print(b, end=' ')
    a,b=b, a+b
```

b)

```
for num in range(3, -4, -1):
    print(num, end=" ")
```

c)

```
#================================
for i in range(1,3):
    for j in range(10, 12):
        print(i, j)
```

d)

```
a='abbabbabbabba'
for i in a:
    print(i, end=' ')
```

e)

```
#==================================
ct = 0
while ct < 2:
    print("Inside while")      #(1)
    ct = ct + 1
else:
    print("Inside else")       #(2)
```

f)

```
birds = ['Sparrow', 'Parrot', 'Koel', 'Pigeon']
for i in range(len(birds)):
    print(birds[i], len(birds[i]))
```

3. The following codes perform a particular task. Identify the logic of the task that it performs.

(a) The code calculates the electricity bill of the user. Identify the logic.

(a)

```
bill=0
unit = int(input("Enter your electric units:"))
if unit<200: bill=0
else: unit=unit-200
if unit<200: bill=bill + unit*3
else:
      unit=unit-200
      bill=bill + 200*3
bill=bill + unit*4
print(bill)
```

(b) The code calculates the grade of a student. Identify the logic.

```
marks = int(input("Enter your Marks:"))
if marks>90:             grade='A'
elif 85<marks<=90:       grade='B'
elif 75<=marks<=85:      grade='C'
elif marks<75:           grade='D'
print(grade)
```

(c) The code calculates travel bill. Identify the logic.

```
bill=0
unit = int(input("Enter distance travelled in km:"))
if unit<=5:  bill= 5 * 10
elif unit<=55: bill= 5 * 10 + (unit-5) * 20
else: bill= 5 * 10 + 50 * 20 + (unit-55) * 15
print(bill)
```

A.6 Bloom Level: Create/Synthesize

Programming Statements

1. Write `if`, `if-else`, `if-elif-else` statements (whichever is best suited) for the following:
   a. To find if a number `a` is greater than `b`
   b. To find if a number `a` is greater than 15
   c. To find if a number `a` is equal to a number `b`
   d. To find if a number `a` is odd
   e. To find if a number `a` is even
   f. To find if a number `a` is odd or even

g. To find if a number `a` is greater than, less than or equal to `b`
h. To find if a number `a` is positive, negative or zero
i. To find if two numbers `a` and `b` are equal or not
j. To compare three numbers and find the largest number and the smallest number
k. To compare three numbers and find the largest number and the smallest number
l. To count number of vowels and consonants in a string
m. To count number of uppercase and lowercase letters in a string
n. To count special characters, vowel and consonants in a string.

2. Write `if` statement for the following: A student wants to apply for a job. The qualification of the student can be Undergraduate, Postgraduate and Doctorate. To apply for the job, the minimum experience required is 3 years for undergraduate, 2 years for postgraduate and 1 year for doctorate.

3. Design `range` function for the following:
   a. Print numbers from 10 to 1
   b. Print numbers from 1 to 10
   c. Print all odd numbers until 50
   d. Print all even numbers until 50
   e. Print multiples of 5 until 50
   f. Print multiples of 5 from 50 to 1
   g. Print the table of 7 from 1 to 70
   h. Print the table of 25 from 25 to 200.

Programming Assignment

1. Check whether a number is even or odd using modulus operator (num & 1 ==0).

2. Check whether a number is even or odd without using modulus operator.

3. Check whether a number is palindrome or not.

4. Check whether a number is perfect or not. Perfect numbers are ones whose sum of the factors is equal to the number itself.

5. Check the marks of the student. If percentage is 75 or above, print "Distinction"; if percentage if 60 to 74, print "First Division"; if percentage if 45 to 59, print "Second division"; else print "Please work hard to improve your scores".

6. Accept a character from the user. If it is in lowercase then convert to upper case and vice-versa.

7. Take salary as input. Apply the rules of income tax calculation. Find the income tax.

8. Find whether a number is positive. If yes, increment the number by one and display the result

9. Find the roots of a quadratic equation.

10. From a given set of numbers, find the maximum number and minimum number.

11. Find the sum of the individual digits of a number.

12. Find the sum of all odd numbers between 1 and *n*.

13. Find the sum of series $1^2 + 2^2 + 3^3 + \dots N$ terms.

14. Find the sum of series $1 + ½ + 1/3 + ¼ + \dots$ *N* terms.

15. Find the sum of all integers between 1 and *n* and are divisible by 7.

16. Print the Fibonacci series up to *n*.

17. Print the first *n* perfect numbers.

18. Print the first n Armstrong numbers.
19. Print the first n prime numbers.
20. Print the integers between 1 and n that are divisible by 9.
21. Print the integers between 1 and n omitting those integers that are divisible by 10.
22. Print the integers between 1 and n that are divisible by 5 but not by 10.
23. Evaluate 1*2*3*4*… n.
24. Print a pyramid of digits as shown:

```
        1
      2 3 2
    3 4 5 4 3
```

25. Print Floyd's triangle.

```
1
2 3
4 5 6
7 8 9 10
```

26. Generate the following patterns:

a)

```
1 2 3 4 5
  1 2 3
    1
```

b)

```
    1
  1 2 3
1 2 3 4 5
  1 2 3
    1
```

Answers

A.1 Bloom Level: Knowledge/Remember

Fill in the blanks

1. header 2. continue 3. break 4. pass
5. iterative 6. iterable 7. target 8. mutable
9. range, sequential 10. 0 11. 9 12. 2
13. Break, continue, pass

True/False

11. False 12. True 13. False 14. False 15. True 16. False 17. False 18. True
19. False 20. True

Multiple Choice Questions (MCQ)

1. (iii) 2. (ii) 3. (iii) 4. (i)

A.3 Bloom Level: Application/Apply

2.

```
Inside while
Inside while
Inside else
```

3. 1 2 5

4. (a) 1 3 (b)

```
0
1
2
3
4
```

(c)

```
1
2
3
4
```

(d) No output

6. Error – n is a str. cannot compare str with int 7. (i) 8. (iv) 9. (i)

A.4 Bloom Level: Analyze

2. 1, 2, 3 and 1, 4
3. 9
4. No. conditions are different
5. (a) `S m a r t` `S m a r t`

(b) 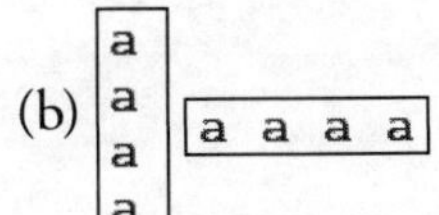

(c)
```
3
6
5
```
```
TypeError: 'int' object is not iterable
```

(d) `12`

(e) `38 5` `38.35`

(f) `5` `5`

A.5 Bloom Level: Evaluate

1. 1, 0 Two times
2. (a)
```
1 1 2 3 5 8
```
(b)
```
3 2 1 0 -1 -2 -3 1 10
```
(c)
```
1 11
2 10
2 11
```
(d)
```
a b b a b b a b b a b b a
```
(e)
```
Inside while
Inside while
Inside else
```
(f)
```
Sparrow 7
Parrot 6
Koel 4
Pigeon 6
```

3. (a)

```
#Accept electric units from user and calculate bill as per following rates.
#First 200 Units      :  Free
#Next 200 Units       :  Rs 3 per day.
#Above 400 Units      :  Rs 4 per day.
#if number of unit is 500 then total bill = 0 + 600 + 400 = 1000
```

(b)

```
#Accept percentage from student, display the grade as follows-
#Marks                         Grade
# > 90                          A
# > 85 and <= 90                B
# >= 75 and <= 85               C
# < 75                          D
```

(c)

```
#Calculate the bill of taxi
#First 5 Km                    Rs 10/km
#Next 50 Km                    Rs 20/km
#After that                    Rs 15/km
```

UNIT III Functions

CHAPTER

7 Function and Module

Contents

7.1 Introduction

In the previous chapters, we have seen the writing of simple programs using data types, variables, constants and statements (Chapter 4), operators and expressions (Chapter 5) and control flow statements (Chapter 6). Most of the real-life problems are much bigger and complex than the programs presented in earlier chapters. As a result, the Python programs written for real-life scenarios become large and complex. Handling large and complex programs becomes difficult. Thus, there is a need to break down the complex problem into simple and manageable tasks. A large and complex program is broken down into many small and manageable program units, also known as ***functions***. In this chapter, we discuss functions. Writing programs using functions makes it easy to manage the programs. Functions can also be reused. As mentioned in the previous chapter, function is also a control flow tool.

Learning Outcomes of this chapter

After completion of the chapter, the learner will be able to:

- Create functions
- Formulate solution to a problem using functions
- Use the user-defined functions
- Use the functions with arguments
- Identify different types of functions
- Create modules
- Create and recognize packages
- Develop programs based on the concepts discussed.

7.2 Need for Functions

A **function** is a group of instructions that perform a specific task.

For handling large and complex programs, there is a need to follow the practices of software engineering for program writing. The software engineering practices used for the development of large and complex programs work on the following principles:

1. **Modularization and divide-and-conquer strategy**
    - A complex problem is divided into small manageable sub-problems.
    - The sub-problems should be easier to manage than the original problem.
    - If the divided sub-problems are still complex, they can be further divided into sub-problems to make them simple.
    - This process continues till the sub-problems are easy to handle.
    - The solutions of sub-problems are combined to form the solution of the original problem.

    The above-defined principles are similar to the ones we follow in real-life scenarios. For example, a project has a Project Manager, having one or more Team Leaders, and who further have a group of programmers working under them. The work is divided among the different teams based on their expertise, and then further divided among the team members. Next, the work done under the different teams is merged to get the final project.

During the development of programs, the users can divide the complex problems into several program units, such that the different units perform specific tasks. The functionality of each program unit is defined in a separate function. The functions perform their own task and interact with other functions, with an aim to solve the complex problem. The functions defined by the users are also referred to as user-defined functions. **Python allows creation of user-defined functions.**

2. **Reusability**

   A functionality that has been developed and tested may be reused instead of creating the same functionality again. Development of functions helps in reusability. The functions developed for specific functionality are tested and kept in the libraries as library functions. Anyone who writes a program and desires a functionality similar to the already-defined library function, can use the library function instead of developing them anew. **Python has a set of defined library functions.**

   In addition to the need and importance of functions as described above, there are other advantages of using functions. Some of the additional advantages are as follows:

   - It creates programs that are more organized and thus easier to read.
   - It improves program maintainability, as programs are organized and easily readable.
   - It facilitates debugging, as it is easier to debug and test an organized program.
   - It facilitates reduction of code redundancy, as reusability of code avoids repetition.
   - It supports information hiding, as reusable functions can be used without understanding the code within it.

   Python supports both user-defined functions and built-in library functions. The functions are discussed in detail in the following sections.

7.3 User-defined Function

During the writing of a program, the functions that are defined, written and developed by the user are called **user-defined functions**. In a program, the user-defined function is first written (Function Definition) and the defined function is invoked (Function call/function use/function invocation). The function that calls/uses/invokes any other function is referred to as **calling function**. The defined function that is being invoked is referred to as **called function**.

When writing functions, the following may be noted:

- The called function may take values as input and it may also return values.
- The variables used within a function have a scope.
- The input values may be provided to function in different ways.

7.4 Function Definition

For implementing the function definition, Python provides the function syntax. The format of *function definition* in Python is as follows:

```
def function_name ([parameters]):
    "function docstring"
    Statements
    [return [expression]]
```

The function definition consists of a header and a body.

```
Header is    def function_name (parameters):
Body is      "function docstring"
             Statements
             [return [expression]]
```

The important points to note about function definition are shown diagrammatically in Figure 7.1:

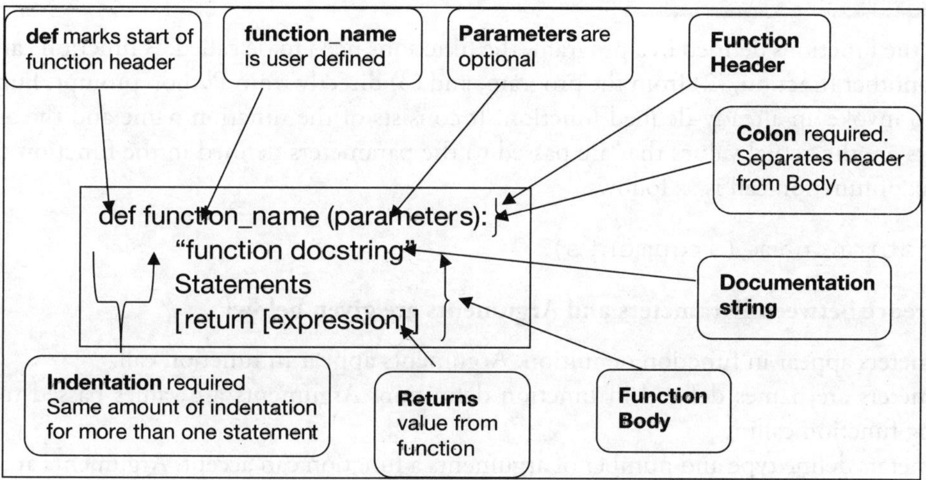

Figure 7.1 Defining a function

The important points to note about *function definition* are as follows:

- Function definition begins with keyword *def* that indicates the start of function. It is followed by function_name and parenthesis ().
- Function_name uniquely identifies a function. Function naming follows the rules of identifier naming in Python.
- Parameters are used to pass value to a function. They are optional.
- Function body may consist of one or more statements. Function body is indented to the same extent for more than one statement.
- Documentation string or *docstring* can be the first statement in a function body. It is a comment about the function. It is optional.
- *Return* statement is used to return value from a function. Return exits a function. Return statement may or may not have arguments. Return is optional.

Let us see an example of a function definition.

In the code below, the function `user_input()` is defined without any parameter, docstring or return. The function accepts integer input from the user in variable "a". It prints the value of "a".

```
# Accept user input
def user_input():
    a = int((input("Enter the number ")))
    print(a)
```

The call and execution of the function is discussed in later sections.

7.5 Function Invocation

For using the functions defined in a program, the functions need to be called. A function can be called (1) from another function, (2) from the program, and (3) directly from Python prompt. Function call is a way to invoke an already-defined function. It consists of the function name and the arguments. Arguments are the actual values that are passed to the parameters defined in the function definition. The syntax of function call is as follows:

```
function_name(arguments)
```

The **difference between Parameters and Arguments are given below:**

- Parameters appear in function definition. Arguments appear in function call.
- Parameters are names defined in function definition. Arguments are values passed to function during function calling.
- Parameters define type and number of arguments a function can accept. Arguments are values for the same.

7.6 The return Statement

The `return` statement is used for returning the result computed in a function to its calling function. The properties of `return` statement are as follows:

- `Return` statement ends execution of the called function and returns the result to the calling function.
- A function can have one or more `return` statements.
- `Return` statement can be anywhere in body of the function.
- Though a function definition may have multiple return statements, during execution, only one return statement executes.
- The `return` statement can have two forms:
  1. Return: It returns a special value None. It ends execution of the called function. The control returns to the calling function.

2. Return (expression): It returns a value from function evaluation. It ends execution of the called function. The control returns to the calling function. The expression value is returned

7.7 Function Input and Output

The functions are classified depending on their input parameters and output, as follows:

- Function with no input and no output
- Function with input but no output
- Function with input and one output
- Function with input and outputs.

7.7.1 Function with No Input and No Output

A function can be defined as that which does not accept any argument and does not return any output.

During function definition, the parameter list is empty.
During function call, the argument list is empty.

Example 7.1: Function to calculate the factorial of 5.

```
# Find factorial of a number
def factorial():  ← 1
    fact = 1
    for i in range(1,6):
        fact *= i
    print("The factorial of ", 5, "is ", fact)  ← 2
factorial()  ← 3
```

Output

The points to be noted in the above code are as follows:

- (1) is the function header with no input parameters.
- (2) is the end of function body (see indentation).
- (3) is the call to the function from the program. To call the function, the name of the function with braces is used.
- (4) is the output when the program snippet is executed.

Let us see another version of the function factorial (Example 7.2).

The function without parameters is also used to write programs having their own input and output. This is largely for the purpose of segregating the functionality of a program.

Example 7.2: Function to calculate factorial of number; the number is accepted from the user inside the function.

```
# Find factorial of a number
def factorial():  ← 1
    a = int((input("Enter the number ")))  ← 2
    fact = 1
    for i in range(1,a+1):
        fact *= i
    print("The factorial of ", a, "is ", fact)  ← 3
factorial()  ← 4
```

Output

```
Enter the number 7
The factorial of  7 is  5040
```

Also, a function can be called from the Python prompt, as shown below.

```
>>> factorial()  ← Function call from Python prompt
Enter the number 6
The factorial of  6 is  720
>>>
```

In the code, the number whose factorial is to be evaluated is taken as input in the function, as in line (2). In this program, the function is like a complete program with its own input and output.

When there is a need to segregate functionality of a program into easy handling routines, functions with no input and no output parameters can be defined. These kinds of function are complete by themselves, in terms of input or output. They help to make the program more readable. Since they do not accept any parameters, they are not flexible, and may have limited functionality.

7.7.2 Function with Input but No Output

The function in Example 7.1 is rigid. A call to the function will always print factorial of 5. It cannot be used to find the factorial of a different number. The function in Example 7.2 has been defined to have complete functionality.

The function for factorial can be made flexible by adding input parameters to it.

During function definition, the parameter list is defined in the braces after the function name.

During function call, the arguments to be passed to the function are defined.

Example 7.3: To find the factorial of a number using argument passing.

```
# Find factorial of a number
def factorial(n):  ← 1
    fact = 1
    for i in range(1,n+1):
        fact *= i
    print("The factorial of ", n, "is ", fact)  ← 2
factorial(7)  ← 3
```

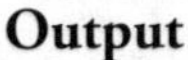

Output

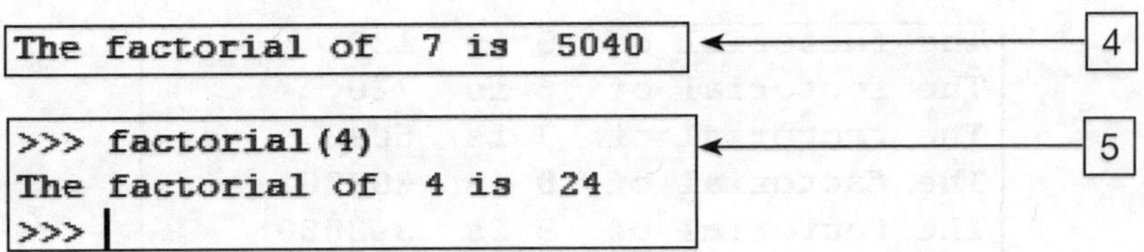

The points to be noted in the above code are as follows:

- (1) is the function header with one input parameter.
- (2) is the end of the function body (see indentation).
- (3) is the call to function from the program. We note that function call has an argument value in braces. During execution, value in function call is passed to a parameter defined in function definition. That is, 7 is passed to function definition parameter "n".
- (4) is the output when the program snippet is executed with value n=7
- (5) is alternative call to function from Python prompt. Here, function call has argument value 4. So, factorial of 4 is evaluated.

We see that since the function accepts input parameter, it is more flexible. The function can be used to calculate the factorial of any number, by using the value in function call.

The number of parameters can be more than one.

7.7.3 Function with Input and One Output

The function in the above programs receives input parameters but they do not return a value; the result of computation is printed within the function. However, the result of the computation may be required in the calling function for further processing.

During function definition, the parameter list is defined in the braces after the function name.

During function call, the arguments to be passed to the function are defined. There is also a place to hold the returned value from the function, like a variable or print statement.

For returning result to the calling function, *return* statement is used in the function.

Example 7.4: To find factorial of numbers with factorial function, input parameter and return value.

```
# Find factorial of a number
def factorial(n):                    ← 1
    fact = 1
    for i in range(1,n+1):
        fact *= i
    return(fact)                     ← 2

for a in (5, 6, 7, 8, 9, 10):
    print("The factorial of ", a, "is ", factorial(a)) ← 3
```

Output

```
The factorial of  5 is  120
The factorial of  6 is  720
The factorial of  7 is  5040
The factorial of  8 is  40320
The factorial of  9 is  362880
The factorial of  10 is  3628800
```

The points to be noted in the above code are as follows:

- Function defines an input parameter "n" (statement 1).
- Function returns a value "fact" (statement 2).
- The calling function calls the function with argument "a" (statement 3).
- Calling function gets a value returned from called function "factorial(a)" (statement 3).
- The returned value is printed at the calling function "print" (statement 3).

7.7.4 Function with More Than One Output

In the earlier sub-section, we noted that even if a function has more than one `return` statement, at any one instance, a function will return a single value.

In order to understand how a function returns more than one output, let us first discuss mutable and immutable objects.

- In Python, almost everything is an object. Variables are actually "names".
- An assignment is the binding of a name to an object.
- Let us understand binding with an example.
  X = "Good"   # (1)
  Y = "Morning"   # (2)
  - In (1), a name X binds to the object "Good".
  - In (2), a name Y binds to the object "Morning".
- In Python, we have two kinds of objects – Mutable objects and Immutable objects.
  - **Mutable objects** can be modified. The type *List, Set, Dict* are mutable. (These are explained in later chapters.)
  - **Immutable objects** once created, cannot be modified. New objects are created when the value of immutable object is to be modified during computation. The type *int, float, str, bool,* and *tuple* are immutable.
- The mutable objects are used for returning more than one output from a function.
  - Calling function passes arguments to called function.
  - In called function, the parameters get updated with the passed arguments. Within the function, during computation the values of parameters get changed.
  - In calling function, if passed arguments are mutable, the changed values of the arguments are reflected here. However, if passed arguments are immutable, the changed values of the arguments are not reflected here.

So, we note that multiple outputs from function are possible **if function call arguments are of type mutable.** `Return` statement can return only one value.

In other languages like C and C++, function calling is defined in terms of call by value and call by reference. In call by value, the arguments in function call are not updated if their value changes inside function definition. In call by reference, the arguments in function call reflect the updated values if their value changes inside function definition. In Python, function call using immutable objects is similar to call by value, and function call using mutable objects, is call by reference.

Let us see an example of mutable objects.

Example 7.5: To find the factorial using list mutable.

```
# Find factorial of a number
def factorial(n):
    fact = 1
    res = []
    for i in n:
        for j in range(1,i+1):
            fact *= j
        res += [fact]
        fact = 1
    n += res          <------ 1
    print("Updated List in Called fucntion \t", n)

numlist = [2, 4, 6, 8]
print("Original List in Calling fucntion \t", numlist)
factorial(numlist)
print("Updated List in Calling function \t", numlist)
```

Output

```
Original List in Calling fucntion        [2, 4, 6, 8]
Updated List in Called fucntion          [2, 4, 6, 8, 2, 24, 720, 40320]
Updated List in Calling function         [2, 4, 6, 8, 2, 24, 720, 40320]
```

In the above program, we see that the arguments passed to the function are of type list, i.e., mutable, so in the calling function, it has updated values for arguments.

Now, if we replace (1) in Example 7.5 by (2) in Example 7.6 as shown below, we see a different result. This is because, when we write `n = n + res`, a new local variable n (discussed in the next section) is created in the function, to which the value is assigned.

Example 7.6: To find the factorial using list mutable but with some side effect.

```
# Find factorial of a number
def factorial(n):
    fact = 1
    res = []
    for i in n:
        for j in range(1,i+1):
            fact *= j
        res += [fact]
        fact = 1
    n = n+ res          <------ 2
    print("Updated List in Called fucntion \t", n)

numlist = [2, 4, 6, 8]
print("Original List in Calling fucntion \t", numlist)
factorial(numlist)
print("Updated List in Calling function \t", numlist)
```

Output

```
Original List in Calling fucntion          [2, 4, 6, 8]
Updated List in Called fucntion            [2, 4, 6, 8, 2, 24, 720, 40320]
Updated List in Calling function           [2, 4, 6, 8]
```

7.8 SCOPE OF VARIABLE

To understand the scope of a variable, the two factors are to be noted:

1. Where is the variable defined?
2. From where can you access the defined variable?

The following subsections discuss the different scope of variables.

7.8.1 Global and Local Variables

A variable in a Python program may be defined inside a function or outside it.

Global variable is a variable defined outside a function.

Local variable is defined inside a function.

The scope of a variable is part of the program from where the variable can be accessed.

The global variable has a global scope. This means that it can be accessed from anywhere in the program, including functions.

The local variable has a scope local to the function in which it is defined. This means that it can be accessed only inside the function in which it is defined. The local variables are active when the function in which it is defined, is called.

When a local variable in a function has the same name as the global variable, then, the local variable is being referred within the function. Or, in other words, within a function, the global variable is hidden by the local variable of same name.

Let us see some examples to understand the concept of local and global variables.

Example 7.7: To show difference between the scope of local and global variables.

```
# Local var prin and global var prin
global_var = 10000 ◄──── 1
def simplevar():
    local_var = 5000 ◄──── 2
    print("Inside function, Local var ", local_var)
    print("Inside function Global var ", global_var)

simplevar()
print("Outside function, Global var ", global_var)
print("Outside function, Local var ", local_var)
```

Output

```
Inside function, Local var  5000
Inside function Global var  10000
Outside function, Global var  10000
Traceback (most recent call last):
  File "C:/Users/dsc/Desktop/mutable.py", line 22, in <module>
    print("Outside function, Local var ", local_var)
NameError: name 'local_var' is not defined
>>>
```

In Example 7.7, we see that global variable is defined at (1) and local variable at (2). The local variable `local_var` does not hold any value outside the function.

Example 7.8: Using global variable value inside a function.

```
# Global var value used inside function
z = 10                                        1
def add(x, y):
    sum = x + y + z                                 2
    print("x =", x, "\ny =", y, "\nz =", z)

add(20, 30)
```

Output

```
x = 20
y = 30
z = 10
```

We note that the global variable defined at (1) is used inside the function at (2). Since we only use the value of global variable, there is no error.

Example 7.9: To assign value to the global variable name inside a function.

```
# Local var prin and global var prin
prin = 10000
def simple_Int(rate, time):
    prin = (prin * rate * time)/100
    print(prin)
    return prin
print(simple_Int(5, 5))
print (prin)
```

Output

```
Traceback (most recent call last):
  File "C:/Users/dsc/Desktop/mutable.py", line 40, in <module>
    print(simple_Int(5, 5))
  File "C:/Users/dsc/Desktop/mutable.py", line 37, in simple_Int
    prin = (prin * rate * time)/100
UnboundLocalError: local variable 'prin' referenced before assignment
>>>
```

In Example 7.9, when we assign value to the global variable name, error is reported. This is because, inside the function, when a variable having the same name as global variable is assigned a value, the variable is treated as local variable inside the function. So, in the program, the local variable, prin, does not have a value, thus the error.

7.8.2 The Global Statement

The global statement is used to assign value to the global variable inside a function. What it means is that a function wants to change the value of the global identifier from within the function scope.

The syntax of the global statement is as follows:

```
global identifier (“,” identifier)*
```

The global statement is used to set a global variable inside a function.

Let us see some examples.

Example 7.10: An example without and with global statement.

```
#without global
x = 5
def f():
    x = 22
    print("Inside function x = ", x)
f()
print("Globally x = ", x)
```

Output

```
Inside function x =  22
Globally x =  5
```

(a)

```
#with global
x = 5
def f():
    global x
    x = 22
    print("Inside function x = ", x)
f()
print("Globally x = ", x)
```

Output

```
Inside function x =  22
Globally x =  22
```

(b)

In Example 7.10(a), we see that when global statement is not used inside the function `f()`, the variable `x` is treated as local. The value of `x` outside the functon remains 5 and does not get updated to 22. However, in Example 7.10(b) when we use global statement, the value of `x` updated within function `f()` is also reflected outside the function. The value of `x` outside the function is updated to 22.

7.8.3 Nested Function

A function definition has a header and a function body. Another function defined within the function body of a function is called *inner* or *nested function.* We can also say that a function defined within another function is a nested function. The function in whose body the nested function is defined is called the *outer function.*

The syntax of nested function is

```
def func1():
    statements
    def func2():
```

In this syntax, we see `func1()` is the outer function and `func2()` is the inner or nested function.

The scope of the variables in nested function is as follows:

- The inner function can access all variables defined within it.
- The inner function can access variables defined within the outer function.
- The outer function cannot access the variables defined within the inner function.

Example 7.11: An example showing nested function.

```
#nested function
def f():
    x = 5
    def g():
        x = 22
        print("Inside Inner Function, x  = ", x)  ← 1
    g()
    print("Inside Outer Function, x = ", x)  ← 2
f()
```

Output

```
Inside Inner Function, x  =  22
Inside Outer Function, x =  5
```

In Example 7.11, we see that a new local variable x gets created. So, the value of x inside the inner loop (1) and inside the outer loop (2) is different.

Example 7.12: An example showing nested function with global statement.

```
#nested function
def f():
    x = 5
    def g():
        global x        <------------ 1
        x = 22
        print("Inside Inner Function, x  = ", x)
    g()
    print("Inside Outer Function, x = ", x)
f()
```

Output

```
Inside Inner Function, x  =  22
Inside Outer Function, x =  5
```

In Example 7.12, we see that though x in the inner function has a global scope (1), x in inner function and outer function do not hold the same value.

Example 7.13: An example showing variables in inner function with scope of variable in outer function.

```
#nested same scope function
def f():
    f.x = 5
    def g():
        f.x = 22
        print("Inside Inner Function, x  = ", f.x)
    g()
    print("Inside Outer Function, x = ", f.x)
f()
```

Output

```
Inside Inner Function, x  =  22
Inside Outer Function, x =  22
```

In Example 7.13, we see that when variable x is defined with function name (f.x), then the variable gets qualified and the scope also gets defined.

Closure: The inner function is a closure if it accesses values from outer local variables.

Example 7.14: An example to show closure.

```
#closure
def f(x):
    def g(y):
        return(x + y)
    print(g(5))
f(10)
```

Output

```
15
```

In Example 7.14, we see that variable x defined in outer function f() is used in inner function g().

7.9 Function Arguments

The arguments are the values passed to the function in a function call. The function arguments are of different kinds as follows:

1. Required Arguments
2. Keyword or Positional Arguments
3. Default Arguments
4. Variable Length Arguments

The following subsections discuss the different types of arguments.

7.9.1 Required Arguments

- Required arguments are mandatory and are passed to the function.
- The arguments passed must match the parameters in function definition.
  - The number of arguments to be passed must be correct.
  - The positional order of argument must be correct.
- For example,

Function definition	Function call
def sum(a, b):	sum(5, 10)
def profile(name, age):	profile("Ashima", 20)
def calculate():	calculate()
def concat(a,b):	concat("Happy", "Birthday")

Example 7.15: Write a function for checking whether a year is a leap year or not. The function should accept an argument. Accept year from the user.

```
#WAP to check whether a year is leap year or not
def check_leap(year):
    if (year%4 == 0 and year%100 != 0 or year %400 ==0):
        print (year , "is a leap year")
    else:
        print(year , "is not a leap year")

check_leap(int(input("Enter the year to check for leap year ")))
```

Output

```
Enter the year to check for leap year 2018
2018 is not a leap year
```

7.9.2 Positional Arguments

- Keyword arguments are mentioned in function call with values.
- Keyword arguments are matched with function parameter by matching the argument and parameter name. Since matching is done by name, the order of arguments may not match with the parameter sequence.
- For example,

Function definition	Function call
`def sum(a, b):`	`sum(a=5, b=10)`
`def profile(name, age):`	`profile(name = "Ashima", age = 20)`
`def calculate():`	`calculate()`
`def concat(a,b):`	`concat(b = "Happy", a = "Birthday")`

The function call using keyword arguments for Example 7.15 is as follows:

```
check_leap(year = int(input("Enter the year to check for leap year ")))
```

7.9.3 Default Arguments

- Default argument is defined in the parameter list of the function definition.
- If function call does not provide an argument value, then the called function assumes the default value. If function call provides an argument value, then default value is overridden.
- The default value to function parameter is assigned using assignment "=" operator.
- For example,

Function definition	Function call
`def sum(a, b=10):`	`sum(5)`
`def profile(name, age=25):`	`profile(name = "Ashima", age = 20)`
`def calculate():`	`calculate()`
`def concat(a="Hello",b="There"):`	`concat()`

Example 7.16: Write a function for checking whether a year is a leap year or not. The function should use default argument.

```
#WAP to check whether a year is leap year or not
def check_leap(year=2000):              ← 1
    if (year%4 == 0 and year%100 != 0 or year %400 ==0):
        print (year , "is a leap year")
    else:
        print(year , "is not a leap year")
check_leap(int(input("Enter the year to check for leap year ")))
check_leap()
```

Output

```
Enter the year to check for leap year 2010
2010 is not a leap year
2000 is a leap year
```

Kindly note that in (1) the default value of `year=2000` is overridden by the passed argument `year=2010`.

7.9.4 Variable Length Arguments

- Variable length arguments are used when it is not known about the exact number of arguments that will be passed to the function.
- In function definition, an asterisk is placed before the variable parameter.
- In function call, zero or any number of values can be passed for variable length argument.
- Before variable argument, there can be a required argument or default argument but not after a variable argument.
- After variable argument, you can have only keyword argument.
- For example,

Function definition	Function call
`def sum(a, *b):`	`sum(5,3,4,5)`
`def profile(name, *age):`	`profile(name = "Ashima")`
`def calculate(*n):`	`calculate(1,2,3,4)`
`def concat(*a, b):`	`concat(1,2,3,b=4)`

Example 7.17: Write a function to check whether a year is a leap year or not. Use variable arguments.

```
#WAP to check whether a year is leap year or not
def check_leap(*yeartup):
    for year in yeartup:
        if (year%4 == 0 and year%100 != 0 or year %400 ==0):
            print (year , "is a leap year")
        else:
            print(year , "is not a leap year")

check_leap(2020, 2017, 2028)
```

Output

```
2020 is a leap year
2017 is not a leap year
2028 is a leap year
```

7.10 THE main() FUNCTION

In the Python program examples, we have seen that we can execute a function by a function call. However, programming languages like C++ and Java need a `main()` function to execute. Using `main()` structures our program and makes the program easier to read for non-Python programmers.

The main function is defined by the name `main()`. The `main()` function helps in organizing the execution of one or more functions in the program.

Example 7.18: WAP to check whether a number is prime or not. Use main().

```
# WAP to check if a number is prime or not
def check_prime(*num):
    for n in num:
        for i in range( 2, n//2 ):
            if n % i == 0:
                print(n, "is not a prime number " )
                break
        else:
            print(n, "is a prime number " )
def main():  <------------ 1
    check_prime()
    check_prime(2, 20, 67, 57, 49)
main() <------------ 2
```

We see that we introduced the `main()` function at (1), from where we made the call to `check_prime()` function. Also we invoked the `main()` function at (2).

7.11 Documentation String

Python allows documentation of modules, functions, classes and methods using docstrings. Docstring is a comment statement that describes what the function does. The comments can be inspected during runtime.

The location of docstrings is as follows:

- In a function, docstring is defined immediately after the function heading.
- In a module, docstring is written at the top of modules. (Modules are discussed further in the chapter.)

Docstring can be accessed using __doc__ attribute on the object during runtime.

Let us see some examples:

We insert docstring in the function factorial, as follows:

```
def factorial(n):
"""This returns factorial of n"""
fact = 1
for i in range(1,n+1):
fact *= i
print("The factorial of ", n, "is ", fact)
```

When we print the _doc_, it appears as follows:

```
>>> import using_main
>>> factorial.__doc__
'This returns factorial of n'
>>>
```

Docstring is printed using the `help()` function as follows:

```
>>> help("using_main")
Help on module using_main:
NAME
    using_main

FUNCTIONS
    choose_func(choice)

    factorial(n)
        This returns factorial of n

    main()

    menu()

    sum_of_digits(n)
        # Find Sum of digits of a number

    user_input()
        # Accept user input
```

Docstring of built-in modules can be printed to understand what the module does. The docstring of time module is shown below:

```
>>> import time
>>> print(time.__doc__)
This module provides various functions to manipulate time values.

There are two standard representations of time.  One is the number
of seconds since the Epoch, in UTC (a.k.a. GMT).  It may be an integer
or a floating point number (to represent fractions of seconds).
The Epoch is system-defined; on Unix, it is generally January 1st, 1970.
The actual value can be retrieved by calling gmtime(0).

The other representation is a tuple of 9 integers giving local time.
The tuple items are:
  year (including century, e.g. 1998)
  month (1-12)
  day (1-31)
  hours (0-23)
  minutes (0-59)
  seconds (0-59)
  weekday (0-6, Monday is 0)
  Julian day (day in the year, 1-366)
  DST (Daylight Savings Time) flag (-1, 0 or 1)
If the DST flag is 0, the time is given in the regular time zone;
if it is 1, the time is given in the DST time zone;
if it is -1, mktime() should guess based on the date and time.

Variables:

timezone -- difference in seconds between UTC and local standard time
altzone -- difference in  seconds between UTC and local DST time
daylight -- whether local time should reflect DST
tzname -- tuple of (standard time zone name, DST time zone name)

Functions:

time() -- return current time in seconds since the Epoch as a float
clock() -- return CPU time since process start as a float
sleep() -- delay for a number of seconds given as a float
gmtime() -- convert seconds since Epoch to UTC tuple
```

7.12 RECURSIVE FUNCTIONS

Until now, we have seen a function calling another function. **Recursive function** is a function that calls itself.

Recursion is a technique to solve problems that can be broken down into similar problems but of smaller size. For example, factorial of a number n can be expressed as n multiplied by factorial $n - 1$ and so on.

Recursion is implemented using recursive function.

While developing recursive programs, the points to be noted are as follows:

- Express the problem as similar problems of smaller size.
- A recursive solution has two parts – base case and recursive case.
- Base case is the condition for termination of recursion. There can be more than one base case.
- Recursive case defines the problem in its own terms but of smaller size.
- For example, the computation of factorial n can be expressed recursively.
  - o Base case: if n == 1, factorial (1) is 1
  - o Recursive case: factorial(n) = n * factorial(n – 1)
- A recursive problem can be expressed as recurrence relation. For example, recurrence relation for factorial of n is as follows:

```
Fact(n)  =       1          for n ==1
    n * fact(n-1)          for n > 1
```

- When writing code for a recursive problem, the function must call itself from within the body of the function.

Example 7.19: Write recursive program for computing the factorial of n.

The recursive program accepts input, calculates factorial recursively and prints output.

```
def fact(n):
    if n == 1:
        return 1
    else:
        return n * fact(n-1)

n = int(input("Enter number "))
print("\nThe factorial of", n, "is", fact(n))
```

Output

```
Enter number 5

The factorial of 5 is 120
>>> |
```

How recursion works: To understand the working of recursion, we take the factorial example. The program has

Base case:
```
if n == 1:
    return 1
```

Recursive case: `return n * fact(n-1)`

or

```
f = n * fact(n-1)
return f
```

Let us understand how recursion works:

Table 7.1 Recursion

main()	fact(5)	fact(4)	fact(3)	fact(2)	fact(1)
Base/ Recursive	f = n*fact(n-1)	f = n*fact(n-1)	f = n*fact(n-1)	f = n*fact(n-1)	return 1
fact(5)	f= 5 * fact(4)	f= 4 * fact(3)	f= 3 * fact(2)	f= 2 * fact(1)	1
120 ⟵	5 * 24 ⟵	4 * 6 ⟵	3 * 2 ⟵	2 * 1 ⟵	1

As shown in Table 7.1, with each recursion, a forward hierarchy is formed with the number multiplied with the recursion value of the smaller number. When factorial of 1 is evaluated, the value is returned in reverse hierarchy.

Note: In Python, a call, whether recursive or not, has the same time and memory space cost. A tail recursion or non-tail recursion has the same cost, in contrast to languages like C programming.

7.13 Anonymous Functions

1. The word anonymous means unnamed. Anonymous functions are defined without a name.
2. Anonymous functions are defined using *lambda* keyword. Other functions are defined using the *def* keyword.
3. Anonymous functions are also called lambda functions.
4. The syntax of lambda function is as follows:

   ```
   lambda arguments: expression
   ```

   - There can be any number of arguments.
   - There is only one expression.
   - The expression is evaluated using the argument values and the result returned.
   - Multiple expressions or commands are not allowed.
   - They can only access variables defined in their parameter list or global variables.
5. Lambda functions are created where they are needed. They are generally used when a nameless function is required for a short duration.
6. Lambda function can be assigned to a variable to give a name.

Let us see some examples:

Example 7.20: Using lambda functions, WAP (a) to find the sum of the square of two numbers (b) for division of two numbers and (c) to find the nth power of any number.

```
f = lambda a, b : a**2 + b**2
print("5 square + 5 square = ", f(5,5))
```

Output

```
5 square + 5 square =  50
```

```
divide = lambda arg1, arg2: arg1/arg2;
print ("10/20 = ", divide( 10, 20 ))
print ("20/20 = ", divide( 20, 20 ))
```

Output

```
10/20 =  0.5
20/20 =  1.0
```

```
#find power of number
double = lambda x, n: x ** n
print("5 to the power 5 is =", double(5,5))
```

Output

```
5 to the power 5 is = 3125
```

7.14 Library Functions

Built-in functions are already built into Python language. Each built-in function performs a specific task. The built-in functions can be used directly by calling them.

`print()` and `input()` functions, which we use for printing output and accepting input from the user, respectively, are built-in functions.

From Python 3.7 onwards, there are 69 built-in functions. A list of the built-in functions in Python and their brief description is given in Table 7.2.

Table 7.2 Built-in functions and their description

Function	Description
abs(number)	Returns the absolute value of a *number*
all(iterable)	Returns True if all elements of the iterable are True
any(iterable)	Returns True if any element of the iterable is True
ascii(object)	Returns string. Printable representation of object
bin(x)	Converts integer to binary string prefix with 0b
bool([x])	Returns Boolean value True or False

(Continued)

Table 7.2 (Continued)

Function	Description
breakpoint()	Drops into the debugger at the call site
bytearray(source[, encoding[, errors]]])	Returns new array of bytes
bytes([source[, encoding[, errors]]])	Returns new byte object with immutable sequence of integers
callable(object)	Return True if object is callable; else false
chr(i)	Returns character whose Unicode is integer i
@classmethod()	Transforms method into class method
compile(source, filename, mode, flags=0, dont_inherit=False, optimize=-1)	Compiles source into a code or object
complex ([real[, imag]])	Creates a complex number
delattr(object, name)	Deletes named attribute from object
dict()	Creates a new Dictionary
dir([object])	Returns names in current local scope
divmod(a,b)	Returns Tuple of Quotient and Remainder
enumerate(iterable, start=0)	Returns Enumerate Object
eval(source[, globals[, locals]])	Executes source as a Python expression
exec(source[, globals[, locals]])	Executes dynamically created program
filter(function, iterable)	Constructs iterator from elements that are true
float([x])	Returns floating point number from number or string x
format(value[, format_spec])	Returns formatted representation of a value
frozenset(iterable)	Returns immutable frozenset object
getattr(object, name[, default])	Returns value of a named object. Name must be a string
globals()	Returns dictionary current global symbol table
hasattr(object, name)	Returns True if object has the specified attribute name
hash(object)	Returns hash value of object
help([object])	Invokes built-in Help system
hex(x)	Converts integer to hexadecimal, prefix 0x
id(object)	Returns identity of object
input([prompt])	Reads and returns a line of string
int(x)	Returns integer from a number or string

(*Continued*)

Table 7.2 (Continued)

Function	Description
isinstance(object, classinfo)	Returns True if object is instance of classinfo
issubclass(object, classinfo)	Returns True if object is subclass of classinfo
iter(iterable)	Returns an iterator over iterable
len(object)	Returns number of items of an object
list(iterable)	Creates list
locals()	Returns dictionary of current local symbol table
map(function, iterable)	Applies function to each iterable. Returns a List
max(iterable), max(a, b, c, …)	Returns largest item of iterable or argument list
memoryview(obj)	Returns memory view of argument
min(iterable), min(a, b, c, …)	Returns smallest item of iterable or argument list
next(iterator[, default])	Retrieves next element from iterator
object()	Creates featureless object
oct(x)	Converts integer to octal. Prefix with 0o
open(file)	Returns File object
ord(char)	Returns Unicode value of one-character string
pow(x,y)	Returns x to power of y
print()	Prints given object
property()	Returns property attribute
range([start,] stop[, step])	Returns list of integers from 0 to (not including) stop
repr(object)	Returns printable string representation of *object*
reversed(seq)	Returns reversed iterator of sequence
round(number[, ndigits])	Returns floating-point number rounded to *n* digits or nearest integer
set()	Returns Python set
setattr(object, name, value)	Sets object's attribute name to the specified value
slice(start, stop[, step])	Creates a slice object specified by range()
sorted(iterable,[, key [, reverse]])	Returns a new sorted list from items in iterable
@staticmethod	Creates static method from a function
str(object)	Returns str version of object

(*Continued*)

Table 7.2 (Continued)

Function	Description
sum(iterable[, start=0])	Returns the sum of all elements of iterable; does not work with strings
super()	Allows you to Refer Parent Class by super
tuple(iterable)	Creates a Tuple
Class type(object)	Returns Type of an Object
vars([object])	Returns __dict__ attribute of a class or object
zip([iter1 [, iter2 [, ...]]])	Makes iterator that aggregates elements from each iterable. Returns iterator of tuples
__import__(name, globals, locals, fromlist=(), level=0)	Function imports module name

The built-in functions are used in the different examples of the book.

7.15 Modules

Python allows re-use of an already-created code. The reusable code could be user-created or already existing in Python library. These are called modules in Python.

- A module may have several items defined within it, like functions, classes and variables. The complete module, or specific function, class or variable can be accessed. (Classes are discussed in later chapters.)
- A program written in Python and saved using *.py* extension is Python module. Thus, any Python program or file can be referenced as a module. Users can create their own modules. For example, a function to find factorial of a number can be defined in a file and saved as *fact.py.* This creates a module *fact* with function factorial.
- Python has a large collection of already-released modules. These modules can be used in the programs. An example is *math* module.
- To use the modules in a program, the modules or items in the modules have to be imported.
- The items in a module can be imported in two ways:
  - o Using `import` statement
  - o Using `from` statement
- Python modules can also be accessed directly from the Python interpreter.

The following sub-sections discuss different aspects of Python module in detail.

7.15.1 The `Import` Statement

The `import` statement allows us to use the module items in a program. When we use `import` statement, the code of module gets executed within the scope of definition. All items in the module are available for use under a separate namespace.

- The syntax of `import` statement is as follows:
  import `modulename, ...`
- The `import` statement is declared at the top of the program code.
- The `import` statement makes the module content available as a separate namespace. To refer to an item of module, the dot notation is used, as follows:
  `modulename.item`
- When a *modulename* is imported, Python interpreter first searches the built-in modules. If it does not find a built-module, then interpreter searches for user-defined file named *modulename.py* in the directory from sys.path variable.
- A module A can be imported and can be used under a different name B, as follows:
  import A as B
- **`Reload()`**: When a module is imported in a script, it gets executed only once. Now, if changes have been made to the module, there is a need to reload the module. For this, the `reload()` function is used. The `reload()` function reloads an already imported module. The syntax of `reload()` function is

```
import importlib
importlib.reload(modulename)
```

- Let us see an example to use `import` statement.

Example 7.21: Write a code to show the use of math module.

Create a Python file *example.py*, shown in (1)
Import the math module, shown in (2)
Use square root function as *math.sqrt(9)*, shown in (3)
We see that `sqrt()`, `factorial()`, `pow()` are functions, however, pi is a variable.

1 → example.py - C:/Users/dsc/Desktop/example.py (3.6.1)

File Edit Format Run Options Window Help

```
import math                                                  ← 2

print("The square root of 9 is ", math.sqrt(9))              ← 3
print("The value of pi is ", math.pi)
print("The factorial of 5 is ", math.factorial(5))
print("The 2 to power 5 is ", math.pow(2,5))
```

Output

```
The square root of 9 is  3.0
The value of pi is  3.141592653589793
The factorial of 5 is  120
The 2 to power 5 is  32.0
>>>
```

7.15.2 The `from..import` Statement

We have seen that an imported module is available in a separate namespace and dot notation is used for referring to an item of module.

In contrast, `from..import` statement allows referring to module items in a program's namespace. This statement copies the items from module to your program namespace. The items can be referred by name instead of the dot notation.

The syntax of `from..import` statement is as follows:

```
from modulename import *
from modulename import item_name1, item_name2, ...
```

The * in first `form` statement, imports all items from *modulename.* Using import statement using * is generally not suggested.

To import specific items, the second `form` statement is used. It allows you to name the items that you want to import from `modulename`.

Example 7.22: Write a code to use `from..import` from math module.

For a number *n*, we find the rounded square root and square. We use `from..import` (1), and module items without dot notation (2).

fromimport.py - C:/Users/dsc/Desktop/fromimport.py (3.6.1)

File Edit Format Run Options Window Help

```
from math import sqrt, pow                                          ← 1

print("N\t", "SQRT(N)\t","POWER(N, 2)")
print("======================================")
for x in range(5, 10):
    print(x, "\t", round(sqrt(x), 2), "\t\t",pow(x,2))              ← 2
```

Output

```
N           SQRT(N)             POWER(N, 2)
================================
5           2.24                25.0
6           2.45                36.0
7           2.65                49.0
8           2.83                64.0
9           3.0                 81.0
>>>
```

Example 7.23 Display power of numbers from 5 to 9 using `import..as` for math module.

Here, we import module math under a different name `mymath`. Then we use `mymath` to access items of math in our program.

```
import math as mymath

print("N\t", "POWER(N, 2)")
print("======================================")
for x in range(5, 10):
    print(x, "\t", mymath.pow(x,2))
```

Output

```
N           POWER(N, 2)
=========================
5           25.0
6           36.0
7           49.0
8           64.0
9           81.0
>>>
```

7.15.3 Creating Your Own Module

In addition to the built-in modules defined in Python library, users can also create their own modules and then import them in other programs.

Example 7.24: Create a Python file with the name *createmodule.py*. Define three functions in it. Write another program, `userdef module.py` and import `createmodule` in it. Show the output.

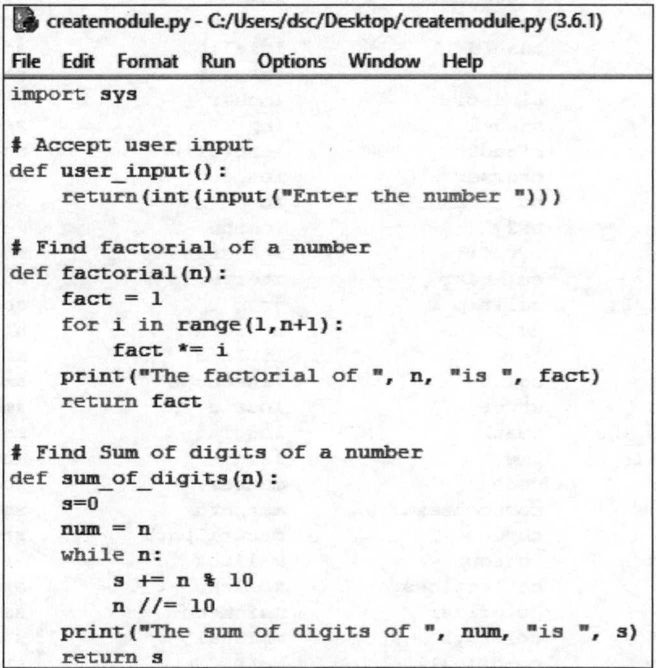

createmodule.py - C:/Users/dsc/Desktop/createmodule.py (3.6.1)

File Edit Format Run Options Window Help

```
import sys

# Accept user input
def user_input():
    return(int(input("Enter the number ")))

# Find factorial of a number
def factorial(n):
    fact = 1
    for i in range(1,n+1):
        fact *= i
    print("The factorial of ", n, "is ", fact)
    return fact

# Find Sum of digits of a number
def sum_of_digits(n):
    s=0
    num = n
    while n:
        s += n % 10
        n //= 10
    print("The sum of digits of ", num, "is ", s)
    return s
```

(a) Defining module

userdef module.py - C:/Users/dsc/Desktop/userdef module.py (3.6.1)

File Edit Format Run Options Window Help

```
import createmodule

createmodule.factorial(createmodule.user_input())
```

(b) Using user defined module

```
Enter the number 8
The factorial of  8 is  40320
>>> |
```

(c) Output of (b)

7.15.4 Using `help()`

An installation of Python software also installs the Python Standard library. The library has several built-in modules. To use any module, there is a need to know the modules available in the library.

- The `help()` function is used to know the modules available in Python.
- The syntax of help function to find modules is as follows:

```
help("modules")
```

- Type the help function in the Python interpreter. It displays the modules available in Python. Figure 7.2 shows one page of the list of displayed modules.

```
>>> help("modules")

Please wait a moment while I gather a list of all available modules...

MathRandom          autocomplete_w      idle                runscript
__future__          autoexpand          idle_test           sched
__main__            base64              idlelib             scrolledlist
_ast                bdb                 imaplib             search
_asyncio            binascii            imghdr              searchbase
_bisect             binhex              imp                 searchengine
_blake2             bisect              importlib           secrets
_bootlocale         browser             inspect             select
_bz2                builtins            io                  selectors
_codecs             bz2                 iomenu              setuptools
_codecs_cn          cProfile            ipaddress           shelve
_codecs_hk          calendar            itertools           shlex
_codecs_iso2022     calltip_w           json                shutil
_codecs_jp          calltips            keyword             signal
_codecs_kr          cgi                 lib2to3             site
_codecs_tw          cgitb               linecache           smtpd
_collections        chunk               locale              smtplib
_collections_abc    cmath               logging             sndhdr
_compat_pickle      cmd                 lzma                socket
_compression        code                macosx              socketserver
_csv                codecontext         macpath             sqlite3
_ctypes             codecs              macurl2path         sre_compile
_ctypes_test        codeop              mailbox             sre_constants
_datetime           collections         mailcap             sre_parse
_decimal            colorizer           mainmenu            ssl
_dummy_thread       colorsys            marshal             stackviewer
_elementtree        compileall          math                stat
_functools          concurrent          mimetypes           statistics
_hashlib            config              mmap                statusbar
_heapq              config_key          module              string
_imp                configdialog        modulefinder        stringprep
_io                 configparser        msilib              struct
_json               contextlib          msvcrt              subprocess
_locale             copy                multicall           sunau
_lsprof             copyreg             multiprocessing     symbol
_lzma               crypt               mutable             symtable
```

Figure. 7.2 Some modules in Python

- The *help* function is also used to find help on any module.

Figure 7.3 shows one page of the details of `time` module.

```
>>> help("time")
Help on built-in module time:

NAME
    time - This module provides various functions to manipulate time values.

DESCRIPTION
    There are two standard representations of time.  One is the number
    of seconds since the Epoch, in UTC (a.k.a. GMT).  It may be an integer
    or a floating point number (to represent fractions of seconds).
    The Epoch is system-defined; on Unix, it is generally January 1st, 1970.
    The actual value can be retrieved by calling gmtime(0).

    The other representation is a tuple of 9 integers giving local time.
    The tuple items are:
      year (including century, e.g. 1998)
      month (1-12)
      day (1-31)
      hours (0-23)
      minutes (0-59)
      seconds (0-59)
      weekday (0-6, Monday is 0)
      Julian day (day in the year, 1-366)
      DST (Daylight Savings Time) flag (-1, 0 or 1)
    If the DST flag is 0, the time is given in the regular time zone;
    if it is 1, the time is given in the DST time zone;
    if it is -1, mktime() should guess based on the date and time.

    Variables:

    timezone -- difference in seconds between UTC and local standard time
    altzone -- difference in  seconds between UTC and local DST time
    daylight -- whether local time should reflect DST
    tzname -- tuple of (standard time zone name, DST time zone name)
```

```
Functions:

time() -- return current time in seconds since the Epoch as a float
clock() -- return CPU time since process start as a float
sleep() -- delay for a number of seconds given as a float
gmtime() -- convert seconds since Epoch to UTC tuple
localtime() -- convert seconds since Epoch to local time tuple
asctime() -- convert time tuple to string
ctime() -- convert time in seconds to string
mktime() -- convert local time tuple to seconds since Epoch
strftime() -- convert time tuple to string according to format specification
strptime() -- parse string to time tuple according to format specification
tzset() -- change the local timezone
```

Figure 7.3 A snapshot of time module

- The `help` function is also used to find help on a user-defined module. Figure 7.24 shows items of user-defined module `createmodule`.

```
>>> help("createmodule")
Help on module createmodule:

NAME
    createmodule

FUNCTIONS
    factorial(n)
        # Find factorial of a number

    fibonacci(n)
        # Find n terms of Fibonacci series

    sum_of_digits(n)
        # Find Sum of digits of a number

    user_input()
        # Accept user input

FILE
    c:\users\dsc\desktop\createmodule.py


>>> |
```

Figure 7.24 Using `help` function for user-defined module

7.15.5 Namespaces

Namespaces are used for making names unique. This is done to avoid any conflict of names. Everything in Python is an object. A name is bound to the object. Python implements namespaces as dictionary. The key-value pair mapping is the name-object pair. Different namespaces can use the same name mapped to a different object. There are different namespaces in Python – Local namespace, Global namespace, and Built-in namespace.

- Local namespace is the local name defined within a function. The scope of local namespace is the function.
- Global namespace includes names that are imported from modules. The scope of global namespace is the program in which you have imported the module.
- Built-in namespace contains built-in functions like `min()`, `max()`.

To get the names of local and global namespaces, the `globals()` and `local()` functions are used. The namespaces are returned depending on the location of the call. The return type is a dictionary.

- **Locals()** called from within function, returns local names accessible from the function.
- **Globals()** called from within function, returns global names accessible globally from the function.

Example 7.25: Write a function to show use of locals in finding factorial of a number.

```
# Find factorial of a number
def factorial(n):
    """This returns factorial of n"""
    print(locals())  <---- 1
    fact = 1
    for i in range(1,n+1):
        fact *= i
    print("The factorial of ", n, "is ", fact)
```

Output

```
This returns factorial of n
Enter the number 3
{'n': 3}  <---- 2
The factorial of  3 is  6
>>>
```

7.15.6 Using __main__

We have seen till now that a program can be run in two ways:

1. As a main program
2. As a module called in another program.

'__main__' in Python is scope of top level code execution.

__name__ == '__main__' is a convention to use. It is used as follows:

```
If __name__ == '__main__'
#code
```

If the module in which the code is defined is executed from standard input, script or interactive mode, then the `if` statement is true. The code in `if` statement executes.

If the module is imported in another program, then the `if` statement is false. So the code within `if` does not execute.

Module checks its own __name__ to know if it is executing in main scope or not.

So,

```
If __name__ == '__main__':
    main()
```

will execute only if the module is not imported.

Let us see an example.

Example 7.26: Write a function to show the use of __main__.

```
import sys
# Accept user input
def user_input():
    return(int(input("Enter the number ")))
# Find factorial of a number
def factorial(n):
    fact = 1
    for i in range(1,n+1):
        fact *= i
    print("The factorial of ", n, "is ", fact)
# Find Sum of digits of a number
def sum_of_digits(n):
    s=0
    num = n
    while n:
        s += n % 10
        n //= 10
    print("The sum of digits of ", num, "is ", s)
def choose_func(choice):
    if choice == 1:
        factorial(user_input())
    elif choice == 2:
        sum_of_digits(user_input())
    else: print("You have entered wrong choice")
def menu():
    print("Enter your choice")
    print("1. Factorial")
    print("2. Sum of digits of a number")
    return(int(input("Enter your choice ")))
def main():
    c = 1
    while c:
        choose_func(menu())
        c = input("Do you want to continue(N/n/no) ")
        if c == "N" or c == "n" or c == "no":
            c = 0
if __name__ == '__main__':
    main()
```

When we execute this file, the main() gets executed.

When this file is imported in another program and a function executed, the main of this file does not get executed.

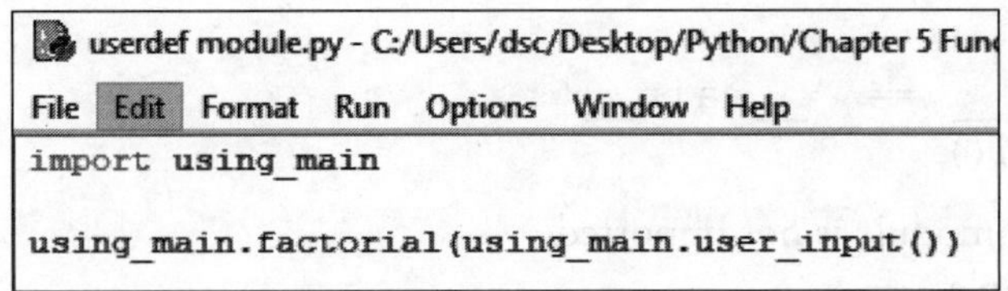

7.16 Comparison Function and Method

The classes and objects are discussed much later. However, as we proceed to the next chapters, we see that both built-in functions and built-in methods are used. Here, we discuss the distinction between them.

There is a thin line between functions and methods. Both functions and methods may be built-in functions or user-defined function. Though function and method look similar, there is a key difference. Table 7.3 depicts the difference between function and method.

Table 7.3 Difference between Function and Method in Python

Feature	Function	Method
Description	Block of code that is called by its name. Helps to implement re-usability. Built-in functions are available in the Python library "Built-in Functions".	It is called by its name, but is associated to an object (dependent). It works on objects of the class Available in respective classes in Python library.
Dependency	Independent	Class-object-method Belongs to a class
Calling	It is called only by its name, as it is defined independently.	It cannot be called by its name only, it is attached to an object. Method is defined within a class and hence they are dependent on that class.
Parameters	Can have parameters Parameters are passed explicitly.	It is implicitly passed to the object on which it is invoked. It can access the data within an object.
Data return	May or may not return any data	May or may not return any data
Data Modification	Functions print or return a value.	It operates on data (instance variables) contained by corresponding class. Method may modify state of an object.

Basic Structure	`def function_name ( arg1, arg2,...):`
	`......`
	`# function body`
	`......`
		`class class_name`
		`def method_name ():`
		`......`
		`# method body`
		`.....`

Example	`>>> abs(99.2)`
	`99.2`
	`>>> abs(-12)`
	`12`
	`>>> max(2, 5, 3,1)`
	`5`
	The functions work independently on data
		`>>> a=[2, 3, 4, 5]`
		`>>> a.append(8)`
		`>>> a`
		`[2, 3, 4, 5, 8]`
		Here, a is an object of type list. The method works on the object a

7.17 Packages

A module in Python is a single file. However, when a large number of files are collectively required to define a project, the packages are created. So similar modules or classes are placed in the same directory to organize them into packages.

To create a package,

- Create a directory having your package name
- Put all files in it
- Create a `__init__.py` file in the directory.

The `__init__.py` file is a way by which Python interpreter knows that the directory is a package and not any ordinary directory.

Let us see an example to create a package as shown in Example 7.27.

Example 7.27: Create a package as follows:

1. Create a directory. Name it "Test".
2. Define the modules. Create two modules `keyword_arg.py` and `using_main.py`.
3. Define `__init__`. Import the modules in it.
4. Define a test program to use the package. Define test.

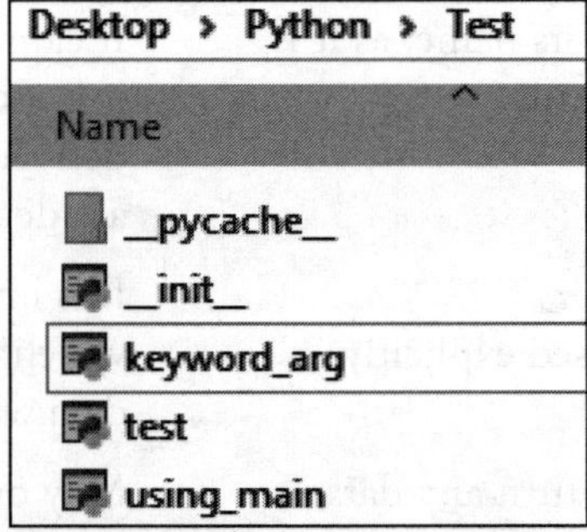

using_main.py - C:\Users\dsc\Desktop\Python\Test\using_main.py (3.6.1)

File Edit Format Run Options Window Help

```
import sys
# Accept user input
def user_input():
    return(int(input("Enter the number ")))
# Find factorial of a number
def factorial(n):
    """This returns factorial of n"""
    print(locals())
    fact = 1
    for i in range(1,n+1):
        fact *= i
    print("The factorial of ", n, "is ", fact)
# Find Sum of digits of a number
def sum_of_digits(n):
```

(a) using_main.py

```
*keyword_arg.py - C:/Users/dsc/Desktop/Python/Test/keyword_arg.py (3.6.1)*
File Edit Format Run Options Window Help

#WAP to check whether a year is leap year or not
def check_leap(year):
    if (year%4 == 0 and year%100 != 0 or year %400 ==0):
        print (year , "is a leap year")
    else:
        print(year , "is not a leap year")

#WAP to print name and age of the user
def print_nameAge(name, age):
    print("Hello!", name, ".", end = " ")
    print("You are sweet", age)
```

(b) keyword_arg.py

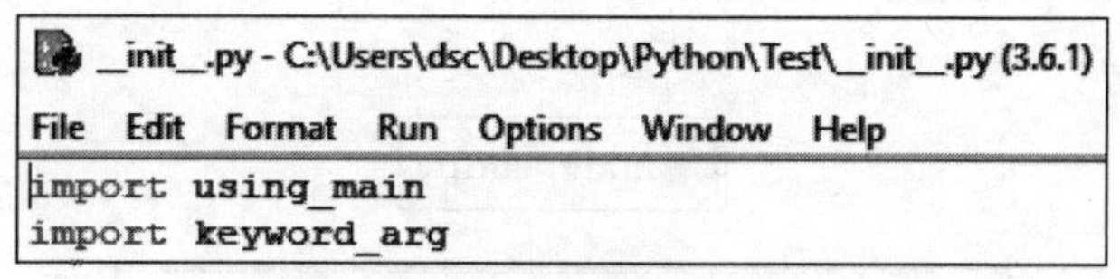

```
_init_.py - C:\Users\dsc\Desktop\Python\Test\_init_.py (3.6.1)
File Edit Format Run Options Window Help
import using_main
import keyword_arg
```

(c) __init__.py

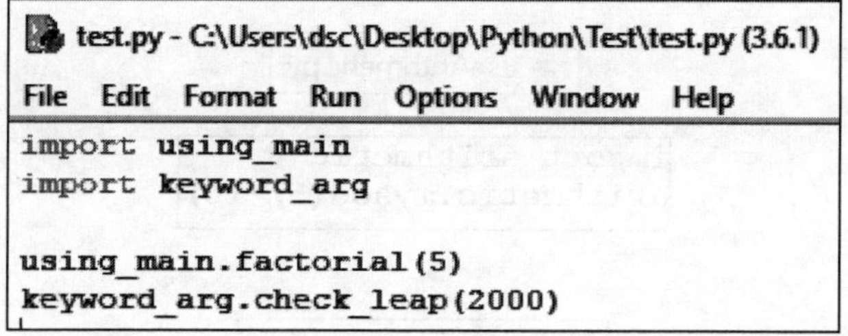

```
test.py - C:\Users\dsc\Desktop\Python\Test\test.py (3.6.1)
File Edit Format Run Options Window Help
import using_main
import keyword_arg

using_main.factorial(5)
keyword_arg.check_leap(2000)
```

(d) test.py

```
{'n': 5}
The factorial of  5 is  120
2000 is a leap year
>>>
```

(e) Output when test is executed

7.18 Comparison – Library, Script, Module, Package

We have already discussed the modules and packages in this chapter. Here, we highlight the difference between script, module, package and library.

Script

- Script contains code written outside the scope of a class or function.
- It is a Python file for direct running.
- When script is run, it must perform a task.

Module

- Module is a Python file that can be a collection of classes, functions and global variables.
- Module has .py extension. It is an executable file.
- It can be imported in scripts or other files.
- Python has several built-in modules, like, math and statistics. Import the module in the program you write, to use the functions of the built-in module.
- You can also create your own module. For example, define a module `arithmetic.py` that performs arithmetic operations on any two integers. Import it in another program and use the defined function `myadd()`.

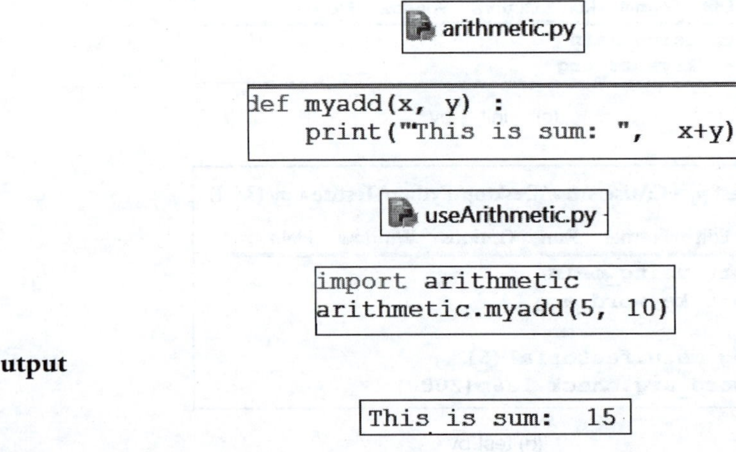

Package

- Package is a collection of related modules that work together to provide functionality.
- Package can be imported. It is a folder.
- The package has a file `_init_` and other files.
- In the example shown below, a package named "test" is shown having four files including the `_init_` and a main file.

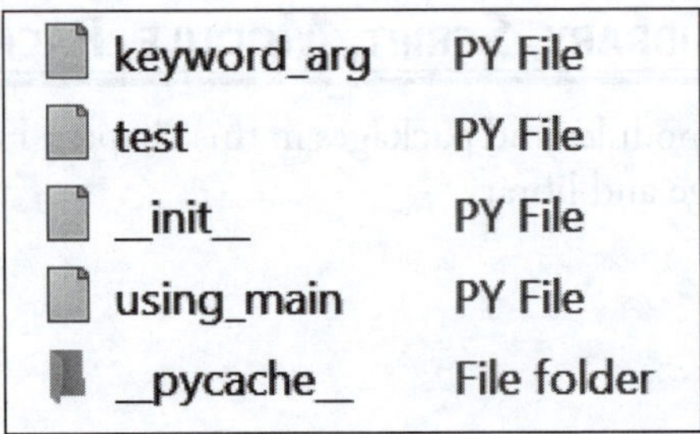

Library

- Library is a collection of codes with related functionality.
- Python Standard Library has hundreds of modules.
- Python Standard Library comes bundled with the installation of Python. Most of the time, you do not have to download it separately.
- Use by importing module from the library and calling the method of the module with `period(.)`.
- The Python Standard Library listing is shown in Annexure 1 of the book.
- In the Example (a) shown below, random module from the library is imported. The function `random()` of the module is used. In the Example (b), math module from the library is imported and the function `sqrt()` is used.

```
>>> import random
>>> random.random()
0.2426005609886973
```

(a)

```
>>> import math
>>> math.sqrt(9)
3.0
```

(b)

7.19 Solved Questions with Explanation

1) Find the output:

```
x = 10
def f1(x):
    print('Inside f1()-x before assign:', x)
    x = 20
    print('Inside f1()-x after assign:', x)
print('Outside f1()-x before call', x)
f1(x)
print('Outside f1()-x after call', x)
```

Output

```
Outside f1()-x before call 10
Inside f1()-x before assign: 10
Inside f1()-x after assign: 20
Outside f1()-x after call 10
```

Explanation: Inside `f1()`, the variable `x` is local, so `x` changed from 10 to 20 inside function, but there is no change of `x` outside `f1()`.

2) Find the output:

```
x = 10
def f1():
    global x
    print('Inside f1()-x before assign:', x)
    x = 20
    print('Inside f1()-x after assign:', x)
print('Outside f1()-x before call', x)
f1()
print('Outside f1()-x after call', x)
```

Output

```
Outside f1()-x before call 10
Inside f1()-x before assign: 10
Inside f1()-x after assign: 20
Outside f1()-x after call 20
```

Explanation: Inside `f1()`, the variable `x` is global, so `x` changed from 10 to 20 inside function and also outside `f1()`.

3) Find the output:

```
def sum_all(*a):
    '''Returns sum of all values'''
    r = 0
    for i in a:
        r += i
    return r
print(sum_all.__doc__)
print(sum_all(2, 4, 6))
print(sum_all(2, 4, 6, 8, 10))
```

Output

```
Returns sum of all values
12
30
```

Explanation: `a` is a variable-length argument. It finds the sum of all values passed to `a`.

4) Find the output:

```
from math import pi
[print(str(round(pi, i))) for i in range(1, 6)]
```

Output

```
3.1
3.14
3.142
3.1416
3.14159
```

Explanation: It prints value of pi rounded from 1 to 5, after the decimal.

5) Find the output:

```
def rec_exp(x, n):
    if n == 0:
        return 1
    elif n % 2 == 0:
        return rec_exp(x*x, n/2)
    else:
        return x * rec_exp(x, n-1)
print(rec_exp(3,4))
```

Output

```
81
```

Explanation: This is a recursive program to find xn.

6) Find the output:

(a)

```
def sum(n):
    if n== 0: return 0
    else:   return n + sum(n-1)
print(sum(int(input("Enter a number:"))))
```

Output

```
Enter a number:5
15
```

Explanation: This is a recursive program to find the sum of first n integers.

6. (b)

```
def sum(n):
    if n== 0: return 0
    else:   return n + sum(n-1)
def trc(f):
    def g(x):
        print(f.__name__, x)
        val = f(x)
        print("return", repr(val))
        return val
    return g
sum = trc(sum)
n1=int(input("Enter a number:"))
print(sum(n1))
```

Output

```
Enter a number:6
sum 6
sum 5
sum 4
sum 3
sum 2
sum 1
sum 0
return 0
return 1
return 3
return 6
return 10
return 15
return 21
21
```

Explanation: This is a recursive program to find the sum of first n integers. This also shows the sequence of calls. The line `sum=trc(sum)` replaces the function `sum` with `trc(sum)`. When a recursive call is made, the new function executes, and it prints trace before calling the original function.

6.(c)

```
def sum(n):
    if n== 0: return 0
    else:   return n + sum(n-1)
def trc(f):
    f.dent = 0
    def g(x):
        print( '|   ' * f.dent + '|--', f.__name__, x)
        f.dent += 1
        val = f(x)
        print('|   ' * f.dent + '|--', 'return', repr(val))
        f.dent -= 1
        return val
    return g
sum = trc(sum)
n1=int(input("Enter a number:"))
print(sum(n1))
```

Output

```
Enter a number:6
|-- sum 6
|   |-- sum 5
|   |   |-- sum 4
|   |   |   |-- sum 3
|   |   |   |   |-- sum 2
|   |   |   |   |   |-- sum 1
|   |   |   |   |   |   |-- sum 0
|   |   |   |   |   |   |   |-- return 0
|   |   |   |   |   |   |-- return 1
|   |   |   |   |   |-- return 3
|   |   |   |   |-- return 6
|   |   |   |-- return 10
|   |   |-- return 15
|   |-- return 21
21
```

Explanation: This is a recursive program to find the sum of first `n` integers. Here `print` statements are defined in such a way that the recursion is visible.

7) Find the output:

```
def t(n,i):
    print(n*i)
    i=i+1
    if i<=10:
        t(n,i)
x=int(input("Enter a number:"))
print(t(x,1))
```

Output

```
Enter a number:6
6
12
18
24
30
36
42
48
54
60
None
```

Explanation: This program finds the first 10 multiples of number. See if you can modify the program so that None is not printed at the end.

7.20 Programming Examples

Program 7.1: WAP to accept input from user and print it.

```
# Accept user input
def user_input():
    a = int((input("Enter the number ")))
    print(a)
user_input()
```

Output

```
Enter the number 5
5
```

```
Enter the number 4
4
```

Program 7.2: WAP to calculate nth power of any number x - find x^n

Function has two parameters. It can be executed for different value of the parameters.

```
# Find x to power n
def power(x, n):
    pow = x
    for i in range(1, n):
        pow *= x
    print("The value of ", x, "to power ", n, "is", pow)
power(2,5)
power(3,5)
power(6,2)
power(10,3)
```

Output

```
The value of  2 to power  5 is 32
The value of  3 to power  5 is 243
The value of  6 to power  2 is 36
The value of  10 to power  3 is 1000
>>> |
```

Program 7.3: WAP to check if a number is odd, even, zero, with function, input parameter and return value.

```
def check_oddeven(n):                              <-- 1
        if n == 0: return("zero")                  <-- 2
        if n%2 == 0:
            return("even")                         <-- 2
        else:
            return("odd")                          <-- 2
for a in (5, 6, 7, 0, 8, 9, 10):
    print("The number", a, "is ", check_oddeven(a))  <-- 3
```

Output

```
The number 5 is  odd
The number 6 is  even
The number 7 is  odd
The number 0 is  zero
The number 8 is  even
The number 9 is  odd
The number 10 is  even
>>>
```

The points to be noted in the above code are as follows:

- The function defines an input parameter "`n`". (1)
- There is more than one `return` statement returning different values. (2)
- The calling function calls the function with argument "`a`". (3)
- A function can return only one value. For a value of calling argument, any one of the `return` statement executes. (2)
- The returned value is printed at the calling function "`print`". (3)

Program 7.4: WAP to compute the LCM of two numbers.

```
# Find the L.C.M. of two input number
def find_LCM(x, y):
   if x > y:   max = x
   else: max = y
   while(True):
       if((max % x == 0) and (max % y == 0)):
           lcm = max; break
       max += 1
   return lcm

print("To find LCM of two numbers")
n1= int(input("Enter the first number:"))
n2= int(input("Enter the second number:") )
print("The L.C.M. is", find_LCM(n1, n2))
```

Output

```
To find LCM of two numbers
Enter the first number:54
Enter the second number:24
The L.C.M. is 216
```

```
To find LCM of two numbers
Enter the first number:10
Enter the second number:21
The L.C.M. is 210
```

```
To find LCM of two numbers
Enter the first number:54
Enter the second number:34
The L.C.M. is 918
```

```
To find LCM of two numbers
Enter the first number:21
Enter the second number:7
The L.C.M. is 21
```

Program 7.5: WAP to calculate simple interest, using function. Use the global statement.

```
# Using global statement
prin = 10000
def simple_Int(rate, time):
    global prin ◄── 1
    prin = (prin * rate * time)/100
    print(prin)
    return prin
print(simple_Int(5, 5))
print (prin)
print("==========")
```

Output

```
2500.0
2500.0
2500.0
==========
```

Program 7.6: WAP to print the name and age of the user. Accept as arguments. Accept input from user.

```
#WAP to print name and age of the user
def print_nameAge(name, age):
    print("Hello!", name, ".", end = " ")
    print("You are sweet", age)
print_nameAge(input("Enter your name "), int(input("Enter your age ")))
```

Output

```
Enter your name Divya
Enter your age 17
Hello! Divya . You are sweet 17
>>> |
```

Program 7.7: WAP to print the name and age of the user. Accept input for only one argument from the user.

```
#WAP to print name and age of the user
def print_nameAge(name, age):
    print("Hello!", name, ".", end = " ")
    print("You are sweet", age)
print_nameAge(input("Enter your name "))
```

Output

```
Enter your name Divya
Traceback (most recent call last):
  File "C:/Users/dsc/Desktop/required-arg.py", line 23, in <module>
    print_nameAge(input("Enter your name "))
TypeError: print_nameAge() missing 1 required positional argument: 'age'
>>> |
```

We see that an error is reported because the number of arguments does not match the number of function parameters.

Program 7.8: WAP to print the name and age of the user. Accept as arguments. Define age as default argument.

```
#WAP to print name and age of the user
def print_nameAge(name, age=16):
    print("Hello!", name, ".", end = " ")
    print("You are sweet", age)
print_nameAge(input("Enter your name "))
print_nameAge(age = int(input("Enter your age ")),
              name = input("Enter your name "))
```

Output

```
Enter your name Nikita
Hello! Nikita . You are sweet 16
Enter your age 20
Enter your name Sonia
Hello! Sonia . You are sweet 20
>>>
```

We see that when an argument is not provided for a parameter, the default argument in the function definition is assumed.

Program 7.9: WAP to check whether a number is prime or not. Use variable arguments.

```
# WAP to check if a number is prime or not
def check_prime(*num):
    for n in num:
        for i in range( 2, n//2 ):
            if n % i == 0:
                print(n, "is not a prime number " )
                break
        else:
            print(n, "is a prime number " )
check_prime()
check_prime(2, 20, 67, 57, 49)
```

Output

```
2 is a prime number
20 is not a prime number
67 is a prime number
57 is not a prime number
49 is not a prime number
>>>
```

We see that when no argument is sent in function call, then nothing happens (`check_prime()`).

Program 7.10: Write a recursive function for computing the factorial of `n`. The user can enter input till they want to continue.

```
def fact(n):
    if n == 1:
        return 1
    else:
        return n * fact(n-1)

ch = "y"
while ch == "y" or ch =="Y":
    n = int(input("Enter number "))
    print("\nThe factorial of", n, "is", fact(n))
    print("==================================")
    ch = input("Do you want to continue Y/y/N/n)")
```

Output

```
Enter number 5

The factorial of 5 is 120
==================================
Do you want to continue Y/y/N/n)n
```

Program 7.11: Write a recursive program for computing the factorial of n. Insert `print` statement to show the recursion.

```
def fact(n):
    print("The value of n is", n)
    if n == 1:
        return 1
    else:
        f = n * fact(n-1)
        print("Recursive cases:", n, "* factorial(",n-1,")=",f)
        return f
ch = "y"
while ch == "y" or ch =="Y":
    n = int(input("Enter number "))
    print("\nThe factorial of", n, "is", fact(n))
    print("==================================")
    ch = input("Do you want to continue Y/y/N/n)")
```

Output

```
Enter number 4
The value of n is 4
The value of n is 3
The value of n is 2
The value of n is 1
Recursive cases: 2 * factorial( 1 )= 2
Recursive cases: 3 * factorial( 2 )= 6
Recursive cases: 4 * factorial( 3 )= 24

The factorial of 4 is 24
==================================
Do you want to continue Y/y/N/n)y
Enter number 6
The value of n is 6
The value of n is 5
The value of n is 4
The value of n is 3
The value of n is 2
The value of n is 1
Recursive cases: 2 * factorial( 1 )= 2
Recursive cases: 3 * factorial( 2 )= 6
Recursive cases: 4 * factorial( 3 )= 24
Recursive cases: 5 * factorial( 4 )= 120
Recursive cases: 6 * factorial( 5 )= 720

The factorial of 6 is 720
==================================
Do you want to continue Y/y/N/n)n
```

Program 7.12: WAP to find the nth power of any number.

```
def double(x, y):
    return x ** y
print("5 to power 5 using def is = ", double(5, 5))
```

Output

```
5 to power 5 using def is =  3125
>>>
```

Program 7.13: Use random module. Create a Python file *example.py*, shown in (1). Import the random module, shown in (2). Use `randint()` to get a random number in specified range 1,5 both 1 and 5 inclusive, shown in (3). Use `randrange()` to return random element from a start, stop, step range. Use step of 3 between any two random numbers. We have used it in for-loop with range 10, so ten random numbers are generated, shown in (4).

1 → exampleRandom.py - C:/Users/dsc/Desktop/exampleRandom.py (3.6.1)

File Edit Format Run Options Window Help

```
import random                              ← 2

for i in range(5):
    print(random.randint(1,5))             ← 3
print("===")
for i in range(10):
    print(random.randrange(1, 20, 3))      ← 4
```

Output

```
4
5
5
4
3
===
1
19
19
7
7
19
19
10
4
13
>>>
```

Program 7.14: Use both math and random module.

More than one module can also be imported. We import both random and math module and generate random number and its square root, five times.

MathRandom.py - C:/Users/dsc/Desktop/MathRandom.py (3.6.1)

File Edit Format Run Options Window Help

```
import random
import math

for i in range(5):
    x = random.randint(1, 20)
    print(x, math.sqrt(x))
```

Output

```
19 4.358898943540674
3 1.7320508075688772
12 3.4641016151377544
14 3.7416573867739413
9 3.0
>>>
```

Program 7.15: Use math module and print the square of integers from 0 to 9, using interactive mode.

```
>>> import math
>>> for i in range(10):
        print(pow(i, 2))


0.0
1.0
4.0
9.0
16.0
25.0
36.0
49.0
64.0
81.0
>>>
```

Program 7.16: Write a program that asks the user for a number n and gives the user the possibility to choose between computing the sum and computing the product of 1, ..., n.

```
import sys
def user_input():
  return(int(input("Enter a number")))
def sum_n(n):
  s=0
  num=n
  while num:
   s+=num
   num-=1
  print("The sum from 1 to ", n, "is", s)
def product_n(n):
  p=1
```

```
  num=n
  while num:
   p *=num
   num-=1
  print("The number from 1 to", num, "is", p)
def choose_func(choice):
  if choice ==1
   sum_n(user_input())
  elif choice ==2:
   product_n(user input())
  else: print(""You have inserted wrong choice")
def menu():
  print("\nSelect any one:)
  print("1. Sum of numbers from 1 to n")
  print("2. Product of numbers from 1 to n")
  return(int(input("Enter your choice")))
def main():
  c = 1
  while c:
   choose_func(menu())
   c = input("Do you want to continue(N/n/no)")
   if c == "N" or c == "n" or c=="no"
      c = 0
if__name__=='__main__'
  main()
```

Output

```
Select any one:
1. Sum of numbers from 1 to n
2. Product of numbers from 1 to n
Enter your choice 1
Enter a number 5
The sum from 1 to 5 is 15
Do you want to continue (N/n/no) y
Select any one:
1. Sum of numbers from 1 to n
2. Product of numbers from 1 to n
Enter your choice 2
Enter a number 5
The product from 1 to 0 is 120
Do you want to continue(N/n/no)n
>>>
```

Summary

- A function is a small and manageable program unit that performs a specific task.
- Python allows both user-defined functions and built-in library functions.
- Function definition and function call are the two main aspects of user-defined functions.
- Function definition is implementation of the function.
- Function call is invocation of the defined function.
- Arguments are values passed during function call and parameters are variable values defined in the function definition.
- A computed result can be returned to the calling function, using `return` statement.
- Functions may take zero or many inputs and provide zero or many outputs.
- Mutable objects are used to return more than one output from a function.
- The variables defined in a function may be local or global variables.
- A function defined in the body of another function is a nested function.
- The arguments passed during function call can be of different kinds – required arguments, keyword arguments, default arguments and variable length arguments.
- `main()` function is used to structure the program.
- Docstrings are comments that can be inspected during runtime.
- Python supports recursive function, where a function calls itself.
- A nameless function required for a short duration can be defined using lambda keyword.
- Built-in functions are pre-defined functions, like `print()`, `input()`.
- Modules are re-usable codes that are user-defined or in the Python library.
- A module may consist of functions, classes and variables.
- `Import` and `from...import` are used to refer to module items in a program.
- The available modules in Python can be known by using `help()` function.
- To avoid name conflict, namespaces are used. `Locals()` and `Globals()` are namespaces in Python.
- `__main__` is used to execute a piece of code if it is run as script and not as imported module.
- Packages allow multiple files to be defined for a project.
- The presence of __init__.py file in a directory tells that it is a package and not any ordinary directory.

Keywords

Function	Return	Local variable
Modularization	Function_name	Global
Divide-conquer strategy	Parameter	Nested function
User-defined function	Argument	Required argument
Reusability	Mutable object	Keyword argument
Library function	Immutable object	Default argument
Function definition	Scope of variable	Variable length argument
Function call	Global variable	Docstring

Recursive function	math module	Local namespace
Recursion	random module	Global namespace
Anonymous function	factorial()	Built-in namespace
Built-in function	Python standard library	Packages
Module	Namespaces	

Programming Language Keywords

`__main__`	`return()`	`module`
`__name__`	`def`	`help()`
`__init__`	`main()`	`lambda`
`__doc__`	`locals()`	`sqrt()`
`reload()`	`globals()`	`pow()`
`randint()`	`import`	
`randrange()`	`from...import`	

Assessment

A.1 Bloom Level: Knowledge/Remember

Review Questions

1. Define – Function, Docstring, Return, Nested function.
2. List two immutable types in Python.
3. List the different kinds of function arguments.
4. What are default arguments?
5. Define anonymous function.
6. Name any three built-in functions.
7. Name the three types of namespaces.
8. What is displayed when `help("modules")` is executed?
9. Match the following:

	Column A		Column B
1	Lambda	a	Docstring
2	def	b	Function
3	__init__	c	Anonymous Function
4	__doc__	d	Packages

Fill in the Blanks

1. ____________ and ___________ are the two aspects of user-defined function.
2. ____ function is function definition.

3. Function body consists of __________ and __________.

4. Function definition begins with the word ______.

5. Function name __________ identifies a function.

6. Arguments are __________ values passed to parameters in function definition.

7. `Return` statement __________ result to calling function.

8. The type __________ and ____ are mutable.

9. __________ objects, when passed as arguments, return more than one output from function.

10. __________ variable is defined outside a function.

11. __________ statement is used to assign value to a global variable inside a function.

12. A function defined within another function is a __________ function.

13. In required arguments, the __________ order of arguments must be correct.

14. __________ arguments are matched with function parameters by matching argument and parameter name.

15. `def fact(n=5):` is a function definition with __________ arguments.

16. In __________ arguments, an asterisk is placed before the variable parameter.

17. Docstring comments are executed during __________.

18. Docstring can be accessed using ______ attribute.

19. A recursive solution has two parts: ________ case and ________ case.

20. Anonymous functions are called using ________ keyword.

21. __________ is the extension name of a file saved as Python module.

22. ___ notation is used to access items of a modules.

23. _____ function is used to find modules available in Python.

24. __________ are used to avoid conflict of names.

25. __________ returns names accessible globally from the function.

State True/False

1. Using of functions facilitate usability of code.
2. Defining functions improve program maintainability.
3. Calling function is the function definition.
4. Arguments are defined in the function definition.
5. A function can have only one `return` statement.
6. A function that does not return any output can be defined.
7. `Int` and `float` types are mutable.
8. Local variable is defined inside a function.
9. The outer function cannot access variables defined within the inner function.

10. Base case is the condition for start of recursion.

11. Lambda function allows multiple expressions.

12. `Print()` is a built-in function.

13. Import statement makes module content available in common namespace.

14. Namespace is implemented as dictionary in Python.

15. Package consists of one file only.

16. Docstring is a comment statement in a function.

Multiple Choice Questions (MCQ)

1. At any given time, the number of `return` statements that can execute in a function is ____.
   (i) 1 (ii) 2
   (iii) 3 (iv) 4

2. Identify the type that is mutable:
   (i) int (ii) Float
   (iii) List (iv) str

3. The attribute using which docstring can be accessed is ____.
   (i) `__doc__` (ii) `__main__`
   (iii) `__name__` (iv) `__init__`

4. In `def power(x, n=3)`, n is a ____.
   (i) Keyword argument
   (ii) Default argument
   (iii) Require Argument
   (iv) Variable-length argument

A.2 Bloom Level: Comprehend/Understand

Review Questions

1. Explain divide-and-conquer strategy for modularization.

2. "Defining functions promote modularity of code". Justify.

3. From software engineering perspective, state the importance of defining functions.

4. State five advantages of using functions.

5. Describe the syntax of function header.

6. Describe the syntax of function body

7. In `def fact(a, *b):` what is the significance of '*'?

8. What is the significance of `main()` function?

9. Why are documentation strings useful?

10. What is the purpose `return` statement?

11. What is the use of global statement?

12. How can more than one value be returned from a function?

13. What is the need of modules?

14. Why are functions needed?

15. How do functions help in handling complexity of the program? Give an example.

16. What is the use of `help()` function?

17. Describe the use of `reload()` function for modules.

18. What is the purpose of Namespaces?

19. What is the significance of __main__ in a Python file?

20. What is the need to define a package?

A.3 Bloom Level: Application/Apply

1. Find errors, and correct the code:

(a)
```
def f1(*a, b):
    print(a, b)
f1(1,2,3,4)
```

(b)
```
def f1(*a, *b):
    print(a, b)
f1(1,2,3,4)
```

(c)
```
def f1(n):
    return n + 25
f1(10)
print(n)
```

2. Fill in the blanks:

(a) This is a code to find square of 5.

```
def pw(b, p):
return b **____      (1)
def sq(x):
return pw(x, ____)    (2)
print(____(5))        (3)
```

(b) This is a code that returns integer remainder of a and b.

```
def rem(a, b):
return a____ b    (1)
print(rem(3,7))
```

3. Match the following:

Function definition	Function call
(i) `def f1(*a):`	(a) `f1()`
(ii) `def f1(a,b):`	(b) `f1 (b = "Good", a = "Morning")`
(iii) `def f1(a, b=60):`	(c) `f1(1,2,3,4)`
(iv) `def f1(a="abc", b="xyz"):`	(d) `f1(4)`

Multiple Choice Questions (MCQ)

1. If `def power(a, *b)` is called by power (2,3,4,5), the values of a and b are:
   (i) a = 2, 3; b = 4, 5
   (ii) a = 2, 3, 4; b = 5
   (iii) a = 2; b = 3, 4, 5
   (iv) a = 2; b = 2, 3, 4, 5

2. If `def power(a, b=10)` is called by `power(2,3)`, the values of a and b are:
   (i) a = 2; b = 3
   (ii) a = 2; b = 10
   (iii) a = 3; b = 10
   (iv) Error in call

3. Identify the correct syntax:
   (i) `def f1(a = 1, b = 2, c):`
   (ii) `def f1(a = 1, b, c = 2):`
   (iii) `def f1(a, b = 1, c):`
   (iv) `def f1(a, b = 1, c = 1):`

4. Identify the correct syntax to call a function:
   (i) `function_name()`
   (ii) `call function_name()`
   (iii) `func function_name()`
   (iv) `function function_name()`

5. Identify the correct syntax to declare a function:
   (i) `def function function_name():`
   (ii) `function function_name():`
   (iii) `def function_name():`
   (iv) `dec function_name():`

6. Find the output:

```
def f1(*a, b):
      print(a, b)
f1(1,2,3,b=4)
```

A.4 Bloom Level: Analyze

1. How are library functions different from user-defined function?

2. List the difference in scope of local and global variables.

3. List differences between parameters and arguments.

4. State the differences between import statement and `from...import` statement.

5. What is the difference between `return` and `return(expression)`.

6. How is local namespace different from global namespace?

7. State and discuss the `recurrence` relation for `factorial(n)`.

8. Show the working of recursion for `factorial(3)`.

9. Identify the line number sequence that will be executed for the following code. Also find the output. (**Hint**: You can use Pythontutor.com/visualize)

```
def f1(a1, a2):
    def f12(b1, b2):
        return b1+b2
    return f12(a1, a2)
ans = f1(10,20)
print(ans)
```

10. Differentiate and analyze the output with justification.

a)

```
t = 10
def f1():
    t = 50
    print(t)

print(t)
f1()
print(t)
```

```
t = 10
def f1():
    global t
    t = 50
    print(t)

print(t)
f1()
print(t)
```

b)

```
a=1; b=2
def f1():
    global b
    a=27; b=72
f1()
print(a)
print(b)
```

```
a=1; b=2
def f1():
    a=27; b=72
f1()
print(a)
print(b)
```

A.5 Bloom Level: Evaluate

1. Evaluate the code for the different function calls.

(i)

```
def f1(a, b=10, c=20):
    print('a:', a, '\tb:', b, '\tc:', c)
```

   (a) `f1(8, 12)`
   (b) `f1(50, c=60)`

(c) f1(c=55, a=75)

(ii)
```
def greet(msg, nt = 1):
    print(msg * nt)
```

(a) greet('Good')
(b) greet('Morning', 5)
(c) greet(4, 'Morning')
(d) greet(4, 5)
(e) greet('Good Morning', 2)

(iii)
```
def mixi(i = 1, j = 2):
    print(i, j)
    i = i + j
    j = j + 1
    print(i, j)
mixi(j = 1, i = 2)
```

(iv)
```
def display(a, n):
    while n > 0:
        print(a,end="")
        n=n-1
display('A',int(input("Enter Iteration number")))
```

What is the output if the user enters 4?

2. For the following lambda functions (i) Identify the task performed, (ii) Find output, (iii) Evaluate the output for different inputs.

(a)
```
x = 10
y = lambda z: z * x
print(y(5))
print(y(2*3/2))
```

(b)
```
A = [lambda x:x**2,lambda x:x**3,lambda x:x**4]
for f1 in A:
   print(f1(5))
```

(c)
```
M = (lambda x, y: x if x < y else y)
M(100, 101)
print(M(x=int(input("Enter first number:")), y=int(input("Enter second number:"))))
```

A.6 Bloom Level: Create/Synthesize

Programming Assignment

1. Create menu-driven programs. Write a program having the common function (i) to (iv).

   i. Function user_input() – accepts input from user. Returns the input value.

   ii. Function `menu()` – displays menu to user. Accepts user choice. Return choice.
   iii. Function `choose_func(choice)` – invokes relevant function depending on value of choice.
   iv. Function `main()` – invoke `menu()` and `choice_func()`. Ask users if they want to continue. Continue executing unless user says No.

2. Write the following functions to choose from in Q1:
   i. Find the sum of first n natural numbers
   ii. Find the sum of the individual digits of a number.
   iii. Find the factorial of a number.
   iv. Find the vales of first n Fibonacci series
   v. Find the reverse of a given number.
   vi. Find the sum of first n odd numbers.

3. Write the following functions to choose from in Q1:
   i. Check whether a given number is prime or not.
   ii. Check whether a number is perfect or not.
   iii. Check whether a number is an Armstrong number.
   iv. Check whether a number is palindrome or not.
   v. Check whether a given year is a leap year or not.
   vi. Check whether a number is even or odd.

4. WAP having functions for a rectangle to: (i) Calculate area, (ii) Calculate perimeter, (iii) Write a function `main()` that invokes the relevant function according to the user's choice.

5. WAP having functions to convert into rupees from (i) dollar, (ii) pound, (iii) euro, (iv) Australian dollar.

6. WAP having functions to convert temperature from Celsius to Fahrenheit and vice-versa.

7. Create a package for the following:
   i. Find the first n perfect numbers.
   ii. Find the first n Armstrong numbers.
   iii. Find the first n prime numbers.

8. Write a module for conversion of numbers. Create function for each: (i) Decimal to Binary, (ii) Binary to Decimal, (iii) Octal to Decimal, (iv) Decimal to Octal, (v) Hexadecimal to Decimal, (vi) Decimal to Hexadecimal. Write a function `display_menu()` that displays the menu and accepts user choice. Send the user choice to another function `convert_menu()` that invokes the relevant function to convert.

ANSWERS

A.1 Bloom Level: Knowledge/Remember

Review Questions

9. (1) c (2) b (3) d (4) a

Fill in the Blanks

1. Function definition, Function call
2. Called
3. Header, Body
4. Def
5. uniquely
6. actual
7. returns
8. List, Set, Dict
9. Mutable
10. Global
11. Global
12. Nested
13. positional
14. keyword
15. default
16. variable-length
17. runtime
18. __doc__
19. Base, Recursive
20. Lambda
21. .py
22. Dot
23. Help()
24. Namespaces
25. `Globals()`

True/False

1. True 2. True 3. False 4. False 5. False 6. True 7. False 8. True
9. True 10. False 11. False 12. True 13. False 14. True 15. False 16. True

Multiple Choice Questions (MCQ)

1. (i) 2. (iii) 3. (i) 4. (ii)

A.3 Bloom Level: Apply

2. (a) p,2, sq (b) % 3. Match the following - (i)-(c) , (ii)-(b), (iii)- (d), (iv)-(a)

Multiple Choice Questions (MCQ)

1. (iii) 2. (i) 3. (iv) 4. (i) 5. (iii) 6. `(1, 2, 3) 4`
7. 8.

A.4 Bloom Level: Analyze

9.
```
#Line Number execution- 1,5,1,2,4,2,3,4,5,6
```

10. (a)
```
10
50
10
```
```
10
50
50
```
(b)
```
1
72
```
```
1
2
```

A.5 Bloom Level: Evaluate

1. (i) (a) `a: 8    b: 12    c: 20` (b) `a: 50    b: 10    c: 60`
   (c) `a: 75    b: 10    c: 55`
   (ii) (a) `Good` (b) `MorningMorningMorningMorningMorning`
   (c) `MorningMorningMorningMorning` (d) `20`
   (e) `Good MorningGood Morning`

(iii)
```
2 1
3 2
```

(iv)
```
Enter Iteration number4
AAAA
```

2. (a)
```
50
30.0
```

(b)
```
25
125
625
```

(c)
```
Enter first number:23
Enter second number:21
21
```

UNIT IV

Sequence, Set and Mapping Type

CHAPTER 8 String

CONTENTS

8.1 Introduction

In the earlier chapters, we have discussed the simple data types like `int` and `float` that cannot be further broken down. Python also has compound data type. The compound data type can be further broken down into smaller pieces. One kind of compound data type is a **sequence data type**. Sequence is a generic term for an ordered collection of objects. Multiple values can be organized and stored efficiently using sequence data type. There are several types of sequences. String, list and tuple are important sequence data type. String is a popular data type and was introduced in the earlier chapters.

String is defined using data type *str*. String is made up of smaller strings that are further made up of characters. We have seen defining of string literal in single, double and triple quotes. We also noted that the characters in a string can be digits, alphabets, symbols and whitespace characters including null. String is an immutable sequence. String can be manipulated and different operations can be performed on string. In this chapter, we discuss the string data type in detail.

Learning Outcomes of this chapter

After completion of the chapter, the learner will be able to:

- Formulate problems having string manipulation
- Use strings in programs
- Use string operators for performing string operations
- Identify different types of string formatting
- Develop programs based on the concepts discussed.

8.2 String: An Overview

- A string is a sequence of characters.
- The characters can be digits, alphabets, symbols and whitespace characters such as newline ('\n') and, tab ('\t') including blank space.
- A string can be empty. An empty string has zero characters.
- In Python, the *str* data type represents string.
- A *str* literal is a sequence of characters enclosed in quotes.
- The quotes can be single quotes ('), double quotes (") or triple quotes ("""). The same type of quote must start and end a string (Figure 8.1).
- The triple quotes are used to span the string across multiple lines.

```
a = "Hello"
b = 'Students'
```

```
e = """The quotes in string can be of the following types
    1. Single quotes
    2. Double quotes
    3. Triple quotes   """
```

Figure 8.1 String literal in Python

8.3 Internal Representation of String

- The characters seen on the screen are stored and manipulated internally in the computer as numbers – a combination of 0s and 1s.
- **Encoding** is the conversion of a character to a number.
- **Decoding** is the conversion of a number to a character.
- ASCII and Unicode are popular encodings that are used.
- **Unicode**
  - o Brings uniformity in coding and includes every character in all languages.
  - o Every character has a unique number irrespective of platform, program and language.
- **Code points** are numerical values that make up code space.
  - o ASCII-7 has 128 code points from $0_{(16)}$ to $7F_{(16)}$
  - o ASCII-8 has 256 code points from $0_{(16)}$ to $FF_{(16)}$
  - o Unicode has 1,114,112 code points from $0_{(16)}$ to $10FFFF_{(16)}$, divided into 17 planes each with 65536 code points. Thus, total is 17 * 65536 = 1,114,112
- Unicode string is a sequence of code points. Encoding involves rules for translating Unicode string to a set of bytes (values 0 to 255) in memory.
- In Python, string is a sequence of Unicode characters.
- String or text has properties like, split, slice, join and add.

8.4 Accessing Characters in String

We know that string is a sequence of characters. We shall now understand enumeration of a string.

- Let us take a string 'Love Yourself'.

L← R

-13	-12	-11	-10	-9	-8	-7	-6	-5	-4	-3	-2	-1
L	O	V	E		Y	O	U	R	S	E	L	F
0	1	2	3	4	5	6	7	8	9	10	11	12

L → R

The characters in the string are enumerated as follows:

- o Left to Right, the characters of a string are enumerated starting from 0.
- o Right to Left, the characters are enumerated starting from –1.
- o Enumeration corresponds to the index. From left to right, the index is 0, 1, 2 … and from right to left, index is –1, –2, –3, …
- o Index starts from 0, so the maximum index of string is 1 less than its length.

8.4.1 Using Indexing

- To access characters in a string, indexing is used.
- Indexing allows to retrieve a part of the string.
- Any character of a string can be accessed by writing the string name followed by index in square brackets.
- Indexing can be done in two ways – Positive indexing and Negative indexing.

- **Positive Indexing:** It starts from the left side of the string starting from 0. For example, if a = "LOVE YOURSELF", a[2] gives the letter "V".

L	O	V	E		Y	O	U	R	S	E	L	F
0	1	2	3	4	5	6	7	8	9	10	11	12

L → R

- **Negative Indexing:** It starts from the right side of the string starting from –1. For example, if a = "LOVE YOURSELF", a[–2] gives the letter "L".

L ← R

–13	–12	–11	–10	–9	–8	–7	–6	–5	–4	–3	–2	–1
L	O	V	E		Y	O	U	R	S	E	L	F

8.4.2 Using Slicing

- **Slicing Operator:** The slicing operator is a square bracket []. It allows creation of a substring from a string. The syntax of slicing operator is
`string[start:end]`
start - index from where the slice starts
end - index where slice ends (excluding end index)
The substring from index *start* to *end–1* is returned. Index *start* and *end* are optional. If omitted, the default value of *start* is 0 and *end* is the last index of the string.
- **Range Indexing:** It allows specifying a range of indexes, to get substrings. All characters starting from index *start* to *end–1* are obtained. For example, if a = "LOVE YOURSELF", a[5:8] gives "YOU".

L	O	V	E		Y	O	U	R	S	E	L	F
0	1	2	3	4	5	6	7	8	9	10	11	12

Example 8.1: (a) Using range indexing (b) Output

```
s = "LOVE YOURSELF"
print("7th Character in LOVE YOURSELF is = ", s[7])
print("7th Character from Last in LOVE YOURSELF is = ", s[-7])
print("Substring from 1 to 7 in LOVE YOURSELF is = ", s[1:7])
```

(a)

```
7th Character in LOVE YOURSELF is =  U
7th Character from Last in LOVE YOURSELF is =  O
Substring from 1 to 7 in LOVE YOURSELF is =  OVE YO
>>> |
```

(b)

- When specifying range indexing, the *start* or *end* index can be omitted.
  - If *start* index is omitted, the substring from beginning of the string till end–1 is returned.
  - If *end* index is omitted, the substring from the start index till the end of the string is returned.

- Index can also be negative. The indexing starts from right to left in negative indexing.
  - o *start* index is lower than *end* index. For example, (–5, –2) start is -5 lower than end -2)

Example 8.2: (a) Using negative index (b) Output

```
sample = "I can change the World"
print(sample[0])
print(sample[0:1])
print(sample[0:7])
print(sample[:7])
print(sample[7:])
print(sample[-5:])
print(sample[:-5])
print(sample[:])
print(sample[5:2])
print(sample[2:-1])
print(sample[-12:-1])
```

(a)

```
I
I
I can c
I can c
hange the World
World
I can change the
I can change the World

can change the Worl
ge the Worl
>>> |
```

(b)

- The index must be an integer, otherwise it will result in *TypeError*.

```
s = "LOVE YOURSELF"
print("7th Character in LOVE YOURSELF is = ", s[7.5])
```

Output

```
Traceback (most recent call last):
  File "C:/Users/dsc/Desktop/access-typeerror.py", line 14, in <module>
    print("7th Character in LOVE YOURSELF is = ", s[7.5])
TypeError: string indices must be integers
>>> |
```

- The index must be in range, otherwise it will result in *IndexError*.
- When we use range to access strings, the following may be noted:
  - o If index range *start* is greater than *end*, no output is displayed.
  - o If index range *start* or *end* is more than the size of the string, there is no error.
  - o If index *start or end* is more than the size of the string, and positive/negative index is used but range is not used, then *IndexError* arises.

Example 8.3: (a) String indexing (b) Output

```
s = "LOVE YOURSELF"
print("Substring [0:10] in LOVE YOURSELF is = ", s[0:10])
print("Substring [-5:-1] Lower Index Less Than Higher is = ", s[-5:-1])
print("Substring [-5:-20] Lower Index Greater Than Higher is = ", s[-5:-20])
print("Substring [-20:-1] Out of Range (Range index)is = ", s[-20:-1])
print("Substring [0:25] Out of Range (Range index) is = ", s[0:25])
print("Substring [20] Out fo Range(Positive/Negative index) is = ", s[20])
```

(a)

```
Substring [0:10] in LOVE YOURSELF is =  LOVE YOURS
Substring [-5:-1] Lower Index Less Than Higher is =  RSEL
Substring [-5:-20] Lower Index Greater Than Higher is =
Substring [-20:-1] Out of Range (Range index)is =  LOVE YOURSEL
Substring [0:25] Out of Range (Range index) is =  LOVE YOURSELF
Traceback (most recent call last):
  File "C:/Users/dsc/Desktop/access-typeerror.py", line 26, in <module>
    print("Substring [20] Out fo Range(Positive/Negative index) is = ", s[20])
IndexError: string index out of range
>>> |
```

(b)

8.4.3 Using Stride with Slicing

- Stride is the third parameter that can be specified, in addition to `start` and `end` index.
- The syntax is
  `String[start: end: stride]`
- Stride specifies the number of characters to move forward after each character retrieval. So, the characters retrieved are: start, start+stride, start+stride+stride, --- end−1. For example,
  S = "LOVE YOURSELF"
  S[1:10:2] will return OEYUS

L	O	V	E		Y	O	U	R	S	E	L	F
0	1	2	3	4	5	6	7	8	9	10	11	12

- The default value of stride is 1. When we do not mention stride, all characters between `start` and `end` are retrieved.
  s[2:4] and s[2:4:1] retrieve same substring from a string s.
- A negative stride will retrieve string from start to end backwards. So, the `start` index must be greater than `end` index, otherwise nothing is returned.

Example 8.4: (a) Using negative stride (b) Output

```
sample = "LOVE YOURSELF"
print("The string is\t", sample)
print("sample[0:4:2]=\t", sample[0:4:2])
print("sample[10:5:-1]=", sample[10:5:-1])
print("sample[5:10:-1]=\t", sample[5:10:-1])
print("sample[3::3]=\t", sample[3::3])
print("sample[3::-3]=\t", sample[3::-3])
print("sample[:10:2]=\t", sample[:10:2])
print("sample[0::1]=\t", sample[0::1])
print("sample[::]=\t", sample[::])
```

(a)

```
The string is        LOVE YOURSELF
sample[0:4:2]=       LV
sample[10:5:-1]=     ESRUO
sample[5:10:-1]=
sample[3::3]=        EOSF
sample[3::-3]=       EL
sample[:10:2]=       LV OR
sample[0::1]=        LOVE YOURSELF
sample[::]=          LOVE YOURSELF
>>> |
```

(b)

8.5 String Mutation: Immutable Strings

- Strings are immutable. This means that when a string has been assigned to a variable, its value cannot be changed. We explain this as follows:
  - o Let us assign s = "Anita". Then an object "Anita" is created and variable s is assigned the object.
  - o When we assign s = "Python", a new object (with a different object-id than the earlier one) is created and the variable s is assigned the object.
  - o We see that when we change a string, the changes do not happen in the same object-id; a new object is created.
  - o So, **strings cannot be updated in place. They are immutable.**

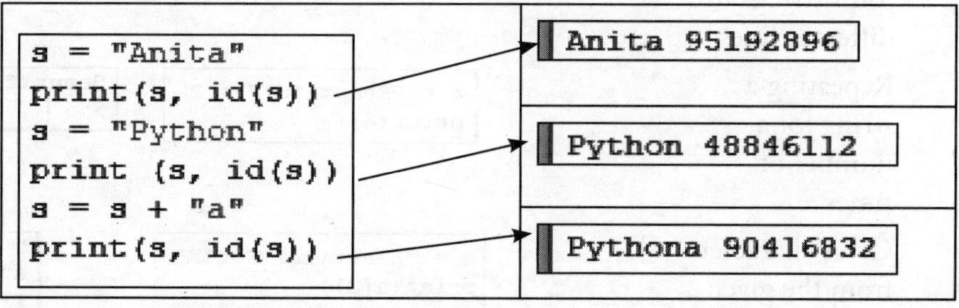

- In the code below, we see that when we print s[2], there is no error and it prints "i". But when we try to change the value of s[2], an error is thrown. This because we cannot change a string. Characters of a string cannot be changed or deleted.

```
s = "Anita"
print(s[2])
s[2] = "a"
print(s[2])
```

```
i
Traceback (most recent call last):
  File "C:\Users\dsc\Desktop\Python\Chapter 6 Strings\string.py", line 3, in <mo
dule>
    s[2] = "a"
TypeError: 'str' object does not support item assignment
>>> |
```

- A string can be deleted. For this, the `del` command is used.
  `del s`
  deletes the string s.

8.6 String Operators

Several operations can be performed on strings. Table 8.1 shows the operations that can be performed on strings.

Table 8.1 String operations

Task	Description	Operator	Example	Output

Concatenation	Joins two or more strings into one string	+	`a = "Love " + "Yourself"`
			`print(a)`
			`a = "Love " "Yourself"`
			`print(a)`
			`a = ("Love "`
			`     "Yourself")`
			`print (a)`
				`Love Yourself`
				`Love Yourself`
				`Love Yourself`
				`>>> |`

		Writes strings together		
	Joins strings in different lines	()		
Repetition	Repeating a string for a number of times	*	`a = "Beautiful" * 2` `print(a)`	`BeautifulBeautiful` `>>> |`

Slice	Gives character from the given index	[]	`a = "Beautiful World"`
			`print(a[3])`
			`print(a[2:6])`
			`print("u" in a)`
			`print("F" not in a)`
			`print("U" in a)`
				`u`
				`auti`
				`True`
				`True`
				`False`
				`>>> |`

Range Slice	Gives characters from the given range	[:]		

(*Continued*)

Table 8.1 (Continued)

Task	Description	Operator	Example	Output
Membership	Returns true if character exists in the given string	in		
	Returns true if character is not in the given string	not in		
Comparison	Compares strings using ASCII values in lexicographic order	> < <= >= != ==		
Ord()	Returns ACSII code of character		`>>> print("j", ord("j"))`	`j 106`
Chr()	Returns character for ASCII code		`>>> print("90", chr(90))`	`90 Z`

Example 8.5: (a) Using string operations (b) Output

```
a = "Beautiful"
al = "BEAUTIFUL"
b = "World"
bl = "world"

print(a, "==",b, ":",  a == b)
print(a, "!=",b, ":",  a != b)
print(a, "==",b, ":",  a == b)
print("ASCII of A = ", ord("A"))
print("ASCII of Z = ", ord("Z"))
print("ASCII of a = ", ord("a"))
print("ASCII of z = ", ord("z"))
print("Lower case letters are \
 lexicographically greater than upper case")
print(a, ">",al, ":",  a > al)
print(al, "<",bl, ":",  al > bl)
```

(a)

```
Beautiful == World : False
Beautiful != World : True
Beautiful == World : False
ASCII of A =  65
ASCII of Z =  90
ASCII of a =  97
ASCII of z =  122
Lower case letters are lexicographically greater than upper case
Beautiful > BEAUTIFUL : True
BEAUTIFUL < world : False
>>> |
```

(b)

8.7 String Traversal and Accumulation

Traversal of string means accessing each element in the string, one by one. Traversal can be done using a loop – `for` loop or `while` loop. Here we show an example to traverse a string using `while` loop and `for` loop.

Output

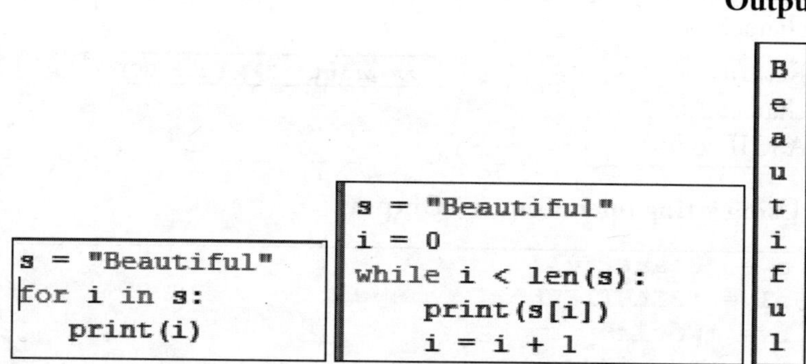

8.8 String Formatting

The string printed in the output can also be formatted. There are different ways of formatting the string, as follows:

- Using Escape characters
- Using percentage sign (%)
- Using Format method

8.8.1 Escape Sequence

The backslash "\" is a special character in Python that is called escape character. It is used for different purposes as follows:

- **Representing whitespace characters** There are certain whitespace characters, like tab, newline and carriage return, that are required to be printed. The escape character is followed by the character to be used. Table 8.2 shows the escape characters and their description.

Table 8.2 Escape characters in Python

Backslash notation	Description
\a	Bell or alert
\b	Backspace
\e	Escape
\f	Form feed
\n	Newline
\r	Carriage return
\s	Space
\t	Horizontal tab
\v	Vertical tab
\x	Character x
\0nn	Character with octal value (n is from 0 to 7)
\xnn	Character with hexadecimal value (n is from 0-9, A-F)

```
print("The character with octal value 45 is = ", "\045")
print("The character with hexadecimal value 50 is = ", "\x50")
```

Output

```
The character with octal value 45 is =  %
The character with hexadecimal value 50 is =  P
>>> 
```

- **Representing a special character as ordinary character** There are certain characters that cannot be printed directly, like single quotes and double quotes. This is because, they already form part of the string syntax to represent a string. So, the escape sequence is used to print such characters. Such characters are prefixed with backslash "\".

Output

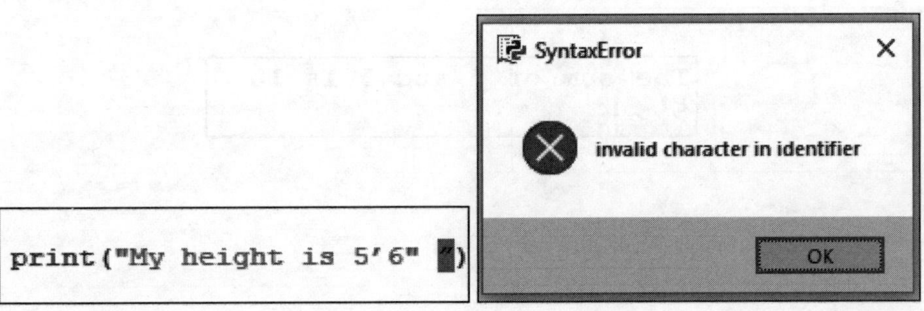

So, when we use escape sequence with double quotes, the output is displayed as follows:

```
print("My height is 5'6\" ")
```

Output

```
My height is 5'6"
>>> |
```

To print a backslash in the output, a double backslash is used.

```
print("The backslash \\ is opposite of slash /")
```

Output

```
The backslash \ is opposite of slash /
```

8.8.2 Formatting Operator

Python has a built-in operator % that is used for formatting. The use of % is a C-style formatting for strings in Python. The % with a character is used for formatting. It is defined as a placeholder for values to be inserted in the string. The values to which format is applied, is defined as a tuple at the end of the string. The use of formatting operator is an old-style of formatting, though it is still used widely.

Let us see an example.

```
print("This is a %s %s" %("Beautiful", "World"))
```

Output

```
This is a Beautiful World
```

```
print("The sum of %d and %d is %d" %(5, 5, 5+5))
```

Output

```
The sum of 5 and 5 is 10
>>> |
```

Table 8.3 shows the list of all symbols that can be used with % for string formatting.

Table 8.3 Symbols used with formatting operator

Format Symbol	Conversion
%c	character
%s	string
%i or %d	signed decimal integer
%u	unsigned decimal integer
%o	octal integer
%x	hexadecimal integer (lowercase letters)
%X	hexadecimal integer (UPPERcase letters)
%e	exponential notation (with lowercase 'e')
%E	exponential notation (with UPPERcase 'E')
%f	floating point real number
%g	shorter of %f and %e
%G	shorter of %f and %E

Also, there are some more symbols as listed in Table 8.4.

Table 8.4 More symbols with formatting operator

Symbol	Functionality
*	argument specifies width or precision
-	left justification
+	display sign
<sp>	leave a blank space before a positive number
#	add octal leading zero ('0') or hexadecimal leading '0x' or '0X', depending on whether 'x' or 'X' were used.
0	pad from left with zeroes (instead of spaces)
%	'%%' gives a single literal '%'
(var)	mapping variable (dictionary arguments)
m.n.	m is minimum total width and n is number of digits to display after decimal point

Some examples of formatting are as follows:

Example 8.6: (a) Using string formatting operators (b) Output

```
print("The sum of %d and %d is %d " % (10, 10, 10+10))
print("The floating point sum of %d and %d is %f" % (-10, -10, -10 + -10))
print("The floating point sum of %d and %d is %2.3f" % (-10, -10, -10 + -10))
print("The number %d in hexadecimal is %X" %(345, 345))
print("The exponential notation of %f is %E" %(12.56700, 12.56700))
print("The exponential notation of %f is %2.3E" %(12.56700, 12.56700))
print("The character %c is a beauty in %s" %("B", "Beautiful"))
```

(a)

```
The sum of 10 and 10 is 20
The floating point sum of -10 and -10 is -20.000000
The floating point sum of -10 and -10 is -20.000
The number 345 in hexadecimal is 159
The exponential notation of 12.567000 is 1.256700E+01
The exponential notation of 12.567000 is 1.257E+01
The character B is a beauty in Beautiful
>>> |
```

(b)

Example 8.7: (a) Print table of 2 and display using string formatting (b) Output

```
#Print table of 2
for i in range(10):
    print("%-4d" "x" "%4d" "    =" "%4d" %(2, i, 2*i))
```

(a)

```
2   x   0   =   0
2   x   1   =   2
2   x   2   =   4
2   x   3   =   6
2   x   4   =   8
2   x   5   =  10
2   x   6   =  12
2   x   7   =  14
2   x   8   =  16
2   x   9   =  18
>>> |
```

(b)

8.8.3 Method `Format()`

String formatting using `format()` method is a new style of formatting. `Format()` is a method of class string in Python. The syntax of the `format()` method is as follows:

```
template.format(p0, p1, p2, ..., k0=v0, k1=v1, ...)
```

- Template is a string that contains fields to be replaced, or embedded in text. The fields to be replaced are written as curly braces{}. The braces act as placeholders or replacement fields that get replaced.
- The syntax contains two kind of arguments – Positional arguments and Keyword arguments.
  - **Positional arguments** are p0, p1, p2, …. They can be accessed with index of argument inside curly braces {index}.
  - **Keyword arguments** are k0, k1, … with values v0, v1,... They are of type key = value. They can be accessed with key of argument inside curly braces {key}.
- Anything that is not in braces is printed as it is.

Let us understand formatting using an example.

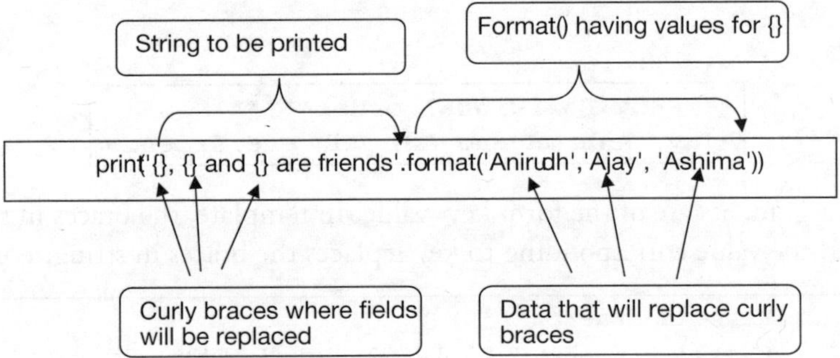

The points to be noted are:

- The string has two parts – template (before dot) and format parts (after dot).
- Template defines the string to be printed. Curly braces are put at positions where the fields are to be formatted. Format has the value of fields that will replace curly brackets at runtime.
- The values defined in format have an index. The first value is index 0, second is index 1, and so on.
- In format, if positional arguments are used in the order they are defined, '{0}{1}{2}', then in template, the index in braces can be omitted. Empty braces are a default option. The `format()` values replace the template braces, in order. The first value replaces the first brace, the second value replaces the second brace, and so on.

```
print("\n*****By default*****")
print('{}, {} and {} are friends'.format('Anirudh','Ajay', 'Ashima'))
```

The output is:

```
*****By default*****
Anirudh, Ajay and Ashima are friends
```

- In format, if positional arguments are to be accessed in a different order, say, '{2}{0}{1}' in the string to be printed, the braces can mention index, i.e., the position order in which values of format will replace the braces in the string. For example,

```
print("\n*****By Positional order*****")
print('{1}, {2} and {0} are friends'.format('Anirudh','Ajay', 'Ashima'))
```

The output is:

```
*****By Positional order*****
Ajay, Ashima and Anirudh are friends
```

- The keyword arguments are of the form key=value. In template, the braces in string mention the key. In format, the value corresponding to key replaces the braces in string. For example,

```
print("\n*****By Keyword order*****")
print('{s}, {n} and {j} are friends'.format(n='Anirudh',j='Ajay', s='Ashima'))
```

The output is:

```
*****By Keyword order*****
Ashima, Anirudh and Ajay are friends
>>>
```

- To print a brace character in the output, a double brace is used, {{ and }}.
- **Optional Format Specification:** The index in curly braces can be followed by a colon and format string. The format string defines the formatting for the field. Tables 8.5 and 8.6 specify some commonly used formatting specifications.
- The field width is always the size of data to be printed, so alignment has no meaning. To use alignment, minimum field width is required to be defined.

Table 8.5 Optional format specifications

Option	Meaning
'<'	Field will be left-aligned. Strings are, by default, left-aligned.
'>'	Field will be right-aligned. Numbers are, by default, right-aligned.
'^'	Field will be centred.
','	Comma for 'thousand' separator is used in numeric.
'0'	Field width will be preceded with 0. Sign-aware zero padding. Only for numeric type of data.
'='	Forces padding to be placed after sign but before digits, like, +00089. Only for numeric type of data.

Table 8.6 Number formatting types (optional)

Type	Meaning
d	Decimal integer
c	Corresponding Unicode character
b	Binary format
o	Octal format
x	Hexadecimal format (lower case)
X	Hexadecimal format (upper case)
e	Exponential notation. (lowercase e)
E	Exponential notation (uppercase E)
f	Displays fixed point number (Default: 6)
F	Same as 'f'. Except displays 'inf' as 'INF' and 'nan' as 'NAN'
g	General format. Rounds number to p significant digits. (Default precision: 6)
G	Same as 'g'. Except switches to 'E' if the number is large.
%	Percentage. Multiplies by 100 and puts % at the end.

Some examples of formatting are as follows:

Example 8.8: (a) Using string formatting types (b) Output

```
print("Padding with Zero. \t{:06d}".format(245))
print("Padding with Zero. \t{:06d}".format(-245))
print("Decimal Number. \t{:d}".format(746))
print("Float Number. \t\t{:f}".format(112.11234))
print("Binary Number.\t\t{0:b}\nOctal Number.\t\t{0:o}\
      \nHexadecimal Number.\t{0:X}".format(10))
print("Float with Padding. \t{:08.3f}".format(12.2346))
print("Show sign. \t\t{:+d} ".format(22))
print("This is ten lakh. \t{:,d}".format(1000000))
print("Exponent Form. \t\t{0:E}".format(1122.879))
print("Round off. \t\t{:0.2f}".format(5/7))
```

(a)

```
Padding with Zero.        000245
Padding with Zero.        -00245
Decimal Number.           746
Float Number.             112.112340
Binary Number.            1010
Octal Number.             12
Hexadecimal Number.       A
Float with Padding.       0012.235
Show sign.                +22
This is ten lakh.         1,000,000
Exponent Form.            1.122879E+03
Round off.                0.71
```

(b)

Example 8.9: (a) Using string alignment format (b) Output

```
print("{:=^30}".format("="))

print("Alignment Left. \n{:12}".format("|Apple|"))
print("Alignment Right. \n{:>12}".format("|Apple|"))
print("Alignment Center. \n{:^12}".format("|Apple|"))
print("Alignment Center with Padding \n{:*^12}".format("Apple"))

print("{:=^30}".format("="))
```

(a)

```
Alignment Left.
|Apple|
Alignment Right.|
     |Apple|
Alignment Center.
   |Apple|
Alignment Center with Padding
***Apple****
```

(b)

Example 8.10: (a) Using string alignment with spacing (b) Output

```
print("Align String. \n|{:^10}|{:^10}|".format('A','Ant'))
print("|{:^10}|{:^10}|".format('B','Bear'))
print("|{:^10}|{:^10}|".format('C','Cat'))
print("|{:^10}|{:^10}|".format('D','Dog'))
print("|{:^10}|{:^10}|".format('E','Elephant'))
print("|{:^10}|{:^10}|".format('F','Frog'))
```

(a)

```
Align String.
|    A     |   Ant    |
|    B     |   Bear   |
|    C     |   Cat    |
|    D     |   Dog    |
|    E     | Elephant |
|    F     |   Frog   |
>>>
```

(b)

8.9 Built-in String Methods

Python supports several built-in methods that can be used with strings. The syntax to use the methods is:

```
str.method()
```

String Methods and the String Module: The string methods in Python 3.x have replaced the earlier String module. Though Python 3.X supports the string module for backward compatibility, you should now use the String Methods and not the String Module.

Table 8.7 lists the built-in string methods.

Table 8.7 Built-in string methods

S. No	Method Name	Syntax and Description
1	**capitalize(...)**	S.capitalize() →str Makes the first character upper case and rest lower case.
2	**casefold(...)**	S.casefold()→ str Returns version of S suitable for caseless comparisons.
3	**center(...)**	S.center(width[, fillchar]) → str S centered in string of length width. Padding is done using fill character (default is space).
4	**count(...)**	S.count(sub[, start[, end]]) → int Returns number of non-overlapping occurrences of substring sub in string S[start:end].
5	**endswith(...)**	S.endswith(suffix[, start[, end]]) → bool Returns True if S ends with specified suffix, False otherwise. With optional start, tests S beginning at start. With optional end, stops comparing S at end. suffix can also be a tuple of strings to try.
6	**expandtabs(...)**	S.expandtabs(tabsize=8) → str Returns copy of S where all tab characters are expanded using spaces. If tabsize 8is not given, a tab size of 8 characters is assumed.
7	**find(...)**	S.find(sub[, start[, end]]) → int Returns lowest index in S where substring sub is found, such that sub is contained within S[start:end]. Returns –1 on failure.
8	**format(...)**	S.format(*args, **kwargs) → str Returns formatted version of S, using substitutions from args and kwargs. The substitutions are identified by {}.
9	**format_map(..)**	S.format_map(mapping) → str Returns formatted version of S, using substitutions from mapping. The substitutions are identified by {}.
10	**index(...)**	S.index(sub[, start[, end]]) → int It is like S.find() but raises ValueError when the substring is not found.
11	**isalnum(...)**	S.isalnum() → bool Returns True if all characters in S are alphanumeric and there is at least one character in S, False otherwise.
12	**isalpha(...)**	S.isalpha() → bool Returns True if all characters in S are alphabetic and there is at least one character in S, False otherwise.

(Continued)

Table 8.7 (Continued)

S. No	Method Name	Syntax and Description
13	**isdecimal(...)**	S.isdecimal() → bool Returns True if there are only decimal characters in S, False otherwise.
14	**isdigit(...)**	S.isdigit() → bool Returns True if all characters in S are digits and there is at least one character in S, False otherwise.
15	**isidentifier(...)**	S.isidentifier() → bool Returns True if S is a valid identifier according to the language definition. Uses keyword.iskeyword() to test for reserved identifiers such as "def" and "class".
16	**islower(...)**	S.islower()→ bool Returns True if all cased characters in S are lowercase and there is at least one cased character in S, False otherwise.
17	**isnumeric(...)**	S.isnumeric() → bool Returns True if there are only numeric characters in S, False otherwise.
18	**isprintable(...)**	S.isprintable() → bool Returns True if all characters in S are considered printable in repr() or S is empty, False otherwise.
19	**isspace(...)**	S.isspace() → bool Returns True if all characters in S are whitespace and there is at least one character in S, False otherwise.
20	**istitle(...)**	S.istitle() → bool Returns True if S is a title cased string and there is at least one character in S, i.e., uppercase and title-case characters may only follow uncased characters and lowercase characters only cased ones. Returns False otherwise.
21	**isupper(...)**	S.isupper()→ bool Returns True if all cased characters in S are uppercase and there is at least one cased character in S, False otherwise.
22	**join(...)**	S.join(iterable) → str Returns a string which is concatenation of strings in iterable. The separator between elements is S.
23	**ljust(...)**	S.ljust(width[, fillchar]) → str Returns S left-justified in a Unicode string of length width. Padding is done using the specified fill character (default is a space).

(*Continued*)

Table 8.7 (Continued)

S. No	Method Name	Syntax and Description
24	**lower(...)**	S.lower() → str Returns a copy of string S converted to lowercase.
25	**lstrip(...)**	S.lstrip([chars]) → str Returns a copy of string S with leading whitespace removed. If chars is given and not None, it removes characters in chars instead.
26	**partition(...)**	S.partition(sep) → (head, sep, tail) Searches for separator sep in S, and returns the part before it, the separator itself, and the part after it. If separator is not found, it returns S and two empty strings.
27	**replace(...)**	S.replace(old, new[, count]) → str Return a copy of S with all occurrences of substring, old replaced by new. If optional argument count is given, only first count occurrences are replaced.
28	**rfind(...)**	S.rfind(sub[, start[, end]]) → int Returns the highest index in S where substring sub is found, such that sub is contained within S[start:end]. Optional arguments start and end are interpreted as in slice notation. Returns -1 on failure.
29	**rindex(...)**	S.rindex(sub[, start[, end]]) → int It is like S.rfind() but raisees ValueError when substring is not found.
30	**rjust(...)**	S.rjust(width[, fillchar]) → str Returns S right-justified in a string of length width. Padding is done using fill character (default is space)
31	**rpartition(...)**	S.rpartition(sep) → (head, sep, tail) Searches for separator sep in S, starting at end of S, and returns the part before it, the separator itself, and the part after it. If separator is not found, it returns two empty strings and S.
32	**rsplit(...)**	S.rsplit(sep=None, maxsplit=-1) → list of strings Returns list of words in S, using sep as delimiter string, starting at the end of string and working to front. If maxsplit is given, at most maxsplit splits are done. If sep is not specified, any whitespace string is a separator.

(*Continued*)

Table 8.7 (Continued)

S. No	Method Name	Syntax and Description
33	rstrip(...)	S.rstrip([chars]) → str Returns a copy of string S with trailing whitespace removed. If chars is given and not None, it removes characters in chars instead.
34	split(...)	S.split(sep=None, maxsplit=-1) → list of strings Returns a list of words in S, using sep as delimiter string. If maxsplit is given, at most maxsplit splits are done. If sep is not specified or is None, any whitespace string is a separator and empty strings are removed from the result.
35	splitlines(...)	S.splitlines([keepends]) → list of strings Returns a list of lines in S, breaking at line boundaries. Line breaks are not included in resulting list unless keepends is given and true.
36	startswith(...)	S.startswith(prefix[, start[, end]]) → bool Returns True if S starts with the specified prefix, False otherwise. With optional start, it tests S beginning at that position. With optional end, it stops comparing S at that position prefix. It can also be a tuple of strings to try.
37	strip(...)	S.strip([chars]) → str Returns a copy of the string S with leading and trailing whitespace removed. If chars is given and not None, it removes characters in chars instead.
38	swapcase(...)	S.swapcase()→ str In S, it swaps uppercase characters to lowercase and vice-versa.
39	title(...)	S.title()→ str Returns a title-cased version of S, i.e., words start with title case characters, all remaining cased characters have lowercase.
40	upper(...)	S.upper()→ str Returns a copy of S converted to uppercase.
41	zfill(...)	S.zfill(width) → str Pads a numeric string S with zeros on left, to fill a field of specified width. S is never truncated.

Some examples are as follows:

Example 8.11: (a) Using string method (b) Output

```
print("{:<20}".format("Capitalize"),"sunIta".capitalize())
print("{:<20}".format("Casefold"),"SUNITA".casefold())
print("{:<20}".format("Center"),"Index".center(30, "="))
s = "abracadabra"
print("++++++++++++++++++++++++++++++++")
print("{:<20}{:<20}".format("**String s = ", s))
print("++++++++++++++++++++++++++++++++")
print("{:<20}".format("Count a in s"), s.count("a"))
print("{:<20}".format("Endswith a in s = "), s.endswith("a"))
print("{:<20}".format("Endswith b in s = "), s.endswith("b"))

p = "Love \tyour \twork"
print("{:<20}".format("Expandtabs 15 = "), p.expandtabs(15))
print("{:<20}".format("Find cad in s"), s.find("cad"))
print("{:<20}".format("Find ced in s"), s.find("ced"))
print("{:<20}".format("Index ced in"), s.index("ced"))
```

(a)

```
Capitalize           Sunita
Casefold             sunita
Center               ============Index=============
++++++++++++++++++++++++++++++++
**String s =         abracadabra
++++++++++++++++++++++++++++++++
Count a in s         5
Endswith a in s =    True
Endswith b in s =    False
Expandtabs 15 =      Love           your           work
Find cad in s        4
Find ced in s        -1
Traceback (most recent call last):
  File "C:\Users\dsc\Desktop\Python\Chapter 6 Strings\string built-in.py", line
16, in <module>
    print("{:<20}".format("Index ced in"), s.index("ced"))
ValueError: substring not found
>>> |
```

(b)

Example 8.12: (a) Using string method (b) Output

```
print("{:<20}".format("Isalnum Earth2018"), "Earth2018".isalnum())
print("{:<20}".format("Isalpha Earth2018"), "Earth2018".isalpha())
print("{:<20}".format("Isdecimal Earth2018"), "Earth2018".isdecimal())
print("{:<20}".format("Isdigit 2018"), "2018".isdigit())
print("{:<20}".format("Isidentifier bool"), "bool".isidentifier())
print("{:<20}".format("Islower Earth2018"), "Earth2018".islower())
print("{:<20}".format("Isspace Earth2018"), "Earth2018".isspace())
print("{:<20}".format("Istitle Earth2018"), "Earth2018".istitle())
print("{:<20}".format("Istitle earth2018"), "earth2018".istitle())
print("{:<20}".format("Isupper Earth2018"), "Earth2018".isupper())
print("{:<20}".format("Isupper EARTH2018"), "EARTH2018".isupper())
```

(a)

```
Isalnum Earth2018     True
Isalpha Earth2018     False
Isdecimal Earth2018   False
Isdigit 2018          True
Isidentifier bool     True
Islower Earth2018     False
Isspace Earth2018     False
Istitle Earth2018     True
Istitle earth2018     False
Isupper Earth2018     False
Isupper EARTH2018     True
>>>
```

(b)

8.10 SOLVED QUESTIONS WITH EXPLANATION

1) Find the output:

```
ct = 0
for c in 'Be kind to people. It does not take much effort':
    if(c == 'o'):
        ct += 1
print(ct,'o letters found')
```

Output

```
5 o letters found
```

Explanation: It counts the number of letter "o" in the string.

2) Find the output:

```
x='This is a good example'
rep='was'
print("The original string is:", x)
print("The replaced striing is:",x.replace('is',rep))
print("The replaced striing is:",x.replace('is',rep,1))
```

Output

```
The original string is: This is a good example
The replaced striing is: Thwas was a good example
The replaced striing is: Thwas is a good example
```

Explanation: The second print replaces all occurrences of the substring in the string. The third print replaces only one occurrence of the substring in the string.

3) Find the output:

```
x = "This is a good example"
print(x.split())
print(x.split(" ",2))
print(x.split(" ",3))
print(x.rsplit(" ",2))
```

Output

```
['This', 'is', 'a', 'good', 'example']
['This', 'is', 'a good example']
['This', 'is', 'a', 'good example']
['This is a', 'good', 'example']
```

Explanation: The first print splits x. The delimiter is space. The second split splits into 3(0,1,2). The third prints into 4. The fourth print splits starting from right side.

4) Find the output:

```
s = input("Enter String:")
print(s[0].upper() + s[1:-1] + s[-1].upper())
```

Output

```
Enter String:be grateful to everyone
Be grateful to everyonE
```

Explanation: It prints the first and last letter in uppercase. The rest of the letters are retained in lower case.

5) Find the output:

```
s = input("Enter String:")
print("The original string is : ", s)
print("String Length:", len(s))
ch = sum(not c.isspace() for c in str(s))
spc = sum(c.isspace() for c in str(s))
print("No. of non-space characters:", ch)
print("No. of Space characters:", spc)
```

Output

```
Enter String:Always remember good things in life
The original string is :  Always remember good things in life
String Length: 35
No. of non-space characters: 30
No. of Space characters: 5
```

Explanation: It prints the number of total characetrs, space characters and non-space characters.

8.11 Programming Examples

Program 8.1: WAP to remove the *n*th letter from the string.

```
def rem_c(s, n):
    r_s = s[:n] + s[n + 1:]
    return r_s

print(rem_c('Programming', 2))
print(rem_c('Confidential', 6))
print(rem_c('Breathe', 5))
```

Output

```
Prgramming
Confidntial
Breate
```

Program 8.2: WAP to find number of occurrences of uppercase and lowercase letters in a string.

```
n_up, n_low = 0,0
def ct_up_low(s):
    global n_up, n_low
    for c in s1:
        if c>='A' and c<='Z': n_up += 1
        if c>='a' and c<='z': n_low += 1
s1=input("Enter the string")
ct_up_low(s1)
print("Input string is: ", s1)
print("Total Number of letters(includes space):", len(s1))
print("Number of letters in Uppercase:", n_up)
print("Number of letters in Lowercase:", n_low)
```

Output

```
Enter the stringA Thing of Beauty is a Joy Forever
Input string is:  A Thing of Beauty is a Joy Forever
Total Number of letters(includes space): 34
Number of letters in Uppercase: 5
Number of letters in Lowercase: 22
>>>
```

Program 8.3: WAP to find the length of each word in a string.

```
# WAP to find length of each word
def f_len_wrd (s):
    s1 = s.split (' ')
    print("String:", s)
    for w1 in s1:
            print("{:<15}{:<0}{:<0}{:<0}".format(w1, "(", len (w1), ")"))
print("="*25)
f_len_wrd("Count your Blessings")
print("="*25)
f_len_wrd("Love Your food and Love Yourself")
print("="*25)
f_len_wrd("Yin and Yang- See the bright side")
print("="*25)
```

Output

```
=========================
String: Count your Blessings
Count          (5)
your           (4)
Blessings      (9)
=========================
String: Love Your food and Love Yourself
Love           (4)
Your           (4)
food           (4)
and            (3)
Love           (4)
Yourself       (8)
=========================
String: Yin and Yang- See the bright side
Yin            (3)
and            (3)
Yang-          (5)
See            (3)
the            (3)
bright         (6)
side           (4)
=========================
```

Program 8.4: WAP to swap the first and last character of a string.

```
def swap_first_last(s):
    if len(s) <= 1:
        return str
    mid = s[1:len(s) - 1]
    return s[len(s) - 1] + mid + s[0]

print(swap_first_last(input("Enter a string:")))
```

Output

```
Enter a string:please be grateful
llease be gratefup
```

```
Enter a string:main is a room
main is a room
```

Program 8.5: WAP to count the number of consonants and vowels in a string.

```
s=input("Enter String:");
vow=0 ; con=0
s.lower()
for i in s:
    if(i in "aeiou"): vow+=1
    else:   con+=1
print("Number of vowels:",vow);
print("Number of consonants:",con);
```

Output

```
Enter String:Love Yourself and Respect Yourself
Number of vowels: 11
Number of consonants: 23
```

```
Enter String:This is a room
Number of vowels: 5
Number of consonants: 9
```

Program 8.6: Given two strings. WAP that efficiently finds the longest common subsequence

A **longest common subsequence (LCS)** is the longest subsequence of elements in the same order which is common in all given input sequences.

Let us take two strings (1) “ABCDEFG” and (2) “ACEFGHI”

The longest subsequence present in both strings is - ACEFG

```
def lcs(S1, S2, x, y):
   L = [[None]*(y+1) for a in range(x+1)]
   for i in range(x+1):
      for j in range(y+1):
         if (i == 0 or j == 0):
            L[i][j] = 0
         elif (S1[i - 1] == S2[j - 1]):
            L[i][j] = L[i - 1][j - 1] + 1
         else:
            L[i][j] = max(L[i - 1][j], L[i][j - 1])
   l = L[x][y]
   LCS = [None] * (l)
   a, b = x, y
   while (a > 0 and b > 0):
      if (S1[a - 1] == S2[b - 1]):
         LCS[l - 1] = S1[a - 1]
         a, b, l  = a - 1, b-1, l-1
      elif (L[a - 1][b] > L[a][b - 1]):
         a = a - 1
      else:
         b = b - 1;
   print("LCS is ", LCS)
   return L[x][y]

S1 = "ABCDEFG"
S2 = "ACEFGHI"
print("S1 = ", S1, "\nS2 = ", S2)
lc = lcs(S1, S2, len(S1), len(S2))
print("Length of LCS is ", lc)
```

Output

```
S1 =  ABCDEFG
S2 =  ACEFGHI
LCS is  ['A', 'C', 'E', 'F', 'G']
Length of LCS is  5
>>>
```

Summary

- A string is a sequence of digits, alphabets, symbols and whitespace characters.
- Conversion of a character to a number is called encoding.
- Conversion of number to a character is called decoding.
- String is a sequence of Unicode characters.
- Indexing allows accessing characters of the string.
- Positive indexing is accessing of string from left to right with index 0, 1, …
- Negative indexing is accessing of string from right to left with index –1, –2, …
- To create a substring from a string, slicing is used.

- Slicing allows specifying a range of index for accessing characters from a string.
- Stride is used to skip characters in between the slice.
- Strings are immutable, i.e., once created, a string cannot be updated in place. Any update of string creates a new string.
- String concatenation, repetition, membership and comparison are some of the operations that can be performed on strings.
- The `for` loop and `while` loop are used to traverse the elements of a string.
- A string can be formatted using escape character, using format operator (%) and using format method.
- The format method uses positional arguments and keyword arguments for formatting.
- There are several built-in string methods that can be used with strings.

Keywords

String	Slicing	Range Slice [:]
Single quotes	Slicing operator []	Membership (in)
Double quotes	Range indexing	Membership (not in)
Triple quotes	TypeError	String comparison
Encoding	IndexError	String Traversal
Decoding	Stride	String formatting
ASCII	Negative stride	Escape characters (\)
Unicode	String update	Formatting operator (%)
Code point	Immutable strings	Positional arguments
String enumeration	Delete string ()	Keyword arguments
Index	String operator	Str.method()
Positive indexing	String concatenation (+)	
Negative indexing	Repetition	

Programming Language Keywords

`[]`	`Del`	`in`
`Chr()`	`not in`	`Str`
`Ord()`	`format`	

Assessment

A.1 Bloom Level: Knowledge/Remember

Review Questions

1. Define – String, Encoding, Decoding.
2. In Python, which encoding is used for string?
3. List three sequence data types.
4. List one mutable sequence data type.

5. List two immutable sequence data types.
6. Can a string be empty?
7. Match the following:

Column A	Column B
1 []	a Concatenation
2 [:]	b Indexing
3 [::]	c Slice Stride
4 +	d Membership
5 *	e Escape character
6 In	f Repetition
7 \	g Range Slice

8. List three ways of formatting a string.
9. List the escape sequence used for horizontal tab.
10. Name three built-in methods for strings and explain their function.

Fill in the Blanks

1. Empty string has ____ characters.
2. Triple quotes are used to span string across ____ lines.
3. ______ and ______ are popular encodings.
4. Each plane in Unicode has _____ code points.
5. The leftmost index of a string, starting from left is _____.
6. The rightmost index of the string, starting from right is ____.
7. The minimum positive index is _____.
8. The indexing in a string can be _____ indexing and ______ indexing.
9. ______ operator allows creating substring from a string.
10. Using _______ returns ASCII code of character.
11. Using ______ returns character for the ASCII code.
12. ______ is used for printing newline in output.
13. ______ is used for printing horizontal ____ in output.
14. Encoding is conversion from _________ to __________.
15. Decoding is conversion from _________ to __________.
16. The number of code points in ASCII-8 are ____________.
17. The number of code points in ASCII-7 are ____________.
18. The number of code points in a plane for Unicode are _____________.
19. The positive indexing starts from ________ to _________.
20. The negative indexing starts from ________ to _________.

State True/False

1. A string cannot be empty.
2. Encoding is conversion of number to character.

3. String can be indexed both from left to right and from right to left.
4. Negative index starts from left to right.
5. [:] is a slice operator.
6. The index to access character in a string must be an integer.
7. * operator is used for concatenation.
8. ASCII of 'A' is 97.
9. Backslash is the escape character.
10. % is formatting operator.
11. < is used to right align in format method.

A.2 Bloom Level: Comprehend/Understand

Review Questions

1. What is the purpose of using triple quotes in string?
2. Explain the difference in Unicode and ASCII encoding for internal representation of string.
3. Explain the meaning of "Strings are immutable".
4. What is the purpose of `del` command?
5. What is the purpose of slicing? Explain with an example.
6. If we want to update a string, is it possible? Explain the reason in support of your answer.
7. Two strings are compared to get the larger string. What is the basis on which the comparison happens?
8. What is the purpose of membership operator? Explain with an example.

A.3 Bloom Level: Application/Apply

Review Question

1. Find errors, and correct the code:

(a)
```
a= "Enjoy  your life"
del a[4]
```

(b)
```
a= "Enjoy  your life"
del a
print(a)
```

(c)
```
print("Written "communications" are easily understood")
```

Fill in the Blanks

1. The slice s[3:6] will retrieve characters in string from index _____ to ______.
2. The `start` and `end` index to access 'ea' from 'beauty' is ____ and _____.
3. The output of s[0:20] on s = "Change the World" is _______.
4. The output of s[−20: −1] on s = "Change the World" is _______.
5. The output of "Good"*3 is _____.
6. The output of "Good" + "Morning" is _____.
7. The output of "Good" "Morning" is _____.
8. The output of "d" *in* "Good" is ___________.

9. The output of "e" *not in* "Good" is ______.

10. Print("{:>10}.format("Python")) will ______ align the word Python.

11. The output of "GOOD" > "good" is ______.

Match the Following

a = "Everything is Energy"
Match the print statements with their output.

Print Statement	Output
(i) print(a[3])	a) ing is Energy
(ii) print(a[0:1])	b) Eeyhn
(iii) print(a[0:7])	c) erything is Energ
(iv) print(a[7:])	d) E
(v) print(a[-5:])	e) r
(vi) print(a[:10:2])	f) nergy
(vii) print(a[::])	g) Everyth
(viii) print(a[2:-1])	h) Everything is Energy

Multiple Choice Questions (MCQ)

1. Identify the invalid string literal.

   (i) "ABC" (ii) "12AB"
   (iii) ABC (iv) "12_AB"

2. The index of 'e' in string 'grateful' is ______.

   (i) 4 (ii) 5
   (iii) 6 (iv) -5

3. A[3] in string A = "Be Strong" is ______.

   (i) S (ii) t
   (iii) Blank (iv) e

4. A[−3] in string A = "Be Strong" is ______.

   (i) n (ii) r
   (iii) o (iv) Blank

Answer 5–8 for the string
s = "Change the World"

5. The output of s[2:5] is ______.

   (i) ange (ii) ang
   (iii) hang (iv) han

6. The output of s[−3] is ______.

   (i) o (ii) r
   (iii) l (iv) g

7. The output of s[0:10:3] is ______.

   (i) Cn e (ii) Cagte
   (iii) Cn t (iv) None

8. The output of s[2:] on string "Beauty" is ______.

(i) a (ii) auty
(iii) aut (iv) error

9. For s = "Change the World", which of the following will result in an error?

(i) s[0:20] (ii) s[-20:0]
(iii) s[-20] (iv) All

10. Identify the correct answer.
S[0:20] when applied on string s = "Beautiful Heart: will give:

(i) Beautiful Heart
(ii) Syntax error
(iii) Index error
(iv) Type error

A.4 Bloom Level: Analyze

1. Explain the difference between positive and negative indexing.
2. What is the difference between positional arguments and keyword argument in method `format()`?
3. When using strings, what is the difference between TypeError and IndexError?
4. Differentiate between s[3:6] and s[3:6:1] when applied on string s = "Beautiful World"
5. Differentiate between the method `capitalize()` and `upper()`. Explain with example.
6. Differentiate and analyze the output with justification.

(i)
```
a1 = "Always admire the blessings of life"
search="e"
```

(a)
```
print(a1.count(search))
```

(b)
```
print(a1.count("e"))
```

(c)
```
print(a1.count('e',0,len(a1)))
```

(ii)
```
a2 = "Awareness is the key to happiness"
search="key"
```

(a)
```
print(a2.find(search))
```

(b)
```
print(a2.find(search,1,len(a1)))
```

(c)
```
print(a2.find(search,18,len(a1)))
```

(iii)
```
a3 = "May God fill us with Peace and Joy forever"
search="Peace"
```

(a)
```
print (a3.index(search))
```

(b)
```
print (a3.index(search,4))
```

(c)
```
print (a3.index(search,25,len(a3)))
```

7. Let s = "Be kind to animals." Write Python statements to get:
s[0], s[0:1], s[0:7], s[:7], s[-7:], s[:-7], s[:], s[8:3], s[8:-1], s[-10:-3]

8. In the string s = "Be nice to yourself" give the output for the following:
S[0:4:2], s[10:4:-1], s[4:10:-1], s[2::3], s[2::-3], s[:10:3], s[2::1], s[::]

A.5 Bloom Level: Evaluate

1. An output is given and print statements for getting that output is also shown.
Output

```
==============================
String= Preserve your legacy
==============================
isupper:        False
```

Code

```
s="Preserve your legacy"
print("="*30)
print("String=", s)
print("="*30)
print("{:<15}".format("isupper:"),s.isupper())
```

Evaluate the following outputs and write the print statememts for the following.

```
capitalize:     Preserve your legacy
partition:      ('Preserve', ' ', 'your legacy')
rjust:          **********Preserve your legacy
ljust:          Preserve your legacy**********
swapcase:       pRESERVE YOUR LEGACY
title:          Preserve Your Legacy
```

2. For the following lambda functions, (i) identify the task performed, (ii) find the output, (iii) evaluate the output for inputs.

(a)
```
s=input("Enter a string:");
l = 0
for i in s:
    if l < 5: print(i)
    l+=1
```

What will be the output if a user enters the string: APPRECIATE?

(b)
```
s="Morning"
x= ("Good" + s) if s == "Morning" else s
print(x);
```

(c)
```
s = input("Enter a string:")
ct=0; nvct=0
for i in s:
    if i in "aeiou": ct+=1
    else: nvct+=1
print(ct, nvct, ct+nvct)
```

What will be the output if a user enters the string: Save the Environment?

(d)

```
s = input("Enter a string:")
print ("String:" + s)
n=input("Enter the character to be removed:")
s1 = s.replace('e', '')
print("String after removal of", n, "character: " + s1)
s1= s.replace('e', '', 1)
print ("String after removal of", n, "character: " + s1)
```

What will be the output if a user enters string: Greet Everyone?
The character to be removed is "e."

(e)

```
def isP(s):
    return s == s[::-1]
s = input("Enter a string:")
ans = isP(s)
if ans:
    print("Yes")
else: print("No")
```

(i) What will be the output if a user enters the string: Greet Everyone?
(ii) What will be the output if a user enters the string: abracadabra?
(iii) What will be the output if a user enters the string: Racecar?
(iv) What will be the output if a user enters the string: Do geese see God?
If answer is No in (iii), what change in the code should be done to get Yes.
If answer is No in (iv), what change in the code should be done to get Yes.

A.6 Bloom Level: Create/Synthesize

Programming Assignment

Apply formatting wherever possible.

1. Specify a Python statement to get the character "a" from the string "Change".
2. Write a statement to print the characters of the string "Grateful".
3. WAP to check if a substring is present in a given string.
4. WAP to print words having even length in a string.
5. WAP to print words having odd length in a string.
6. WAP to print words having length greater than or equal to *n* in a string. Accept *n* from user.
7. WAP with functions defined for problems (4), (5), (6). Define a menu to accept user choice.
8. WAP to accept two strings. Find how many characters are matching in the two strings.
9. WAP to remove all duplicate characters in a given string.
10. WAP to find the sum of the ASCII number of each character in a string.
11. WAP to count the number of words in the string and tell whether they are odd or even.
12. WAP to reverse a string.
13. WAP to count occurrences of each word in a string.

Answers

A.1 Bloom Level: Knowledge/Remember

Review Questions

6. (1) b (2) g (3) c (4) a (5) f (6) d (7) e

Fill in the Blanks

1. zero **2.** multiple **3.** ASCII, Unicode **4.** 65536
5. zero **6.** –1 **7.** zero
8. positive, negative **9.** Slice **10.** `Ord()` **11.** `Chr()`
12. \n **13.** \t **14.** character, number
15. number, character **16.** 256 **17.** 128 **18.** 65536
19. left, right **20.** right, left

True/False

1. False **2.** False **3.** True **4.** False **5.** True **6.** True **7.** False **8.** False
9. True **10.** True **11.** False **12.**

A.3 Bloom Level: Apply

Review Question

1. (a)
```
TypeError: 'str' object doesn't support item deletion
```
1. (b)
```
NameError: name 'a' is not defined
```
1. (c)
```
SyntaxError: invalid syntax
```
```
print ("Written \"communications\" are easily understood")
```
1. False **2.** True **3.** False **4.** **5.** **6.** **7.** **8.**

Fill in the Blanks

1. 3, 5 **2.** 1,3 **3.** Change the World
4. Change the Worl **5.** GoodGoodGood **6.** GoodMorning
7. Good Morning **8.** True **9.** True
10. right **11.** False **12.**

Match the Following

1. (i)– (e), (ii)– (d), (iii)– (g), (iv)– (a), (v)– (f), (vi)– (b), (vii)– (h), (viii)– (c)

Multiple Choice Questions (MCQ)

1. (iii) **2.** (i) **3.** (i) **4.** (iii) **5.** (ii) **6.** (ii) **7.** (i) **8.** (ii)
9. (iii) **10.** (ii)

A.4 Bloom Level: Analyze

5. (i) (a) 4 (b) 4 (c) 4

5. (ii) (a) 17 (b) 17 (c) –1

5. (iii) (a) 21 (b) 21 (c)

```
ValueError: substring not found
```

A.5 Bloom Level: Evaluate

1.

```
print("{:<15}".format("capitalize:"), s.capitalize())
print("{:<15}".format("partition:"), s.partition(" "))
print("{:<15}".format("rjust:"),s.rjust(30,"*"))
print("{:<15}".format("ljust:"),s.ljust(30, "*"))
print("{:<15}".format("swapcase:"), s.swapcase())
print("{:<15}".format("title:"), s.title())
```

2. (a) Prints the first five letters of the input string.

(b) GoodMorning

(c)

```
Enter a string:Save the environment
7 13 20
```

(d)

```
String:Greet Everyone
Enter the character to be removed:e
String after removal of e character: Grt Evryon
String after removal of e character: Gret Everyone
```

(e) (iii), (iv)

```
s=s.lower()
s=s.replace(" ", "")
```

CHAPTER

9 List and Tuple

Contents

9.1 INTRODUCTION

In the previous chapter, we discussed one of the sequences – String. Here, we discuss two other sequences – List and Tuple. List and tuple are ways to represent a collection of objects. They are different from strings. List and tuple are made up of elements or items that are values of any data type. The collection keeps values together and operations can be performed on them readily. Tuple is an immutable sequence, and List is mutable sequence. The operations on string discussed in the last chapter, namely, membership operator, length function, index, slice and stride, apply to list and tuple too.

In this chapter, we discuss the list and tuple in detail. The ways of accessing the elements, the operations that can be performed on them and the built-in methods and functions are discussed here.

Learning Outcomes of this chapter

After completion of the chapter, the learner will be able to:

- Perform basic operations on list and tuple
- Use list and tuple in programs
- Use operators for performing operations on list and tuple
- Formulate programs using built-in list and tuple type methods
- Develop programs based on the concepts discussed.

9.2 LISTS: AN OVERVIEW

- List is an ordered collection of objects. The objects are called items or elements of list.
- List is created in square brackets []. The elements or items of a list are defined within the square brackets, separated by comma.
  List1 = ["a", "e", "i", "o", "u"]
  List2 = [1, 5, 10, 20]
- The items in a list can be of different types. So, a list may have items that are a mix of type integers, strings and other data types. For example, in List1, "Apple" and "Banana" are strings but 25 and 30 are integers.
  List1 = ["Apple, "Banana", 25, 30]
- List may be empty. An empty list has zero items.
  List1 = []
- List can have another list as an item in it. These are called nested lists. For example, [3,9,27] is a list defined within a list List1.
  List1 = ["brinjal", "potato", [3, 9, 27], "tomato"]
- The items in a list are accessed using index.
- Lists are compared using ASCII values in lexicographic order.

```
L1 = [1, 5, 10, 20]
L2 = [1, 5]
print(L1>L2)
```

Output

```
True
```

```
L1 = ["a", "e", "i"]
L2 = ["a", "e", "u"]
print(L1>L2)
```

Output

```
False
```

- ***List is mutable*** unlike strings. Thus, the elements of a list can be changed in place.
- List data type is an essential part of Python scripting.

Example 9.1: (a) Example of mutable list (b) Output

```
L1 = [1,5, 10, 20]
L2 = [10, "Apple", 20, "Banana"]
L3 = ["Grateful", "Strong", "Passion", "Smile", "Mastery"]
L4 = [["Anushka",1100], ["Akanksha", 1101], ["Akriti", 1102]]

print("L1= ", L1)
print("L2= ", L2)
print("L3= ", L3)
print("L4= ", L4)
```

(a)

```
L1=  [1, 5, 10, 20]
L2=  [10, 'Apple', 20, 'Banana']
L3=  ['Grateful', 'Strong', 'Passion', 'Smile', 'Mastery']
L4=  [['Anushka', 1100], ['Akanksha', 1101], ['Akriti', 1102]]
```

(a)

9.3 Access Elements in List

Since list is a sequence type, indexing, slicing, and stride with slicing work in the same way for list as they work for the string. The elements of list are enumerated similar to strings. The indexing, slicing and stride with slicing have been discussed in detail in the context of strings. Here, we discuss them in the context of lists. We shall now understand enumeration of list.

- The elements of list are enumerated as follows:
    - o Left to Right, the elements are enumerated starting from 0.
    - o Right to Left, the elements are enumerated starting from –1.
    - o Enumeration corresponds to the index. From left to right, the index is 0, 1, 2 … and from right to left, index is –1, –2, –3, …

- The enumeration of a list L = ["Apple", "Banana", 100, 50] is depicted below.

L ← R

–4	–3	–2	–1
Apple	Banana	100	50
0	1	2	3

L → R

9.3.1 Indexing

- Indexing is used for accessing elements in the list. For this, the list name followed by index in square brackets is used.
- Indexing is of two kinds – Positive indexing and Negative indexing.
- **Positive Indexing:** It is from left to right, starting from index 0. For example, if L = ["Apple", "Banana", 100, 50], L[2] is 100.

Apple	Banana	100	50
0	1	2	3

- **Negative Indexing:** It is from right to left, starting from index –1. For example, if L = ["Apple", "Banana", 100, 50], L[–3] is Banana.

–4	–3	–2	–1
Apple	Banana	100	50

9.3.2 Slicing

- ***Slicing operator*** is used for creating a sublist from a list. The syntax of slicing operator is

  list[start:end]
  start - index from where the slice starts
  end - index till where the slice ends (excluding end index)
  The list from index *start* to *end–1* is returned.
- The *start* and *end* index are optional. If they are omitted, the default value of *start* is 0 and *end* is the last index of the list.
- **Range Indexing** allows specifying a range of indexes. It uses the slicing operator to get a sublist. For example, if L = ["Apple", "Banana", 100, 50], L[1: 3] gives ["Banana", 100].

Apple	Banana	100	50
0	1	2	3

Example 9.2: (a) Range indexing in list (b) Output

```
months = ["Jan", "Feb", "Mar", "Apr", "May", "June", "Jul", "Aug", "Sep"]
print("months=", months)
print("7th Element is = ", months[7])
print("7th Element from Last is = ", months[-7])
print("Sublist from 1 to 7 is = ", months[1:7])
```

(a)

```
months= ['Jan', 'Feb', 'Mar', 'Apr', 'May', 'June', 'Jul', 'Aug', 'Sep'
7th Element is =  Aug
7th Element from Last is =  Mar
Sublist from 1 to 7 is =  ['Feb', 'Mar', 'Apr', 'May', 'June', 'Jul']
```

(b)

- Omitting either start or end index is allowed.
  - o If *start* index is omitted, the list from the beginning until end–1 is returned.
  - o If *end* index is omitted, the list from start index until end of list is returned.
- Negative index can be used to start from right to left.
  - o *start* index is lower than *end* index. For example, start is –5 which is lower than end of –2)

Example 9.3: (a) Using Slicing operator (b) Output

```
months = ["Jan", "Feb", "Mar", "Apr", "May", "June", "Jul", "Aug", "Sep"]
print("months[0]=\t", months[0])
print("months[0:1]=\t",months[0:1])
print("months[0:6]=\t",months[0:6])
print("months[:7]=\t",months[:7])
print("months[7:]=\t",months[7:])
print("months[-5:]=\t",months[-5:])
print("months[:-5]=\t",months[:-5])
print("months[:]=\t",months[:])
print("months[5:2]=\t",months[5:2])
print("months[2:-1]=\t",months[2:-1])
print("months[-12:-1]=\t",months[-12:-1])
```

(a)

```
months[0]=        Jan
months[0:1]=      ['Jan']
months[0:6]=      ['Jan', 'Feb', 'Mar', 'Apr', 'May', 'June']
months[:7]=       ['Jan', 'Feb', 'Mar', 'Apr', 'May', 'June', 'Jul']
months[7:]=       ['Aug', 'Sep']
months[-5:]=      ['May', 'June', 'Jul', 'Aug', 'Sep']
months[:-5]=      ['Jan', 'Feb', 'Mar', 'Apr']
months[:]=        ['Jan', 'Feb', 'Mar', 'Apr', 'May', 'June', 'Jul', 'Aug', 'Sep']
months[5:2]=      []
months[2:-1]=     ['Mar', 'Apr', 'May', 'June', 'Jul', 'Aug']
months[-12:-1]=   ['Jan', 'Feb', 'Mar', 'Apr', 'May', 'June', 'Jul', 'Aug']
```

(b)

- The index must be an integer; otherwise, it will result in TypeError.

Example 9.4: (a) Using non-integer index (b) Output

```
months = ["Jan", "Feb", "Mar", "Apr", "May", "June", "Jul", "Aug", "Sep"]
print("months=", months)
print("7th Element in months is = ", months[7.5])
```

(a)

```
months= ['Jan', 'Feb', 'Mar', 'Apr', 'May', 'June', 'Jul', 'Aug', 'Sep']
Traceback (most recent call last):
  File "C:/Users/Admin/Desktop/operator.py", line 15, in <module>
    print("7th Element in months is = ", months[7.5])
TypeError: list indices must be integers or slices, not float
```

(b)

- Regarding usage of index range to access lists, the following may be noted:
  - If *start* is greater than *end*, and range is used, no output is displayed.
  - If *start* or *end* index is more than the size of list, and range is used, no error is displayed.
  - If *start* or *end* index is more than the size of list, and positive/negative index is used but range is not used, then *IndexError* arises.

Example 9.5: (a) Using range index (b) Output

```
allmonths = ["Jan", "Feb", "Mar", "Apr", "May", "June", "Jul", "Aug", "Sep",
          "Oct", "Nov", "Dec"]
print("SubList[0:10]= ", allmonths[0:10])
print("SubList[-5:-1]= ", allmonths[-5:-1])
print("SubList[-5:-20]= ", allmonths[-5:-20])
print("SubList[-20:-1]= ", allmonths[-20:-1])
print("SubList[0:25]= ", allmonths[0:25])
print("SubList[20]= ", allmonths[20])
print("SubList[-20]= ", allmonths[-20])
```

(a)

```
SubList[0:10]=  ['Jan', 'Feb', 'Mar', 'Apr', 'May', 'June', 'Jul', 'Aug', 'Sep', 'Oct']
SubList[-5:-1]=  ['Aug', 'Sep', 'Oct', 'Nov']
SubList[-5:-20]=  []
SubList[-20:-1]=  ['Jan', 'Feb', 'Mar', 'Apr', 'May', 'June', 'Jul', 'Aug', 'Sep', 'Oct', 'Nov']
SubList[0:25]=  ['Jan', 'Feb', 'Mar', 'Apr', 'May', 'June', 'Jul', 'Aug', 'Sep', 'Oct', 'Nov', 'Dec']
Traceback (most recent call last):
  File "C:/Users/Admin/Desktop/access-typeerror.py", line 27, in <module>
    print("SubList[20]= ", allmonths[20])
IndexError: list index out of range
```

(b)

9.3.3 Stride with Slicing

- In addition to start and end index, a third parameter, stride, can be specified. The syntax is List[start: end: stride]
- Stride specifies the number of elements to move forward from, after each element retrieval. So, the elements retrieved are – start, start + stride, start + stride + stride, ___ end – 1. For example, if L = ["Apple", "Banana", 100, 50] then, L[1:4:2] will give the result as ["Banana", 50]. Here, L[1] is "Banana" and after stride 2, it is 50.
- The default value of stride is 1. So, when stride is not mentioned, all elements between start and end are retrieved.
  L[2:4] and L[2:4:1] retrieve the same sublist from a list L.
- A negative stride retrieves list from start to end backwards. So, the start index must be greater than end index, otherwise nothing is returned.

Example 9.6: (a) Using stride with slicing in list (b) Output

```
months = ["Jan", "Feb", "Mar", "Apr", "May", "June", "Jul", "Aug", "Sep"]
print("List months =\t", months)
print("months[0:4:2]=\t", months[0:4:2])
print("months[10:5:-1]=", months[10:5:-1])
print("months[5:10:-1]=", months[5:10:-1])
print("months[3::3]=\t", months[3::3])
print("months[3::-3]=\t", months[3::-3])
print("months[:10:2]=\t", months[:10:2])
print("months[0::1]=\t", months[0::1])
print("months[::]=\t", months[::])
```

(a)

```
List months =    ['Jan', 'Feb', 'Mar', 'Apr', 'May', 'June', 'Jul', 'Aug', 'Sep']
months[0:4:2]=   ['Jan', 'Mar']
months[10:5:-1]= ['Sep', 'Aug', 'Jul']
months[5:10:-1]= []
months[3::3]=    ['Apr', 'Jul']
months[3::-3]=   ['Apr', 'Jan']
months[:10:2]=   ['Jan', 'Mar', 'May', 'Jul', 'Sep']
months[0::1]=    ['Jan', 'Feb', 'Mar', 'Apr', 'May', 'June', 'Jul', 'Aug', 'Sep']
months[::]=      ['Jan', 'Feb', 'Mar', 'Apr', 'May', 'June', 'Jul', 'Aug', 'Sep']
```

(b)

9.4 BUILT-IN LIST TYPE METHODS

Python supports several built-in methods that can be used with lists. The syntax to use the methods is:

```
list.method()
```

Table 9.1 lists the built-in list methods along with their syntax and description.

Table 9.1 Built-in list methods

S. no	Method name	Syntax and description
1	**append(...)**	append(x:object):None Adds element x to the end of the list. Returns None.
2	**count(...)**	count(x:object):int Returns number of times the element x appears in list.
3	**extend(...)**	extend(l:list):None Appends all elements in l to list. Returns None.
4	**index(...)**	index(x: object):int Returns index of first occurrence of element x in list
5	**insert(...)**	insert(index: int, x:object):None Inserts element x at a given index. The first element in list has index 0. Returns None
6	**remove(...)**	remove(x:object):None Removes the first occurrence of element x from list. Returns None
7	**reverse(...)**	reverse():None Reverses the list. Returns None
8	**sort(...)**	sort(): None Sorts elements in list in ascending order. Returns None.
9	**pop(...)**	pop(i): object Removes element at position I and returns it. If I is not specified, `pop()` removes and returns the last element in the list.

Example 9.7: (a) Using the list methods (b) Output

```
science = ["phy", "chem", "bot", "zoo"]
arts = ["eco", "eng", "math"]
leapyear = [2000, 2004, 2008, 2012, 2016, 2020]
print("science=", science)
science.append("comp")
print("science after append=", science)
print("\narts=", arts)
arts.extend(["geo", "math", "eco"])
print("arts after extend=", arts)
arts.insert(3, "phil")
print("arts after insert=", arts)
print("math count=", arts.count("math"))
science.sort()
print("\nscience after sort=", science)
science.reverse()
print("science after reverse=", science)
print("\nleapyear=\t", leapyear)
print("index of 2004 =\t", leapyear.index(2004))
leapyear.remove(2008)
print("remove 2008 =\t", leapyear)
print("pop 2=\t\t", leapyear.pop(2))
```

(a)

```
science= ['phy', 'chem', 'bot', 'zoo']
science after append= ['phy', 'chem', 'bot', 'zoo', 'comp']

arts= ['eco', 'eng', 'math']
arts after extend= ['eco', 'eng', 'math', 'geo', 'math', 'eco']
arts after insert= ['eco', 'eng', 'math', 'phil', 'geo', 'math', 'eco']
math count= 2

science after sort= ['bot', 'chem', 'comp', 'phy', 'zoo']
science after reverse= ['zoo', 'phy', 'comp', 'chem', 'bot']

leapyear=         [2000, 2004, 2008, 2012, 2016, 2020]
index of 2004 =   1
remove 2008 =     [2000, 2004, 2012, 2016, 2020]
pop 2=            2012
```

(b)

9.5 Basic Operations on Lists: List Is Mutable

Lists are mutable. This means a list can be updated in place. Therefore, operations like, add element to list, delete an element from the list, and update a list, can be performed on it. We can explain the following operations on lists:

- Add, Update, Delete and Search element
- Copy or Clone list
- Repeat List, Traverse List and other operations

9.5.1 Add Element

- To add an element to the list, plus (+) sign is used. Both the operands must be a list.

  In the following example, we define the element u as a list ["u"] and then add the two lists.

```
L1 = ["a","e", "i", "o"]
print("L1=", L1)
L1 = L1 + ["u"]
print("L1 after add element =", L1)
```

Output

```
L1= ['a', 'e', 'i', 'o']
L1 after add element = ['a', 'e', 'i', 'o', 'u']
```

If we add a string to a list, then error is displayed.

```
L1 = ["a","e", "i", "o"]
```

```
L1 = L1 + "u"
print("L1 after add element =", L1)
```

Output

```
Traceback (most recent call last):
  File "C:/Users/Admin/Desktop/Python/Chapter 7 Lists/operations.py", line 5, in <module>
    L1 = L1 + "u"
TypeError: can only concatenate list (not "str") to list
```

- To add a character directly to a list, use `append()`, `extend()` and `insert()` methods.

```
L1 = ["a","e", "i", "o"]
print("L1=", L1)
L1.append("u")
print("L1 after append u =", L1)
L1.insert(2, "x")
print("L1 after insert x =", L1)
L1.extend("p")
print("L1 after extend p =", L1)
```

Output

```
L1= ['a', 'e', 'i', 'o']
L1 after append u = ['a', 'e', 'i', 'o', 'u']
L1 after insert x = ['a', 'e', 'x', 'i', 'o', 'u']
L1 after extend p = ['a', 'e', 'x', 'i', 'o', 'u', 'p']
```

- Let us now see the difference between `append()` and `extend()` when they are used with two lists.

  Let us take list A1 and A2. We append A2 to A1 and extend A1 with A2.
  - o When we append A2 to A1, the list A2 gets added as an element in A1.
  - o When we extend A1 with A2, the elements of list A2 get added to list A1.

  An example is shown below:

A1= [“a”, “b”, “c”] A2 = [“d”, “e”]	
A1.append(A2)	A1.extend(A2)
Output: [“a”, “b”, “c”, [“d”, “e”]]	Output: [“a”, “b”, “c”, “d”, “e”]
A1[3] is [“d”, “e”]	A1[3] is “d”

  We note that both `append()` and `extend()` apply at the end of the list. Also, if A2 were not a list but an element, then the difference between `append()` and `extend()` will not be visible.

- `Insert()` allows an element to be inserted in the list at a particular index. This shifts the elements of the list to make space for the inserted element.

  In the example shown below, `L1.insert(0, "x")`, inserts the character "x" at index 0 in the list L1.

```
L1 = ["a","e", "i", "o"]
print("L1=", L1)
L1.append(["a", "b"])
print("L1 after append =", L1)
L1.insert(0, "x")
print("L1 after insert x =", L1)
L1.extend(["p", "q"])
print("L1 after extend =", L1)
```

Output

```
L1= ['a', 'e', 'i', 'o']
L1 after append = ['a', 'e', 'i', 'o', ['a', 'b']]
L1 after insert x = ['x', 'a', 'e', 'i', 'o', ['a', 'b']]
L1 after extend = ['x', 'a', 'e', 'i', 'o', ['a', 'b'], 'p', 'q']
```

9.5.2 Update Element

- To update an element or more than one element, we provide the updated value at the index using assignment operator. For example, we update the L1[1] from "e" to "u", as shown below:

```
L1 = ["a","e", "i", "o"]
print("L1=", L1)
L1[1] = "u"
print("L1 after update element =", L1)
```

Output

```
L1= ['a', 'e', 'i', 'o']
L1 after update element = ['a', 'u', 'i', 'o']
```

9.5.3 Delete Element and List

- To delete one or more than one element, we use `del` command. The syntax of `del` command is

```
del list_name[index]
```

The element at the index in list_name is deleted.

```
L1 = ["a","e", "i", "o"]
print("L1=", L1)
del L1[1]
print("L1 after delete element =", L1)
```

Output

```
L1= ['a', 'e', 'i', 'o']
L1 after delete element = ['a', 'i', 'o']
```

- If the index is not known, an element in a list can be deleted using `remove()` method. Here, we specify the elements to be removed.

```
L1 = ["a","e", "i", "o"]
print("L1=", L1)
L1.remove("e")
print("L1 after delete element =", L1)
```

Output

```
L1= ['a', 'e', 'i', 'o']
L1 after delete element = ['a', 'i', 'o']
```

- The `del` command is also used to delete a list.

```
del list_name
```

will delete the list.

9.5.4 Search Element (`in` operator)

- The `in` operator is used for searching elements in a list.
- The syntax of `in` operator is:

```
element in list_name
```

- If the element is present in the list, True is returned; else, False is returned. For example,

```
L1 = ["a","e", "i", "o"]
print("L1=", L1)
print("u in L1 is=", "u" in L1)
print("o in L1 is=", "o" in L1)
```

Output

```
L1= ['a', 'e', 'i', 'o']
u in L1 is= False
o in L1 is= True
```

- The `not in` operator is used to check if an element is not in a list. The syntax of `not in` operator is:

```
element not in list_name
```

- If the element is not in the list, True is returned, else False is returned. For example,

```
L1 = ["a","e", "i", "o"]
print("L1=", L1)
print("u not in L1 is=", "u" not in L1)
print("o not in L1 is=", "o" not in L1)
```

Output

```
L1= ['a', 'e', 'i', 'o']
u not in L1 is= True
o not in L1 is= False
```

9.5.5 Copy or Clone List

- A list can be copied and cloned. Copy a list is different from Clone a list.
- **Copy a list** creates a copy of the original list. Copy creates a reference to the original list. Both the copy list and original list refer to the same memory location. Therefore, any change in the list is reflected both for original list and copy list. For example, a list is copied using *L1 = L2*, where L1 and L2 are both lists. Any change made to the elements of the list is reflected in both L1 and L2.

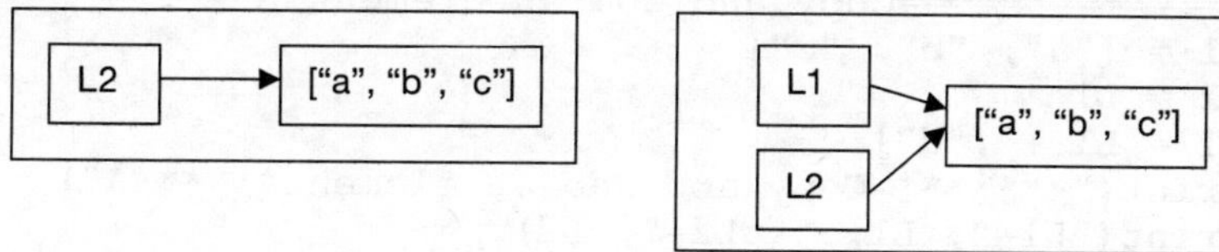

We see in the code below that the id of copy list and original list is the same.

Example 9.8: (a) Using copy a list (b) Output

```
#Copy
L1 = ["a", "b", "c"]
L2 = L1
print("L1=", L1, "\tL2=", L2)
print("id(L1)=", id(L1), "\tid(L2)=", id(L2))
```

(a)

```
L1= ['a', 'b', 'c']      L2= ['a', 'b', 'c']
id(L1)= 2159389361792    id(L2)= 2159389361792
```

(b)

- **Copy and update an element:** If we update an element of the list, there is no change in the copy list and original list. For example, in the following code, the "b" is updated by "d". We see that the id of the copy list and original list is same.

Example 9.9: (a) Using copy and update an element (b) Output

```
#============Copy and update an element==========
L1 = ["a", "b", "c"]
L2 = L1
L2[1] = "d"
print("******* Copy and update an element*******")
print("L1=", L1, "\tL2=", L2)
print("id(L1)=", id(L1), "\tid(L2)=", id(L2))
```

(a)

```
******* Copy and update an element*******
L1= ['a', 'd', 'c']      L2= ['a', 'd', 'c']
id(L1)= 2159420620992   id(L2)= 2159420620992
```

(b)

- **Copy and add a list element:** If we add a new element to list using assignment, then a new list is created. The list now has a new reference. For example, in the following code, ["d"] is added to L1. We see that the id of the copy list and original list are different.

Example 9.10: (a) Using copy and add a list element (b) Output

```
#============Copy and add an element===========
L1 = ["a", "b", "c"]
L2 = L1
L1 = L1 + ["d"]
print("******* Copy and add an element*******")
print("L1=", L1, "\tL2=", L2)
print("id(L1)=", id(L1), "\tid(L2)=", id(L2))
```

(a)

```
******* Copy and add an element*******
L1= ['a', 'b', 'c', 'd']          L2= ['a', 'b', 'c']
id(L1)= 2159389365376   id(L2)= 2159389361792
```

(b)

- **Clone a list** is used if we want to modify a list and also save an original copy of the list. A clone creates a copy of the list instead of creating reference to the list. **Slice operator** is used for cloning a list. Any change in original list or clone list does not affect the other. In the following example, we see that when an element is changed in L2, L1 is not affected.

Example 9.11: (a) Using clone a list (b) Output

```
L1 = ["a", "b", "c"]
L2 = L1[:]
print("L1=", L1)
print("L2=", L2)
print("id(L1)=", id(L1), "id(L2)=", id(L2))
L2[1] = "d"
print("******* Change an element of list*******")
print("L1=", L1)
print("L2=", L2)
print("id(L1)=", id(L1), "id(L2)=", id(L2))
```

(a)

```
L1= ['a', 'b', 'c']
L2= ['a', 'b', 'c']
id(L1)= 34941248 id(L2)= 34941368
******* Change an element of list*******
L1= ['a', 'b', 'c']
L2= ['a', 'd', 'c']
id(L1)= 34941248 id(L2)= 34941368
```

L1 does not change

(b)

- **Copy a list using `list()` method:** In this case, a separate list is created with a different id.

Example 9.12: (a) Using copy and add a list element (b) Output

```
L1 = ["a", "b", "c"]
L2 = list(L1)
print("L1=", L1)
print("L2=", L2)
print("id(L1)=", id(L1), "id(L2)=", id(L2))
L2[1] = "d"
print("******* Change an element of list*******")
print("L1=", L1)
print("L2=", L2)
print("id(L1)=", id(L1), "id(L2)=", id(L2))
```

(a)

```
L1= ['a', 'b', 'c']
L2= ['a', 'b', 'c']
id(L1)= 32858400 id(L2)= 32564208
******* Change an element of list*******
L1= ['a', 'b', 'c']
L2= ['a', 'd', 'c']
id(L1)= 32858400 id(L2)= 32564208
```

(b)

- **Copy a list using `copy()` method of the copy module:** This makes a shallow copy, meaning that it will not clone the child objects. So, if a list has a sublist within it, the sublist is not cloned. This is called shallow copy. In the example below, we see that when we change an element of the sublist, the change is reflected in both lists.

Example 9.13: (a) Using `copy()` method to copy a list (b) Output

```
from copy import copy
L1 = ["a", "b", ["p", "q"], "c"]
L2 = copy(L1)
print("L1=", L1)
print("L2=", L2)
print("id(L1)=", id(L1), "id(L2)=", id(L2))
L2[2][0] = "d"
print("******* Change an element of list*******")
print("L1=", L1)
print("L2=", L2)
print("id(L1)=", id(L1), "id(L2)=", id(L2))
```

Both lists change

(a)

```
L1= ['a', 'b', ['p', 'q'], 'c']
L2= ['a', 'b', ['p', 'q'], 'c']
id(L1)= 32835864 id(L2)= 32858400
******* Change an element of list*******
L1= ['a', 'b', ['d', 'q'], 'c']
L2= ['a', 'b', ['d', 'q'], 'c']
id(L1)= 32835864 id(L2)= 32858400
```

(b)

- **Copy a list using `deepcopy()` method of the copy module:** This makes a deep copy, meaning that it will clone the child objects also. So, if a list has a sublist within it, the sublist is also cloned. The clone is independent of the original. This is called deep copy. In the example below, we see that when we change an element of the sublist, the change is not reflected in the original list.

Example 9.14: (a) Using `deepcopy()` method to copy a list (b) Output

```
from copy import deepcopy
L1 = ["a", "b", ["p", "q"], "c"]
L2 = deepcopy(L1)
print("L1=", L1)
print("L2=", L2)
print("id(L1)=", id(L1), "id(L2)=", id(L2))
L2[2][0] = "d"
print("******* Change an element of list*******")
print("L1=", L1)
print("L2=", L2)
print("id(L1)=", id(L1), "id(L2)=", id(L2))
```

(a)

```
L1= ['a', 'b', ['p', 'q'], 'c']
L2= ['a', 'b', ['p', 'q'], 'c']
id(L1)= 32835824 id(L2)= 32835864
******* Change an element of list*******
L1= ['a', 'b', ['p', 'q'], 'c']
L2= ['a', 'b', ['d', 'q'], 'c']
id(L1)= 32835824 id(L2)= 32835864
```

Only one list changes

(b)

9.5.6 Repeat List (* operator)

- The "*" operator is used to replicate elements in a list.
- The syntax is:

```
List_name * integer
```

The elements in list list_name gets replicated, integer number of times.

```
L1 = ["a", "e", "i"]
print("List=", L1)
print("List replicated 3 times =", L1 * 3)
```

Output

```
List= ['a', 'e', 'i']
List replicated 3 times = ['a', 'e', 'i', 'a', 'e', 'i', 'a', 'e', 'i']
```

9.5.7 Built-in List Function

- In addition to the built-in methods, Python defines functions that can operate on the list.
- The commonly used functions are shown in Table 9.2:

Table 9.2 Commonly used Python functions

Method name	Description
len(L1)	Length of list L1, i.e. number of elements in L1
min(L1)	Smallest element in list L1
max(L1)	Largest element in list L1
sum(L1)	Sum of all numbers in list L1

- Let us see some examples:

Example 9.15: (a) Using list methods (b) Output

```
L1 = [1, 5, 10, 20]
print("L1=", L1)
print("Length L1=", len(L1))
print("Max in L1=", max(L1))
print("Min in L1 =", min(L1))
print("Sum of L1=", sum(L1))
```

(a)

```
L1= [1, 5, 10, 20]
Length L1= 4
Max in L1= 20
Min in L1 = 1
Sum of L1= 36
```

(b)

Example 9.16: (a) Using list method to find sum of charaters (b) Output
Here, an error occurs when we find the sum of characters.

```
L1= [1, 5, 10, 20]
Length L1= 4
Max in L1= 20
Min in L1 = 1
Sum of L1= 36
```

(a)

```
L1= ['a', 'e', 'i']
Length L1= 3
Max in L1= i
Min in L1 =  a
Traceback (most recent call last):
  File "C:/Users/Admin/Desktop/operations.py", line 95, in <module>
    print("Sum in L1=", sum(L1))
TypeError: unsupported operand type(s) for +: 'int' and 'str'
```

(b)

9.5.8 Traverse List

- Traversal of list is accessing each element in list, one by one.
- Traversal is done using a loop – `for` loop or `while` loop.

```
L1 = ["a", "e", "i"]
print("List=", L1)
for i in L1:
    print(i)
```

```
L1 = ["a", "e", "i"]
print("List=", L1)
i = 0
while i <len(L1):
    print("L1[", i, "]=", L1[i])
```

Output

```
List= ['a', 'e', 'i']
a
e
i
```

```
List= ['a', 'e', 'i']
L1[ 0 ]= a
L1[ 1 ]= e
L1[ 2 ]= i
```

9.6 List Comprehension

- List comprehension is used for creating new lists from an existing list.
- The new list is a result of transformation applied to an existing list.
- List comprehension is an alternative way to create lists.
- The advantage of list comprehension is that only a few lines of code are required as the syntax is concise.
- Common application of list comprehension: The elements of a list are the outcome of an operation applied to each member of the iterable. In other words, it creates sublist from these elements when a certain condition is true.
- List comprehension uses set notation form (as in mathematics). For example, in Maths, to get the square of a number, we write as follows:

$$A = \{x^2 \mid x \in N\}$$

which means, set A consists of the square of number x, for x belongs to a set of natural numbers.
- The syntax for list comprehension is:

```
List_var = [x for x in iterable]
```

The iterable can be a list or any other iterable.

Let us now discuss an example, using (1) list comprehension, and (2) using initialization and append. We create a list having the letters in word "Computer".

Example 9.17: (a) Using list comprehension (b) Output

Using list comprehension	Using list initialization and append

`letter = [a for a in "Computer"]`
`print (letter)`
	`letter = []`
	`for a in "Computer":`
	`    letter.append(a)`
	`print(letter)`

(a)

```
['C', 'o', 'm', 'p', 'u', 't', 'e', 'r']
```

(b)

We see that the output is same, but list comprehension gives us a compact and succinct code. Let us see another example to create a list of square of numbers from 0 to 9.

```
num = [x**2 for x in range(10)]
print (num)
```

```
[0, 1, 4, 9, 16, 25, 36, 49, 64, 81]
```

- List comprehension can also use **if-statement** to modify the output when creating a new list.

```
letter = [a for a in "Computer" if a in ["a", "e", "i", "o", "u"]]
print (letter)

num = [x**2 for x in range(10) if x%2==0]
print (num)
```

Output

```
['o', 'u', 'e']
[0, 4, 16, 36, 64]
```

As we see in the examples, for every item, the `if` condition is applied and if the answer is True, then the item is included in the list. The first example puts only vowels to the list and second example puts square of even numbers to the list.

- List comprehension can also use **nested if-statement** to modify the output when creating a new list. For example, the below list has the square of numbers divisible by 2 and 4.

```
num = [x**2 for x in range(10) if x%2==0 if x%4 == 0]
print (num)
```

Output

```
[0, 16, 64]
```

- List comprehension can also have **nested `for` loops.** They are useful for performing multiple iterations. For example, multiply elements of two lists. The output is 1*2, 1*3, 1*2, 2*4, 2*3, 2*2, 3*4, 3*3, 3*2.

```
num = [x* y for x in range(1, 4) for y in range(4, 1, -1)]
print (num)
```

Output

```
[4, 3, 2, 8, 6, 4, 12, 9, 6]
```

9.7 Tuple: An Overview

- Tuple is an ordered collection of objects. The objects are called items or elements of tuple.
- Tuple is created in two ways: (1) comma separated values, and (2) comma separated values in parenthesis ().
  T1 = 1, 5, 10, 20
  T2 = ("a", "e", "i", "o", "u")
  T3 = "a", "b", "c"
- The items in tuple need not be of the same type. This means that a tuple may have items that are a mix of type integers, strings and other data types.
  T1 = ("a", "b", 20, 25)
- Tuple may be empty. An empty tuple has zero items.
  T1 = ()
- Tuple with only one value has to include a comma at end. If we do not include comma, then type string is created.
  T1 = ("a",)
- Tuple can also have another tuple as an item in it. These are called nested tuples.
  T1 = ("a", "b", ("a", "b"))
- The items in a tuple can be accessed using index.
- Tuple is compared using ASCII values in lexicographic order.

```
print((1, 2, 3)>(1, 3, 4))
print(("a",)>("A",))
```

Output

```
False
True
```

- ***Tuple is immutable*** unlike lists. Tuples are read-only. This means tuples cannot be changed in place.
- **Difference between tuple and list**
  - o Tuple is immutable. They cannot be changed in place. List is mutable.
  - o Tuple is written in parenthesis. List is written in square bracket.
- **Advantages of tuple over list**
  - o Generally, tuple is used for heterogeneous datatypes; list is used for homogeneous datatypes.
  - o Data written using tuple remains write-protected (cannot be changed).

  Some examples of tuple:

Example 9.18: (a) Using a tuple (b) Output

```
T1 = (2, 4, 6, 8, 10)
T2 = (2, "Rivers", 4, "Lakes")
T3 = ("Ganga", "Yamuna", "Saraswati", "Godavari")
T4 = (("Aarti", 10), ("Deepak", 20), ("Akash", 30))
T5 = 1, 2, 3, 4, 5
print("T1= ", T1)
print("T2= ", T2)
print("T3= ", T3)
print("T4= ", T4)
print("T5= ", T5)
```

(a)

```
T1=   (2, 4, 6, 8, 10)
T2=   (2, 'Rivers', 4, 'Lakes')
T3=   ('Ganga', 'Yamuna', 'Saraswati', 'Godavari')
T4=   (('Aarti', 10), ('Deepak', 20), ('Akash', 30))
T5=   (1, 2, 3, 4, 5)
```

(b)

9.8 Access Elements in Tuple

We know that tuple, list and string are sequences. So, indexing, slicing, stride with slicing work in the same way for tuple as they work for the string and list. The elements of a tuple are enumerated similar to those of string and list. The indexing, slicing and stride with slicing have been discussed in detail in the context of strings. We present here a brief overview in context of tuple. We shall now understand enumeration of tuple.

- The enumeration of a tuple T = ("a", "b", "c", 10, 20, 30) is depicted below.

L ← R

-6	-5	-4	-3	-2	-1
a	b	c	10	20	30
0	1	2	3	4	5

L → R

- The elements of tuple are enumerated as follows:
  - o Left to Right, the elements are enumerated starting from 0.
  - o Right to Left, the elements are enumerated starting from –1.
  - o Enumeration corresponds to the index. From left to right, the index is 0, 1, 2 … and from right to left, the index is –1, –2, –3, …

9.8.1 Indexing

- Indexing is used for accessing elements in the tuple.
- An element of tuple is accessed by writing the tuple name followed by index in square brackets.
- **Positive Indexing:** It is from left to right, starting from 0. For example, if T = ("a", "b", "c", 10, 20, 30), T[2] gives c.

a	b	c	10	20	30
0	1	2	3	4	5

- **Negative Indexing:** It is from right to left, starting from –1. For example, if T = ("a", "b", "c", 10, 20, 30), T[–2] gives 20.

-6	-5	-4	-3	-2	-1
a	b	c	10	20	30

9.8.2 Slicing

- **Slicing operator** is used to get selected elements from a tuple. The syntax of slicing operator is

  tuple[start:end]

  start – index from where the slice starts
  end – index till where the slice ends (excluding end index)
  The tuple from index *start* to *end–1* is returned.

- The *start* and *end* index are optional. If they are omitted, the default value of *start* is 0 and *end* is the last index of tuple.
- **Range Indexing:** It allows specifying a range of indexes. All elements starting from *start* to *end–1* are obtained. For example, if T = ("a", "b", "c", 10, 20, 30), T[1:4] gives ('b', 'c', 10).

a	b	c	10	20	30
0	1	2	3	4	5

- The index can be specified where either start or end index are omitted.
  - o If *start* index is omitted, elements from beginning of tuple till end–1 is returned.
  - o If *end* index is omitted, elements from start index till end of tuple is returned.
- The index can be negative. The indexing starts from right to left in negative indexing.
  - o *start* index is lower than *end* index. For example, start is –5, which is lower than end, which is –2.
- The index must be an integer; otherwise it will result in TypeError.
- The index must be in range; otherwise it will result in IndexError.
- When we use range to access tuple, the following may be noted:
  - o If index range *start* is greater than *end*, no output is displayed.
  - o If index range *start* or *end* is more than the size of the tuple, there is no error.
  - o If *start* or *end* index is more than the size of the tuple, and positive/negative index is used but range is not used, then IndexError arises.

9.8.3 Stride with Slicing

- In addition to start and end index, a third parameter, stride, can also be specified. The syntax is

  `Tuple[start: end: stride]`

- The stride specifies the number of elements to move forward from, after each element retrieval. So the elements retrieved are – start, start + stride, start + stride + stride, ___ end – 1. For example,
  T = ("a", "b", "c", 10, 20, 30)
  T[1:5:2] will return ['b', 10]
- The default value of stride is 1. So when we do not mention stride, all elements between start and end are retrieved.
  T[2:4] and T[2:4:1] retrieve the same tuple from T.
- A negative stride will retrieve elements from `start` to `end` backwards. So, the start index must be greater than end index; otherwise nothing is returned.

9.9 Built-in Tuple Type Methods

Tuples are immutable, so methods to add or delete elements from tuple are not available. Python supports only two built-in methods that can be used with tuples. The syntax to use the methods is:

```
tuple.method()
```

Table 9.3 lists the built-in tuple methods along with their description.

Table 9.3 Built-in tuple methods

S. no	Method name	Description
1	count(x)	Return occurrences of x in the tuple
2	index(x)	Return index of first occurrence of x in tuple

```
T1 = ("a", "e", "i", "o", "u", "e", "i", "e", "i")
print("T1=", T1)
print("Count of e=", T1.count("e"))
print("Index of i=", T1.index("i"))
```

Output

```
T1= ('a', 'e', 'i', 'o', 'u', 'e', 'i', 'e', 'i')
Count of e= 3
Index of i= 2
```

9.10 Basic Operations on Tuple: Tuple Is Immutable

- Tuples are immutable. This means tuples cannot be updated in place. So, add, update and delete element cannot be applied to tuples.

  The following code gives an error:

```
T = ("a", "b", "c", 10, 20, 30)
T[20] = 50
```

Output

```
Traceback (most recent call last):
  File "C:/Users/Admin/Desktop/tuple-intro.py", line 24, in <module>
    T[20] = 50
TypeError: 'tuple' object does not support item assignment
```

- The following operations are applied to tuple:
  - o Concatenate, delete tuple
  - o Search element, Repeat tuple, Tuple comparison
  - o Tuple assignment, Traverse tuple and other operations

9.10.1 Concatenate Tuple (+ operator)

- The (+) operator is used to concatenate tuple.

```
T1 = ("cat", "bat", "rat")
T2 = (10, 20, 30)
T = T1 + T2
print("T1=", T1)
print("T2=", T2)
print("T1+T2=", T)
```

Output

```
T1= ('cat', 'bat', 'rat')
T2= (10, 20, 30)
T1+T2= ('cat', 'bat', 'rat', 10, 20, 30)
```

- The (+) operator is used to concatenate a string to tuple.

```
T1 = ("cat", "bat", "rat")
print("T1=", T1)
print("The animals in T1 are " + T1[0] + " and " + T1[2])
```

Output

```
T1= ('cat', 'bat', 'rat')
The animals in T1 are cat and rat
```

9.10.2 Delete Tuple

- The `del` command is also used to delete a tuple.

del tuple_name

will delete the tuple.
If we try to print the tuple after deletion, an exception is raised, since the tuple does not exist.

```
T1 = ("cat", "bat", "rat")
del T1
print(T1)
```

Output

```
Traceback (most recent call last):
  File "C:/Users/Admin/Desktop/tuple-intro.py", line 42, in <module>
    print(T1)
NameError: name 'T1' is not defined
>>>
```

9.10.3 Search Element (in operator)

- The in operator is used to search for elements in a tuple.
- The syntax of in operator is:

```
element in tuple_name
```

- If the element is present in tuple, True is returned else False is returned. For example,

```
T1 = ("cat", "bat", "rat")
print("T1=", T1)
print("fat in T1=", "fat" in T1)
print("bat in T1=", "bat" in T1)
```

Output

```
T1= ('cat', 'bat', 'rat')
fat in T1= False
bat in T1= True
```

- The not in operator is used to check if element not in tuple. The syntax of not in operator is:

```
element not in tuple_name
```

- If the element is not in tuple, True is returned, else False is returned. For example,

```
T1 = ("cat", "bat", "rat")
print("T1=", T1)
print("fat not in T1=", "fat" not in T1)
print("bat not in T1=", "bat" not in T1)
```

Output

```
T1= ('cat', 'bat', 'rat')
fat not in T1= True
bat not in T1= False
```

9.10.4 Repeat Tuple (* operator)

- The "*" operator is used to replicate elements in tuple.
- The syntax is,

```
Tuple_name * integer
```

The elements in tuple tuple_name gets replicated integer number of times.

```
T1 = ("cat", "bat", "rat")
T2 = T1 * 2
print("T1=", T1)
print("T2=T1*2=", T2)
```

Output

```
T1= ('cat', 'bat', 'rat')
T2=T1*2= ('cat', 'bat', 'rat', 'cat', 'bat', 'rat')
```

9.10.5 Tuple Assignment

- Tuple assignment is a unique feature.
- A tuple can be on the left side of an assignment
- If left side is more than one variable, tuple assignment allows assigning more than one variable in single statement.
- How it works is:
  - o Left side is tuple of variables; Right side is tuple of values.
  - o All expressions on right side are evaluated before any assignment.
  - o Each value on right is assigned to a variable in left, in a sequence.
- Let us see some examples:

Example 9.19: We see that the three elements of the tuple are assigned to the three variables – Name, Age and Country, in a sequence.

```
T1 = ("Akriti", 20, "India")
print("T1=", T1)
Name, Age, Country = T1
print("Name=", Name, "\nAge=", Age, "\nCountry=", Country)
```

(a)

```
T1= ('Akriti', 20, 'India')
Name= Akriti
Age= 20
Country= India
```

(b)

Example 9.20: Swapping values of two variables. Conventionally, we use a temporary variable for swapping values.

```
temp = x
x = y
y = x
```

In Python, this can be done in a single statement using tuple assignment.

```
y, x = x, y
```

```
x = 5
y =10
print("Before Swap:\t", "x =", x, "\ty =", y)
y, x = x, y
print("After Swap:\t", "x =", x, "y =", y)
```

(a)

```
Before Swap:      x = 5  y = 10
After Swap:       x = 10 y = 5
```

(b)

- The right side can be any sequence – string, tuple or list. Tuple assignment can be used to split values; for example, splitting an email address into user name and domain

```
email = "goel.anita@gmail.com"
print("Email address=", email)
user_name, domain_name = email.split("@")
print("User_name=", user_name, "\nDomain_name=", domain_name)
```

Output

```
Email address= goel.anita@gmail.com
User_name= goel.anita
Domain_name= gmail.com
```

- The number of variables on the right and left side should be same; otherwise, ValueError is reported

```
T1 = ("Akriti", 20, "India")
print("T1=", T1)
Name, Age = T1
print("Name=", Name, "\nAge=", Age, "\nCountry=", Country)
```

Output

```
T1= ('Akriti', 20, 'India')
Traceback (most recent call last):
  File "C:/Users/Admin/Desktop/tuple-intro.py", line 104, in <module>
    Name, Age = T1
ValueError: too many values to unpack (expected 2)
```

9.10.6 Built-in Tuple Functions

- In addition to the built-in methods, Python defines functions that can operate on the tuples.
- The commonly used functions are shown Table 9.4:

Table 9.4 Built-in tuple functions in Python

Method Name	Description
`len(tuple)`	Returns length of tuple
`min(tuple)`	Returns smallest element in tuple
`max(tuple)`	Returns largest element in tuple
`tuple(list)`	Converts a list into tuple

- Let us see some examples. We can see that when a list is converted to tuple, the brackets change.

Example 9.21: (a) Converting a list to a tuple (b) Output

```
T1 = ("table", "chair", "rack")
T2 = ("cat", "bat", "rat")
print("Tuple T1=", T1)
print("Tuple T2=", T2)
print("Length T1=", len(T1))
print("Max in T1=", max(T1))
print("Min in T1 = ", min(T1))
print("Tuple([1, 2, 3])=", tuple([1, 2, 3]))
```

(a)

```
Tuple T1= ('table', 'chair', 'rack')
Tuple T2= ('cat', 'bat', 'rat')
Length T1= 3
Max in T1= table
Min in T1 =  chair
Tuple([1, 2, 3])= (1, 2, 3)
```

(b)

9.10.7 Traverse Tuple

- Traversal of tuple is accessing each element in tuple, one by one.
- Traversal is done using a loop – `for` loop or `while` loop.

Example 9.22: (a) Traverse a tuple using `for` loop (b) Output

```
T1 = ("table", "chair", "rack")
print("Tuple=", T1)
for i in T1:
    print(i)
```

(a)

```
Tuple= ('table', 'chair', 'rack')
table
chair
rack
```

(b)

Example 9.23: (a) Traverse a tuple using `while` loop (b) Output

```
T1 = ("table", "chair", "rack")
print("Tuple=", T1)
i = 0
while i <len(T1):
    print("T1[", i, "]=", T1[i])
    i = i+1
```

(a)

```
Tuple= ('table', 'chair', 'rack')
T1[ 0 ]= table
T1[ 1 ]= chair
T1[ 2 ]= rack
```

(b)

9.11 Array: An Overview

- Array is an ordered collection of objects. Every object of an array is of the same data type. For example, an array of integers, array of string, and array of float.
- The objects are called elements of array.
- Arrays are used when many variables of the same type are needed.
- The elements of an array are stored at contiguous memory locations. The position of each element is calculated by adding an offset to a base value (first element of array).
- Array is created by importing the array module. The syntax to create an array is:
  ```
  from array import *
  array_name = array(typecode, [elements])
  ```
  where, `array_name` is user-defined name for array; `typecode` defines the type of elements stored in the array; `elements` is the comma-separated elements of the array.
  The typecodes are:

Typecode	Value
b	signed integer of size 1 byte
B	unsigned integer of size 1 byte
c	character of size 1 byte
u	Unicode character of size 2 byte
i	signed integer of size 2 bytes
I	unsigned integer of size 2 bytes
h	signed short integer of size 2 bytes
H	unsigned short integer of size 2 bytes
l	signed long integer of size 4 bytes
L	unsigned long integer of size 4 bytes
q	signed long integer of size 8 bytes
Q	unsigned long integer of size 8 bytes
f	floating-point of size 4 bytes
d	floating-point of size 8 bytes

- The elements of an array are accessed using index. The index starts from 0. The length of the array defines the number of elements stored in the array. For example,

```
from array import *

a1 = array('d', [1.1, 1.2, 1.3])
a2 = array('i', [1, 2, 3, -10, -20])
print(a1)
print(a1[0])
print(a2[3])
```

```
array('d', [1.1, 1.2, 1.3])
1.1
-10
```

Output

In the example,
Line 1: import array
Line 3: array declaration of type float
Line 4: array declaration of type integer
Line 5: Printing the array
Line 6, 7: Accessing elements of array

- An array can be empty. It can be defined without any elements as:
  `array_name = array(typecode)`
- ***Array is mutable***. Thus, the elements of array can be changed in place.
- **List and Array**
  - o Both list and array are ordered sequence of elements. Both are mutable.
  - o List stores elements of different data types. Arrays store elements of the same data type.
  - o List can be treated as array. The data type of the elements of list cannot be constrained to the same data type.

9.11.1 Basic Operations on Arrays

Several operations can be performed on arrays. Table 9.5 shows the operations that can be performed on arrays.

Table 9.5 Array operations

Operation: function	Example	Output
Length of array: `len()`	from array import * a1 = array('i', [10, 20, 30, 40, 50]) print(a1) print("Length of array is:", len(a1))	array('i', [10, 20, 30, 40, 50]) Length of array is: 5
Add element: `insert(index, value)`	from array import * a1 = array('i', [10, 20, 30, 40, 50]) print("Before Insertion:\n", a1) a1.insert(2, 25) print("After Insertion: \n",a1)	Before Insertion: array('i', [10, 20, 30, 40, 50]) After Insertion: array('i', [10, 20, 25, 30, 40, 50])
Add new element at end `Append(element)`	from array import * a1 = array('i', [10, 20, 30, 20, 20]) a1.append(51) print(a1)	array('i', [10, 20, 30, 20, 20, 51])
Add more than one element at end `Extend(elements)`	from array import * a1 = array('i', [10, 20, 30, 20, 20]) a1.extend([61, 71, 81]) print(a1)	array('i', [10, 20, 30, 20, 20, 61, 71, 81])

(Continued)

Table 9.5 (Continued)

Operation: function	Example	Output
Update element `[]`	from array import * a1 = array('i', [10, 20, 30, 20, 20]) a1[3] = 40 print(a1)	array('i', [10, 20, 30, 40, 20])
Delete element: `remove(element)` Removes first instance of element	from array import * a1 = array('i', [10, 20, 30, 20, 20]) print("Before Remove:\n", a1) a1.remove(20) print("After Remove 20: \n",a1)	Before Remove: array('i', [10, 20, 30, 20, 20]) After Remove 20: array('i', [10, 30, 20, 20])
Delete element: `pop(index)`	from array import * a1 = array('i', [10, 20, 30, 40, 50]) print("Before pop:\n", a1) a1.pop(2) print("After pop 2: \n",a1)	Before pop: array('i', [10, 20, 30, 40, 50]) After pop 2: array('i', [10, 20, 40, 50])
Concatenate arrays: +	from array import * a1 = array('d', [1.1, 1.2, 1.3]) a2 = array('d', [1.0, 2.0, 3.3, -20.7]) print(a1+a2)	array('d', [1.1, 1.2, 1.3, 1.0, 2.0, 3.3, -20.7])
Traverse array: `For-loop`	from array import * a1 = array('i', [10, 20, 30, 40]) for x in a1: print(x)	10 20 30 40
Reverse array: `reverse()`	from array import * a1 = array('i', [10, 20, 30, 40, 50] a1.reverse() print(a1)	array('i', [50, 40, 30, 20, 10])
Count occurrence of element: `count(element)`	from array import * a1 = array('i', [10, 20, 30, 20, 20]) print(a1.count(20))	3
Slicing an array :	from array import * a1 = array('i', [10, 20, 30, 20, 20]) print(a1[:3]) #first three print(a1[2:4]) # from index 2 to 4-1	array('i', [10, 20, 30]) array('i', [30, 20])

9.11.2 Two-dimension Arrays and Operations

- Two-dimension array is one array within another. It represents a table with rows and columns.
- The position of an element is referred by two indices.
- The syntax to create a 2-dim array is-
  `array_name=[n_rows][n_columns]`
  where, `array_name` is user defined array name; `n_rows` and `n_columns` are the number of rows and columns, respectively, in the array.
- The elements of array can be accessed using row and column indices.
  `array_name[row_index][col_index]`
  where `array_name` is the array›s name, row_ind is the row index of the element, and col_ind is the column index of the element.
- For example, a 3×3 matrix can be represented using a 2-dim array.

We present an example that performs different operations on a 2-dim array, like, create array, print array, access a row of array, access a single element of array, insert, update, delete, append elements in array and slicing a two-dimension array.

Example 9.24: (a) Operations on a 2-dim array (b) Output

```
from array import *
#========= Function to print array
def print_arr(x1):
    for i in range(len(x1)):
        for j in range(len(x1[0])):
            print(x1[i][j], end = " ")
        print()
#========= Create array
size = int(input())
x1 = []
for i in range(size):
    x1.append([int(j) for j in input().split()]
for r in x1:
    print(r)
#========= Another way to create array
n = int(input())
x1 = []
for i in range(n):
    row = input().split()
    for i in range(len(row)):
        row[i] = int(row[i])
    x1.append(row)
for r in x1:
    print(r)
```

```
#=====Access a row
#x1 = [ [10, 20, 30], [40, 50, 60]]
print("The array x1 = : ")
print("Row 0=",x1[0])
print("Row 1=",x1[1])

#=====Access Single element
print("Element at [1][0]=",x1[1][0])

#========== insert elements
x1.insert(1, [11, 22, 33])
print("Array after insertion of elements: ")
print_arr(x1)

#=========update element
x1[0] = [5, 10, 15]
print("After Updation: ")
print_arr(x1)

#===========delete elements
del(x1[1])
print("Array Deletion: ")
print_arr(x1)

#=============append elements
x1.append([1,2, 3])
print("Array Append: ")
print_arr(x1)

#==========slicing array
x2 = x1[1:2]         #index 1 to 2
print("Array Slicing: ")
print("Slice x1[1:2]= ", x2)
x2 = x1[:1]          #index 0 to 1
print("Slice x1[:1]= ", x2)
```

Output

```
4
1 2 3
2 3 4
3 4 5
4 5 6
[1, 2, 3]
[2, 3, 4]
[3, 4, 5]
[4, 5, 6]
4
11 22 33
22 33 44
33 44 55
44 55 666
[11, 22, 33]
[22, 33, 44]
[33, 44, 55]
[44, 55, 666]
The array x1 = :
Row 0= [11, 22, 33]
Row 1= [22, 33, 44]
Element at [1][0]= 22
```

```
Array after insertion of
element
11 22 33
11 22 33
22 33 44
33 44 55
44 55 666
After Updation:
5 10 15
11 22 33
22 33 44
33 44 55
44 55 666
Array Deletion:
5 10 15
22 33 44
33 44 55
44 55 666
Array Append:
5 10 15
22 33 44
33 44 55
44 55 666
1 2 3
Array Slicing:
Slice x1[1:2]= [[22, 33,
44]]
Slice x1[:1]= [[5, 10, 15]]
>>>
```

9.11.3 Passing Arrays to Function

- Arrays can also be passed as parameter to a function.
- This need arises when you want the function to execute on all members of the array.
- To pass an array to a function, the following steps may be taken:
  - Create an array
  - Define a function that takes array as an argument
  - Call the function by passing array as an argument.

- In Example 9.24, the array x1 is passed as an argument to the function `print_arr()` as `def print_arr(x1):`

9.12 SOLVED QUESTIONS WITH EXPLANATION

1. Find the output:

```
Day = ["Mon","Tues", "Wed", "Thurs", "Fri", "Sat", "Sun"]
print("=====================================")
print("(i)   Day:\t", Day)
print("(ii) Day[0]:\t", Day[0])
print("(iii)Day[6]:\t", Day[6])
print("(iv) Day[0:1]:\t", Day[0:1])
print("(v)   Day[-6]:\t", Day[-6])
print("(vi) Day[-5:]:\t",Day[-5:])
print("(vii)Day[1:5]:\t",Day[1:5])
print("(viii)Day[:]:\t",Day[:])
print("(ix) Day[6:2]:\t",Day[6:2])
print("(x)   Day[3:-2]:\t",Day[3:-2])
print("(xi) Day[-6:-1]:",Day[-6:-1])
print("(xii)Day[6:3:-1]:",Day[6:3:-1])
print("(xiii)Day[8:3:-1]:",Day[8:3:-1])
print("(xiv)Day[2::2]:\t",Day[2::2])
print("(xv) Day[4::-2]:",Day[4::-2])
print("(xvi)Day[0::1]:\t",Day[0::1])
print("=====================================")
```

Output

```
=====================================
(i)  Day:           ['Mon', 'Tues', 'Wed', 'Thurs', 'Fri', 'Sat', 'Sun']
(ii) Day[0]:        Mon
(iii)Day[6]:        Sun
(iv) Day[0:1]:      ['Mon']
(v)  Day[-6]:       Tues
(vi) Day[-5:]:      ['Wed', 'Thurs', 'Fri', 'Sat', 'Sun']
(vii)Day[1:5]:      ['Tues', 'Wed', 'Thurs', 'Fri']
(viii)Day[:]:       ['Mon', 'Tues', 'Wed', 'Thurs', 'Fri', 'Sat', 'Sun']
(ix) Day[6:2]:      []
(x)  Day[3:-2]:     ['Thurs', 'Fri']
(xi) Day[-6:-1]: ['Tues', 'Wed', 'Thurs', 'Fri', 'Sat']
(xii)Day[6:3:-1]: ['Sun', 'Sat', 'Fri']
(xiii)Day[8:3:-1]: ['Sun', 'Sat', 'Fri']
(xiv)Day[2::2]:     ['Wed', 'Fri', 'Sun']
(xv) Day[4::-2]: ['Fri', 'Wed', 'Mon']
(xvi)Day[0::1]:     ['Mon', 'Tues', 'Wed', 'Thurs', 'Fri', 'Sat', 'Sun']
=====================================
```

2. Find the output:

```
L = [a for a in "Morning"]
print (L)
```

Output

```
['M', 'o', 'r', 'n', 'i', 'n', 'g']
```

Explanation: It splits a string into characters.

3. Find the output:

```
x = [a*a for a in range(5)]
print(x)
```

Output

```
[0, 1, 4, 9, 16]
```

Explanation: It finds the square of each number from 0 to 4.

4. Find the output:

```
#This is cartesian product of AxB
Name = ["Asha", "Usha", "Disha"]
Roll_no = [1, 2, 3]
Name_roll = [(x, y) for x in Name for y in Roll_no]
print(Name_roll)
```

Output

```
[('Asha', 1), ('Asha', 2), ('Asha', 3), ('Usha', 1), ('Usha', 2), ('Usha', 3), (
'Disha', 1), ('Disha', 2), ('Disha', 3)]
```

Explanation: It finds the cartesian product of name and roll_no.

5. Find the output:

```
#What is returned when the following code is run?
print((66, 4, 17, 4) < (66, 4, 16, 5))
```

Output

```
False
```

Explanation: It compares the values. 17 is greater than 16.

6. Find the output:

```
#What is the value of a[1:-1] if it exists?
a = (1, 2, 3, 4)
print(a[1:-1])
```

Output

```
(2, 3)
```

Explanation: It prints from the second element (index 1) to the last−1 element of the list. Last index is (−1).

7. Find the output:

```
#What is printed when the following code is written?
a = ['Enjoy', 'Yourself']
a1, a2 = a
print(a2)
```

Output

```
Yourself
```

Explanation: It assigns each string to a varaible. The variable a2 is assigned to the second string.

8. Find the output:

```
def LongestWrd(lst):
    wLen = []
    for i in lst:
        wLen.append((len(i), i))
    wLen.sort()
    return wLen[-1][0], wLen[-1][1]
ans = LongestWrd(["Always", "be", "grateful"])
print("The word \"", ans[1], "\" is longest, with length:", ans[0])
```

Output

```
The word " grateful " is longest, with length:
```

Explanation: The fiunction first creates a list with the length of each word and the word. The list is then sorted. The last element in the sorted list is the largest element and last−1 is the length of the element.

9. Find the output:

```
lst = [(1, 2, 3, 4), (2, 4, 5, 7), (10, 11, 12, 13), (0, 12, 11, 23, 1)]
print("Original list:\n", lst)

lst.sort(key = lambda m : max(m), reverse = True)
print("Tuples sorted by maximum element:\n", lst)
```

Output

```
Original list:
 [(1, 2, 3, 4), (2, 4, 5, 7), (10, 11, 12, 13), (0, 12, 11, 23, 1)]
Tuples sorted by maximum element:
 [(0, 12, 11, 23, 1), (10, 11, 12, 13), (2, 4, 5, 7), (1, 2, 3, 4)]
```

Explanation: This program sorts the tuples by the maximum element.

10. Find the output:

```
lst = [1,2,3,4,5,6,7,8,9,10]
print(lst, id(lst))
lst.reverse()
print(lst, id(lst))
rev_lst = list(reversed(lst))
print(rev_lst, id(rev_lst))
```

Output

```
[1, 2, 3, 4, 5, 6, 7, 8, 9, 10] 2339620242432
[10, 9, 8, 7, 6, 5, 4, 3, 2, 1] 2339620242432
[1, 2, 3, 4, 5, 6, 7, 8, 9, 10] 2339616462016
```

Explanation: This program reverses a list. `Reverse()` is a method that reverses the list in place. So, we see that the first and second id in the print statement is same. `Reversed()` returns an iterable of a list in reverse order; a new list is created.

9.13 Programming Examples

Program 9.1: WAP to check if all elements of the tuple are same or not.

```
#WAP to check if all elements of the tuple are same
# all() is an in-built function

T1 = (77, 77, 77, 77, 77, 77)
x = all(i == T1[0] for i in T1)
print(x)
```

Output

```
True
```

Program 9.2: WAP to find the maximum number in a list using list comprehension.

```
#Find maximum number in a list using list comprehension

L1= [10, 20, -90, 8]
max=L1[0]
max=[a for a in L1 if a> max]
print(max)
```

Output

```
[20]
```

Program 9.3: WAP to find words having length more than n using list comprehension.

```
#Find words having length more than n using List Comprehension
s="A thing of beauty is joy for ever"
n=3
L1= s.split()
print("String: ", L1)
L2=[]
L2.append([a for a in L1 if len(a)> n])
print(L2)
```

Output

```
String:  ['A', 'thing', 'of', 'beauty', 'is', 'joy', 'for', 'ever']
[['thing', 'beauty', 'ever']]
```

Program 9.4: WAP to sort tuple of tuples by second item.

```
#Sort tuple of tuples by 2nd item
T1 = (("Smile", 3), ("Beautiful", 20), ("Makes", 5), ("Look", 11), ("You", 9))
T1 = tuple(sorted(list(T1), key=lambda x: x[1]))
print(T1)
```

Output

```
(('Smile', 3), ('Makes', 5), ('You', 9), ('Look', 11), ('Beautiful', 20))
```

Program 9.5: WAP to create arrays using list.

```
#Lists can be used to create arrays
# Python does not have built-in arrays
a = [[1, 2, 3, 4],
     [5, 6, 7, 8],
     [9, 0, 1, 2],
     [3, 4, 5, 6]]

for i in range(0, 4):
   print(a[i].pop(-1))
```

Output

```
4
8
2
6
```

Program 9.6: WAP to move all zero digits to the end or beginning of a list of numbers.

```
#WAP to move all zero digits to end/beginning of list of numbers
def zbeg(lst):
    zero_beg = sorted(lst, key=lambda x: not x, reverse=True)
    return zero_beg
def zend(lst):
    zero_end = sorted(lst, key=lambda x: not x)
    return zero_end
lst = [2, 4, 6, 0, 0, 0, 8, 10, 0, 0, 12, 0, 14, 0, 45]
print("List: ", "\t\t", lst)
print("List(0 in end): ", zend(lst))
print("List(0 in begin):", zbeg(lst))
```

Output

```
List:             [2, 4, 6, 0, 0, 0, 8, 10, 0, 0, 12, 0, 14, 0, 45]
List(0 in end):   [2, 4, 6, 8, 10, 12, 14, 45, 0, 0, 0, 0, 0, 0, 0]
List(0 in begin): [0, 0, 0, 0, 0, 0, 0, 2, 4, 6, 8, 10, 12, 14, 45]
```

Program 9.7: WAP to find the dimension of a matrix.

```
#WAP to find dimension of the matrix
def mat_dim(lst):
    Nrow = len(lst)
    Ncol = len(lst[0])
    return Nrow,Ncol
def print_mat(lst):
    print("Matrix:")
    for a in lst:
        print("\t",a)

lst = [[1,2,3],[2,4,6], [10,20,30]]
print_mat(lst)
print("Matrix Dimension", mat_dim(lst))
lst = [[11, 22],[55, 66]]
print_mat(lst)
print("Matrix Dimension", mat_dim(lst))
```

Output

```
Matrix:
         [1, 2, 3]
         [2, 4, 6]
         [10, 20, 30]
Matrix Dimension (3, 3)
Matrix:
         [11, 22]
         [55, 66]
Matrix Dimension (2, 2)
```

Program 9.8: WAP to pair up two consecutive elements of a list.

```
#WAP to pair up two consecutive elements of a given list
def pair_list(lst):
    pLst = [[lst[i], lst[i+1]] for i in range(0,len(lst)-1,2)]
    return pLst
lst =  [1,2,3,4,5,6]
print("Original Lists:", lst)
print("Paired up List:", pair_list(lst))

lst =  ["Love", "Yourself", "Smile", "Please", "Show", "Gratitude"]
print("\nOriginal Lists:", lst)
print("\nPaired up List:", pair_list(lst))
```

Output

```
Original Lists: [1, 2, 3, 4, 5, 6]
Paired up List: [[1, 2], [3, 4], [5, 6]]
```

```
Original Lists: ['Love', 'Yourself', 'Smile', 'Please', 'Show', 'Gratitude']

Paired up List: [['Love', 'Yourself'], ['Smile', 'Please'], ['Show', 'Gratitude'
]]
```

Program 9.9: WAP to create a list of integers, float and string from a list of mixed values.

```
#WAP to create a list of integers, float ans string from a list of mixed values
def iLst(lst):
    return [lst for lst in lst if isinstance(lst, int)]
def fLst(lst):
    return [lst for lst in lst if isinstance(lst, float)]
lst = [3.14, 2.2, 2, 3, -3, 3.0, "Mixed", 0, "Int"]
def sLst(lst):
    return [lst for lst in lst if isinstance(lst, str)]
lst = [3.14, 2.2, 2, 3, -3, 3.0, "Mixed", 0, "Int"]
print("List:", lst, "\n")
print("Integer List:", iLst(lst))
print("Float List:", fLst(lst))
print("String List:", sLst(lst))
```

Output

```
List: [3.14, 2.2, 2, 3, -3, 3.0, 'Mixed', 0, 'Int']

Integer List: [2, 3, -3, 0]
Float List: [3.14, 2.2, 3.0]
String List: ['Mixed', 'Int']
```

Program 9.10: WAP to reverse a sentence.

```
#WAP to reverse sentence
def revSen(st):
    wd = st.split(' ')
    rev_st = ' '.join(reversed(wd))
    return rev_st
#if __name__ == "__main__":
s = input("Enter String:")
print(revSen(s))
```

Output

```
Enter String:Smile makes you look Beautiful
Beautiful look you makes Smile
```

```
Enter String:Green World
World Green
```

Program 9.11: WAP to count the total characters, non-space characters and space characters in a string.

```
s1 = 'Gratitude is the key     to    success'
print("String: " + str(s1))
ans1 = sum(not ch.isspace() for ch in s1)
ans2 = sum(ch.isspace() for ch in s1)
print("Total character:", len(s1))
print("No. of non-Space characters: " + str(ans1))
print("No. of space characters: " + str(ans2))
```

```
String: Gratitude is the key     to    success
Total character: 38
No. of non-Space characters: 26
No. of space characters: 12
```

Program 9.12: Write a program using function that checks whether an element occurs in a list.

```
def create_list():
    c = 1
    L1 = []
    while c:
      L1 = L1 + [input("Enter elements for list ")]
      c = input("Do you want to continue(N/n/no) ")
      if c == "N" or c == "n" or c == "no":
         c = 0
      print ("The list is=", L1)
    return(L1)
def check_elem(L1):
   c = 1
   while c:
      print(input("Enter an element to search ") in L1)
      c = input("Do you want to search another element(N/n/no) ")
      if c == "N" or c == "n" or c == "no":
         c = 0
def main():
   L1 = create_list()
   check_elem(L1)

if __name__ =='__main__':
   main()
```

Output

```
Enter elements for list 3
Do you want to continue(N/n/no) y
The list is= ['3']
Enter elements for list 4
Do you want to continue(N/n/no) y
The list is= ['3', '4']
Enter elements for list 6
Do you want to continue(N/n/no) y
The list is= ['3', '4', '6']
Enter elements for list 8
Do you want to continue(N/n/no) y
The list is= ['3', '4', '6', '8']
Enter elements for list g
Do you want to continue(N/n/no) y
The list is= ['3', '4', '6', '8', 'g']
Enter elements for list jk
Do you want to continue(N/n/no) n
The list is= ['3', '4', '6', '8', 'g', 'jk']
Enter an element to search 4
True
Do you want to search another element(N/n/no) y
Enter an element to search gh
False
Do you want to search another element(N/n/no) y
Enter an element to search jk
True
Do you want to search another element(N/n/no) n
>>>
```

Program 9.13: Write a program using three functions that computes the sum of the numbers in a list: using a `for` loop, a `while` loop and recursion.

```
def create_list():
    c, L1 = 1, []
    while c:
      L1 = L1 + [int(input("Enter elements for list "))]
      c = input("Do you want to continue(N/n/no) ")
      if c == "N" or c == "n" or c == "no":
          c = 0
      print ("The list is=", L1)
    return(L1)
```

```
def sum_forloop(L1):
    sum = 0
    for i in L1:
        sum += i
    return(sum)

def sum_whileloop(L1):
    sum, i = 0, 0
    while (i <len(L1)):
        sum += L1[i]
        i= i + 1
    return(sum)

def sum_recursion(L1, n):
    if n== 0:
      return 0
    else:
        return L1[n-1] + sum_recursion(L1, n-1)
```

```
def main():
    L1 = create_list()
    print("Sum of elements using for loop is = ", sum_forloop(L1))
    print("Sum of elements using while loop is = ", sum_whileloop(L1))
    print("Sum of elements using recursion is = ", sum_recursion(L1, len(L1)))

if __name__ == '__main__':
    main()
```

Output

```
Enter elements for list 1
Do you want to continue(N/n/no) y
The list is= [1]
Enter elements for list 2
Do you want to continue(N/n/no) y
The list is= [1, 2]
Enter elements for list 3
Do you want to continue(N/n/no) y
The list is= [1, 2, 3]
Enter elements for list 6
Do you want to continue(N/n/no) y
The list is= [1, 2, 3, 6]
Enter elements for list 9
Do you want to continue(N/n/no) y
The list is= [1, 2, 3, 6, 9]
Enter elements for list 20
Do you want to continue(N/n/no) n
The list is= [1, 2, 3, 6, 9, 20]
Sum of elements using for loop is =  41
Sum of elements using while loop is =  41
Sum of elements using recursion is =  41
>>>
```

Summary

- Lists are an ordered collection of items or elements.
- The items in a list need not be of the same type.
- A list defined within another list is a nested list.
- Lists are mutable.
- To access elements of a list, indexing, slicing, and stride with slicing are used.
- Positive indexing allows access of list from left to right, starting from 0. Negative indexing allows access to list starting from right to left, starting with index −1.
- Slicing allows specifying start and end index to get sublist from a list.
- Stride with slicing allows skipping of elements in between, start and end slice.
- There are several built-in methods like `append()` and `count()` that are used with lists.
- List is mutable, so elements can be added to list, an element can be updated and elements can be deleted from list.
- The `in` operator is used for searching an element in a list or tuple.
- A clone of list creates a separate copy of the list. Any update on copy does not update the original list.
- Shallow copy does not clone a nested list. Deep copy clones nested lists.
- Repetition of list or tuple is done using "*" operator.
- `Len()`, `min()`, `max()` and `sum()` are some list functions in Python.
- List comprehension applies a transformation to an existing list and creates a new list.
- Tuples are an ordered collection of objects created in parenthesis ().
- Like lists, elements of tuple are accessed using indexing, slicing and stride with slicing.
- Tuples are immutable, so elements cannot be added, deleted or updated.
- `Count()` and `index()` are built-in tuple methods.
- The + operator is used to concatenate lists and tuples.
- Tuple assignment allows assigning more than one variable in a single statement.
- `Len()`, `min()`, `max()`, `tuple(list)` are some functions that operate on tuples.

Keywords

Lists	TypeError	Copy list
Elements	IndexError	Clone list
Items	Stride with slicing [::]	Deep copy list
Mutable lists	Built-in list methods	List method
Enumeration	Concatenate (+)	Length of list
Indexing []	Repeat (*)	List comprehension
Positive indexing	Search (`in, not in`)	Tuple
Negative indexing	Traverse	Immutable tuples
Slicing	Update list	Built-in tuple methods
Slicing operator [:]	Delete list element	Delete tuple (`del`)
Range Indexing	Delete list (`del`)	Tuple assignment

Programming Language Keywords

```
copy()              list.extend(list)        min(list)
deepcopy()          list.index(x)            min(tuple)
len(list)           list.insert(index, x)    sum(list)
len(tuple)          list.remove(x)           tuple(list)
list()              list.reverse()           tuple.count(x)
list.append(x)      list.sort() max(list)    tuple.index(x)
list.count(x)       max(tuple)
```

Assessment

A.1 Bloom Level: Knowledge/Remember

Review Questions

1. Define – List, Nested list.
2. Is list mutable?
3. How many elements are there in an empty list?
4. Give an example of nested list.
5. List the operator used in searching for an element in a list.
6. A `copy()` is to shallow copy as ________ is to `deepcopy()`.
7. Name three built-in methods for lists and explain their functions.
8. Define a tuple.
9. Is tuple mutable?
10. Name two built-in methods for tuple.

Fill in the Blanks

1. ________and ________ are ordered collection of objects.
2. An empty list has ______ items.
3. A list defined within another list is called a ________ list.
4. From left to right, list enumeration starts with index _____.
5. From right to left, list enumeration starts with index ______.
6. TypeError in list accessing arises if the index is not of type ________.
7. If index for list is not in range, an error __________ is thrown.
8. A list can be cloned using ______ operator.
9. If we want to modify a list and also keep a copy of the original list, then we must _____ the list.
10. ______ copy will not clone the nested lists.
11. ______ copy will clone the nested lists.
12. The syntax – `x for x in iterable` is for ______________.
13. ___________ error is reported if number of variables on left side and right side is not same in tuple assignment.

State True/False

1. The index for accessing list can be of any data type.
2. The 'not in' operator gives False if element is not in the list.
3. List comprehension uses mathematical set notation form.
4. In a tuple assignment, each value on the right is assigned to a variable on the left.
5. The `copy()` method makes a clone.
6. The `deepcopy()` method does not make a clone.
7. Tuple is an ordered collection of objects.
8. For concatenation of two tuples, the * operator can be used.
9. For deleting a tuple, the – operator is used.
10. Data written using tuple remains write-protected.

A.2 Bloom Level: Comprehend/Understand

Review Questions

1. "Lists are mutable." Explain the statement.
2. Describe the following ways of accessing elements of list.
   (i) Index (ii) Slice
   (iii) Stride with slice
3. Explain indexing with example. When does IndexError arise?
4. Describe the meaning of the following methods of list:
   `append(), count(), extend(), index(), insert(), remove(), reverse(0), sort(), pop()`
5. Explain the following functions of a list:
   `Len(), min(), max(), sum()`
6. What is the purpose of list comprehension?
7. What is the advantage of using list comprehension?
8. "Tuples are read only." Explain the statement.
9. What are the advantages of tuple over list?
10. Describe the meaning of the following methods of tuple: `count()`, `index()`
11. What is the purpose of slicing? Explain with an example.

A.3 Bloom Level: Application/Apply

Review Question

1. Find errors, and correct the code:
   (a)

```
a=[1,2,3,4,5, 6]
a[::2]=10,20,30,40,50
print(a)
```

   (b) This is the code to swap two tuples. Find the error.

```
T1 = (11, 22)
T2 = (99, 88)
T1, T2 == T2, T1
print("T1: ",T1)
print("T2: ", T2)
```

   (c) This is the code to print[4, 3, 2] in output. Find the error.

```
a=[1,2,3,4,5]
print(a[-3:0:-1])
```

(d) Code to concatenate elements of two tuples.

```
a = [7, 14]
b = (21, 27)
[print(x) for x in [a + b]]
```

Fill in the Blanks

1. For a list L1, the L1[2:5] gives _____ number of items.
2. Let L1 = [1, 2, 3] and L2 = [4, 5], L1 + L2 will give ___________.
3. Let L1 = [1, 2, 3, 4, 5], after del L1[2], the list will be ___________.
4. The output of ["a", "b"] * 2 is _________.
5. If L1=["a", "b", "c"], len(L1) is _________.
6. If L1 = ["a", "b", "A", "B"], min(L1) is ________.
7. If L1 = ["a", "b", "A", "B"], max(L1) is ________.
8. If L1 = ["a", "b", "A", "B"], sum(L1) is ________.
9. If T1 = (1, 2, 1, 2, 3, 1), then T1.count(1) is _______.
10. If x = 5, y=6, after x, y = y, x the values of x is ______ and y is ______.

State True/False

1. ["a", "b", 1, 2] cannot be stored in a list as the items are not of same type.
2. [2, 5] > [1. 6] is True.
3. ["a", "e"] > ["a", "u"] is True.
4. For any list L, L[4:6] and L[4:6:1] will give same output.
5. Let L1 = [1, 2, 3], L1 + 4 will give [1, 2, 3, 4].
6. If L1 = [1, 2, 3], del L1 will delete the list L1.
7. If L1 = [1, 2, 3], del L1[1] or remove[1] will give same output.
8. If L1 = [1, 2, 3], 3 *in* L1 gives result True.
9. L1 and L2 are two lists. After executing L1 = L2, the id of L1 and the id of L2 will be same.
10. L1 and L2 are two lists. After executing L1 = L2[:], the id of L1 and the id of L2 will be same.
11. Let L1= [1, 2, 3]; after L2 = L1 and L2 = L1[:], the content of list L2 is same as L1.
12. If L2 = list(L1), the id of L2 and L1 are same.
13. If L1 = ["a", "b', "c", "D"], min(L1) is "D"
14. T1 = 2, 5 is an incorrect definition of tuple.
15. ("d)>("D") will return True
16. Let T1 = (1, 2, 3, 4, 5); after T1[2] =6, T1 will be (1, 2, 6, 4, 5)
17. Tuple (L2), where L2 is a list, will convert L2 into tuple.

Multiple Choice Questions (MCQ)

Answer Questions 1–10 for the list L1 = [["a", 1], ["b", 2], ["c", 3], "d"]

1. The number of elements in L1 is ______.
   (i) 5 (ii) 4
   (iii) 7 (iv) 8

2. The index of "d" in L1 is _____.
   (i) 3 (ii) 4
   (iii) –2 (iv) 6

3. The element at index –2, i.e., L[–2] is ______.
   (i) ["b", 2] (ii) "d"
   (iii) ["c", 3] (iv) 3

4. L[2] is ______.
   (i) ["b", 2] (ii) ["c", 3]
   (iii) "b" (iv) "c", 3

5. L[1:2] is ______.
   (i) ["a", 1]
   (ii) [["b", 2], ["c", 3]]
   (iii) ["b", 2]
   (iv) [1, "b"]

6. L[-3:-1] gives ______.
   (i) ["b", 2]
   (ii) [["b", 2], ["c", 3]]
   (iii) [["b", 2], ["c", 3], "d"]
   (iv) [["c", 3], "d"]

7. L[2:0] gives ______.
   (i) Error
   (ii) Null list
   (iii) [["c", 3], ["b", 2], ["a", 1]]
   (iv) [["a", 1], ["b", 2], ["c", 3]]

8. L[5] gives ______.
   (i) Null list (ii) IndexError
   (iii) TypeError (iv) No output

9. L[1:10] gives ______.
   (i) Null list
   (ii) IndexError
   (iii) [["b", 2], ["c", 3], "d"]
   (iv) [["a", 1], ["b", 2], ["c", 3], "d"]

10. L[3::-2] gives ______.
    (i) ["d", ["b", 2]] (ii) Error
    (iii) ["d"] (iv) ["d", ["c", 3]]

11. Let L1 = [1, 5, 10, 15, 20]. L1.index(15) is _____.
    (i) 4 (ii) 3
    (iii) –5 (iv) –4

12. Let L1 = [1, 5, 10, 15, 20]. L1.count(1) is _____.
    (i) 1 (ii) 2
    (iii) 3 (iv) 4

Answer Questions 13–15 for the list L1 = ["a", "e", "i"] and L2 = ["o", "u"]

13. L1.append(L2) gives _____.
    (i) [["a", "e", "i"] ["o", "u"]]
    (ii) ["a", "e", "i", "o", "u"]
    (iii) ["a", "e", "i",["o", "u"]]
    (iv) [["a", "e", "i"], "o", "u"]

14. L1.extend(L2) gives _____.
    (i) [["a", "e", "i"] ["o", "u"]]
    (ii) ["a", "e", "i", "o", "u"]
    (iii) ["a", "e", "i",["o", "u"]]
    (iv) [["a", "e", "i"], "o", "u"]

15. If L1[1] = "u", then L1 will be _____.
    (i) ["a", "e", "u", "i"]
    (ii) ["a", "u", "e", "i"]
    (iii) ["a", "u", "i"]
    (iv) Error

Answer Questions 16–17 for the list L1 = ["a", "b", ["c", "d"]]

16. If L2 = deepcopy[L1]
    L2[2][1] = "e"
    The list L1 is _____.
    (i) ["a", "b", ["c", "d"]]
    (ii) ["a", "b", ["c", "e"]]
    (iii) Error
    (iv) ["a", "b", ["c", "d"], "e"]

17. If L2 = copy[L1]
L2[2][1] = "e"
The list L1 is ____.
   (i) ["a", "b", ["c", "d"]]
   (ii) ["a", "b", ["c", "e"]]
   (iii) Error
   (iv) ["a", "b", ["c", "d"], "e"]

18. If T1 = [1, 2, 1, 2, 3, 1], L1.index(1) is ____.
   (i) 0
   (ii) 2
   (iii) 0, 2, 5
   (iv) -1

A.4 Bloom Level: Analyze

1. Explain the difference between the following:
   (i) `del()` and `remove()`
   (ii) `in` and `not in`
   (iii) Copy list and Clone list
   (iv) Shallow copy and Deep copy
   (v) Mutable and Immutable
   (vi) List and Tuple
   (vii) L2 = L1 and L2 = L1[:] if L1 and L2 are lists.

2. Explain the difference between append list and extend list.

3. Analyze the following code. Identify the error in the given code. How can you correct the error?

```
T1 = (1,) * 3
print(T1)
T1[0] = 2
print(T1)
```

4. Analyze the following code. What is the output? Justify.

```
T1 = ((1, 2),) * 5
print(len(T1))
```

5. Analyze the difference in L1, L2 and L3. What is the output? Justify.

```
L1= ["Parrot", "Pigeon", "Peacock", "Parakeet"]
L2 = L1
L3=L1[:]

L2[0] = "Sparrow"
L3[1] = "SkyLark"
print(L1, "\n", L2, "\n", L3)
```

6. Analyze the following code. Is the output shown here correct? Justify your answer.

```
T1 = (1, 2, 3, 4, 5)
T1[1] = 10
print(T1)
```

```
(1, 10, 2, 3, 4, 5)
```

7. Differentiate and analyze the output, with justification.

(i)

(a)

```
T1 = (11, [22, 33], 44, 55)
print(id(T1))
T1[1][0] = 222
print(id(T1))
print(T1)
```

(b)

```
T1 = (11, (22, 33), 44, 55)
print(id(T1))
T1[1][0] = 222
print(id(T1))
print(T1)
```

(ii)

(a)

```
a = 'a', 'b'
print(type(a))
b = ('a', 'b')
print (a == b)
```

(b)

```
a='a'
print(type(a))
b = ('a', 'b')
print (a == b)
```

(iii)

(a)

```
L1 = []
L1.append([1, [2, 3], 4])
L1.extend([7, 8, 9])
print(L1)
print(L1[0][1][1])
print( L1[2])
print("sum:", L1[0][1][1] + L1[2])
```

(b)
```
L1 = [11, 22]
L1.append([1, [2, 3], 4])
L1.extend([7, 8, 9])
print(L1)
print(L1[2][1][1])
print( L1[2])
print(L1[2][1][1] + L1[2])
```

A.5 Bloom Level: Evaluate

1. Evaluate the following code. (i) Which of the two options give the same output? (ii) What is the output of the same options? (iii) How does the output of the other two options differ from the same output?

```
T1 = (22, 33, 44, 55, 66)
```

(a)
```
print(T1[:-2])
```
(b)
```
print(T1[0:4])
```
(c)
```
print(T1[0:3])
```
(d)
```
print(T1[-4:])
```

2. Evaluate the code. (i) What is the task performed? (2) What is the output?

(a)
```
T1 = (10, 11, 12, 13, 14, 15)
print(T1[::-1])
```

(b)
```
T1 = (101, 201, 301, 401, 501)
x1, x2, x3, x4, x5 = T1
print(x1)
print(x2)
print(x3)
print(x4)
print(x5)
```

(c)
```
#What is the type of the output
T1 = ("Blessing", [11, 22, 33], (15, 25, 35, 45))
print(T1[0], type(T1[0]))
print(T1[1][1], type(T1[1][1]))
print(T1[1], type(T1[1]))
print(T1[2], type(T1[2]))
```

3. Evaluate the code for the following.
(i) Identify the task performed.
(ii) Find the output.

(a)
```
tuple1 = (11, 22, 33, 44, 55, 66)
tuple2 = tuple1[3:-1]
print(tuple2)
```

(b)
```
T1 = (25, 35, 25, 45, 25, 55, 25)
print(T1.count(25))
```

(c)
```
T1 = ("World", [10, 20], (11, 22), (3, 6, 9))
print(T1[2][1])
```

(d)
```
T1 = (50, )
print(type(T1))
print(T1)

T1 = (50)
print(type(T1))
print(T1)
```

A.6 Bloom Level: Create/Synthesize

Programming Assignment

Apply formatting, wherever possible.

1. WAP to interchange the first and second last element of a list.
2. WAP to check if an element exists in a list.
3. WAP to reverse a list.
4. WAP to find the sum of elements in a list.
5. WAP to check if a list is empty or not.
6. WAP that takes two lists and returns True if they have at least one common member.
7. WAP to shuffle and print a specified list. (**Hint**: Use from random import shuffle, `shuffle(list)`)
8. WAP to check whether a list contains a sublist.
9. WAP to compute the difference between two lists. (**Hint**: Use from collections import `Counter, counter()`)
10. WAP to convert a list of characters into a string.
11. WAP to remove duplicates from a list of lists. (**Hint**: Use `itertools.groupby()`)
12. WAP to find all tuples having *k* elements, from a list of tuple.
13. WAP to sort a list of tuples.
14. WAP to convert a tuple to a string.
15. WAP to remove empty tuples from a list of tuples.
16. WAP to convert a string to a tuple.
17. Convert Celsius to Fahrenheit using list comprehension.
18. Evaluate x**2 + y**2 = z**2 using list comprehension for x, y, z in range 20.
19. Using list comprehension, compare two lists. If list is not equal, combine the elements of the list.
20. Using list comprehension, do the following:
    (i) Create list with values doubled.
    (ii) Print only positive values in list.
    (iii) Apply function `round()` to all elements of float list.
    (iv) Create tuple, (x, x**2) for integers 1 to 10.

ANSWERS

A1. Bloom Level: Knowledge/Remember

Fill in the Blanks

1. List, Tuple	2. Zero	3. Nested	4. 0
5. -1	6. Integer	7. Indexerror	8. Slice
9. Clone	10. Shallow	11. Deep	
12. List comprehension	13. Value	14.	15.
			16.

True/False

1. False	2. False	3. True	4. False	5. False	6. False	7. True	8. False
9. False	10. True	11.	12.				

A3. Bloom Level: Apply

Review Question

1. (a) `ValueError: attempt to assign sequence of size 5 to extended slice of size`

   (b) `== sign instead of =`

   (c) Error. It prints [3, 2]. Correct `print(a[3:0:-1])`

   (d) `cannot concatenate list to tuple`

Fill in the Blanks

1. 3	**2.** [1, 2, 3, 4, 5]	**3.** [1, 2, 4, 5]	**4.** ["a", "b", "a", "b"]
5. 3	**6.** 'A'	**7.** 'b'	**8.** Typeerror or error
9. 3	**10.** 6, 5	**11.**	**12.**

True/False

1. False	**2.** True	**3.** False	**4.** True	**5.** False	**6.** True	**7.** True	**8.** True
9. True	**10.** False	**11.** True	**12.** False	**13.** True	**14.** False	**15.** True	**16.** False
17. True							

Multiple Choice Questions (MCQ)

1. (ii)	**2.** (i)	**3.** (iii)	**4.** (ii)	**5.** (iii)	**6.** (ii)	**7.** (ii)	**8.** (ii)
9. (iii)	**10.** (i)	**11.** (ii)	**12.** (i)	**13.** (iii)	**14.** (ii)	**15.** (iii)	**16.** (i)
17. (ii)	**18.** (i)						

A4. Bloom Level: Analyze

3. `TypeError: 'tuple' object does not support item assignment`

4. `5`

5.
```
['Sparrow', 'Pigeon', 'Peacock', 'Parakeet']
 ['Sparrow', 'Pigeon', 'Peacock', 'Parakeet']
 ['Parrot', 'SkyLark', 'Peacock', 'Parakeet']
```

6. No. `TypeError: 'tuple' object does not support item assignment`

7. (i)
```
2689899173104
2689899173104
(11, [222, 33], 44, 55)
```

```
2689899173184
Traceback (most recent call last):
  File "C:/Users/Anita Goel/Desktop/Python/Chapter 9 Lists/
ne 12, in <module>
    T1[1][0] = 222
TypeError: 'tuple' object does not support item assignment
```

(ii)

```
<class 'tuple'>
True
```

```
<class 'str'>
False
```

```
[[1, [2, 3], 4], 7, 8, 9]
3
8
sum: 11
```

(iii)

```
[11, 22, [1, [2, 3], 4], 7, 8, 9]
3
[1, [2, 3], 4]
Traceback (most recent call last):
  File "C:/Users/Anita Goel/Desktop/Python/Chapter 9 Lists/List
ne 44, in <module>
    print(L1[2][1][1] + L1[2])
TypeError: unsupported operand type(s) for +: 'int' and 'list'
```

A5. Bloom Level: Evaluate

1. 1,3

```
(22, 33, 44)
(22, 33, 44, 55)
(22, 33, 44)
(33, 44, 55, 66)
```

2. (a) Reverse the elements of the tuple.

```
(15, 14, 13, 12, 11, 10)
```

(b)

```
101
201
301
401
501
```

(c)

```
Blessing <class 'str'>
22 <class 'int'>
[11, 22, 33] <class 'list'>
(15, 25, 35, 45) <class 'tuple'>
```

The tuple T1 is unpacked into five variables.

3. (a)

```
Copy element 44 into a new tuple===========(44, 55)
```

```
(44, 55)
```

(b)

```
#Counts the number of occurrences of item 25 from a tuple 4
```

```
4
```

(c)

```
#Which element does it access- value 22 from the following tuple.
```

```
22
```

(d)

```
#Create a tuple with single item 50- <class 'tuple'>(50,)
```

```
#<class 'int'>50
```

```
<class 'tuple'>
(50,)
<class 'int'>
50
```

```
<class 'tuple'>
(50,)
<class 'int'>
50
False
(2, 3)
Yourself
```

CHAPTER

10 Set and Dictionary

Contents

10.1 Introduction

The earlier chapters discussed the three sequence types – string, list and tuple. A key feature of the sequence type is that it is an ordered collection of objects. In this chapter, we shall discuss the two compound types – set and dictionary. Set data type and dictionary data type are an unordered collection of objects, i.e., there is no order among the objects. Therefore, set and dictionary are different from sequence type. The sets in Python work like mathematical sets; the operations that can be performed on mathematical sets can be performed on set data type. Dictionary is different from other data types. Dictionary is a mapping type and it is indexed by keys. It is a key-value pair.

In this chapter, we discuss the set and dictionary in Python. The ways of accessing the elements, the operations that can be performed on them and built-in methods and functions are discussed here.

Learning Outcomes of this chapter

After completion of the chapter, the learner will be able to:

- Understand the set type and mapping type
- Perform basic operations on Set and Dictionary
- Use set and dictionary in programs
- Use operators for performing operations on set and dictionary
- Formulate programs using built-in set and dictionary type methods
- Develop programs based on the concepts discussed.

10.2 Set: An Overview

- Set is an unordered collection of objects.
- The objects are also called items or elements of the set.
- Set is created in curly brackets {}.
- The elements or items of a set are defined within the curly brackets, separated by comma. The ordering of set elements is arbitrary.

Code	Output
`Set1 = {"a", "e", "i", "o", "u"}`	`{'a', 'o', 'i', 'e', 'u'}`
`Set2 = {1, 2, 3, 4, 5}`	`{1, 2, 3, 4, 5}`

- The items in set need not be of the same type. This means that a set may have items that are a mix of type integer, float, string and other data types.

Code	Output
`Set1 = {"a", "b", 1.1, 2, 2.2, 3}`	`{'a', 2, 3, 'b', 1.1, 2.2}`
`Set2 = {1, 2, (1, 2, 3)}`	`{1, 2, (1, 2, 3)}`

- Set is also defined using the built-in function `set()`.
- A set may be empty. An empty set has zero items.
  - Creating an empty set with curly braces defines an empty dictionary and NOT a set.
  - To create an empty set, `set()` function is used with no arguments.

Code	Output
`a= {}` `print (type (a))`	`<class 'diet'>`
`a = set ()` `print (type (a))`	`<class 'set'>`

- Every element in a set is unique. Set does not have duplicates.
- Set can be defined from list, tuple or string using `set()` function. The set will be created with the elements of the string, tuple and list.

Code	Output
`S1 = set([1, 2, 3, 1, 2])` `print ("S1=", S1)`	`S1= {1, 2, 3}`
`S1 = set ({1, 2, 3, 1, 2 })` `print ("S1=", S1}`	`S1= {1, 2, 3}`
`S1 = set ("Grateful")` `print ("S1=", S1)`	`S1={'r','e','G','l','u','f','t','a'}`
`S1= {1, 2, 2, 3, 4, 4}`	`{1, 2, 3, 4}`

- Set is mutable. Elements can be added and removed from a set.
  - However, every element in a set is immutable, i.e., it cannot be changed.
  - Set **cannot** have mutable items like list, set or dictionary, as elements. A TypeError is reported.

  Code

```
Setl = {1, [1, 2, 3], 3, 4, 4}

print (Setl)
```

  Output

```
Traceback (most recent call last):
  File "C:/Users/Admin/Desktop/set-overview.py", line 13, in <module>
    Setl = {1, [1, 2, 3], 3, 4, 4}
TypeError: unhashable type: 'list'
```

- Sets are unordered, so indexing has no meaning. Thus, an element of a set cannot be accessed using indexing or slicing.

10.3 Built-in Set Type Methods

Python supports several built-in methods that can be used with sets. The syntax to use the methods is:

```
set.method()
```

Table 10.1 lists the built-in set methods along with their description.

Table 10.1 Built-in Set methods

	Python Set Methods	
S. No	**Method**	**Description**
1	`add()`	Adds one element to the set
2	`clear()`	Removes all elements from the set
3	`copy()`	Returns shallow copy of the set
4	`difference()`	Returns difference of two or more sets as a new set
5	`difference_update()`	Removes all elements of another set from this set
6	`discard()`	Removes element from a set if it is a member. (It does nothing if the element is not in the set)
7	`intersection()`	Returns intersection of two sets as a new set
8	`intersection_update()`	Updates set with intersection of itself and another
9	`isdisjoint()`	Returns True if two sets have null intersection
10	`issubset()`	Returns True if another set contains this set
11	`issuperset()`	Returns True if this set contains another set
12	`pop()`	Removes and returns arbitrary set element. Raises KeyError if set is empty
13	`remove()`	Removes element from the set. If element is not a member, it raises KeyError
14	`symmetric_difference()`	Returns symmetric difference of two sets as a new set
15	`symmetric_difference_update()`	Updates set with symmetric difference of itself and another
16	`union()`	Returns union of sets in a new set
17	`update()`	Updates set with union of itself and others

The usage of the built-in methods is discussed in the next section.

10.4 Basic Operations on Sets: Sets are Mutable

- Sets are mutable; elements can be added or deleted from set.
- We explain the following operations on sets:
  - Add, Delete and Search element
  - Copy set
  - Set mathematical operations – union, intersection etc.
  - Traverse Set and other operations

10.4.1 Add Element

- Only immutable elements can be added to the set.
- To add elements to set, `add()` and `update()` methods are used.
- `add()` adds a single element to the set.
  - If an already existing element is added, there is no effect.
  - If two or more elements are added, error is raised.

Example 10.1: (a) Add an element in a set (b) Output

```
S1 = {"Violet", "Indigo", "Blue", "Green"}
print("S1 =", S1)
S1.add("Yellow")
print("S1 - add()=", S1)
S1.add("Blue")
print("S1 - add() duplicate =", S1)
S1.add("Orange", "Red")
print("S1 - add() Two items =", S1)
```

(a)

```
S1 = {'Indigo', 'Green', 'Blue', 'Violet'}
S1 - add()= {'Yellow', 'Green', 'Blue', 'Violet', 'Indigo'}
S1 - add() duplicate = {'Yellow', 'Green', 'Blue', 'Violet', 'Indigo'}
Traceback (most recent call last):
  File "C:/Users/Admin/Desktop/set-overview.py", line 37, in <module>
    S1.add("Orange", "Red")
TypeError: add() takes exactly one argument (2 given)
```

(b)

- `update()` adds multiple elements to the set.
  - The iterables – list, tuple and string, and other sets can be argument to `update()`.
  - It takes each element from the iterable and adds to the set.
  - If an already existing element is added, there is no effect.

Example 10.2: (a) Using `update()` on a set (b) Output

```
S1 = {"Violet", "Blue"}
print("S1 =", S1)
S1.update("Pink")
print("S1-update()String=", S1)
S1.update(["Orange", "Red"])
print("S1-update()List =", S1)
S1.update(("Yellow", "Magenta"))
print("S1-update()Tuple =", S1)
```

(a)

```
S1 = {'Violet', 'Blue'}
S1-update()String= {'k', 'P', 'Blue', 'Violet', 'n', 'i'}
S1-update()List = {'k', 'P', 'Blue', 'Orange', 'Violet', 'n', 'i', 'Red'}
S1-update()Tuple = {'k', 'P', 'Blue', 'Orange', 'Violet', 'Yellow', 'n', '
Magenta', 'i', 'Red'}
```

(b)

10.4.2 Delete Elements

- To delete elements from set, `discard()`, `remove()`, `clear()` and `pop()` methods are used.
- `discard()` deletes an element if it exists. If the element does not exist, `discard()` will not do anything.

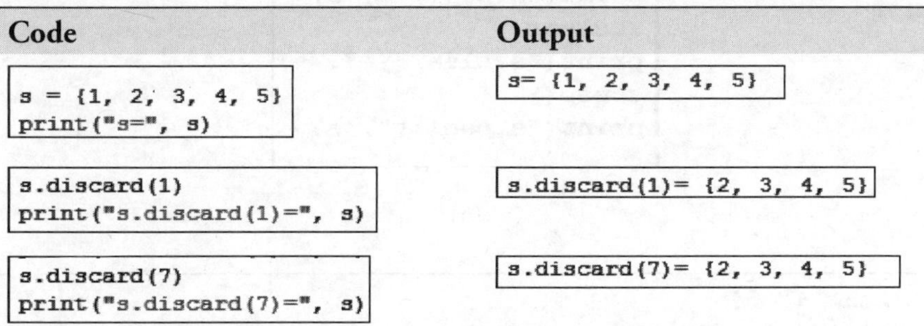

Code	Output
`s = {1, 2, 3, 4, 5}` `print("s=", s)`	`s= {1, 2, 3, 4, 5}`
`s.discard(1)` `print("s.discard(1)=", s)`	`s.discard(1)= {2, 3, 4, 5}`
`s.discard(7)` `print("s.discard(7)=", s)`	`s.discard(7)= {2, 3, 4, 5}`

- `remove()` deletes an element if it exists. If element does not exist, `remove()` will raise KeyError.

Example 10.3: (a) Using `remove()` on a set (b) Output

```
s = {1, 2, 3, 4, 5}
print("s =", s)
s.remove(1)
print("s.remove(1)=", s)
s.remove(7)
print("s.remove(7)=", s)
```

(a)

```
s = {1, 2, 3, 4, 5}
s.remove(1)= {2, 3, 4, 5}
Traceback (most recent call last):
  File "C:/Users/Admin/Desktop/set-overview.py", line 72, in <module>
    s.remove(7)
KeyError: 7
```

(b)

- `clear()` deletes all elements from the set.

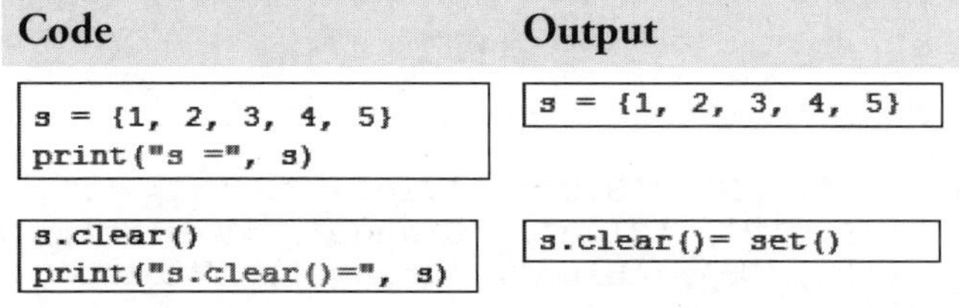

Code	Output
`s = {1, 2, 3, 4, 5}` `print("s =", s)`	`s = {1, 2, 3, 4, 5}`
`s.clear()` `print("s.clear()=", s)`	`s.clear()= set()`

- `pop()` deletes an arbitrary element from the set, since set is unordered. If set is empty, `pop()` will raise KeyError.

Example 10.4: (a) Using `pop()` on a set (b) Output

```
s = {1, 2, 3, 4, 5}
print("s =", s)
s.pop()
print("s.pop()=", s)
s.clear()
print("s.clear()=", s)
s.pop()
print("s.pop()=", s)
```

(a)

```
s = {1, 2, 3, 4, 5}
s.pop()= {2, 3, 4, 5}
s.clear()= set()
Traceback (most recent call last):
  File "C:/Users/Admin/Desktop/set-overview.py", line 74, in <module>
    s.pop()
KeyError: 'pop from an empty set'
```

(b)

10.4.3 Search Element (in) Operator

- The in operator is used to search for elements in a set.
- The syntax of in operator is:
  `element in set_name`
- If element is present in set, True is returned; else False is returned. For example,

Code	Output
`s = {1, 2, 3, 4, 5}` `print("s = ", s)`	`s = {1, 2, 3, 4, 5}`
`print("2 in s =", 2 in s)`	`2 in s = True`
`print("8 in s =", 8 in s)`	`8 in s = False`

- The not in operator is used to check if element is not in set. The syntax of not in operator is:
  `element not in set_name`
- If element is not in set, True is returned; else False is returned. For example,

Code	Output
`s = {1, 2, 3, 4, 5}` `print("s = ", s)`	`s = {1, 2, 3, 4, 5}`
`print("2 not in s =", 2 not in s)`	`2 not in s = False`
`print("8 not in s =", 8 not in s)`	`8 not in s = True`

10.4.4 Copy Set

- A set is copied using assignment statement, copy() and set() method.
- **Assignment operator** *(=)* creates a new pointer to the same set. So, any change in set will be reflected in both original and assigned set.

Example 10.5: (a) Using assignment on a set (b) Output

```
s = {1, 2, 3, 4, 5}
print("s =", s)
sassign = s
print("sAssign =", sassign)
s.add(7)
print("s after add =", s)
print("sAssign after add=", sassign)
```

(a)

```
s = {1, 2, 3, 4, 5}
sAssign = {1, 2, 3, 4, 5}
s after add = {1, 2, 3, 4, 5, 7}
sAssign after add= {1, 2, 3, 4, 5, 7}
```

(b)

- `copy()` makes a shallow copy. Meaning thereby that it will copy the set. So, any change in original set will be reflected in only the original set but not in the copied set. Also, any change in copied set will be reflected only in the copied set but not in the original set.

Example 10.6: (a) Using `copy()` to make shallow copy (b) Output

```
s = {1, 2, 3, 4, 5}
print("s =", s)
scopy = s.copy()
print("sCopy =", scopy)
s.add(7)
print("s after add =", s)
print("sCopy after add=", scopy)
```

(a)

```
s = {1, 2, 3, 4, 5}
sCopy = {1, 2, 3, 4, 5}
s after add = {1, 2, 3, 4, 5, 7}
sCopy after add= {1, 2, 3, 4, 5}
```

(b)

- `set()` makes a shallow copy. Meaning thereby that it will copy the set. So, any change in original set will be reflected in only the original set but not in the copied set. Also, any change in copied set will be reflected only in the copied set but not in the original set.

Example 10.7: (a) Using `set()` to make shallow copy (b) Output

```
n = {1, 2, 3, 4, 5}
nclone = set(n)
print("Original Set:\t", n)
print("Copy Set:\t", nclone)
print("="*10, "After add element in set", "="*10)
n.add((6))
nclone.add((7))
print("Original Set-Add 6:\t",n)
print("Copy Set-Add 7:\t\t", nclone)
```

(a)

```
Original Set:     {1, 2, 3, 4, 5}
Copy Set:         {1, 2, 3, 4, 5}
========== After add element in set ==========
Original Set-Add 6:       {1, 2, 3, 4, 5, 6}
Copy Set-Add 7:           {1, 2, 3, 4, 5, 7}
```

(b)

10.4.5 Set Mathematical Operations

- Mathematical set operations like set union, intersection and difference can be performed on a set. Let us understand the set operations on the following set.

```
s = {1, 2, 3, 4, 5, 6}
s_even = {2, 4, 6, 8, 10}
s_odd = {1, 3, 5, 7, 9}
print("s =\t\t", s)
print("s_even =\t", s_even)
```

Output

```
s =              {1, 2, 3, 4, 5, 6}
s_even =         {2, 4, 6, 8, 10}
```

- **union() or pipe operator (|)** creates union of two sets. The syntax is `s1.union(s2)`.
The output is all elements that are in s1 or in s2, without duplicates.

```
print("\ns union s_even =", s.union(s_even))
print("s | s_even =\t", s |(s_even))
```

Output

```
s union s_even = {1, 2, 3, 4, 5, 6, 8, 10}
s | s_even =     {1, 2, 3, 4, 5, 6, 8, 10}
```

- **intersection() or ampersand operator (&)** creates intersection of two sets. The syntax is
`s1.intersection(s2)`.
The output is all elements that are common in s1 and s2.

```
print("\ns intersection s_even =\t", s.intersection(s_even))
print("s & s_even =\t\t", s &(s_even))
```

Output

```
s intersection s_even =   {2, 4, 6}
s & s_even =              {2, 4, 6}
```

- **`intersection_update()`** is like `intersection()` but it works like, `x = x & y`, i.e., the result of intersection is assigned to the first set.
- **`difference()` or operator `(-)`** finds the difference of two sets. The syntax is `s1.difference(s2)`.
  The output is all elements that are in s1 but not in s2.

```
print("\ns difference s_even =\t", s.difference(s_even))
print("s - s_even =\t\t", s -(s_even))
print("s - s_even - s_odd =\t", s -s_even- s_odd)
print("s =\t\t", s)
```

Output

```
s difference s_even =     {1, 3, 5}
s - s_even =              {1, 3, 5}
s - s_even - s_odd =      set()
s =                 {1, 2, 3, 4, 5, 6}
```

s does not change

- **`difference_update()`** is like `difference()` but it works like, x = x – y, i.e., the result of difference is assigned to the first set.

```
s.difference_update(s_even)
print("\ns After difference_update s_even =", s)
```

Output

```
s After difference_update s_even = {1, 3, 5}
```

s is updated

- **`symmetric_difference()`** returns elements not common in both sets. The syntax is `s1.symmetric_difference(s2)`.
  The output is all elements that are in s1 and s2 but not in both.

```
s = {1, 2, 3, 4, 5, 6}
s_even = {2, 4, 6, 8, 10}
print("\ns symmetric difference s_even =",
        s.symmetric_difference(s_even))
print("s ^ s_even =\t\t\t", s ^ s_even)
print("s =\t\t\t\t", s)
```

Output

```
s symmetric difference s_even = {1, 3, 5, 8, 10}
s ^ s_even =                    {1, 3, 5, 8, 10}
s =                             {1, 2, 3, 4, 5, 6}
```

s does not change

- **`symmetric_difference_update()`** is like `symmetric_difference()` but it works like,
`x = x ^ y`, i.e., the result of symmetric difference is assigned to the first set.
This method returns None. It updates the set with which it is called.

```
s = {1, 2, 3, 4, 5, 6}
s_even = {2, 4, 6, 8, 10}
print("\ns symmetric difference update s_even =\t",
      s.symmetric_difference_update(s_even))
print("s =\t\t\t\t", s)
```

Output

```
s symmetric difference update s_even =   None
s =                                      {1, 3, 5, 8, 10}
```

s is updated

- **`isdisjoint()`** checks if two sets have null intersection. The syntax is
`s1.isdisjoint(s2)`.
The output is True if s1 and s2 do not have any common elements; otherwise False.
An example:

```
s1 = {"a", "b", "c", "d", "e"}
s2 = {"a", "e"}
print("s1=", s1)
print("s2=", s2)
print("s1.isdisjoint(s2) =",s1.isdisjoint(s2) )
```

Output

```
s1= {'c', 'a', 'e', 'b', 'd'}
s2= {'a', 'e'}
s1.isdisjoint(s2) = False
```

- **`issubset()` or operator (<=)** checks if a set is a subset of another set. Set s1 is a subset of s2 if all elements of s1 are in s2. The syntax is
`s1.issubset(s2)`.
If s1 is subset of s2, the output is True; else False.
The operator (<=) is also used for checking the subset of a set.

The operator (<) is used for checking **proper subset** of a set. Set s1 is a proper subset of s2 if all elements of s1 are in s2, and s1 and s2 are not equal.

Example 10.8: Using < operator to check for proper subset of a set (b) Output

```
s1 = {"a", "b", "c", "d", "e"}
s2 = {"a", "e"}
print("s1=", s1)
print("s2=", s2)
print("s1.issubset(s2) =",s1.issubset(s2) )
print("s2.issubset(s1) =", s2.issubset(s1))
print("s1 < s2 =", s1<s2)
print("s1 <= s2 =", s1<=s2)
print("s2 < s1 =", s2<s1)
print("s2 <= s1 =", s2<=s1)
print()
```

(a)

```
s1= {'b', 'c', 'a', 'e', 'd'}
s2= {'a', 'e'}
s1.issubset(s2) = False
s2.issubset(s1) = True
s1 < s2 = False
s1 <= s2 = False
s2 < s1 = True
s2 <= s1 = True
```

(b)

- **`issuperset()` or operator `(>=)`** checks if a set is a superset of another set. Set s1 is a superset of s2 if all elements of s2 are in s1. The syntax is `s1.issuperset(s2)`.
  If s1 is superset of s2, output is True; else False.
  The operator (>=) is also used for checking superset of a set.
  The operator (>) is used for checking **proper superset** of a set. Set s1 is a proper superset of s2 if all elements of s2 are in s1, and s1 and s2 are not equal.

Example 10.9: Using > operator to check for proper subset of a set (b) Output

```
s1 = {"a", "b", "c", "d", "e"}
s2 = {"a", "e"}
print("s1=", s1)
print("s2=", s2)
print("s1.issuperset(s2) =",s1.issuperset(s2) )
print("s2.issuperset(s1) =", s2.issuperset(s1))
print("s1 > s2 =", s1 > s2)
print("s1 >= s2 =", s1 >= s2)
print("s2 > s1 =", s2 > s1)
print("s2 >= s1 =", s2 >= s1)
```

(a)

```
s1= {'b', 'c', 'a', 'e', 'd'}
s2= {'a', 'e'}
s1.issuperset(s2) = True
s2.issuperset(s1) = False
s1 > s2 = True
s1 >= s2 = True
s2 > s1 = False
s2 >= s1 = False
```

(b)

10.4.6 Built-in Set Function

- In addition to the built-in methods, Python defines functions that can operate on the set.
- The commonly used functions are shown below:

Function	Description
all()	Returns True if all elements of set are true (or if set is empty).
any()	Returns True if any element of set is true. If set is empty, return False.
enumerate()	Returns an enumerate object. It contains index and value of all items of set as a pair.
len()	Returns length (number of items) in set.
max()	Returns largest item in set.
min()	Returns smallest item in set.
sorted()	Returns a new sorted list from elements in set (does not sort-set itself).
sum()	Returns sum of all elements in set

- Let us see an example:

Example 10.10: Using built-in set functions (b) Output

```
S1 = {3, 27, 9, 81}
S2 = set()
print("S1=", S1)
print("S2=", S2)
print("all(S1) =", all(S1))
print("all(S2) =", all(S2))
print("any(S1) =", any(S1))
print("any(S2) =", any(S2))
print("set(enumerate(S1)) =", set(enumerate(S1)))
print("set(enumerate(S1, 10)) =", set(enumerate(S1, 10)))
print("len(S1) =", len(S1))
print("max(S1) =", max(S1))
print("min(S1) =", min(S1))
print("sorted(S1) =", sorted(S1))
print("S1 =", S1)
print("sum(S1) =", sum(S1))
```

(a)

```
S1= {27, 9, 3, 81}
S2= set()
all(S1) = True
all(S2) = True
any(S1) = True
any(S2) = False
set(enumerate(S1)) = {(0, 27), (3, 81), (2, 3), (1, 9)}
set(enumerate(S1, 10)) = {(13, 81), (11, 9), (10, 27), (12, 3)}
len(S1) = 4
max(S1) = 81
min(S1) = 3
sorted(S1) = [3, 9, 27, 81]
S1 = {27, 9, 3, 81}
sum(S1) = 120
```


(b)

10.4.7 Traverse Set

- Traversal of set is accessing each element in a set, one by one.
- Traversal is done using `for` loop.

Example 10.11: (a) Traverse a set using for-loop (b) Output

```
days = {"Mon", "Tues", "Wed", "Thurs", "Fri", "Sat", "Sun"}
print("days =", days)
for x in days:
    print(x)
```

(a)

```
days = {'Thurs', 'Mon', 'Wed', 'Fri', 'Sat', 'Tues', 'Sun'}
Thurs
Mon
Wed
Fri
Sat
Tues
Sun
```

(b)

10.5 Frozenset

- Python has another set type called frozenset.
- Set is mutable, i.e., we can add and remove elements from the set using set methods like `add()` and `remove()`.
- Frozenset is immutable. The content of frozenset cannot be altered, once created.

- Frozensets are immutable sets.
- Though we discuss dictionary in the next section, here we shall discuss frozenset for dictionary.
  - o Mutable types do not have hash value, so they cannot be used as dictionary key.
  - o Set is unhashable and thus cannot be used as dictionary key.
  - o Frozenset is hashable and thus can be used as dictionary key.
- If we try to change an element of frozenset, it gives AttributeError.

Example 10.12: (a) Using set and frozenset (b) Output

```
s1 = {1, 2,3, 4}
print(s1)
s1.add(5)
print(s1)
```

(a)

```
{1, 2, 3, 4}
{1, 2, 3, 4, 5}
```

(b)

```
s2 = frozenset([1, 2,3, 4])
print(s2)
s2.add(5)
print(s2)
```

(c)

```
frozenset({1, 2, 3, 4})
Traceback (most recent call last):
  File "C:/Users/Admin/Desktop/set function.py", line 35, in <module>
    s2.add(5)
AttributeError: 'frozenset' object has no attribute 'add'
```

(d)

10.6 Set Comprehension

- Set comprehension is similar to list comprehension. Set comprehension uses curly braces for set.
- The syntax for set comprehension is:
  `set_var = {x for x in iterable}`
  The iterable is a set.

Example 10.13: (a) Using set comprehension (b) Output

```
nsquare = {n**2 for n in range(10)}
print(nsquare)
```

(a)

```
{0, 1, 64, 4, 36, 9, 16, 49, 81, 25}
```

(b)

10.7 Dictionary: An Overview

- Dictionary is an unordered collection of objects.
- The objects are also called items or elements of dictionary.
- Dictionary is a mapping type, which means that it maps key to value.
- Each element of dictionary is a key-value pair.
- Dictionary is created by placing comma-separated elements in curly braces {}.
- An element is a key-value pair. A key is separated from value by a colon (:). In a key-value pair, the first part is key and the second is value.
  `D1 = {1: "Jan", 2: "Feb", 3: "Mar"}`
  `print(D1)` it will give

```
{1: 'Jan', 2: 'Feb', 3: 'Mar'}
```

  In D1, 1: "Jan" key is 1 and "Jan" is value.
- Key in a dictionary is unique (no duplicate key). If a key is duplicated, the last value of the key is considered.

```
D1 = {'MONTH' : 'Jan', 'MONTH' : 'Feb', 'month' : 'Mar'}
print(D1)
```


Output

```
{'MONTH': 'Feb', 'month': 'Mar'}
```

- The value in the key-value pair can repeat.

```
D1 = {'Month' : 'Jan', 'MONTH' : 'Jan', 'month' : 'Mar'}
print(D1)
```

Output

```
{'Month': 'Jan', 'MONTH': 'Jan', 'month': 'Mar'}
```

- Key must be of type immutable, i.e., string, number, tuple; value can be of any data type.
- Key is case-sensitive. For example, key 'Month', 'MONTH' and 'month' are different.

```
D1 = {'Month' : 'Jan', 'MONTH' : 'Feb', 'month' : 'Mar'}
print(D1)
```

Output

```
{'Month': 'Jan', 'MONTH': 'Feb', 'month': 'Mar'}
```

- Value in dictionary need not be of the same type. It can be a mix of integers, strings and other data types.
  D1 = {"human": "person", "Gender": ["F", "M"]}
  print(D1) it will give
  Output

```
{'human': 'person', 'Gender': ['F', 'M']}
```

- A dictionary may be empty. An empty dictionary has zero items.
  D1 = {}
  print(D1) will give

```
{}
```

- A dictionary can have another dictionary inside it. These are called nested dictionary.
  D1 = {1: {'Name': 'Preeti', 'Roll no': 10},
  2: {'Name': 'Neelima', 'Roll no': 11}}
  print(D1) will give
  Output

```
{1: {'Name': 'Preeti', 'Roll no': 10}, 2: {'Name': 'Neelima', 'Roll no': 11}}
```

- The value from the key-value pair in dictionary is accessed using the following syntax:
  dict_name[key]
  It gives the value corresponding to the key.

Example 10.14: (a) Print values in a dictionary (b) Output

```
D1 = {1 : "Jan", 2 : "Feb", 3 : "Mar"}
print("1st Month=", D1[1])
print("2nd Month=", D1[2])
print("3rd Month=", D1[3])
```

(a)

```
1st Month= Jan
2nd Month= Feb
3rd Month= Mar
```

(b)

Example 10.15: (a)Print value of a key in dictionary (b) Output

```
D1 = {'MONTH' : 'Jan', 'MONTH' : 'Feb', 'month' : 'Mar'}
print(D1['MONTH'])
```

(a)

```
Feb
```

(b)

- Dictionary can also be created using built-in function `dict()`.
  dict_name = dict()

```
season = dict()
season[1] = 'Autumn'
season[2] = 'Summer'
season[3] = 'Spring'
season[4] = 'Winter'
print(season)
```

Output

```
{1: 'Autumn', 2: 'Summer', 3: 'Spring', 4: 'Winter'}
```

10.8 Built-in Dictionary Type Methods

Python supports built-in methods that can be used with dictionary. The syntax to use the methods is:

`dictionary.method()`

Table 10.2 lists the built-in dictionary methods along with their description.

Table 10.2 Built-in dictionary methods

S. no.	Method	Description
1	`clear()`	Removes all items from dictionary
2	`copy()`	Returns shallow copy of dictionary
3	`fromkeys(seq[, v])`	Returns new dictionary with keys from seq and value equal to v (default is None)
4	`get(key[,d])`	Returns value of key. If key does not exist, it returns d (default is None)
5	`items()`	Returns list of dictionary items (key, value)
6	`keys()`	Returns list of dictionary keys
7	`pop(key[,d])`	Removes item with key and returns its value or d if key is not found. If d is not provided and key is not found, raises KeyError
8	`popitem()`	Removes and returns an arbitrary item (key, value) Raises KeyError if dictionary is empty.
9	`setdefault(key[,d])`	If key is in dictionary, returns its value. If not, inserts key with value of d and returns d (defaults to None)
10	`update([other])`	Updates dictionary with key/value pairs from *other*, overwriting existing keys.
11	`values()`	Returns list of dictionary values

Example 10.16: (a) Using built-in dictionary methods (b) Output

```
season = {1: 'Autumn', 2: 'Summer', 3: 'Spring', 4: 'Winter'}
print("season =", season)
s = season.copy()
print("copy s =", s)
print("get(1) =", season.get(1))
print("get(10) =", season.get(10))

print("items() =", season.items())

print("keys() =", season.keys())

print("setdefault() =", season.setdefault(3))

print("values() = ", season.values())

a = ('A', 'B', 'C', 'D')
s = {}.fromkeys(a)
print("fromkeys() =", s)

print("pop(1) =", season.pop(1))
print("popitem() =", season.popitem())
```

(a)

```
season = {1: 'Autumn', 2: 'Summer', 3: 'Spring', 4: 'Winter'}
copy s = {1: 'Autumn', 2: 'Summer', 3: 'Spring', 4: 'Winter'}
get(1) = Autumn
get(10) = None
items() = dict_items([(1, 'Autumn'), (2, 'Summer'), (3, 'Spring'), (4, 'Winter')
])
keys() = dict_keys([1, 2, 3, 4])
setdefault() = Spring
values() =  dict_values(['Autumn', 'Summer', 'Spring', 'Winter'])
fromkeys() = {'A': None, 'B': None, 'C': None, 'D': None}
pop(1) = Autumn
popitem() = (4, 'Winter')
```

(b)

10.9 Basic Operations on Dictionary

- Dictionary is mutable. This means dictionary can be updated in place.
- We explain the following operations on dictionary:
  - o Update dictionary, Delete element

- Search element, Built-in dictionary functions
- Traverse dictionary

10.9.1 Update Dictionary

- New items can be added to dictionary. Value of existing items can be modified.
- If key already exists in dictionary, then its value gets updated; otherwise, the key-value pair adds to the dictionary.

Example 10.17: (a) Update a dictionary (b) Output

```
D1 = {1 : "Jan", 2 : "Feb", 3 : "Mar"}
print("D1 =\t\t", D1)
D1[4] = 'Apr'
print("D1 add element =", D1)
D1[4] = 'May'
print("D1 change value =", D1)
```

(a)

```
D1 =               {1: 'Jan', 2: 'Feb', 3: 'Mar'}
D1 add element = {1: 'Jan', 2: 'Feb', 3: 'Mar', 4: 'Apr'}
D1 change value = {1: 'Jan', 2: 'Feb', 3: 'Mar', 4: 'May'}
```

(b)

10.9.2 Delete Elements

- Individual elements can be removed from dictionary.
- **del** command deletes an individual element of dictionary.
  `del dict_name[element_key]`
- **pop()** method deletes a particular element of dictionary.
  `dict_name.pop([element_key])`
- **popitem()** method deletes an arbitrary element of dictionary.
  `dict_name.popitem()`
- **del** command deletes entire dictionary.
  `del dict_name`

  If we try to print the dictionary after deletion, an exception is raised, since the dictionary does not exist.
- **Clear()** method deletes all elements of dictionary.
  `dict_name.clear()`

Example 10.18: (a) Deleting elements in a dictionary (b) Output

```
D1 = {1 : "Jan", 2 : "Feb", 3 : "Mar", 4 : "Apr"}
print("D1 =\t\t", D1)
del D1[2]
print("del D1[2] =\t", D1)
D1.pop(1)
print("D1.pop(1) =\t", D1)
D1.popitem()
print("D1.popitem =\t", D1)
D1.clear()
print("D1.clear() =\t", D1)
del D1
print("del D1 =\t\t", D1)
```

(a)

```
D1 =                {1: 'Jan', 2: 'Feb', 3: 'Mar', 4: 'Apr'}
del D1[2] =         {1: 'Jan', 3: 'Mar', 4: 'Apr'}
D1.pop(1) =         {3: 'Mar', 4: 'Apr'}
D1.popitem =        {3: 'Mar'}
D1.clear() =        {}
Traceback (most recent call last):
  File "C:/Users/anita/Desktop/dict-operations.py", line 23, in <module>
    print("del D1 =\t\t", D1)
NameError: name 'D1' is not defined
```

(b)

10.9.3 Search Element (in operator)

- The `in` operator is used to search for a key in a dictionary. It does not search for a value.
- The syntax of **`in`** operator is:
  element in dict_name
- If an element is present in dictionary, True is returned; else False is returned.
- The **`not in`** operator is used to check if a key is not in dictionary. The syntax of **`not in`** operator is:
  key not in dict_name
- If an element is not in dictionary, True is returned; else False is returned.

Example 10.19: (a) Searching an element in dictionary (b) Output

```
D1 = {1 : "Jan", 2 : "Feb", 3 : "Mar", 4 : "Apr"}
print("D1 =\t\t", D1)
print("1 in D1 =\t", 1 in D1)
print("1 not in D1 =\t", 1 not in D1)
print("10 in D1 =\t", 10 in D1)
```

(a)

```
D1 =              {1: 'Jan', 2: 'Feb', 3: 'Mar', 4: 'Apr'}
1 in D1 =         True
1 not in D1 =     False
10 in D1 =        False
```

(b)

10.9.4 Built-in Dictionary Functions

- In addition to built-in methods, Python defines functions that can operate on dictionary.
- The commonly used functions are shown below:

Method name	Description
`len(dict)`	Gives total length of dictionary, i.e., number of items in dictionary
`str(dict)`	Gives printable string representation of dictionary
`type(variable)`	Returns type of passed variable. If passed variable is in dictionary, then it returns dictionary type

Let us see some examples.

Example 10.20: (a) Using built-in dictionary functions (b) Output

```
D1 = {1 : "Jan", 2 : "Feb", 3 : "Mar", 4 : "Apr"}
print("D1 =\t\t", D1)
print("len(D1) =\t", len(D1))
print("type(D1) =\t", type(D1))
print("str(D1) =\t", str(D1))
```

(a)

```
D1 =              {1: 'Jan', 2: 'Feb', 3: 'Mar', 4: 'Apr'}
len(D1) =         4
type(D1) =        <class 'dict'>
str(D1) =         {1: 'Jan', 2: 'Feb', 3: 'Mar', 4: 'Apr'}
```

(b)

10.9.5 Traverse Dictionary

- Traversal of dictionary is accessing each key in dictionary, one by one.
- Dictionary does not keep the order of elements stored in it.
- Traversal is done using a loop – `for` loop or `while` loop.

Example 10.21: (a) Traversing a dictionary (b) Output

```
D1 = {1 : "Jan", 2 : "Feb", 3 : "Mar", 4 : "Apr"}
for i in D1:
    print("D1 =\t", D1[i])
print("=====================")
for i,j in D1.items():
    print("D1 =\t", i, j)
```

(a)

```
D1 =      Jan
D1 =      Feb
D1 =      Mar
D1 =      Apr
=====================
D1 =      1 Jan
D1 =      2 Feb
D1 =      3 Mar
D1 =      4 Apr
```

(b)

10.10 Comparison – List, Tuple, Set, Dictionary

In Python, Collection is a container that is used for the storing of data of different types, such as list, set, tuple and dictionary. Collection is a built-in collection. The Python Collection module provides additional data structures to facilitate the storage for collection of data.

Here we compare the key features of list, tuple, set and dictionary.

Table 10.3 Feature comparison of list, tuple, set and dictionary

Feature	List	Tuple	Set	Dictionary
Definition	Collection of items that are ordered	Collection of items that are ordered	Collection of unordered and unindexed items.	Key-Value Pair. Collection that is unordered, changeable and indexed.
Homogeneity	Non-homogeneous	Non-homogeneous	Non-homogeneous	Non-homogeneous
Representation structure	Elements in single row and multiple rows and columns	Elements in single row and multiple rows and columns	Elements in single row	Elements in key-value pairs

(*Contnued*)

Table 10.3 (Contnued)

Feature	List	Tuple	Set	Dictionary
Symbolic Representation	[]	()	{}	{}
Duplicate elements	Allowed	Allowed	Not allowed	Keys are not duplicated
Example	[1, 2, 3, 4, 5]	(1, 2, 3, 4, 5)	{1, 2, 3, 4, 5}	{1:'x', 2:'y', 3: 'z'}
Creation	`list()` function	`tuple()` function	`set()` function	`dict()` function.
Mutable/ Immutable	Mutable	Immutable	Mutable	Mutable. Keys are not duplicated
Ordered	Yes	Yes	No	Yes
Benefit	Lists are like arrays declared in other languages	Faster than lists Used for protection against accidental changes in data	Not faster than lists Benefit in membership testing	Tuple can be used as keys in dictionary
Add element	`append()` adds a single item at end of list	Immutable. Element cannot be added	`add()`	`update()` updates dictionary with key-value pairs
Sort	sort()	Immutable. Cannot be sorted.	Unordered. Cannot be sorted	`sorted()` sorts keys in dictionary
Search	`index()`	`index()`	Set is unordered. Index cannot be retrieved	Using `get()` returns value of item with key
Count	`count()`	`count()`	No duplicates. No `count()`	Not defined
Reverse	`reverse()`	Not defined. Immutable.	Not defined. Unordered.	Not defined. Items are in key-value pairs

10.11 Solved Questions with Explanation

1. Find the output:

```
s1 = {"a", "b", "c", "d", "e"}
s2 = {"p", "q"}
print("s1=", s1)
print("s2=", s2)
print("s1.isdisjoint(s2) =",s1.isdisjoint(s2) )
```

Output

```
s1= {'c', 'a', 'e', 'b', 'd'}
s2= {'p', 'q'}
s1.isdisjoint(s2) = True
```

Explanation: It finds if any element is common in the two sets. Uses `isdisjoint()`.

2. Find the output:

```
pow = {2, 4, 8, 16, 32}
print("pow =", pow)
for x in pow:
    print(x)
```

Output

```
pow = {32, 2, 4, 8, 16}
32
2
4
8
16
```

Explanation: It prints the elements of the set as a set and as elements.

3. Find the output:

```
s = {x for x in "Beautiful World"
        if x  not in {'a', 'e', 'i', 'o', 'u'}}
print(s)
```

Output

```
{' ', 'W', 'f', 't', 'd', 'B', 'l', 'r'}
```

Explanation: It prints the elements of the string that are not vowels.

4. Find the output:

```
primes = {x for x in range(2, 51)
            if all(x%y for y in range(2, min(x, 11)))}
print(primes)
```

Output

```
{2, 3, 5, 37, 7, 41, 11, 43, 13, 47, 17, 19, 23, 29, 31}
```

Explanation: It uses set comprehension to print prime numbers between 2 and 50.

5. Find the output:

```
#WAP to match key values in two dictionaries.
x = {'k1': 10, 'k2': 30, 'k3': 20}
y = {'k1': 10, 'k2': 20}
for (key, value) in set(x.items()) & set(y.items()):
    print('%s: %s is present in both x and y' % (key, value))
```

Output

```
k1: 10 is present in both x and y
```

Explanation: It matches key values in two dictionaries.

6. Find the output:

```
#WAP to filter a dictionary based on values.
price_list = {'Mango': 75, 'Apple': 120, 'Grapes': 175, 'Pear': 90}
print("Price_List:", price_list)
print("Price greater than 100:")
ans = {k:val for (k, val) in price_list.items() if val >= 100}
print(ans)
```

Output

```
Price_List: {'Mango': 75, 'Apple': 120, 'Grapes': 175, 'Pear': 90}
Price greater than 100:
{'Apple': 120, 'Grapes': 175}
```

Explanation: It finds the values in a dictionary based on a condition.

7. Find the output:

```
#WAP to get the maximum and minimum value in a dictionary.
d1 = {'1':300, '2':1234, '3': 432, '4':230}
k_max = max(d1.keys(), key=(lambda k: d1[k]))
k_min = min(d1.keys(), key=(lambda k: d1[k]))
print('Maximum Value: ',d1[k_max])
print('Minimum Value: ',d1[k_min])
```

Output

```
Maximum Value:  1234
Minimum Value:  230
```

Explanation: It finds the maximum and minimum value in a dictionary.

8. Find the output:

```
list = [1,2,3,4,5,6,7]
dict_list = {v:v**3 for v in list if v%2 == 0}
print("Dictionary:", dict_list)
```

Output

```
Dictionary: {2: 8, 4: 64, 6: 216}
```

Explanation: It creates dictionary from a list having key as number and value as cube of the number, for even numbers.

9. Find the output:

```
dict_sq = {n: n*n for n in range(1, 11)}
print(dict_sq)
```

Output

```
{1: 1, 2: 4, 3: 9, 4: 16, 5: 25, 6: 36, 7: 49, 8: 64, 9: 81, 10: 100}
```

Explanation: It creates dictionary with number and its square from 1 to 10.

10. Find the output:

```
#Convert to Rupees
doll_price = {'Pen': 1.10, 'Pencil': 0.50, 'Eraser': 1.2}
doll_to_rup = 75
rup_price = {k: v*doll_to_rup for (k, v) in doll_price.items()}
print(rup_price)
```

Output

```
{'Pen': 82.5, 'Pencil': 37.5, 'Eraser': 90.0}
```

Explanation: It converts dictionary values to rupees from dollar.

11. Find the output.

```
#grades
marks= {'English': 75, 'Maths': 90, 'Science': 88, 'Hindi': 70}
grade = {k: ('A' if v >=90 else ('B' if 80<v<90 else ('C')))
        for (k, v) in marks.items()}
print(grade)
```

Output

```
{'English': 'C', 'Maths': 'A', 'Science': 'B', 'Hindi': 'C'}
```

Explanation: It uses dictionary comprehension to assign grades based on the marks.

10.12 Programming Examples

Program 10.1: WAP to count the number of vowels in a string using set.

```
# WAP to count vowel in a string using set
def v_ct(s):
    cnt = 0
    vowl = set("AEIOUaeiou")
    for c in s:
        if c in vowl:
            cnt=cnt+1
    print("No. of vowels :", cnt)
s=input("Enter a String:")
v_ct(s)
```

Output

```
Enter a String:This is a book
No. of vowels : 5
```

```
Enter a String:This is a beautiful world
No. of vowels : 9
```

Program 10.2: WAP to check if a string is a pangram.

```
#WAP to check if the given string is pangram or not.
#Pangram-A sentence in which every letter of alphabetis used at least once.
#Use ascii_lowercase of string. Returns lowercase letters a to z as string.

from string import ascii_lowercase
def pangm_chk(s):
    return set(ascii_lowercase) - set(s.lower()) == set([])

s1 ="The five boxing wizards jump quickly"
s2 ="Farmer jack realized that big yellow quilts were expensive"
if(pangm_chk(s1)== True):
    print("String is a pangram")
else:
    print("String is not a pangram")
print(len(s1))
if(pangm_chk(s2)== True):
    print("String is a pangram")
else:
    print("String is not a pangram")
print(len(s2))
```

Output

```
String is a pangram
36
String is a pangram
58
```

Program 10.3: WAP to find elements in a set that are not in another set.

```
#WAP to find elements in a set that are not in another set.
#Create set from user input
def get_lst():
    lst = []
    while True:
        inp_val =int(input("Enter Element:"))
        if inp_val != -1:
            lst.append(inp_val)
        else:   break
    return(lst)
print("Enter elements for Set 1. Enter -1 to stop")
s1 = set(get_lst())
print("Enter elements for Set 2. Enter -1 to stop")
s2 = set(get_lst())
print("Set 1=",s1)
print("Set 2=", s2)
print("="*20)
print("Set 1-Set 2=", s1-s2)
print("Set 2-Set 1=", s2-s1)
```

Output

```
Enter elements for Set 1. Enter -1 to stop
Enter Element:2
Enter Element:3
Enter Element:4
Enter Element:5
Enter Element:6
Enter Element:-1
Enter elements for Set 2. Enter -1 to stop
Enter Element:1
Enter Element:3
Enter Element:5
Enter Element:7
Enter Element:9
Enter Element:-1
Set 1= {2, 3, 4, 5, 6}
Set 2= {1, 3, 5, 7, 9}
====================
Set 1-Set 2= {2, 4, 6}
Set 2-Set 1= {1, 9, 7}
```

Program 10.4: WAP to create a sequence of key-value pairs into a dictionary of lists.

```
#WAP to create a dictionary grouping
#a sequence of key-value pairs into a dictionary of lists.
def group_dict(l):
    ans = {}
    for k, v in l:
         ans.setdefault(k, []).append(v)
    return ans
color = [('Red', 1), ('Pink', 2), ('Orange', 3), ('Pink', 4), ('Red', 1)]
print("Dictionary:\n", color)
print("Dictionary of list:\n", group_dict(color))
```

Output

```
Dictionary:
 [('Red', 1), ('Pink', 2), ('Orange', 3), ('Pink', 4), ('Red', 1)]
Dictionary of list:
 {'Red': [1, 1], 'Pink': [2, 4], 'Orange': [3]}
```

Program 10.5: WAP to find duplicate sets in a list of sets.

```
# WAP to find duplicate sets in list of sets
# Using Counter() + frozenset() to get frequency
from collections import Counter
lst = [{1, 3, 5, 7}, {7, 3, 1, 5}, {2, 2, 4, 6}, {2, 4, 6}, {7, 8, 9}]
print("List:" + str(lst))
freq = Counter(frozenset(s_lst) for s_lst in lst)
ans = []
for k, v in freq.items():
    if v > 1 :  ans.append(k)
print("Duplicate List : " + str(ans))

#List:[{1, 3, 5, 7}, {1, 3, 5, 7}, {2, 4, 6}, {2, 4, 6}, {8, 9, 7}]
#Duplicate List : [frozenset({1, 3, 5, 7}), frozenset({2, 4, 6})]
```

Output

```
List:[{1, 3, 5, 7}, {1, 3, 5, 7}, {2, 4, 6}, {2, 4, 6}, {8, 9, 7}]
Duplicate List : [frozenset({1, 3, 5, 7}), frozenset({2, 4, 6})]
```

Program 10.6: WAP to check if a set is superset of itself and of any other set.

```
#WAP to check if a given set is superset of itself
#and superset of another given set.

n1 = {1, 2, 3, 4, 5, 7}
n2 = {2, 4, 5}
print("n1 a superset of itself:", n1.issuperset(n1))
print("n1 = ", n1)
print("n2 = ", n2)
print("n1 is superset of n2:", n1>n2)
```

Output

```
n1 a superset of itself: True
n1 =  {1, 2, 3, 4, 5, 7}
n2 =  {2, 4, 5}
n1 is superset of n2: True
```

Summary

- Set is an unordered collection of objects. The ordering of elements is arbitrary.
- Set does not have duplicate elements.
- Set is mutable but every element of a set is immutable.
- Sets are unordered. Thus, an element of a set cannot be changed using indexing or slicing.
- Several built-in methods can be used with sets.
- The methods – `discard()`, `remove()`, `clear()` and `pop()` are used to delete elements from a set.
- The `in` operator is used to search for elements in a set.
- Mathematical operations like set union, intersection and difference can be performed on a set.
- Python has built-in functions that can operate on the set.
- Frozenset is immutable. The content of frozenset cannot be altered, once created.
- Frozenset is hashable and thus can be used as dictionary key. Set is unhashable
- Dictionary is an unordered collection of objects.
- Dictionary is a mapping type, an element is a key-value pair.
- Key, in a dictionary, is unique.
- Dictionary keys are case sensitive.
- Python supports built-in methods that can be used with dictionary.
- Dictionary is mutable. This means dictionary can be updated in place.
- The `in` operator is used to search for a key in a dictionary. It does not search for a value.
- Python defines functions that can operate on the dictionary.

Keywords

Built-in Function
Built-in methods
copy set
del
Dictionary
dictionary.clear()
dictionary.copy()
dictionary.fromkeys()
dictionary.get()
dictionary.items()
dictionary.keys()
dictionary.pop()
dictionary.popitem()
dictionary.setdefault()
dictionary.update()
dictionary.values()
frozen set
hashable
Immutable
in operator
intersection_update()
Key-value
len(dict)Mapping
Mutable
pipe operator (|)
Set
Set comprehension
Set Mathematical Operations
set.add()
set.clear()
set.copy()
set.difference()
set.difference_update()
set.discard()
set.intersection()
set.intersection_update()

set.issubset()
set.issuperset()
set.pop()
set.remove()
set.symmetric_difference()
set.symmetric_difference_update()
set.union()
set.update()
type(variable)
unordered

Programming Language Keywords

```
add()
all()
any()
clear()
copy()
Dict()
difference()
difference_update()
discard()
enumerate()
intersection()
intersection_update()
isdisjoint()
issubset()
issuperset()
len()
len(dict)
max()
min()
pop()
remove()
sorted()
str(dict)
sum()
symmetric_difference()
symmetric_difference_update()
union()
update()
```

Assessment

A.1 Bloom Level: Knowledge/Remember

Review Questions

1. Define – Set, Dictionary, Frozenset.
2. List any two methods using which elements can be added to a set.
3. List three built-in methods that operate on a set.
4. List the different ways for adding elements to a set.
5. List the different ways for deleting elements from a set.
6. List three ways using which a set can be copied.
7. List three built-in set functions.
8. Identify the mutable – Set, Frozenset, Dictionary.
9. List three built-in methods that operate on dictionary.
10. Match the following set operations with their operator:

Column A	Column B
1 Union	a -
2 Intersection	b ^
3 Difference	c <=
4 Symmetric Difference	d >=
5 issubset	e &
6 issuperset	f |

Fill in the blanks

1. Set is an ______ collection of objects.
2. An ______ set has zero elements.
3. _____ function is used to create empty set.
4. The built-in methods _____ and _____ are used to add elements to the set.
5. ______ method adds a single element to the set.
6. ______ method adds multiple elements to the set.
7. If an element does not exist in the set, ______ method will raise an error.
8. ______ method deletes all elements from the set.
9. ______ method deletes an arbitrary element from the set.
10. ______ method is used for making shallow copy of the set.
11. ______ set is immutable.
12. ________ is an unordered collection of objects.
13. Each element of a dictionary is ________ pair.

State True/False

1. The ordering of a set element is defined.
2. Set contains only unique elements.
3. Tuple can be added to set.
4. If an element is not in the set, `discard()` method will raise an error.
5. In dictionary, a key is separated from its value by a semicolon(;).
6. Keys in dictionary are case sensitive.
7. Nested dictionary is not allowed in Python.
8. A key can be modified in a dictionary.
9. Duplicate keys are not allowed in dictionary.
10. Once created, the content of frozenset cannot be altered.

Multiple Choice Questions (MCQ)

1. The braces to define the set are:
   (i) [] (ii) {}
   (iii) () (iv) [{}]
2. To add a single element to a set, use the function:
   (i) `add()` (ii) `update()`
   (iii) `insert()` (iv) `pop()`
3. If an element to be deleted from a set does not exist, a KeyError is raised. The method used is:
   (i) `discard()` (ii) `remove()`
   (iii) `clear()` (iv) `pop()`
4. To delete an arbitrary element from a set, use:
   (i) `discard()` (ii) `remove()`
   (iii) `clear()` (iv) `pop()`
5. Identify the correct Venn diagram for the set operation – Set Union.

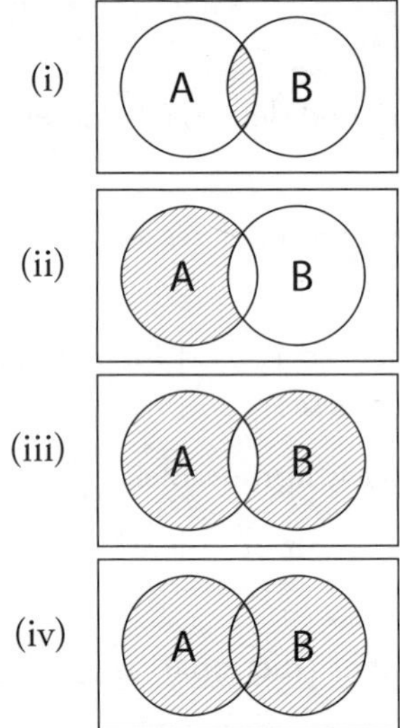

6. Identify the correct Venn diagram for the set operation – Set Intersection.

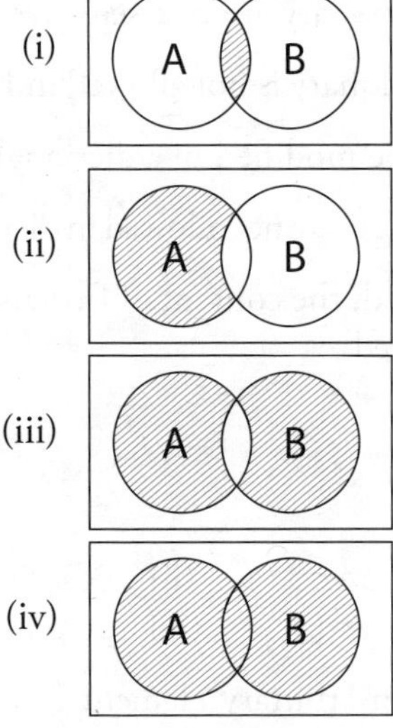

7. Identify the correct Venn diagram for the set operation – Set Difference.

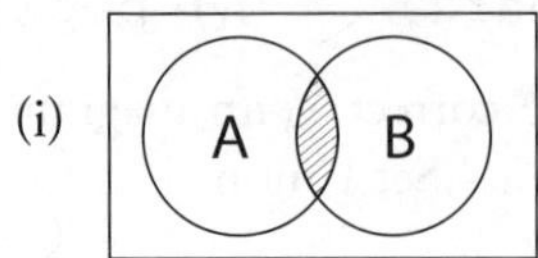

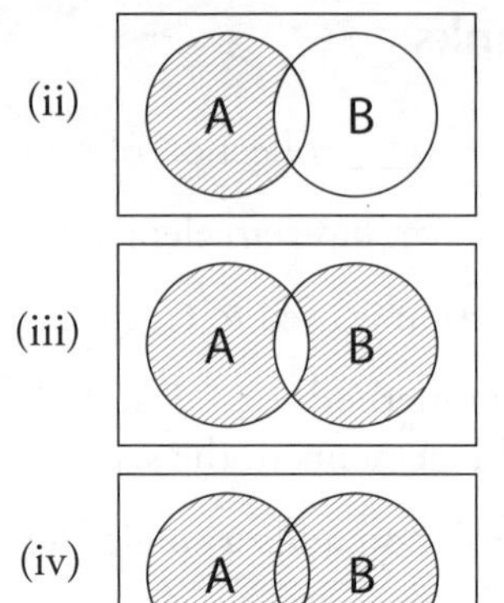

8. Identify the correct Venn diagram for the set operation – Set Symmetric Difference.

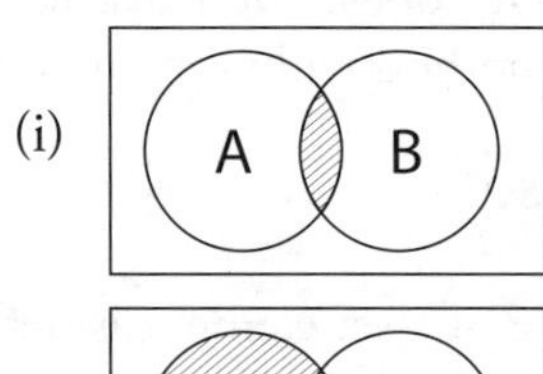

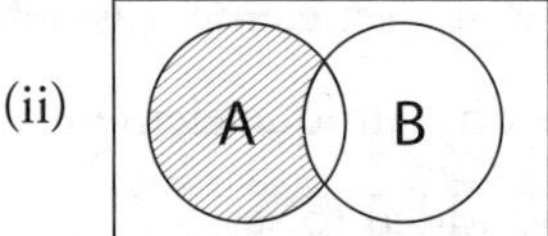

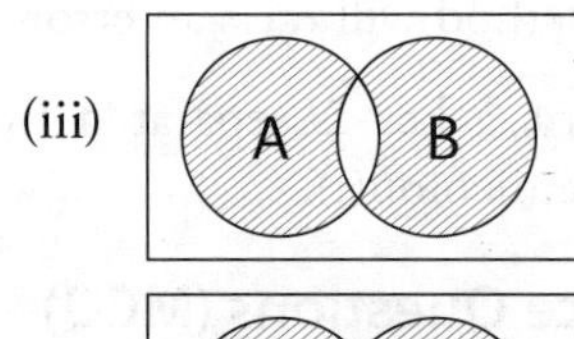

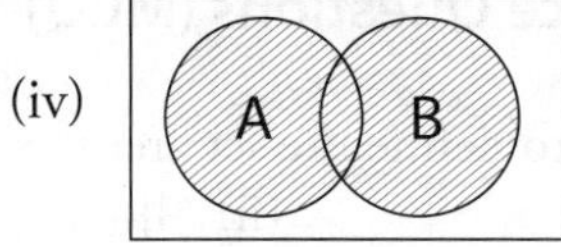

9. The error that appears if we try to change an element of frozenset:
   (i) AttributeError (ii) TypeError
   (iii) KeyError (iv) NameError

10. To delete an arbitrary element of dictionary, we use:
   (i) `popitem()` (ii) `pop()`
   (iii) `clear()` (iv) `del`

A.2 Bloom Level: Comprehend/Understand

Review Questions

1. "Set is mutable but every element in set is immutable". Explain the statement.
2. Describe the meaning of following built-in set methods:
`add(), clear(), copy(), difference(), difference_update(), discard(), intersection(), intersection_update(), isdisjoint(), issubset(), issuperset(), pop(), remove(), symmetric_difference(), symmetric_difference_update()`
3. Explain the following functions of a set:
`all(), any(), enumerate(), len(), max(), min(), sorted(), sum()`
4. Describe the meaning of the following built-in dictionary methods:
`clear(), copy(), fromkeys(), get(), items(), keys(), pop(), popitem(), setdefault(), update(), values()`
5. What is the purpose of set comprehension?
6. What is the advantage of using set comprehension?
7. What is a mapping type?
8. Describe the different ways in which an element can be deleted from a set.
9. Describe the different ways in which an element can be added to a set?
10. Explain the different ways to make a shallow copy of a set.
11. Explain the different ways to copy a set such that any change is reflected in both the original set and copy set.
12. Explain why an element cannot be added to a frozenset.
13. Can a key of dictionary be of type list? Justify your answer.
14. Describe the different ways to delete an element from a dictionary.

A.3 Bloom Level: Application/Apply

Review Question

1. Find the errors, and correct the code:
   (a) This is the code to find the sum of all items in a dictionary. Find the error and correct it.

```
d1 = {'k1':200,'k2':-10,'k3':200}
print(sum(d1.key()))
```

   (b) This is the code to merge the contents of two dictionaries. Find the error and correct it.

```
d1 = {'a1': 10, 'a2': 20}
d2 = {'b1': 30, 'b2': 40}
d = d1.copy()
d = d2.copy()
print(d)
```

   (c) This is the code to add two elements to a set. Find the error and correct it.

```
S1=set(['a','b','c'])
S1.add('d', 'e')
print(S1)
```

   (d) This is the code to print all set members except vowels. Find the error and correct it.

```
s=set('Eva, can I see bees in a cave?')
print("S=", s)
s1 = {x for x in s if x in 'aeiou'}
print("S1=", s1)
```

Fill in the blanks

1. The output of
   `S1 = set({1. 2. 1, 2})`
   is set ________.

2. If `S = {}.` The command `print(type(S))` will give output as ________.

3. If `S = set {}.` The command `print(type(S))` will give output as ________.

4. Let `S = {1, 2, 3}`, then `2 in S` will give output as ________.

5. Let `S1 = {1, 2, 3}`
   `S2 = S1`
   `S1.add(4)`
   The output of `print(S1)` is ________ and `print(S2)` is ______.

6. `S1 = {1, 2, 3}`
   `S2 = S1.copy()`
   `S1. add(4)`
   The output of `print(S1)` is ________.

7. In Q 6, the output of `print(S2)` is ________.

8. S1 = {x, y, z}
   S2 = {x, p, q}
   The output of S1.isdisjoint(S2) is ________.

9. In Q 8, The output of S1.issubset(S2) is ________.

10. S1 = {1, 2, 3, 4, 5}
    S2 = {2, 4}
    The output of S1.issuperset(S2) is ________.

Answer 11-19 for the set
`S1 = {1, 2, 3, 4, 5}`

11. All(S1) is ________.
12. Any(S1) is ________.
13. Len(S1) is ________.
14. max(S1) is ________.
15. Min(S1) is ________.
16. Sorted(S1) is ________.
17. Sum(S1) is ________.
18. Set(enumerate(S1)) is ________.
19. Set(enumerate(S1, 5)) is ________.
20. `power = (x**2) for x in range(5))`
    `print(power)`
    The output is ________.

Multiple Choice Questions (MCQ)

1. The output of `S1 = set("Good")` is ______.
   (i) Error
   (ii) {'G', 'o', 'o', 'd'}
   (iii) {'G', 'o', 'd'}
   (iv) {}

2. The output of `S1 = {1, [1, 2], 2}` is ______.
   (i) Error
   (ii) {1, 2}
   (iii) {1, [1, 2],2}
   (iv) {[1, 2]}

3. The output of `S1 = {1, 2, 3, 4}`
   `S1.add(5, 6)`
   (i) Error
   (ii) {1, 2, 3, 4, 5, 6}
   (iii) {1, 2, 3, 4, {5, 6}}
   (iv) {{1, 2, 3, 4}, {5, 6}}

4. The output of `S = {'A', 'B'}` `S.update(('C', 'D'))`
   (i) Error
   (ii) {'A', 'B', 'C', 'D'}
   (iii) {'A', 'B', {'C', 'D'}}
   (iv) {'A', 'B', ('C', 'D')}

Answer 5–12 for the two sets
s1 = {1, 2, 3, 4, 5, 6, 7}
s2= {1, 3, 5, 7, 11, 13}

5. (s1 |(s2)) is ______.
   (i) {1, 2, 3, 4, 5, 6, 7, 11, 13}
   (ii) {1, 2, 5, 1, 3, 4, 3, 5, 6, 7, 7, 11, 13}
   (iii) {1, 2, 5, 1, 3, 4, 6, 7, 7, 11, 13}
   (iv) {1, 2, 5, 3, 4, 3, 5, 6, 7, 11, 13}

6. (s1 &(s2)) is ______.
   (i) {1, 3, 5, 7}
   (ii) {1,1, 3, 3, 5, 5, 7,7}
   (iii) {1, 3, 5}
   (iv) {1,1, 3, 3, 5, 5}

7. (s1–s2) is ______.
   (i) {11, 13}
   (ii) {2, 4, 6}
   (iii) {2, 4, 6, 11, 13}
   (iv) {1, 3, 5, 7}

8. (s2-s1) is ______.
   (i) {2, 4, 6}
   (ii) {11, 13}
   (iii) {2, 4, 6, 11, 13}
   (iv) {1, 3, 5, 7}

9. (s1 ^ s2) is ______.
   (i) {2, 4, 6, 11, 13}
   (ii) {1, 3, 5, 7}
   (iii) {2, 4, 6}
   (iv) {11, 13}

10. (s1.intersection_update(s2)). What is the value of s1?
   (i) {2, 4, 6}
   (ii) {11, 13}
   (iii) {1, 3, 5, 7}
   (iv) {1, 3, 5, 7, 11, 13}

11. (s1.difference_update(s2)). What is the value of s1?
   (i) {11, 13}
   (ii) {2, 4, 6}
   (iii) {2, 4, 6, 11, 13}
   (iv) {1, 3, 5, 7}

12. (s1.symmetric_difference_update(s2)). What is the value of s1?
   (i) {2, 4, 6, 11, 13}
   (ii) {1, 3, 5, 7}
   (iii) {2, 4, 6}
   (iv) {11, 13}

Answer 13–20 for the dictionary:
quality = {1: 'Wisdom', 2: 'Hardwork', 3: 'Intelligent', 4: 'Knowledge'}

13. (quality.get(1)) is:
   (i) Wisdom
   (ii) Hardwork
   (iii) 1:Wisdom
   (iv) 'Wisdom'

14. (quality.get(10)) is:
   (i) Knowledge
   (ii) None
   (iii) Error
   (iv) Wisdom

15. (quality.items()) is:
   (i) dict_items([(1, 'Wisdom'), (2, 'Hardwork'), (3, 'Intelligent'), (4, 'Knowledge')])
   (ii) [(1, 'Wisdom'), (2, 'Hardwork'), (3, 'Intelligent'), (4, 'Knowledge')]
   (iii) ([(1, 'Wisdom'), (2, 'Hardwork'), (3, 'Intelligent'), (4, 'Knowledge')])
   (iv) (1, 'Wisdom'), (2, 'Hardwork'), (3, 'Intelligent'), (4, 'Knowledge')

16. (quality.keys()) is:
   (i) ([1, 2, 3, 4])
   (ii) [1, 2, 3, 4]
   (iii) dict_keys(1, 2, 3, 4)
   (iv) dict_keys([1, 2, 3, 4])

17. (quality.setdefault(3)) is:
    (i) Intelligent
    (ii) Hardwork
    (iii) Wisdom
    (iv) True

18. (quality.values()) is:
    (i) dict_values(['Wisdom', 'Hardwork', 'Intelligent', 'Knowledge'])
    (ii) dict_items(['Wisdom', 'Hardwork', 'Intelligent', 'Knowledge'])
    (iii) dict(['Wisdom', 'Hardwork', 'Intelligent', 'Knowledge'])
    (iv) (['Wisdom', 'Hardwork', 'Intelligent', 'Knowledge'])

19. (quality.pop(1)) is:
    (i) Hardwork
    (ii) Wisdom
    (iii) {Wisdom}
    (iv) {Hardwork}

20. (quality.pop(10)) is:
    (i) IndexError
    (ii) None
    (iii) KeyError
    (iv) DataError

A.4 Bloom Level: Analyze

1. Explain the difference between the following:
    (i) `add()` and `update()`
    (ii) `discard()` and `remove()`
    (iii) `intersection()` and `intersection_update()`
    (iv) `difference()` and `difference_update()`
    (v) `difference()` and `symmetric_difference()`
    (vi) `symmetric_difference()` and `symmetric_difference_update()`
    (vii) `all()` and `any()`
    (viii) `set` and `frozenset`
    (ix) `del()` and `pop()`
    (x) `pop()` and `popitem()`

2. `{1, 2, (1, 2)}` is not a valid set. Is it True or False?

3. Let `S1 = {1, 2, 3}`, then `2 not in S1` will give output as False. Is it True or False?

4. `D = {'A': 1, 'a':2}` will give an error in output. Is it True or False?

5. Analyze the following code. What is the task performed? What is the output?

(a)
```
t1 = set(('a','b','c','d'))
print(t1)
```

(b)
```
l1=set(['A','E','I'])
print(l1)
```

(c)
```
s1 = set('This is a string')
print(s1)
```

(d)
```
l1=set(['B','O','B','B','Y'])
print(l1)
```

(e)
```
a = set('abracadabra')
print(a)
```

(f)
```
l1=set(['B','O','B','B','Y'])
l1.update(['e','f'])
print (l1)
```

(g)
```
Vehicles = {"Car", "Truck", "Tempo"}
if "Car" in Vehicles:
    print("Yes, Car is in Vehicles")
```

6. Analyze the difference in (i) and (ii). What is the output? Justify.

(i)
```
d1 = {'c1': [5, 4, 1], 'c3': [7, 3, 4], 'c2': [5, 8, 4]}
d1_sot = {a: sorted(b) for a, b in d1.items()}
print(d1_sot)
```

(ii)
```
d1 = {'c1': [5, 4, 1], 'c3': [7, 3, 4], 'c2': [5, 8, 4]}
d1_sot = sorted(d1.items(), key=lambda x:x[0])
print(d1_sot)
```

7. Differentiate and analyze the output with justification:

(a)
```
s1={1,2, 3, 4, 5,6 }
s2=s1
s2.add(7)
print("s1=", s1)
print("s2=", s2)
```

(b)
```
s1={1,2, 3, 4, 5,6
s2=s1
s2={7}
print("s1=", s1)
print("s2=", s2)
```

(c)
```
s1={1,2, 3, 4, 5,6 }
s2=s1.copy()
s2={7}
print("s1=", s1)
print("s2=", s2)
```

(d)
```
s1={1,2, 3, 4, 5,6 }
s2=s1.copy()
s2.add(7)
print("s1=", s1)
print("s2=", s2)
```

(e)
```
s1={1,2, 3, 4, 5,6 }
s2=set(s1)
s2={7}
print("s1=", s1)
print("s2=", s2)
```

(f)
```
s1={1,2, 3, 4, 5,6 }
s2=set(s1)
s2.add(7)
print("s1=", s1)
print("s2=", s2)
```

A.5 Bloom Level: Evaluate

1. Evaluate the following code. (i) Which of the two options give the same output? (ii) What is the output of the same options? (iii) What is the task performed by each option?

```
d1 = { 'India' : 'New Delhi',
       'Japan': 'Tokyo',
       'Australia' : 'Canberra'}
d2 = { 'Ireland' : 'Dublin',
       'Kenya' : 'Nairobi',
       'Japan' : 'Washington'  }
```

(a)
```
d1.update(d2)
print(d1)
```

(b)
```
m = {**d1, **d2}
print(m)
```

(c)
```
k = dict(list(d1.items()) + list(d2.items()))
print(k)
```

(d)
```
b= dict(d1, **d2)
print(b)
```

2. Evaluate the code. (i) What is the task performed? (ii) What is the output?

(a)
```
str_set = 'pqr'
num_set = {10, 20}
num_set.update(str_set)
print('num_set =', num_set)
```

(b)
```
dict_1 = {'Python': 1, 'Prog
num_set = {'a', 'b'}
num_set.update(dict_1)
print('num_set =', num_set)
```

(c)

```
x = {100, 200, 300, 400}
y = {200, 250, 260, 270}
print("Set x:", x)
print("Set y:", y)
print("="*20)
print(x.isdisjoint(y))
```

(d)

```
x = {100, 200, 300, 400}
y = {240, 250, 260, 270}
print("Set x:", x)
print("Set y:", y)
print("="*20)
print(x.isdisjoint(y))
```

(e)

```
l1 = [2, 4, 6, 8, 10]
l2 = [1, 2, 3, 4, 5, 8]
l1_l2 = list(set(l1) - set(l2))
l2_l1 = list(set(l2) - set(l1))
diff = l1_l2 + l2_l1
print(diff)
```

3. Evaluate the code for the following: (i) Identify the task performed. (ii) Find the output. Discuss how the output is different in (a), (b) and (c).

(a)

```
d1 = {'Animal': 'Cow', 'Sound': 'Moo','Animal': 'Dog', 'Sound': 'Bark',
      'Animal': 'Cat', 'Sound': 'Purr','Animal': 'Rat', 'Sound': 'Squeak'}
print(d1)
```

(b)

```
d1 = {'Cow':'Moo','Dog':'Bark','Cat':'Purr','Rat':'Squeak'}
print("="*20)
print ("{:<10} {:<10}".format('Animal', 'Sound'))
print("="*20)
for key, value in d1.items():
    print ("{:<10} {:<10}".format(key, value))
print("="*20)
```

(c)

```
d1 = {  1: ["Cow", "Moo"],
        2: ['Dog', "Bark"],
        3: ['Cat', "Purr"],
        4: ['Rat', "Squeak"]}
print("="*30)
print ("{:<10} {:<10}{:<10}".format('Key', 'Animal', 'Sound'))
print("="*30)
for key, value in d1.items():
    name, sound = value
    print ("{:<10}{:<10} {:<10}".format(key, name, sound))
```

A.6 Bloom Level: Create/Synthesize

Programming Assignment

Apply formatting wherever possible.

1. WAP to remove duplicates from a list. (**Hint**: Use set)
2. Create a dictionary to store the names of animals and their sounds. Write at least 5 entries. Do the following:
   a) Print the output as "Dog sound is Bark" for all animals and their sounds.
   b) Modify the sound of an animal.
   c) Modify the name of an animal and its sound.
   d) Add a new animal and its sound.
   e) Remove an animal and its sound.

f) Create a menu-driven program for the same.

3. WAP to create and display all combinations of letters, selecting each letter from a different key in a dictionary.

4. WAP to print a dictionary in table format.

5. WAP to remove spaces from dictionary keys.

6. WAP to count the number of items in a dictionary value that is a list.

7. Define a Fruit set containing fruit names. Add a fruit name to the Fruit set. Create a menu-driven program to (i) Add a new fruit, (2) Remove a fruit, (3) Reply suitably if a duplicate fruit is added, (4) Update the spelling of a fruit, (5) Print the names of all fruits.
   - From the fruit set create a dictionary that has fruit name as in Fruit set and the color of the fruit, for a key-value pair.

8. Define a Vegetable set containing the names of vegetables. Add two vegetable names to the set.

9. Create a dictionary showing your subject and grade in all the semesters. Print the highest grade.
   - Change one subject from the current subjects. Let the grade be your expected grade.
   - Calculate how many grades you get: "A" – 2 subjects. "B" – 1 subject.
   - Empty the dictionary.

10. Remove all duplicates from a given string in Python. Use set.

11. WAP to get the difference between two lists. Use set.

12. WAP to get unique values from a list. Use set.

13. WAP to convert a list of multiple integers into a single integer.

14. WAP to find the intersection of two lists using set.

15. WAP to print the size of the dictionary in bytes. (**Hint**: Use `sys.getsizeof()`)

16. Using set comprehension, do the following:
    (i) Create a set with values doubled.
    (ii) Create a set from a string.
    (iii) Print only positive values in a set.
    (iv) Apply function `round()` to all float elements of a set.

Answers

A.1 Bloom Level: Knowledge/Remember

Review Questions

7. (1 – f, 2 – e, 3 – a, 4 – b, 5 – c, 6 – d)

Fill in the Blanks

1. unordered	2. empty	3. `Set()`	4. `add(), update()`
5. `Add()`	6. `Update( )`	7. `remove()`	8. `Clear()`

9. `Pop()` 10. `Copy()` 11. Frozen 12. `Dictionary`
13. `key-value`

True/False

1. False 2. True 3. True 4. False 5. False 6. True 7. False 8. False
9. True 10. True

Multiple Choice Questions (MCQ)

1. (ii) 2. (i) 3. (ii) 4. (iv) 5. (iv) 6. (i) 7. (ii) 8. (iii)
9. (i) 10. (i)

A.3 Bloom Level: Apply

Review Question

1. (a) `print(sum(d1.values()))` (b) `d.update(d2)`
   (c) `S1.update('d', 'e')` (d) `a = {x for x in s if x not in 'aeiou'}`

Fill in the blanks

1. {1,2} 2. <class 'dict'> 3. <class 'set'> 4. True
5. {1,2,3,4}{1,2,3,4} 6. {1,2,3,4} 7. {1,2,3} 8. False 9. False
10. True 11. True 12. True 13. 5
14. 5 15. 1 16. [1, 2, 3, 4, 5] 17. 15
18. {(0, 1), (1, 2), (4, 5), (2, 3), (3, 4)} 19. {(7, 3), (9, 5), (6, 2), (5, 1), (8, 4)}
20. {0, 1, 4, 9, 16}

Multiple Choice Questions (MCQ)

1. (iii) 2. (i) 3. (i) 4. (ii) 5. (i) 6. (i) 7. (ii) 8. (ii)
9. (i) 10. (iii) 11. (ii) 12. (i) 13. (i) 14. (ii) 15. (i) 16. (iv)
17. (i) 18. (iii) 19. (ii) 20. (iii)

A.4 Bloom Level: Analyze

2. False 3. False 4. False

5. (a) Creating set from a tuple `{'a','b','c','d'}`
   (b) Creating set from list `{'E', 'A', 'I'}`
   (c) Create set from string.

   `{' ', 'n', 'h', 'g', 't', 'i', 'r', 'a', 'T', 's'}`

   (d) Create a set from a list with duplicate items. `{'Y', 'B', 'Q'}`
   (e) Find unique letters in the set. `{'b', 'r', 'a', 'd', 'c'}`
   (f) Adding multiple items to a set. `{'f', 'e', 'O', 'Y', 'B'}`

(g) Check if element is present in Vehicles set.
```
Yes, Car is in Vehicles
```

6. (i)
```
{'c1': [1, 4, 5], 'c3': [3, 4, 7], 'c2': [4, 5, 8]}
```
(ii)
```
[('c1', [5, 4, 1]), ('c2', [5, 8, 4]), ('c3', [7, 3, 4])]
```

7. (a)
```
s1= {1, 2, 3, 4, 5, 6, 7}
s2= {1, 2, 3, 4, 5, 6, 7}
```
(b)
```
s1= {1, 2, 3, 4, 5, 6}
s2= {7}
```
(c)
```
s1= {1, 2, 3, 4, 5, 6}
s2= {7}
```
(d)
```
s1= {1, 2, 3, 4, 5, 6}
s2= {1, 2, 3, 4, 5, 6, 7}
```
(e)
```
s1= {1, 2, 3, 4, 5, 6}
s2= {7}
```
(f)
```
s1= {1, 2, 3, 4, 5, 6}
s2= {1, 2, 3, 4, 5, 6, 7}
```

A.5 Bloom Level: Evaluate

1. (a)
```
{'India': 'New Delhi', 'Japan': 'Washington', 'Australia': 'Canberra', 'Ir
eland': 'Dublin', 'Kenya': 'Nairobi'}
```
(b)
```
{'India': 'New Delhi', 'Japan': 'Washington', 'Australia': 'Canberra', 'Ir
eland': 'Dublin', 'Kenya': 'Nairobi'}
```
(c)
```
{'India': 'New Delhi', 'Japan': 'Washington', 'Australia': 'Canberra', 'Ir
eland': 'Dublin', 'Kenya': 'Nairobi'}
```
(d)
```
{'India': 'New Delhi', 'Japan': 'Washington', 'Australia': 'Canberra', 'Ir
eland': 'Dublin', 'Kenya': 'Nairobi'}
```

2. (a) Add elements of string and dictionary to the set.
```
num_set = {'p', 10, 20, 'q', 'r'}
```
(b) Add keys of dictionary to the set.
```
num_set = {'a', 'b', 'Programming', 'Python'}
```
(c) Check if two sets are disjoint or not.
```
Set x: {200, 100, 400, 300}
Set y: {200, 250, 260, 270}
====================
False
```
(d) Check if two sets are disjoint or not.
```
Set x: {200, 100, 400, 300}
Set y: {240, 250, 260, 270}
====================
True
```
(e) Find the difference between two lists using set.
```
[10, 6, 1, 3, 5]
```

3. (a)
```
{'Animal': 'Rat', 'Sound': 'Squeak'}
```
(b)
```
====================
Animal      Sound
====================
Cow         Moo
Dog         Bark
Cat         Purr
Rat         Squeak
====================
```
(c)
```
================================
Key         Animal      Sound
================================
1           Cow         Moo
2           Dog         Bark
3           Cat         Purr
4           Rat         Squeak
```

CHAPTER

11 Files

Contents

11.1 Introduction

Let us reflect on the steps that are followed while writing a Python program – start from the Python interface, create a new file, write the Python program, and save the file. The next time, when we start the computer, we look for the saved program file in directory and open the program. Thus, we see that saving a program file stores it on the hard disk (non-volatile memory) for future use.

Let us now reflect on the steps followed while executing a Python program – the program executes, data is entered from the interface, and the result is displayed. During execution of the program, the data is temporarily stored in RAM (volatile memory). The next time, when we execute the same program, the data has to be entered again. This is because we did not save the data on the hard disk.

However, there may be a need to store the data too. For example, consider the names and addresses of all the students in a class. The data needs to be stored on the hard disk, so that it is available next time during the execution. Thus, data is stored in files.

Handling of file requires creating or opening a file, performing operations on the file, like read and write and then closing the files. In this chapter, we discuss the defining of file and directory paths, opening and closing of files, and, reading and writing data to files.

Learning Outcomes of this chapter

After completion of the chapter, the learner will be able to:

- Understand the file type
- Perform basic operations on files
- Formulate file paths
- Use files in programs
- Formulate programs using built-in file type methods
- Develop programs based on the concepts discussed.

11.2 Files: An Overview

- File is used for storing of the data, permanently. File is non-volatile.
- The data in a file is stored on a device like a disk.
- On the disk, file is a named location to store data.
- In Python, files can store data in two formats – text and binary.

11.2.1 Types of Files

In Python, the files that store data are of two kinds:

1. Text files, and
2. Binary files.

Text-files are human-readable, simple text file.

- It represents content in string (str) format.
- It is a sequence of lines. Each line may have one or more characters.
- The lines are terminated with end-of-line character, like comma and newline.

- It does the Unicode encoding and decoding automatically.
- All text, ASCII and any 8-bit encoding is Unicode.
- Text files can be opened in any text editor.
- Some examples of text files are: web files (.html, .json, .xml); source files (.py, .java); documents (.txt); tables (.csv); configuration files (.reg, .ini).

Binary files are computer-readable files.

- It represents content in special string (bytes) format.
- The content is not human-readable.
- The content is read by programs that can understand the file structure and interpret it.
- Some examples of binary files are: image files (.jpg, .png); video files (.mp4, .avi); audio files (.mp3, .wav); database files (.mdb, .sqlite); executable files (.exe, .dll); archive files (.zip, .rar)
- The binary files have a specific format. To read a binary file, special software is required. For example, video editor software for videos, photo editor software for images, and audio editor software for audio files.

It is suggested to use `bytes` string for binary files and `str` string for text files. Also, opening a binary data file in text mode is not suggested because text file implements Unicode encoding.

11.2.2 File Path

- A file has a name and a path.
- The file name is specified by the creator of the file.
- File path is the location of the file on the computer. For example, a file named a1.py is stored in the following path on my computer having Windows operating system.

  "C:\Users\Anita Goel\Desktop\Python\a1.py"

The above path means that we have a hierarchy of folders and finally the Python folder has the file a1.py. Folders can contain both other folders and files.

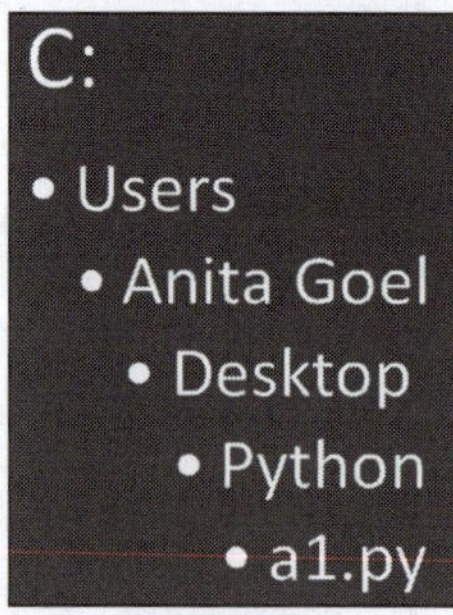

In this path, the C: is the root folder. In Windows, the root folder is the drive name and the folder separator is backslash. In OSX and Linux, the root folder is / and folder separator is forward slash.

For a Python program to work in all operating systems, the `os.path.join()` is used when defining the path. This is discussed later in the chapter.

11.2.3 Relative and Absolute Path

Current working directory is the folder where the Python program is executing. If full path name is not specified implicitly, the file is in the current working directory. A file path that is not specified from the root is taken to be under the current working directory.

To find the current working directory, Python has several methods like, `os.getcwd()`, `pathlib.Path.cwd`, discussed later in the chapter.

- In Python, paths are specified in two ways:
  1. Absolute path, and
  2. Relative path
- Absolute path begins with the root folder. For example, "C:\Anita Goel\Python \break.py" is an absolute path.
- Relative path begins from the current working directory. The current working directory is the folder from where the Python program is executing. To get the full path of the file, the path from the root to the current working directory is joined with the name of the file. For example, in a Python program if we specify the file path as "break.py", it means it is a relative path, i.e., the break.py is relative to the current working directory "C:\Anita Goel\Python".

When specifying file paths in a Python program, either use the absolute path; or if relative path is used, take care that the file is in the current working directory.

11.3 BASIC OPERATIONS ON FILES

- Files can be read and written to.
- We explain the following operations on files:
  - o Open and close file
  - o File encoding
  - o Read from file
  - o Write to file
  - o Rename a file or delete a file

11.3.1 Open File

The built-in function `open()` is provided in Python to open a file. The syntax of `open()` is,

```
file_object = open("filename", "mode")
```

In the syntax,

- **`filename`** is name of the file to be opened. It must be of type string. `filename` may include directory path if file is not in current working directory.
- **`file_object`** is the returned variable. It is also called **file object, file pointer or file handle**. It contains information about the file that has been opened. There are methods and attributes that are used on `file_object` to gather information and manipulate the opened file. Some of the file object attributes are listed in Table 11.1.

Table 11.1 File attributes and their description

Attribute	Description
<file_obj.closed>	Returns True if file is closed, otherwise false
<file_obj.mode>	Returns access mode in which the file is opened
<file_obj.name>	Returns name of file

- **mode** is the way a file is to be opened, like read, write or append. Specifying access mode is optional. By default, mode is read text data (r). The access modes can be summarized as
  - r/w/a – read/write/append in text mode
  - rb/wb/ab – read/write/append in binary mode
  - r+/w+/a+ – read and write/write and read/append and read in text mode
  - rb+/wb+/ab+ – read and write/write and read/append and read in binary mode
  - x – exclusive create

  The access modes and their description are shown in Table 11.2.

  In text mode, strings are read from the file. In binary mode, bytes are returned from the file. Byte mode is used with non-text files, like image file or executable file.

Table 11.2 Access modes for opening a file

Mode	Description
t	Open file in text mode. (Default)
r	Open file for reading in text mode. (Default)
w	Open file for writing. If file does not exist, create a new file; if file exists, overwrite file.
a	Open file to append at end of file, if file exists. If file does not exist, new file is created
b	Open file in binary mode.
rb	Open file for reading in binary mode.
wb	Open file for writing in binary mode. If file does not exist, create a new file; if file exists, overwrite file.
ab	Open file to append at end of file in binary mode, if file exists. If file does not exist, create a new file.
+	Open file for updating (reading and writing).
r+	Open file for both reading and writing.
w+	Open file for writing and reading. If file does not exist, create a new file; if file exists, overwrite file.

(*Continued*)

Table 11.2 (Continued)

Mode	Description
a+	Open file to append at end of file and reading, if file exists. If file does not exist, create a new file.
rb+	Open file for both reading and writing in binary format.
wb+	Open file for writing and reading in binary format. If file does not exist, create a new file; if file exists, overwrite file.
ab+	Open file to append at the end of file and read in binary format, if file exists. If file does not exist, create a new file.
x	Open file for exclusive creation. If file already exists, the operation fails.

- `with` clause can also be used to open a file. The syntax of `open()` with `with` clause is:
  `with open(filename, mode) as file_object:`

```
with open('file1.txt', mode ='w', encoding = 'utf-8') as f1:
```

Example 11.1: (a) File open in write mode (b) Output

```
f1 = open("file1.txt", "w")
print("1.   f1 in write mode =", f1)
```

(a)

```
1.   f1 in write mode = <_io.TextIOWrapper name='file1.txt' mode='w' encoding='c
p1252'>
```

(b)

Example 11.2: (a) File open with Path in write mode (b) Output

```
# escape every backslash (\ is special character in Python)
f2 = open("C:\\Python\\file2.txt", "w")
print("2.   f2 opened in specified path =", f2)
```

(a)

```
2.   f2 opened in specified path = <_io.TextIOWrapper name='C:\\Python\\file2.tx
t' mode='w' encoding='cp1252'>
```

(b)

Example 11.3: (a) File open in rb mode (b) Output

```
f1 = open("file1.txt", "rb")
print("3.   f1 in rb mode =\t", f1)
```

(a)

```
3.    fl in rb mode =      <_io.BufferedReader name='filel.txt'>
```

(b)

Example 11.4: (a) File open in r+b mode (b) Output

```
fl = open("filel.txt", "r+b")
print("4.    fl in r+b mode =", fl)
```

(a)

```
4.    fl in r+b mode = < io.BufferedRandom name='filel.txt'>
```

(b)

Example 11.5: (a) File open using Default mode (b) Output

```
fl = open("filel.txt")
print("5.    fl in default mode =", fl)
```

(a)

```
5.    fl in default mode = <_io.TextIOWrapper name='filel.txt' mode='r' encoding=
'cp1252'>
```

(b)

Example 11.6: (a) File Handle Attributes (b) Output

```
#file handle attributes
fl = open("filel.txt", "w")
print("fl write,encoding cp1252 =", fl)
print("File name =", fl.name)
print("File closed =", fl.closed)
print("Opening mode =", fl.mode)
```

(a)

```
fl write,encoding cp1252 = <_io.TextIOWrapper name='filel.txt' mode='w' encoding
='cp1252'>
File name = filel.txt
File closed = False
Opening mode = w
```

(b)

11.3.2 File Encoding

Encoding is converting text data to binary data (in bytes). **Decoding** is the reverse process; it converts binary data to text data. Python has Unicode (utf-8) `strings` and `byte` class. By default, Python represents strings in Unicode (utf-8). Therefore, by default, char 'a' does not represent ASCII value 97. In case a file is to be used in text mode, there is a need to mention the encoding type.

- Python stores a file in bytes, on the disk. When files have to be written or read, they have to be encoded and decoded.
- By default, encoding is platform-dependent: <cp1252> for windows and <utf-8> for Linux.
- If encoding type is not specified, then the code may behave differently for different platforms. It is recommended to use the encoding type in the open statement.

Example 11.7: (a) File open() with Encoding CP1252 (default in windows) (b) Output

```
#encoding
f1 = open("file1.txt", "w")
print("f1 write,encoding cp1252 =", f1)
```

(a)

```
f1 write,encoding cp1252 = <_io.TextIOWrapper name='file1.txt' mode='w' encoding
='cp1252'>
```

(b)

Example 11.8 (a) File open() with Encoding UTF-8 (b) Output

```
f1 = open("file1.txt", "w", encoding = 'utf-8')
print("f1 write, encoding utf-8 =", f1)
```

(a)

```
f1 write, encoding utf-8 = <_io.TextIOWrapper name='file1.txt' mode='w' encoding
='utf-8'>
```

(b)

11.3.3 Close File

The files that are opened have to be closed. This is required so that the resources held by the file are released. After the file is closed, no more reading or writing can be done on the file. The built-in function close() is provided in Python to close a file. The syntax of close() is:

```
file_object.close()
```

where, file_object is the file to be closed.

- A file gets closed automatically, if file_object variable is assigned to another file. However, it is suggested to use the close() statement explicitly, to close a file.

Example 11.9: (a) File `close()` (b) Output

```
#file close
f1 = open("file1.txt", "w")
print("File name =", f1.name)
print("File closed =", f1.closed)
print("==============================")
f1.close()
print("File closed =", f1.closed)
```

(a)

```
File name = file1.txt
File closed = False
==============================
File closed = True
```

(b)

- A file can be closed using `with` clause. The file gets closed by itself when the code in `with` clause executes. In this case, there is no need to use `close()` method.

Example 11.10: (a) File `close()` and `with` clause (b) Output

```
#file close with
with open('file1.txt', mode ='w', encoding = 'utf-8') as f1:
    print("f1 closed INSIDE WITH =", f1.closed)
print("f1 closed OUTSIDE WITH =", f1.closed)
```

(a)

```
f1 closed INSIDE WITH = False
f1 closed OUTSIDE WITH = True
```

(b)

11.3.4 Write to File

The files that have been opened do not have any content in it. The content has to be written to the file. The write operation is performed on a file for writing content to a file. The built-in function `write()` is provided in Python for writing to a file. The syntax of `write()` is:

```
file_object.write(string)
```

- **`file_object`** is the file to be written to.
- **`string`** is to be written to file. The string can have both binary and text data.
- **`write()`** method writes string to open file. It does not add newline character (\n) to the end of string. The programmer must use newline character to separate lines stored in the file.

Example 11.11: (a) Writing to file without newline character (b) Output

```
#file write without newline
with open('file1.txt', mode ='w', encoding = 'utf-8') as f1:
    f1.write("Be Happy")
    f1.write("Be Loving")
print("****File write without newline****")
with open('file1.txt', mode ='r', encoding = 'utf-8') as f1:
    print(f1.read())
```

(a)

```
****File write without newline****
Be HappyBe Loving
```

(b)

The output is without newline, i.e., Python does not add newline character by itself.

Example 11.12: (a) Writing to file with newline character

```
#file write with newline
with open('file1.txt', mode ='w', encoding = 'utf-8') as f1:
    f1.write("Be Happy\n")
    f1.write("Be Loving\n")
print("****File write with newline****")
with open('file1.txt', mode ='r', encoding = 'utf-8') as f1:
    print(f1.read())
```

(a)

```
****File write with newline****
Be Happy
Be Loving
```

(b)

- The access mode for writing to file is:
  - 'w' for writing (If file already exists, the file is overwritten. If file does not exist, new file is created.)
  - 'a' for append (write more content at the end of current data in file).
  - 'x' for exclusive creation. (If file already exists, it will not write to the file. It will create and write if the file does not already exist.)

Example 11.13: (a) Append to file with newline character (b) Output

```
with open('filel.txt', mode ='w', encoding = 'utf-8') as fl:
    fl.write("Be Happy\n")
    fl.write("Be Loving\n")
with open('filel.txt', mode ='r', encoding = 'utf-8') as fl:
    print(fl.read())
fl = open('filel.txt', mode ='a', encoding = 'utf-8')
fl.write("Be Happy and Loving\n")
fl.close()

fl = open('filel.txt', mode ='r', encoding = 'utf-8')
print("****File append with newline****")
print(fl.read())
fl.close()
```

(a)

```
Be Happy
Be Loving

****File append with newline****
Be Happy
Be Loving
Be Happy and Loving
```

(b)

The output shows that data is appended to the end of file.

11.3.5 Read from File

The files that have been written to, are required to be read. The `read` operation is required to be performed on a file to read content from a file. The built-in function `read()` is provided in Python to read from a file. The syntax of `read()` is:

```
file_object.read[size]
```

- **`file_object`** is the file to be read from.
- **`size`** is the number of bytes to read. The `size` is optional. If `size` is not specified, the file is read till the end of file.
- **`read()`** method reads the entire content of file. The type is a string. The string can be binary data or text data. The access mode for reading from a file is 'r'.

Example 11.14: (a) Read from file (b) Output

```
#file read
with open('myprog.txt', 'w') as f:
   f.write("1:Beautiful World\n")
   f.write("2:Be Grateful\n")
   f.write("3a:Love Yourself\t")
   f.write("3b:Live Life\n")

with open("myprog.txt", "r") as f:
    print("First 4 data:\t", f.read(4))      #read first 4 data
    print("Next 5 data:\t", f.read(5))      #read next 5 data
    print("Rest of File:\t", f.read())      #read rest of the data till eof
    print("Read all data:\t", f.read())      #all data read-returns empty string
```

(a)

```
First 4 data:     1:Be
Next 5 data:      autif
Rest of File:     ul World
2:Be Grateful
3a:Love Yourself          3b:Live Life

Read all data:
```

(b)

In the above example, the `read` without parameter (third) reads the rest of the string till the end of file (eof). So, the last `read` prints an empty string in the output.

A few other ways of reading are:

- **`read(integer)`** reads the integer number of characters from the file.
- **`readline()`** reads a single line from the open file. The type is a string. The line is read till end of line including the newline character(\n).
- **`readlines()`** reads all content of the file. The type is a list. A line is identified by a line break.
- **Using `for` loop to read file, line by line:** The content of the file is read by iterating through the file, line by line. Here, a blank line is printed after each line because lines in the file have newline character and `print` prints on a new line. To avoid extra blank line, use `print()` end parameter.

Example 11.15: (a) Readline from File (b) Output

```
with open('myprog.txt', 'w') as f:
   f.write("1:Beautiful World\n")
   f.write("2:Be Grateful\n")
   f.write("3a:Love Yourself\t")
   f.write("3b:Live Life\n")
   #without new line character
   f.write("3c:Love Yourself")
   f.write("3d:Live Life")
```

(a)

```
#read reads entire content of file
print("==========Read()===============")
with open("myprog.txt", "r") as f:
    file_content = f.read()
    print(file_content)
    print(type(file_content))
#readline reads one line
print("==========Readline()============")
with open("myprog.txt", "r") as f:
    file_content = f.readline()
    print(file_content)
    print(type(file_content))
#readlines read all lines
print("==========Readlines()============")
with open("myprog.txt", "r") as f:
    file_content = f.readlines()
    print(file_content)
    print(type(file_content))
#read in for-loop with blank lines
print("==========for loop with blank lines=========")
with open("myprog.txt", "r") as f:
    for line in f:
        print(line)
#read in for-loop without blank lines
print("==========for loop without blank lines=========")
with open("myprog.txt", "r") as f:
    for line in f:
        print(line, end='')
```

(a)

```
==========Read()===============
1:Beautiful World
2:Be Grateful
3a:Love Yourself        3b:Live Life
3c:Love Yourself3d:Live Life
<class 'str'>
==========Readline()============
1:Beautiful World

<class 'str'>
==========Readlines()============
['1:Beautiful World\n', '2:Be Grateful\n', '3a:Love Yourself\t3b:Live Life\n', '
3c:Love Yourself3d:Live Life']
<class 'list'>
==========for loop with blank lines=========
1:Beautiful World

2:Be Grateful

3a:Love Yourself        3b:Live Life

3c:Love Yourself3d:Live Life
==========for loop without blank lines=========
1:Beautiful World
2:Be Grateful
3a:Love Yourself        3b:Live Life
3c:Love Yourself3d:Live Life
>>>
```

(b)

11.3.6 File Positions

A file that is open has the current position of the file handle or file pointer at 0. However, as we read from the file, the current position shifts accordingly.

- **`tell()`** provides current position of the file pointer of a file. The syntax of `tell()` is – `file_object.tell()`
    - o **`tell()`** method returns an integer. It tells the position of `file_object` from beginning of the file, in bytes. So, the next read or write happens at that position.
- **`seek()`** allows to change the current position of the file pointer. The syntax of `seek()` is – `file_object.seek(offset[,from])`.
    - o **`seek()`** method changes the current position of the file pointer; `offset` is the number of bytes to be moved; `from` is the reference position from where the bytes are to be moved. The value of `from` indicates the reference position as follows:
        - 0 – Beginning of file
        - 1 – Current position
        - 2 – End of file

By default, the `from` argument is set to 0.

In text mode, the `from` argument cannot be 1 or 2, except when the `offset` is 0.

In binary mode, the `from` argument can be 0, 1 or 2, and the `offset` can be negative, accordingly.

Example 11.16: (a) File positions (b) Output

```
with open('myprog1.txt', 'w') as f:
    f.write("1:Be an amazing person\n")
    f.write("2:Always inspire others\n")
    f.write("3:Be more kind\n")
    f.write("4:Simplify your life\n")
    f.write("5:Be more courageous\n")

#read reads entire content of file
print("===========Read()================")
with open("myprog1.txt", "r") as f:
     print("The first 12 characters are= ", f.read(12))
     # check current position of file pointer
     print("Current Position of file pointer= ", f.tell())
     # Reposition the file pointer
     print("Reposition file pointer at location= ", f.seek(6, 0))
     print("Starting from 6th character= \n", f.read())
```

(a)

```
The first 12 characters are=  1:Be an amaz
Current Position of file pointer=  12
Reposition file pointer at location=  6
Starting from 6th character=
 n amazing person
2:Always inspire others
3:Be more kind
4:Simplify your life
5:Be more courageous

>>> |
```

(b)

11.3.7 Renaming and Deleting Files

The Python `os` module has several functions that can be used to perform operations on the file. To use the methods, the `os` module is required to be imported in the file. To import, the following statement is used:

```
import os
```

- **`rename()`** method in `os` module allows renaming of a file. The syntax is
  `os.rename(current_file_name,new_file_name).`
- **`remove()`** method in `os` module allows deleting of a file. The syntax is
  `os.remove(file_name).`

Example 11.17: File renaming and deletion

```
import os
# Rename a file from myprog.txt to myprog-a.txt
os.rename( "myprog.txt", "myprog-a.txt" )

#Delete file
os.remove( "myprog-a.txt" )
```

Output

The files in the folder are as shown: (a) myprog.txt (b) myprog.txt renamed to myprog-a.txt (c) myprog-a.txt deleted.

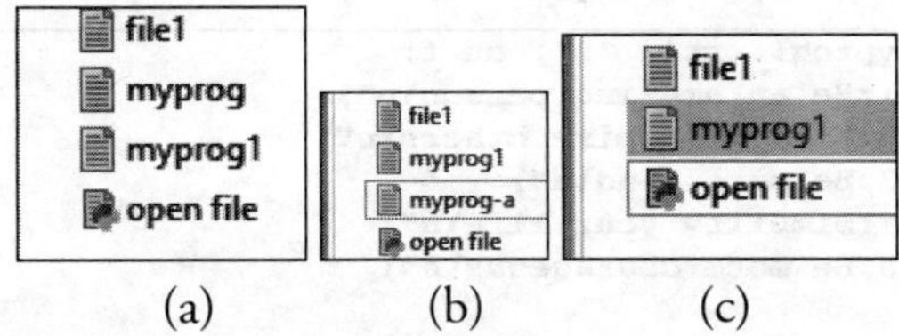

(a) (b) (c)

11.4 Memory Management Operations

Memory management involves managing of the computer memory. The tasks that need to be performed are –

- Allocation of memory – Allocating memory to the variables at runtime when a request is received.
- Deallocation of memory – Freeing the allocated memory when the program does not need it anymore.

In Python, memory allocation and deallocation are automatic. The memory manager is responsible for tasks such as periodically running to clean up memory, allocate, and manage the memory.

Python manages objects by using reference counting. The reference count value increases when a variable is assigned. The reference count value decreases when the object's reference goes out of scope or an object is deleted.

To manage the memory, the memory manager performs the following tasks:

- It keeps track of the number of references to each object in the program.

- If object's reference count is zero, the **Python Garbage Collector** (part of memory manager) is activated.
- Garbage Collector automatically frees the memory from the object.
- *Garbage Collection* is the process of freeing the blocks of memory that are no longer used.

11.5 CSV FILE

- A CSV file (Comma Separated Values file) is a plain text file that uses structuring to arrange tabular data.
- Each field of the tabular data is separated by a *delimiter* (comma, generally).
- A CSV file is saved with.***csv*** file extension.
- CSV is a common format for spreadsheet and database. It is supported by many applications.
- CSV file is used for handling large amounts of data. It contains text data – ASCII or Unicode characters.
- The structure of a csv file is:

```
Column_1_name, column_2_name, column_3_name
row_1_data_1, row_1_data_2 row_1_data_3
row_2_data_1, row_2_data_2 row_2_data_3
```

- Python has a module called *csv* for handling of the CSV files.

11.5.1 Reading Data from a CSV file

- The reader class from the *csv* module is used for reading data from a CSV file.
- The steps are –
  - o Open the CSV file using the `open()` method in 'r' mode. It is suggested that `with` keyword be used for `open()` to simplify exception handling and to close the CSV file automatically.
  - o A file object is returned. It is passed to the reader.
  - o Read by using `reader()` method of CSV module.
  - o It returns the reader object that iterates over lines in the CSV file.
- The syntax of the csv.reader is:

  `csv.reader(csvfile, dialect='excel', **fmtparams`

  `where,`

  `csvfile` is an object

  d*ialect* is optional. It defines parameters specific to a particular CSV dialect.

  `fmtparams` is optional. It is used to override individual formatting parameters in the current dialect.

Example 11.18: (a) Read CSV file (b) File Stud_data.csv (c) Output

```
import csv

with open('Stud_data.csv', mode ='r') as fp1:
  csvData = csv.reader(fp1)
  for rows in csvData:
        print(rows)
```

(a)

Output

1	Roll No	Name	Date of Birth	City
2	1001	Asha	01-01-2000	Delhi
3	1002	Usha	02-02-2000	Chennai
4	1003	Isha	03-02-2000	Mumbai
5	1004	Misha	04-03-2000	Udaipur
6	1005	Disha	05-03-2000	Jaipur
7	1006	Pasha	06-04-2000	Noida
8	1007	Maasha	08-05-2000	Lucknow
9	1008	Nisha	09-06-2000	Ahmedabad
10	1009	Risha	11-07-2000	Benguluru
11	1010	Sasha	12-08-2000	Kochi

(b)

Output

```
['Roll No', 'Name', 'Date of Birth', 'City']
['1001', 'Asha', '01-01-2000', 'Delhi']
['1002', 'Usha', '02-02-2000', 'Chennai']
['1003', 'Isha', '03-02-2000', 'Mumbai']
['1004', 'Misha', '04-03-2000', 'Udaipur']
['1005', 'Disha', '05-03-2000', 'Jaipur']
['1006', 'Pasha', '06-04-2000', 'Noida']
['1007', 'Maasha', '08-05-2000', 'Lucknow']
['1008', 'Nisha', '09-06-2000', 'Ahmedabad']
['1009', 'Risha', '11-07-2000', 'Benguluru']
['1010', 'Sasha', '12-08-2000', 'Kochi']
```

(c)

In this program, we understand the different statements:
Line 3: The CSV file is opened using `with` clause. File object `fp1` is returned.
Line 4: File object `fp1` is passed to the csv.reader. It returns reader object `csvData`.
Line 5, 6: Print the file from `csvData`.

11.5.2 Writing Data to a CSV file

- The writer class from the *csv* module is used for writing data to a CSV file.
- The steps are –
  - o Open the CSV file using the `open()` method in 'w' mode. It is suggested that `with` keyword be used for `open()` to simplify exception handling and to close the CSV file automatically.
  - o A file object is returned. It is passed to the writer.
  - o Write by using `writer()` method of CSV module.
  - o Use `writerow()` and `writerows()` method of *writer* to write the file content.
- The syntax of the csv.writer is:

```
csv.writer(csvfile, dialect='excel', **fmtparams)
```

where,

csvfile is an object

dialect is optional. It defines parameters specific to a particular CSV dialect.

fmtparams is optional. It is used to override individual formatting parameters in the current dialect.

- csv.writer provides two methods for writing to CSV – writerow() and writerows().
  - o writerow() writes a single row at a time. It is used to write Field row.
    Syntax: writerow(fields)
  - o writerows() writes multiple rows at a time. It is used to write rows list.
    Syntax: writerows(rows)

Example 11.19: (a) Write to CSV file (b) Output

```
import csv

heading = ['Name', 'Branch', 'Year', 'CGPA']
rows = [ ['Asha', 'COMP', '1', '9.9'], ['Usha', 'COMP', '2', '8.1'],
         ['Isha', 'COMP', '2', '9.5'], ['Pasha', 'IT', '1', '9.5'],
         ['Nisha', 'IT', '3', '8.8'], ['Sasha', 'COMP', '2', '9.0']]

newFile = "Stud1_data.csv"
with open(newFile, 'w', newline='') as fp1:
    x = csv.writer(fp1)
    x.writerow(heading)
    x.writerows(rows)
with open('Stud1_data.csv', mode ='r')as fp2:
  csvData = csv.reader(fp2)
  for r1 in csvData:
      print(r1)
```

(a)

Output

```
['Name', 'Branch', 'Year', 'CGPA']
['Asha', 'COMP', '1', '9.9']
['Usha', 'COMP', '2', '8.1']
['Isha', 'COMP', '2', '9.5']
['Pasha', 'IT', '1', '9.5']
['Nisha', 'IT', '3', '8.8']
['Sasha', 'COMP', '2', '9.0']
```

(b)

11.6 File Methods – IO Module

The io module is present in the Python Standard Library, under the Generic Operating System Services. The io module provides the core tools for working with the streams. The io module provides Python's main facilities for dealing with various types of I/O. An object belonging to either text or binary I/O, is a file object.

There are several built-in methods that can be used with the `file_object`. Some methods like, `open()` and `read()` have already been used. A list of methods that can be used with `file_object` is shown in Table 11.3.

Table 11.3 File methods

Method	Description
`close()`	Closes an open file.
`fileno()`	Returns an integer number (file descriptor) of the file.
`flush()`	Flushes write buffer of file stream.
`read(n)`	Reads n characters from file. Reads till end of file if it is negative or None.
`write(s)`	Writes string s to file. Returns the number of characters written.
`readline(n=-1)`	Reads and returns one line from file. Reads at most n bytes, if specified.
`readlines(n=-1)`	Reads and returns a list of lines from file. Reads at most n bytes/character if specified.
`writelines(lines)`	Writes a list of lines to file.
`isatty()`	Returns True if file stream is interactive.
`readable()`	Returns True if file stream can be read from.
`writable()`	Returns True if file stream can be written to.
`seekable()`	Returns True if file stream supports random access.
`truncate(size=None)`	Resizes file stream to size bytes. If size is not specified, it resizes to current location.
`seek(offset, from)`	Changes file position to offset bytes, in reference to from (start, current, end).
`tell()`	Returns current file location.

11.7 Directory Methods – OS Module

The `os` module is present in the Python Standard Library, under the `Generic Operating System Services`. The `os` module provides the miscellaneous operating system interfaces and provides a portable way of using operating system-dependent functionality.

A directory is a collection of files and folders. The Python `os` module provides methods that operate on directory. A list of methods that can be used with directory is shown in Table 11.4.

Table 11.4 Directory methods

Method	Syntax	Description
getcwd()	`os.getcwd()`	Displays the current working directory as a string.
mkdir()	`os.mkdir('new_dir_ name')`	Creates a new directory in current working directory, with new name.
rmdir()	`os.rmdir(file_name)`	Removes empty directory of specified name. Removes contents of directory before using this method, else error is thrown.
listdir()	`os.listdir([path])`	Displays the list of files and subdirectories in path or in current working directory, if path not specified.
chdir()	`os.getchdir('new_dir_ name'`	Changes current directory to name specified in argument.
rename()	`os.rename(current_ file_name,new_file_ name)`	Renames directory or file from current name to new name.
scandir()	`os.scandir(path='.')`	Returns iterator of `os.DirEntry` objects corresponding to entries in directory given by path.

Example 11.20: Directory methods on interactive surface

```
>>> os.getcwd()
'C:\\Dr Anita Aggarwal Goel\\Python\\Chapter 11. Files'
>>> os.chdir('C:\Dr Anita Aggarwal Goel\Python Examples')
>>> os.getcwd()
'C:\\Dr Anita Aggarwal Goel\\Python Examples'
>>> os.listdir()
['access-typeerror.py', 'createmodule.py', 'example.py', 'exampleRandom.py', 'fr
omimport.py', 'MathRandom.py', 'module.py', 'mutable.py', 'required-arg.py', 'us
erdef module.py']
```

```
>>> os.mkdir('Sample')
>>> os.listdir()
['access-typeerror.py', 'createmodule.py', 'example.py', 'exampleRandom.py', 'fr
omimport.py', 'MathRandom.py', 'module.py', 'mutable.py', 'required-arg.py', 'Sa
mple', 'userdef module.py']
>>> os.chdir('Sample')
>>> os.getcwd()
'C:\\Dr Anita Aggarwal Goel\\Python Examples\\Sample'
```

```
>>> os.chdir('C:\\Dr Anita Aggarwal Goel\\Python Examples')
>>> os.rename('Sample', 'Sample_new')
>>> os.listdir()
['access-typeerror.py', 'createmodule.py', 'example.py', 'exampleRandom.py', 'fr
omimport.py', 'MathRandom.py', 'module.py', 'mutable.py', 'required-arg.py', 'Sa
mple_new', 'userdef module.py']
>>>
```

```
>>> os.rmdir('Sample_new')
>>> os.listdir()
['access-typeerror.py', 'createmodule.py', 'example.py', 'exampleRandom.py', 'fr
omimport.py', 'MathRandom.py', 'module.py', 'mutable.py', 'required-arg.py', 'us
erdef module.py']
>>>
```

Example 11.21: (a) Display all the files (excluding directories) in the given path "C:\Anita Goel\Python" (b) Output

```
import os

with os.scandir("C:\Anita Goel\Python") as x:
    for f1 in x:
        if f1.is_file():
            print(f1.name)
```

(a)

```
break.py
Built-in function.py
continue.py
for.py
nested.py
pass.py
tempo.py
tep.py
userdef module.py
while.py
```

(b)

11.8 File Paths – os.path and pathlib Module

The `os.path` and `pathlib` module are present in the Python Standard Library, under the `File and Directory Access`. Both `os.path` and `pathlib` are used for working with file paths.

`os.path` module provides common pathname manipulations. It implements some useful functions on pathnames. This module is procedural and uses functions. All the functions in `os.path` accept either bytes or string objects as parameters. The result is an object of same type, if a path or file name is returned. Applications may represent file names as (Unicode) character strings. To use the functions of `os.path`, you may import `os.path` and call functions as `os.path.xxx`. For path representation, `os.path` requires function nesting, i.e., nested string function calls. Traditionally, the file paths are represented as text strings, in Python. The support is provided by the `os.path` module. However, paths are not strings.

`pathlib` module provides object-oriented file system paths and uses classes. `pathlib` is newer, and was introduced in Python 3.4. In `pathlib`, the focus is on the `Path` object. Any functionality that we need can be accessed as either attributes or methods on `Path` object. `Pathlib` has all the functionality of `os.path`. Moreover, `pathlib` is a built-in package, so it is installed with the Python package. When using the module, import the class `Path` from `pathlib`, i.e., from `pathlib`, import `Path`. Using `Path` allows chaining of methods and attributes on Path object to get path representation.

Here, we show the usage of `os.path` and `pathlib` to perform different operations on the file paths.

- **Get current working directory**

```
import os
path = os.getcwd()
print(path)
```

```
from pathlib import Path
path = Path.cwd()
print(path)
```

Output from both cases:

```
C:\Anita Goel\Python\Chapter 11. Files
```

- **Create File Path:** The Windows operating system uses \ as a separator in paths. The Linux operating system uses / as a separator in paths. Both `os.path` and `pathlib` offer portable ways to construct paths. `os.path` uses join with expanduser. `Pathlib` uses home().

```
import os
path= os.path.join(os.path.expanduser('~'), 'sample', 'f1.txt')
print(path)
```

```
from pathlib import Path
path = Path.home()/'sample'/'f1.txt'
print(path)
```

Output from both cases:

```
C:\Users\Anita Goel\sample\f1.txt
```

- **Create Home directory**

```
import os
path = os.path.expanduser('~')
print(path)
```

```
from pathlib import Path
path = Path.home()
print(path)
```

Output from both cases

```
C:\Users\Anita Goel
```

- **Make Directory**

```
import os
path = os.path.join(os.path.expanduser('~'), 'pqr')
os.mkdir(path)
print(path)
```

Output

```
C:\Users\Anita Goel\pqr
```

```
from pathlib import Path
path = Path.home()/'test-path'
path.mkdir()
print(path)
```

Output

```
C:\Users\Anita Goel\test-path
```

Make Directory. Check directory already exists.

```
from pathlib import Path
path = Path.home()/'test-path'/'abc'
path.mkdir(parents=True, exist_ok=True)
print(path)
```

Output

```
C:\Users\Anita Goel\test-path\abc
```

- **Write data to files:** This has been already explained in the previous section.
    - o With `os.path`, create file path, `path`. Use `open()` in write mode. Write with `file_object.write()`. For example,
      ```
      with open(path, 'w') as file1:
          file1.write(str(test))
      ```
    - o With `pathlib`, create file path, `path`. Write with `path.write_text()`. For example, path.write_text(str(test))
- **Appending data to file:** This has been already explained in the previous section.
    - o With `os.path`, create file path, `path`. Use `open()` in append mode. Append with `file_object.write()`. For example,
      ```
      with open(path, 'a') as file1:
          file1.write(str(test)+'\n')
      ```
    - o With `pathlib`, create file path, `path`. Use `path.open()` in append mode. Append with `file_object.write()`. For example,

```
with path.open('a') as file1:
    file1.write(str(test)+'\n')
```

- **Read from text files:** This has been explained in the previous section.
  - o With os.path, create file path, path. Use open() in read mode. Read with file_object.read(). For example,
    ```
    with open(path, 'r') as file1:
        x = file1.read()
    ```
  - o With pathlib, create file path, path. Use path.read_text() to read the file directly. For example,
    ```
    x = path.read_text()
    ```

Remove Files and Directories

Python allows removal of file, removal of empty directory and removal of non-empty directory. The commands for removal are shown below.

To remove a file or directory, specify the path and use a suitable command. There is not much difference between os and pathlib except for defining the path.

Action	os.path	pathlib
Remove empty directory	os.rmdir	path.rmdir
Remove File	os.remove	path.unlink
Remove non-empty Directory	shutil.rmtree	shutil.rmtree

11.9 Solved Questions with Explanation

1. Find the output:

```
f1=open("sample4.txt","a+")
line= "This is a new line."
f1.write(line)
f1.seek(0)
print(f1.read())
f1.close()
```

Output

```
Love Yourself
Live with gratitude
Be compassionate
Live with dignity
Count your Blessings
Let us Enjoy life
Believe your intuition
This is a new line.
```

Explanation: It opens an existing file "sample4.txt" and appends a new line to the file.

2. Find the output:

```
def file_word_count():
    f1 = open("sample4.txt","r")
    word_ct = 0
    f1_data = f1.read()
    all_words = f1_data.split()
    for word in all_words:
        if word =="with" or word =="your":
           word_ct += 1
    print("Occurrence of /""with/"" and /""your/"" :", word_ct)
    f1.close()
file_word_count()
```

Output

```
Occurrence of /with/ and /your/ : 4
```

Explanation: It reads lines from text file "sample4.txt" and finds occurrences of the words, "with" and "your".

3. Find the output:

```
import os.path
open('sample5.txt', 'w')
print(os.path.isfile('sample5.txt'))
```

Output

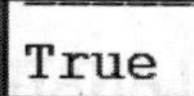

```
True
```

Explanation: It tests whether a specified file exists or not. It uses isfile(filename).

4. Find the output:

```
from collections import Counter
def word_count(file):
    with open(file) as f1:
        return Counter(f1.read().split())
print("Total number of each word in file :")
print(word_count("sample4.txt"))
```

Output

```
Total number of each word in file :
Counter({'Live': 2, 'with': 2, 'your': 2, 'is': 2, 'a': 2, 'new': 2, 'Love': 1,
'Yourself': 1, 'gratitude': 1, 'Be': 1, 'compassionate': 1, 'dignity': 1, 'Count
': 1, 'Blessings': 1, 'Let': 1, 'us': 1, 'Enjoy': 1, 'life': 1, 'Believe': 1, 'i
ntuition': 1, 'This': 1, 'line.This': 1, 'line.': 1})
```

Explanation: It calculates the frequency of all words in a file. It uses Counter from Collections for counting. `f1.read().split()` splits the content of the file into words.

5. Find the output:

```
d1 = {'Name': "Akshat", 'Marks' :78}
with open('file.txt','w+') as f1:
    f1.write(str(d1))
    f1.seek(0)
    print(f1.read())
```

Output

```
{'Name': 'Akshat', 'Marks': 78}
```

Explanation: It stores the content of dictionary to a file. Since a string can be written to a file, the conent is first converted into string and then written to the file.

6. Find the output:

```
s1 = 'Live'
f1 = open("sample4.txt", "r")
read_f1 = f1.read()
if s1 in read_f1:
    print('String', "\"", s1, "\"", 'Found In File')
else:
    print('String', s1 , 'Not Found')
f1.close()
```

Output

```
String " Live " Found In File
```

Explanation: It searches for the presence of a string in the file.

11.10 Programming Examples

Program 11.1: WAP to create a file "sample4.txt" having multiple sentences. Print the content of the file.

```
with open('sample4.txt', 'w') as f:
    f.write("Love Yourself\n")
    f.write("Live with gratitude\n")
    f.write("Be compassionate\n")
    f.write("Live with dignity\n")
    f.write("Count your Blessings\n")
    f.write("Let us Enjoy life\n")
    f.write("Believe your intuition\n")
def read_file():
    f1 = open("sample4.txt","r")
    print("="*30); print("File Content"); print("="*30)
    for one_line in f1:
        print(one_line, end="")
    print("="*30)
    f1.close()
read_file()
```

Output

```
==============================
File Content
==============================
Love Yourself
Live with gratitude
Be compassionate
Live with dignity
Count your Blessings
Let us Enjoy life
Believe your intuition
==============================
```

Program 11.2: WAP to count the number of lines in the file "sample4.txt" that do not start with the alphabet "L".

```
def line_count():
    f1 = open("sample4.txt","r")
    count=0
    print("Lines not starting with L"); print("="*30)
    for one_line in f1:
        if one_line[0] not in 'L':
            print(one_line)
            count+= 1
    print("="*30)
    f1.close()
    print("No of lines not starting with 'L'=",count)
line_count()
```

Output

```
Lines not starting with L
==============================
Be compassionate

Count your Blessings

Believe your intuition

==============================
No of lines not starting with 'L'= 3
```

Program 11.3: WAP to display all words in the file "sample4.txt" and also the total count of the words.

```
def file_word_count():
    f1 = open("sample4.txt","r")
    word_ct = 0
    f1_data = f1.read()
    all_words = f1_data.split()
    for a_word in all_words:
        print(a_word)
        word_ct += 1
    print("Number of words:",word_ct)
    f1.close()
file_word_count()
```

Output

```
Love
Yourself
Live
with
gratitude
Be
compassionate
Live
with
dignity
Count
your
Blessings
Let
us
Enjoy
life
Believe
your
intuition
Number of words: 20
>>> |
```

Program 11.4: WAP to find the longest word in the file "sample4.txt".

```
#4. WAP to find the longest words in file sample4.txt.

def file_longest_word(file):
    with open(file, 'r') as f1:
        all_words = f1.read().split()
    max_wd_len = len(max(all_words, key=len))
    return [w for w in all_words if len(w) == max_wd_len]
print("Longest word is", file_longest_word('sample4.txt'))
```

Output

```
Longest word is ['compassionate']
```

Program 11.5: WAP to find the number of different kinds of files in the directory.

```
# List number of different kinds of file in directory
# .iterdir() iterates over all files in directory.
# collections.Counter class- count no. of files of each filetype
# Parts of path
#    .name: filename without directory
#    .parent: directory having file/parent directory
#    .stem: filename without suffix
#    .suffix: file extension
#    .anchor: part of path before directories
```

```
import collections
from pathlib import Path

path = Path().home()
print("path=", path)
print("path name=", path.name)
print("path stem=", path.stem)
print("path suffix=", path.suffix)
print("path parent=", path.parent)
print("path parent parent=", path.parent.parent)
print("path anchor=", path.anchor)

print("\npath cwd=", Path.cwd())
print(collections.Counter(p.suffix for p in Path.cwd().iterdir()))
```

Output

```
path= C:\Users\Anita Goel
path name= Anita Goel
path stem= Anita Goel
path suffix=
path parent= C:\Users
path parent parent= C:\
path anchor= C:\

path cwd= C:\Anita Goel\Python\Chapter 11. Files
Counter({'.txt': 9, '.py': 8, '': 1})
```

Program 11.6: WAP to find the number of different kinds of files in the directory.

```
#How to compare two text files in python, line by line.

f1 = open("sample2.txt", "r")
f2 = open("sample3.txt", "r")

i = 0
for l1 in f1:
    i += 1
    for l2 in f2:
        if l1 == l2:
            print("Line ", i, "is identical to:", l2)
        else:
            print("Line ", i, ":")
            print("\tFile 1:", l1, end='')
            print("\tFile 2:", l2, end='')
        break
f1.close()
f2.close()
```

Output

```
Line  1 :
        File 1: Save the Environment
        File 2: This is a different line
Line  2 is identical to: The sky is beautiful

Line  3 is identical to: Plant more trees

Line  4 is identical to: Keep the rivers clean
```

Program 11.7: WAP that reads a file and copies alternative lines to another file.

```
fr = open('sample4.txt', 'r')
fw = open('sample5.txt', 'w+')

fr_content = fr.readlines()
print("="*30); print("File Content: sample4.txt"); print("="*30)
for x in fr_content:
    print(x, end="")
for i in range(0, len(fr_content)):
    if(i%2 != 0):
        fw.write(fr_content[i])
fw.seek(0)
fw_content = fw.read()
print("="*30); print("File Content: sample5.txt"); print("="*30)
print(fw_content)
fr.close()
fw.close()
```

Output

```
File Content: sample4.txt
==============================
Love Yourself
Live with gratitude
Be compassionate
Live with dignity
Count your Blessings
Let us Enjoy life
Believe your intuition
==============================
File Content: sample5.txt
==============================
Live with gratitude
Live with dignity
Let us Enjoy life
```

Summary

- A file is used for storing data permanently on a device such as a disk.
- There are two types of files in Python – text file and binary file.
- Text files represent content in string (str) format. Unicode is used for encoding and decoding.
- Binary files represent content in string (bytes) format. It is not human-readable.
- A file has two properties – filename and file path.
- An object belonging to either text or binary I/O is a file object.
- Current working directory is the folder where the Python program is executing.
- Absolute path begins with the root folder.
- Relative path begins from the current working directory.
- A file can be opened in a simple or combination of modes to read, write and append for both text and binary files.
- Image files and executable files are some examples of files stored in binary mode.
- Encoding is the process to convert text data to binary data.
- Decoding is the process to convert binary data to text data.
- Strings are represented in Unicode (utf-8).
- All open files must be closed to enable the release of resources held by the file.
- There are three modes to write to a file: `w`, `a`, `x`.
- There are options to read `n` number of characters, a complete line or a complete file.
- The current position of the file pointer is provided by `tell()`.
- To change the current position of the file pointer, use `seek()`.
- A file can be renamed and removed.
- There are several built-in file methods that operate on the file object.
- Directory is a collection of files and folders.
- `io` module provides tools for working with streams.
- `os` module has methods that operate on a directory.
- `os.path` module uses functions and provides common pathname manipulations.
- `pathlib` module uses classes and provides object-oriented file system path. The focus is on the `Path` object.

Keywords

File	file path	Delete a file
Text file	Absolute path	File Position
Binary file	Relative path	import os
Unicode	Open file	os module
Encoding	Close file	io module
Decoding	File object	File method
Str	File Access Mode	Directory
Bytes	Read from file	Directory method
Root folder	Write to file	File path
Currentworking directory	Rename a file	os.path module

Pathlib module	Append to file	Remove File
Home directory	Remove empty directory	

PROGRAMMING LANGUAGE KEYWORDS

getcwd()	seek()	truncate()
<file_obj.closed>	rename()	mkdir()
<file_obj.mode>	remove()	rmdir()
<file_obj.name>	fileno()	listdir()
with open()	flush()	chdir()
close()	read()	scandir()
write()	writelines()	os.rmdir()
read()	isatty()	path.rmdir()
readline()	readable()	os.remove()
readlines()	writable()	path.unlink()
tell()	seekable()	shutil.rmtree

ASSESSMENT

A.1 Bloom Level: Knowledge/Remember

Review Questions

1. Define – File, Text file, Binary file, Relative path, Absolute path, File object, Current working directory, file path, Encoding, Decoding.
2. List the two formats in which the files are defined in Python.
3. List two methods used for finding the current working directory.
4. List some examples of file extensions of text file type.
5. List some examples of file extensions of binary file type.
6. Name one text file termination character.
7. List the three modes in which a file can be opened.
8. List the syntax to: (i) rename a file, and (ii) remove a file.
9. List the features of writing to a file in `w`, `a` and `x` mode.
10. Match the following in reference to `seek()`, the current position from where the byte is to be moved.

	Column A		Column B
1	0	a	End of file
2	1	b	Current position
3	2	c	Beginning of file

Fill in the Blanks

1. A file is primarily stored on a ________.
2. Files store data in two formats – ________ and ________.

3. Text file is represented in ________ format.
4. ___________ encoding is used for text file.
5. __________ file content is not human readable.
6. In Windows, for defining the file path, ________ slash is used.
7. ___________ path begins with the current working directory.
8. In text mode, the default mode of a file is __________.
9. ________ is used for reading a single-line form an open file.
10. `Tell()` provides current position of the file pointer in _________.
11. ________ allows changing the current position of the file pointer.
12. The _______ module in Python Standard Library provides tools for working with streams.
13. _________ module provides object-oriented file system paths.
14. To use the `pathlib` for defining paths, use the first statement as _________.
15. To use the functions of os.path, define the first statement as _________.
16. The process of converting text data to binary data is called _______.
17. In Windows operating system, the default encoding for a file is _______.
18. In Linux operating system, the default encoding for a file is _______.

State True/False

1. `Readlines()` reads one line from an open file.
2. The default current position of the file pointer is 0.
3. In a file, the value of char 'e' is 101.
4. Encoding is platform independent.
5. `write()` writes to a file but does not add newline character to the end of the string.
6. The process of converting binary data to text data is called decoding.
7. The default mode to open a file is binary mode.
8. The os module in Python Standard Library provides miscellaneous operating system interfaces.
9. Binary file is represented in bytes format.
10. In Linux, for defining the file path, back slash is used.

Multiple Choice Questions (MCQ)

1. A file is to be opened for reading in binary mode. Use the mode _______.
   (i) r (ii) rb
   (iii) ab (iv) ab+
2. If file exists, open file to append at the end of file, otherwise create a new file. Use the mode _____.
   (i) a (ii) w
   (iii) w+ (iv) x
3. If file exists, the operation fails; otherwise create a new file. Use the mode _____.
   (i) a (ii) w
   (iii) w+ (iv) x

4. To open a file for both reading and writing text, use the mode ______.
   (i) r+ (ii) rb+
   (iii) r (iv) w

5. `readlines()` to read from a file will read ______.
   (i) n number of lines
   (ii) single line
   (iii) all content
   (iv) five lines

6. Get the current working directory using the method ______.
   (i) `listdir()`
   (ii) `scandir()`
   (iii) `chdir()`
   (iv) `getcwd()`

7. To change the current directory use the method ______.
   (i) `listdir()`
   (ii) `scandir()`
   (iii) `chdir()`
   (iv) `getcwd()`

8. To remove a non-empty directory, use the method ______.
   (i) `os.rmdir`
   (ii) `os.remove`
   (iii) `shutil.rmtree`
   (iv) `path.unlink`

A.2 Bloom Level: Comprehend/Understand

Review Questions

1. Describe the features of a text file.
2. Describe the features of a binary file.
3. Why are files needed?
4. Can you read a binary data file in text mode? Justify your answer.
5. From the following file extensions, identify the text and binary files.
   .json, .java, .exe, .png, .csv, .zip, .reg, .mdb
6. Write the syntax of `with` clause. Describe its purpose.
7. What is the need to specify encoding in an open statement?
8. What is the need to close a file?
9. Describe the meaning of following built-in file methods:
   `close()`, `fileno()`, `flush()`, `read(n)`, `write(s)`, `readline(n=-1)`, `readlines(n=-1)`, `writelines(lines)`, `isatty()`, `readable()`, `writable()`, `seekable()`, `truncate(size=None)`, `seek(offset, from)`, `tell()`
10. Explain the following built-in directory methods:
    `getcwd()`, `mkdir()`, `rmdir()`, `listdir()`, `chdir()`, `rename()`, `scandir()`
11. Explain the following `os.path` methods:
    `os.rmdir. os.remove`, `shutil.rmtree`
12. Explain the following `pathlib` methods:
    `path.rmdir. path.unlink`, `shutil.rmtree`
13. Describe the different ways in which a `char` can be written at the start of a file.
14. Why is it better to use `pathlib` for defining file paths rather than `os.path`?
15. Is it better to use absolute path or relative path? Discuss.

A.3 Bloom Level: Application/Apply

1. Find the output for the following:
   `if f1=open("abc.txt". "w")`
   `f1.mode` will return ________.
   `f1.name` will return ________.
   `f1.closed` will return __________.

2. What is the output of statement (1) and statement (2)?

```
with    open    ("abc.txt",
mode='w') as f1:
   print(f1.closed) #(1)
   print(f1.closed) #(2)
```

3. What is the new filename in the following rename statement?
   `os.rename("x.py", "y.py")`

4. Find the output of the following code:
   (a)

```
with open('sample2.txt', 'w') as f:
    f.write("Save the Environment\n")
    f.write("The sky i sbeautiful\n")

with open("sample2.txt", "rb") as f:
    print("1.\t", f.read(10))              #(1)
    print("2.\t", f.tell())                #(2)
    f.seek(-2,1)                           #(3)
    print("3.\t", f.tell())                #(4)
```

   (b) Content of sample2.txt:

```
Save the Environment
The sky is beautiful
Plant more trees
Keep the rivers clean
```

```
f1 = open('sample2.txt')
data = f1.readlines()
print(data)
print(data[0])
print(data[0:2])
```

5. Find the output at statement#(1) to statement #(10) in the following code:

```
with open('sample1.txt', 'w') as f:
   f.write("1:Gorgeous\n")
   f.write("2:Beautiful\n")
   f.write("3a:Smart\t")
   f.write("3b:Living\n")

with open("sample1.txt", "r") as f:
    print("1.\t", f.read(2))             #(1)
    print("2.\t", f.read(8))             #(2)
    print("3.\t", f.tell())              #(3)
    f.seek(4)
    print("4.\t", f.tell())              #(4)
    print("5.\t", f.readline())          #(5)
    print("6.\t", f.read(9))             #(6)
    f.seek(0, 2)
    print("7.\t", f.tell())              #(7)
    print("8.\t", f.read())              #(8)
    f.seek(20,0)
    print("9.\t", f.tell())              #(9)
    print("10.\t", f.read())             #(10)
```

6. Find errors, and correct the code:
(a)

```
with open('sample2.txt', 'w') as f:
   f.write("Save the Environment\n")
   f.write("The sky i sbeautiful\n")

with open("sample2.txt", "r") as f:
    print("1.\t", f.read(10))          #(1)
    print("2.\t", f.tell())            #(2)
    f.seek(4,1)                        #(3)
    print("3.\t", f.tell())            #(4)
```

(b)

```
with open('sample2.txt', 'w') as f:
   f.write("Save the Environment\n")
   f.write("The sky i sbeautiful\n")

with open("sample2.txt", "r") as f:
    print("1.\t", f.read(10))          #(1)
    print("2.\t", f.tell())            #(2)
    f.seek(-2,1)                       #(3)
    print("3.\t", f.tell())            #(4)
```

(c) This is the code to replace all newlines with blanks in a file. The content of the file is shown before the execution of the code. After the code is executed, the file is empty. Find the error in the code and correct it.
Content of sample2.txt:

```
Save the Environment
The sky is beautiful
```

```
with open('sample2.txt', 'w+') as f1:
    f1_data = f1.read().replace('\n', ' ')
    f1.write(f1_data)
    print(f1_data)
```

(d) This is the code to insert a new content at the first position in the file. After the code is executed, an error is thrown. Find the error in the code and correct it.

```
f = open("sample2.txt" , "r+")
file_data = f.readline()
print(file_data)
f.close()

file_data.insert(1 , "New line inserted!\n")
f = open("sample2.txt" , "w")
f.writelines(file_data)
f.close()

f = open("sample2.txt" , "r+")
file_data = f.readlines()
print(file_data)
f.close()
```

A.4 Bloom Level: Analyze

1. Explain the difference between the following:
   (i) Text file and Binary file
   (ii) Relative file path and Absolute file path
   (iii) `readline()` and `readlines()`
   (iv) w, a, x modes when writing to a file.
   (v) os.path and `pathlib`.
2. Differentiate between the following modes:
   (a) r and r+
   (b) w and w+
   (c) a and a+
   (d) r+ and w+
3. Analyze the following codes. What is the task performed? What is the output?
   (a)

```
import os
os.rename( "sample1.txt", "sample1copy.txt" )
```

   (b)

```
f1 = open("sample1copy.txt", "rb")
print("f1 in rb mode =\t", f1)
```

   (c)

```
from pathlib import Path
path = Path.home()/'sample'
path.mkdir()
print(path)
```

   (d)

```
import os
path= os.path.join(os.path.expanduser('~'), 'sample2.txt')
print("path=", path)
with open(path, 'a') as f1:
    f1.write(str("extended")+'\n')
with open(path, 'r') as f1:
    print(f1.readlines())
```

4. Analyze the difference between (i) and (ii). What is the output? Justify.
   (i)

```
f1 = open("file1.txt", "rb")
print("1.   f1 in rb mode =\t", f1)
```

   (ii)

```
f1 = open("file1.txt", "r")
print("1.   f1 in r mode =\t", f1)
```

5. Identify the output. Analyze it and justify.
   (a) The file "sample2.txt" opened in w+ mode does not exist before the following code is executed.

```
with open('sample2.txt', 'w+') as f:
    f.write("Save the Environment\n")
    f.write("The sky i sbeautiful\n")

with open("sample2.txt", "rb") as f:
    print("1.\t", f.read(10))          #(1)
    print("2.\t", f.tell())            #(2)
```

(b) The file "sample2.txt" opened in r+ mode does not exist before the following code is executed.

```
with open('sample2.txt', 'r+') as f:
    f.write("Save the Environment\n")
    f.write("The sky i sbeautiful\n")

with open("sample2.txt", "rb") as f:
    print("1.\t", f.read(10))          #(1)
    print("2.\t", f.tell())            #(2)
```

(c) Diffferentiate between (i) and (ii).

(i)

```
with open('sample2.txt', 'rb+') as f:
    f.write(b"Save the Environment\n")
    f.write(b"The sky is beautiful\n")
    print("1.\t", f.tell())            #(1)
    print("2.\t", f.read(10))          #(2)
    print("3.\t", f.tell())            #(3)

with open('sample2.txt', 'rb+') as f:
    f.write(b"Save the Environment\n")
    f.write(b"The sky is beautiful\n")
    print("1.\t", f.tell())            #(1)
with open("sample2.txt", "rb") as f:
    print(f.readlines())
    print("2.\t", f.read(10))          #(2)
    print("3.\t", f.tell())            #(3)
```

(ii)

```
with open('sample2.txt', 'r+') as f:
    f.write("Save the Environment\n")
    f.write("The sky is beautiful\n")
    print("1.\t", f.tell())            #(1)
    print("2.\t", f.read(10))          #(2)
    print("3.\t", f.tell())            #(3)

with open('sample2.txt', 'r+') as f:
    f.write("Save the Environment\n")
    f.write("The sky is beautiful\n")
    print("1.\t", f.tell())            #(1)
with open("sample2.txt", "r") as f:
    print(f.readlines())
    print("2.\t", f.read(10))          #(2)
    print("3.\t", f.tell())            #(3)
```

A.5 Bloom Level: Evaluate

1. Evaluate the following file path and answer the questions below.
   "C:/Desktop/Python/abc.py"
   a) Directory of abc.py
   b) Filename
   c) Parent directory of abc.py
   d) Number of sub-directories of C: in the file path
   e) List of sub-directories of C: in the file path
   f) Operating system on the machine
   g) Draw the hierarchy of folders
   h) Identify the root folder.

2. Evaluate the following code. (i) What is the content of file sample2.txt at line #1, 2, 3, 4? What is printed in the output at line # 1, 2, 3, 4? Analyze the output with reason.

```
with open('sample2.txt', 'w') as f:
    f.write("Save the Environment\n")
    f.write("The sky is beautiful\n")
    f.write("Plant more trees\n")
    f.write("Keep the rivers clean\n")                    #(1)

with open('sample2.txt', 'r') as f1:
     f1_data = f1.read().replace('\n', ' ')
     print(f1_data)                                        #(2)

with open('sample2.txt', 'r+') as f1:
     f1_data = f1.read().replace('\n', ' ')
     f1.write(f1_data)
     print(f1_data)                                        #(3)

with open('sample2.txt', 'w+') as f1:
     f1_data = f1.read().replace('\n', ' ')
     f1.write(f1_data)
     print(f1_data)                                        #(4)
```

3. Evaluate the code. (i) What is the task performed? (2) What is the output?
   (a)

```
from pathlib import Path
s1 = Path('sample2.txt').stat().st_size
print(s1)
```

   (b)

```
import os
s1 = os.path.getsize('sample2.txt')
print(s1)
```

   (c)

```
with open('sample2.txt', "r") as f1:
    f1_content = f1.readlines()
    for line in f1_content:
        wrds = line.split()
        print (wrds)
```

(d)

```
f1 = open('sample5.txt', "w+")
print("Is sample5.txt readable: ", f1.readable())
print("Is sample5.txt writeable: ",f1.writable())
print("File no:", f1.fileno())
f1.close()
```

(e)

```
f1 = open('sample5.txt', "wb+")
data= "Everything is Energy"
f1_encode = data.encode("ASCII")
f1.write(f1_encode)

f1.seek(0)
f1_bin_data = f1.read()
print("Binary Data:\t", f1_bin_data)

f1_txt_datan = f1_bin_data.decode("ASCII")
print("Text data:\t", f1_txt_datan)
```

4. Evaluate the code for the following. (i) Identify the task performed. (ii) Find the output. Discuss how the task performed by the code can be done in a different way.

(a)

```
with open('sample2.txt','r') as f1, open('sample3.txt','a') as f2:
    for line in f1:
        f2.write(line)
```

(b)

```
with open("sample2.txt") as f1, open("sample3.txt") as f2:
   f1_content = f1.readline()
   f2_content = f2.readline()
   print(f1_content, f2_content)
```

(c)

```
def file_no_lines(file1):
    with open(file1) as f1:
        for count,line in enumerate(f1):
            print(count, line)
            pass
    return count + 1
print("Number of lines in file: ",file_no_lines("sample2.txt"))
```

A.6 Bloom Level: Create/Synthesize

Programming Assignment

1. WAP to read the first n lines of a file.
2. WAP to append text to a file and display the text.
3. WAP to read the last n lines of a file.
4. WAP to read a file line by line and store it into a list.
5. WAP to read a file line by line and store it into a variable.
6. WAP to read a file line by line and store it into an array.
7. WAP to find the length of each word in a file.
8. WAP to count the number of lines in a text file.
9. WAP to count the frequency of words in a file.
10. WAP to get the file size of a plain file.
11. WAP to write a list to a file.
12. WAP to copy the content of a file to another file
13. WAP to combine each line from the first file with the corresponding line in the second file.
14. WAP to read a random line from a file.
15. WAP to assess if a file is closed or not.
16. WAP to remove newline characters from a file.
17. WAP that takes a text file as input and returns the number of words of a given text file.
18. WAP to extract characters from various text files and put them into a list.
19. WAP to count words in a text file those are ending with alphabet "e".
20. WAP to count the uppercase characters in a text file.
21. WAP to read lines from a text file and display the words that are less than 4 characters.
22. WAP to create a binary file having the details of the students (20 students). It must contain – Roll no., Name, Fees, Course, Marks. Perform the following operations:
    - Calculate total fees of all students.
    - Display the details of the file for the Roll No. x.
    - Display the details of the file for the students having marks more than 75%.
23. WAP to create a file having the details of the books issued to the students in a library (20 students). It must contain – Roll no., Name, No_book_issued. Perform the following operations:
    - List all students who have more than two books issued.
    - What is the total number of books issued to all the students?

Answers

A.1 Bloom Level: Knowledge/Remember

Review Questions

10. (1)-(c), (2)-(b), (3)-(a)

Fill in the Blanks

1. disk **2.** text, binary **3.** str **4.** unicode
5. binary **6.** back **7.** relative **8.** read
9. readline() **10.** bytes **11.** seek() **12.** io
13. `pathlib` **14.** from `pathlib` import path **15.** import os
16. encoding **17.** <cp1252> **18.** <utf-8>

True/False

1. False **2.** True **3.** False **4.** False **5.** True **6.** True **7.** False **8.** True
9. True **10.** False

Multiple Choice Questions (MCQ)

1. (ii) **2.** (i) **3.** (iv) **4.** (i) **5.** (iii) **6.** (iv) **7.** (iii) **8.** (iii)

A.3 Bloom Level: Apply

1. w, abc.txt, False **2.** False; True

3. `y.py`

4. (a)

```
1.        b'Save the E'
2.        10
3.        8
```

(b)

```
['Save the Environment\n', 'The sky is beautiful\n', 'Plant more trees\n', 'Keep
 the rivers clean\n']
First line:  Save the Environment

First Two lines: ['Save the Environment\n', 'The sky is beautiful\n']
```

5.

```
1.        1:
2.        Gorgeous
3.        10
4.        4
5.        rgeous

6.        2:Beautif
7.        45
8.
9.        20
10.       ful
3a:Smart          3b:Living
```

6. (a)

Use binary mode

```
    f.seek(4,1)
io.UnsupportedOperation: can't do nonzero cur-relative seeks
```

(b)

Use binary mode

```
    f.seek(-2,1)                          #(3)
io.UnsupportedOperation: can't do nonzero cur-relative seeks
```

(c)

Replace w+ with r+.

(d) Use `readlines()` instead of `readline()`. `readlines()` returns a list. `readline()` returns a string.
A str object has no insert() method but a list object does.

```
['Save the Environment\n', 'The sky is beautiful\n', 'Plant more trees\n', 'Keep
 the rivers clean\n']
['Save the Environment\n', 'New line inserted!\n', 'The sky is beautiful\n', 'Pl
ant more trees\n', 'Keep the rivers clean\n']
```

A.4 Bloom Level: Analyze

3. (a) Renames the file sample1.txt to sample1copy.txt

(b)

```
f1 in rb mode =  <_io.BufferedReader name='sample1copy.txt'>
```

(c)

```
C:\Users\Anita Goel\sample
```

(d)

```
path= C:\Users\Anita Goel\sample2.txt
['extended\n']
```

4.

```
1.    f1 in rb mode =     <_io.BufferedReader name='file1.txt'>
1.    f1 in r mode =      <_io.TextIOWrapper name='file1.txt' mode='r' encoding='
cp1252'>
```

5. (a)

```
1.       b'Save the E'
2.       10
```

(b)

```
FileNotFoundError: [Errno 2] No such file or directory: 'sample2.txt'
```

(c)

```
1.       42
2.       b'\r\n\r\n'
3.       46
1.       42
[b'Save the Environment\n', b'The sky is beautiful\n', b'\r\n', b'\r\n']
2.       b''
3.       46
```

```
1.       44
2.

3.       46
1.       44
['Save the Environment\n', 'The sky is beautiful\n', '\n']
2.
3.       46
```

A.5 Bloom Level: Evaluate

1.

Directory of abc.py	`C:/Desktop/Python`
Filename	`abc.py`
Parent directory of abc.py	`Python`
Number of sub-directories of C: in the file path	2
List of sub-directories of C: in the file path	`Desktop, Python`
Operating system on the machine	Windows
Identify root folder.	C:

2. #1 File:

```
Save the Environment
The sky is beautiful
Plant more trees
Keep the rivers clean
```

Printed: nothing

#2 File: same as (#1).

Printed

```
Save the Environment The sky is beautiful Plant more trees Keep the rivers clean
```

#3 File:

```
Save the Environment
The sky is beautiful
Plant more trees
Keep the rivers clean
Save the Environment The sky is beautiful Plant more trees Keep the rivers clean
```

Printed:

```
Save the Environment The sky is beautiful Plant more trees Keep the rivers clean
```

#4 File: blank file

Printed: blank line

w+ deletes all the old content from text file and save new text in the file.

3. (a) `166` Finds the size of the file.

(b) `166` Finds the size of the file.

(c) Splits the content of file into words.

```
['Save', 'the', 'Environment']
['The', 'sky', 'is', 'beautiful']
['Plant', 'more', 'trees']
['Keep', 'the', 'rivers', 'clean']
['Save', 'the', 'Environment', 'The', 'sky', 'is', 'beautiful', 'Plant', 'more',
 'trees', 'Keep', 'the', 'rivers', 'clean']
```

(d) Checks the file – readable, writable and file no.

```
Is sample5.txt readable:  True
Is sample5.txt writeable:  True
File no: 4
```

(e) Does encoding–decoding for binary data.

```
Binary Data:     b'Everything is Energy'
Text data:       Everything is Energy
```

4. (a) Writes the content of f1 to f2.
(b) Opens two files in reading mode. Prints one line each.
(c) Counts the number of lines in the file.

```
0 Save the Environment

1 The sky is beautiful

2 Plant more trees

3 Keep the rivers clean

Number of lines in file:  4
```

CHAPTER 12

Error and Exception Handling

Contents

12.1 Introduction

In compiled languages like C++, some errors get detected during compilation and others during execution of the program. Python is an interpretive language. When a Python program is executed, it is translated into byte code. If there is an error in the program whereby the rules of the language are not followed, then the byte code is not generated and a syntax error appears. The program has to be corrected and then executed again, until there is no syntax error in the program under execution. The syntactically correct program is executed.

During execution of a syntactically correct program, an exception may occur. An exception is an unusual circumstance and when it arises, it results in abrupt termination of execution of the program. For a graceful termination of the program, in cases where exception may arise, there is a need for handling the exception in a program. Exception handling allows a program to be terminated normally, with an appropriate message, when an exception occurs.

In this chapter, we discuss the different kinds of errors, built-in exceptions, handling of exceptions and use of assertion for debugging in Python.

Learning Outcomes of this chapter

After completion of the chapter, the learner will be able to:

- Understand syntax errors
- Understand exception
- Handle the exceptions
- Use assertions in programs
- Formulate programs using exception handling
- Develop programs by incorporating the concepts discussed.

12.2 Syntax Error

In context of a programming language, **syntax** is a set of rules for the grammar and spelling of language, i.e., rules that define structure of the language. Syntax involves rules relating to the structure of symbols, punctuation, and the words used, such as naming conventions and reserved words. A program written in Python must follow the syntax of the Python programming language. While writing a Python program, the programmer must pay attention to the syntax of the Python language.

Syntax error is an error in syntax of the Python code written by the programmer. Syntax error appears in a program when the rules of writing the Python program have not been followed. It means the syntax provided by the Python language has been violated. Syntax error may appear due to several reasons. Some examples are listed below:

- Spelling mistake in reserved word (writing fr instead of for in `for` statement)
- Wrong syntax (not putting colon after the control statements, missing quotes in print-statement, missing a closing bracket)
- Indentation error (indentation not in alignment with the code); and many more.

Syntax error in a Python program is caught by the Python interpreter during execution.

- Python is an interpretive language. The interpreter works by first parsing the Python program and then converting it into byte code.
- If during parsing, a syntax error is found, the code is not successfully parsed.
- When syntax error appears in the Python program, the interpreter tries to show where the error has occurred. A red-colored bar can be seen at the line having the error. A pop-up window, SyntaxError, appears and shows a message of invalid syntax. Figure 12.1 shows a snapshot of a code where the colon is missing at the end of `for`-statement. A SyntaxError window is displayed.

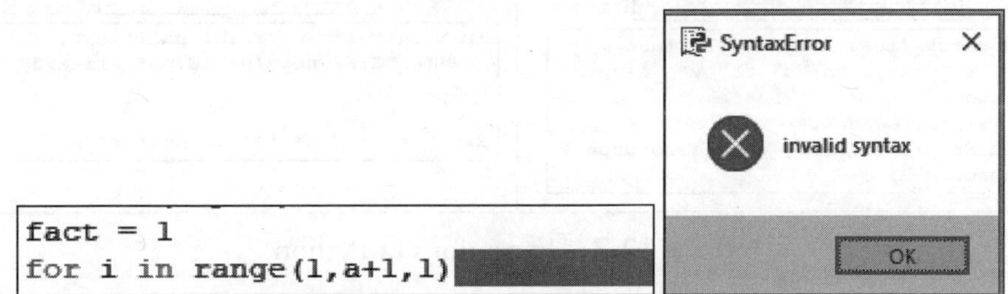

Figure 12.1 An example with syntax error

- The syntax error needs to be fixed by the programmer for successful execution of the program.
- When there are no syntax errors in the program, the Python program executes successfully.

12.3 Exceptions: An Overview

Exceptions handle the errors that occur during the execution of Python programs. Exceptions do not happen because of syntax error. Syntactically, the code is correct. During execution of the program, some unusual condition may arise in the program that results in an error and cannot be handled by the system. This interrupts the flow of execution of the program. An exception occurs and stops further execution of the program. We have already encountered exceptions (Figure 12.2) in our earlier chapters. Some cases are:

- Accessing array index that is out of range (Exception: IndexError)
- Applying an operation to an object of inappropriate type (Exception: TypeError)
- Passing value of an argument that is incorrect (Exception: ValueError)
- Not finding a variable in local or global space (Exception: NameError).

Some errors in the programs related to files are as follows:

- Open a file. File not found for reading. `IOError "No such file or directory"`
  ```
  f = open ("abc.txt")
  ```
- Open a file. Encoding not defined. `UnicodeDecodeError:`
  ```
  f = open('abc.txt') # encoding= 'utf-8' not defined
  x = f.read()
  ```

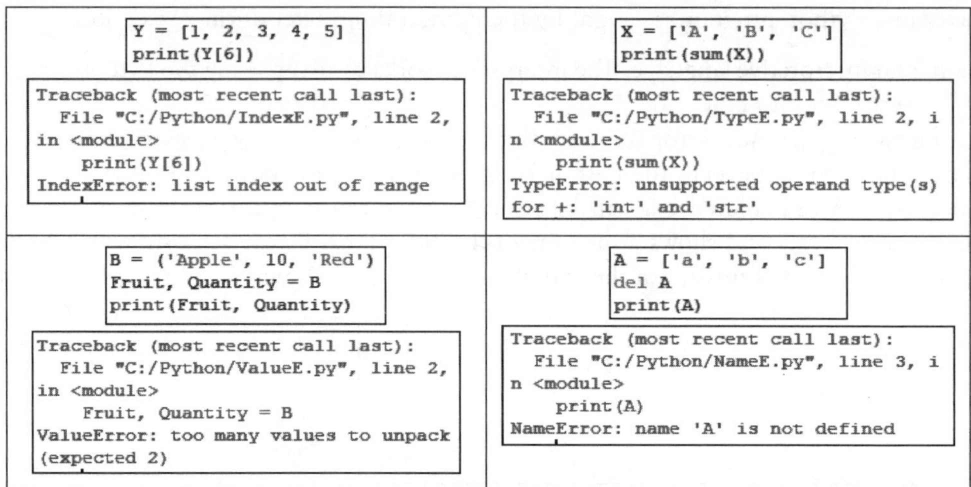

Figure 12.2 Exceptions in Python

- Write float data to file. `TypeError: expected a character buffer object`

```
pi = 3.141592
f1 = open('abc.txt', 'w')
f1.write(pi)  # f1.write(str(pi)
```

Until now, we have seen that when an error occurs, Python reports the exception on the screen and execution of the program terminates. Also, as a result of exception, a program may crash, resulting in data loss, or it may corrupt the data.

Exceptions need to be handled. Python provides a way to handle the exception so that execution of the program does not stop abruptly, and the rest of the code is executed without any interruption. For this, Python has an error-handling framework and a set of pre-defined exceptions. A Python programmer needs to include the error handling code in the program for the possible exception situations. Some key points for exception handling are as follows:

- An exception is a Python object that represents an error.
- Exception is a value (object) raised (thrown) automatically by Python. It signals occurrence of exception condition. As a result, the program proceeds to handle the exception that is generated.
- *Raise* or *throw* exception is the task of generating an exception.
- *Catching* an exception means responding to the exception.
- *Handling* an exception means defining what to do when an exception is caught. Different types of exceptions may require different actions.
- Python provides different kinds of exceptions for the different types of errors. The relevant exception is raised based on the type of error.
- Python provides *built-in exceptions* and also allows users to define their own exceptions.

We discuss how to handle exceptions, so that we can correct the error and continue with execution of the program, or, we may terminate the program gracefully, maybe by displaying the appropriate message.

12.4 Built-in Exceptions

Built-in exceptions are handled by the Python software itself. Python has built-in exceptions of different types. The type of exception helps in identifying the cause of the error. Table 12.1 shows some standard exceptions in Python along with their cause of error.

Table 12.1 Some standard exceptions and cause for error

Exception	Cause of Error
AssertionError	Raised when *assert* statement fails
ImportError	Raised when the import statement fails
IndexError	Raised when index is out of range
KeyError	Raised when a key is not found in dictionary
KeyboardInterrupt	Raised when the user hits Ctrl+C or delete
NameError	Raised when a variable is not found in local/global scope
OSError	Raised when system operation causes system-related error
RuntimeError	Raised when error does not fall under any other category
SystemError	Raised when interpreter detects internal error
TypeError	Raised when operation is applied to object of incorrect type
UnicodeError	Raised when Unicode-related encoding/decoding error occurs
ValueError	Raised when function gets argument of correct type but improper value
ZeroDivisionError	Raised when the denominator of division is zero

The built-in exceptions in Python are structured hierarchically. Table 12.2 shows the hierarchy of built-in exceptions. We note that all exceptions inherit from `BaseException`. For example, `NameError` inherits from `Exception` and also from `BaseException`. However, most exceptions inherit from `Exception`.

Different types of exceptions are generated so that cause of the error is reported appropriately. For example, `TypeError` occurs when an operation or function is applied to an object of incorrect type; for example, when a list is passed instead of a float. `ValueError` occurs when a built-in operation or function gets an argument of right type but wrong value; for example, negative values instead of positive.

Table 12.2 Python Built-in Exceptions

`BaseException`
- `SystemExit`
- `KeyboardInterrupt`
- `GeneratorExit`

(Continued)

Table 12.2 (Continued)

- `Exception`
    - `StopIteration`
    - `StopAsyncIteration`
    - `ArithmeticError`
        - `FloatingPointError, OverflowError, ZeroDivisionError`
    - `AssertionError`
    - `AttributeError`
    - `BufferError`
    - `EOFError`
    - `ImportError`
        - `ModuleNoteFoundError`
    - `LookupError`
        - `IndexError, KeyError`
    - `MemoryError`
    - `NameError`
        - `UnboundLocalError`
    - `OSError`
        - `BlockingIOError`
        - `ChildProcessError`
        - `ConnectionError`
        - `BrokenPipeError, ConnectionAbortedError`
        - `ConnectionRefusedError, ConnectionResetError`
        - `FileExistsError`
        - `FileNotFoundError`
        - `InterruptedError`
        - `IsADirectoryError`
        - `NotADirectoryError`
        - `PermissionError`
        - `ProcessLookupError`
        - `TimeoutError`
- `ReferenceError`
- `RuntimeError`
    - `NotImplementedError, RecursionError`
- `SyntaxError`
    - `IndentationError`
        - `TabError`
- `SystemError`
- `TypeError`
- `ValueError`
    - `UnicodeError`
        - `UnicodeDecodeError, UnicodeEncodeError,`
        - `UnicodeTranslateError`

(Continued)

Table 12.2 (Continued)

- `Warning`
  - o `DeprecationWarning, PendingDeprecationWarning`
  - o `RuntimeWarning, SyntaxWarning`
  - o `UserWarning, FutureWarning, ImportWarning`
  - o `UnicodeWarning, BytesWarningException, ResourceWarning`

Source: https://docs.python.org/3/library/exceptions.html#base-classes

12.5 Catching and Handling Exceptions

Python allows programmers to define their own exception, in addition to the built-in exception. Programmers can identify the cause of error and define their own exception. The exceptions can be caught and handled so that the programs do not crash. Handling of exceptions may involve displaying appropriate error message to the user or may be even fixing the problem that is causing the error.

Exception handling in Python is similar to that in Java. Java uses try-catch block to catch and handle exceptions. Python provides `try-except` block to catch and handle exceptions.

The `try-except` block has the following variations:

1. Try-except with exception
2. Try-except with no exception
3. Try-except with multiple exceptions
4. Try-except-else
5. Try-except-finally

The exception handling and `try-except` block variations are discussed in the following subsection.

12.5.1 `Try-except` Block

The format of `try-except` block in Python is as follows:

```
try:
     try_body
except exceptionType1 as var1:
     exceptionHandleCode1
except exceptionType2 as var2:
     exceptionHandleCode2
     .
     .
     .
except:
     default_exceptionHandleCode
else:
     else_body
finally:
     finally_body
```

The important points to note about `try-except` block are as follows:

- **`try` statement** allows testing of `try-code` for errors.
  - o `try-body`: The code that has a potential to cause error is written in `try-body`.
  - o When the `try` statement executes, the `try-body` is executed. The result of execution is either error or no error.
    - ▪ If no error occurs, all `except-statement` are skipped. The control comes to next statement following `try-except` block.
    - ▪ If error occurs, an exception is thrown. The rest of `try-body` is skipped. Depending on how `try-except` block is written, the exception handling varies.
- `try` statement can have any number of `except` statements, to throw different types of exceptions.
- **`except`** statement handles the error.
  - o `exceptionType1, exceptionType2` are the types of exception to be caught.
  - o `exceptionHandleCode1, exceptionHandleCode2` are the codes to be executed for handling their respective exception types.
- **`except` with one exception:** The exception thrown is matched with `exceptionType1`.
  - o If it matches, the exception is handled. `exceptionHandleCode1` is executed.
  - o If it does not match, it is passed to the outer `try` statement. If no handler is found, the exception is unhandled and the execution of the program stops.
- **`except` with multiple exceptions** is searched sequentially to match thrown exception with `exceptionType1, exceptionType2,` and so on.
  - o If it matches, the corresponding `exceptionHandleCode1, exceptionHandleCode2,`... is executed.
  - o If it does not match, it is passed to the outer `try` statement. If no handler is found, the exception is unhandled and the execution of the program stops.
- **`except` without exception** is the last statement of `try-except`. It is used to handle all types of exceptions. It executes if any earlier exception type does not match. Then `default_exceptionHandleCode` is executed.
- **`except` exception with argument** provides additional information about the error. The argument or variable (var1, var2, ...) specifies the cause of error.
- **`else`** statement specifies `else-body`, where any code that is to be executed is processed if there are no exceptions from `try` block. **`else`** statement is written after all `except` statements. **`else`** statement is executed if `try` statement does not throw any error.
- **`finally`** statement always executes, irrespective of the result of `try` and `except` statements. It executes after the `try`, `except` and `else` have got executed. **`finally`** statement defines `finally_body`, where any code that is required to clean the exception handling, like close files, or other variables is specified.

It may be noted that after executing code in the `except` statement, execution of the rest of program continues normally.

Let us take an example: Writing a program for factorial of *n*. As we understand, *n* must be positive. When we write a program, we have the following possibilities for handling the error arising due to non-positive number entered by the user.

- *Case 1:* Report error on screen. Program ends abruptly.
- *Case 2:* Catch error – correct error – continue execution.
- *Case 3:* Catch error – terminate the program gracefully.

Example 12.1: Write the factorial program for Case 1. The program ends abruptly in case of an error. A character is input and ValueError is reported. Program execution stops.

```
#==============================================================
#Factorial =Case 1:Report error on screen. Program ends abruptly.
#==============================================================

f1 = int(input("Enter a number:"))
if (f1 > 0):
    fact = 1
    for x in range(1, f1+1):
        fact *= x
    print(f1, "! = %i" %fact)
```

```
Enter a number:8
8 ! = 40320
>>>
======= RESTART: C:\Anita Goel\Python\Chapter 12. Exceptions\Exception.py =====
Enter a number:-7
>>>
======= RESTART: C:\Anita Goel\Python\Chapter 12. Exceptions\Exception.py =====
Enter a number:k
Traceback (most recent call last):
  File "C:\Anita Goel\Python\Chapter 12. Exceptions\Exception.py", line 11, in <
module>
    f1 = int(input("Enter a number:"))
ValueError: invalid literal for int() with base 10: 'k'
```

Example 12.2: Write the factorial program for Case 2. The program catches any error in the input and asks the user to correct the input error. When the correct value is entered, the result is printed.

```
#==============================================================
# Factorial =Case 2: Catch error-correct error-continue execution===
#==============================================================
while True:
    try:
        f1 = int(input("Enter a number:"))
        if (f1 >= 0):
            break
        else:
            print("Please enter only positive number")
    except Exception:
            print("Please enter number only")

fact = 1
for x in range(1, f1+1):
    fact *= x
print(f1, "! = %i" %fact)
```

```
Enter a number:7
7 ! = 5040
```

```
Enter a number:-7
Please enter only positiv
Enter a number:7
7 ! = 5040
```

```
Enter a number:k
Please enter number only
Enter a number:9
9 ! = 362880
```

Example 12.3: Write the factorial program for Case 3. The program catches any error in the input, raises an exception and terminates the program gracefully.

```
#======================================================================
# Factorial =Case 3:Catch error - terminate the program gracefully.===
#======================================================================

try:
    f1 = int(input("Enter a number:"))
    if (f1 < 0):
        print("Please enter only positive number")
    else:
        fact = 1
        for x in range(1, f1+1):
            fact *= x
        print(f1, "! = %i" %fact)
except Exception:
        print("Please enter number only")
```

```
Enter a number:7
7 ! = 5040
```

```
Enter a number:-8
Please enter only positive number
```

```
Enter a number:k
Please enter number only
```

Example 12.4: Open a file in `try` statement. The code must close the file, always.

```
try:
    f = open("test.txt",encoding = 'utf-8')

finally:
    f.close()
```

Tip

User-defined exception should be made subclass of `Exception` and not `BaseException`.

This is because `KeyboardException` is not a subclass of `Exception`. So, exception handling code will not be triggered if user interrupts code using ctrl-c

12.6 Raising Exceptions

Python allows the user to raise an exception explicitly. For this, a `raise` statement is provided in Python. Exception is an object generated automatically with `raise` statement. The syntax of `raise` statement is:

```
raise [exception [, args [, traceback]]]
```

In the syntax,
`exception` is type of exception.
`args` is value for exception argument.
`traceback` is traceback object used for exception.

After an exception is raised, the execution of the program proceeds differently. After the `raise` statement is executed, it looks for the handler (starting from where it was raised to the top level of the program). If handler is found, it is invoked and executed; if not found, the program aborts with an error message.

Raise exception is not required for built-in exceptions. It is used when you define own exceptions unique to your program (discussed in the next section).

Let us now see some examples of `raise` statement.

Example 12.5: Write the factorial program using the raise exception.
In the program, we see that we raise ValueError in the factorial function which gets caught in the `try-except` statement.

```
#==============================================================
# Factorial with raise
#==============================================================
def factorial(n):
    n = int(n)
    if n < 0:
        raise ValueError()
    if n == 0:
        return 1
    else:
        return n * factorial(n-1)

x = input("Enter a number: ")
try:
    y = factorial(x)
except ValueError:
    print("Pl. enter positive number")
except:
    print("An error occurred!")
    raise
else:
    print("{x}! = {y}".format(x=x, y=y))
```

```
Enter a number: -7
Pl. enter positive number
```

```
Enter a number: 9
9! = 362880
```

```
Enter a number: k
Pl. enter positive number
```

Example 12.6: Write a program to raise an exception if the number is positive.

```
#===========================================================
# raise EXception
#===========================================================

def func1(n):
   if n > 1:
      raise Exception(n)
   return n
try:

   i = int(input("Enter a number: "))
   x = func1(i)
   print ("n = ",x)
except Exception as e:
   print ("Caught the exception:",e.args[0])
```

```
Enter a number: -9
n =  -9
```

```
Enter a number: 8
Caught the exception: 8
```

12.7 USER-DEFINED EXCEPTIONS

Python allows users to define their own exceptions. The syntax of defining the exception is:

```
class MyDefError(Exception):
   pass
```

Defining a class like this, inherits all methods and variables from the Exception class. This exception can be raised, caught and handled like the built-in exceptions.

To see the variables and methods that you want to override, get help from - help(Exception) or dir('Exception') or help(dir('Exception'))

Object-oriented Programming is discussed in the next chapter.

12.8 ASSERTIONS

Assertion is a debugging expression used for self-checking of the program. It is used by the programmer for knowing the internal state of the program during testing, like value of variables and control condition. It is not meant for the user of the program. It is meant for the programmer. Some key points for assertion are as follows:

- Assertion is a condition or a Boolean expression.
- Assertion evaluates to either True or False.

- Assertion is written in the program to be always True.
- If assertion is True, nothing happens.
- If assertion is False, error is thrown. The program execution stops.
- Assertions are used to check for errors, like, type of parameter, pre-condition and conditional values.
- Assertions can be turned off after successfully checking the program during testing.

The syntax of assert statement is:

```
assert Expression[, Arguments]
```

In the syntax,
`Expression` evaluates to a Boolean (True or False)
`Arguments` are error messages
When assertion fails, AssertionError is thrown.

Example 12.7: Write a program to find the square of a positive number. Use assertion to check that the number is positive.

```
def square(x):
    assert x>=0, 'Enter only positive numbers'
    return x*x
i = int(input("Enter a number: "))
n = square(i)
print("Square of", i, ": ", n)
```

```
Enter a number: 8
Square of 8 :  64
>>>
```

```
Enter a number: -9
Traceback (most recent call last):
AssertionError: Enter only positive numbers
```

12.9 Solved Questions with Explanation

1. Some codes with bugs are provided here. Also a message is provided to be printed to handle exception handling. Insert exception handling with the message at the correct position in the code, so that the code teminates gracefully in case of any error.

(i) *IndexError*

message = "Index out of range"

```
x=[10, 20, 30]
try:
    print(x[4])
```

Explanation

```
x=[10, 20, 30]
try:
     print(x[4])
except IndexError as error:
     message="Index out of range"
     print(message)
```

(ii) BaseException Error

message="Cannot add int and string".

a="Hello World!"

try:

a + 10

print(message)

Explanation

```
a="Good Morning!"
try:
   a + 10
except Exception:
   message= "Cannot add int and string"
   print(message)
```

(iii) ZeroDivisionError

message="division by zero"

a = 10

b = 0

try:

ans= a/b

except ZeroDivisionError:

Explanation

```
a = 10
b = 0
try:
     ans= a/b
except ZeroDivisionError:
     message = "Division by zero"
     print(message)
```

2. Identify the reason for the error. Use exception handling in the code.

(i)

```
animals = ["lion", "tiger", "leopard", "horse", "cow", "cat"]
x = []
for i in animals:
    x.append(x[4])
```

Explanation: An error will occur as x is empty and we are trying to access x[4].

```
animals = ["lion", "tiger", "leopard", "horse", "cow", "cat"]
x = []
try:
    for i in animals:
        x.append(x[4])
except:
    print("An error occured")
```

(ii)

```
def total(n):
    return sum(n)
def avg(sum, n):
    return sum / n
def complete(list):
    for i in list:
        print(i, "Average=", avg(total(i), len(i)))
a = [10, 20, 30, 40, 50]
b = [100, 200, 300, 400, 500]
c = []
x = [a, b, c]
complete(x)
```

Explanation: An error will occur as c is empty and when average is calculated, it will be division by zero.

```
def total(n):
    return sum(n)
def avg(sum, n):
    return sum / n
def complete(list):
    try:
        for i in list:
            print(i, "Average=", avg(total(i), len(i)))
    except ZeroDivisionError:
        pass
a = [10, 20, 30, 40, 50]
b = [100, 200, 300, 400, 500]
c = []
x = [a, b, c]
complete(x)
```

(iii)

```
age = int(input("Enter the age:"))
if(age>18):
    print("the age is valid")
```

Explanation: An error will occur if user enters a non-integer number. We raise exception with multiple arguments that are returned as a tuple. They are accessed via args variable of error

```
try:
    age = int(input("Enter the age:"))
    if(age<18):
        raise ValueError("You entered", age, "age less than 18")
    else:
        print("the age is valid")
except ValueError as e:
    print("Error: {0} {2}: {1}".
          format(e.args[0], e.args[1], e.args[2]))
```

```
Enter the age:2
Error: You entered age less than 18: 2
```

3. Explain the difference in the output of the two codes.

```
a = int(input("Enter a positive integer: "))
if a <= 0:
    raise ValueError("That is not a positive number!")
```

```
try:
    a = int(input("Enter a positive integer: "))
    if a <= 0:
        raise ValueError("That is not a positive number!")
except ValueError as ve:
    print(ve)
```

Explanation: If the error is raised but not caught, then the error is displayed after the Traceback statement. The output of the two codes when a non-positive integer is entered is shown below.

```
Enter a positive integer: -4
Traceback (most recent call last):
```

```
ValueError: That is not a positive number!
```

```
Enter a positive integer: -4
That is not a positive number!
```

4. Find the syntax error in the code.

```
data = 50
try:
    data = data/10
except ZeroDivisionError:
    print("Sorry! You cannot divide by 0")
finally:
    print("Yippe! I am done")
else:
    print('Division successful ', end = '')
```

Explanation: The `else` block after the `finally` is not allowed.

5. Identify the redundant code.

(i)

```
x = [1, 2, 3]
y = 0
try:
    y = x[3]
except IndexError:
    print("First except")
except:
    print("Second except")
```

(ii)

```
x = [1, 2, 3, 4]
try:
    x = x[5]/0
except (IndexError, ZeroDivisionError):
    print("First Except")
else:
    print("Second Except")
finally:
    print("Finally!")
```

Explanation: In both the codes, at a time, only one exception is caught. The second exception in (i) and `else` in (ii) are redundant.

12.10 Programming Examples

Program 12.1: WAP to accept two numbers n1 and n2 from the user. Find the output n1/n2. Check for and catch the exception that occurs if n2 is zero, n1 or n2 is not an integer and also any other error that may arise.

```
try:
    n1 = int(input("Enter a n1: "))
    n2 = int(input("Enter a n2: "))
    ans = n1 / n2
    print("The output of", n1, "/", n2, "=", ans)

except ZeroDivisionError:
    print("Exception: Divide ny zero")
except ValueError:
    print("Exception: Only Integer Division")
except:
    print("There was some error")
```

Output

```
Enter a n1: 9
Enter a n2: 0
Exception: Divide ny zero
```

```
Enter a n1: 8
Enter a n2: 2
The output of 8 / 2 = 4.0
```

```
Enter a n1: 8.9
Exception: Only Integer Division
```

```
Enter a n1: h
Exception: Only Integer Division
```

```
Enter a n1: 7
Enter a n2: -1
The output of 7 / -1 = -7.0
```

Program 12.2: WAP to raise an error if the correct range of month (>=1 and <=12) is not entered by the user.

```
def getMonth(m):
  try:
     if m<1 or m>12:
        raise ValueError("Invalid")
     print(m)
  except ValueError as e:
     print(e)
getMonth(int(input("Enter month=")))
```

Output

```
Enter month=4
4
```

```
Enter month=19
Invalid
```

Program 12.3: WAP to calculate simple interest. The rate of interest must not be more than 100.

```
def simple_interest(amt, yr, rt):
    try:
        if rt > 100:
            raise ValueError(rt)
        si = (amt * yr * rt) / 100
        print("Simple Interest= ", si)
        return si
    except ValueError:
        print("Interest rate cannot be more than 100. You entered=", rt)
simple_interest(200, 5, 5)
simple_interest(200, 6, 200)
```

Output

```
Simple Interest=  50.0
Interest rate cannot be more than 100. You entered= 200
```


```
Simple Interest=  50.0
Interest rate cannot be more than 100. You entered= 200
```

Program 12.4: WAP to count the number of lines in the file "file1.txt" that do not start with alphabet "L".

Content of file1.txt

```
Life is so beautiful
There is green grass
Life is happy
Life is grateful
Life is compassionate
Earth is brown
Air is pure
Water is bl
Lessons are learnt form life
Let us celebrate life
```

```
def f_ct_lines(lst):
  ct = 0
  for line in lst:
    if line[0] == "L":
      ct += 1
  return ct

try:
  f1 = open("file1.txt", "r")
  f1_list = f1.readlines()
  print("Number of lines starting with L = ", f_ct_lines(f1_list))
except IOError:
  print ("Error: Cannot find file or read data")
```

Output

```
Number of lines starting with L = 6
```

When the file file1.txt is deleted, then the output is as follows:

```
Error: Cannot find file or read data
```

Program 12.5: WAP to find the factorial of a number. Use exception handling.

```
def fact(n):
    while n > 0:
        return n * fact(n-1)
    return 1
def inpt():
    try:
        print("Factorial=", fact(int(input("Enter number for factorial: "))))
    except ValueError:
        print("Pl. enter a number. Try again.")
        return inpt()
if __name__ == '__main__':
    inpt()
```

Output

```
Enter number for factorial: 6
Factorial= 720
```

```
Enter number for factorial: 1
Factorial= 1
```

```
Enter number for factorial: -4
Factorial= 1
```

```
Enter number for factorial: f
Pl. enter a number. Try again.
Enter number for factorial: t
Pl. enter a number. Try again.
Enter number for factorial: 8
Factorial= 40320
```

Summary

- Syntax is the set of rules for grammar and spelling of a language, i.e., rules that define the structure of the language.
- Syntax errors appear during execution of a program when rules of writing the Python program have not been followed.
- Some examples of syntax errors are – spelling mistake in reserved word, incorrect punctuation, indentation error, and empty block.
- Syntax errors are caught by Python interpreter and are to be corrected by the programmer.
- Exception is an unusual condition that may arise during the execution of a syntactically correct program and results in an error, not handled by the system.
- Some examples of exception are – IndexError, TypeError, ValueError and NameError.
- Python allows handling of exception so that execution of the program does not stop abruptly, and rest of the code is executed.
- Built-in exceptions are standard exceptions in Python for a cause of error.
- `try-except` block is used for catching and handling exceptions.
- `try-except` block has several variations – with exception, with no exception, with multiple exceptions, `try-except-else`, and `try-except-finally`.
- `raise` statement allows the user to raise an exception, explicitly.
- User-defined exception allows users to define their own exceptions.
- Assertion is self-checking a debugging expression to know the internal state of a program during testing. It is used by the programmer to check the program.

Keywords

Syntax	Type Error	Base Exception
Syntax error	Value Error	try-except
Indentation error	Name Error	try-statement
Exception	Raise Exception	User-Defined Exception
Index Error	Built-in exception	Assertion

Programming Language Keywords

```
getcwd()                BaseException
file_obj.closed         Exception
SyntaxError             Try
IndexError              except
TypeError               finally
ValueError              else
NameError               raise
IOError                 assert
```

Assessment

A.1 Bloom Level: Knowledge/Remember

Review Questions

1. Define – Syntax, Syntax error, Exception, Assertion, Built-in exception.
2. What is the need for exception handling?
3. Name the two main kinds of errors.
4. Name some reasons for syntax error.
5. What is indentation error?
6. How do you know that a Python code is successfully parsed?
7. Can assertions be turned off?
8. List three situations in a program when an exception can occur.
9. Match the following:

Type of error		Reason for error
(i) IndexError	a	Not finding a variable
(ii) TypeError	b	Passing value of argument that is incorrect
(iii) ValueError	c	Accessing array index out of range
(iv) NameError	d	Applying operation to an object of inappropriate type

Fill in the Blanks

1. Generally, a _______ color bar can be seen at the line having a syntax error.
2. Python interpreter parses the Python program into ________ code.
3. ____________ occur when some unusual condition arises in a program and results in an error.
4. "No such file or directory" is an ________ error.
5. An exception is a Python __________.
6. __________ exception performs the task of generating an exception.
7. All exceptions inherit from built-in class __________.
8. ____________ statement is executed if the `try` statement does not throw any error.
9. ____________ is used by the program to know the internal state of the program during testing.

10. Assertion is meant for the ____________ during testing.

11. Assertion evaluates to either ____________ or ____________.

State True/False

1. Syntax error appears in a program when the rules of Python language are followed.
2. Python interpreter does not show where the syntax error has occurred.
3. Syntax error is found during parsing of the Python program.
4. Exceptions occur due to syntax error.
5. A program may crash if exceptions are not handled properly.
6. `Try` statement can have only one `except` statement.
7. `Finally` statement always executes.
8. `Raise` exception is required for built-in exceptions.
9. Assertion is not meant for the user of a program.

Multiple Choice Questions (MCQ)

1. Which one of the following is not an example of wrong syntax?
   (i) Colon after control statement
   (ii) Missing quotes in print statement
   (iii) Array index out of range
   (iv) Missing closing bracket.
2. Find the odd one out. Syntax involves rules related to:
   (i) Symbol
   (ii) Punctuation
   (iii) Reserved words
   (iv) Division by zero.
3. Spelling mistake in a reserved word is a kind of ________.
   (i) SyntaxError
   (ii) IOError
   (iii) Indentation error
   (iv) NameError
4. If you want to close all files in the program, the best part of the `try-except` block is ________,
   (i) `try-body` (ii) `except`
   (iii) `else` (iv) `finally`
5. Assertion is a/an ________.
   (i) `try` statement
   (ii) exception
   (iii) Boolean expression
   (iv) Syntax error

A.2 Bloom Level: Comprehend/Understand

Review Questions

1. Explain the working of the Python interpreter.
2. Why do exceptions occur?
3. Under what circumstances does syntax error occur?
4. What are built-in exceptions? Explain with examples.
5. Describe the syntax of the `try-except` block?
6. What is the need to specify `else` part in a `try-except` statement?
7. In a `try-except` block, when does the `else` statement execute?

8. Explain what happens if the `try` statement does not throw any error.

9. What is the need to specify `finally` in a `try-except` statement?

10. What is the purpose of `raise` statement?

11. What are user-defined exceptions. Explain with an example.

12. Describe the syntax of `raise` statement.

13. Describe the syntax of assertion statement.

14. What is the purpose of assertion statement in a program?

15. Explain what happens when an assertion is False?

A.3 Bloom Level: Application/Apply

1. Find output for the following:

(i)

```
try:
  f = open("test1.txt")
  f.write("Beautiful World")
except:
  print("Cannot be written. Some error")
finally:
  f.close()
```

(ii)

```
x = "good"
if not type(x) is int:
  raise TypeError("x is not an integer")
```

(iii)

```
try:
  print(x)
except:
  print("An exception occurred")
```

(iv)

```
#check divide by 0
x = 10
y = 0
assert y != 0, "**Division by zero**"
print(x/y)
```

(v)

```
#==============================
def avg(marks):
    assert len(marks) != 0,"**List is empty**"
    return sum(marks)/len(marks)
marks1 = [10, 20, 30, 40, 50]
print("Avg cost 1:",avg(marks1))
marks2 = []
print("Avg cost 2:",avg(marks2))
```

2. Find the errors, and correct the code:

(i)

```
def a():
    try:
          f(x, 4)
    finally:
          print('finally -after f')
a()
```

(ii

```
a=0
while not a:
    try:
        f1 = input("Enter file name")
        f2 = open(f1, 'r')
    except:
        print("Input file not found")
```

(iii)

```
a = 0
while not a:
    try:
        n=int(input("Enter a number"))
        while n%2==0:
            print("Hello")
        a = 1
    except ValueError:
        print("Not a")
```

(iv)

```
def avg(marks):
    assert len(marks) != 0
    return sum(marks)/len(marks)
i = int(input("Enter a number: "))
mark1 = [i]
print("Average of mark1:",avg(mark1))
```

(v)

```
def fun1()
    a = "Good Morning"
    print(a)
     return a
```

A.4 Bloom Level: Analyze

1. Explain the difference between the following:
   (i) Exception and Assertion
   (ii) ValueError and IndexError
   (iii) Syntax error and Exception
   (iv) Built-in exception and User-defined exception
   (v) `else` and `finally`

2. Analyze the difference between (i) and (ii). What is the output? What is the content of files `testfile` and `testfile1`? Analyze the difference between the outputs and the content of the files. Assume that the files `testfile` and `testfile1` do not exist, initially.

(i)

```
try:
   fh = open("testfile", "a")
   fh.write("This is my test file for exception handling!!")
except IOError:
   print ("Error: can\'t find file or read data")
else:
   print ("Written content in the file successfully")
   fh.close()
try:
   fh = open("testfile", "a")
   fh.write("This is my test file for exception handling!!")
except IOError:
   print ("Error: can\'t find file or read data")
else:
   print ("Written content in the file successfully")
   fh.close()
```

(ii)
```
try:
    fh = open("testfile1", "w")
    fh.write("This is my test file for exception handling!!")
except IOError:
    print ("Error: can\'t find file or read data")
else:
    print ("Written content in the file successfully")
    fh.close()
try:
    fh = open("testfile1", "w")
    fh.write("This is my test file for exception handling!!")
except IOError:
    print ("Error: can\'t find file or read data")
else:
    print ("Written content in the file successfully")
    fh.close()
```

3. Analyze the difference between (i) and (ii). What is the output and the reasons for difference in the output? Assume that the files `tfile1` and `tfile2` do not exist, initially.

(i)
```
try:
    tf = open("tfile1", "r")
    tf.write("Write to tfile1")
finally:
    print ("tfile1 is getting closed")
    tf.close()
```

(ii)
```
try:
    tf = open("tfile2", "r")
    try:
        tf.write("Write to tfile2")
    finally:
        print ("tfile2 is getting closed")
        tf.close()
except IOError:
    print ("Error: Cannot find tfile2")
```

4. Analyze the following code. What is the task performed? What will be the output when (i) file `f1.txt` is found and (2) file `f1.txt` is not found? In what cases will the `except` part of the code execute?

```
try:
    fp = open("f1.txt","r")
    try:
        fp.write("You can write on me")
    finally:
        fp.close()
        print("The file has been closed")
except:
    print("Error: I cannot read the file")
```

5. Differentiate between the following codes. What is being demonstrated by the two codes. What is the output in both cases?

(i)

```
data = 100
try:
    data = data/0
except ZeroDivisionError:
    print('Sorry! You cannot divide by 0')
else:
    print('Yippie! I am success', data)
```

(ii)

```
try:
    data = data/5
except:
    print('Inside except block')
else:
    print('Yippie! I am success', data)
```

A.5 Bloom Level: Evaluate

1. What kind of errors will be reported? Justify your answer.

(i)

```
x = [1, 2, 3]
print(x[3])
```

(ii)

```
int('22.44')
```

(iii)

```
Print("Beautiful World")
```

(iv)

```
print("Beautiful world)
```

(v)

```
x1 = ['Apple', 'Ball', 'Comb']
del x1
print(x1)
```

(vi)

```
a = 5
b = 6
assert a>b, 'a is greater than b'
```

2. Evaluate the following three codes. What is the output of codes? Justify the use of exception in the three codes and suggest any changes that can be made. Which exception statement will be executed in the three codes?

(i)

```
#Code 1================================
def f():
    a = int("Cat")
try:
    f()
except ValueError as e:
    print("Calling Function=", e)
print("1=====Proceed Further======")
```

(ii)

```
#Code 2=====================================
def f():
    try:
        a = int("Cat")
    except ValueError as e:
        print("In function-ValueError=", e)
try:
    f()
except ValueError as e:
    print("Calling function=", e)
print("2=====Proceed Further======")
```

(iii)
```
#Code 3==================================
def f():
    try:
        a = int("Cat")
    except ValueError as e:
        print("In function-ValueError=", e)
        raise ValueError(e)
try:
    f()
except ValueError as e:
    print("Raised ValueError=", e)
print("3=====Proceed Further======")
```

3. Evaluate the following code. What is the task performed? What is the output of the code? Is the result calculated for all six values? Is the result printed for all six values? Justify your answer.

```
result = [80, 75, 60, 55, 42, 44]
success = 45
for i in result:
        assert i >= 45, str(i) + " is Fail"
        print (str(i) + " is Pass" )
```

A.6 Bloom Level: Create/Synthesize

Programming Assignment

1. For all the programs that you have written so far in the previous chapters, do the following:
    - o Identify the conditions that can result in Exception.
    - o Handle these conditions using exception handling.
    - o Programs must end during execution, in a graceful manner, i.e., handle abrupt end of program, program crash etc.

P.S. For all the programs that you write, now on, write the programs using exception handling.

Answers

A.1 Bloom Level: Knowledge/Remember

Review Questions

9. (i)-(c) (ii)-(d) (iii)-(2) (iv)-(a)

Fill in the Blanks

1. red	2. byte	3. Exceptions	4. IO
5. object	6. `Raise`	7. `BaseException`	8. `Else`
9. Assertion	10. Programmer	11. True, False	

True/False

1. False **2.** False **3.** True **4.** False **5.** True **6.** False **7.** True **8.** False
9. True

Multiple Choice Questions (MCQ)

1. (iii) **2.** (iv) **3.** (i) **4.** (iv) **5.** (iii)

A.3 Bloom Level: Apply

1. (i)
```
Cannot be written. Some error
  NameError: name 'f' is not defined
```

(ii)
```
#TypeError: x is not an integer
```

(iii)
```
An exception occurred
```

(iv
```
#AssertionError: **Division by zero**
```

(v)
```
Avg cost 1: 30.0
```

```
AssertionError: **List is empty**
```

2. (i)
```
finally -after f
```

```
NameError: name 'f' is not defined
```

(ii)
```
this is run in infinite loop unless the file is found.
```

(iii)
```
Hello is printed infinite number of times
```

(iv) The assertion error will never occur. If the input is not correct then it will result in ValueEerror

```
Enter a number: y
Traceback (most recent call last)
```

```
    i = int(input("Enter a number: "))
ValueError: invalid literal for int() with base 10: 'y'
```

```
Enter a number: 20
Average of mark1: 20.0
```

```
Enter a number: 0
Average of mark1: 0.0
```

(v) There are two syntax errors. (1) No semicolon in `def` statement (2) Wrong indentation in `return` statement. If both errors are corrected, then no output will be printed as the function is not called.

A.4 Bloom Level: Analyze

2.

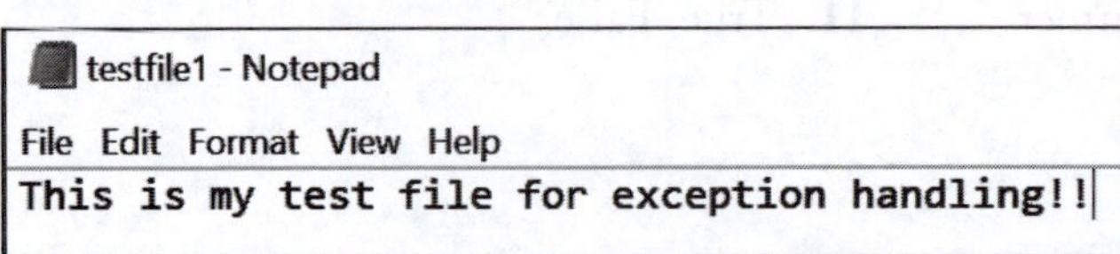

testfile - Notepad

File Edit Format View Help

```
This is my test file for exception handling!!This is my test file for exception handling!!
```

3.
```
Traceback (most recent call last):
  File "C:\Anita Goel\Python\Chapter 12. Exceptions\Solved eg.py", line 28, in
<module>
    tf.close()
NameError: name 'tf' is not defined
```

```
>>>
====== RESTART: C:\Anita Goel\Python\Chapter 12. Exceptions\Solved eg.py =====
Error: Cannot find tfile2
```

4. File found
```
The file has been closed
Error: I cannot read the file
```

File Not Found
```
Error: I cannot read the file
```

If the file is found, then execution will enter the inner try. There is a `write` statement but the file is opened in `read` mode. The `finally` will execute and the file will be closed and message is printed as in `print` statement. Then the `print` in the `except` part is executed.
If file is not found, then execution will not enter the inner `try` statement. The `except` statement is exceuted and the `print` in the `except` part is executed.

5.
```
Error: I cannot read the file
```

The first code only tests for division by zero. Since the `try` code is dividing by zero, the `except` part will always be excuted. The second code will handle any kind of execption in the `execpt` block. The first code will print the content of `print` statement in ZeroDivisionError. The `else` part will never be excuted. The second code will print the `else` part if there is no error in the `try` code.

A.5 Bloom Level: Evaluate

1. (i)
```
IndexError: list index out of range
```

(ii)
```
ValueError: invalid literal for int() with base 10: '22.44'
```

(iii)
```
NameError: name 'Print' is not defined
```

(iv)
```
SyntaxError: EOL while scanning string literal
```

(v)
```
AssertionError: a is greater than b
```

(vi)
```
NameError: name 'x1' is not defined
```

2.
```
Calling Function= invalid literal for int() with base 10: 'Cat'
1=====Proceed Further======
```

```
In function-ValueError= invalid literal for int() with base 10: 'Cat'
2=====Proceed Further======
```

```
In function-ValueError= invalid literal for int() with base 10: 'Cat'
Raised ValueError= invalid literal for int() with base 10: 'Cat'
3=====Proceed Further======
```

3.
```
80 is Pass
75 is Pass
60 is Pass
55 is Pass
```

```
Traceback (most recent call last):
```

```
AssertionError: 42 is Fail
```

UNIT V
Object-Oriented Programming

CHAPTER 13 Classes and Objects

Contents

13.1 Introduction

In the chapters till now, we have followed the procedural programming, where we write a Python program by dividing a task into a set of functions and modules, which are created based on the desired functionality and are tightly woven. We have understood the nuances of writing a Python program in procedural programming.

Python is an object-oriented language. So, Python provides the features for writing an object-oriented program. The object-oriented program is different from a procedural program. In object-oriented programming, a program is written based on the concept of objects and the interaction between the objects.

In this chapter, we focus on writing the Python program using object-oriented programming. We discuss the concepts and elaborate on the features provided by the Python language for the same.

Learning Outcomes of this chapter

After completion of the chapter, the learner will be able to:

- Understand the classes, objects and methods
- Understand working with objects
- Use methods with different types of arguments
- Formulate programs using object-oriented concepts
- Develop programs by incorporating the concepts discussed.

13.2 Classes and Objects

- In object-oriented programming, *class* is the basic building block.
- A class consists of: (i) Data attributes, and (ii) Methods that operate on the data attributes defined in the class.
- *Object* is a runtime instance of a class. An object has a (i) state, and (ii) behavior. The state of an object is defined by the data attributes. The behavior of an object is defined by the methods. The data attributes can be modified by the methods defined in the class.
- Class is a template for a set of objects that share common data attributes and common behavior. Each object of a class has a unique identity.
- Encapsulation, inheritance and polymorphism are the three unique features of object-oriented programming.
- Encapsulation facilitates data hiding. The encapsulation feature hides the data attributes, as it prevents direct access to the data attributes from outside the class.
- Inheritance is a feature that allows a new class to be derived from an already existing class.
- Polymorphism means many (poly) forms. This feature allows an object to have many forms. It allows an object to respond to a message in different ways.

13.3 Class Definition

In Python, *class* is a data type. A class is defined using *class* statement. The syntax is:

```
class ClassName:
        class-body
```

- `Class-body` is a set of Python statements defining the assignments of a variable or data attribute, and the methods. `class-body` is indented below the class header.
- `ClassName` is an identifier. It is the name of the class. Conventionally, class identifier is capitalized with each word (ClassName).
- Python allows `class-body` to be a single `pass` statement. An example of class definition with a single `pass` statement is:

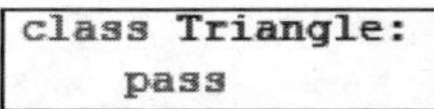

```
class Triangle:
    pass
```

To understand Python classes, we contrast them with the defining of Java or C++ classes. In Java and C++, the data attributes and functions are declared in the class definition. The attributes and functions are accessed from the objects of the class. However, Python allows creation of data attributes and functions on the fly. Python does not require explicit defining of variables or method definitions. They do not have to be declared in the class definition. (Class definition can simply define `pass` statement in class-body.)

> **Do You know**
>
> All in-built data types are classes in Python.

13.4 Object Creation

For a class defined in Python, an instance of the class can be created. The created instance is also referred to as an object of the class. The syntax to create class object is:

```
class_obj = ClassName()
```

An object can access the data attributes or methods of a class using the dot notation. The syntax is:

```
class_obj.var
class_obj.method()
```

An example of object creation is as follows:

Example 13.1: Create a class Factorial.

```
class Factorial:
    pass

my_fact = Factorial()
my_fact.n = 6
print('Factorial of', my_fact.n, 'is = ', 2*3*4*5*my_fact.n)
```

```
Factorial of 6 is =  720
```

In this program, we understand the different statements:
Line 1: Class declaration
Line 4: An object `my_fact` of the class Factorial is created.
Line 5: The object creates an object variable n and assigns value to it.
Line 6: Factorial of n is printed.

13.5 Variables – Object, Class and Local

Python allows three kinds of variables to be defined with reference to a class:

1. Object Variable or Instance Variable,
2. Variable or Local Variable, and
3. Class Variable.

Here, we discuss the three kinds of variables.

Object variable

An object variable is defined with an object of class using the dot and a value can be assigned to the variable. The syntax to create an object variable is:

```
class_obj.variable = value
```

A class can have several objects or instances. Each object has its own copy of the object variable.

An object variable is referred as `class_obj.variable,` both when assigning value to the variable and when accessing the variable.

Let us take an example.

Example 13.2: Define a class Square that calculates the area of a square. Show the use of object variable.

```
class Square:
    def area (self,s):
        self.side = s
        print("self.side=", self.side)
obj1 = Square()
obj1.area(10)
obj2 = Square()
obj1.area(20)
```

Output

```
self.side= 10
self.side= 20
```

We see that in the example above, `side` is an object variable.
Every object or instance has its own copy of `side`.
When `obj1.area()` is called, then the output of `self.side` is 10.

When `obj2.area()` is called, then `self.side` is 20.

Local Variables

A local variable is also referred to as a variable. A local variable is defined locally within a function of a class. It is not attached to an object.

Let us take an example.

Example 13.3: Define a class Square that calculates area of the square. Show the use of local variable.

```
class Square:
    def area (self):
        s = 8
        print("Square Side =", s, "Area =", s*s)
sq1 = Square()
sq1.area()
print(sq1.s)
```

Output

```
Square Side = 8 Area = 64
Traceback (most recent call last):
  File "C:\Anita Goel\Python\Chapter 13 Classes and Objects\Chapter Running prog
rams.py", line 41, in <module>
    print(sq1.s)
AttributeError: 'Square' object has no attribute 's'
```

We see that in the above example, we define a function `area()` within a class Square.

s is a local variable defined within the function `area()`.

s is not attached to self – the object that will invoke the class.

So, when we try to print `sq1.s` from outside the function, an `AttributeError` is thrown because `s` is not an object variable, but a local variable defined in function `area()`.

So, `s` cannot be accessed from outside the class function.

However, `s` can be accessed from within the class function (used in print statement within class function).

Class Variables

A class variable is defined within the class but outside all functions of the class. Thus, it is common to all objects of the class. The class variables are generally used when there is a need to perform a task on all objects of the class, for example, to count the number of objects invoking the class. The syntax of class variable is:

```
Class. class_var
```

- `Class_var` is class variable defined in `Class`.
- It is not defined within any method.

Let us take an example.

Example 13.4: Define a class Square that calculates area of a square. It takes the side as an input from the user. Users can continue to enter sides as many times as they wish. Find the number of objects for which the area has been calculated. Use Class variable.

```
class Square:
    ct = 0
    def area (self, s):
        self.side = s
        Square.ct = Square.ct +1
        print("Square Side =", self.side, "Area =", self.side*self.side)
a=1
while (a):
    x = int(input("Enter Length of Square side= "))
    sql = Square()
    sql.area(x)
    a = int(input("\nDo you want to continue(Enter 0 to exit) "))
print("\nSquare class has been called with", Square.ct, "objects")
```

Output

```
Enter Length of Square side= 5
Square Side = 5 Area = 25

Do you want to continue(Enter 0 to exit) 4
Enter Length of Square side= 56
Square Side = 56 Area = 3136

Do you want to continue(Enter 0 to exit) 0

Square class has been called with 2 objects
```

In the above example, we note the following:

- `ct` is a class variable defined within the class but outside any function of the class.
- `ct` is accessed as `Square.ct`
- `ct` is used for counting the number of objects that have invoked the class.

13.6 Methods

Methods are defined as functions in a class. Once defined, they can be invoked from the objects of the class. The syntax of method invocation is – object followed by a period followed by the method to be invoked.

```
class_obj.functionName()
```

where,
`class_obj` is an object of a class.
`functionName()` is a function defined in a class whose object is `class_obj`.
The methods defined in a class has `self` as the first argument. Also, the method `__init__` is defined in a class for initializing variables, and `__del__` is defined to destroy the created object. We discuss them in the following subsections.

13.6.1 Self as Argument

Every method defined within a class must include the first parameter as `self` in its argument list. This is even if the method does not have any other argument. When an object calls a method, the object is bound to the method by `self`; thus, the code in method can refer to the object by name.

Let us see an example.

Example 13.5: Define a class Square that calculates area of the square. Use `self` as an argument.

```
class Square:
    def area(self, s):
        self.side = s
        print('Square Side = ', self.side, 'Area = ', self.side*self.side)

sq = Square()
sq.area(5)
```

Output

```
Square Side =  5 Area =  25
```

We note the following:

- `self` is an argument in function definition.
- `s` is a local variable defined in function definition. The scope of the variable is only in this function. It cannot be accessed from outside the function.
- `side` is an object variable. It gets bound to the object that invoked this method.

All features of Python functions, like default arguments and keyword arguments can be used with Methods. In the following code, we see that default argument is defined (s=2). When the function is not called with the argument, the variable takes default argument; else the value is passed as the argument is used.

Example 13.6: Default argument in a class definition

```
class Square:
    def area(self, s=2):
        self.side = s
        print('Square Side = ', self.side, 'Area = ', self.side*self.side)

sq = Square()
sq.area(5)
sq.area()
```

Output

```
Square Side =  5 Area =  25
Square Side =  2 Area =  4
```

13.6.2 Method __init__()

Constructor is a special method in Python that is called when an object of a class is created. The task of the constructor is to initialize the object. Constructors also check if there are enough resources for the object, during the start, to perform its task.

Constructors must be included in Python classes. However, if no constructor is included, Python initializes the object, by default.

- In Python, `__init__()` function works like a constructor.
- `__init__()` only initializes the data attributes of the class.
- A Python program has only one `__init__()` function.
- Any data attribute defined within `__init__()` is created automatically.

The syntax of `__init__()` function is:

```
def __init__(self, [arguments]):
    body
```

- The statements that are required to be executed during initialization can be written in this method. The `__init__()` method executes by itself when an object is created.
- Python allows initialization of objects using the `__init__` method in class-body.
- Whenever a new object of class is created, the `__init__()` function gets executed by itself, with the object that invokes the method as its first argument.
- The `__init__()` function can take arguments also.

Let us see an example.

Example 13.7: Using the method `__init__()`

```
1 class Square:
2     def __init__(self):
3         self.side = 10
4 sq = Square()
5 print('Square Side = ', sq.side, 'Area = ', sq.side*sq.side)
6 sq.side = 15
7 print('Square Side = ', sq.side, 'Area = ', sq.side*sq.side)
8 sq.side = 20
9 print('Square Side = ', sq.side, 'Area = ', sq.side*sq.side)
```

Output

```
Square Side =  10 Area =  100
Square Side =  15 Area =  225
Square Side =  20 Area =  400
```

The points to be noted are:

- `self` is always the first argument of `__init__`.
- When a new object is created, `self` is set to that object. (3)
- `self.side` is an object variable created automatically. No declaration is required.
- An object/instance is created. (4)
- Since `sq.side` is already initialized in `self`, the print statement takes the value defined in `self`, i.e., 10. (3)
- The value of object can be overwritten (6, 8) and after each overwrite, the updated value is considered. (7, 9)

Objects are **mutable**. This means that the state of the object can be changed. The state of the object is defined by the value it holds for the object variable. In the above example, we see that for object `sq`, the value of `side` is updated and the latest value holds.

Without `__init__()`

When a class is created without the constructor, `__init__()` method, Python initializes the object by itself, as can be seen in Example 13.5, which has no `__init__()` method.

13.6.3 Method `__del__()`

Destructor is used to destroy an object. The task of destructor is to release the memory occupied by the object, when the object is no longer used.

Python keeps track of the number of references to an object. The references to an object can increase due to assignment, such as obj1 = obj2. An object is destroyed when the number of references to the object become zero. Python uses two methods for destructor, each having a different purpose.

- `del objectname` is used to decrement the reference count for `objectname` by 1.
- `__del__()` method is used for destroying the object when the refernce count of the object is zero.

The syntax of `__def__()` function is:

```
def __del__(self):
    body
```

- The statements that are required to be executed when the object is to be destroyed can be written in this method.
- This function executes by itself when the reference count of the object becomes zero.

Let us see an example.

Example 13.8: Using the method `__del__()`

```
class Square:
    def __init__(self, s, id):
        self.side = s
        self.id = id
        print("Object id = ", self.id)
    def area(self):
        ar = self.side * self.side
        print("Area of square with side", self.side, "is =", ar)
    def __del__(self):
        print("The destroyed object has id =", self.id)

sq1 = Square(5, "12A")
sq2 = sq1
sq1.area()
del sq1
print("===Still one more object to go=====")
del sq2
```

Output

```
Object id =  12A
Area of square with side 5 is = 25
====Still one more object to go=====
The destroyed object has id = 12A
```

In the example, we see that an object sq1 is created having one more reference sq2. When we delete the two objects, the `__del__()` is invoked automatically.

However, in Python, it is not necessary to define a destructor, explicitly. If `__del__()` function is not specified, Python uses automatic memory management. It keeps track of the number of references to the object. When the reference to object reaches zero, Python relcaims the memory of the object.

It is a good practice, to define both the constructor and destructor in a program.

13.7 Encapsulation: Private and Public Members

Encapsulation means information hiding. Encapsulation hides implementation details of the class.

It separates implementation of the class from its interface. The separation of interface from implementation allows changes to be made in implementation of the class without affecting the interface. The effect of changes is restricted to the class itself.

- A class encapsulates data and methods. Interaction with the class is through the methods defined in the class. Python incorporates encapsulation in two ways:
    1. Data hiding, and
    2. Method hiding
- For this, Python uses the terminology of private members and public member.
- A **private member** is accessible from within the class in which it is declared. It is not visible or accessible from outside the class in which it is declared.
- In contrast, a **public member** is visible and accessible from both inside the class in which it is declared and from outside the class.
- Both, data and methods can be public or private.
- **By default, all members are public.**
- Python allows defining of private member by naming the data attribute or method with a double underscore prefix. `__attributename and __methodname.`

Data Hiding

In the following code, the variable `__side` is a private data member. We access it from outside the class in `print` statement; in the output, we see that an error occurs.

Let us see an example.

Example 13.9: Accessing a private data member of a class from outside the class

```
class Square:
    def __init__(self):
        self.__side = 1

sq = Square()
print("Sqaure side =", sq.side, "Area = ", sq.side*sq.side)
```

Output

```
Traceback (most recent call last):
  File "C:\Anita Goel\Python\Chapter 13 Classes and Objects\Chapter Running prog
rams.py", line 130, in <module>
    print("Sqaure side =", sq.side, "Area = ", sq.side*sq.side)
AttributeError: 'Square' object has no attribute 'side'
```

Method Hiding

In the following code, the method `__area` is a private method. We access it from outside the class. In the output, we see that an error occurs.

Let us see an example.

Example 13.10: Accessing a private method of a class from outside the class

```
class Square:
    def __init__(self, s):
        self.__side = s
    def __area(self):
        ar = self.__side * self.__side
        print("Area of square with side= ", self.side, "is =", ar)
sq = Square(5)
sq.area()
```

Output

```
Traceback (most recent call last):
  File "C:\Anita Goel\Python\Chapter 13 Classes and Objects\Chapter Running prog
rams.py", line 143, in <module>
    sq.area()
AttributeError: 'Square' object has no attribute 'area'
```

Accessing Private Data and Method from outside the class

The data and methods are declared private, so that they are not accessible from outside the class. However, if there is a need to access the private data members from outside the class, Python allows that too. For this, the private data or method is accessed as:

`object._className__attributeName`

`object._className__methodName`

i.e., `object.underscore classname doubleunderscore` method or attribute name

Let us see an example.

Example 13.11: Allowing access to a private data member of a class from outside the class

```
class Square:
    def __init__(self):
        self.__side = 10

sq = Square()
print("Square side =", sq._Square__side,
      "Area = ", sq._Square__side*sq._Square__side)
```

Output

```
Square side = 10 Area =  100
```

Let us see another example.

Example 13.12: Allowing access to a private method of a class from outside the class

```
class Square:
    def __init__(self, s):
        self.__side = s
    def __area(self):
        ar = self.__side * self.__side
        print("Area of square with side = ", self.__side, "is =", ar)
sq = Square(5)
sq._Square__area()
```

Output

```
Area of square with side =  5 is = 25
```

When writing a program, the programmer must try to make all data members private, and all methods required for internal working of the program as private. The methods that are to be accessible from outside the class, should be made public.

13.8 Working with Objects

Till now, we have written programs where we create an object of a class, to access the class. We have seen the creation of an object, variables that can be accessed via the object, the methods of the class accessible via the object, and also, how to access the class via the created object.

Here, we focus on using an object as a parameter, i.e., object as an argument to a method of a class and also as return value from a method. We also see how the different methods defined within a class can invoke each other.

13.8.1 Object as Argument to Method

An object can be passed as an argument to a method. In such cases, the method works on the object that is passed.

Let us see an example.

Example 13.13: Calculate area of a rectangle using object as an argument to a method.

```
class Rectangle:
    def area(self, obj):
        print("Side 1 of rectangle = ", obj.side1)
        print("Side 2 of rectangle = ", obj.side2)
        ar = obj.side1 * obj.side2
        print("Area of rectangle = ", ar)
rect = Rectangle()
rect.side1 = int(input("Enter side 1 of rectangle = "))
rect.side2 = int(input("Enter side 2 of rectangle = "))
rect.area(rect)
```

Output

```
Enter side 1 of rectangle = 23
Enter side 2 of rectangle = 12
Side 1 of rectangle =  23
Side 2 of rectangle =  12
Area of rectangle =  276
```

In the example, we see that:

- An object `rect` of class `Rectangle` is defined and two parameters `side1` and `side2` are defined and assigned values.
- The object `rect` is passed as argument to `area()`. The method `area()` calculates the area of the object by using `side1` and `side2` of the object `rect` and prints the output.

13.8.2 Object as Return Value from Method

A function defined in a class can also return an object. In the following example we see that a class `Rectangle` computes the area of a rectangle. We define a function `incr_side()` that increments the side length of the rectangle and returns an object of `Rectangle` with the incremented size.

Let us see an example.

Example 13.14: Calculate area of a rectangle. (1) Take sides as input from the user, (2) Pass the object as an argument to a method, (3) Return an object as an argument from a method.

```
class Rectangle:
    def __init__(self):
        self.side1 = 5
        self.side2 = 10
    def area(self, obj):
        print("Side 1 of rectangle = ", obj.side1)
        print("Side 2 of rectangle = ", obj.side2,"\n")
        ar = obj.side1 * obj.side2
        print("Area of rectangle = ", ar, "\n")
    def incr_side(self, obj):
        obj.side1 = obj.side1 + 5
        obj.side2 = obj.side2 + 5
        return(obj)

rect1 = Rectangle()
rect1.side1 = int(input("Enter side 1 of rectangle = "))
rect1.side2 = int(input("Enter side 2 of rectangle = "))
rect1.area(rect1)

rect1.incr_side(rect1)
rect1.area(rect1)
```

Output

```
Side 1 of rectangle =  5
Side 2 of rectangle =  10

Area of rectangle =  50

Side 1 of rectangle =  10
Side 2 of rectangle =  15

Area of rectangle =  150
```

13.8.3 Calling a Class Method from Another Class Method

A method of a class can be called using `self` from another method of the class.

Let us see an example.

Example 13.15. Calculate the area of a square. Include (1) constructor, (2) a method to calculate area, (3) a method `output()` that prints output and is invoked by `area()`.

```
class Square:
    def __init__(self, s):
        self.__side = s
    def area(self):
        ar = self.__side * self.__side
        self.output(ar)
    def output(self, area):
        print("Area of square with side = ", self.__side, "is =", area)
sq = Square(10)
sq.area()
```

Output

```
Area of square with side =  10 is = 100
```

In the code, we see that the method `output()` is called from another method `area()`.

13.9 Built-in Class Attributes and Functions

Python provides built-in attribute and functions that can be used with classes and objects. Python provides two kinds of built-in attributes:

1. Built-in class attributes, and
2. Built-in object methods.

Built-in Class Attributes

There are several built-in attributes that are associated with a class. They can be used to get more information about the class. Since these attributes work on a class, the built-in attributes can be accessed using the dot operator, i.e., `class_name.built_in attribute`.

The built-in attributes are as follows:

- **`__doc__`** – It displays documentation string of the class, if given; otherwise none.
- **`__name__`** – It displays name of the class.
- **`__module__`** – It displays name of the module in which the class is defined. In interactive mode, the module name is __main__.
- **`__bases__`** – It displays tuple containing the base class in order of their occurrence in the list of base classes.
- **`__dict__`** – It displays dictionary containing the class namespace.

Let us see an example that uses the built-in class attributes.

Example 13.16: Calculate the factorial of n. Include (1) constructor, (2) a method for input, output, and to calculate factorial, (3) use the built-in attributes of the class factorial.

```
class Factorial:
    def __init__(self):
        self.ft = 1
    def input(self):
        print("Program to Factorial of n")
        return(int(input("Enter the number ")))
    def fact(self, n):
        for i in range (1, n+1):
            self.ft = self.ft * i
    def output(self):
        print("Factorial =", self.ft)
my_fact = Factorial()
my_fact.fact(my_fact.input())
my_fact.output()
print("Factorial.__doc__:", Factorial.__doc__)
print("\nFactorial.__name__:", Factorial.__name__)
print("\nFactorial.__module__:", Factorial.__module__)
print("\nFactorial.__bases__:", Factorial.__bases__)
print("\nFactorial.__dict__:", Factorial.__dict__)
```

Output

```
Program to Factorial of n
Enter the number 5
Factorial = 120
Factorial.__doc__: None

Factorial.__name__: Factorial

Factorial.__module__: __main__

Factorial.__bases__: (<class 'object'>,)

Factorial.__dict__: {'__module__': '__main__', '__init__': <function Factorial.
__init__ at 0x0000025AAF6B1160>, 'input': <function Factorial.input at 0x0000025A
AF6B11F0>, 'fact': <function Factorial.fact at 0x0000025AAF6B1280>, 'output': <f
unction Factorial.output at 0x0000025AAF6B1310>, '__dict__': <attribute '__dict_
_' of 'Factorial' objects>, '__weakref__': <attribute '__weakref__' of 'Factoria
l' objects>, '__doc__': None}
```

Built-in object methods

Python is an object-oriented language. There are several built-in functions, as discussed in Chapter 7, Table 7.2, that work on objects and attributes of a class. These functions can be used from outside the class to check whether an object has an attribute present, get value of the attribute, set value of the attribute and delete the attribute. Since these are built-in functions and not functions defined within a class, the dot operator is not used for accessing them. These methods also work on the classes and objects created by the user. Table 13.1 shows the syntax and the task performed by some of the methods.

Table 13.1 Built-in functions for objects and their description

Function	Description
`ascii(object)`	Returns string. Printable representation of object
`callable(object)`	Returns True if object is callable; else false
`@classmethod()`	Transforms method into class method
`delattr(object, name)`	Deletes attribute `name` of the `object`. Once deleted, the attribute does not exist for class or object
`dir([object])`	Returns names in current local scope
`getattr(object, name[default])`	To get value of the `name` attribute of `object`. Name must be string. If the attribute does not exist then an exception is thrown. So, `default` is the value that can be specified. If attribute does not exist, the default value is displayed instead of throwing of exception.
`hasattr(object, name)`	True if object has the `name` attribute.
`hash(object)`	Returns hash value of object
`help([object])`	Invokes built-in Help System
`id(object)`	Returns Identity of object
`isinstance(object, classinfo)`	Returns True if object is instance of classinfo
`issubclass(object, classinfo)`	Return True if object is subclass of classinfo
`len(object)`	Returns the number of items of an object
`memoryview(obj)`	Returns memory view of argument
`object()`	Creates featureless object
`repr(object)`	Returns printable string representation of object
`reversed(seq)`	Returns reversed iterator of sequence
`setattr(object, name, value)`	Sets the attribute `name` with `value` for the `object`. If attribute `name` does not exist, it creates the attribute.
`@staticmethod`	Creates static method from a function
`str(object)`	Returns str version of object
`super()`	Allows you to Refer Parent Class by super
`Class type(object)`	Returns Type of an Object
`vars([object])`	Returns __dict__ attribute of a class or object
`repr(object)`	Returns printable string representation of object

Let us see an example.

Example 13.17: Calculate the factorial of n and use built-in methods – `hasattr`, `getattr`, `delattr`.

```
class Factorial:
    def __init__(self):
        self.ft = 1
    def fact(self, n):
        for i in range (1, n+1):
            self.ft = self.ft * i
    def output(self):
        print("Factorial =", self.ft)

my_fact = Factorial()
x = int(input("Enter the number "))
my_fact.fact(x)
my_fact.output()
print("hasattr: ft ", hasattr(my_fact, "ft"))
print("getattr: ft ", getattr(my_fact, "ft"))
print("delattr: ft", delattr(my_fact, "ft"))
my_fact.fact(x)
```

Output

```
Enter the number 6
Factorial = 720
hasattr: ft  True
getattr: ft  720
delattr: ft None
```

```
Traceback (most recent call last):
```

```
    self.ft = self.ft * i
AttributeError: 'Factorial' object has no attribute 'ft'
```

In the above example, we see that when the attribute `ft` is deleted using `delattr`, then an error is thrown when we try to print the factorial.

13.10 Class Method and Static Method

We have seen that methods belonging to a class are invoked by objects of the class using the syntax `object.methodName()`. Since they are invoked from class object, `self` is by default their first argument.

Class methods are different. They are bound to the class but not to the object of the class. Class methods cannot modify the state of an object of class. Class methods can be used to access and modify the state of class. They can be used to modify the class variable. The modified class state applies to all the objects of class.

To define a class method, the `@classmethod` decorator is used just before the class method. Class methods have the class name `cls` and the arguments. The syntax for defining class method is:

```
@classmethod
def class_method(cls, arguments):
    body
```

Let us see an example.

Example 13.18: Calculate the factorial of n. Define a class method that compares the two sides of rectangle. An object is instantiated only if the two sides are different; otherwise a message is displayed that it is a square.

```
class Rectangle:
    def __init__(self, s1, s2):
        self.side1 = s1
        self.side2 = s2
    def area(self):
        print("Length = ", self.side1)
        print("Breadth = ", self.side2,"\n")
        ar = self.side1 * self.side2
        self.output(ar)
    def output(self, ar):
        print("Area of rectangle = ", ar, "\n")
    @classmethod
    def isEqualSide(cls, side1, side2):
        return(side1==side2)

s1 = int(input("Enter Length of Rectangle="))
s2 = int(input("Enter Breadth of Rectangle="))
if Rectangle.isEqualSide(s1, s2) == 0:
    rect1 = Rectangle(s1, s2)
    rect1.area()
else:
    print("This is a square")
```

Output

```
Enter Length of Rectangle=5
Enter Breadth of Rectangle=6
Length =  5
Breadth =  6

Area of rectangle =  30
```

```
Enter Length of Rectangle=5
Enter Breadth of Rectangle=5
This is a square
```

Static methods are called without an object of the class. They are bound to the class and not to the object of class. Therefore, static methods cannot modify the state of object. They do not know anything about the class. Static methods just work with the parameters. We note that static methods are different from class methods, because class methods work with the class (cls) itself.) but static methods do not work with the class.

To define a static method, the `@staticmethod` decorator is used just before the static method. The syntax for defining static method is:

```
@staticmethod
def static_method(arguments):
    body
```

Let us see an example.

Example 13.19: Define a class that finds the average marks of all the students.

```
class Result:
    count = 0
    total = 0
    def __init__(self, mks):
        self.marks = mks
        Result.count = Result.count + 1
        Result.total = Result.total + self.marks
    @staticmethod
    def average():
        return(Result.total/Result.count)

n = int(input("Enter total number of students= "))
for i in range(n):
    m = int(input("Enter Marks of Student = "))
    s1 = Result(m)
print("The average marks of", i+1, "students is = ", Result.average())
```

Output

```
Enter total number of students= 3
Enter Marks of Student = 10
Enter Marks of Student = 20
Enter Marks of Student = 30
The average marks of 3 students is =  20.0
```

13.11 GETTERS, SETTERS AND @PROPERTY

Data encapsulation does not allow direct access to the attributes defined in the class, from outside the class. To get or set attributes of the class, the getter and setter methods are used. The **getter** method gets value of an attribute of the class, from outside the class. By this way, we are able to get the values of private variables in a class. The **setter** method sets value for an attribute of the class. The values for private variables can be set from outside the class.

Python allows two ways for accessing private variables in a class from outside the class:

1. **Define functions (as we have done earlier) as getter and setter methods.**

Let us see an example.

Example 13.20: Define a class Square having private variables. Use getter and setter methods to access the private variables from outside the class.

```
class Square:
    def __init__(self, s):
        self.__side = s
    def area(self):
        ar = self.__side * self.__side
        print("Area of square with side = ", self.__side, "is =", ar)
#getter method
    def get_side(self):
        return self.__side
#setter method
    def set_side(self, val):
        self.__side = val
sq = Square(5)

sq.area()
print("*"*20)
sq.set_side(10)
print("Setter: Side of Square=", sq.get_side())
print("Getter: Side of Square=", sq.get_side())
sq.area()
print("*"*20)
sq.set_side(20)
print("Setter: Side of Square=", sq.get_side())
print("Getter: Side of Square=", sq.get_side())
sq.area()
```

```
Area of square with side =  5 is = 25
********************
Setter: Side of Square= 10
Getter: Side of Square= 10
Area of square with side =  10 is = 100
********************
Setter: Side of Square= 20
Getter: Side of Square= 20
Area of square with side =  20 is = 400
```

In the example, we see that a method `get_side()` is defined as getter method and `set_side` is defined as setter method. The getter and setter method allows us to access the private variables from outside the class.

2. Use property decorator (@property)

The property decorator is the Python way to allow access to the getters and setters via the object of the class using the dot notation.

The syntax of the @property is:

`@property(fget=None, fset=None, fdel=None, doc)`

`fget` is the function to get value of an attribute.
`fset` is the function to set value of an attribute.
`fdel` is the function to delete an attribute.
`Doc` is a string for the property's docstring.
The dot notation is used to access the property.
Let us see an example:

Example 13.21. Define a class Square having private variables. Use @property to access the attributes of the class.

```
1  class Square:
2      def __init__(self, s):
3          self.__side = s
4      def area(self):
5          ar = self.__side * self.__side
6          print("Area of square with side = ", self.__side, "is =", ar)
7  #getter method
8      def get_side(self):
9          print("In getter-------", self.__side)
10         return self.__side
11 #setter method
12     def set_side(self, val):
13         print("In setter-------", val)
14         self.__side = val
15     value = property(get_side, set_side)
16
17 sq = Square(5)
18 print(sq.value)
19 sq.area()
20
21 sq.value = 20
22 print(sq.value)
23 sq.area()
24
```

Here we see that

- Lines 8–10 define the getter method.
- Lines 12–14 define the setter method.
- Line 15 defines the property.
- When Lines 18 and 22 are executed, the `fget` function `get_side` of property is executed.
- When Line 21 is executed, the `fset` function `set_side` of property is executed.

```
In getter------- 5
5
Area of square with side =  5 is = 25
In setter------- 20
In getter------- 20
20
Area of square with side =  20 is = 400
```

13.12 Solved Questions with Explanation

1. Find the output:

   (i)

```
class Customer:
  def __init__(self, cust_id, age):
    self.cust_id = cust_id
    self.age = age

def change(cust2):
  cust2=Customer(100,30)

cust1=Customer(101,25)
change(cust1)
print(cust1.age)
```

Answer 25

Explanation: The new value of 30 assigned in method `change()` will not be reflected back in the calling program. So, cust1.age retains the original value 25 even after change.

(ii)

```
class Learner:
    def __init__(self, id):
        self.id = id

x1 = Learner(55)
x1.__dict__['age'] = 25
print (x1.__dict__)
print (x1.age + len(x1.__dict__))
```

Answer

```
{'id': 55, 'age': 25}
27
```

Explanation: The `__dict__` gives the key–value pair. The first one is id and second is age. The length of the dict is 2(1- id, 2-age).

(iii)

```
class Student:
    ct = 0
    def __init__(self):
        ct = 0
        ct = ct + 1
    @staticmethod
    def count():
        return(Student.ct)

n = int(input("Enter total number of students= "))
for i in range(n):
    s1 = Student()
print("The average marks of", i+1, "students is = ", Student.count())
```

Answer

```
Enter total number of students= 3
The average marks of 3 students is =  0
```

Explanation: The ct defined in `__init__` is a local variable. The ct defined in class is a global variable. The increment of ct is for the local variable. The Student.ct will access the global variable whose value is 0.

2. Explain the difference in the output of the two codes.

(i)

```
class Counter:
    def __init__(self):
        self.ctr = 0

def increment(c, n):
        c.ctr += 1
        n += 1

sampleCtr = Counter()
n = 0
for i in range(0, 100):
    increment(sampleCtr , n)
print("Sample Counter =", sampleCtr .ctr, ", N =", n)
```

(ii)

```
class Counter:
    def __init__(self):
        self.ctr = 0

def increment(c, n):
        c.ctr += 1
        c.n += 1

sampleCtr = Counter()
sampleCtr.n = 0
for i in range(0, 100):
    increment(sampleCtr, n)
print("Sample Counter =", sampleCtr.ctr, ", N =", sampleCtr.n)
```

```
Sample Counter = 100 , N = 0
Sample Counter = 100 , N = 100
```

Explanation: In (i) n is not a variable defined in the class. The value of n incremented in `increment()` is reflected in the output.

In (ii) n is a variable of the class. The value of n incremented in `increment()` is reflected in the output.

3. Identify the error and reason for the error. Correct the code.

(i)

```
class S1:
    def __init__(self, x):
        self.a = x

    def print(self):
        print(a)

s1 = S1("A Code Snippet")
s1.print()
```

Output

```
    print(a)
NameError: name 'a' is not defined
```

Explanation
Here, the variable 'a' should be self.a.
Corrected Code

```
class S1:
    def __init__(self, x):
        self.a = x

    def print(self):
        print(self.a)

s1 = S1("A Code Snippet")
s1.print()
```

Output

```
A Code Snippet
```

(ii)

```
class Test:
    def __init__(self):
        self.a = 1
        self.__b = 1

    def getB(self):
        return self.__b

val = Test()
print(val.b)
```

Output

```
AttributeError: 'Test' object has no attribute 'b'
```

Explanation: Here, the Test object has b as a private variable. So it is not accessible from outside the class.
Corrected Code

```
class Test:
    def __init__(self):
        self.b = 1
        self.__b = 1

    def getB(self):
        return self.__b

val = Test()
print(val.getB())
```

Output

```
1
```

(iii)

```
class Result:
    count = 0
    total = 0
    def __init__(self, mks):
        self.marks = mks
        count = count + 1
        Result.total = Result.total + self.marks
    @staticmethod
    def average():
        return(Result.total/Result.count)

n = int(input("Enter total number of students= "))
for i in range(n):
    m = int(input("Enter Marks of Student = "))
    s1 = Result(m)
print("The average marks of", i+1, "students is = ", Result.average())
```

Output

```
    count = count + 1
UnboundLocalError: local variable 'count' referenced before assignment
```

Here, count is seen as a local variable and it is not iniitialized.
But we see that count is a class variable.

Corrected Code

```
class Result:
    count = 0
    total = 0
    def __init__(self, mks):
        self.marks = mks
        Result.count = Result.count + 1
        Result.total = Result.total + self.marks
    @staticmethod
    def average():
        return(Result.total/Result.count)

n = int(input("Enter total number of students= "))
for i in range(n):
    m = int(input("Enter Marks of Student = "))
    s1 = Result(m)
print("The average marks of", i+1, "students is = ", Result.average())
```

Output

```
Enter total number of students= 3
Enter Marks of Student = 76
Enter Marks of Student = 77
Enter Marks of Student = 87
The average marks of 3 students is =  80.0
```

4. Create a class called 'Computer' with attributes as price and brand. A method that changes price of object. This method is outside the class. An instance of class is created. The price of the computer is changed and the output is printed as:

```
Computer Price: 75000
```

Rearrange the code to get the above output.

```
class Computer:
self.prc = price
def change_price(comp_obj):
comp_obj.prc = 75000
self.brnd = brand
def __init__(self, price, brand):
c1 = Computer(70000, "BrandX")
print ("Computer Price:", c1.prc)
change_price(c1)
```

Answer

```
class Computer:
    def __init__(self, price, brand):
        self.prc = price
        self.brnd = brand

def change_price(comp_obj):
        comp_obj.prc = 75000

c1 = Computer(70000, "BrandX")
change_price(c1)
print ("Computer Price:", c1.prc)
```

Output

```
Computer Price: 75000
```

5. Write codes for the following:
   (i) Create an object 'r1' for the class 'Rectangle' having two sides s1 and s2.

```
class Rectangle:
  def __init__(self):
   self.s1= ""
   self.s2=0.0

r1 = Rectangle()
```

(ii) Create a class called 'Students' without any attributes or method.

```
class Students:
    pass
```

(iii) Create a class 'Student'. Define its constructor and destructor.

```
class Student:
    def __init__(self, rno, n, a):
        self.roll_no = rno
        self.name = n
        self. age = a
        print("The created object is: ", self.roll_no)
    def __del__(self):
        print("The object estroyed is: ", self.roll_no)

s1 = Student('1A', "Anita", 25)
del(s1)
```

Output

```
The created object is:  1A
The object estroyed is:  1A
```

(iv) Create a class 'Color'. Define a private method 'change_color() to change the color of the object. Access the method from outside the class.

```
class Color:
    def __init__(self, clr):
        self.color = clr

    def __change_color(obj):
        obj.color = 'Red'

c1 = Color('Brown')
c1._Color__change_color()
print ("new Color:", c1.color)
```

Output

```
new Color: Red
```

13.13 Programming Examples

Program 13.1: Define a class Temperature that converts temperature from Celsius to Fahrenheit and vice-versa.

```
class Temperature:
    def __init__(self):
        cel_temp = 0.0
        fah_temp = 0.0
    def cel_fah(self, cel_temp):
        fah_temp =  (cel_temp * 9/5) + 32
        print ('The %.2f degree Celsius is equal to: %.2f Fahrenheit'  %(cel_temp, fah_temp))
    def fah_cel(slef, fah_temp):
        cel_temp = (fah_temp - 32) * 5/9
        print ('The %.2f degree Fahrenheit is equal to: %.2f Celsius'  %(fah_temp, cel_temp))

t1 = Temperature()
t1.cel_fah(float(input("Pl. enter the Celsius temperature = ")))
t1.fah_cel(float(input("Pl. enter the Fahrenheit temperature = ")))
```

Output

```
Pl. enter the Celsius temperature = 30
The 30.00 degree Celsius is equal to: 86.00 Fahrenheit
Pl. enter the Fahrenheit temperature = 98
The 98.00 degree Fahrenheit is equal to: 36.67 Celsius
```

Program 13.2: Define a class that calculates x to the power n.

```
class Power:
    def __init__(self):
        self.x = 1
        self. n = 1
    def calc(self):
        self.power = self.x ** self.n
        print("The", self.x, "to power ", self.n, "is ", self.power)
    def input_data(self):
        self.x = int(input("Enter the value of x = "))
        self.n = int(input("Enter the value of n = "))

p1 = Power()
p1.input_data()
p1.calc()
```

Output

```
Enter the value of x = 3
Enter the value of n = 4
The 3 to power  4 is  81
```

Program 13.3: WAP to create a class Triangle. Take the three angles of the triangle as input. Check whether the triangle is equilateral, isosceles or scalene.

```
class CheckTriangle:
    def __init__(self, a1=60, a2=60, a3=60):
        self.ang1=a1
        self.ang2=a2
        self.ang3=a3
        no_sides = 3
    def check_data(self):
        if self.ang1 + self.ang2 + self.ang3 ==180:
            if self.ang1 == self.ang2 == self.ang3:
                print("The triangle is equilateral")
            elif (self.ang1 == self.ang2) or (self.ang1 == self.ang3) or (self.ang2 == self.ang3):
                print("The triangle is Isoceles")
            else:
                print("The triangle is Scalene")
        else:
            print("The total of the angles is not 180")
    def input_data(self):
       print("Pl. enter the angles of the Triangle")
       self.ang1 = int(input("Angle 1="))
       self.ang2 = int(input("Angle 2="))
       self.ang3 = int(input("Angle 3="))

t1 = CheckTriangle()
t1.input_data()
t1.check_data()
```

Output

```
Pl. enter the angles of the Triangle
Angle 1=30
Angle 2=30
Angle 3=120
The triangle is Isoceles
```

```
Pl. enter the angles of the Triangle
Angle 1=55
Angle 2=44
Angle 3=55
The total of the angles is not 180°
```

```
Pl. enter the angles of the Triangle
Angle 1=34
Angle 2=66
Angle 3=80
The triangle is Scalene
```

```
Pl. enter the angles of the Triangle
Angle 1=60
Angle 2=60
Angle 3=60
The triangle is equilateral
```

Program 13.4: WAP to create a class Account. Define the methods to deposit and withdraw from the account. Show the account details in dictionary form.

```
class Account:
    def create_acct(self):
        self.id = 0
        self.bal = 0

    def deposit(self, id, amt):
        self.id = id
        self.bal = self.bal + amt
        print("Deposit=", self.bal)

    def withdraw(self, id, amt):
        self.bal = self.bal - amt
        print("Withdraw=", self.bal)

a1 = Account()
a1.create_acct()
a1.deposit(1, 100)
a2 = Account()
a2.create_acct()
a2.deposit(2, 200)
a2.withdraw(2, 50)
print(a1.__dict__)
print(a2.__dict__)
```

Output

```
Deposit= 100
Deposit= 200
Withdraw= 150
{'id': 1, 'bal': 100}
{'id': 2, 'bal': 150}
```

Program 13.5: WAP to define a class Square. Create two objects of the class. Compare the objects for their side length. Also print the string representation of one of the objects.

```
class Square:
    def __init__(self, s):
        self.side = s
    def __repr__(self):
        return repr(self.side)
    def __cmp__(self, obj):
        return self.side - obj.side
    def area_sq(self):
        ar = self.side * self.side
        print("Area of square with side", self.side, "is", ar)
```

```
sq1 = Square(10)
sq1.area_sq()
sq2 = Square(50)
sq2.area_sq()
print("The string rep. of object sq1 - ", repr(sq1))
print("The comparison of object sq1 and sq2 is = ", sq1.__cmp__(sq2))
```

Output

```
Area of square with side 10 is 100
Area of square with side 50 is 2500
The string rep. of object sq1 -  10
The comparison of object sq1 and sq2 is =  -40
```

SUMMARY

- Class is the basic building block. It consists of data attributes and methods.
- Object is a runtime instance of a class.
- An object has a unique identity, state and behavior.
- Encapsulation, inheritance and polymorphism are unique features of object-oriented programming.
- In Python, class is a data type and is defined using class statement.
- An object variable is defined with an object of class.
- Methods are defined as functions in a class.
- An object can access the data attributes or methods of a class using the dot notation.
- A local variable is not attached to an object and is defined locally within a class function.
- A class variable is defined within a class but outside all functions of the class.
- The methods in a class have *self* as first argument.
- Python has functions for constructor and destructor.
- Objects are mutable.
- Python incorporates encapsulation by defining private members and public methods.
- A private member is accessible from within the class in which it is declared.
- A public member is accessible from both inside and outside the class in which it is declared.
- An object can be passed as an argument to a method of a class.
- An object can be a return value from a method.
- A method in a class can call another method in the same class.
- Python provides built-in attributes and functions to be used with classes and objects.
- Class method is bound to the class but not to an object of the class.
- Static method is called without an object of the class. They do not work with the class.
- The getter and setter methods are used to get or set attributes of a class.
- The property decorator allows access to getters and setters via the class object.

KEYWORDS

Class
Object
Data attribute
Method
State
Encapsulation
Inheritance
Polymorphism
Object variable
Local Variable
Class Variable
Constructor
Destructor
Private members
Public members
Data Hiding
Method Hiding
Object as Argument
Object as Return Value
Built-in class attribute
Built-in object method
Class method
Static method
Getter
Setter
Property decorator

PROGRAMMING LANGUAGE KEYWORDS

```
class
self
__init__()
__del__()
__doc__
__name__
__module__
__bases__
__dict__
__attributename
__methodname
ascii()
callable()
@classmethod()
delattr()
dir()
getattr()
hasattr()
hash()
help()
id(object)
isinstance()
issubclass()
len()
memoryview()
object()
repr()
reversed()
setattr()
@staticmethod
str()
super()
tuple()
class type()
vars()
repr()
@property
@classmethod
@staticmethod
```

ASSESSMENT

A.1 Bloom Level: Knowledge/Remember

Review Questions

1. Define: Class, Object, Encapsulation, Inheritance, Polymorphism.
2. List the three unique features of object-oriented programming.
3. What is a local variable?
4. When is a destructor called?
5. When is a constructor called?
6. How many constructors can be defined in a class?
7. List the methods used for constructor and destructor.
8. List the statement for creating multiple references to an object.
9. State the relation between the number of references and destruction of an object.

10. What is a private member of a class?
11. What is a public member of a class?
12. List three built-in class attributes.
13. What is the variable type that can be used to count the number of objects invoking a class?
14. List the built-in object method to:
    (i) Delete attribute of an object
    (ii) Return identity of an object
    (iii) Return string version of an object
    (iv) Check if object has an attribute
    (v) Return number of items of an object.
15. Match the following:

	Description		Name
(a)	Static attributes are accessed using	(i)	Class attributes
(b)	Prevent access to a data outside the class	(ii)	@staticmethod
(c)	Adding a double underscore (__) changes the name of attribute to	(iii)	Classname__ attribute
(d)	Create shared attributes by placing them directly inside the class and not inside the constructor. The shared attributes are	(iv)	Class Name
(e)	Decorator method helps to access the specified method using the class objects	(v)	Encapsulation

Fill in the blanks

1. _______ is the basic building block in object-oriented programming.
2. A class consists of _________________ and _________.
3. The _________ of an object is defined by the data attributes defined in the class.
4. Class is a _____________ for a set of objects.
5. ______________ feature facilitates data hiding.
6. In Python, a class is defined using ___________ statement.
7. A _____________ variable is defined locally within the function of a class.
8. A method defined in a class is invoked from the _____________ of the class.
9. ___________ is the first parameter in the argument list of the class.
10. ______ is used to decrement reference count for an object.
11. ___________ built-in attribute is used for displaying the dictionary containing the class namespace.
12. ____________ decorator is used for defining a class method.
13. A Python program can have ________ `__init__()` function.
14. Encapsulation allows hiding of ________ and _____________.
15. By default, all members of a class are ____________.
16. To prevent direct access to a method from outside the class, define it as ___________.

State True/False

1. Data attributes are runtime instance of a class.
2. Polymorphism feature allows a new class to be derived from an existing class.
3. An object of a class responds to a message in different ways.
4. Python requires explicit defining of variables or method definitions.
5. Each object has its own copy of object variable.
6. Class variable is common to all objects of a class.
7. If a constructor is not defined explicitly, Python initializes the object by itself.
8. There can be only one reference to an object.
9. A public method is visible only inside the class.
10. An object can be passed as an argument to a method.
11. A class cannot return an object.
12. Class method is bound to the object of the class.
13. Static methods do not work with a class.

Multiple Choice Questions (MCQ)

1. The correct way to define an object of a class ABC is ________.
   (i) x = ABC
   (ii) x = ABC()
   (iii) x = new ABC
   (iv) x = new ABC ()
2. The correct way to define a class X is ________.
   (i) class X
   (ii) class X:
   (iii) class X():
   (iv) new class X:
3. The constructor of a class is defined as ________.
   (i) _init_
   (ii) __init__
   (iii) __init()__
   (iv) __init__()
4. A private data attribute `fact` in a class is defined as ________.
   (i) _fact
   (ii) __fact
   (iii) _fact_
   (iv) __fact__
5. The statement `obj1.Fibo.__n` allows access to:
   (i) Public variable n from object obj1 of class Fibo from outside the class
   (ii) Private variable n from object obj1 of class Fibo from inside the class
   (iii) Public variable n from object obj1 of class Fibo from inside the class
   (iv) Private variable n from object obj1 of class Fibo from outside the class.
6. An object is passed as an argument to a method as ________.
   (i) r1.area(r1)
   (ii) r1.area(_r1)
   (iii) r1.area(__r1)
   (iv) r1.area.(r1)
7. The correct way to call a class method `m1` from another class method is ________.

(i) self.m1()
(ii) m1.self
(iii) self.m1
(iv) m1().self

A.2 Bloom Level: Comprehend/Understand

Review Questions

1. Explain the purpose of `self`, `__init__()`, `__del__()`.
2. Explain the following built-in class attributes:
   `__name__`, `__doc__`, `__module__`, `__bases__`, `__dict__`.
3. Describe the meaning of following built-in object methods.
   `ascii(object)`, `callable(object)`, `@classmethod()`, `delattr(object, name)`, `dir([object])`, `getattr(object, name[, default])`, `hasattr(object, name)`, `hash(object)`, `help([object])`, `id(object)`, `isinstance(object, classinfo)`, `issubclass(object, classinfo)`, `len(object)`, `memoryview(obj)`, `object()`, `repr(object)`, `reversed(seq)`, `setattr(object, name, value)`, `@staticmethod`, `str(object)`, `super()`, `Class type(object)`, `vars([object])`, `repr(object)`.
4. Describe the syntax for the following:
   (i) Create an instance of a class
   (ii) Define a class
   (iii) Create an object variable of a class
   (iv) Access a method of a class
   (v) Define a constructor
   (vi) Define a private data attribute
   (vii) Access private member from outside the class
   (viii) Built-in class attributes.
5. What is the purpose of class method, static method, and @classmethod, getter, setter, property decorator?
6. Define a property decorator to access attribute of a class.
7. What is the purpose of a destructor?
8. What is the purpose of a constructor?
9. Is it better to use private member or public member in a class? Discuss.
10. When is a need to declare a static method or a class method? Explain with examples.

A.3 Bloom Level: Application/Apply

1. (i)

```
class a1:
    def __init__(self,x="Beautiful World!"):
        self.x=x
    def disp(self):
        print(self.x)
obj=a1()
obj.disp()
```

(ii)

```
class a2:
    def __init__(self, x1, x2, x3):
        self.x = x1 + x2 + x3
a = a2(2, 4, 6)
setattr(a, 'x', getattr(a,'x')+1)
print(a.x)
```

(iii)

```
class a3:
    def __init__(self,x):
        self.x = x
    def display(self):
        print(self.x)
obj=a3("Hello")
obj.display()
```

(iv)

```
class X:
    stud_id = 10
    stud_name = "Filler"
    def __init__(self, i, n):
        stud_id = i
        stud_name = n
        print (stud_id, stud_name)
s1 = X(5, "Refill")
print(s1.stud_id, s1.stud_name)
```

(v)

```
class Sales:
    def __init__(self, id):
        self.id = id
        id = 100
val = Sales(123)
print(val.id)
```

2. Find the errors and correct the code in the following:

(i)

```
class a4:
    def __init__(self):
        self.x = 100
        self.update(self.x)
    def update(self, y):
        y = y + 100
ob1 = a4()
print(" obj1.x=", ob1.x)
print(" obj1.y=", ob1.y)
```

(ii)

```
class test:
    def __init__(self,a):
        self.a = a

    def display(self):
        print(self.a)
obj=test()
obj.display()
```

(iii)

```
class Test1:
    @classmethod
    def isEqual(x, y):
        return(x == y)
print(Test1.isEqual(5, 10))
```

(iv)

```
class Test1:
    def get_date(self):
        self.__date = 5
        return self.__date
t1 = Test1()
print(t1.__date)
```

(v)

```
class Student:
    total_height = 0
    count = 0
    def __init__(self,name, height):
        self.name = name
        self.__height = height
        count = count + 1
        total_height = total_height + self_height
    @staticmethod
    def average():
        return(total_heightcount)

s1 = Student("Akshita",165.0)
s2 = Student("Ashima",170.0)
s3 = Student("Anuradha",155.0)
print(Student.avg())
print("Student Name: ",s1.name)
print("Student Height: ", s1.__height)
```

A.4 Bloom Level: Analyze

1. Explain the difference between the following:
   (i) Class and Object
   (ii) Object variable and Class variable
   (iii) Constructor and Destructor
   (iv) Private member and Public member
   (v) Class method and Static method
   (vi) `del obj` and `__del__()`

2. What is the difference when r1 and r2 are objects?
   (i) r2 = r1.calc(r1)
   (ii) r1.calc(r1)

3. Analyze the following code. What is the task performed by (i) and (ii)? What is the output? Is the output for the two codes same? If not, explain the difference in the output and the reasons for the same.

(i)

```
class a4:
    def __init__(self):
        self.x = 100
        self.update(self.x)
    def update(self, y):
        y = y + 100
        self.y = y
ob1 = a4()
print(" obj1.x=", ob1.x)
print(" obj1.y=", ob1.y)
```

(ii)

```
class a4:
    def __init__(self):
        self.x = 100
        self.update(self.x)
    def update(self, y):
        y = y + 100
ob1 = a4()
print(" obj1.x=", ob1.x)
print(" obj1.y=", ob1.y)
```

4. Analyze the difference between (i) and (ii). What is the output and the reasons for difference in the output?

(i)

```
class Student:
    def __init__(self, stud_id, stud_name, stud_section):
        self.stud_id = stud_id
        self.stud_name = stud_name
        self.stud_section = stud_section
s1 = Student('XYZ11', 'Ashima Anirudh', 'A')
print(Student.__dict__)
print(Student.__name__)
```

(ii)

```
class Student:
    def __init__(self, stud_id, stud_name, stud_section):
        self.stud_id = stud_id
        self.stud_name = stud_name
        self.stud_section = stud_section
s1 = Student('XYZ11', 'Ashima Anirudh', 'A')
print(s1.__dict__)
print(s1.__name__)
```

5. Differentiate between the following codes. What is being demonstrated by the two codes? What is the output in both cases? Give reasons for the difference in outputs.

(i)

```
class Test1:
  def __init__(self,n):
    self.marks=n

  def set_marks(self,n):
    marks=n

  def get_marks(self):
    return self.marks

obj=Test1(90)
print(obj.get_marks())
obj.set_marks(100)
print(obj.get_marks())
```

(ii)

```
class Test2:
  def __init__(self,n):
    self.marks=n

  def set_marks(self,n):
    self.marks=n

  def get_marks(self):
    return self.marks

obj=Test2(90)
print(obj.get_marks())
obj.set_marks(100)
print(obj.get_marks())
```

A.5 Bloom Level: Evaluate

1. The desired output from the code is given. However, on executing the code, an error is reported. Evaluate the code and identify the kind of error that will be reported in the following code. Justify your answer. Correct the code so that the desired output is displayed.

```
class Person:
  def __init__(self,name, weight):
    self.name=name
    self.__weight=weight
  def get_weight(self):
    return self.__weight

p1 = Person("Sapna", 50.00)
print("Person name:", p1.__name)
print("Person weight:", p1.__weight)
```

Desired Output:

```
Person name: Sapna
Person weight: 50.0
```

2. Evaluate the following code. What is the output of the two print statements? What output does the `__dict__` display? What is the justification for the obtained output?

```
class sweets:
    def __init__(self, price):
        self.price = price
obj = sweets(400)
obj.qty=15
obj.bags=2
print(obj.__dict__)
print(obj.qty+len(obj.__dict__))
```

3. Evaluate the code. What is the task performed? What is the output of the two print statements in the code? Is it the same or are they different? Justify your answer?

```
class First:
    def __init__(self):
        pass

    def test(self):
        print(__name__)

obj = First()
obj.test()
print(First.__name__)
```

4. Evaluate the two codes. Identify the task performed. Will both the codes give the same output or different output? Justify your answer.

(i)

```
class Candidate:
    def __init__(self, cand_id, age):
        self.cand_id = cand_id
        self.age = age

def change(c1):
    c1 = Candidate(10, 35)
    print("age= ", c1.age)
    print("In called id= ", id(c1))

c1=Candidate(9, 25)
print("In call 1 id= ", id(c1))
change(c1)
print("In call 2 id= ", id(c1))
print("age= ", c1.age)
```

(ii)

```
class Candidate:
    def __init__(self, cand_id, age):
        self.cand_id = cand_id
        self.age = age

    def change(self, c1):
        c1.cand_id = 10
        c1.age = 35
        print("age= ", c1.age)
        print("In called id= ", id(c1))

c1=Candidate(9, 25)
print("In call 1 id= ", id(c1))
c1.change(c1)
print("In call 2 id= ", id(c1))
print("age= ", c1.age)
```

A.6 Bloom Level: Create/Synthesize

Programming Assignment

1. For all the programs that you have written so far in the previous chapters, do the following:
   - o Create classes. Define functions within classes.
   - o Use constructor and destructor to initialize and destroy the objects.
2. Create a class Square. Create an instance of the class. Display the namespace of the instance.
3. Create a class named Student. Display the type of the class. Display the `__dict__` attribute keys and the value of the __module__ attribute of the class.
4. Create a class named Student. Let it have three attributes: `student_id`, `student_name` and `student_marks`. Create 10 objects. Modify the marks of the fifth student.
5. Create a class named Student. Let it have three attributes: `student_id`, `student_name` and `student_marks`. Create 10 objects. Add a new attribute `student_grade`. Display all the attributes and their values for all the students.
6. Create the following classes:
   - o Rectangle
   - o Square
   - o Quadrilateral
   - o Triangle

   Include functions to accept the data from the user; calculate area; and calculate perimeter. Include methods to compare two objects of the same class.
7. Create a class that has two methods to accept the string and print the string in lowercase.
8. Define a class Student to store name and marks in three subjects for 100 students. You may read the data from a file. Use a class variable to store the highest marks achieved in each subject and the average marks of the class for each subject.

9. Create a class that reverses a string, word by word.

10. Create a class as follows:
    - o Define a class "Champion". Make all the attributes private. The attributes are – name and gender.
    - o Define getter and setter for the name and gender attribute.
    - o Define rules to identify a champion (**Hint:** Run speed, race length, etc.). Create a method for the same.
    - o Create an object 'ob1' with the name as 'Shradha' and gender 'Female'. Check whether ob1 is a champion or not.

Answers

A.1 Bloom Level: Knowledge/Remember

Review Questions

15. (a)– (iv), (b) – (v), (c) – (iii), (d) – (i) (e) – (ii)

Fill in the Blanks

1. Class **2.** data attributes, methods **3.** state **4.** template
5. Encapsulation **6.** class **7.** local **8.** object
9. Self **10.** `del` **11.** `__dict__`
12. @classmethod **13.** one **14.** data, method
15. public **16.** private

True/False

1. False **2.** False **3.** True **4.** False **5.** True **6.** True **7.** True **8.** False
9. False **10.** True **11.** False **12.** False **13.** True

Multiple Choice Questions (MCQ)

1. (ii) **2.** (ii) **3.** (iv) **4.** (ii) **5.** (iv) **6.** (i) **7.** (i)

A.3 Bloom Level: Application/Apply

1.

(i)
```
Beautiful World!
```

(ii)
```
13
```

(iii)
```
Hello
```

(iv)
```
5 Refill
10 Filler
```

(v)
```
123
```

2.

(i)
```
AttributeError: 'a4' object has no attribute 'y'
```

(ii)
```
TypeError: __init__() missing 1 required positional argument: 'a'
```

(iii)
```
TypeError: isEqual() takes 2 positional arguments but 3 were given
```

(iv)
```
AttributeError: 'Test1' object has no attribute '__date'
```

(v)
```
    count = count + 1
UnboundLocalError: local variable 'count' referenced before assignment
```

A.4 Bloom Level: Analyze

2. (i) returns an object and pass an object

(ii) pass an object

3.

(i)
```
obj1.x= 100
obj1.y= 200
```

(ii)
```
obj1.x= 100
```

```
    print(" obj1.y=", ob1.y)
AttributeError: 'a4' object has no attribute 'y'
```

4.

(i)
```
{'__module__': '__main__', '__init__': <function Student.__init__ at 0x000002D13CB640D0>, '__di
ct__': <attribute '__dict__' of 'Student' objects>, '__weakref__': <attribute '__weakref__' of 'Student'
objects>, '__doc__': None}
Student
```

```
{'stud_id': 'XYZ11', 'stud_name': 'Ashima Anirudh', 'stud_section': 'A'}
```

(ii)
```
    print(s1.__name__)
AttributeError: 'Student' object has no attribute '__name__'
>>>
```

5.

(i)
```
90
90
```

(ii)
```
90
100
```

A.5 Bloom Level: Evaluate

2.

```
{'price': 400, 'qty': 15, 'bags': 2}
18
```

3.

```
__main__
First
```

4.

(i)

```
In call 1 id= 2588212316432
age= 35
In called id= 2588213002000
In call 2 id= 2588212316432
age= 25
```

(ii)

```
In call 1 id= 2588213002000
age= 35
In called id= 2588213002000
In call 2 id= 2588213002000
age= 35
```

CHAPTER 14 Inheritance and Polymorphism

CONTENTS

14.1 Introduction

In the previous chapter, we were introduced to object-oriented programming. We understood that encapsulation, inheritance, and polymorphism are the three unique features of object-oriented programming. We also discussed the object, class, and encapsulation. Abstraction is another feature of object-oriented programming that hides details at the design level and shows the essential information. In this chapter we shall study about inheritance, polymorphism and abstraction features in detail. We shall examine the different types of inheritance and overriding of the methods in the inherited class and explore how abstraction is implemented in Python. We also learn about the overloading of operators and the overloading of functions.

Learning Outcomes of this chapter

After completion of the chapter, the learner will be able to:

- Understand the concept of inheritance and use it in programs
- Understand the concept of polymorphism and use it in programs
- Formulate programs with different levels of inheritance
- Use abstraction while writing programs
- Formulate programs with method overriding
- Use methods with function and operator overloading
- Develop programs by incorporating the concepts discussed.

14.2 Inheritance Relationship

Inheritance allows a new class (derived class) to be created by inheriting data and methods from an already existing class (base class). The already existing class is called **base class or superclass**. The class that inherits from the base class is called **derived class or subclass.**

- Derived class inherits attributes and methods defined in the base class. Thus, inheritance facilitates **reusability** since functionality of existing classes is re-used by derived classes. Inheritance results in code reusability; therefore it is an important feature.
- Inheritance is known as a parent–child relationship, where the base class or superclass is referred to as parent, and, derived class or subclass is referred to as a child.
- Inheritance is **is-a** relationship between subclass and superclass. A subclass is a specific instance of superclass. Some examples of inheritance are:
    - o Square is-a Shape; Shape is superclass, Square is subclass. Square is-a kind of Shape.
    - o Teacher is-a Employee is-a Person
    - o Car is-a land vehicle is-a Vehicle
    - o Harmonium is-a Wind Instrument is-a Musical Instrument.

  In Python, the syntax to define inheritance is as follows:

```
Class Base_class:
   Base_class-body
Class Derived_class(Base_class):
   Derived_class-body
```

where,

`Base_class` is base class from which derived class inherits.

`Base_class-body` is the code of `Base_class`

`Derived_class` is the name of derived class.

`Derived_class-body` is the code of `Derived_class`

The important points to note about *inheritance* are shown diagrammatically in Figure 14.1:

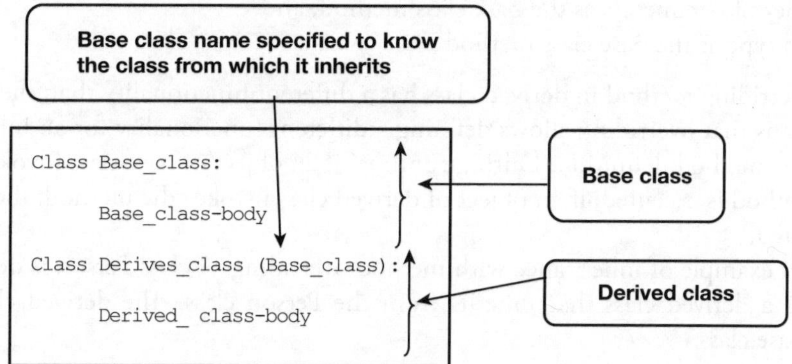

Figure 14.1 Inheritance – definition

The important points to note about *inheritance definition* are as follows:

- Base class and Derived class are two separate classes.
- Each class has its own body.
- Derived class has base class name as argument. It shows that derived class inherits from base class.

The methods of base class can also be accessed from derived class. There are two ways to access methods of base class from the derived class:

1. Using **super** keyword. The syntax of super keyword is –
   `super().<method_name>`
2. Using name of base class. The syntax is –
   `Base_class.<method_name>`

Derived class, in an inheritance hierarchy, can have three types of attributes and methods:
(1) New, (2) Inherited, and (3) Overriding.

- **New** – Derived class may add its own new attributes and methods. The new methods defined in the derived class have different name and functionality than methods defined in the base class.
- **Inherited** – Derived class (subclass) inherits attributes and methods of base class (superclass). The methods defined in base class are inherited methods in derived class. The inherited methods can be invoked from derived class. This means that an attribute or method defined in base class and not in derived class, can be invoked from an object of derived class. In Example 14.1, we see that method `getName()` is defined only in the base class (Line 9) but is invoked from object `p2` of derived class (Line 29).
- **Overriding** – Derived class may override some or all attributes and methods inherited from base class. The overriding method is discussed, in detail, in the next section.

14.3 Method Overriding

Method overriding means that a method defined in base class is also defined (overridden) in the derived class with the same method name.

The overriding method in derived class has –

1) same name as a method defined in base class;
2) same number of parameters as the base class method; and,
3) same return type as the base class method.

However, the overriding method in derived class has a different functionality than the method of the base class. It means that overriding allows defining a different functionality for an inherited method but with the same method definition. During runtime, if an object of base class invokes the method, the base class method is executed; if an object of derived class invokes the method, then derived class method is executed.

Let us see an example of inheritance with method overriding. A class Person is defined. Another class Manager is a derived class that inherits from the Person class. The derived class overrides a method of the base class.

Example 14.1: Inheritance relationship: Person–Manager

```
class Person:
    def __init__(self, n, ag, addr):
        self.name = n
        self.age = ag
        self.address = addr
    def getDetail(self):
        print("Name: ", self.name)
        print("Age : ", self.age, '\nAddress: ', self.address)
    def getName(self):
        print("Name: ", self.name)

class Manager(Person):
    def __init__(self, n, ag, addr, idn, divi):
        super().__init__(n, ag, addr)
        self.id = idn
        self.division = divi
    def getDetail(self):
        super().getDetail()
        print("Manager ID: ", self.id)
        print("Division: ", self.division)

p1 = Person("Akash", 20, "New Delhi")
print("--------------------------------------------")
print("Details of Person are-")
print("--------------------------------------------")
p1.getDetail()
p2 = Manager("Prabhat", 20, "NCR", 1100, "IT")
print("\n****************************")
p2.getName()
print("*****************************")
print("--------------------------------------------")
print("Details of Manager are-")
print("--------------------------------------------")
p2.getDetail()
```

Output

```
------------------------------------------
Details of Person are-
------------------------------------------
Name:  Akash
Age :  20
Address:  New Delhi

******************************
Name:  Prabhat
******************************
------------------------------------------
Details of Manager are-
------------------------------------------
Name:  Prabhat
Age :  20
Address:  NCR
Manager ID:  1100
Division:  IT
>>>
```

In this program, we understand the different statements:

Line 6, 17: Name of overriding method `getDetail(self)` is same in superclass and subclass.

Line 7–8, 18–20: Functionality of overriding method is different in superclass and subclass.

Line 22, 26, 6: Object p1 of class `Person` created; `p1.getDetail()` executes; method of class `Person` is invoked.

Line 27, 24, 17: Object p2 of class `Manager` created; `p2.getDetail()` executes; method of class `Manager` is invoked.

14.4 Types of Inheritance

Inheritance facilitates:

- *Specialization* that allows extending the functionality of an existing class, and
- *Generalization* that allows sharing commonality between two or more classes.

Python supports different kinds of inheritance, as follows:

- Single Inheritance
- Multiple Inheritance
- Multi-level Inheritance
- Multi-path Inheritance

The different types on inheritance are discussed in the following subsections.

14.4.1 Single Inheritance

Single inheritance allows a subclass to inherit data and method from a single superclass. For example, Person–Employee. An Employee is-a Person. Employee inherits the attributes and methods of Person.

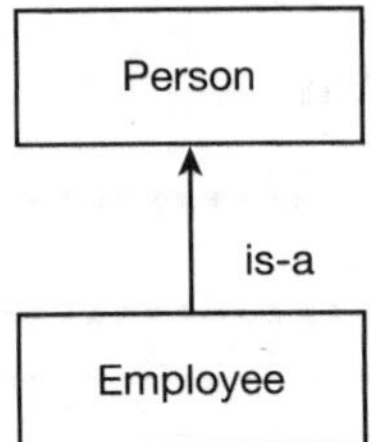

Figure 14.2 Example of single inheritance

Let us see an example of single inheritance (Figure 14.2). A class Person is defined. Another class Employee is a derived class that inherits from the Person class.

Example 14.2: Single inheritance

```
class Person:
    def __init__(self, name, age, addr):
        self.name = name
        self.age = age
        self.address = addr
    def getDetail(self):
        print("Name= ", self.name, "\nAge = ", self.age,'\nAddress = ', self.address)

class Employee(Person):
    def __init__(self, name, age, addr, id, dept, sal):
        super().__init__(name, age, addr)
        self.id = id
        self.department = dept
        self.salary = sal
    def EmpDetail(self):
        super().getDetail()
        print("Employee ID= ", self.id)
        print("Employee Department = ", self.department)
        print("Employee Salary = ", self.salary)

p1 = Person("Akash", 20, "New Delhi")
print("*"*10, "Person Details ", "*"*10)
p1.getDetail()
p2 = Employee("Prabhat", 20, "NCR", 1100, "IT", 25000)
print("*"*10, "Employee Details", "*"*10)
p2.EmpDetail()
```

Output

```
********** Person Details  **********
Name= Akash
Age = 20
Address = New Delhi
********** Employee Details **********
Name= Prabhat
Age = 20
Address = NCR
Employee ID= 1100
Employee Department = IT
Employee Salary = 25000
```

In this program, we understand the different statements:

Line 9: In `class Employee(Person)` declaration, class `Employee` inherits from class `Person`.

Line 11: `super().__init__(name, age, addr)`

`Employee` explicitly calls `init()` of superclass to initialize attributes defined in `Person`. If not called, the attributes of `Person` in `Employee` will remain undefined. Initialization can also be done using `Person.__init__(name, age, addr)`.

Line 16: Access the methods defined in class `Person` from class `Employee`.

`super().getDetail()` to access `getDetail()` method of superclass.

14.4.2 Multi-level Inheritance

In multi-level inheritance, a derived class inherits from an already-derived class. In Figure 14.3, we see that Class C inherits from class B, which inherits from Class A.

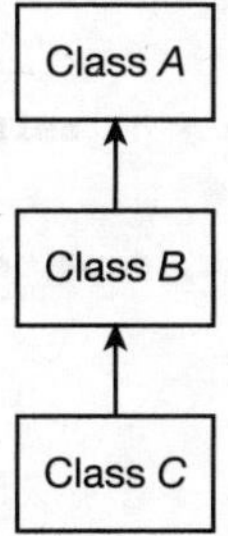

Figure 14.3 Multi-level inheritance: Inheritance from an already-derived class

In Python, the syntax to define multi-level inheritance is as follows:

```
Class Base_class:
    Base_class-body
Class Derived_class1(Base_class):
    Derived_class1-body
Class Derived_class2(Derived_class1):
    Derived_class2-body
```

The important points to note about *multi-level inheritance definition* are as follows:

- `Base_class`, `Derived_class1` and `Derived_class2` are separate classes.
- Each class has its own body.
- `Derived_class1` has the name of base class as argument. `Derived_class2` has `Derived_class1` name as argument It shows multi-level hierarchy.
- Further, the level of hierarchy may be extended, if required.

Let us understand multi-level inheritance with an example. A Part-time Employee is-a Employee is-a Person. Part-time-Employee inherits the attributes and methods of Employee, which in turn inherits the attributes and methods of Person (Figure 14.4). Example 14.3 shows the Python code for the same.

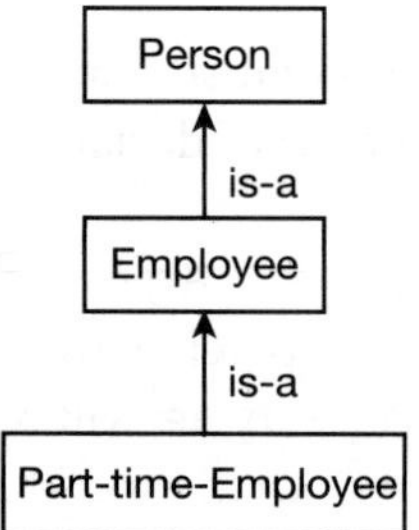

Figure 14.4 Example of multi-level inheritance

Example 14.3: Multi-level inheritance

```
class Person:
    def __init__(self, name, age, addr):
        self.name = name
        self.age = age
        self.address = addr
    def getDetail(self):
        print("Name= ", self.name, "\tAge = ", self.age, '\tAddress = ', self.address)

class Employee(Person):
    def __init__(self, name, age, addr, id, dept, sal):
        super().__init__(name, age, addr)
        self.id = id
        self.department = dept
        self.salary = sal
    def EmpDetail(self):
        super().getDetail()
        print("Emp. ID= ", self.id, "\tDept.= ", self.department, "\tSalary = ", self.salary)
    def EmpSalary(self):
        print("Employee Salary = ", self.salary)

class Part_Time_Employee(Employee):
    def __init__(self, name, age, addr, id, dept, hourly_rate, no_hours, no_days):
        super().__init__(name, age, addr, id, dept, hourly_rate, )
        self.no_of_hours = no_hours
        self.no_of_days = no_days
        self.salary = self.no_of_hours * self.no_of_days * hourly_rate
    def EmpDetail(self):
        super().EmpDetail()

```

```
30 p1 = Person("Akash", 20, "New Delhi")
31 print("*"*10, "Person Details ", "*"*10)
32 p1.getDetail()
33
34 p2 = Employee("Prakash", 25, "Mumbai", "E1000", "Marketing", 30000 )
35 print("*"*10, "Employee Details ", "*"*10)
36 p2.EmpDetail()
37
38 p3 = Part_Time_Employee("Sarvprakash", 30, "NCR", "P1100", "IT", 100, 8, 30)
39 print("*"*10, "Part-Time Employee Details", "*"*10)
40 p3.EmpDetail()
```

Output

```
********** Person Details  **********
Name=  Akash     Age =  20        Address =  New Delhi
********** Employee Details  **********
Name=  Prakash  Age =  25         Address =  Mumbai
Emp. ID=  E1000          Dept.=  Marketing          Salary =  30000
********** Part-Time Employee Details **********
Name=  Sarvprakash       Age =  30         Address =  NCR
Emp. ID=  P1100          Dept.=  IT         Salary =  24000
>>>
```

In this program, we understand the different statements:

Line 5, 17: `Part_Time_Employee` inherits from `Employee`, which further inherits from `Person`.

Line 11, 23: `EmpDetail()` of class `Employee` is overridden in class `Part_Time_Employee`.

Line 16: `getDetail()` of class `Person` is invoked from `Part_Time_Employee`.

14.4.3 Multiple Inheritance

In multiple inheritance, a derived class inherits from more than one base class. In Figure 14.5, we see that Class C inherits from two classes, Class A and Class B.

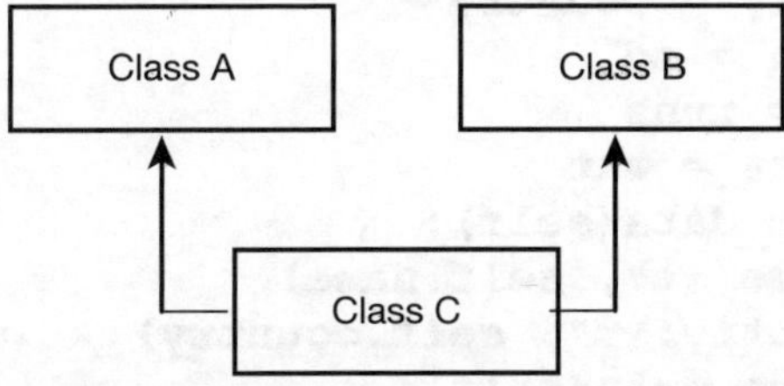

Figure 14.5 Multiple inheritance

In Python, the syntax to define multiple inheritance is as follows:

```
Class Base_class1:
     Base_class1-body
Class Base_class2:
     Base_class2-body
Class Derived_class(Base_class1, Base_class2):
     Derived_class-body
```

The important points to note about *multiple inheritance definition* are as follows:

- `Base_class1, Base_class2 and Derived_class` are separate classes.
- Each class has its own body.
- Derived class has names of base class as argument. It shows that derived class inherits from two base classes.
- Derived class may inherit from more than one base class.

Let us understand multiple inheritance with an example. A class `Bowler` provides the bowling data of a cricket player. A class `Batsman` provides the batting data of a cricket player. The class `Player` inherits from class `Bowler and Batsman`. The class `Player` provides the complete details of a cricket player (Figure 14.6). Example 14.4 shows the Python code for the same.

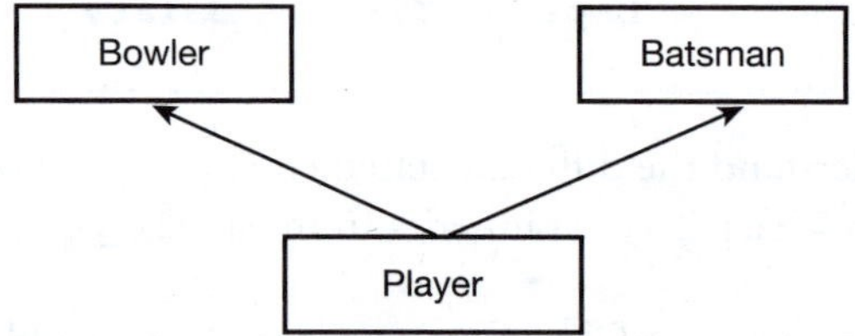

Figure 14.6 Example of multiple inheritance

Example 14.4: Multiple inheritance

```
class Bowler:
    def __init__(self, name, country, md,  runs, wkt):
        self.name = name
        self.country = country
        self.maiden = md
        self.runs = runs
        self.wickets = wkt
    def disp_bowler_data(self):
        print ("Name:\t", self.name)
        print("Country:\t", self.country)
    def disp_bowling_data(self):
        print("Bowling Data:", "\t Maiden Overs:", self.maiden,
              "\t Runs:", self.runs, "\t Wickets:",self.wickets)
class Batsman:
    def __init__(self, name, country, rn, scr):
        self.name = name
        self.country = country
```

```
        self.runs = rn
        self.max_score = scr
    def get_bat_data(self, rn, scr):
        self.runs = rn
        self.max_score = scr
    def disp_batsman_data(self):
        print ("Name:\t", self.name)
        print("Country:\t", self.country)
    def disp_batting_data(self):
        print("Batting Data:", "\t Runs:", self.runs,
              "\t Highest Score:" ,self.max_score)
class Player(Batsman, Bowler):
    def __init__(self, name, country, md,  runs, wkt, rn, scr):
        Bowler.__init__(self,  name, country, md,  runs, wkt)
        Batsman.__init__(self, name, country, rn, scr)
    def disp_all_data(self):
        self.disp_batsman_data()
        super().disp_bowling_data()
        super().disp_batting_data()

b1 = Bowler("Akash", "India", 1, 45, 3)
print("*"*5, "Bowler Stats", "*"*5)
b1.disp_bowler_data()
b1.disp_bowling_data()

b2 = Batsman("Akash", "India", 66, 121)
print("*"*5, "Batsman Stats", "*"*5)
b2.disp_batsman_data()
b2.disp_batting_data()

b3 = Player("Akash", "India", 1, 45, 3,66, 121 )
print("*"*5, "Player Stats", "*"*5)
b3.disp_all_data()
```

Output

```
***** Bowler Stats *****
Name:    Akash
Country:            India
Bowling Data:     Maiden Overs: 1          Runs: 45          Wickets: 3
***** Batsman Stats *****
Name:    Akash
Country:            India
Batting Data:     Runs: 66          Highest Score: 121
***** Player Stats *****
Name:    Akash
Country:            India
Bowling Data:     Maiden Overs: 1          Runs: 66          Wickets: 3
Batting Data:     Runs: 66          Highest Score: 121
>>>
```

In this program, we understand the different statements:
Line 29: `Player` inherits from two superclass – `Bowler` and `Batsman`.
Line 31, 32: `__init__()` of both superclass are invoked.
Line 34, 35, 36: Methods in the class `Player` invoke the methods of both the superclass.

14.4.4 Multi-path Inheritance

Multi-path or hybrid inheritance is a combination of single and multiple inheritance. A derived class inherits from two already derived classes (multiple inheritance), which inherit from a base class (single inheritance). In Figure 14.7, we see that Class B and Class C inherit from Class A, and Class D inherits from Class B and Class C. Hybrid inheritance forms a grandparent-parent-child relationship.

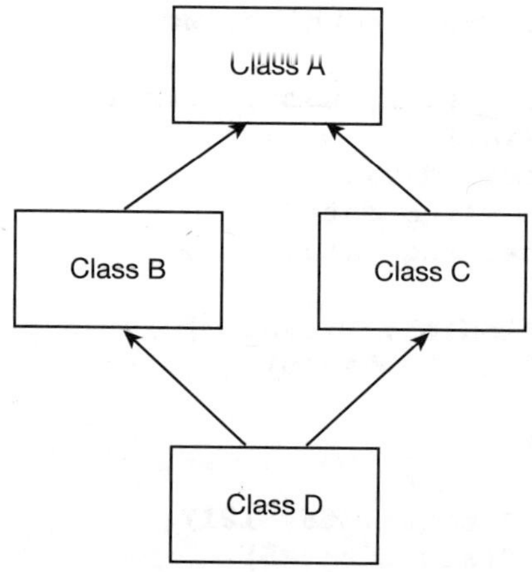

Figure 14.7 Multi-path inheritance

```
Class Base_class:
     Base_class-body
Class Derived_class1(Base_class):
     Derived_class1-body
Class Derived_class2(Base_class):
     Derived_class2-body
Class Derived_class3(Derived_class1, Derived_class2):
     Derived_class3-body
```

In Python, the syntax to define hybrid inheritance is as follows:

Let us understand multi-path inheritance with an example. A class `Student` defines the details of the student. A student has both sports and academic results. Two classes inherit from the class `Student` – `Academic` and `Sports`. The class `Academic` gives the academic result of the student and class `Sports` gives the sport result of the student. The class `Student_Result` inherits from two both `Academic` and `Sports` to give the result of the student.

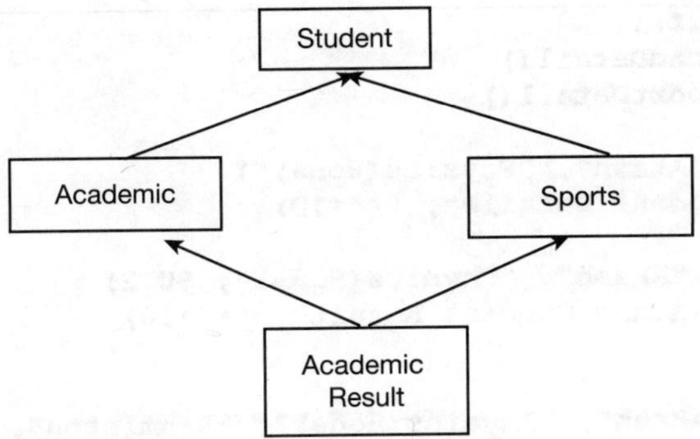

Figure 14.8 Example of multi-path inheritance

Example 14.5: Multi-path inheritance

```
class Student:
    def __init__(self, rno, name, course):
        self.roll_no = rno
        self.name = name
        self.course = course
    def getDetail(self):
        print("Roll Number =", self.roll_no, "\nName= ",
              self.name, '\nCourse = ', self.course)
class Academic(Student):
    def __init__(self, rno, name, course, acad_marks):
        Student.__init__(self, rno, name, course)
        self.acad_marks = acad_marks
    def AcadDetail(self):
        print("Academic Marks = ", self.acad_marks)

class Sports(Student):
    def __init__(self, rno, name, course, sp_name, sp_marks):
        Student.__init__(self, rno, name, course)
        self.sp_name = sp_name
        self.sp_marks = sp_marks
    def getDetail(self):
        super().getDetail()
    def SportDetail(self):
        print("Sports Name = ", self.sp_name)
        print("Sports Marks = ", self.sp_marks)

class Result_Student(Academic, Sports):
    def __init__(self, rno, name, course, acad_marks,  sp_name, sp_marks):
        Academic. __init__(self, rno, name, course, acad_marks)
        Sports.__init__(self, rno, name, course,  sp_name, sp_marks)
```

```
31     def Result(self):
32         super().AcadDetail()
33         super().SportDetail()
34
35 p1 = Student(11, "Akash", "Physics(Hons)")
36 print("*"*10, "Student Details", "*"*10)
37 p1.getDetail()
38 p2 = Academic(11, "Akash", "Physics(Hons)", 90.2)
39 print("*"*10, "Academic Student Result", "*"*10)
40 p2.getDetail()
41 p2.AcadDetail()
42 p3 = Sports(11, "Akash", "Physics(Hons)", "Badminton", 88)
43 print("*"*10, " Sports Student Result", "*"*10)
44 p3.getDetail()
45 p3.SportDetail()
46 p4 = Result_Student(11, "Akash", "Physics(Hons)", 90.2, "Badminton", 88)
47 print("*"*10, " Student Result", "*"*10)
48 p4.getDetail()
49 p4.Result()
```

Output

```
********** Student Details **********
Roll Number = 11
Name=  Akash
Course =  Physics(Hons)
********** Academic Student Result **********
Roll Number = 11
Name=  Akash
Course =  Physics(Hons)
Academic Marks =  90.2
**********  Sports Student Result **********
Roll Number = 11
Name=  Akash
Course =  Physics(Hons)
Sports Name =  Badminton
Sports Marks =  88
**********  Student Result **********
Roll Number = 11
Name=  Akash
Course =  Physics(Hons)
Academic Marks =  90.2
Sports Name =  Badminton
Sports Marks =  88
>>>
```

In this program, we understand the different statements:

Line 9, 16: Class `Academic` and `Sports` inherit from class `Student`.

Line 27: Class `Result_Student` inherits from two superclass – `Academic` and `Sports`.

Line 32, 33: Methods in class `Result_Student` invoke the methods of both the superclass.

14.5 Inheritance and Access Control

In an inheritance hierarchy, access to the variables, classes, function, and methods along the hierarchy are controlled via the access control attributes – public, private, protected, and internal.

- *Public* access is for any class that calls it. An object defined outside the class can access public members of the class. In an inheritance hierarchy, the derived class or any other class can access the public members of the base class.
- *Private* access is for the class that defines it. Private members cannot be accessed from outside the class. In an inheritance hierarchy, the derived class cannot access private members of the base class but can access rest of the data members and methods of the base class.
- *Protected* access is for the class that defines it and the class that inherits from it. Protected members of a class can be accessed from the class that defines it and from the class that is derived from it. In an inheritance hierarchy, protected members behave like private members for the class in which they are defined but they can be inherited and accessed from the derived class also. However, protected members cannot be accessed from any other class.
- *Internal* is for calling from within the package. By default, the access control attribute is set to internal.

Python does not support the keywords – public, private and protected. Instead, the private, public and protected members are defined as:

- Private member by naming the data attribute or method with a double underscore prefix. `__attributename` and `__methodname`. For example, __sum, __x.
- Protected member by naming the data attribute or method with a single underscore prefix. `_attributename` and `_methodname`. For example, _sum, _x.
- Public member by naming the data attribute or method with no prefix. `attributename` and `methodname`. For example, sum, x.

Let us understand access control attributes with an example.

Example 14.6: Access control in inheritance hierarchy

```
class Person:
    name = None                 # public data member
    _age = None                 # protected data member
    __marks = None              # private data member

    def __init__(self, n, a, m):
        self.name = n
        self._age = a
        self.__marks = m

    def displayPublic(self):                              # public function
        print("The public attribute is", self.name)  # accessing public data member

    def _displayProtected(self):                          # protected function
      print("The protected attribute is", self._age) # accessing protected data member

    def __displayPrivate(self):                           # private function
        print("The private attribute is", self.__marks) # accessing private data member

```

```
20      def accessPrivate(self):                          # public function
21          self.__displayPrivate()                       # accessing private function
22
23 class Student(Person):
24     def __init__(self, v1, v2, v3):
25         Person.__init__(self, v1, v2, v3)
26
27     def accessProtected(self):                      # public function
28         self._displayProtected()
29
30 obj = Student("Asha", 4, 25)                        # creating object of derived class
31 obj.displayPublic()
32 obj.accessProtected()
33 obj.accessPrivate()
34 print("Object is accessing protected member:", obj._age)
35
36 #print(obj.__marks)      #AttributeError: 'Student' object has no attribute '__marks'
37 #obj.__displayPrivate() #AttributeError: 'Student' object has no attribute '__displayPrivate
```

Output

```
The public attribute is Asha
The protected attribute is 4
The private attribute is 25
Object is accessing protected member: 4
>>>
```

In this program, we understand the different statements:

Line 2, 3, 4: A public, protected and private data member is defined.

Line 11, 14, 17: Functions to access the data members.

Line 31, 32, 33: Public and protected functions called by the object of derived class, Student.

Line 36, 37: These statements, when included, displays an Attribute error because private members of base class are being accessed from derived class.

14.6 Method Resolution Order

- Method Resolution Order (MRO) is used in inheritance.
- In a hierarchy of classes, MRO looks for the order in which a method is searched in a hierarchy.
- MRO is useful in single inheritance but particularly useful in multi-level, multi-path and multiple inheritance. This is because a method may be inherited in multiple classes in the hierarchy.
- The method or attribute is searched first from the bottom to the top. This means, the method is searched in the current class; if not found, then it is searched in the parent class, and so on.
- In case a class has multiple super classes, then it is searched from left to right.
- Also, the order of hierarchy is followed.
- To see the order of the method resolution, Python provides an attribute and a method:
    - __mro__ Attribute
    - mro() Method

  Using these in the `print` statement, we can display the order in which the methods are resolved.

  `print(object-classname.__mro__)`

```
print(object-classname.mro())
```

Let us understand with examples.

Example 14.7(a): MRO in single inheritance

```
class A:
  def method(self):
    print("class A")
class B(A):
  def method(self):
    print("class B")

b = B()
b.method()
print(B.mro())
```

Output

```
class B
[<class '__main__.B'>, <class '__main__.A'>, <class 'object'>]
```

This is a case of single inheritance. When the `b.method()` is called, the method is searched in class B. If found, it is executed; else, it is searched in the superclass, i.e., class A. The class "object" is the superclass of all classes, so it is executed last. The MRO in the above example is B → A

Example 14.7(b): MRO in multiple inheritance

```
class A:
  def method(self):
    print("class A")
class B:
  pass
class C(B, A):
  pass

c = C()
c.method()
print(C.mro())
```

Output

```
class A
[<class '__main__.C'>, <class '__main__.B'>, <class '__main__.A'>, <cl
ass 'object'>]
```

This is a case of multiple inheritance. When the `c.method()` is called, the method is searched in class C. If found, it is executed; else, it is searched in the superclass, i.e., class B because this class appears first in the class C declaration and then in class A. The MRO in this case is C → B → A

Example 14.7(c): MRO in multi-path inheritance

```
class A:
  def method(self):
    print("class A")
class B:
  def method(self):
    print("class B")
class C(A, B):
  pass
class D(C, B):
  pass

d = D()
d.method()
print(D.mro())
```

Output

```
class A
[<class '__main__.D'>, <class '__main__.C'>, <class '__main__.A'>, <cl
ass '__main__.B'>, <class 'object'>]
```

When the `d.method()` is called, the method is searched in class D. If found, it is executed; else, it is searched in the superclass, i.e., class C because this class appears first in the class C declaration. In Python 3, the next search is in class A first and then in class B, because both classes D and C inherit from class B (as also shown in the diagram). The MRO in this case is D → C → A → B

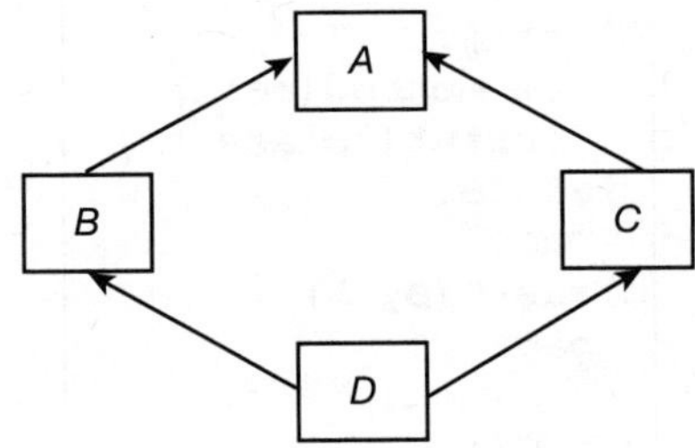

Example 14.7(d): MRO in multi-path inheritance

```
class A:
    def myname(self):
        print("class A")
class B(A):
    def myname(self):
        print("class B")
class C(A):
    def myname(self):
        print("class C")
class D(B, C):
    pass

print(D.__mro__)
```

Output

```
(<class '__main__.D'>, <class '__main__.B'>, <class '__main__.C'>, <cl
ass '__main__.A'>, <class 'object'>)
```

When the `d.method()` is called, the method is searched in class D. If found, it is executed; else it is searched in the superclass, i.e., class B because this class appears first in the class D declaration. In Python 3, the next search is in class C first (left to right) and then in class A. The MRO in this case is D → B → C → A

14.6.1 Invocation of Constructor and Destructor in Hierarchy

In Python, `__init__()` and `__del__()` methods are used for constructor and destructor, respectively.

- The constructor and destructor execute automatically when an object of the class is created.
- In an inheritance hierarchy, if the child class has an `__init__()` defined, then the `__init__()` of parent class does not get executed by itself. The `__init__()` of the parent has to be explicitly called from the `__init__()` of the child class.
- Another alternative is to use the `super` keyword in the child for executing the `__init__()` of the parent.
- The sequence of execution of the constructor and destructor obeys the MRO.

14.7 Composition and Aggregation Relationship

Both Composition and Aggregation are types of association which are used to represent the relationship between two classes.

14.7.1 Composition

Composition is one of the ways to represent relationships in a problem domain. Composition models relationships among the parts of a whole component. An object is composed from other objects. By using composition, we can structure an object in parts. The reason for structuring may be to describe object in detail, or to increase understanding. For example, a Person object is composed with the objects – Head, Heart, Arms, and Legs.

- Composition models the ***part-of*** relationship.
- A complex object can be created by combining objects of different types.
- In a composition, there is a parent–child relationship. The class refers to other class, i.e., parent. The class that is being referred in parent is the child.
- In a composition, parent and child are tightly coupled. The entities in the relationship cannot exist independently. The child cannot exist without the parent. All the entities are dependent on each other. Any entity cannot exist without the other entity.
- The composition relationship in UML (Unified Modeling Language) is represented as shown in Figure 14.9.

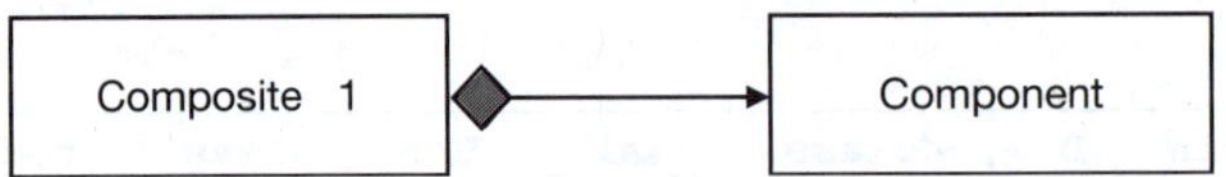

Figure 14.9 Composition relationship in UML

The class that contains objects of other classes is the composite. The class used to create more complex types is the component. An arrow connects the composite and the component. The cardinality at composite indicates the number of instances the composite will contain.

- Some examples of composition relationship are:
  - Car–Engine relationship: An engine is a part of Car.
  - Person–Heart relationship: A heart is a part of the Person.
  - Building–Room relationship: A room is a part of the Building.

  Let us understand composition relationship with an example.

Example 14.8: Composition relationship

```
1 #====composition==========================
2 class Salary:
3     def __init__(self, basic, emol):
4         self.pay = basic
5         self.emolument = emol
6     def annual_salary(self):
7         return (self.pay*12)+self.emolument
8 
9 class Employee:
10    def __init__(self, name, age, basic, emol):
11        self.name = name
12        self.age = age
13        self.obj_salary = Salary(basic, emol)  # composition
14
15    def yearly_sal(self):
16        return self.obj_salary.annual_salary()
17
18 emp = Employee('Asha', 28, 150000, 100000)
19 print(emp.yearly_sal())
```

Output

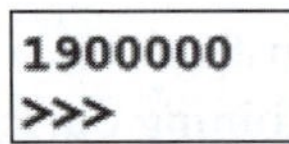

```
1900000
>>>
```

In this program, we understand the different statements:
Line 2-7: Class Salary is defined.
Line 9-16: Class Employee is defined.
Line 13: Salary class method is called from within the class.
Line 18: An instance of Employee is created.

In the above code, we see that we have called the method of a different class from inside another class using the concept of composition.

14.7.2 Aggregation

Aggregation is another way to represent relationships in a problem domain. In aggregation relationship, a complex object can be created by combining objects of different types. For example, the objects – man, woman and child exist independently, but Family object is created to express the joining of these objects. An aggregate object is represented as a union of several objects.

- Aggregation models the ***has-a*** relationship.
- It is a one-way relationship. For example, Department and Students; Student and Address. A department has students; a student has an address. These relationships are not true vice-versa.
- Aggregation is a form of composition where the two entities in the relationship can exist independently.
- The entities are loosely coupled. If one entity is deleted, the other can exist.
- The aggregation relationship in UML (Unified Modeling Language) is represented as shown in Figure 14.10.

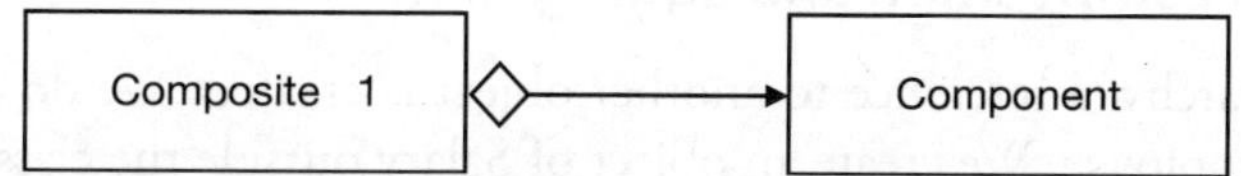

Figure 14.10 Aggregation relationship in UML

An arrow connects the composite and the component. The arrow has an empty diamond at composite side. The cardinality at composite indicates the number of instances the composite will contain.

- Some examples of aggregation relationship are:
  - Student–Address relationship: A student has an address.
  - Company–Employee relationship: A company has employees.

Let us understand aggregation relationship with an example.

Example 14.9: Aggregation relationship

```
# ==========Aggregation
class Salary:
    def __init__(self, basic, emol):
        self.pay = basic
        self.emolument = emol
    def annual_salary(self):
        return (self.pay*12)+self.emolument

class Employee:
    def __init__(self, name, age, sal):
        self.name = name
        self.age = age
        self.aggregate_salary = sal    # Aggregation

    def yearly_sal(self):
        return self.aggregate_salary.annual_salary()

obj_sal = Salary(150000, 100000)
emp = Employee('Asha', 28, obj_sal)
print(emp.yearly_sal())
```

Output

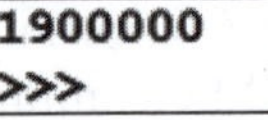

```
1900000
>>>
```

In this program, we understand the different statements:
Line 2–7: Class Salary is defined.
Line 9–16: Class Employee is defined.
Line 13: Employee salary is calculated from aggregation.
Line 18: An object of Salary class is created from outside the class Employee.
Line 19: The object is passed as a parameter `obj_sal`.
Line 18: An instance of Employee is created.
We note that the output from using the aggregation and composition is same.

Difference between composition and aggregation

- In aggregation hierarchy, a reference to another object is created. We do not create an object of Salary inside the Employee. We create an object of Salary outside the class and pass as parameter to Employee. Even if we delete the Employee, object of Salary will exist.
- In a composition hierarchy, we create a child within the parent. We initialize Salary within Employee. If Employee is deleted, the object of Salary defined inside Employee also gets deleted.

14.8 Abstract Class and Metaclass

14.8.1 Abstract Class

- In object-oriented programming, ***abstraction*** is a feature that is used for hiding internal details of a class from the users. For example, in a car music system, one can select a particular channel from the dashboard without bothering about its internal working.
- In Python, abstraction is implemented using the ***abstract class***.
- An abstract class cannot be instantiated. It means that one cannot create an object or instance of an abstract class. However, an abstract class can be extended, i.e., a new class can inherit from an abstract class.
- The methods and properties defined in abstract class are called *abstract methods* and *abstract properties*. An abstract method is without an implementation.
- The derived class or subclass that inherits the abstract methods and properties are required to implement them in order to be able to create objects from it.
- An abstract class may or may not include an abstract method. But an abstract method needs to be declared in an abstract class. In other words, a class that contains one or more abstract methods is called an abstract class.
- An abstract class is used for creating a blueprint for the classes that inherit from it. Its purpose is to define how classes that inherit from the abstract class should look like, i.e., what methods and properties they are expected to have. It is generally used when we design large programs that need to have common interface definitions for different implementations.

- Python does not support abstract classes directly.
- In Python, the module `abc` (abstract base class) is used for defining abstract classes. The `abc` module provides infrastructure for defining abstract base classes. To define an abstract method, the `@abstractmethod` decorator is used. In addition to abstract method, an abstract attribute can also be defined using the decorator `@abstractproperty`. The class that inherits it includes the decorator `@property`.

The syntax to define abstract class is:

```
from abc import ABC
class AbstractClassName(ABC):
    pass
from abc import ABC, abstractmethod
class AbstractClassName(ABC):
    @abstractmethod
    def abstract_method(self):
    pass
@abstractproperty
    def abstract_property(self):
    pass
```

- Use the `from` statement to import ABC class and from the `abc` module. The import of `abstractmethod` allows using the `@abstractmethod` decorator of `abc` module.
- `AbstractClassName` is an identifier. It is the name of the abstract class defined by the user.
- `abstract_method` is an identifier for the abstract method defined by the user.
- An abstract method does not have an implementation, so a single `pass` statement is used.
- `abstract_property` is an identifier for the abstract attribute defined by the user.
- An abstract property does not have an implementation, so a single `pass` statement is used.

Let us understand abstract class with an example.

Example 14.10: Abstract class

```
from abc import ABC, abstractmethod, abstractproperty

class Figure(ABC):
    def __init__(self, fig_name):
        self.fig_name = fig_name

    @abstractproperty
    def sides(self):
        pass
    @abstractmethod
    def area(self):
        pass

```

```
14 class Square(Figure):
15     def __init__(self, side):
16         super().__init__("Square")
17         self.side = side
18     @property
19     def sides(self):
20         print("I am a Square. I have four sides")
21     def area(self):
22         print("Area of square with side", self.side, "is "
23                     ,self.side*self.side)
24 circle = Square(5)
25 circle.sides
26 circle.area()
```

Output

```
I am a Square. I have four sides
Area of square with side 5 is  25
>>>
```

In this program, we understand the different statements:
Line 1: The import statement is used.
Line 3: The Class Figure inherits from ABC.
Line 7: The @abstractproperty is used.
Line 9: The @abstractmethod is used.
Line 14: The Class Square inherits from Class Figure.
Line 18: The @property is used for defining the inherited abstract attribute.
Line 25: The sides is invoked as an attribute.

14.8.2 Metaclass

- In Python, everything is an object. A class is also an object.
- Every object has a type. Thus, a class also has a type.
- The type of class is "type", where "type" is a metaclass and all classes are instances of "type". Just as an object of a class is its instance, similarly, all classes in Python are an instance of metaclass "type".
- Let us take an example. We see that type of the class C1 is "type". Also, type of all types is also "type".

```
class C1:
    pass
x = C1()
print("type x=", type(x))
print("\ntype C1=", type(C1))

print("\ntype dict=", type(dict))
print("type int=", type(int))
print("type tuple=", type(tuple))
print("type list=", type(list))
```

Output

```
type x= <class '__main__.C1'>

type C1= <class 'type'>

type dict= <class 'type'>
type int= <class 'type'>
type tuple= <class 'type'>
type list= <class 'type'>
>>>
```

- The syntax to create metaclass using `type()` is –
  `class_name = type(<name>, <bases>, <dct>)`
  where,
  `<name>` is the class name.
  `<bases>` is a tuple of base class from which this class will inherit.
  `<dct>` is a dictionary that has the definition of class.
- In Python, classes can be created dynamically. A class can be created using the following two ways:

```
class C1(object):
    a = 5
print("C1=", C1, " C1.a=", C1.a)
```

```
C1 = type("C1", (), {"a":5})
print("C1=", C1, " C1.a=", C1.a)
```

Output

```
C1= <class '__main__.C1'> C1.a= 5
```

```
C1= <class '__main__.C1'> C1.a= 5
```

- A new class can inherit from the already defined class as follows:

```
C2 = type("C2", (C1,), {})
print("C2=", C2, " C2.a=", C2.a)
```

The output is:

```
C2= <class '__main__.C2'> C2.a= 5
```

We see that the class C2 inherits Class C1.

- Generally, metaclass is not used.

14.9 Polymorphism and Method Overloading

14.9.1 Polymorphism

Polymorphism means many forms. Polymorphism allows different objects to respond to the same message in different ways.

- Polymorphism is divided into two parts:
  - Static polymorphism, and Dynamic polymorphism
- ***Static polymorphism*** involves binding of functions or methods based on number, type and sequence of their arguments.
  - Static binding occurs at compile-time. The parameters are defined in function declaration; so the function can be bound to the calls at compile time.
  - It is also called as early binding. It means that when the program is executed, the function calls are already bound to the appropriate functions.
- ***Dynamic polymorphism*** refers to an entity, like function or object changing its form depending on the circumstances.
  - Dynamic binding occurs at runtime. It refers to resolution of the method invocation call to their associated methods at runtime.
  - It is also called late binding. It means the resolution of the function to its associated method happens at runtime instead of compile time.
  - This feature increases flexibility of the program. It allows a method to be invoked depending on the object executing the method invocation call at runtime.
- Polymorphism is implemented in two ways:
  - Method overloading
  - Operator overloading
- In method overloading, two or more methods or functions have the same name. The difference is in the parameters that they take as input values.
- In operator overloading, an operator can behave differently with different built-in types.

14.9.2 Method Overloading

- In method overloading, three changes can be made to the parameters:
  - The number of parameters can be different. For example, two functions can be defined with name `add()` that adds integers; one function takes 2 integers as parameters, and another takes 3 integers as parameters.
  - The data type of parameters can be different. For example, one function adds integers, and another one with same name adds an integer and a float.
  - The order of parameters can be different.

- By default, Python does not support method overloading. Two methods cannot have the same name in Python. Though Python allows a method to be overloaded, it is the latest defined method that gets executed. This is because in Python, everything is an object including the class or an object. Just like an assignment, if we write two function definitions with the same name, the second definition replaces the first one.

```
def add(a, b):
    p = a + b
    print(p)

def add(a, b, c):
    p = a + b + c
    print(p)

add(4, 5)
add(4, 5, 5)
```

```
def add(a, b):
    p = a + b
    print(p)

def add(a, b, c):
    p = a + b + c
    print(p)

add(4, 5, 5)
```

Output

```
   add(4, 5)
TypeError: add() missing 1 required positional argument: 'c'
```

```
14
```

- We achieve method overloading in Python in the following ways:
    - o By setting the default value of a parameter. In the following code, we see that c is set to 0. So, there is no error during the execution of the code.

```
def add(a, b, c=0):
    p = a + b + c
    print(p)

add(4, 5)
add(4, 5, 5)
```

Output

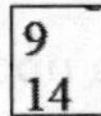

```
9
14
```

- o By using Multiple Dispatch Decorator (This is not discussed here).

14.10 OPERATOR OVERLOADING

In Python, operator overloading allows overriding the functionality of a built-in operator such as, +, *, in the user-defined classes.

- An extended meaning is provided to an operator beyond their predefined meaning.
- The operators work for built-in types (`int, str, list`) but behave differently with different built-in types.

- Because of operator overloading, an operator behaves differently depending on the operands on which the operator is applied. For example, "+" operator when applied on integers, adds the integers; "+" operator applied on strings, concatenates the strings; "+" operator applied on lists, merges the two lists. Here, the "+" operator is overloaded by the objects of the class `int`, `str` and `list`. Another example is of the "*" operator. When applied on numbers, it multiplies them, and when applied on list or string, it is used as repetition operator.

```
1 print(type(1), 1 + 2)
2 print(type("1"), "1" + "2")
3 print(type([1]), [1] + [2])
4
5 print(3 * 4)
6 print("Happy"*4)
```

Output

```
<class 'int'> 3
<class 'str'> 12
<class 'list'> [1, 2]
12
HappyHappyHappyHappy
```

Line 1: Adds two integers.
Line 2: Adds two strings.
Line 3: Adds two lists.
Line 5 Multiplies two integers.
Line 6: Repeats the string.

- Python provides some special functions for operator overloading. These functions are invoked automatically when they are associated with an operator. For example, when we use the "+" operator, the function `__add__()` is invoked. Table 14.1 lists special methods for the different operators.
- For user-defined classes, the behavior of an operator can be changed by defining functionality of the special methods. For example, we can use "+" operator to add two complex objects.
- In operator overloading, Python does not allow changing of number of operands for an operator. For example, the unary operator will have only one operand and cannot be overloaded as binary operator.

Let us understand operator overloading with an example. A class complex performs addition and subtraction of two complex numbers (user-defined class) using operator overloading.

Example 14.11: Operator overloading

```
class complex:
    def __init__(self, x, y):
        self.x = x
        self.y = y

    def __add__(self, other):
        return self.x + other.x, self.y + other.y
    def __sub__(self, other):
        return self.x - other.x, self.y - other.y

def choose_func(choice):
    obj1 = complex(2, 4)
    obj2 = complex(6, 8)
    if choice == 1:
        obj3 = obj1 + obj2
        print(obj3)
    elif choice == 2:
        obj3 = obj1 - obj2
        print(obj3)
    else: print("You have entered wrong choice")

def menu():
    print("Enter your choice")
    print("1. Add complex numbers")
    print("2. Subtract complex numbers")
    return(int(input("Enter your choice ")))

def main():
    c = 1
    while c:
        choose_func(menu())
        c = input("Do you want to continue(N/n/no) ")
        if c == "N" or c == "n" or c == "no":
            c = 0
if __name__ == '__main__':
    main()
```

Output

```
Enter your choice
1. Add complex numbers
2. Subtract complex numbers
Enter your choice 1
(8, 12)
Do you want to continue(N/n/no) y
Enter your choice
1. Add complex numbers
2. Subtract complex numbers
Enter your choice 2
(-4, -4)
Do you want to continue(N/n/no) n
>>>
```

In this program, we understand the different statements:

Line 6, 8: Special methods `__add__` and `__sub__` have been redefined to add and subtract, respectively, two complex objects.

Line 15: Operator overloading. When line 15 executes, `__add__` method gets invoked for the operator "+".

Line 18: Operator overloading. When line 18 executes, `__sub__` method gets invoked for the operator "-".

Table 14.1 Special methods

Binary operators

Operator	Method name
+	`__add__`(self, other)
–	`__sub__`(self, other)
*	`__mul__`(self, other)
/	`__truediv__`(self, other)
//	`__floordiv__`(self, other)
%	`__mod__`(self, other)
**	`__pow__`(self, other)
>>	`__rshift__`(self, other)
<<	`__lshift__`(self, other)
&	`__and__`(self, other)
|	`__or__`(self, other)
^	`__xor__`(self, other)

Assignment operators

Operator	Method name
-=	`__isub__`(self, other)
+=	`__iadd__`(self, other)
*=	`__imul__`(self, other)
/=	`__idiv__`(self, other)
//=	`__ifloordiv__`(self, other)
%=	`__imod__`(self, other)
**=	`__ipow__`(self, other)
>>=	`__irshift__`(self, other)
<<=	`__ilshift__`(self, other)
&=	`__iand__`(self, other)
|=	`__ior__`(self, other)
^=	`__ixor__`(self, other)

Comparison operators

Operator	Method name
<	`__lt__`(self, other)
>	`__gt__`(self, other)
<=	`__le__`(self, other)
>=	`__ge__`(self, other)
==	`__eq__`(self, other)
!=	`__ne__`(self, other)

Unary operators

Operator	Method name
–	`__neg__`(self)
+	`__pos__`(self)
~	`__invert__`(self)

The advantages of operator overloading are:

- Using the operators improves the readability of the code.
- The behavior of objects is consistent for both the built-in types and user-defined types.
- The code becomes simple to write.

14.11 Solved Questions with Explanation

1. Draw inheritance diagram to indicate the following:
   (i) x is an instance of class B.
   (ii) B is an instance of the type metaclass.
   (iii) type is also an instance of type metaclass, so it is an instance of itself.

Answer

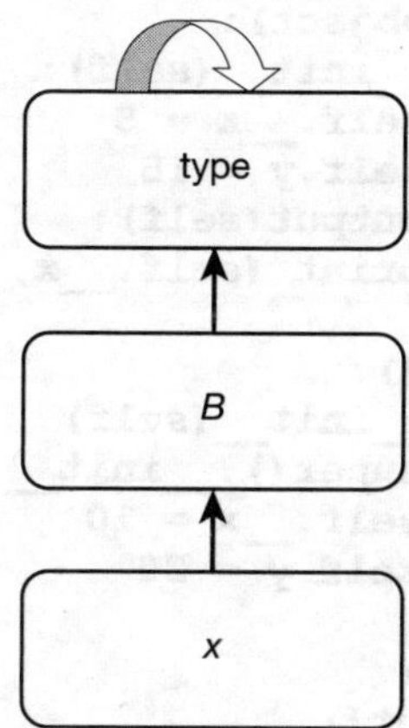

2. Find the output:
   (i)

```
class A:
    pass
class B(A):
    pass
obj1=B()
print(isinstance(obj1,A))
```

Answer: `True`

Explanation: `isinstance()` function works on principle of is-a relationship. `isinstance()` returns True if classinfo argument of `isinstance()` is the object class's parent class.

(ii)

```
class A:
    def A1(self):
        return 'B'
    def A2(self):
        return 'A'

class B(A):
    def A2(self):
        return 'B'

obj1=A()
obj2=B()
print(obj1.A2(), obj2.A2())
```

Answer: A B

Explanation: obj1.A2() will execute the A2 method in class A. Class B inherits from class A, but class B has an overriding method A2(). So obj2.A2() will execute the A2() method in B.

(iii)

```
class A(object):
    def __init__(self):
        self.__x = 5
        self.y = 15
    def output(self):
        print (self.__x, self.y)

class B(A):
    def __init__(self):
        super().__init__()
        self.__x = 10
        self.y = 30

obj = B()
obj.output()
```

Answer: 5 30

Explanation: self.__x is a private variable. The initialization in class A by self.__x =5 cannot be overridden by self.__x = 10 in class B. self.y is a public variable, so initialization self.y = 15 is overridden in class B by self.y = 30.

3. Identify the error and reason for the error. Correct the code.

(i)

```
class A:
    def __init__(self):
        self.x = 0
class B(A):
    def __init__(self):
        self.y = 1
def main():
    obj = B()
    print(obj.x, obj.y)

main()
```

Answer

Output

```
AttributeError: 'B' object has no attribute 'x'
```

The variable x is not initialized in B. To correct it, invoke the init() of A using super().

Corrected code

```
class A:
    def __init__(self):
        self.x = 0
class B(A):
    def __init__(self):
        super().__init__()
        self.y = 1

def main():
    obj = B()
    print(obj.x, obj.y)

main()
```

Output

```
0 1
```

(ii)

```
class A:
    def __init__(self):
        self.__x = 1
class B(A):
    def display(self):
        print(self.__x)
def main():
    obj = B()
    obj.display()
main()
```

Answer

Output

```
AttributeError: 'B' object has no attribute '_B__x'
```

self.__x is a private variable. The variable x is not accessible in B. To access variable x in B declare it as a protected variable.

Corrected code

```
class A:
    def __init__(self):
        self._x = 1
class B(A):
    def display(self):
        print(self._x)
def main():
    obj = B()
    obj.display()
main()
```

Output

```
1
```

(iii)

```
fruit_list = ["apple", "strawberry", "mango"]
fruit_list +="pineapple"
print(fruit_list)
```

Answer

Output

```
TypeError: can only concatenate list (not "str") to list
```

There is an error because only a list can be added to a list. "pineapple" is a string.

Corrected code

We write a program in whiuch the addition operator is overloaded.

```
class A:
    def __init__(self, a):
        self.a = a
    def __add__(self, other):
        temp = [other]
        temp = self.a + temp
        return(temp)
ob1 = A(["apple", "strawberry", "mango"])
ob2 = "pineapple"
print(ob1+ob2)
```

Output

```
['apple', 'strawberry', 'mango', 'pineapple']
```

4. Explain the difference in the output of the two codes.

(i)

```
class A1:
    def __new__(self):
        self.__init__(self)
        print("A1: new()")
    def __init__(self):
        print("A1: init()")
class A2(A1):
    def __init__(self):
        print("A2: init()")
def main():
    obj1 = A2()
    obj2 = A1()
main()
```

(ii)

```
class A1:
    def __new__(self):
        self.__init__(self)
        print("A1: new()")
    def __init__(self):
        print("A1: init()")
class A2(A1):
    def __new__(self):
       print("A2: new()")
       return self
    def __init__(self):
        print("A2: init()")
def main():
    obj1 = A2()
    obj2 = A1()
main()
```

Output

```
A2: init()
A1: new()
A1: init()
A1: new()
```

```
A2: new()
A1: init()
A1: new()
```

Answer: In (i), `new()` of A1 is not overridden in A2. First, `init()` of A2 is invoked and then the inherited method `new()` of A1 is invoked. Then `init()` and `new()` of A1 are invoked.

In (ii), `new()` of A2 in invoked. Then `init()` and `new()` of A1 are invoked.

5. Define a class "Triangle" with attribute as three sides and method as `area()`. The area of a triangle is calculated by using Heron's formula: Area = $\sqrt{(s(s-a)(s-b)(s-c)}$ where s is $(a + b + c)/2$.
Define a class "Equilateral_Triangle" that inherits from class "Triangle", where both attributes and method of class Triangle are inherited. Since all sides of equilateral triangle are equal, length of only one side is provided to the constructor.
Modify the class "Equilateral_Triangle" by overriding the method `area()` that calculates area of equilateral triangle using `area=√3/4a2`.
Answer:

```
import math

class Triangle:
    def __init__(self, a, b, c):
        self.s1=a
        self.s2=b
        self.s3=c
    def area(self):
        s = (self.s1 + self.s2 + self.s3)/2
        area=math.sqrt(s*(s-self.s1)*(s-self.s2)*(s-self.s3))
        return area
if __name__=='__main__':
    t1=Triangle(5,13,17)
    print ('Area of triangle = ',t1.area())
```

Output

```
Area of triangle =  22.18529918662356
```

Inherit all members of class Trianle in class Equilateral_Triangle

```
class Equilateral_Triangle(Triangle):
    def __init__(self, a):
        s1 = a
        s2 = a
        s3 = a
        super().__init__(s1, s2, s3)

t2=Equilateral_Triangle(15)
print ('Area of Equilateral Triangle = ',t2.area())
```

Output

```
Area of Equilateral Triangle =  97.42785792574934
```

Overriding method area() in class Equilateral_Triangle.

```
class Equilateral_Triangle(Triangle):
    def __init__(self, a):
        s1 = a
        s2 = a
        s3 = a
        super().__init__(s1, s2, s3)
    def area(self):
        area=math.sqrt(3)*pow(self.s1, 2) / 4
        return area
t2=Equilateral_Triangle(15)
print ('Area of Equilateral Triangle = ',t2.area())
```

Output

```
Area of Equilateral Triangle =  97.42785792574934
```

6. Write codes for the following:

(i) Merge two lists using operator overloading of "+".

```
L1 = [1,2,3,4]
L2 = [10,20,30,40]
print(L1 + L2)
```

Output

```
[1, 2, 3, 4, 10, 20, 30, 40]
```

(ii) Create an object of derived class. Use `isinstance()` to check whether this object is an instance of the base class or not. (**Hint**: `isinstance()` works on the principle of is-a relationship. It returns True if classinfo argument of `instance()` is the object's class's parent class).

```
class A:
        pass
class B(A):
        pass
obj=B()
print(isinstance(obj,A))
```

Output

```
True
```

(iii) Define a class hierarchy A-parent, B inherits from A, C inherits from B. Define a method `__str__()` in A that returns the string "Happy". Both the classes B and C should also return the string "Happy" when their instance is created.

```
class A:
  def __str__(self):
    return "Happy"
class B(A):
  def __init__(self):
    super().__init__()
class C(B):
  def __init__(self):
    super().__init__()

def main():
  b = B()
  a = A()
  c = C()
  print(a, b, c)
main()
```

Output

```
Happy Happy Happy
```

14.12 PROGRAMMING EXAMPLES

Program 14.1: WAP to overload equality and less than operator.

```
class A:
    def __init__(self, a):
        self.a = a
    def __lt__(self, other):
        if(self.a < other.a):
            return "Object 1 < Object 2"
        else:
            return "Object 2  < Object 1"
    def __eq__(self, other):
        if(self.a == other.a):
            return "Both objects are equal"
        else:
            return "Both objects are not equal"

ob1 = A(10)
ob2 = A(20)
print(ob1 < ob2)
print(ob1 == ob2)

ob3 = A(25)
ob4 = A(25)
print(ob3 == ob4)
```

Output

```
Object 1 < Object 2
Both objects are not equal
Both objects are equal
```

Program 14.2: Create a class Profit that accepts profit from the user. Create class Loss that accepts loss from the user. Create a class BalanceSheet that inherits from both classes Profit and Loss and calculates the balance. It has two methods `getBalance()` and `printBalance()`.

```
class Profit:
    def getProfit(self):
        self._profit=int(input("Enter Profit: "))

class Loss:
    def getLoss(self):
        self._loss=int(input("Enter Loss: "))

class BalanceSheet(Profit, Loss):
    def getBalance(self):
        self.getProfit()
        self.getLoss()
        self.__balance=self._profit - self._loss
        return self.__balance
    def printBalance(self):
        print("Profit:",self._profit)
        print("Loss:",self._loss)
        print("Balance:",self.__balance)

user1 = BalanceSheet()
user1.getBalance()
print("==========")
user1.printBalance()
```

Output

```
Enter Profit: 15
Enter Loss: 4
==========
Profit: 15
Loss: 4
Balance: 11
```

Program 14.3: WAP to extend the abstract class Polygon as given below, by the class Triangle. For class Triangle, write methods for no_of_sides and area. Print the area of the Triangle.

```
class Polygon(ABC):
    @abstractmethod
    def no_of_sides(self):
        pass
    @abstractmethod
    def area(self):
        pass
```

class Triangle(Polygon):

```
from abc import ABC, abstractmethod
import math
class Polygon(ABC):
    @abstractmethod
    def no_of_sides(self):
        pass
    @abstractmethod
    def area(self):
        pass
class Triangle(Polygon):
    def no_of_sides(self, a, b, c):
        self.s1 = a
        self.s2 = b
        self.s3 = c
    def area(self):
        s = (self.s1 + self.s2 + self.s3)/2
        area=math.sqrt(s*(s-self.s1)*(s-self.s2)*(s-self.s3))
        return area
t1 = Triangle()
t1.no_of_sides(20, 40, 50)
print("Area of Triangle = ", t1.area())
```

Output

```
Area of Triangle =  379.9671038392666
```

Program 14.4: WAP using composite relationship as follows: Create a class Student having constructor (student id) and a method `reg_num()` that returns student id and department id. Create a class Department with constructor having the id and an instance of class Student as parameters and define a method `stud_reg()` that invokes `reg_num()` of Student. In main, create an instance of Student and pass value of stud_id as parameter. Create an instance of class Department. Print the `stud_reg()`.

```
class Student:
    def __init__(self, id):
        self._id = id
    def reg_num(self, dept_id):
        return 'Stud_id is ' + str(self._id) + ' and Dept_id is ' + dept_id

class Department:
    def __init__(self, id, stud):
        self._id = id
        self._stud = stud
    def stud_reg(self):
        return self._stud.reg_num(self._id)

if __name__ == '__main__':
    s1 = Student(2)
    d1 = Department('Maths', s1)
    print(d1.stud_reg())
```

Output

```
Stud_id is 2 and Dept_id is Maths
```

Program 14.5: Create a class Rectangle having following methods: `init()`, `perimeter()`, `area()`, and `display()`. Create a class Cuboid that inherits from Rectangle. Include methods – `init()`, `print_height()` and `volume()`. In main, create an instance of rectangle and print its length, breadth, area and perimeter. Create an instance of Cuboid and print its height and volume.

```
class Rectangle:
    def __init__(self, length, breadth):
        self.length = length
        self.breadth = breadth
    def perimeter(self):
        return 2*(self.length + self.breadth)
    def area(self):
        return self.length*self.breadth
    def display(self):
        print("Rectangle Length: ", self.length)
        print("Rectangle Breadth:  ", self.breadth)
        print("Perimeter: ", self.perimeter())
        print("Area: ", self.area())

class Cuboid(Rectangle):
    def __init__(self, length, breadth, height):
        Rectangle.__init__(self, length, breadth)
        self.height = height
    def print_height(self):
        print("Cuboid Height: ", self. height)
    def volume(self):
        return 2*(self.length*self.breadth + self.length*self.height
                  + self.breadth*self.height)

r1 = Rectangle(10, 20)
r1.display()
print("============")
c1 = Cuboid(10, 20, 30)
c1. print_height()
print("Cubioid Volume: " , c1.volume())
```

Output

```
Rectangle Length:  10
Rectangle Breadth:   20
Perimeter:  60
Area:  200
============
Cuboid Height:  30
Cubioid Volume:  2200
```

Summary

- In an inheritance hierarchy, base class is an already-existing class and derived class inherits from base class.
- Base class is called superclass or parent and derived class is called subclass or child.
- Inheritance is is-a relationship and promotes reusability.
- Derived class can have three types of methods – new, inherited, and overriding.
- Method overriding allows defining a method with same name in both base and derived class.
- Python supports single inheritance, multiple inheritance, multi-level inheritance and multi-path inheritance.
- Single inheritance allows a subclass to inherit data and method from a base class.
- Multi-level inheritance allows a derived class to inherit from a derived class.
- Multiple inheritance allows derived class to inherit from more than one base class.
- Multi-path inheritance is a combination of single and multiple inheritance. It forms a grandparent-parent-child relationship.
- Public access allows a derived class to access public member of base class.
- Private access does not allow a derived class to access private members of base class.
- Protected access allows protected members to be accessed from the derived class.
- Internal is the default access control attribute.
- Method Resolution Order looks for the order in which a method is searched in a hierarchy.
- Composition models the part-of relationship.
- Aggregation models the has-a relationship.
- Abstraction feature is used for hiding internal details of a class from the users.
- Abstraction is implemented using module abc (abstract base class), to define abstract class.
- Static polymorphism and dynamic polymorphism are the two types of polymorphism.
- Static polymorphism happens at compile time and dynamic polymorphism, at runtime.
- Polymorphism is implemented using method overloading and operator overloading.
- Python provides some special functions for operator overloading.

Keywords

Inheritance
Base class
Superclass
Derived class
Subclass
Reusability
Parent-child
Is-a
Inherited Method
Overriding Method
Method overriding
Specialization
Generalization

Single Inheritance
Multiple Inheritance
Multilevel Inheritance
Multipath Inheritance
Access control
Public
Private
Protected
Internal
Method Resolution Order (MRO)
Composition
Part-of

Aggregation
Has-a
Composite
Component
Abstract class
Abstraction
Abstract method
Abstract property
Metaclass
Static polymorphism
Dynamic polymorphism
Static binding
Dynamic binding

Method Overloading
Operator Overloading
Multiple Dispatch
abc (abstract base class)

Programming Language Keywords

`super()`
`abc`
`@abstractmethod`
`@abstractproperty`
`@property`
`__mro__`
`mro()`

Assessment

A.1 Bloom Level: Knowledge/Remember

Review Questions

1. Define – Inheritance, Derived class, Base class, Superclass, Subclass, Abstraction, Static polymorphism, Dynamic polymorphism.
2. What are the two ways to access methods of the base class and the derived class?
3. What is method overriding?
4. What is the use of `super()` method?
5. What is an inherited method?
6. What is an overriding method?
7. Name the four kinds of inheritance.
8. What is single inheritance, multiple inheritance, multi-level inheritance, and multi-path inheritance?
9. Illustrate graphically – single inheritance, multiple inheritance, multi-path inheritance, and multi-level inheritance.
10. What is access control? What is private, public, and protected access control?
11. What is method Resolution Order?
12. What is composition relationship and aggregation relationship?
13. Give an example for abstraction.
14. When should you use an abstract class?
15. What is a metaclass?
16. Name the two kinds of polymorphism.
17. Name two ways to implement polymorphism.
18. What is operator overloading and method overloading?
19. List the three changes that can be made to the parameters of method overloading.
20. List the special functions for operator overloading for the following operators:
    (i) *
    (ii) <<
    (iii) >
    (iv) +=
21. Match the following:

(a)	Is-a relationship	(i)	Private member
(b)	Has-a relationship	(ii)	Protected member
(c)	Part-of relationship	(iii)	Abstract class
(d)	_attributename	(iv)	Aggregation
(e)	__attributename	(v)	Inheritance
(f)	abc	(vi)	Composition

Fill in the blanks

1. The class that inherits from superclass is called ________.
2. The derived class can have three types of method – ____________, ___________, and ________.
3. Superclass is also called as _________ class.
4. ______________ allows sharing commonality between two or more classes.
5. In multi-level inheritance, a derived class inherits from an already __________ class.
6. ______________ inheritance forms a grandparent–parent–child relationship.
7. A derived class cannot access ____________ members of the base class.
8. Aggregation models the __________ relationship.
9. In Python, abstraction is implemented using the ____________ class.
10. The module ____________ is used for defining abstract classes.
11. In Python, every object has a ___________.
12. Dynamic binding occurs at _________ time.

State True/False

1. In method overriding, the derived class has a different return type than the base class method.
2. In inheritance, overriding method in derived class has a different functionality than the method of the base class.
3. Specialization allows extending the functionality of an existing class.
4. In multiple inheritance, a derived class inherits from more than one base class.
5. Protected members of the class can be accessed from all classes except from derived class.
6. The `__init__()` of parent has to be explicitly called from the `__init__()` of child class.
7. In a composition relationship, parent and child are loosely coupled.
8. An abstract class cannot be instantiated.
9. Static binding occurs at compile-time.
10. By default, Python supports method overloading.

Multiple Choice Questions (MCQ)

1. Identify the protected member.
   (i) __sum (ii) _sum
   (iii) sum (iv) sum__
2. Identify the private member.
   (i) `x()__` (ii) `__x()`
   (iii) `_x()` (iv) `x()`
3. Car–Engine relationship is:
   (i) Single inheritance
   (ii) Composition
   (iii) Aggregation
   (iv) is-a

4. An inheritance hierarchy A→B→C→D is:
   (i) Single inheritance
   (ii) Multiple inheritance
   (iii) Multi-level inheritance
   (iv) Multi-path inheritance

5. If a = A(), then the correct way to call the mro method is:
   (i) `a.mro()`
   (ii) `A().mro()`
   (iii) `A.mro()`
   (iv) `A().mro`

6. Identify the statement that is NOT true about abstract class.
   (i) A class which contains one or more abstract methods is called an abstract class.
   (ii) An abstract class has both declaration and implementation.
   (iii) Abstract classes are classes that you cannot create instances from.
   (iv) By default, Python does not provide abstract classes.

A.2 Bloom Level: Comprehension/Understand

Review Questions

1. "Inheritance facilitates reusability". Explain.
2. Explain the following built-in class attributes and methods: `__mro__`, `mro()`, `@abstractproperty`, `@abstractmethod`
3. Describe the meaning of following special methods: `__add__(self, other)`, `__sub__(self, other)`. `__mul__(self, other)`, `__truediv__(self, other)`, `__floordiv__(self, other)`, `__mod__(self, other)`, `__pow__(self, other)`, `__rshift__(self, other)`, `__lshift__(self, other)`, `__and__(self, other)`, `__or__(self, other)`, `__xor__(self, other)`, `__lt__(self, other)`, `__gt__(self, other)`, `__le__(self, other)`, `__ge__(self, other)`, `__eq__(self, other)`, `__ne__(self, other)`, `__isub__(self, other)`, `__iadd__(self, other)`, `__imul__(self, other)`, `__idiv__(self, other)`, `__ifloordiv__(self, other)`, `__imod__(self, other)` `__ipow__(self, other)`, `__irshift__(self, other)`, `__ilshift__(self, other)`, `__iand__(self, other)`, `__ior__(self, other)`, `__neg__(self)`, `__pos__(self)`, `__invert__(self)`
4. Describe the syntax for the following:
   (i) Access base class from derived class
   (ii) Single inheritance
   (iii) Multiple inheritance
   (iv) Multi-level inheritance
   (v) Multi-path inheritance
   (vi) Abstract class
   (vii) Create metaclass using type
5. What is the purpose of protected access control?

6. What is the purpose of abstraction? Explain with examples.
7. What is the purpose of using an abstract class? Explain.
8. "An abstract method is without an implementation." Explain.
9. How are metaclass and type related?
10. Explain the method resolution order in Python.

A.3 Bloom Level: Application/Apply

1. Identify whether the following are composition, aggregation or inheritance (single, multiple, multi-level, multi-path) relationship:
   (i) Teacher–Employee–Person
   (ii) Harmonium–Wind Instrument
   (iii) Person–Employee
   (iv) Person–Employee–Part-time Employee
   (v) Person–Heart
   (vi) Student–Address
   (vii) Ferrari–Car
   (viii) Car–Wheel
   (ix) Teacher-in-charge is a faculty member of the college.
   (x) Teacher-in-charge and teachers have i-card to enter the college.

2. Find output for the codes:

(i)

```
class A:
    def __init__(self, x = 5, y = 10):
        self.x = x
        self.y = y
    def __str__(self):
        return "X"
    def __eq__(self, num ):
        return self.x * self.y == num.x * num.y
def main():
    a = A(2, 4)
    b = A(4, 2)
    print(a == b)

main()
```

(ii)

```
class A:
    def __init__(self,x):
        self.x = x
    def ct(self,x):
        self.x = self.x+1

class B(A):
    def __init__(self, y=0):
        A.__init__(self, 3)
        self.y = y
    def ct(self):
        self.y += 1

def main():
    b1 = B()
    b1.ct()
    print(b1.x, b1.y)
main()
```

(iii)

```
class A:
    def __init__(self):
        print('Init: class A')
    def method(self, b):
        print('Print class A:', b)

class B(A):
    def __init__(self):
        print('Init: class B')
        super().__init__()
    def method(self, b):
        print('Print class B:', b)
        super().method(b + 1)

class C(B):
    def __init__(self):
        print('Init: class C')
        super().__init__()
    def method(self, b):
        print('Print class C:', b)
        super().method(b + 1)

if __name__ == '__main__':
    c = C()
    c.method(1)
```

(iv)

```
class Person:
    def __init__(self, p_name, p_age):
        self.name = p_name
        self.age = p_age
    def display_name(self):
        print("Name: ", self.name)
    def display_age(self):
        print("Age: ", self.age)

class Student(Person):
    def __init__(self, s_name, s_age, s_id):
        super().__init__(s_name, s_age)
        self.stud_id = s_id
    def get_id(self):
        return self.stud_id

p1 = Person("Akshita", 20)
p1.display_name()
p1.display_age()
print("=========")
s1 = Student("Meghna", 21, "S111")
print("Id: ", s1.get_id())
s1.display_name()
print("=========")
```

(v)

```
class A:
    x_a = 5
    def __init__(self, x, y):
        self.x = x
        self.y = y
    def method1(self):
        self.w = 1

class B:
    x_b = 10
    def __init__(self,z):
        self.z = z
    def method1(self):
        self.z = self.z + B.x_b
        print("z=", z)

class C(A,B):
    x_c = 15
    def __init__(self, x, y, z, w):
        A.__init__(self, x, y)
        B.__init__(self,z)
        self.w = w
    def method1(self):
        super().method1()
        print("C: x= ", self.x, "y= ", self.y)
        print("C: z= ", self.z, "w= ", self.w)
        A.x_a = B.x_b + C.x_c
        print("A.x_a= ", A.x_a)
        print("C.x_a= ", C.x_a)

c1=C(2, 4, 6, 8)
c1.method1()
```

3. Find errors, and correct the code:

(i)

```
from abc import ABC,abstractmethod

class Animal(ABC):
    @abstractmethod
    def sound(self):
        pass
class Human(Animal):
    def sound(self):
        print("Speak")

class Dog(Animal):
    def sound(self):
        print("Bark")

class Lion(Animal):
    def sound(self):
        print("Roar")

c=Animal()
```

(ii)

```
class Test:
        def __init__(self):
            self.a = 1
            self.__b = 1
        def get(self):
            return self.__b

t1 = Test()
t1.a=45
print(t1.a, t1.b)
```

(iii)

```
class Parent:
    def __init__(self, num):
        self.n1 = num

class Child(Parent):
    def __init__(self, num):
        self.n2 = num*5
    def show(self):
        print(self.n1, self.n2)

c1 = Child(20)
c1.show()
```

4. Define a class First that has:
   (a) Constructor that initializes variable x to 5, and private variable y to 5.
   (b) A method get_y() that returns the value of the private variable.

   Create an instance of the class and print the value of the private variable y.

A.4 Bloom Level: Analyze

1. Explain difference between the following:
   (i) Single inheritance and Multiple inheritance
   (ii) Multi-level inheritance and Multi-path inheritance
   (iii) Single inheritance and Multi-level inheritance
   (iv) Inheritance and Composition relationship
   (v) Composition and Aggregation
   (vi) Private, Public and Protected access control
   (vii) Static polymorphism and Dynamic polymorphism.
2. What is the type of inheritance in code (i) and code (ii)? Draw a diagram to show the inheritance.

   (i)

```
class A():
    pass
class B():
    pass
class C(A, B):
    pass
class D(B, C):
    pass
```

   (ii)

```
class P():
    pass
class Q(P):
    pass
class R(P):
    pass
class S(Q, P):
    pass
```

3. Analyze the following code. What is the output? Is the output for the two codes same? If not, explain the difference in the output and the reasons for the difference.

   (i)

```
import abc
from abc import ABC, abstractmethod

class parent(ABC):
    @abc.abstractproperty
    def name(self):
        return "Parent"
class child(parent):
    @property
    def name(self):
        return "Child"

try:
    r =parent()
    print( r.name)
except Exception as err:
    print (err)

r = child()
print (r.name)
```

   (ii)

```
import abc
from abc import ABC, abstractmethod

class parent(ABC):
    @abc.abstractproperty
    def name(self):
        return "Parent"
class child(parent):
    @property
    def name(self):
        return "Child"

r =parent()
print( r.name)
r = child()
print (r.name)
```

4. Analyze the difference between (i) and (ii). What is the output and the reasons for difference in the output?

(i)

```
import abc
from abc import ABC
class Figure(ABC):
    def __init__(self, name):
        self.name = name
    @abc.abstractmethod
    def no_of_sides(self):
        pass

class Square(Figure):
    def __init__(self, side):
        super().__init__("Square")
        self.side = side
    @property
    def no_of_sides(self):
        print("Square: Four sides")

circle = Square(5)
circle.no_of_sides()
```

(ii)

```
import abc
from abc import ABC
class Figure(ABC):
    def __init__(self, name):
        self.name = name
    @abc.abstractproperty
    def no_of_sides(self):
        pass

class Square(Figure):
    def __init__(self, side):
        super().__init__("Square")
        self.side = side
    @property
    def no_of_sides(self):
        print("Square: Four sides")

circle = Square(5)
circle.no_of_sides()
```

5. The code finds if the first object is less than the second object.
   a) What is the output in the three cases?
   b) Which of the following codes displays the correct answer?
   c) Give reasons for the difference in outputs.

(i)

```
class compare1:
    def __init__(self, x):
        self.x = x
    def __lt__(self, other):
        if self.x < other.x:
            return False
        else:
            return True
a1 = compare1(5)
a2 = compare1(10)
print("a1 < a2 = ", a1 < a2)
```

(ii)

```
class compare2:
    def __init__(self, x):
        self.x = x
    def __lt__(self, other):
        if self.x < other.x:
            return True
        else:
            return False
a1 = compare2(5)
a2 = compare2(10)
print("a1 < a2 = ", a1 < a2)
```

(iii)

```
class compare3:
    def __init__(self, x):
        self.x = x
    def __less__(self, other):
        if self.x < other.x:
            return True
        else:
            return False
a1 = compare3(5)
a2 = compare3(10)
print("a1 < a2 = ", a1 < a2)
```

A.5 Bloom Level: Evaluate

1. The desired output from the code is given. However, on executing the code, error is reported. Evaluate and identify the kind of error that will be reported in the following code. Justify your answer. Correct the code so that the desired output is displayed.

```
from abc import ABC, abstractmethod

class Employee(ABC):
    def __init__(self, name):
        self.name = name
    @abstractmethod
    def get_salary(self):
        pass

class FulltimeEmployee(Employee):
    def __init__(self, name, salary):
        super().__init__(name)
        self.salary = salary
    def get_salary(self):
        return self.salary

class HourlyEmployee(Employee):
    def __init__(self, name, hours_worked, rate):
        super().__init__(name)
        self.hours_worked = hours_worked
        self.rate = rate
    def get_salary(self):
        return self.hours_worked * self.rate
```

```
class Payroll:
    def __init__(self):
        self.employee_list = []
    def add(self, employee):
        self.employee_list.append(employee)
    def print(self):
        for e in self.employee_list:
            print(f"{e.name} \t Rs.{e.get_salary()}")

p1 = Payroll()
p1.add(FulltimeEmployee('Ashok Mittal', 10000))
p1.add(FulltimeEmployee('Prachi Jain', 11500))
p1.add(HourlyEmployee('Sonali Singh', 150, 50))
p1.add(HourlyEmployee('Parna Das', 115, 50))
p1.print()
```

Desired Output

```
Ashok Mittal                Rs. 10000
Prachi Jain                 Rs. 11500
Sonali Singh                Rs. 7500
Parna Das                   Rs. 5750
```

2. Evaluate the following code.
   (a) Which operator does the code overload?
   (b) Which special method is used for operator overloading?
   (c) What output does the print statement display?

```
class A:
    def __init__(self, a):
        self.a = a
    def __invert__(self):
        return "This overloads the operator"

ob1 = A(2)
print(~ob1)
```

3. Evaluate the code. What is the task performed? What is the output? What is the purpose of `__add__`, `__eq__` and `__str__` methods? Where is the `__str__` method used. When objects are added, what is added in the result? When the objects are compared, what is being compared? Justify your answer.

```
class Fruit:
  def __init__(self, weight, name = "none"):
    self.name = name;
    self.weight = weight;

  def __add__(self, x):
    if isinstance (x, Fruit):
      return Fruit(self.weight + x.weight)
    if isinstance (x, int):
      return Fruit(self.weight + x, self.name)

  def __eq__(self, x):
    if self.name == x.name:
      print("Same Fruits")
    else:
      print("Different Fruits: ", self.name, "and", x.name, )

  def __str__(self):
    if self.name == "none":
      return "Weight: {0}\n".format(self.weight)
    else:
      return "Name: {0} \tWeight: {1}\n".format(self.name, self.weight)

a = Fruit(50, "Mango")
b = Fruit(10, "Banana")
c = Fruit(120)
print(a, b, c)
print(a + b + c)
a == b
```

4. Evaluate the code. Identify the task performed. Draw the inheritance diagram for the code. Identify the inherited, overridden and new attributes and methods in the two classes. Write the output of the code. Justify your answer.

```
class Vehicle:
    def __init__(self, name, color, price):
        self.name = name
        self.color = color
        self.price = price
    def show(self):
        print('Details:', self.name, self.color, self.price)
    def max_speed(self):
        pass
    def change_gear(self):
       pass

class Car(Vehicle):
    def max_speed(self):
        pass
    def change_gear(self):
        pass

car = Car('Car A1', 'White', 100000)
car.show()
car.max_speed()
car.change_gear()

vehicle = Vehicle('Truck T1', 'Brown', 65000)
vehicle.show()
vehicle.max_speed()
vehicle.change_gear()
```

A.6 Bloom Level: Create/Synthesize

Programming Assignment

1. Create the following inheritance hierarchy with the following methods:
   class Person(object):
   def __init__(self, name):
   def getName(self):
   def isEmployee(self):
   class Employee(Person):
   def isEmployee(self):
   Create a driver code that creates objects of both classes and prints the name of employee.

2. Create the following multi-level inheritance hierarchy and the driver program:
   Class: Employee
   getEmployee() - gets user input from id, name and salary.
   printEmployeeDetails()
   getSalary() - return salary
   Class: Perks inherits from Employee
   calcPerks() - calculates perks.
   putPerks() - print perks.
   totalPerks() - return total perks.

Class : NetSalary inherits from Perks
getTotal() - calculate Salary using perks and base salary.
showTotal() - prints total salary.

3. Create the following multi-path inheritance hierarchy and the driver program.
   a) Create a class Square with attributes – side
   b) Create a class Triangle with attributes – base and height; method to calculate area
   c) Create a class RightPyramid. Right pyramid is a pyramid with a square base, built from a Triangle and Square. It inherits from both classes. It has an attribute slant_height, initializes and calculates area. The general formula for **total surface area** of a regular pyramid is 0.5 * perimeter * slant_height + base area.

4. Create a class Circle. It contains:
   a) Private attributes: radius (type double) default value 2.0 and color (type String), with default value "green".
   b) Overloaded constructors: (i) default constructor with no argument, and (ii) constructor which takes a double argument for radius.
   c) Pubic methods: `getRadius()` – returns radius of circle, and `getArea()` – returns area of circle.

   Create a class cuboid that inherits from the circle. And create a driver program for the same.

5. Create a class Rectangle and a class Cuboid that inherits from the class Rectangle. Create methods Area and Volume in class Rectangle and override them in the class Cuboid.

6. Create the following hierarchy and a driver program to execute it.
   - Class Furniture having protected members – color, width, height
   - Class Bookshelf inherits from Furniture. New attributes – No. of shelves, method `acceptdata()`, `display_data()`.
   - Class Chair inherits from Furniture. New attribute – No of legs. Method `acceptData()`, `displayData()`.

7. Create the following hierarchy and a driver program to execute it.
   - Create a class Publication. Attributes – title, price
   - Class Book inherits from Publication. Attribute – pageCount.
   - Each class has `getdata()` and `putdata()` methods.

8. Create the following inheritance hierarchy:
   - BankAccount – SavingsAccount – FeeSavingsAccount
   - Employee – FullTimeEmployee – PartTimeEmployee
   - Staff – Teacher, Officer, Typist
   - Furniture – WoodenFurniture – WoodenChair; Furniture – PlasticFurniture – PlasticChair
   - Animal – Mammal – Cow; Animal – Herbivores – Cow
   - Figure – Rectangle, Square, Triangle – Closed Figure
   - Bank Account – Loan, Interest, Brokerage

   Define the classes with suitable attributes and methods. Use method overriding where possible. Use abstract class where possible. Use `super()` to invoke constructor of the parent. Write the driver programs.

9. Write the implementation of special methods for the following tasks:
   - Compare two complex numbers

- Compare two sentences
- Compare two lists, tuples, dictionary
- Add two lists, tuples, complex numbers, rational numbers, strings
- Check if a number is an integer or rational
- Compare two objects of a particular type
- Apply left shift and right shift of words on a sentence
- Apply minus to remove a word from a string
- Use invert to change case of letters of a word – uppercase to lowercase and vice-versa.

10. Create composition hierarchies with suitable attributes and methods. Create a driver program to execute them.
- Salary – Employee
- Human – Heart, Lungs
- Car – Engine
- House – Rooms

11. Create aggregation hierarchies with suitable attributes and methods. Create a driver program to execute them.
- Student–Address
- Company–Employee

Answers

A.1 Bloom Level: Knowledge/Remember

Review Questions

20. (a)– (v), (b) – (iv), (c) – (vi), (d) – (ii) (e) – (i), (f) – (iii)

Fill in the Blanks

1. subclass **2.** new, inherited, overriding **3.** base **4.** generalization **5.** derived
6. multipath **7.** private **8.** has-a **9.** abstract **10.** abc
11. type **12.** run

True/False

1. False **2.** True **3.** True **4.** False **5.** False **6.** True **7.** False
8. True **9.** True **10.** False

Multiple Choice Questions (MCQ)

1. (ii) **2.** (ii) **3.** (ii) **4.** (iii) **5.** (iii) **6.** (ii)

A3. Bloom Level: Application/Apply

1.

(i) Multiple inheritance
(ii) Single inheritance
(iii) Single inheritance
(iv) Multiple inheritance
(v) Composition
(vi) Aggregation
(vii) Single Inheritance
(viii) Composition
(ix) Single Inheritance
(x) Aggregation

2.

i.

```
True
```

ii.

```
3 1
```

iii.

```
Init: class C
Init: class B
Init: class A
Print class C: 1
Print class B: 2
Print class A: 3
```

iv.

```
Name:  Akshita
Age:  20
========
Id:  S111
Name:  Meghna
========
```

v.

```
C: x=  2 y=  4
C: z=  6 w=  1
A.x_a=  25
C.x_a=  25
```

3.

(i)

```
AttributeError: 'a4' object has no attribute 'y'
```

(ii)

```
TypeError: __init__() missing 1 required positional argument: 'a'
```

(iii)

```
TypeError: isEqual() takes 2 positional arguments but 3 were given
```

(iv)

```
AttributeError: 'Test1' object has no attribute '__date'
```

(v)

```
    count = count + 1
UnboundLocalError: local variable 'count' referenced before assignment
```

4.

(i)

```
TypeError: Can't instantiate abstract class Animal with abstract method sound
```

(ii)

```
AttributeError: 'Test' object has no attribute 'b'
```

(iii)

```
AttributeError: 'Child' object has no attribute 'n1'
```

5.

```
class First:
  def __init__(self):
    self.x = 5
    self.__y = 5
  def get_y(self):
    return self.__y
val = First()
print(val.get_y())
```

A.4 Bloom Level: Analyze

2. (i) Multipath inheritance

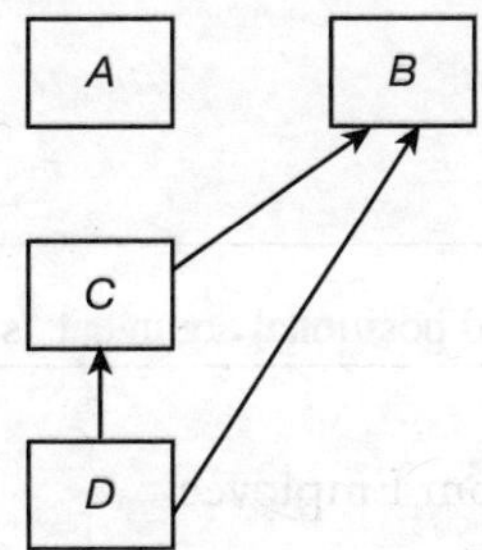

(ii) Multiple inheritance

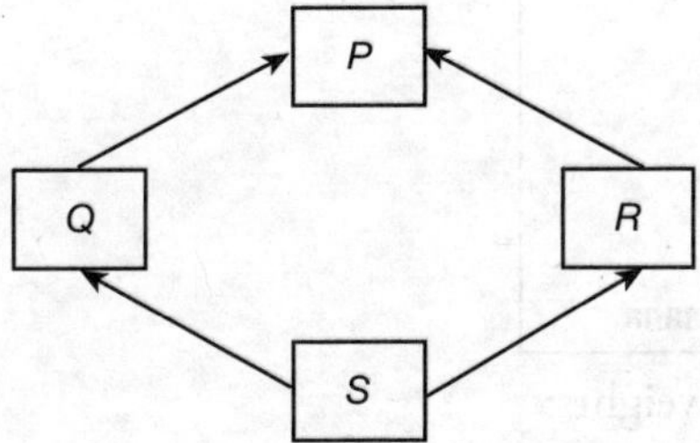

3. (i) **Output**

```
Can't instantiate abstract class parent with abstract method name
Child
```

(ii) **Output**

```
TypeError: Can't instantiate abstract class parent with abstract method name
```

The output of the two codes is not same. In code (i), the call to parent is enclosed in try-except. The error is printed and the exceution of the rest of the program continues. In (ii), the error occurs and execution stops.

4. (i)

```
Square: Four sides
```

(ii)

```
    circle.no_of_sides()
TypeError: 'NoneType' object is not callable
```

In (i), no_of_sides() is defined in @abc.abstractmethod and in (ii), in @abc.abstractproperty.

5.

```
a1 < a2 = False
```

```
a1 < a2 = True
```

```
TypeError: '<' not supported between instances of 'compare3' and 'compare3'
```

(I) Displays correct answer

In (i), the answer is False because the `if` statement compares the objects and if the first object is less than the second, it displays False.

In (ii), the answer is correct.

In (iii), `__less__()` is not a special method. So a TypeError is displayed.

A.5 Bloom Level: Evaluate

1. **Error**

```
    super().__init__(name)
TypeError: __init__() missing 1 required positional argument: 'salary'
```

Correction

HourlyEmployee should inherit from Employee

```
class HourlyEmployee(Employee):
```

3.

```
Name: Mango         Weight: 50
 Name: Banana       Weight: 10
 Weight: 120

Weight: 180

Different Fruits:  Mango and Banana
```

Comparing names and not weights:

Overloading `__str__()` to use `print(Fruit)`:

4.

```
Details: Car A1 White 100000
Details: Truck T1 Brown 65000
```

CHAPTER 15 GUI Programming – Tkinter

Contents

15.1 INTRODUCTION

Graphical User Interface (GUI) applications are desktop applications that help to interact with the computer. GUI applications can be activated with mouse, keyboard or touch. In addition to GUI, there is also Command Line Interface (CLI). CLI requires writing the command for executing an application. Commonly, we interact with the computer via GUI applications, like, text editors, browsers and games. GUI applications have visuals in it.

For developing GUI applications, Python provides interfaces to several GUI libraries and toolkits. Some of the key Python interfaces provided for different GUI toolkits are as follows:

- Tkinter – Python interface to Tk GUI toolkit.
- wxPython – Python interface for wxWidgets GUI toolkit.
- PyQt – Python interface for Qt GUI library.
- Kivy – Python interface for mobile applications.

Tkinter is simple to use and is popular among the learners and developers. In this chapter, we discuss the Python Tkinter interface to develop GUI applications.

Learning outcomes of this chapter

After completion of the chapter, the learner will be able to:

- Understand Tkinter concepts – (1) Widgets and their attributes, (2) Geometry management, and (3) Event handling
- Create GUI interfaces
- Create Events in the application
- Create Event Handlers to take action on the occurrence of events
- Create both simple and complex GUI applications.

15.2 TKINTER – PYTHON INTERFACE TO TK

- Tk is primary GUI toolkit. Tk is simple and is used to build GUIs that run on most platforms. Tk toolkit was originally designed for Tool Command Language (TCL). Tk is popular and is ported in many scripting languages like Perl, Ruby and Python.
- Tkinter is the default GUI library of Python. Tkinter is based on Tk toolkit. We access Tk from Python interface called Tkinter (short for "Tk interface"). Tkinter provides an object-oriented interface to Tk GUI toolkit.
- Python's Tkinter is used for building GUI applications in Python.
- To check whether Tkinter is available on your Python interpreter, type the following:

```
>>> import tkinter
```

- With Python 3, it gets installed by default. You need not worry!

15.3 Building Application Using Tkinter

Let us start by understanding the process of GUI application development in Python.

- There is a **top-level window** on which the other objects are built. It is defined as:

```
window = Tk()
window.title("GUI") #displays this title on the window
```

- There are several GUI components on the top-level window, called ***widgets.*** Some of the widgets are: button, label, message, listbox and combobox. The widgets are placed on the top-level window at specified locations. For example,

```
labl = Label(window, text="Hello") # a label is drawn on the window
lbl.pack()      # location of widget label
```

- The widgets have some behavior. For example, a button can be pressed, and an entry can be filled with data by the user. These are called **events** that occur during interaction with the user. In Python, there are broadly two kinds of events – from mouse and from keyboard.
- The processing of GUI applications is event-driven. The response to an event is called a **callback**, i.e., it specifies what action is to be taken if a button is pressed.
- A GUI application runs like a client–server application. When we start a Python GUI application, it establishes a top-level window and arranges all widgets. The application runs in an infinite loop waiting for an event to occur. When an event occurs, the event is handled. In Python, an infinite loop is created by using

```
Window.mainloop()      #run an infinite loop
```

Broadly, there are four steps that are required to create a Tkinter application. The steps are as follows:

- Import the Tkinter module `(import tkinter)`.
- Create a main window for GUI application. This window will contain all objects of GUI application.
- Build the GUI components and functionality on the main window. (Add Widgets)
- Enter the main event loop. The loop runs infinitely in the backend and tells the code to keep displaying the window, until the window is closed manually.

An example is shown below:

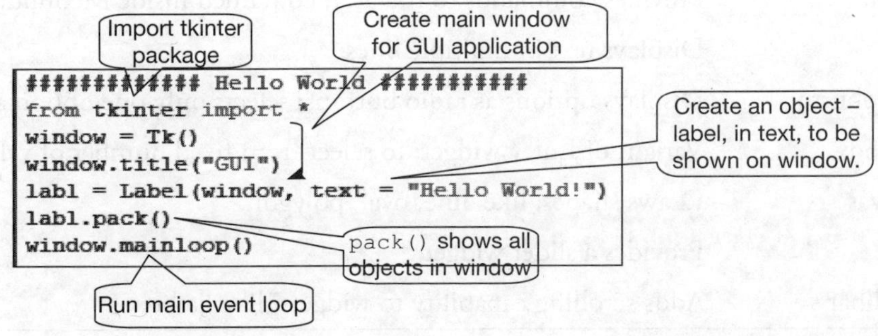

The output is as follows:

15.4 Tkinter Widgets, Attributes and Geometry Manager

In a Tkinter application, the things that you see on the screen, like button, labels, scrollbars and text entry are called **widgets**. The widgets are also referred to as controls or windows. Widgets in Tkinter are similar to tag elements in HTML. In Python software, there are classes to represent button, frame, text, and so on. The widgets are objects or instances of these classes.

The Python widgets can be broadly categorized into:

- *Interactive widgets* that require the user to interact with the widget for selection or data entry.
- *Display Information widgets* for displaying information to the user.
- *Grouping widgets* for grouping several widgets together.

Table 15.1 lists the key widgets along with their brief description. The widgets are discussed in detail in the next section.

Table 15.1 Tkinter widgets and their description

S. No	Widget	Description
Interactive		
1	Button	Displays buttons in application.
2	Checkbutton	Displays options as checkboxes; selects multiple options at a time.
3	Entry	Displays single-line text field to accept values from the user.
4	Listbox	Provides a list of options to the user.
5	Menubutton	Displays menus in the application.
6	Menu	Provides commands to the user, contained inside Menubutton.
7	Text	Displays text in multiple lines.
8	Radiobutton	Displays options as radio buttons; selects only one option at a time.
9	Spinbox	Variant of Entry widget; to select from fixed number of values.
10	Canvas	Draws shapes, like, line, oval, polygon.
11	Scale	Provides a slider widget.
12	Scrollbar	Adds scrolling capability to widgets, like listbox.

(*Continued*)

Table 15.1 (Continued)

S. No	Widget	Description
Display information		
13	Label	Provides single-line caption or images for other widgets.
14	Message	Displays multiline text fields to accept values from the user.
For grouping		
15	Frame	Container widget. To organize other widgets.
16	LabelFrame	Container widget. For spacer in complex window layouts.
17	PanedWindow	Container widget. For multiple panes, horizontally or vertically.
18	Toplevel	Provides a separate window container.

Standard Attributes

There are several attributes that are common to all widgets. These are also called standard attributes. The common attributes are as given in Table 15.2.

Table 15.2 Standard attributes of widgets

S. No.	Attribute	Description
1	Dimension	Describes length, width, and other dimensions of widgets. An integer is considered to be in pixels.
2	Color	Specifies colors in two ways: (1) Hexadecimal string specifying proportion of red, green and blue. For example, "#000000" for black, and "#00ffff" for cyan. (2) Color names like white, black, blue, magenta, dark blue. "fg" and "bg" are used to specify foreground and background color.
3	Font	Specifies font family, size in points, and style modifiers, like bold, italic and underline. For example, font=("Courier", "16", "bold")
4	Anchor	Specify position of text relative to a reference point. Anchor attributes are: NW, N, NE, W, CENTER, E, SW, S, and SE. NW N NE W CENTER E SW S SE

(*Continued*)

Table 15.2 (Continued)

S. No.	Attribute	Description
5	Relief styles	Specifies 3-dimension effect around widget. The attributes are – FLAT, RAISED, SUNKEN, GROOVE, RIDGE 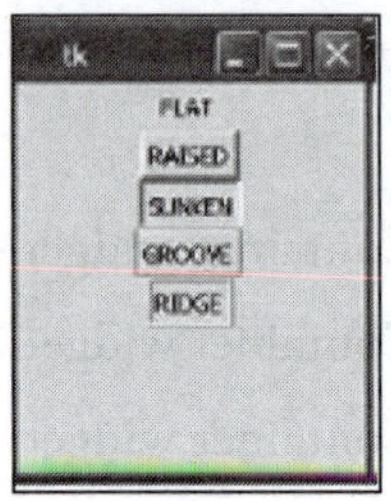
6	Bitmaps	Displays bitmap – "error", "hourglass", "info", "question", "warning" 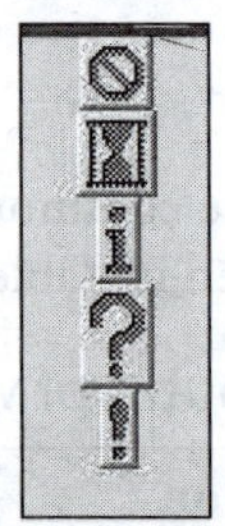 Also, "gray75", "gray50", "gray25", "gray12", "questhead"
7	Cursors	Specify a different mouse cursor. Examples are, "arrow", "circle", "clock", "heart", "man", "plus", "spider", "star", "watch".

Geometry Management

It is used for organizing the widgets in the parent widget area (also the top-level window). For this, Tkinter has Geometry Manager classes as follows:

- `pack()` organizes widgets in blocks before placing them in the parent widget.
- `grid()` organizes widgets in a table-like structure in parent widget.
- `place()` organizes widgets by placing them at specific positions in parent widget.

Event Handler

An *event* is a stimulus for an application. An event may occur in many ways, like,

- o User presses a key.
- o User clicks mouse on a widget.
- o User hovers the mouse on a widget.

Callback or *Event Handler* is a code (function, method, lambda expression) that is to be run in response to an event. Callback or command handler can be defined as a free-standing function or as a class member. The widgets can specify their handlers. Command handlers use the syntax,

```
command = function_name
```

In the next section, we shall study about using the widgets.

15.5 Using Tkinter Widgets and Event Handlers

We shall now understand the different widgets and write GUI applications using them. The functionality of each widget is highlighted, the attributes are used with the widgets and also the location of widgets in an application is decided. After discussing the three widgets – label, button and frame, we discuss the event handlers. Then the rest of the widgets are discussed. We also present several examples of GUI applications.

15.5.1 Label Widget

Label is used to create texts and images. It is a single definition. Label is used for displaying information to the user. Let us see some examples:

Label using font attribute

By default, the labels will be located at the center in first line.

Example 15.1: Create a Label "Let's Start Using Tkinter" with font "Arial Bold", size 30.

```
############# Label with Font ###########
from tkinter import *
top = Tk()
top.title("GUI")
L1 = Label(top, text = "Let's Start Using tkinter",
                       font=("Arial Bold", 30))
L1.pack()
top.mainloop()
```

Label using `grid()` and font attribute with color

Example 15.2: Create a Label "Hello" with font "Times", size 20 in bold italics. The background color of label is blue and foreground color is red. The label should appear at row 1 and column 1.

```
########### Label with color and grid ############
from tkinter import *
top = Tk()
top.title("GUI")
a2 = Label(top, text = "Hello",fg="red",bg="blue",
                    font=("Times", "20", "bold italic" ))
a2.grid(column=1, row=1)
top.mainloop()
```

Label using `geometry()` and font attribute

`Geometry()` is used to create a window of specified size. For example, geometry('200x100') will create a window of size 200 pixels in width and 100 pixels in height.

Example 15.3: Create a Label "Hello" with font "Times", size 20 in bold italics. The background color of label is blue and foreground color is red. Create a window of size 200x100. The label should appear at row 1 and column 1.

```
########### Label Using color and geometry ############
from tkinter import *
top = Tk()
top.title("GUI")
a2 = Label(top, text = "Hello",fg="red",bg="blue",
                    font=("Times", "20", "bold italic" ))
top.geometry('200x100')
a2.grid(column=1, row=1)
top.mainloop()
```

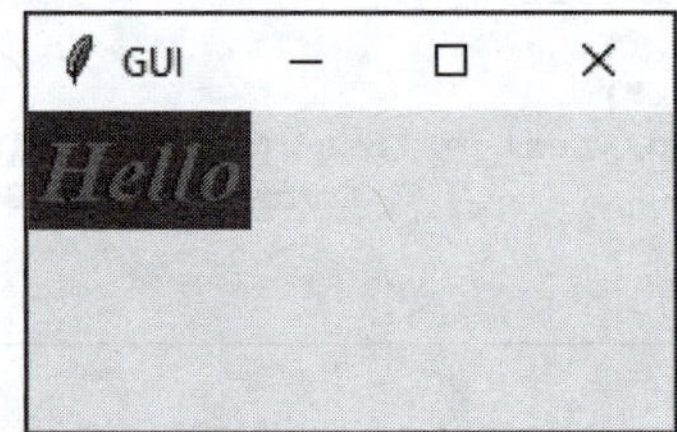

15.5.2 Button Widget

Button can contain text and images. Button can be clicked by the user. A Python method can be linked to a button, so that on click, the method gets executed.

Example 15.4: Create a Button "Enter" with raised relief. The background color of the button is yellow and the foreground color is green.

```
########### Button using relief=raised ############
from tkinter import *
import tkinter
top = Tk()
top.title("GUI")

btl = Button (top, text="Enter", relief = RAISED, fg="green", bg="yellow")
btl.pack()
top.mainloop()
```

Output

15.5.3 Frame Widget

Frame widget works like a container to group and organize other widgets. Within a frame, the position of other widgets can be arranged. Frame is a rectangular area.

Example 15.5: Create two frames – upper and lower. In the upper frame, create three buttons. In the lower frame, create one button.

```
########## Frame ############
from tkinter import *
top = Tk()
topFrame = Frame(top)
topFrame.pack()

bottomFrame = Frame(top)
bottomFrame.pack(side = BOTTOM )

bt1 = Button(topFrame, text = "Red", fg = "red", bg = "cyan")
bt1.pack(side = LEFT)
bt2 = Button(topFrame, text = "Brown", fg="brown", bg = "Yellow")
bt2.pack(side = LEFT )
bt3 = Button(topFrame, text = "Blue", fg = "blue", bg = "pink")
bt3.pack(side = LEFT )
bt4 = Button(bottomFrame, text = "Black", fg = "black", bg = "White")
bt4.pack(side = BOTTOM)

top.mainloop()
```

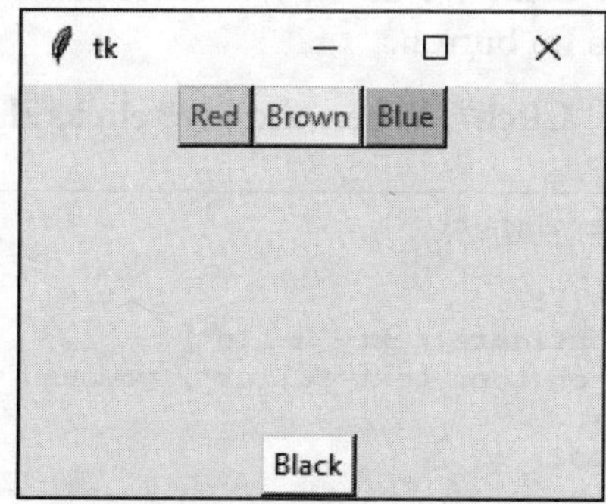

15.5.4 Event Handlers

There are two ways of event handling – (1) `callback()`, (2) `bind()`. We have already defined the command `callback`. Here, we see some examples of the command callback. We also discuss the `bind()` method.

Example 15.6: To change the color of background and foreground of the button on click.

In the code, we see that when the user clicks the button, an event occurs. In response to the event, the function "clicked" is executed (command=clicked). `clicked()` is a function which changes the color of the button.

Configure is used when the size or color of the widget is changed.

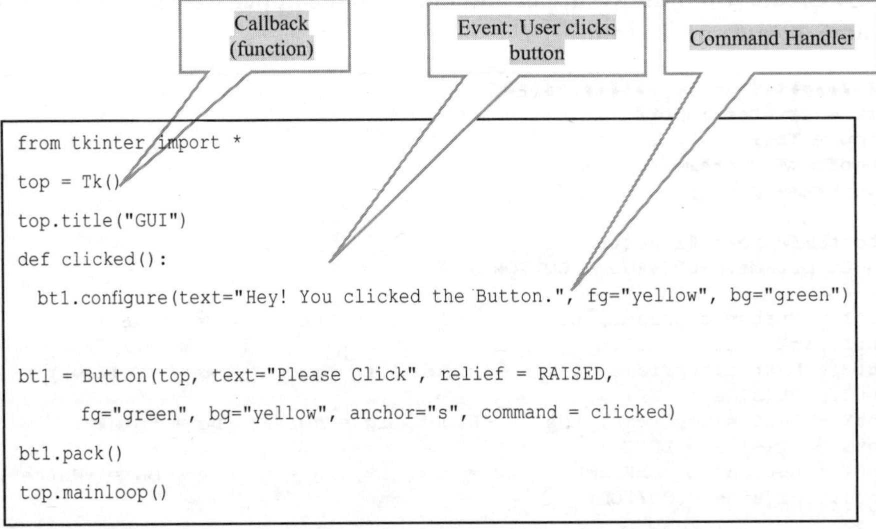

Button with an event when it is clicked: We use parameter `command`, which calls the `clicked()` function on button click. We define a function `clicked()`. The `configure` on button is used to define the action on button.

Example 15.7: Create a Button "Click". When the user clicks the button, then the button displays "Hello".

```
from tkinter import *
top = Tk()
def clicked():
    but1.configure(text="Hello")
but1 = Button(top, text="Click", command = clicked)
but1.pack()
top.mainloop()
```

Output

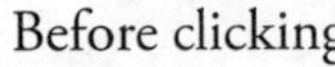
Before clicking

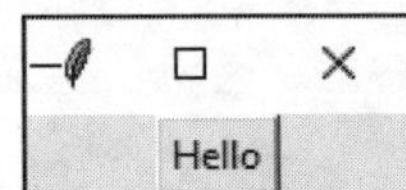

After clicking

Example 15.8: To quit the application on clicking a button.

```
########### root.quit #################
from tkinter import *
top = Tk()
Button(top, text='Click', command=top.quit).pack()
top.mainloop()
```

Output

Click

Example 15.9: To display "Hello! How do you do!" every time the button is clicked.

```
########### Command = Hello #################
from tkinter import *
top = Tk()

def hello():
    Label(top, text = "Hello! How do you do!").pack()
Button(top, text = "Please Click", command = hello).pack()
top.mainloop()
```

Output

Please Click
Hello! How do you do!
Hello! How do you do!
Hello! How do you do!
Hello! How do you do!
Hello! How do you do!

Binding is the act of linking the occurrence of an event to the event handler. The syntax is –

`widget.bind(event, handler)`

If an event matching the event description (as shown in Table 15.3) occurs in the widget, the given handler is called with an object describing the event. For each widget, functions and methods can be bound to events. A description of event attributes is given in Table 15.4.

Table 15.3 Events and bindings

	Event	Binding
	<Button-1>	Left mouse button
	<Button-2>	Middle mouse button (on 3-button mouse)
	<Button-3>	Rightmost mouse button
	<B1-Motion>	Mouse moved with left button depressed
	<ButtonRelease-1>	Left button released
	<Double-Button-1>	Double click on button 1
	<Enter>	Mouse pointer entered widget
	<Leave>	Mouse pointer left the widget
Keyboard Events	<FocusIn>	Keyboard focus moved to a widget
	<FocusOut>	Keyboard focus moved to another widget
	<Return>	Enter key depressed
	<Key>	A key was depressed
	<Shift-Up>	Up arrow while holding Shift key
	<Configure>	To change widget size or location

Table 15.4 Attributes of Events

Event attributes	Description
widget	Widget which generated this event. It is not a name. It is set for all events
x, y	Current mouse position in pixels
x_root, y_root	Current mouse position relative to upper left corner of the screen, in pixels.
char	Character code as a string (keyboard events)
keysym	Key symbol (keyboard events)
keycode	Key code (keyboard events)
num	Button number (mouse button events only)
width, height	New size of widget in pixels (Configure events)
type	Event type

Example 15.10: Create a button with a foreground and background color. When the mouse enters the button, change the color of the button. When the mouse leaves the button, the button is displayed with original color.

```
################ Mouse over ################
from tkinter import *
top = Tk()
top.title("GUI")
def chgcolor(event):
    btl.configure(fg="red", bg="cyan")
def orgcolor(event):
    btl.configure(fg="green", bg="yellow")

btl = Button(top, text="Please Click", relief = RAISED,
             fg="green", bg="yellow", anchor="s")
btl.bind("<Enter>", chgcolor)
btl.bind("<Leave>", orgcolor)
btl.pack()
top.mainloop()
```

Output

Example 15.11: Create three buttons having text "ONE", "TWO" and "THREE". On click of a button, call the same method with the number of the button clicked.

In cases where the same function is a callback with different parameter value, it is suggested to use `lambda` function. The `lambda` expression creates a link between the callback function and Tkinter.

```
from tkinter import *
top = Tk()
top.title("GUI")
def callback(num):
    Label(top, text = "You pressed Button " + str(num)).pack()
Button(text="ONE", command=lambda: callback(1)).pack()
Button(text="TWO", command=lambda: callback(2)).pack()
Button(text="THREE",command=lambda: callback(3)).pack()
top.mainloop()
```

Output

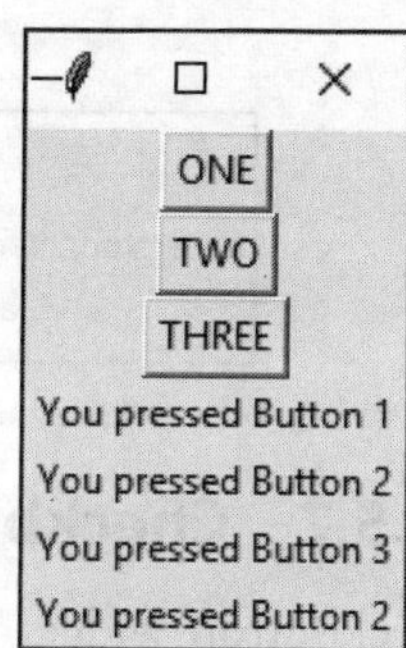

15.5.5 Message Widget

The message widget displays text. It provides multiline displays that cannot be modified.

Example 15.12: Create a message "Hello! This is a message". The background color of the message is yellow.

```
########## Message ############
from tkinter import *
top = Tk()
lbl = Message(top, text="Good Morning",
              bg = "yellow", relief = RAISED )
lbl.pack()
top.mainloop()
```

Output

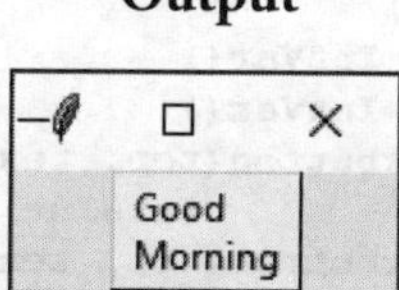

15.5.6 Entry Widget

Entry widget is used to create input fields for taking text input.

Example 15.13: Display label "Enter Your Name" in col 1, row 1. Display entry box of width 20 in col 2, row 1. Display button "Done" in col 2, row 2. When the button is clicked, the text entered by the user is displayed as "Welcome to …" in col 1, row 3, in Times font of size 15 having foreground color as yellow and background color as red.

```
########## Entry widget with response ############
from tkinter import *
top = Tk()
def clicked():
        disp = "Welcome to " + el.get()
        tl.grid(column= 1,row=3)
        tl.configure(text= disp, fg="yellow", bg="red", font=("Times", "15"))
tl = Label(top, text = "Enter Your Name")
tl.grid(column= 1,row=1)
el = Entry(top, width=20)
el.grid(column= 2,row=1)
bt = Button (top, text="Done", command=clicked)
bt.grid(column= 2,row=2)
top.mainloop()
```

Output

15.5.7 Checkbutton Widget

Checkbutton widget is used to display multiple options as toggle buttons. One or more than one button can be selected by the user, by clicking on the buttons. Text or image can both be used.

Example 15.14: Display two checkbuttons: (1) First checkbutton displaying "Peacock" written in blue on a pink background, (2) Second checkbutton displaying "Parrot" written in blue on a yellow background. They should have integer value 0 if not selected and 1 if selected. The height of each button is 5 and width is 20.

```
########## Checkbutton ############
from tkinter import *
top = Tk()
chkvar1 = IntVar()
chkvar2 = IntVar()
C1 = Checkbutton(top, text = "Peacock",fg = "blue", bg = "pink", variable = chkvar1
                 onvalue = 1, offvalue = 0,height=5, width=20)
C2 = Checkbutton(top, text = "Parrot", fg = "blue", bg = "yellow", variable = chkva
                 onvalue = 1, offvalue = 0, height=5, width=20)
C1.pack()
C2.pack()
top.mainloop()
```

Output

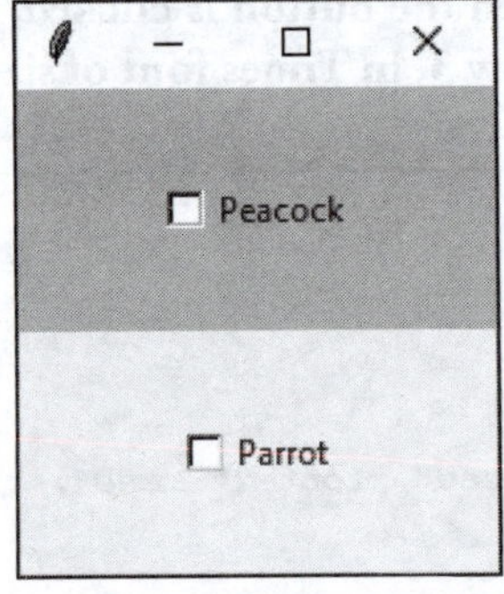

Before selection

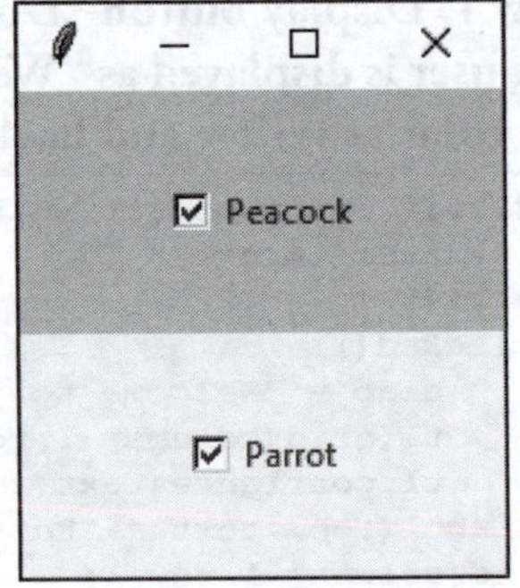

After selection

15.5.8 Toplevel Widget

Toplevel widgets are used for displaying top level windows. Top-level widgets do not have a parent. Top level windows are managed directly, by Windows Manager. They are used for pop-up or grouping widgets on a window. An application can have any number of top-level windows.

Example 15.15: Create a Button "Click" and place it at (50, 50). Define a function `click()` that creates a new window and displays "Hello! How are you!" as a label.

```
########## Toplevel ############
from tkinter import *
root = Tk()

def click():
    top = Toplevel(root)
    L1 = Label(top, text="Hello! How are You!")
    L1.pack()
    top.mainloop()
bt = Button(root, text = "click", command = click)
bt.place(x=50,y=50)
root.mainloop()
```

Output

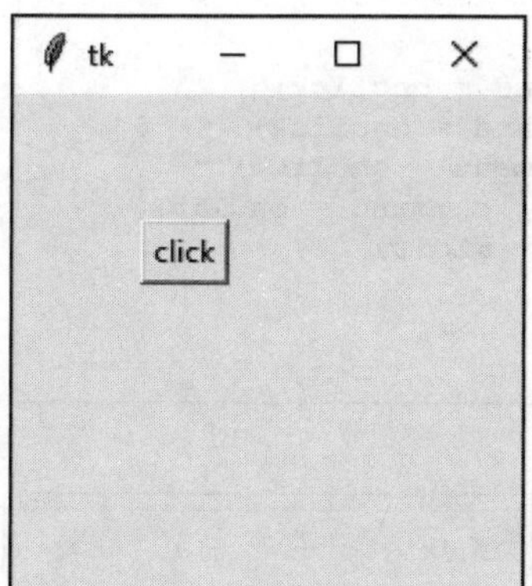

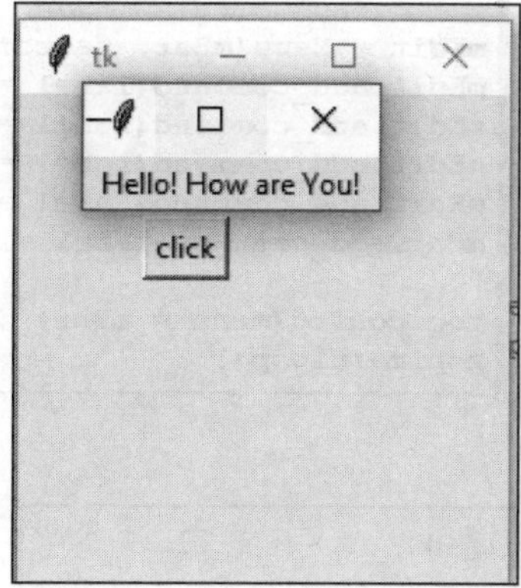

On clicking button "click"

15.5.9 Menu Widget

In a drop-down menu, there are two things:

1) `menu` button that is always displayed on the screen, and
2) `menu` that lists the options for the user to choose. The `menu` appears after the user clicks on the `menu` button.

Menu widget allows to create menus. Tearoff = 0 or 1 is used with menu. If tearoff is 1, it allows to separate the window having the choices. If the user clicks on the dotted line, a new window containing the choices appears. The menu may appear as top-level, pop-up or pull-down.

Example 15.16: Display two menu bars – File and Edit. On click, the menu bars should display: (1) File menu bar – New File, Open…, OpenModule…, Recent Files, Module Browser and Path Browser. Draw a horizontal line and then display option – Exit. (2) Edit menu bar – Cut, Copy, Paste and Select All. If you click on any options, then it should display a window showing the message, "Sorry! Only Sample."

```
########## Menu ############
from tkinter import *
top = Tk()
def onclick():
   popup = Toplevel(top)
   bt = Button(popup, text="Sorry! Only Sample")
   bt.pack()
mBar = Menu(top)
mFile = Menu(mBar, tearoff = 0)
mFile.add_command(label = "New File", command = onclick)
mFile.add_command(label = "Open...", command = onclick)
mFile.add_command(label = "Open Module...", command = onclick)
mFile.add_command(label = "Recent Files", command = onclick)
mFile.add_command(label = "Module Browser", command = onclick)
mFile.add_command(label = "Path Browser", command = onclick)
mFile.add_separator()
mFile.add_command(label = "Exit", command = top.quit)
mBar.add_cascade(label = "File", menu = mFile)

mEdit = Menu(mBar, tearoff=0)
mEdit.add_command(label = "Cut", command = onclick)
mEdit.add_command(label = "Copy", command = onclick)
mEdit.add_command(label = "Paste", command = onclick)
mEdit.add_command(label = "Select All", command = onclick)
mBar.add_cascade(label = "Edit", menu = mEdit)

top.config(menu = mBar)
top.mainloop()
```

Output

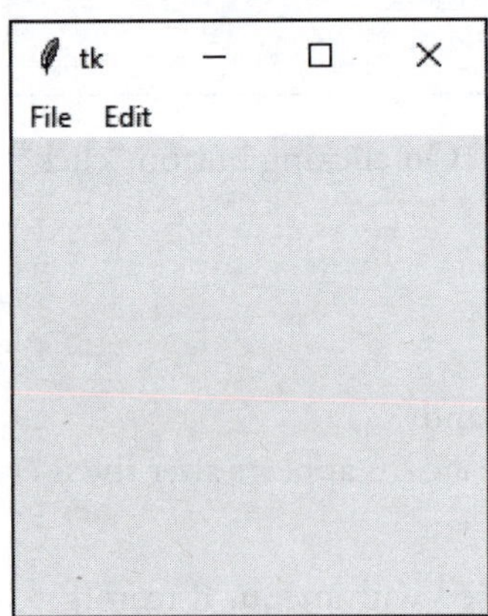

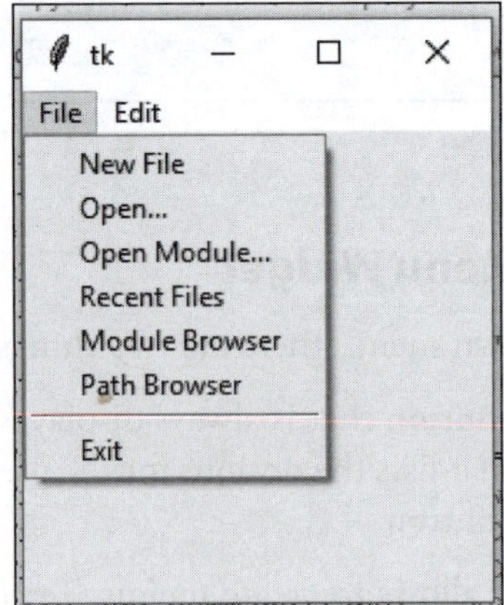

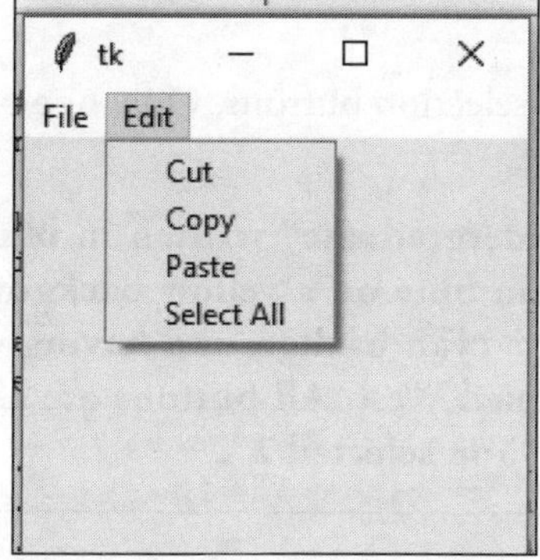

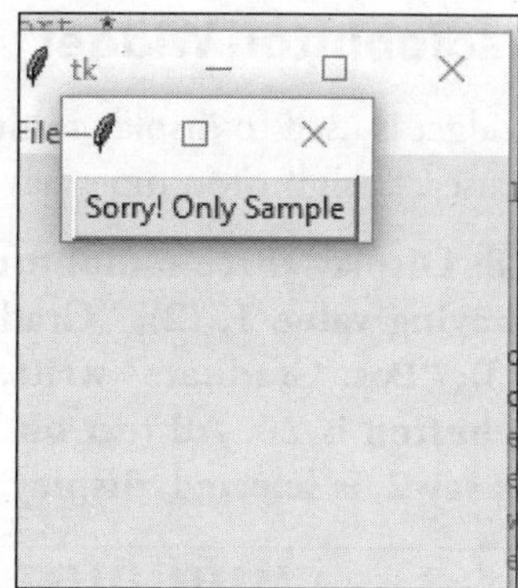

15.5.10 Menubutton Widget

Menubutton is used with menu widget. The menubutton is displayed on screen, all the time, even when the menu is displayed.

Example 15.17: Display a menubutton "Breakfast Menu". On click, a drop-down menu without tearoff must appear. The menu must display four options – Idli Sambhar, Onion Kachori, Chole Bhature and Cheese Sandwich.

```
########## Menubutton ############
from tkinter import *
top = Tk()

mBut =  Menubutton(top, text = "BreakFast Menu", relief = GROOVE )
mBut.grid()
mBut.menu   =  Menu (mBut, tearoff = 0 )
mBut["menu"]   =  mBut.menu

iVar   = IntVar()
oVar = IntVar()
coVar = IntVar()
chVar = IntVar()
mBut.menu.add_checkbutton(label = "IdliSambhar", variable = iVar)
mBut.menu.add_checkbutton(label = "Onion Kachori", variable = oVar)
mBut.menu.add_checkbutton(label = "Chole Bhature", variable = coVar)
mBut.menu.add_checkbutton(label = "Cheese Sandwich", variable = chVar)
mBut.pack()
top.mainloop()
```

Output

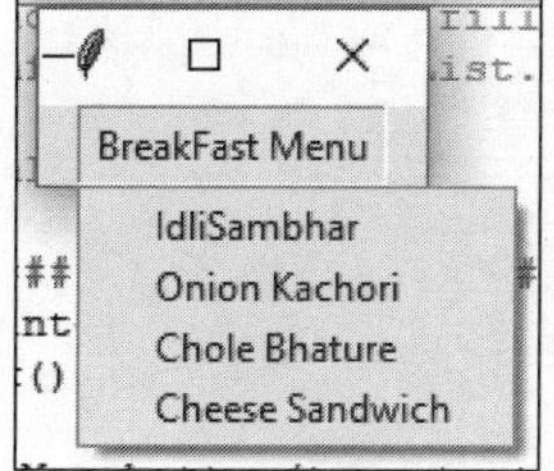

15.5.11 Radiobutton Widget

Radiobutton widget is used to display multiple options as selection buttons. Only one button can be selected by the user. Each button must have a unique value.

Example 15.18: Display three radiobuttons – (1) "Undergraduate" written in blue on a pink background, having value 1, (2); "Graduate" written in blue on a yellow background having value 2, and (3); "Post Graduate" written in black on a cyan background having value 3. The width of each button is 20. All text on buttons is aligned West. All buttons are aligned West. After a button, say 2, is selected, display the selection, "You selected 2".

```
########## Radiobutton ############
from tkinter import *
top = Tk()
def choice():
    ans = "Great! You selected " + str(var.get())
    label.config(text = ans)

var = IntVar()
RB1 = Radiobutton(top, text = "1. Under Graduate", fg = "blue", bg = "pink",anchor = W,
                  variable = var, value = 1, command = choice, width = 20)
RB2 = Radiobutton(top, text = "2. Graduate", fg = "blue", bg = "yellow", anchor = W,
                  variable = var, value = 2, command = choice, width = 20)
RB3 = Radiobutton(top, text = "3. Post Graduate",fg = "black", bg = "cyan", anchor = W,
                  variable = var, value = 3,command = choice, width = 20)
RB1.pack(anchor = W )
RB2.pack(anchor = W )
RB3.pack(anchor = W)

label = Label(top)
label.pack()
top.mainloop()
```

Output

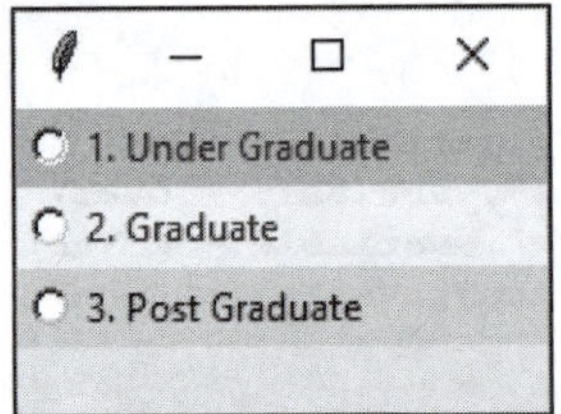

Before selection

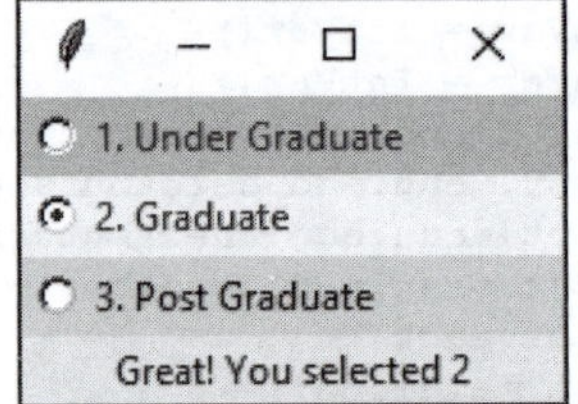

After selection

15.5.12 Scale Widget

Scale widget provides a slider having value range. The user can use the slider to select a value.

Example 15.19: Display an integer scale. Display a button "Get scale value". When a user moves the slider and clicks on the button, it should display the value at which the slider is located.

```
########## Scale ############
from tkinter import *
top = Tk()
def sel():
    val = "Scale Value = " + str(var.get())
    label.config(text = val, fg = "cyan", bg = "black", )

var = IntVar()
scale = Scale(top, variable = var )
scale.pack(anchor = CENTER)

button = Button(top, text = "Get Value of Scale",
                fg = "black", bg = "cyan", command = sel)
button.pack(anchor = CENTER)

label = Label(top)
label.pack()
top.mainloop()
```

Output

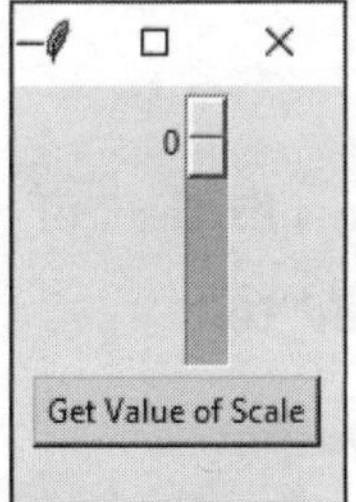

Before selection

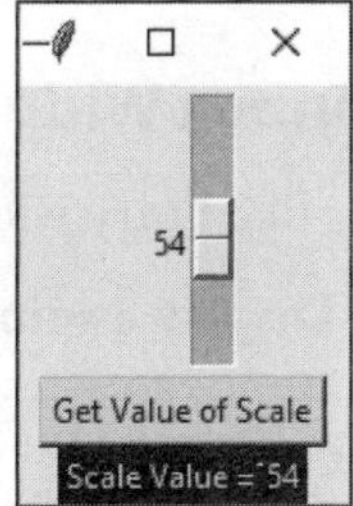

After selection

15.5.13 Listbox Widget

Listbox widget displays a list of items. The user can select from the listed items. The user can select more than one item.

Example 15.20: Display a list of names of your six friends.

```
########## Listbox ############
from tkinter import *
top = Tk()

Lbl = Listbox(top)
Lbl.insert(1, "Ashish")
Lbl.insert(2, "Rajesh")
Lbl.insert(3, "Anirudh")
Lbl.insert(4, "Anand")
Lbl.insert(5, "Rahul")
Lbl.insert(6, "Ajay")

Lbl.pack(side = LEFT)
top.mainloop()
```

Output

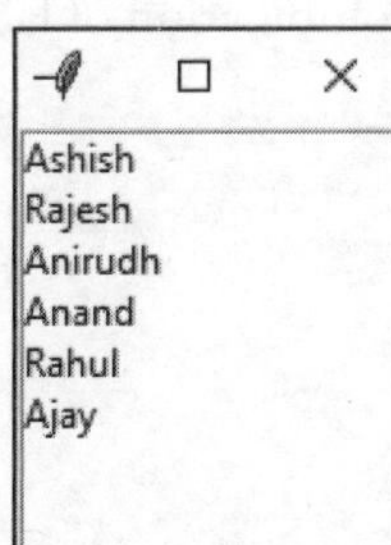

15.5.14 Scrollbar Widget

Scrollbar widget displays a scroll bar. It can be used with Listbox, Text and Canvas for vertical scrolls. It is used with Entry widget for horizontal scroll.

Example 15.21: Display numbers from 1 to 50 in listbox. Include a scrollbar.

```
########## Listbox and Scrollbar ############
from tkinter import *
top = Tk()

sBar = Scrollbar(top)
sBar.pack(side = RIGHT, fill = Y)

sList = Listbox(top, yscrollcommand = sBar.set)
for line in range(50):
   sList.insert(END, "Number = " + str(line))

sList.pack(side = LEFT, fill = BOTH )
sBar.config(command = sList.yview )

top.mainloop()
```

Output

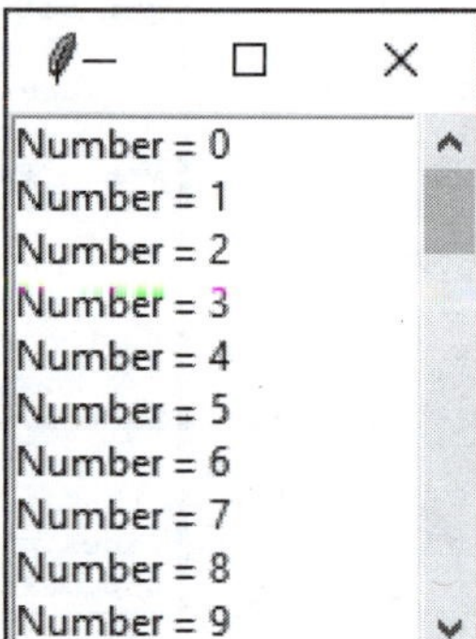

15.5.15 Spinbox Widget

Spinbox widget is like Entry widget, but selection can be made from a fixed set of values.

Example 15.22: Display a spinbox with values ranging from 1 and 10.

```
########## Spinbox ############
from tkinter import *
top = Tk()

w = Spinbox(top, from_ = 1, to = 10)
w.pack()

mainloop()
```

Output

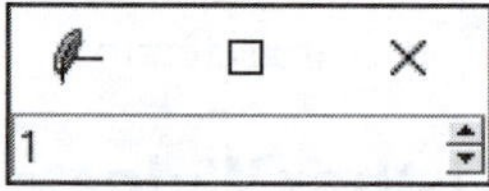

15.5.16 Labelframe Widget

Labelframe is a combination of label and frame. It possesses the features of a frame. It can also display labels.

Example 15.23: Display two frames with labels.

```
########## Labelframe ############
from tkinter import *
root = Tk()

topframe = LabelFrame(root, text = "This is a LabelFrame")
topframe.pack(fill = "both", expand = "yes")
top = Label(topframe, text = "This is top frame")
top.pack()

bottomframe = LabelFrame(root)
bottomframe.pack(fill = "both", expand = "yes")
bottom = Label(bottomframe, text = "This is bottom frame")
bottom.pack()

root.mainloop()
```

Output

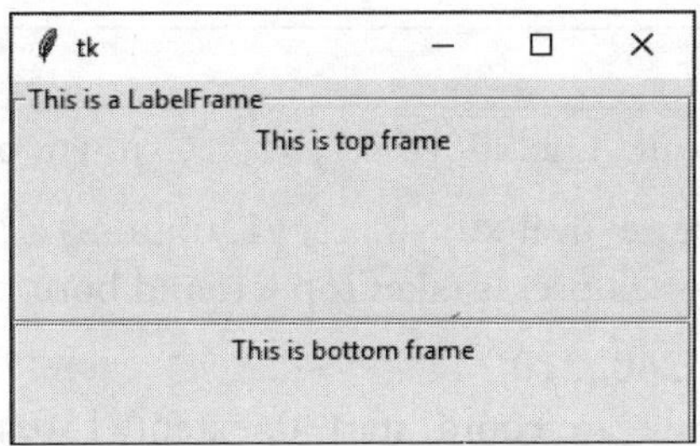

15.5.17 PanedWindow Widget

PanedWindow widget is a container for multiple panes. The panes can be arranged both horizontally and vertically. PanedWindow can contain any number of panes. A pane can contain only one widget. The separation between the panes can be moved to resize the panes.

Example 15.24: Display three paned windows, with the left pane displayed full-length and the right pane divided into two and placed at the top and bottom, respectively.

```
########## PanedWindow ############
from tkinter import *

pw1 = PanedWindow()
pw1.pack(fill = BOTH, expand = 1)

left = Entry(pw1, bd = 8, bg="yellow")
pw1.add(left)

pw2 = PanedWindow(pw1, orient = VERTICAL)
pw1.add(pw2)

top = Label(pw2, text="This is Paned Window",
            font=("Arial", "16", "bold italic" ))
pw2.add(top)

bottom = Button(pw2, text = "DONE",
                relief = RAISED, fg = "white", bg = "blue")
pw2.add(bottom)
mainloop()
```

Output

15.5.18 Canvas Widget

Canvas widget provides a rectangular area for drawings. Other widgets, drawings and frames can be placed on a Canvas. The standard items supported by Canvas widget are shown in Table 15.5.

Table 15.5 Items supported by Canvas widget

Item	Command
Line	line = canvas.create_line(x0, y0, x1, y1, … xn, yn, option)
Oval	oval = canvas.create_oval(x0, y0, x1, y1, options) Used for circle or ellipse. It takes top left and bottom right corners.
Arc	coord = 10, 50, 240, 210 arc = canvas.create_arc(coord, start=0, extent=150, fill=”blue”
Image	filename = PhotoImage(file= “sunshine.gif”) image = canvas.create_image(50, 50, anchor = NE, image = filename) (BitmapImage or PhotoImage classes)
Polygon	oval = canvas.create_polygon(x0, y0, x1, y1, …xn, yn, options) (atleast 3 vertices)

Example 15.25: Define a canvas of size 300x300. Create a kite as shown below.

```
########## Canvas ############
from tkinter import *
top = Tk()

C = Canvas(top, bg = "pink", height = 300, width = 300)

oval = C.create_polygon(100,100,200,200,0,200, fill="red")
oval = C.create_polygon(100,100,0,0,0,200, fill="yellow")
oval = C.create_polygon(100,100,0,0,200,0, fill="blue")
oval = C.create_polygon(100,100,200, 0,200, 200, fill="green")
oval = C.create_oval(75,75,150,150, fill="cyan")
kite = C.create_polygon(200,200,200,250,250,225, fill="orange")

C.pack()
top.mainloop()
```

Output

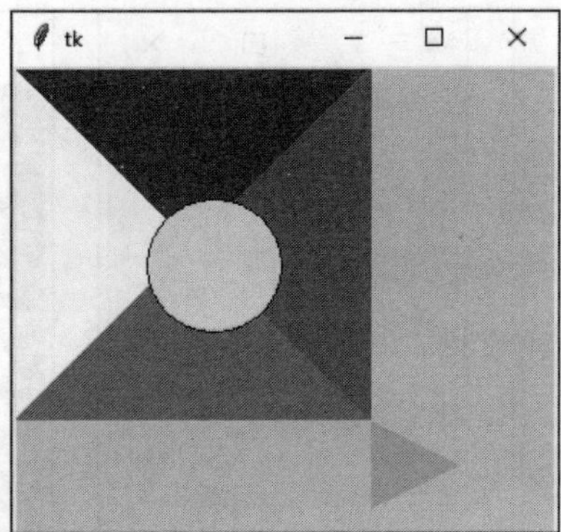

15.6 Programming Examples

To create a GUI application, first identify the following:

- Widgets to be used
- Location of the widgets
- Color of the widgets
- Action to be taken on a click, data entry.

Program 15.1: Create an image with background color "yellow" above the text "Change Background Color". When the user clicks on the image, the color of the background toggles between red and blue.

To place the image above the button, use "compound =TOP" attribute of the button. The compound option controls how to combine text and image location. It has values – TOP, BOTTOM, LEFT, RIGHT, and CENTER. If top is used, image is on top of the text, and so on. If CENTER is used, then text is on the image.

```
############# PhotoImage click change bg color ############
from tkinter import *
btl_flag = True
def clickl():
    global btl_flag
    if btl_flag:
        btl.config(bg="red")
        btl_flag = False
    else:
        btl.config(bg="blue")
        btl_flag = True
root = Tk()
frml = Frame(root)
frml.pack(side=TOP)
imgl = PhotoImage(file="Hibiscus.gif")
btl = Button(frml, compound=TOP, width=150, height=200, image=imgl,
        text="Change Background color", bg="yellow", command=clickl)
btl.pack(side=LEFT, padx=3, pady=3)
btl.image = imgl
root.mainloop()
```

Output

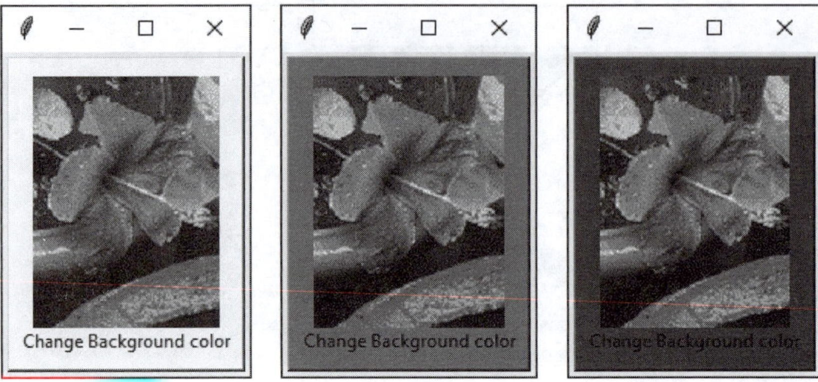

Program 15.2: Create an interface to accept a number from the user and display if the number is a palindrome or not.

```
from tkinter import *
from tkinter import ttk

def palindrm(*args):
        value = float(num.get())
        tmp=value
        opp=0
        while(value>0):
            dig=value%10
            opp=opp*10+dig
            value=value//10
        if(tmp==opp):
            ansl.set("It is a palindrome!")
        else:
            ansl.set("It is not a palindrome!")


root = Tk()
root.title("Palindrome")

framel = Frame(root, padx=10, pady=10)
framel.grid(column=0, row=0, sticky=(N, W, E, S))

num = StringVar()
ansl = StringVar()
num_data = Entry(framel, width=6, textvariable=num)
num_data.grid(column=2, row=1, sticky=(W, E))

Label(framel, textvariable=ansl).grid(column=2, row=3, sticky=(W, E))
Button(framel, text="Check", command=palindrm).grid(column=2, row=2, sticky=W)
Label(framel, text="Enter Number").grid(column=1, row=1, sticky=W)
Label(framel, text="Answer: ").grid(column=1, row=3, sticky=W)

for child in framel.winfo_children(): child.grid_configure(padx=5, pady=5)

num_data.focus()
root.bind('<Return>', palindrm)
root.mainloop()
```

Output

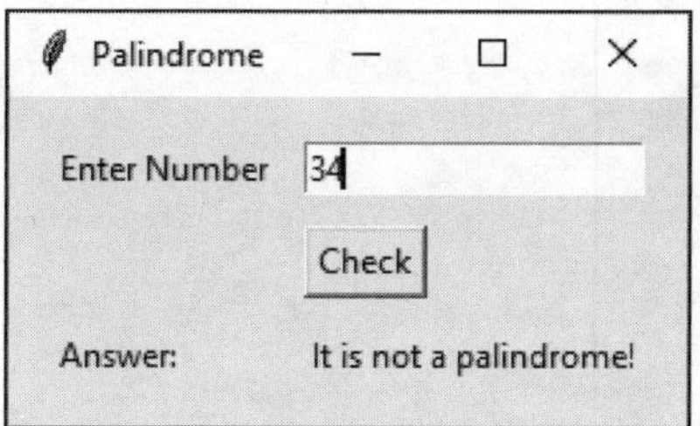

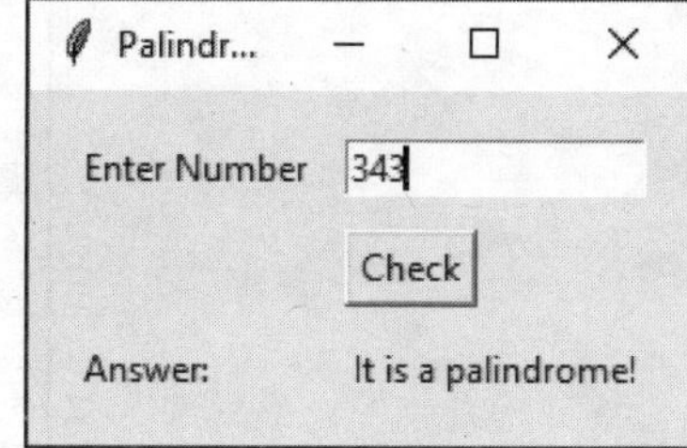

Program 15.3: Create a Button "Please Click" having raised relief. The background color of the button is yellow and foreground color is green. When the user clicks the button, then another button appears with text: "Hey! You clicked the Button". The background color of the button is green and foreground color is yellow.

```
########### Button using command ############
from tkinter import *
top = Tk()
top.title("GUI")
def clicked():
    btl.configure(text="Hey! You clicked the Button.", fg="yellow", bg="green")

btl = Button(top, text="Please Click", relief = RAISED,
             fg="green", bg="yellow", anchor="s", command = clicked)
btl.pack()
top.mainloop()
```

Output

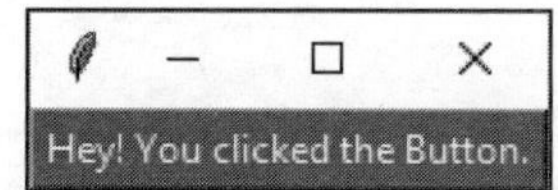

Program 15.4: Display the location at which mouse is clicked. Also, display the character clicked on the keyboard.

```
################# Event binding to Frame #################
from tkinter import *
root = Tk()

def keyloc(event):
    Label(root, text = "You pressed key " + repr(event.char)).pack()
def butlloc(event):
    frame.focus_set()
    loc = "Click (x, y) = (" + repr(event.x) + ", " + repr(event.y)+")"
    Label(root, text = loc ).pack()

frame = Frame(root, width=150, height=150)
frame.bind("<Key>", keyloc)
frame.bind("<Button-1>", butlloc)
frame.pack()
root.mainloop()
```

Output

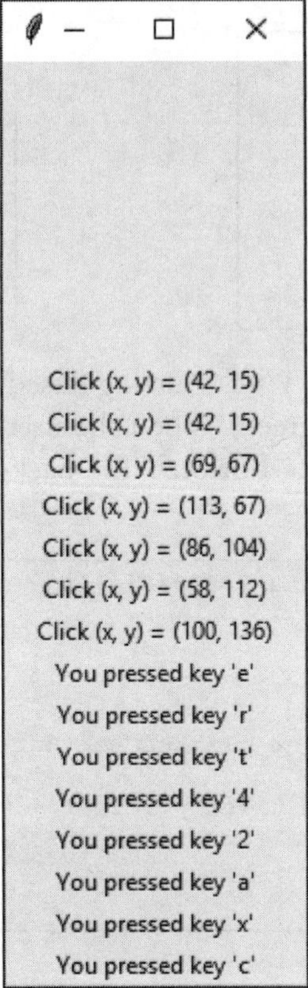

Summary

- Python provides Tkinter as an interface to Tk GUI toolkit.
- In Python, Tkinter is used for building GUI applications.
- To create a Tkinter application, four steps are required to be followed – (1) Import Tkinter, (2) Create main window, (3) Build GUI components on main window, and (4) Execute main event loop, so that a window is displayed until the user closes it.
- There are several widgets that can be used in a GUI application, such as label, button, message and radiobutton.
- The widgets are of different kinds, for example, container widgets, interactive widgets and widgets for displaying information.
- The interactive widgets are – Button, Checkbutton, Entry, Listbox, Menubutton, Menu, Text, Radiobutton, Spinbox, Canvas, Scale and Scrollbar.
- Label and Message are widgets for displaying information.
- Event occurs when an action is taken from mouse or keyboard.
- Event handling is done using command `callback()` and `bind()`.
- Binding connects an occurrence of movement of mouse or keyboard to its handler.
- Frame, LabelFrame, PanedWindow and Toplevel are widgets for grouping other widgets.

- Dimension, color, anchor, relief, font, bitmap and cursor are some of the standard attributes that are common to all widgets.
- `Pack()`, `grid()` and `place()` are used for organizing widgets in parent widget area.

KEYWORDS

Button	Label	CLI
Event	Message	Tkinter
Event Handler	Frame	Tk GUI toolkit
Callback	LabelFrame	wxPython
Bind()	PanedWindow	wxWidgets GUI toolkit
Command	Toplevel	PyQt
Checkbutton	Dimension	Qt GUI library
Entry	Color	Kivy
Listbox	Anchor	TCL
Menubutton	Relief	Widgets
Menu	Font	Attributes
Text	Bitmap	Geometry Manager
Radiobutton	cursor	FLAT
Spinbox	Pack()	RAISED
Canvas	grid()	SUNKEN
Scale	place()	GROOVE
Scrollbar	GUI	RIDGE

ASSESSMENT

A.1 Bloom Level: Knowledge/Remember

Review Questions

1. Give the full forms of – GUI, CLI, TCL.
2. What is the purpose of using Tkinter interface?
3. What is the purpose of – (1) Tkinter, (2) wxPython, (3) PyQt, (4) Kivy.
4. List the four steps to be followed for creating a Tkinter application.
5. Name five interactive widgets.
6. Name two widgets that can display information, but cannot accept input.
7. Name two container widgets.
8. List the options for anchor attribute.
9. What is Geometry management?
10. When are the sources of event occurrence?
11. What is a callback?

Fill in the Blanks

1. Shapes like polygon can be drawn on _________ in Tkinter.
2. ____________ provides a slider widget.

3. __________ widget is for accepting single-line text values from a user.
4. ____________ widget is a variant of Entry widget.
5. ___________ specifies the position of text relative to a reference point for a widget.
6. There are ________ anchor attributes.
7. ____________ organizes widgets in a table-like structure.
8. `Window.mainloop()` runs ______________ in a GUI application.
9. `Bind()` links an __________ to an event handler.
10. <Enter> and <Leave> events are linked to ___________ pointer.

State True/False

1. Tk toolkit is not designed for Tool Command Language.
2. Label provides multiline fields to accept values from users.
3. Radiobutton allows selection of one option at a time.
4. Checkbutton allows selection of multiple options at a time.
5. The dimension of widgets is considered in pixels.
6. Anchor specifies three-dimension effect around widgets.
7. `Place()` organizes widgets in blocks before placing them in parent widget.
8. Flat, Raised and Sunken are options for anchor attributes.
9. Specifying cursor as clock is allowed.
10. Display of hourglass symbol is done using bitmap.
11. A lambda expression can be a callback.

Multiple Choice Questions (MCQ)

1. Identify a container widget.
   (i) Entry
   (ii) Label
   (iii) Scale
   (iv) PanedWindow
2. Identify the widget that is used for organizing other widgets.
   (i) Frame (ii) Message
   (iii) Scrollbar (iv) Button
3. For relief style attributes, find the odd one out.
   (i) Raised (ii) Sunken
   (iii) Flat (iv) Ground
4. The error bitmap is displayed as _____.
   (i) (ii)
   (iii) (iv)
5. Identify the widget not used for Geometry Management.
   (i) `pick()` (ii) `pack()`
   (iii) `place()` (iv) `grid()`
6. The command to create a window in Tkinter is _______.
   (i) `top = new window()`
   (ii) `top = window()`
   (iii) `top = Tk()`
   (iv) `top = new Tk()`
7. The command to create main event loop in Tkinter is _______.
   (i) `top.loop()`
   (ii) `top.loopmain()`

(iii) `top.mainloop()`
(iv) `top.mainloop`

8. How do you create a label under a parent window?
(i) Lbl = Label(text="Hello")
(ii) Lbl = Label(text="Hello", font="Arial bold")
(iii) Lbl = Label(window, text="Hello")
(iv) Lbl = Label(text="Hello", bg = "red")

9. The command to draw a line from 50, 50 to 200, 200 is _______.
(i) Canvas.create_line(50, 50, 150, 150)
(ii) Canvas.create_line(50, 50, 200, 200)
(iii) Canvas.create_line(200, 200, 50, 50)
(iv) Canvas.create_line(50, 200, 50, 200)

10. If you want to place a label at row 2 column 1, which container will you use?
(i) `pack()` (ii) `grid()`
(iii) `place()` (iv) `pick()`

11. The option that you will use to place a component across multiple rows, when using a grid manager is _______.
(i) row (ii) rowlength
(iii) rowlines (iv) rowspan

12. In Python Tkinter, an image can be created using _______.
(i) im = PhotoImage(filename)
(ii) im = PhotoImage(image=filename)
(iii) im = PhotoImage(file = filename)
(iv) im = PhotoImage(photo=filrname)

13. In Python Tkinter, the syntax for writing command is _______.
(i) Command = function_name
(ii) Command: function_name
(iii) Command:= function_name
(iv) Command:: function_name

14. In Python Tkinter, the <Button-1> event occurs when _______.
(i) Right mouse button is clicked
(ii) Left mouse button is clicked
(iii) Middle mouse button is clicked
(iv) the mouse button is double-clicked

A.2 Bloom Level: Create/Synthesize

Programming Assignment

1. Create a Student Registration form.
2. Create a login screen of your email account.
3. Create a GUI application to accept a number and display its factorial.
4. Create an image that changes its color on click.
5. Create the File menu of Word software.
6. Create a directory-like structure.
7. Create a Report Card format.
8. Draw a circle. Create a slider such that when the user moves the slider, the size of the circle changes.
9. Make a book cover.
10. Make a magazine cover.
11. Create a restaurant billing interface where thr user selects the food item. Then the bill is generated.
12. Create a graphics splash. (Use at least 10 colors, 10 geometry shapes, 2 images and 2 frames.)

13. Display an image. Ask the user to select a type of frame, like rectangle, circle or hexagon. Display the image in the selected frame.

14. Create a distance–time calculator.

15. Create an interface to accept an amount from a user in Indian currency. Display the choices of currency conversion. Let the user select a currency. Display the amount in the selected currency.

Enter Amount (rupees)		Converted ( )
[ ]		[ ]
Select currency		
○ Dollar	○ Pound	○ Euro

Answers

A.1 Bloom Level: Knowledge/Remember

Review Questions

1. Canvas	**2.** Scale	**3.** Entry	**4.** Spinbox
5. Anchor	**6.** nine	7. `grid()`	**8.** infinitely
9. Event	**10.** Mouse		

True/False

1. False	**2.** False	**3.** True	**4.** True	**5.** True	**6.** False	**7.** False	**8.** False
9. True	**10.** True	**11.** True					

Multiple Choice Questions (MCQ)

1. (iv)	**2.** (i)	**3.** (iv)	**4.** (iii)	**5.** (i)	**6.** (iii)	**7.** (iii)	**8.** (iii)
9. (ii)	**10.** (ii)	**11.** (iv)	**12.** (iii)	**13.** (i)	**14.** (ii)		

CHAPTER

16 Python Libraries

Contents

16.1 Introduction

A library is a collection of pre-compiled and reusable functions and routines that can be referenced in a program. An open-source library has an open-source license, normally, General Public License (GPU). The users of open-source library can modify the library without permission and the users are free to run, share and modify the contents of the library.

Python has several open-source libraries that play a critical role in machine learning and data science for data preprocessing, data modeling and data visualization. A library consists of several modules and each module has a specific purpose. Several operations can be performed using the methods defined in the modules. Thus. the writing of programs using the methods becomes easier. It also becomes easier to automate the tasks; the size of programs is reduced and it helps to provide insight into the data, with less effort.

There are several open-source libraries in Python. In this chapter, we discuss in detail, three libraries – NumPy, Pandas, and Matplotlib.

Learning Outcomes of this chapter

After completion of the chapter, the learner will be able to:

- Understand the open-source libraries in Python
- Understand the libraries for data preprocessing, modeling and visualization
- Use NumPy for the manipulation of arrays and tables
- Formulate programs for manipulation of NumPy arrays
- Use Pandas methods and operations for working on Series and DataFrame
- Use Matplotlib for the visualization of data.

16.2 Libraries in Python

Python library is a collection of related modules. The modules can be used in different programs, repeatedly. The reuse of modules makes programming convenient and simpler for the programmer. Whenever there is a need to use a module, the programmer can import the module from the library. For importing, the reserved word `import` is used.

- Python libraries are popularly used in fields such as machine learning and data science.
- Some of the libraries of Python are:
    - **Python standard library**: It consists of more than 200 core modules for performing common tasks, such as send email and read JSON data. The Standard Library gets installed at the time of installation of Python; so, its modules can be used when needed without having to download them again.
    - **Open-source libraries:** Python provides several open-source libraries (Fig. 16.1). Each library has its own code. Several libraries exist for working on data, such as NumPy, Pandas, Matplotlib, SciPy, and Scikit learn. These libraries provide a comprehensive set of tools for working with the data and they have to be installed at the time of use.

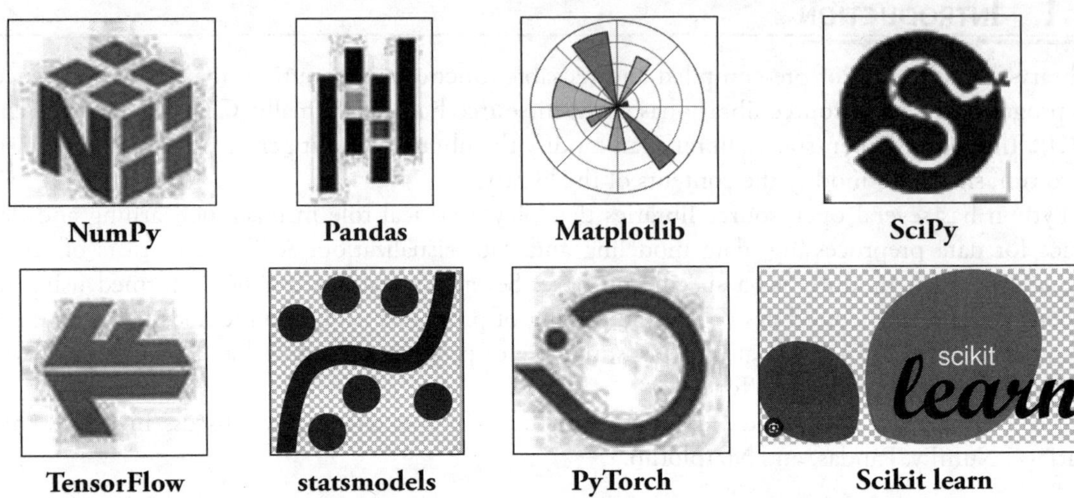

Figure 16.1 Python open-source libraries

16.3 Data Preprocessing, Modeling and Visualization

The open-source Python libraries are required for various purposes:

- o Data Preprocessing,
- o Data Modelling, and
- o Data Visualization.

Data Preprocessing

Data Preprocessing provides insight into the data and for making informed decisions. It helps to ensure data quality, data consistency and data accuracy. It involves tasks like:

- o *Data accuracy:* Identify and handle missing or duplicate data.
- o *Data suitability:* Eliminate errors.
- o *Handling outliers:* The results get skewed due to outliers.
- o *Feature scaling:* To ensure that all features have the same scale.
- o *Encoding categorical data:* To convert into numerical data.
- o *Reduce dimensionality:* To reduce data dimension, so that it is easier to model.

For data preprocessing, various techniques are used on the data. It involves three steps: (1) Data Cleaning, (2) Data Transformation, and (3) Data Selection.

Data cleaning involves various techniques that can be used to identify and handle missing or erroneous data. Some of the tasks in data cleaning are:

- o Handling duplicates to improve accuracy of result and reduce error risk.
- o Handling missing data by deleting, providing input or replacing it with mean or median.
- o Handling outliers by techniques such as replacing outliers with missing data.

- o Normalizing data by scaling the data to a common scale.
- o Encoding categorical data into numerical data by one-hot encoding.
- o Feature selection to reduce dimensionality.
- o Handling data errors such as data entry or formatting errors using data validation.

Data transformation is the process to convert data from one format to another. It helps to improve the quality of data. Some techniques for data transformation are:

- o *Scaling*: Rescaling the data to a common scale, such as between 0 and 1.
- o *Normalization*: Transforming the data so that it has a normal distribution.
- o *Aggregation*: Combining multiple data points into a single data point.
- o *Discretization*: Converting continuous data into categorical data.
- o *Encoding*: Converting categorical data into numerical data.
- o *Feature engineering*: Creating new features from existing features.

- ***Data selection*** is the process of selecting a subset of data from a larger dataset based on a criterion. It reduces the size of the dataset. The techniques for data selection are:
  - o *Random sampling*: Selecting a random subset of data from the larger dataset.
  - o *Stratified sampling*: Dividing dataset into subgroups based on a specific variable and then selecting a random sample from each subgroup.
  - o *Feature selection*: Selecting the subset of features from a dataset by relevance to task.
  - o *Instance selection*: Selecting the subset of instance from a dataset by relevance to task.
- `NumPy, Pandas,` and `Matplotlib` are some popular libraries for data preprocessing. These libraries provide various functions and methods that make it easier to perform data preprocessing tasks efficiently and effectively.

Data Modeling

Data modeling focuses on transforming raw data into structural data that helps in deriving meaningful insights from the data.

- o For this, there is a need to decide the break-up of data into multiple tables and establish the relationships between the tables.
- o It allows data analysis to use data in decision-making processes.
- o It maps the types of data and where it is stored within systems.
- o It illustrates relationships between data types and groups and organizes data by establishing formats and attributes.

`statsmodels` is a library of Python for data modeling.

- o It is used to explore data, estimate statistical models, and for statistical testing.
- o It is suited for complex calculations, like linear and Bayesian models.
- o It allows to build generalized models and run statistical tests.
- o It has good compatibility with other Python libraries and tools.
- o `statsmodels` is built on top of libraries like NumPy, Pandas, and Matplotlib.

Data Visualization

Data visualization deals with visual representation of data.

- o It plots the data, graphically. It is easy to get inferences from the data.
- o It provides visual summary of the data.
- o There are several libraries for data visualization, such as Matplotlib, Seaborn and Plotly.
- o The libraries provide features to create informative and customized plots for presenting the data simply and effectively.
- o `Matplotlib, Seaborn,` and `Plotly` are some libraries for data visualization.

Here, we discuss in detail three open-source Python libraries – `NumPy, Pandas` and `Matplotlib`.

16.4 NumPy: Basics

NumPy name stands for "Numerical Python". It is a popular scientific library for programming in Python. NumPy is a library for working with arrays. It is a commonly used, freely available machine learning library for numerical computing that supports large matrices and multi-dimensional data. It consists of in-built mathematical functions for easy computations. NumPy is used for data analysis. Several other libraries, like Pandas, Matplotlib, SciPy and scikit-learn are built on top of this library. It has tools to work with arrays and mathematical functions, to manipulate the data.

- An ***array*** is a collection of homogeneous (same data type) elements.
- An array may have one or more dimensions.
- ***Vector*** is an array of one dimension.
- ***Matrix*** is an array of two dimensions.
- Some properties of homogeneous multidimensional matrices are:
  - o It is a table of elements.
  - o All elements are of the same type.
  - o It is indexed by a tuple of non-negative integers.
- ***Axes*** – It is the dimension of the matrix. For example,
  - o An array `[20, 41]` has one axis, with two elements in it, and length of 2.
  - o An array `[[1, 0, 1],`
    `[2, 3, 6]]`
    has 2 axes. The length of first axis (row) is 2, and the length of second axis (column) is 3.
- ***Rank*** – It is the number of axes.
- ***ndarray*** or *N*-dimensional array is the array object in NumPy.
- Some basic array operations that can be performed using NumPy are – add, slice, multiply, flatten, reshape, and index.

NumPy Arrays and Python Lists

- In Python, lists act as arrays that can store elements of various types.
- NumPy is faster than lists, generally fifty times faster. NumPy arrays are preferred over Python lists when mathematical operations are to be performed on a large amount of data.

- o Lists are an array of pointers. Each pointer points to a memory location that stores the element detail, such as number of bytes and value. Though advantageous, the overhead of pointer for memory and computation is huge when storing arrays (large collection). Also, most details are redundant when all objects of the list are of same type.
- o In NumPy, all elements are of the same type. The NumPy arrays are stored continuously in memory, unlike lists. This behavior is called locality of reference. Since the arrays are stored continuously, manipulation is efficient, particularly on arrays of large size. Also, with NumPy arrays, element-wise operations can be performed, which is not possible using lists.

16.4.1 Import NumPy as np

On downloading Anaconda, the NumPy library comes pre-installed. In case NumPy needs to be installed separately, it can be done by the following command:

```
pip install numpy
```

A common way to use the installed NumPy library in a Python code is to import the library. For doing this, you need not write the word "numpy" each time you use the library; you can use `np`. So, include the following statement at the beginning of each Python file:

import numpy as np

where, `np` is the common abbreviation used by the Python community for `numpy`.

Some of the key benefits of importing NumPy are:

- Its functions are very fast compared to the regular Python functions.
- It allows performing of common mathematical operations such as array functions, linear algebra, random number generation, polynomials and Fourier transforms much faster than regular Python functions.
- It can vectorize the code. As a result, a single operation can be applied to multiple elements of the array simultaneously. This feature is useful while working on large datasets.
- It is interoperable with other Python packages, like Pandas and Matplotlib, which makes it useful for data analysis tasks.

16.4.2 `ndarray`: Multidimensional Array Object

- `ndarray` is the *N*-dimensional array object of NumPy. It is a homogeneous array and has elements of the same data type.
- `ndarray` objects are created from NumPy's ndarray class.
- It allows you to perform mathematical operations on a whole block of data, in the same way as you perform on each element of the array.
- The `numpy.array` is different from the Standard Python Library class `array.array`. The `array.array` handles only one-dimensional arrays.
- The important attributes of `ndarray` object are:
  - o `ndarray.ndim` – dimension of array (number of axes).
  - o `ndarray.shape` – tuple indicating size of each dimension. For a matrix with *n* rows and *m* columns, shape is (*n*, *m*).
  - o `ndarray.size` – total number of elements of the array.

- o `ndarray.dtype` – data type of elements of the array.
- o `ndarray.itemsize` – size of each element of the array, in bytes. For example, itemsize is 8 for array elements of type float64.
- o `ndarray.data` – buffer object pointing to the start of the array data.

Example 16.1: (a) Using ndarray object (b) Output

```
a = np.arange(1, 11)
print("Array= \n",a)
print("Shape= ",a.shape)
print("Dimension= ",a.ndim)
print("Data type= ",a.dtype.name)
print("Size of element(in bytes)= ",a.itemsize)
print("Size of array= ",a.size)
print("Buffer object start of data= ",a.data)
print("Type= ",type(a))
```

(a)

```
Array=
 [ 1  2  3  4  5  6  7  8  9 10]
Shape=  (10,)
Dimension=  1
Data type=  int32
Size of element(in bytes)=  4
Size of array=  10
Buffer object start of data=  <memory at 0x0000018D8FD2C880>
Type=  <class 'numpy.ndarray'>
```

(b)

16.5 Creation of NumPy Arrays and Vector

There are several ways to create arrays. To create an array and use its methods, first we need to import the NumPy library. Let us see the different ways to create an array.

16.5.1 Using `array()` Function

A way to create an array is by using the array function of NumPy. The function `np.array()` is used for the creation of NumPy arrays.

- It accepts a sequence type (list or tuple) object.
- It creates a NumPy array with the data. The data in `ndarray` is referred to as an array.
- The type of array is based on the type of array elements. By default, the `dtype` of created array is float64. The `dtype` can also be specified explicitly.
- A sequence is transformed to one-dimension array; sequence of sequence to two-dimensional array, sequence of sequence of sequence into three-dimensional arrays, and so on.
- A 1-dimension array is returned as rows.

- A 2-dimension array is returned as matrix.
- When a 2-dimension array is created, the elements of the list or tuple are also a list or tuple.

Example 16.2: (a) Using `np.array()` to create arrays (b) Output

```
1 import numpy as np
2
3 a = np.array([1, 2, 5])
4 print("Array a from integer list = ",a,"Data type= ",a.dtype)
5 b = np.array([1.2, 3.9, 5.7])
6 c = np.array([[1, 2], [3, 4]])
7 print("2-dim array from list       = \n", c, "shape= ", c.shape)
8 print("Array b from float list     = ",b, "Data type= ",b.dtype)
9 print("1-dim array from tuple      = ",np.array((1, 3, 5, 9)))
10 print("2-dim array from tuple     = \n",
11                     np.array([(1.8, 20, 30), (44, 55, 66)]))
12 a = np.array(2, 4, 6, 8)
```

(a)

```
Array a from integer list =  [1 2 5] Data type=  int32
2-dim array from list      =
 [[1 2]
 [3 4]] shape=  (2, 2)
Array b from float list    =  [1.2 3.9 5.7] Data type=  float64
1-dim array from tuple     =  [1 3 5 9]
2-dim array from tuple     =
 [[ 1.8 20.   30. ]
 [44.   55.   66. ]]
```

```
TypeError: array() takes from 1 to 2 positional arguments but
4 were given
```

(b)

We see that on execution of line 12, a `TypeError` occurs. This is because, the elements of the array must be a list or tuple.

16.5.2 Using Other Array Functions

In addition to the `array()` function of NumPy, several other functions can be used for creation of new arrays. `zeros()`, `ones()`, `empty()`, and `arange()` are some of the functions for the creation of arrays. Table 16.1 shows the use of the functions to create arrays. The application of these functions to create array is shown in Example 16.3.

Table 16.1 Functions to create arrays and their description

Function	Description
`zeros()`	Create array filled with 0's. By default, data type of array created is float.

(Continued)

Table 16.1 (Continued)

Function	Description
`ones()`	Create array filled with 1's By default, data type of array created is float.
`empty()`	Create an array with random content.
`identity()`	Create a square array with 1 on main diagonal and 0 elsewhere.
`full(shape,fill_value)`	Create array of given shape, filled with `fill_value`. For 1-dimension array, shape is an integer. For n-dimension array, shape is as per the tuple passed.
`np.arange(start, stop, step, dtype)`	Create an array in a range of integer elements. Start – optional. It is the start of interval; default is 0. Stop – mandatory. It is the end of interval. The elements are one less than the stop. Step – optional. It is the spacing between values; default is 1. If step is specified, then start must also be given.
`np.linspace(start, stop, no_of_elements)`	Create array with floating-point values, in a specified interval.
`np.random.randn(d0, d1,..., dn)`	Create array of given shape, elements are from standard normal distribution (random values from (0,1))

Example 16.3: (a) Using other functions to create arrays (b) Output

```
import numpy as np
print("*" * 30)
print("np.zeros((2))    =", np.zeros(2))
print("np.zeros((3, 4))\n", np.zeros((3, 4)))
print("np.zeros((3, 4, dtype=int 32))\n", np.zeros((3, 4), dtype=np.int32))
print("np.ones((2))     =",np.ones(2))
print("np.ones((2, 3, 4,dtype=int 32))\n",np.ones((2, 3, 4), dtype=np.int32))
print("np.empty(2)      =",np.empty(2))
print("np.empty(2, 3)\n",np.empty((2, 3)) )
print("*" * 30)
print("np.identity(4, dtype=int32)\n",np.identity(4, dtype=np.int32))
print("*" * 30)
print("np.full(4, 3)    =",np.full(4, 3))
print("np.full(2, 3), 10)    \n",np.full((2, 3), 10))
print("np.full(2, 2), 1.5)    \n",np.full((2, 2), 1.5))
print("*" * 30)
print("arange(4)             = ", np.arange(4))
print("arange(2, 9)          = ", np.arange(2, 9))
print("arange(10, 30, 5) = ", np.arange(10, 30, 5))
print("arange(0, 2, 0.3) = ",np.arange(0, 2, 0.3) )
print("*" * 30)
print("linspace(0, 10, 5) = ", np.linspace(0, 10, num=5))
print("linspace(0, 2, 9)         = ",np.linspace(0, 2, 9))
print("*" * 30)
print("randn()     = ", np.random.randn())
print("randn(4)    = ", np.random.randn(4))
print("randn(2, 4) \n", np.random.randn(2, 4))
```

(a)

```
np.zeros((2))    = [0. 0.]
np.zeros((3, 4))
 [[0. 0. 0. 0.]
 [0.  0.  0.  0.]
 [0.  0.  0.  0.]]
np.zeros((3, 4, dtype=int 32))
 [[0 0 0 0]
 [0 0 0 0]
 [0 0 0 0]]
np.ones((2))     = [1. 1.]
np.ones((2, 3, 4,dtype=int 32))
 [[[1 1 1 1]
  [1 1 1 1]
  [1 1 1 1]]

 [[1 1 1 1]
  [1 1 1 1]
  [1 1 1 1]]]
np.empty(2)      = [1. 1.]
np.empty(2, 3)
 [[0. 0. 0.]
 [0.  0.  0.]]
*******************************
np.identity(4, dtype=int32)
 [[1 0 0 0]
 [0 1 0 0]
 [0 0 1 0]
 [0 0 0 1]]
*******************************
```

```
np.full(4, 3)     = [3 3 3 3]
np.full(2, 3), 10)
 [[10 10 10]
 [10 10 10]]
np.full(2, 2), 1.5)
 [[1.5 1.5]
 [1.5 1.5]]
*******************************
arange(4)           =  [0 1 2 3]
arange(2, 9)        =  [2 3 4 5 6 7 8]
arange(10, 30, 5) =  [10 15 20 25]
arange(0, 2, 0.3) =  [0.  0.3 0.6 0.9 1.2 1.5 1.8]
*******************************
linspace(0, 10, 5) =  [ 0.   2.5  5.   7.5 10. ]
linspace(0, 2, 9)       =  [0.    0.25 0.5  0.75 1.    1.25 1.5
1.75 2.  ]
*******************************
randn()    =  -0.9809738465332963
randn(4)   =  [ 0.44038912  0.01135801 -1.16131181  1.19980143]
randn(2, 4)
 [[-0.24499492  0.63926458  0.90686809 -0.58536913]
 [ 0.55096535  0.77737444 -0.00534649 -0.13289023]]
```

(b)

16.5.3 Creation of Vectors

A vector is a single-dimension array. A vector can be horizontal or vertical. A horizontal vector is also known as row vector. A vertical vector is a column vector. A vector is created using `np.array()` method of Python. A vector has both magnitude and direction.

Row Vector: To create a row vector, we create a 1-dimension array with one row.

Example 16.4: (a) Creating row vector (b) Output

```
import numpy as np
vec_row = np.array([1, 2, 3])
print("Vector Row = ", vec_row)
print("Dimension= ", vec_row.ndim, "Shape = ", vec_row.shape)
```

(a)

```
Vector Row =  [1 2 3]
Dimension=  1 Shape =  (3,)
```

(b)

Column Vector: To create a column vector, we create a 2-dimension array with one column. It may be noted that a column vector is 2-dimensional.

Example 16.5: (a) Creating column vector (b) Output

```
import numpy as np
vec_col = np.array([[1],[2],[3]])
print("Vector Column = \n", vec_col)
print("Dimension= ", vec_col.ndim, "Shape = ",vec_col.shape)
```

(a)

```
Vector Column =
 [[1]
 [2]
 [3]]
Dimension=  2 Shape =  (3, 1)
```

(b)

16.6 Manipulation of NumPy Arrays

The NumPy array can be manipulated in different ways as follows:

- Operations that can be applied on an array, like sort an array or concatenate multiple arrays.
- Arrays can be sliced to view selected sections of array. Since a view is provided, so the array is not modified permanently.
- Subset and filtering can be done to extract specific elements from the array based on some Boolean conditions.

- Linear algebra operations can be performed.

We discuss array manipulation in the following subsections.

16.6.1 Array Operations to Update an Array

There are several operations that can be performed to update the array. Some of the operations are – sort an array, concatenate two arrays, reshape and flatten an array, and append elements to an existing array. Let us discuss them here.

- **sort()**: To sort an array, where axis, kind, and order can also be specified.

```
a1 = np.array([5, 3, 4, 2, 1, 6, 8, 7 ,9, 10])
print("Original Array = ", a1)
print("Sorted Array   = ", np.sort(a1))
a2 = np.array([[10, 6, 4, 8],
               [5, 7, 3, 9]])
print("Original Array = \n", a2)
print('Column Sort:','\n',np.sort(a2, kind='mergesort',axis=1))
print('Row Sort:','\n',np.sort(a2, kind='mergesort',axis=0))
```

Output

```
Original Array =  [ 5  3  4  2  1  6  8  7  9 10]
Sorted Array   =  [ 1  2  3  4  5  6  7  8  9 10]
Original Array =
 [[10  6  4  8]
 [ 5  7  3  9]]
Column Sort:
 [[ 4  6  8 10]
 [ 3  5  7  9]]
Row Sort:
 [[ 5  6  3  8]
 [10  7  4  9]]
```

- **concatenate()**: To concatenate arrays where axis, kind, and order can be specified.

```
a = np.array([1, 3, 5, 7, 9])
b = np.array([2, 4, 6, 8, 10])
print("Array a = ", a)
print("Array b = ", b)
print("Concat a and b = ", np.concatenate((a, b)))

a1 = np.array([[2, 4], [6, 8]])
a2 = np.array([[10, 12]])
print("Array a1 = \n", a1)
print("Array a2 = ", a2)
print("Concat a1 and a2 = \n",np.concatenate((a1,a2), axis=0))
```

Output

```
Array a =  [1 3 5 7 9]
Array b =  [ 2  4  6  8 10]
Concat a and b =  [ 1  3  5  7  9  2  4  6  8 10]
Array a1 =
 [[2 4]
 [6 8]]
Array a2 =  [[10 12]]
Concat a1 and a2 =
 [[ 2  4]
 [ 6  8]
 [10 12]]
```

- `reshape()`: To reshape an array without changing the data. The original and the reshaped array have the same number of elements.

```
1 import numpy as np
2 a1 = np.arange(8)
3 print("Original Array = ", a1)
4 a2 = a1.reshape(4, 2)
5 print("Reshaped Array = \n", a2)
6 print("Further reshape = \n", np.reshape(a2, newshape=(2, 4), order='C'))
7 print("Four rows :\n",np.reshape(a1,(4,-1)))
8 print("Four columns :\n",np.reshape(a1,(-1,4)))
```

Output

```
Original Array =  [0 1 2 3 4 5 6 7]
Reshaped Array =
 [[0 1]
 [2 3]
 [4 5]
 [6 7]]
Further reshape =
 [[0 1 2 3]
 [4 5 6 7]]
Four rows :
 [[0 1]
 [2 3]
 [4 5]
 [6 7]]
Four columns :
 [[0 1 2 3]
 [4 5 6 7]]
```

In this program, we understand the different statements:

Line 6: newshape allows to specify the new shape.

Lines 7, 8: When reshaping, you can use –1 if you are unsure about the shape of any of the axis. On seeing –1, NumPy automatically calculates the shape.

- **`flatten array`:** To get a copy of array into one dimension. It accepts order argument. Use 'C' for row-major order (default); 'F' for column-major order. It returns a copy of the original array.

```
import numpy as np
a1 = np.ones((3,3))
print("Array a = \n", a1)
a2 = a1.flatten()
print("Shape of a = ", a1.shape)
print('Shape after flatten :',a2.shape)
print("Array after Flatten = ", a2)
```

Output

```
Array a =
 [[1. 1. 1.]
 [1. 1. 1.]
 [1. 1. 1.]]
Shape of a =  (3, 3)
Shape after flatten : (9,)
Array after Flatten =  [1. 1. 1. 1. 1. 1. 1. 1. 1.]
```

- **`append()`:** To add new elements at the end of array.

```
import numpy as np
a1 = np.array([[2,4],
              [6,8]])
print("Original array = \n",a1)
print("Array after append =  \n", np.append(a1,[[10,20]], axis=0))
```

Output

```
Original array =
 [[2 4]
 [6 8]]
Array after append =
 [[ 2  4]
 [ 6  8]
 [10 20]]
```

- **`transpose()`:** To swap row values with column values, and column values with row values.

```
a1 = np.array([[2, 4, 6],
               [1, 3, 5]])
a2 = np.transpose(a1)
print("Original Matrix: Shape is ",a1.shape,'\n',a1)
print("Transposed Matrix: Shape is",a2.shape,'\n',a2)
```

Output

```
Original Matrix: Shape is  (2, 3)
 [[2 4 6]
 [1 3 5]]
Transposed Matrix: Shape is (3, 2)
 [[2 1]
 [4 3]
 [6 5]]
```

16.6.2 Array Indexing and Slicing in NumPy

- Indexing and slicing are used to access the elements of NumPy arrays.
- Indexing and slicing NumPy arrays is done in the same way as you do for Python lists.
- *Slicing* allows to extract part of an array, using : notation.
- *Indexing* is done using the location of array elements. It begins with 0 and uses square bracket [] notation.
- *Boolean array indexing* is same as indexing but elements are picked from array based on specific condition.
- The slicing has already been explained in detail in the earlier chapters. So, we skip the explanation here.

Example 16.6: (a) Slicing an array (b) Output

```
import numpy as np

data = np.array([[1, 2, 3],
                 [4, 5, 6],
                 [7, 8, 9]])
print("Array= \n",data, "Shape = ", data.shape)
print("data[1]= ", data[1])   #select element
print("data[-1]= ",data[-1])# select element from end
print("data[0:2]=\n ",data[0:2]) #select element from 0 to end-1
print("data[:]= \n",data[:])      #select all
print("data[0:-1]= \n",data[0:-1]) #select element from 0 to end-1
print("data[:3]=\n ",data[:3])   #select element from 0 to end-1
print("data[1:]=\n ",data[1:]) #select element from 1 to end
print("data[2:-1]= ",data[2:-1]) #select element from 2 to end
print("data[-2:1]=\n ",data[-2:]) #select element from start to end
print("data[::-1]= \n",data[::-1]) # select all elements in reverse order
```

(a)

```
Array=
 [[1 2 3]
 [4 5 6]
 [7 8 9]] Shape =  (3, 3)
data[1]=  [4 5 6]
data[-1]=  [7 8 9]
data[0:2]=
  [[1 2 3]
 [4 5 6]]
data[:]=
 [[1 2 3]
 [4 5 6]
 [7 8 9]]
data[0:-1]=
 [[1 2 3]
 [4 5 6]]
data[:3]=
  [[1 2 3]
 [4 5 6]
 [7 8 9]]
data[1:]=
  [[4 5 6]
 [7 8 9]]
data[2:-1]=  []
data[-2:1]=
  [[4 5 6]
 [7 8 9]]
data[::-1]=
 [[7 8 9]
 [4 5 6]
 [1 2 3]]
```

(b)

Example 16.7: (a) Boolean array indexing (b) Output

```
import numpy as np
arr = np.array([[1, 3, 5, 7], [2, 4, 6, 8], [9, 10, 11, 12]])
print("Array= \n", arr)
print("Array element < 6 = ", arr[arr < 6])
great_six = (arr >= 6)
print("Array elemnt >=6 = ", arr[great_six])
div_by_5 = arr[arr%5==0]
print("Array elements divisible by 5 = ", div_by_5)
arr_range = arr[(arr > 5) & (arr < 15)]
print("Array in range 5 and 15 = ", arr_range)
two_cond = ((arr >= 5) & (arr%5==0))
print("Array >= 5 and divisible by 5 = \n", arr[two_cond])
```

(a)

```
Array=
 [[ 1  3  5  7]
 [ 2  4  6  8]
 [ 9 10 11 12]]
Array element < 6 =  [1 3 5 2 4]
Array elemnt >=6 =  [ 7  6  8  9 10 11 12]
Array elements divisible by 5 =  [ 5 10]
Array in range 5 and 15 =  [ 7  6  8  9 10 11 12]
Array >= 5 and divisible by 5 =
 [ 5 10]
```

(b)

16.6.3 Mathematical Operations with NumPy Arrays

Several arithmetic operations can be performed on the NumPy arrays. These operations include – `np.add()`, `np.subtract()`, `np.multiply()`, and `np.divide()`. A **universal function or ufunc** performs element-wise operations on data in `ndarray`. Because of vectorization, the operations work on the entire array with a single operation; otherwise, there would have been a need to use looping. The vectorized operations are faster than the looping ones.

Example 16.8: (a) Arithmetic operations (b) Output

```
import numpy as np
x = np.array([[1,2], [3,4]])
y = np.array([[6,7], [8,9]])
print("Array x = \n", x)
print("Array y = \n", y)
print("Element-wise Subtract y-x :\n",y-x)
print("Element-wise Add  x+y:\n",x+y)
print("Element-wise Divide y/x:\n",y/x)
print("Element-wise Power y**x:\n",y**x)
print("Element-wise Remainder y%x:\n",y%x)
```

(a)

```
Array x =
 [[1 2]
 [3 4]]
Array y =
 [[6 7]
 [8 9]]
Element-wise Subtract y-x :
 [[5 5]
 [5 5]]
Element-wise Add  x+y:
 [[ 7  9]
 [11 13]]
Element-wise Divide y/x:
 [[6.         3.5       ]
 [2.66666667 2.25      ]]
Element-wise Power y**x:
 [[   6   49]
 [ 512 6561]]
Element-wise Remainder y%x:
 [[0 1]
 [2 1]]
```

(b)

There are several statistical functions for NumPy arrays – Min, max sum, mean std, median.

Example 16.9: (a) Statistical functions (b) Output

```
1 import numpy as np
2 x = np.arange(5,14)
3 print("x = ", x)
4 print('Mean :',np.mean(x))
5 print('Median :',np.median(x))
6 print('Standard deviation :',np.std(x))
7
8 x1 = np.array([[1,6, 5], [4,3,7]])
9 print("x1 = \n", x1)
10 print("Min axis 0 = ",np.min(x1,axis=0))
11 print("Index- min axis 0 = ",np.argmin(x1,axis=0))
12 print("Max axis 1 = ",np.max(x1,axis=1))
13 print("Index- max axis 1 = ",np.argmax(x1,axis=1))
```

(a)

```
x =  [ 5  6  7  8  9 10 11 12 13]
Mean : 9.0
Median : 9.0
Standard deviation : 2.581988897471611
x1 =
 [[1 6 5]
 [4 3 7]]
Min axis 0 =  [1 3 5]
Index- min axis 0 =  [0 1 0]
Max axis 1 =  [6 7]
Index- max axis 1 =  [1 2]
```

(b)

At lines from 10–13, the use of `axis` keyword specifies the dimension of array that will be collapsed. `axis=0` specifies that the first axis (rows) will be collapsed. For 2-dimension array, the values within each column will be aggregated.

16.6.4 Linear Algebra

- Linear algebra is a branch of mathematics that deals with linear equations and their representation using matrices.
- `numpy.linalg` is a package in NumPy for NumPy Linear Algebra. It contains all the functions necessary for linear algebra.
- NumPy provides functions for common linear algebra tasks, such as:
  - o rank, determinant, trace of an array
  - o eigen values of matrices, decompositions

- matrix product, vector product, matrix exponentiation
- solving linear equations

Table 16.2 Functions for Linear Algebra and their description

Function	Description
`dot()`	Calculate dot product of two arrays
`vdot()`	Calculate dot product of two vectors
`cross()`	Calculate cross product of two vectors
`inner()`	Calculate inner product of two arrays (Sum of products of their corresponding entries)
`outer()`	Calculate outer product of two arrays (Product of all possible pairs of their entries)
`det()`	Calculate determinant of matrix
`solve()`	Solve linear matrix equation
`trace()`	Calculate sum of diagonal elements
`matmul()`	Calculate matrix multiplication of two arrays
`linalg.inv()`	Calculate multiplicative inverse of a matrix
`linalg.qr()`	Compute QR factorization of matrix
`linalg.svd()`	Compute singular value decomposition
`Linalg.eig()`	Compute eigenvalues and right eigenvectors of a square array
`Linalg.eigvals()`	Compute eigenvalues of a general matrix

Eigenvalues are a unique set of scalar values connected to a set of linear equations that are most likely seen in matrix equations. ***Eigenvector*** is a non-zero vector that changes at most by a scalar factor when a linear transformation is applied to it. It is represented by lambda (λ).

For a matrix P, x is eigenvector and λ is the eigenvalue for its transformation P.

$$Px = \lambda x$$

The `eig()` function of `linalg` library gives eigenvalues and eigenvectors of an array.

A popular application of eigenvalues and eigenvectors is decomposition of a square matrix.

Example 16.9: (a) Linear algebra function (b) Output

```
import numpy as np
a1 = np.array([[1, 2], [3, 4]])
a2 = np.array([[10, 20], [30, 40]])
print("Array a1 = \n", a1)
print("Array a2 = \n", a2)
print("Dot(a1, a2)       :\n", np.dot(a1, a2))
print("vdot(a1, a2)      :", np.vdot(a1, a2))
print("Trace(a1)         :", np.trace(a1))
print("Matmul(a1, a2) :\n", np.matmul(a1, a2))
print("Inner(a1, a2)     :\n", np.inner(a1, a2))
print("Outer(a1, a2)     :\n", np.outer(a1, a2))
print("\nCross(a1, a2): ", np.cross(a1, a2))

print("Determinant(a1):", np.linalg.det(a1))
print("Inverse(a1)       :\n", np.linalg.inv(a1))
print("Solve(a1, a2)     :\n", np.linalg.solve(a1, a2))
P, Q = np.linalg.eig(a1)
print("Eigen Values(a1): \n", P)
print("Eigen Vectors(a1): \n", Q)
```

(a)

```
Array a1 =
 [[1 2]
 [3 4]]
Array a2 =
 [[10 20]
 [30 40]]
Dot(a1, a2)      :
 [[ 70 100]
 [150 220]]
vdot(a1, a2)     : 300
Trace(a1)        : 5
Matmul(a1, a2) :
 [[ 70 100]
 [150 220]]
Inner(a1, a2)    :
 [[ 50 110]
 [110 250]]
Outer(a1, a2)    :
 [[ 10  20  30  40]
 [ 20  40  60  80]
 [ 30  60  90 120]
 [ 40  80 120 160]]
```

```
Cross(a1, a2):  [0 0]
Determinant(a1): -2.0000000000000004
Inverse(a1)      :
 [[-2.   1. ]
 [ 1.5 -0.5]]
Solve(a1, a2)    :
 [[10.  0.]
 [ 0. 10.]]
Eigen Values(a1):
  [-0.37228132  5.37228132]
Eigen Vectors(a1):
  [[-0.82456484 -0.41597356]
 [ 0.56576746 -0.90937671]]
```

(b)

16.7 Pandas: Basics

Pandas is a popular library for data analysis and manipulation. It is an open-source machine learning library. It provides flexible high-level data structures and several analysis tools.

- It is used for working with datasets. It has data structures for storing and processing large datasets.
- It has tools for data cleaning, aggregation, and transformation.
- Pandas is a fast, powerful, flexible and easy-to-use data analysis library.
- Pandas is built on top of NumPy.
- Pandas works with tabular heterogeneous data. In contrast, NumPy works with homogeneous numerical data.
- Pandas supports operations like sorting, re-indexing, concatenation, conversion of data, visualization, and aggregation.
- It is used in academic and commercial areas, like, statistics and finance.

16.7.1 Import Pandas as pd

A common way to use Pandas in a Python code is to import the library. For doing this, you need not write the word 'Pandas' each time you use the library; you can use `pd`. So, include the following statement at the beginning of each Python file, as follows:

import pandas as pd

where, `pd` is the common abbreviation used by the Python community for pandas.

The standard Python does not come with an installed Pandas module. However, on downloading Anaconda, Pandas is installed by default. In case you want to install Pandas, you can do so by the following command:

```
pip install pandas
```

Some of the key benefits of importing Pandas are:

- The functions, classes and sub-packages in Pandas library can be accessed as: `pd.namespace`.
- Pandas has two main data structures for storing and manipulating data:
  - **Series:** A 1-dimension data structure. It is a single column of data.
  - **DataFrame:** A 2-dimension data structure. It is a sheet with rows and columns.
- Pandas functions are very fast compared to the regular Python functions.
- It has functions to perform mathematical operations, like array functions, linear algebra, random number generation, polynomials and Fourier transforms.
- It can vectorize the code. As a result, a single operation can be applied to multiple elements of the array simultaneously. This feature is useful while working on large datasets.
- It is interoperable with other Python packages like Matplotlib, which makes it useful for data analysis tasks.

16.7.2 Features of Pandas

- The main features provided by Pandas fall into three categories:
  - o Data cleaning,
  - o Data transformation, and
  - o Data wrangling.
- **Data cleaning** provides tools for cleaning the data. It has methods to handle missing data, remove duplicates, and replace values. Some methods provided by Pandas are:
  - o `dropna()` to drop any rows or columns that contain missing data.
  - o `fillna()` to fill missing data with a specified value.
  - o `drop_duplicates()` to removes duplicate rows from a DataFrame.
  - o `replace()` to replace specific values with new values.
- **Data transformation** makes the data more suitable for analysis or modeling. Pandas provides several methods for transforming data:
  - o `loc[]` to select rows and columns by label.
  - o `iloc[]` to select rows and columns by index.
  - o `sort_values()` to sort a DataFrame by one or more columns or indices.
  - o `groupby()` to group a DataFrame by one or more variables. Aggregate operations can be performed on a group, like sum and mean.
- **Data wrangling** is the act of processing data, like merging, grouping, and concatenating. It allows merging or joining of two or more datasets based on a common column or key. Pandas provides several methods for merging and joining data, including:
  - o `merge()` to merge two DataFrames based on a common column or key.
  - o `join()` to join two DataFrames based on their indices.
  - o `concat()` to concatenate multiple DataFrames along an axis.

16.8 Pandas Series

The `Series` object represents one-dimensional data structures in Pandas. There are two main components of a Series – data and index. The data are values in 1-dimension.

The series is composed of two arrays associated with each other. The main array (array of values) holds *one-dimensional data* to which each element contained within the other array (array of labels) is associated by a label, called the *index*. To see the two arrays that make up the series, individually, call the *index* and *values* attributes of the series. Because a series is one-dimensional, it has a single axis (dimension) – index, and, values of index – 0, 1, 2, 3, which are called axis labels.

16.8.1 Creation of Series

The syntax for creating a Pandas Series is:

```
pd.Series(data=…, index=…, dtype=…, name=…)
```

where, the Series class constructor is called with the arguments.
`data` can be any of – one-dimension ndarray, Python list, Python dictionary, or Scalar value.

`index` is optional. If not specified, a default index from 0 to $n - 1$ is created, where n is length of data.

`dtype` is datatype of the data (Series values). The values can be of type – string, integer, float, and Boolean. It is optional. You may specify datatype of Series values when it is created.

A series can be created using different ways:

- Using a one-dimension ndarray
- Using a Pythion list
- Using a Python dictionary
- Using a Scalar value.

When defining a Series, `index` is optional.

- If index is not specified, then by default, Pandas assigns numerical values starting from 0 as labels. The labels correspond to indexes (position in array) of elements in the series.
- Specify index during the series creation, to define meaningful labels. Labels are defined as a list of same length as of the values array.

Use `ser.index` and `ser.values` to display index and values of a Series, respectively.

Example 16.9: (a) Creation of series (b) Output

```
import pandas as pd
import numpy as np
#=========Create using 1-dim ndarray=========
an_array = np.arange(2, 12, 2)
ser_1 = pd. Series(an_array)
print("*****Series using ndarray: \n", ser_1)
#=======Create using 1-dim ndarray with index==
an_array = np.arange(1, 10, 2)
ser_2 = pd.Series(an_array, index=["I", "II", "III", "IV", "V"])
print("*****Series using ndarray:\n", ser_2)
print("Series Index=", ser_2.index)
print("Series Values = ", ser_2.values)
#====Create using list=====================
alist = [5, 10, 15, 20, 25]
ser_3 = pd.Series(alist, index=["I", "II", "III", "IV", "V"])
print("*****Series using list:\n", ser_3)
#====Create using dictionary================
dict_1 = {"First":1, "Second":2, "Third":3 }
ser_4 = pd. Series(dict_1)
print("*****Series using dictionary:\n",ser_4)
#====Create using scalar value==============
import numpy as np
ser_5 = pd. Series(5.3)
print("*****Series using scalar value:\n",ser_5)
```

(a)

```
*****Series using ndarray:
 0    2
1     4
2     6
3     8
4    10
dtype: int32
*****Series using ndarray:
 I      1
II     3
III    5
IV     7
V      9
dtype: int32
Series Index= Index(['I', 'II', 'III', 'IV', 'V'], dtype='ob
ject')
Series Values =   [1 3 5 7 9]
*****Series using list:
 I       5
II     10
III    15
IV     20
V      25
dtype: int64
```

```
*****Series using dictionary:
 First     1
Second    2
Third     3
dtype: int64
*****Series using scalar value:
 0     5.3
dtype: float64
```

(b)

In this program, we understand the different statements:

Lines 4–6: Creates a series from 1-dim ndarray of first five even numbers.

Lines 8–12: Creates a series from 1-dim ndarray with index specified.

Lines 14–16: Creates a series using a Python list, where index is also specified.

Lines 18–20: Creates series using dictionary. For the key–value pair in dictionary, the key forms the index and values are the data.

Lines 22–24: Creates series from scalar value.

16.8.2 Operations on Series

The indexing and slicing that are applicable to NumPy arrays can be extended to the series because Pandas library is built on top of NumPy. The following operations can be performed as we do for NumPy arrays.

- Select a single element. Use index number or index label of the series.
- Select a range of elements. Use slice notation.
- Select multiple elements. Use index numbers.
- Use conditions and Boolean operators to select elements from a series.
- Change value of an element. Series are mutable.
- Perform arithmetic operations.
- Use statistical functions, like mean.

Example 16.10: (a) Operations on series (b) Output

```
import pandas as pd
import numpy as np

an_array = np.arange(1, 10, 2)
ser_2 = pd.Series(an_array, index=["I", "II", "III", "IV", "V"])
print("*****Series using ndarray: \n", ser_2)
print("*****Series ser_2[2]=", ser_2[2])
print("*****Series ser_2[II]=",ser_2["II"])
print("*****Series ser_2[0:3]:\n",ser_2[0:3])
print("*****Series ser_2[[1,3,4]]:\n",ser_2[[1, 3, 4]])
print("*****Series ser_2[[I,III,V]]:\n",ser_2[["I", "III", "V"]])
print("*****Series ser_2 < 7 = \n", ser_2[ser_2 < 7])
print("*****Series ser_2 >2 and <9: \n", ser_2[(ser_2 > 2) &(ser_2 <9)])
ser_2[1:4] = 50
print("Series ser_2[2:4} = 50:\n", ser_2)
print("*****Series ser_2*2=\n",ser_2*2)
print("*****Series ser_2.mean()=",ser_2.mean())
```

(a)

```
*****Series using ndarray:
 I      1
II      3
III     5
IV      7
V       9
dtype: int32
```

```
*****Series ser_2[2]= 5
*****Series ser_2[II]= 3
*****Series ser_2[0:3]:
 I      1
II      3
III     5
dtype: int32
```

```
*****Series ser_2[[1,3,4]]:
 II     3
IV    7
V     9
dtype: int32
*****Series ser_2[[I,III,V]]:
 I      1
III    5
V      9
dtype: int32
*****Series ser_2 < 7 =
 I      1
II     3
III    5
dtype: int32
*****Series ser_2 >2 and <9:
 II     3
III    5
IV     7
dtype: int32
Series ser_2[2:4} = 50:
 I       1
II      50
III     50
IV      50
V        9
dtype: int32
```

```
*****Series ser_2*2=
 I       2
II     100
III    100
IV     100
V       18
dtype: int32
*****Series ser_2.mean()= 32.0
```

(b)

16.9 PANDAS DATAFRAME

- A DataFrame is a two-dimensional data structure composed of rows and columns, like a spreadsheet or SQL table.
- Each column of a DataFrame is a Pandas series.
- The columns are of the same length, but they can be of different datatypes – float, int, bool.
- DataFrames are both value-mutable and size-mutable. In contrast, a Series is only value-mutable. Thus, operations can be performed that can alter values or add/delete columns to/from the DataFrame.
- DataFrame consists of three components – Two-dimensional data (Values), Row index, and Column index
- The label in first array is associated with row. The label of second array is associated with column. The row axis is axis 0; the column axis is axis 1.
- DataFrame class constructor accepts different types of arguments – two-dimensional ndarray, dictionary of dictionaries, dictionary of lists, and dictionary of series.
- Row label index and column labels can be specified along with the data. If not specified, they are generated from the input data.

16.9.1 Creation of DataFrame

The syntax for creating a Pandas DataFrame is:

`pd.DataFrame(data=…, index=…, columns=…)`

where, the DataFrame class constructor is called with the arguments.
`data` can be any of – one-dimension ndarray, Python list, Python dictionary, or Scalar value.
`index` is optional. If not specified, default index from 0 to *n* – 1 is created, where *n* is length of data.
`columns` is name of columns.

A DataFrame can be created using different ways, using:

- Two-dimension ndarray.
- A dictionary of dictionaries – Column names are created from keys of the main dictionary, and row index is created from keys of the sub-dictionaries.
- A dictionary list – The components that make up DataFrame can be seen by using values, index and columns attributes of DataFrame.
- A dictionary of series.
- A file or table – It supports many file formats, like, csv, excel, sql, and json. Each format is accessed with a prefix read_*, and is used for reading a file into a DataFrame.
    - o `read_csv()` to read comma-separated values (csv) file or a text file
    - o `read_excel()` to read an Excel file
    - o `read_html()` to read HTML tables
    - o `read_sql()` to read SQL query or database table.

Example 16.11: (a) Creation of DataFrame (b) Output

```
import pandas as pd
import numpy as np
#=========Create using 1-dim ndarray==========
arr = np.array([[160, 65], [156, 66], [165, 55], [156, 80]])
df1 = pd. DataFrame(arr, index =["Asha", "Usha", "Isha", "Disha"],
                    columns =["Height", "Weight"])
print("\n****df1:Create using 1-dim ndarray\n",df1)
print("df1.values:\n", df1.values)
print("df1.index: \n", df1.index)
print("df1.columns:\n", df1.columns)
#=========Create using dictionary of dictionaries==========
dict2 = {"Name":{"A": "Asha", "U":"Usha", "I": "Isha", "D": "Disha"},
         "Height":{"A": 160, "U":156, "D":165, "I":156},
         "Weight":{"A": 65, "U":66, "D":55, "I":80}}
df2 = pd. DataFrame(dict2)
print("\n****df2:Create using dictionary of dictionaries\n",df2)

#=========Create using dictionary list==========
dict3 = {"Name": ["Asha", "Usha", "Isha", "Disha"],
         "Height":[160, 156, 165, 156],
         "Weight":{65, 66, 55, 80}}
df3 = pd. DataFrame(dict2, index=["A", "U", "I", "D"])
print("\n****df3:Create using dictionary list\n",df3)
print("df3.values:\n", df3.values)
print("df3.index: ", df3.index)
print("df3.columns:", df3.columns)
print("type(df3.values):", type(df3.values))
print("df3.values.ndim:", df3.values.ndim)
print("df3.values.shape:", df3.values.shape)
```

```
#=========Create using dictionary of Series==========
s1 = pd.Series(["Asha", "Usha", "Isha", "Disha"],index=["A", "U", "D", "I"]
s2 = pd.Series([160, 156, 165, 156], index=["A", "U", "D", "I"])
s3 = pd.Series([65, 66, 55, 80], index=["A", "U", "D", "I"])
dict4 = {"Name": s1, "Height": s2, "Weight":s3}
df4 = pd. DataFrame(dict4)
print("\n****df4:Create using dictionary of Series\n",df4)
col_1 = df4["Name"]
print("First Column: \n", col_1)
#=========read_csv file==========
data =  pd.read_csv('data.txt', sep=",")
print(data)
```

(a)

```
****df1:Create using 1-dim ndarray
        Height  Weight
Asha     160      65
Usha     156      66
Isha     165      55
Disha    156      80
df1.values:
 [[160  65]
 [156  66]
 [165  55]
 [156  80]]
df1.index:
 Index(['Asha', 'Usha', 'Isha', 'Disha'], dtype='object')
df1.columns:
 Index(['Height', 'Weight'], dtype='object')

****df2:Create using dictionary of dictionaries
    Name  Height  Weight
A   Asha     160      65
U   Usha     156      66
I   Isha     156      80
D  Disha     165      55

****df3:Create using dictionary list
    Name  Height  Weight
A   Asha    160      65
U   Usha    156      66
I   Isha    156      80
D  Disha    165      55
```

```
df3.values:
 [['Asha' 160 65]
 ['Usha' 156 66]
 ['Isha' 156 80]
 ['Disha' 165 55]]
df3.index:  Index(['A', 'U', 'I', 'D'], dtype='object')
df3.columns: Index(['Name', 'Height', 'Weight'], dtype='object')
type(df3.values): <class 'numpy.ndarray'>
df3.values.ndim: 2
df3.values.shape: (4, 3)

****df4:Create using dictionary of Series
     Name  Height  Weight
A   Asha      160      65
U   Usha      156      66
D   Isha      165      55
I  Disha      156      80
First Column:
 A     Asha
U     Usha
D     Isha
I    Disha
Name: Name, dtype: object
```

```
     key1 key2  value1  value2
0   first    A      10      20
1   first    B      30      40
2   first    C      50      60
3   first    D      70      80
4  second    A      90     100
5  second    B     110     120
6  second    C     130     140
7  second    D     150     160
```

(b)

16.9.2 Operations on a DataFrame

Several operations can be performed on dataframes. The operations can be divided into different categories, such as for data inspection, data slicing and extraction, data cleaning and transformation, and data wrangling, as shown in Table 16.3.

Table 16.3 Functions for operation on DataFrame and their description

Function	Description
Data Inspection	
`df.head(n)`	View first *n* rows
`df.tail(n)`	View last *n* rows

(*Continued*)

Table 16.3 (Continued)

Function	Description
`df.index`	Change index
`df.shape()`	Check shape
`df.dtypes`	Check data types of columns
`df.columns`	Print columns
`df.values`	Print table values
`df.describe()`	Get statistical summary (count, mean, standard deviation, min, 25%, 50%, 75%, max)
Data Slicing and Extraction	
`df.iloc[]` `df.iloc[1,:]`	Select data by row and column labels
`df.loc[idx_name]`	Select data by index
`df['col_name'].value_counts()`	Count number of values
Data Cleaning and Transformation	
`df.drop(['col1', 'col2'], axis = 1, inplace = true)`	Drop columns
`df.isnull().sum()`	Check number of missing values in each column
`df.dropna(inplace=true)`	Drop rows with missing values
`df.fillna(df.median(),inplace=true)` `df.fillna(df.mean(),inplace=true)` `df.fillna(0, inplace=true)`	Fill missing values with median, mean or constant
`df['col'] = df['col'].astype('float')`	Change data type of a column
`df.sort_values()`	Sort record by any column
`df.rename(col={'old': 'new'}, inplace=true)`	Rename a column
`df.replace(-99, np.nan)`	Replace values
`df.drop_duplicates()`	Remove duplicates
Data Wrangling	
`df.groupby('emp_name')`	Group data into categories
`pd.merge(df1, df2, on='emp_id')`	Merge two data frames
`pd.concat([df1, df2])`	Concatenate data frames

Example 16.12: (a) Operations on DataFrames (b) Output

```
import pandas as pd
import numpy as np
import math
#==========Operations on DataFrame==========================
data = {'VEGETABLE':['Brinjal', 'Brinjal', 'Tomato', 'LadyFinger',
                     'Cabbage', 'Cauliflower', 'Raddish', 'Carrot'],
        'COLOR': ['Purple', 'Wheatish', 'Red', 'Green',
                  'Green','White','Orange', 'White'],
        'SHAPE': ['Elongate', 'Round', 'Round', 'Taper Small',
                  'Big Round','Flower Round', 'Taper mid', 'Taper Long'],
        'QUANTITY': [5, 10, np.nan, 1, 2, 3, 2, np.nan]}
df = pd.DataFrame(data,index = np.arange(1,9))
print("*****df*****\n", df)
#*********Data Inspection
print("*****df.index*****\n",df.index)
print("*****df.shape*****\n",df.shape)
print("*****df.dtypes*****\n",df.dtypes)
print("*****df.columns*****\n",df.columns)
print("*****df.values*****\n",df.values)
print("*****df.head(3)*****\n", df.head(3))
print("*****df.tail(3)*****\n", df.tail(3))
print("*****df.describe*****\n",df.describe())
#*********Data Slicing and Extraction
print("\n*****df.iloc[2:6]*****\n",df.iloc[2:6])
print("\n*****df.iloc[1,:]*****\n",df.iloc[1,:])
print("\n*****df.loc[5]*****\n",df.loc[5])
print("\n**df['COLOR'].value_counts()**\n",df['COLOR'].value_counts())
#********Data Cleaning and Transformation
print("\n**df.drop([‘Color’]**\n",df.drop(['COLOR'], axis = 1))
print(df)
print("\n*****df.isnull().sum()*****\n",df.isnull().sum())
print("\n*****df.fillna(0)*****\n",df.fillna(0, inplace=True))
print("\n**df.dropna(inplace=true)**\n",df.dropna(inplace=True))
print(df)
df = df.astype({'QUANTITY':'int'})
print("\n*****df.QUANTITY.astype('int')*****\n",df)
temp1 = df.sort_values(by=['VEGETABLE'])
print("\n**df.sort_values('VEGETABLE')**\n",temp1)
temp2 = df.rename(columns={'QUANTITY': 'QTY'})
print("\n**df.rename{'QUANTITY':'QTY'}**\n",temp2)
print("\n*****df.replace*****\n",df.replace(-99, np.nan))
temp3 = df.drop_duplicates(subset=['QUANTITY'])
print("\n**df.drop_duplicates()**\n",temp3)
#********Data Wrangling
data1 = {'VEGETABLE': ['Beans', 'Peas', 'Capsicum'],
         'COLOR': ['Green', 'Green', 'Yellow'],
         'SHAPE': ['Taper Small', 'Taper Small', 'Oval'],
         'QUANTITY': [2, 10, 15]}
df1 = pd.DataFrame(data1,index = np.arange(1,4))

print("\n**df.groupby(QUANTITY)**\n",df.groupby("QUANTITY").indices)
df2 = pd.merge(df, df1, on = 'COLOR')
print("\n*****df.iloc[2:6]*****\n",df2)
print(pd.concat([df, df1]))
```

(a)

```
*****df*****
      VEGETABLE     COLOR          SHAPE  QUANTITY
1       Brinjal    Purple       Elongate       5.0
2       Brinjal  Wheatish          Round      10.0
3        Tomato       Red          Round       NaN
4    LadyFinger     Green    Taper Small       1.0
5       Cabbage     Green      Big Round       2.0
6   Cauliflower     White   Flower Round       3.0
7       Raddish    Orange      Taper mid       2.0
8        Carrot     White     Taper Long       NaN
```

Output: Data Inspection

```
*****df.index*****
 Index([1, 2, 3, 4, 5, 6, 7, 8], dtype='int32')
*****df.shape*****
 (8, 4)
*****df.dtypes*****
 VEGETABLE     object
COLOR          object
SHAPE          object
QUANTITY      float64
dtype: object
*****df.columns*****
 Index(['VEGETABLE', 'COLOR', 'SHAPE', 'QUANTITY'], dtype='object')
*****df.values*****
 [['Brinjal' 'Purple' 'Elongate' 5.0]
 ['Brinjal' 'Wheatish' 'Round' 10.0]
 ['Tomato' 'Red' 'Round' nan]
 ['LadyFinger' 'Green' 'Taper Small' 1.0]
 ['Cabbage' 'Green' 'Big Round' 2.0]
 ['Cauliflower' 'White' 'Flower Round' 3.0]
 ['Raddish' 'Orange' 'Taper mid' 2.0]
 ['Carrot' 'White' 'Taper Long' nan]]
```

```
*****df.head(3)*****
  VEGETABLE     COLOR     SHAPE  QUANTITY
1   Brinjal    Purple  Elongate       5.0
2   Brinjal  Wheatish     Round      10.0
3    Tomato       Red     Round       NaN
*****df.tail(3)*****
      VEGETABLE   COLOR          SHAPE  QUANTITY
6   Cauliflower   White   Flower Round       3.0
7       Raddish  Orange      Taper mid       2.0
8        Carrot   White     Taper Long       NaN
```

```
*****df.describe*****
        QUANTITY
count   6.000000
mean    3.833333
std     3.311596
min     1.000000
25%     2.000000
50%     2.500000
75%     4.500000
max    10.000000
```

Output: Data Slicing and Extraction

```
*****df.iloc[2:6]*****
     VEGETABLE  COLOR          SHAPE  QUANTITY
3       Tomato    Red          Round       NaN
4   LadyFinger  Green    Taper Small       1.0
5      Cabbage  Green      Big Round       2.0
6  Cauliflower  White   Flower Round       3.0

*****df.iloc[1,:]*****
```

```
VEGETABLE     Brinjal
COLOR        Wheatish
SHAPE           Round
QUANTITY         10.0
Name: 2, dtype: object

*****df.loc[5]*****
VEGETABLE     Cabbage
COLOR           Green
SHAPE       Big Round
QUANTITY          2.0
Name: 5, dtype: object

*****df['COLOR'].value_counts()*****
COLOR
Green       2
White       2
Purple      1
Wheatish    1
Red         1
Orange      1
Name: count, dtype: int64
```

Output: Data Cleaning and Transformation

```
*****df.drop(['Color']*****
     VEGETABLE         SHAPE  QUANTITY
1      Brinjal      Elongate       5.0
2      Brinjal         Round      10.0
3       Tomato         Round       NaN
4   LadyFinger   Taper Small       1.0
5      Cabbage     Big Round       2.0
6  Cauliflower  Flower Round       3.0
7      Raddish     Taper mid       2.0
8       Carrot    Taper Long       NaN
     VEGETABLE     COLOR          SHAPE  QUANTITY
1      Brinjal    Purple       Elongate       5.0
2      Brinjal  Wheatish          Round      10.0
3       Tomato       Red          Round       NaN
4   LadyFinger     Green    Taper Small       1.0
5      Cabbage     Green      Big Round       2.0
6  Cauliflower     White   Flower Round       3.0
7      Raddish    Orange      Taper mid       2.0
8       Carrot     White     Taper Long       NaN
```

```
*****df.isnull().sum()*****
 VEGETABLE    0
COLOR         0
SHAPE         0
QUANTITY      2
dtype: int64

*****df.fillna(0)*****
 None
```

```
**df.dropna(inplace=true)**
 None
      VEGETABLE     COLOR          SHAPE  QUANTITY
1       Brinjal    Purple       Elongate       5.0
2       Brinjal  Wheatish          Round      10.0
3        Tomato       Red          Round       0.0
4    LadyFinger     Green    Taper Small       1.0
5       Cabbage     Green      Big Round       2.0
6   Cauliflower     White   Flower Round       3.0
7       Raddish    Orange      Taper mid       2.0
8        Carrot     White     Taper Long       0.0

*****df.QUANTITY.astype('int')*****
      VEGETABLE     COLOR          SHAPE  QUANTITY
1       Brinjal    Purple       Elongate         5
2       Brinjal  Wheatish          Round        10
3        Tomato       Red          Round         0
4    LadyFinger     Green    Taper Small         1
5       Cabbage     Green      Big Round         2
6   Cauliflower     White   Flower Round         3
7       Raddish    Orange      Taper mid         2
8        Carrot     White     Taper Long         0
```

```
**df.sort_values('VEGETABLE')**
      VEGETABLE     COLOR          SHAPE  QUANTITY
1       Brinjal    Purple       Elongate         5
2       Brinjal  Wheatish          Round        10
5       Cabbage     Green      Big Round         2
8        Carrot     White     Taper Long         0
6   Cauliflower     White   Flower Round         3
4    LadyFinger     Green    Taper Small         1
7       Raddish    Orange      Taper mid         2
3        Tomato       Red          Round         0

**df.rename{'QUANTITY':'QTY'}**
      VEGETABLE     COLOR          SHAPE  QTY
1       Brinjal    Purple       Elongate    5
2       Brinjal  Wheatish          Round   10
3        Tomato       Red          Round    0
4    LadyFinger     Green    Taper Small    1
5       Cabbage     Green      Big Round    2
6   Cauliflower     White   Flower Round    3
7       Raddish    Orange      Taper mid    2
8        Carrot     White     Taper Long    0
```

```
*****df.replace*****
      VEGETABLE     COLOR          SHAPE  QUANTITY
1       Brinjal    Purple       Elongate         5
2       Brinjal  Wheatish          Round        10
3        Tomato       Red          Round         0
4    LadyFinger     Green    Taper Small         1
5       Cabbage     Green      Big Round         2
6   Cauliflower     White   Flower Round         3
7       Raddish    Orange      Taper mid         2
8        Carrot     White     Taper Long         0

**df.drop_duplicates()**
      VEGETABLE     COLOR          SHAPE  QUANTITY
1       Brinjal    Purple       Elongate         5
2       Brinjal  Wheatish          Round        10
3        Tomato       Red          Round         0
4    LadyFinger     Green    Taper Small         1
5       Cabbage     Green      Big Round         2
6   Cauliflower     White   Flower Round         3
```

Output: Data Wrangling

```
*****df.groupby('QUANTITY')*****
 {0: array([2, 7], dtype=int64), 1: array([3], dtype=int64), 2: array([4,
6], dtype=int64), 3: array([5], dtype=int64), 5: array([0], dtype=int64),
10: array([1], dtype=int64)}

*****df.iloc[2:6]*****
  VEGETABLE_x  COLOR      SHAPE_x  ...  VEGETABLE_y    SHAPE_y QUANTITY
_y
0  LadyFinger  Green  Taper Small  ...        Beans  Taper Small
2
1  LadyFinger  Green  Taper Small  ...         Peas  Taper Small        1
0
2     Cabbage  Green    Big Round  ...        Beans  Taper Small
2
3     Cabbage  Green    Big Round  ...         Peas  Taper Small        1
0

[4 rows x 7 columns]
     VEGETABLE      COLOR         SHAPE  QUANTITY
1      Brinjal     Purple      Elongate         5
2      Brinjal  Wheatish          Round        10
3       Tomato        Red         Round         0
4   LadyFinger      Green   Taper Small         1
5      Cabbage      Green     Big Round         2
6  Cauliflower      White  Flower Round         3
7      Raddish     Orange     Taper mid         2
8       Carrot      White    Taper Long         0
1        Beans      Green   Taper Small         2
2         Peas      Green   Taper Small        10
3     Capsicum     Yellow          Oval        15
```

(b)

16.10 Matplotlib: Basics

Matplotlib is a popular library for data visualization. It is an open-source, 2D plotting library for numerical data.

- It is used in data analysis. The data is transformed into graphics.
- It is used for plotting figures, like pie chart, histogram, scatterplot, and graphs.
- `pyplot` is a state-based interface of Matplotlib. It provides an interface like MATLAB.
- `pyplot` allows to plot figures such as line plot, scatter plot, and histogram.
- `Matplotlib pyplot` interface enables creation of visualizations with a few lines of code.
- Several customization options for the plots exist, like, color, marker, annotation, and legends.
- Matplotlib can be integrated easily with libraries, like NumPy and Pandas. The data can be visualized from the data analysis tools. It is user-friendly, flexible, and customizable.
- It also allows 3-D plot by importing the `mplot3d toolkit`, from Matplotlib package.

16.10.1 Import matplotlib.pyplot as plt

A common way to use Matplotlib in a Python code is to import the library. For doing this, you need not write `matplotlib` each time you use the library; you can use `plt`. So, include the following statement at the beginning of each Python file, as follows:

import matplotlib.pyplot as plt

where, `plt` is common abbreviation used by Python community for `matplotlib pyplot.`

The standard Python does not come with an installed Matplotlib module. Matplotlib is simple to install. You can do by the following command:

pip install matplotlib

In case you are using Anaconda, you can install Matplotlib using the following command:

conda install matplotlib

Some of the key benefits of importing `matplotlib.pyplot` are:

- `pyplot` provides functions to add plot elements, like lines, images, and text to the axes in the current figure.
- Several Matplotlib utilities are present in the pyplot submodule.
- `pyplot` supports popular plots such as bar graph, pie chart, histogram, line chart, and scatter plot.
- `pyplot` provides easy-to-use interface for making different kinds of plots. The interface provides high-level method for drawing graphs with little coding.

16.10.2 Figure in Matplotlib

- Figure object is a bounded space. It is a canvas that holds the graphs or plots.
- It is the top-level container for all the plot elements.
- The graphs and plots in Matplotlib are plotted within a figure.
- A figure contains one or more than one axes or plots.
- When a graph is plotted, the figure is generated automatically, on which the plot is drawn.
- Multiple figures can be created, the properties of figures can be changed, and subplots can be added to the figure.

The function used for creating a new figure is: `matplotlib.pyplot.figure()`.

`plt` is a common alias of `matplotlib.pyplot.` To use the `figure()` function in a code, the following syntax is used:

```
import matplotlib.pyplot as plt
plt.figure(num=None,figsize=None,     dpi=None,     facecolor=None,
edgecolor=None,frameon=True,FigureClass=<class 'matplotlib.figure.
Figure'>, clear=False, **kwargs)
```

where,

- o `num` is provided, and a figure with this id already exists.
- o `figsize` specifies width, height in inches. It is of type float.
- o `dpi` is resolution of the figure.
- o `facecolor` is background color.
- o `edgecolor` is border color.
- o `frameon` suppresses figure frame.
- o `FigureClass` uses custom figure instance.
- o `clear`: If True and figure already exists, then it is cleared.
- o `Return` returns the values that follow it.
- o `figure`: The returned figure instance is passed to new_figure_manager in backend.

The properties of `figure()` function like size, dpi, face color, edge color, can be changed. For this, pass the parameters with specific values.

16.11 CREATION OF FIGURE

The different parameters of figure and axes are discussed here.

- **Axes:** It is a fixed reference line for the measurement of coordinates. A figure contains usually more than one axes (plots) and it may contain two or three in case of three-dimensional structure or objects. It also sets the location of the figure. Each axis has a title, an X–label, and Y–label.
  - o To add axis use:
    ```
    plt.axes(*args, **kwargs)
    ```
  - o Limits may be set. Either none or all of the limits must be given.
    ```
    ax.set(xlim=(xmin, xmax), ylim=(ymin, ymax))
    ```
  - o To add axes to the current figure:
    ```
    plt.axes(arg=None,projection=None,xlabel=None,ylabel=None,
    title=None)
    ```
  - o Some examples:
    ```
    fig,ax = plt.subplots(1,1)
    ax.hist(marks,bins=n_bins,color='red',edgecolor='black')
    ax.set_title("Histogram")
    ax.set_xlabel('Marks')
    ax.set_ylabel('Number of Students')
    ax = plt.axes()
    ax.bar(X,data[0],color='black',width=0.2, label='Asha')
    ```
- **Label:** It is used to assign names to x-axis and y-axis or title of the plot.
  - o To assign labels use the following functions for *x* and *y* axis,
    ```
    plt.xlabel(xlabel, fontdict=None, labelpad=None)
    plt.ylabel(ylabel, fontdict=None, labelpad=None)
    ```

- An example:
```
plt.xlabel('Students')
plt.ylabel('Marks')
```

- **Ticks**: Ticks are markers which help to denote data points on the axes. For a 2-D plot, there is x-tick and y-tick.
  - The following function may be used for assigning ticks.
    ```
    plt.xticks(ticks=None, labels=None, **kwargs)
    ```
    where,
    `ticks` is tick location.
    `label` is the label to place at given ticks location.
    `**kwargs` is text properties to control label appearance.
  - Some examples:
    ```
    plt.xticks(x, ('Asha', 'Usha', 'Isha'))
    plt.yticks(np.arange(0, 350, 40))
    ```
- **Legend**: To label data series plotted on a graph. Legends help to understand the plotted data.
  - To add a legend, use this function:
    ```
    plt.legend(['label1','label2'],facecolor=None,loc='upper
    center',shadow=True,edgecolor=None,title=None))
    ```
  - To locate string in different locations of graph use loc = '— —'
    The different options are:
    best, upper right, upper left, lower left, lower right, right, center left, center right
    lower center, upper center, center.
  - Some examples:
    ```
    plt.legend(['Data 1', 'Data 2'], loc=4)
    plt.legend(loc='best')
    plt.legend()
    ```
- **Grid lines:** They are lines that cross the chart plot to show axis divisions. The lines help the viewer to see the value that is represented by an unlabeled data point. Grid lines come in two types: major and minor.
  - To add grid lines, use this function:
    ```
    plt.grid(b=None, which='major', axis='both', **kwargs)
    ```
  - An example:
    ```
    ax.grid(b=True,color='grey',linestyle='-',linewidth=2,
    which='both', axis='both')
    ```
- **Markers**: The plotted points are called markers.
  - It allows you to set the marker style, marker edge color (mec), marker fill color (mfc) and much more. Black color is represented as 'k'.
  - Some examples:
    ```
    plt.plot(data1,color='black',marker='o', mec='k',mfc='r')
    plt.plot(data2,color='red',marker='o', mec='r',mfc='k')
    ```

- Some important functions are:
  - o `plt.show()`: to display the figure.
  - o `plt.savefig()`: to save any figure.
  - o `plt.title()` : to set title for the axes in any figure.
  - o `plt.annotate()` : to add any comment or text or any arrows /marks in the figure.

When we plot a single graph using `plt` such as `plt.bar(...)`, a `Figure` instance is created implicitly, and an `axes` inside the Figure object is created.

For example, when a figure is created as:

```
fig=plt.figure(figsize=[5,7],facecolor='blue',
edgecolor='black',dpi=360)
```

The output is:

```
<Figure size 1800x2520 with 0 Axes>
```

Thus, a new figure of size 1800x2520 is created.

16.12 VISUALIZATION USING MATPLOTLIB

- There are many Matplotlib plots which are used in Machine Learning for analysis and visualization. We discuss the following common plots here:
  - o Line chart
  - o Scatter plot
  - o Bar plot
  - o Histogram
  - o Pie chart
  - o Box plot
  - o Stem plot
  - o Heatmap

16.12.1 Line Plot

- A line plot displays information as a series of data points connected by a straight line.
- Each data point is called 'marker' that is plotted and relates to a line.
- It can be plotted using `matplotlib.pyplot.plot()` function.

  ```
  plt.plot(x,y, scalex=True, scaley=True, data=None, color=None)
  ```

  - o Some examples:

  ```
  plt.plot(np.arange(10),data1,color="black",linewidth=2)
  plt.plot(np.random.rand(20))
  plt.plot(x, y)
  ```

- **Area plot** is based on line plot. It displays quantitative data. The area between axis and line is shown as colored. It is useful for comparing two or more quantities in a graph.

Example 16.13: (a) Line plots (b) Output

```
import pandas as pd
import numpy as np
import matplotlib.pyplot as plt
#========Line Plot - Simple==========================
data1 = [2, 6, 9, 10, 8, 13, 10, 13, 15, 10]
#marker:ms-marker size, mec-marker edgecolor, mfc-marker fillcolor
plt.plot(data1, color='black',marker = 'o', mec = 'k',mfc = 'r')
plt.savefig('line1.png', dpi=300, bbox_inches='tight')
plt.show()
#=========Line Plot - Multiple===================
data2 = [5, 8, 11, 14, 6, 15, 8, 9, 5, 12]
plt.plot(data1, color='black',marker = 'o', mec = 'k',mfc = 'r')
plt.plot(data2, color='red',marker = 'o', mec = 'r',mfc = 'k',alpha=0.5)
plt.title('Line Plot - Multiple')
plt.ylabel('x-axis')
plt.xlabel('y-axis')
plt.legend(['Data 1', 'Data 2'], loc=4)
plt.show()
#=========Line Plot - Multiple sin wave=============
fig1 = plt.figure()
axs = plt.axes()
axs.grid(color='k', linestyle='--', linewidth=2,alpha=0.1)
x = np.linspace(0, 15, 1000)
plt.plot(x, np.sin(x - 0), color='black',alpha=0.5,label='sin x')
plt.plot(x, np.sin(x - 0.5), color='orange',label='sin(x-0.5)')
plt.plot(x, np.sin(x - 1),color='red' ,label='sin(x-1)')
plt.legend(loc='best')
plt.show()
```

```
#=========Area Plot=====================
plt.fill_between(np.arange(10),data1, color="orange", alpha=0.5)
plt.plot(np.arange(10), data1, color="black", alpha=0.6, linewidth=2)
plt.title('Area Plot')
plt.tick_params(labelsize=10)
plt.xlabel('x-axis')
plt.ylabel('y-axis')
plt.show()
```

(a)

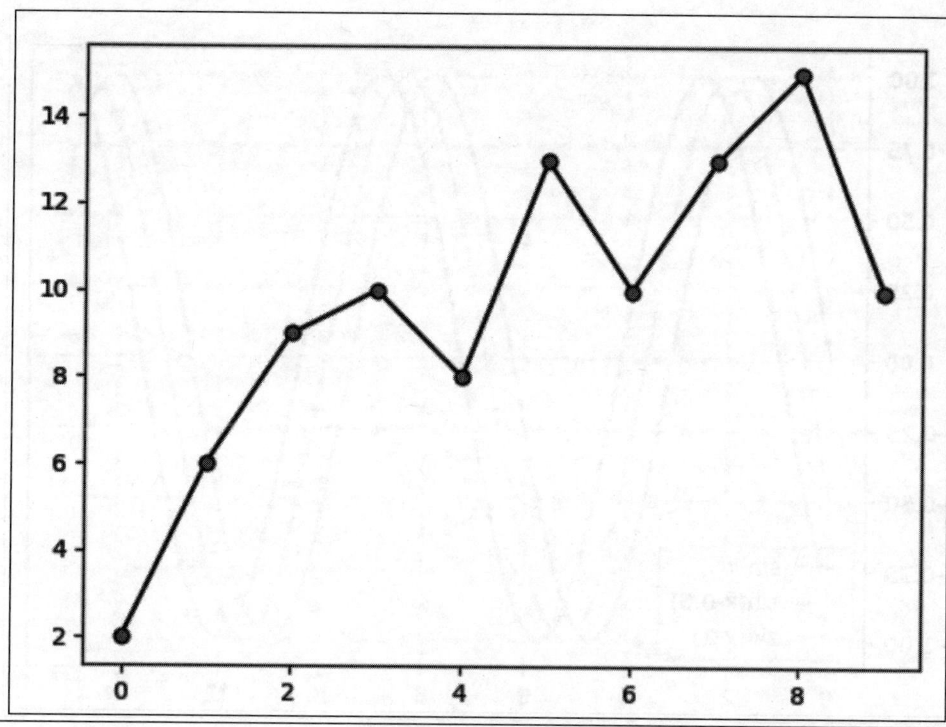
14
12
10
8
6
4
2
0
2
4
6
8

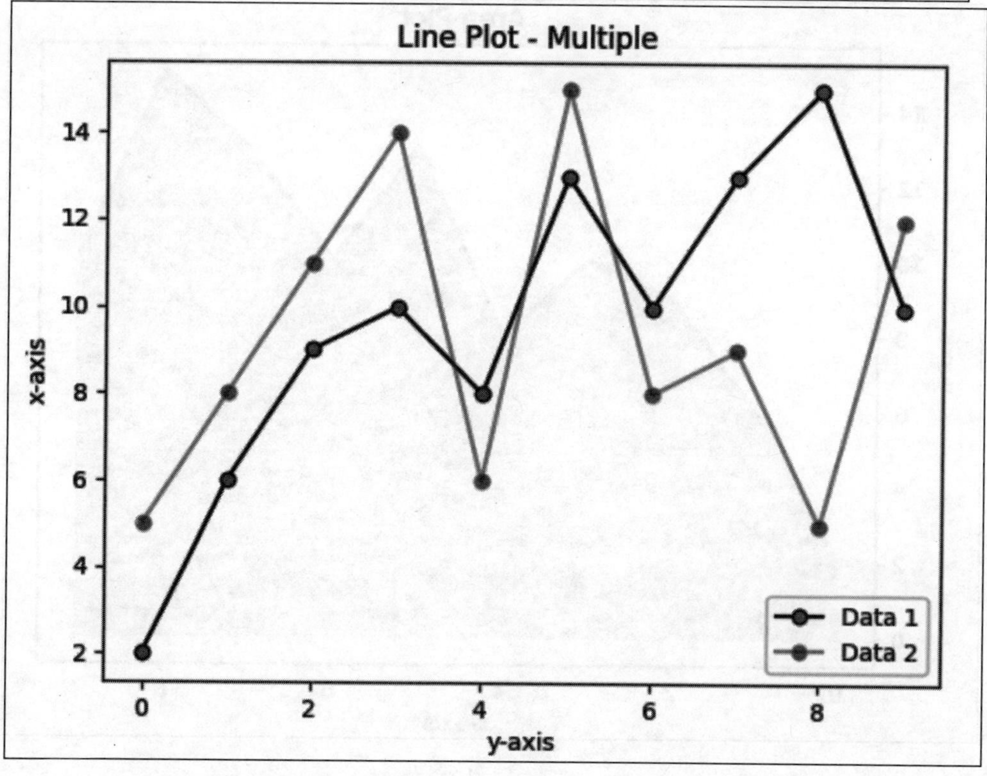
Line Plot - Multiple
x-axis
y-axis
Data 1
Data 2
14
12
10
8
6
4
2
0
2
4
6
8

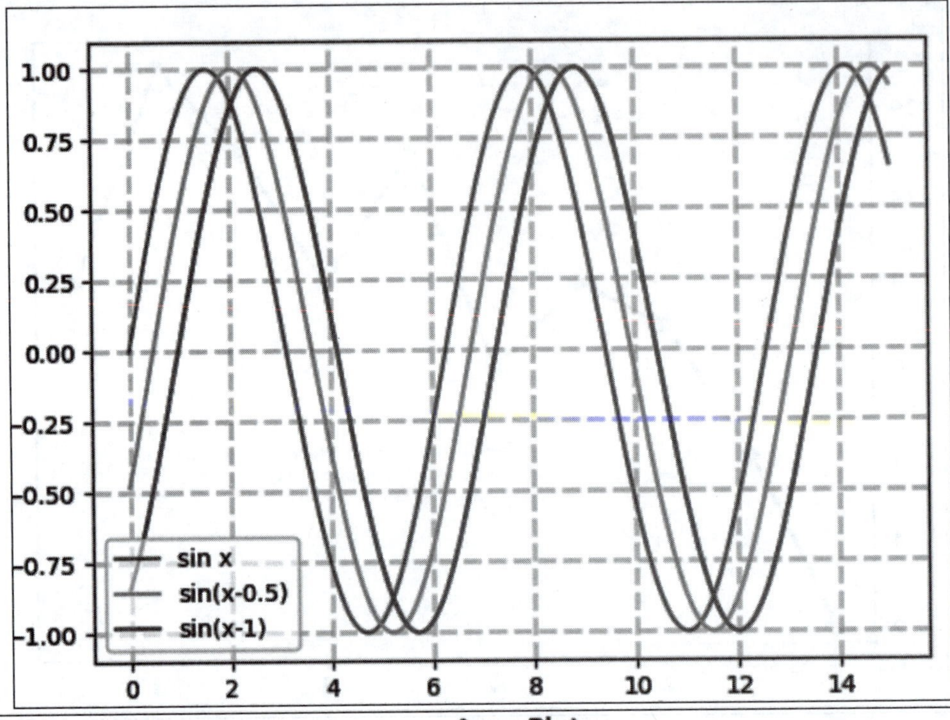
1.00
0.75
0.50
0.25
0.00
-0.25
-0.50
-0.75
-1.00
sin x
sin(x-0.5)
sin(x-1)
0
2
4
6
8
10
12
14

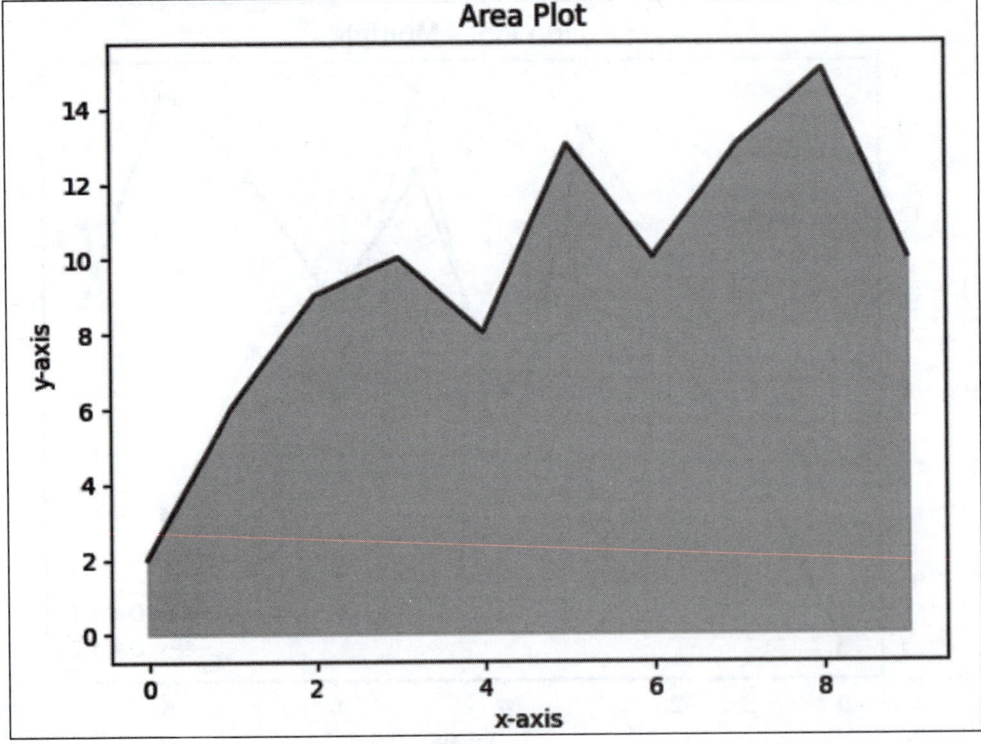
Area Plot
14
12
10
8
6
4
2
0
y-axis
0
2
4
6
8
x-axis

(b)

16.12.2 Scatter Plot

- It shows the relationship between two or more variables.
- It displays the value of variables in two dimensions.
- The data is scattered and not confined to a range.
- The data of each variable is represented by a different color.
- Each dot represents an observation.
- It can be plotted using `matplotlib.pyplot.scatter()` function.
  `plt.scatter(x, y, s=None, c=None, marker=None, cmap=None, norm=None, vmin=None, vmax=None, alpha=None, linewidths=None, verts=None, edgecolors=None,data=None)`

Example 16.14: (a) Scatter plots (b) Output

```
import pandas as pd
import numpy as np
import matplotlib.pyplot as plt

np.random.seed(19680801)
N = 75
x = np.random.rand(N)
y = np.random.rand(N)
plt.scatter(x, y,c='black')
plt.show()
plt.scatter(x, y, s=(30 * x)**2, c='red') #bubble
plt.show()
```

(a)

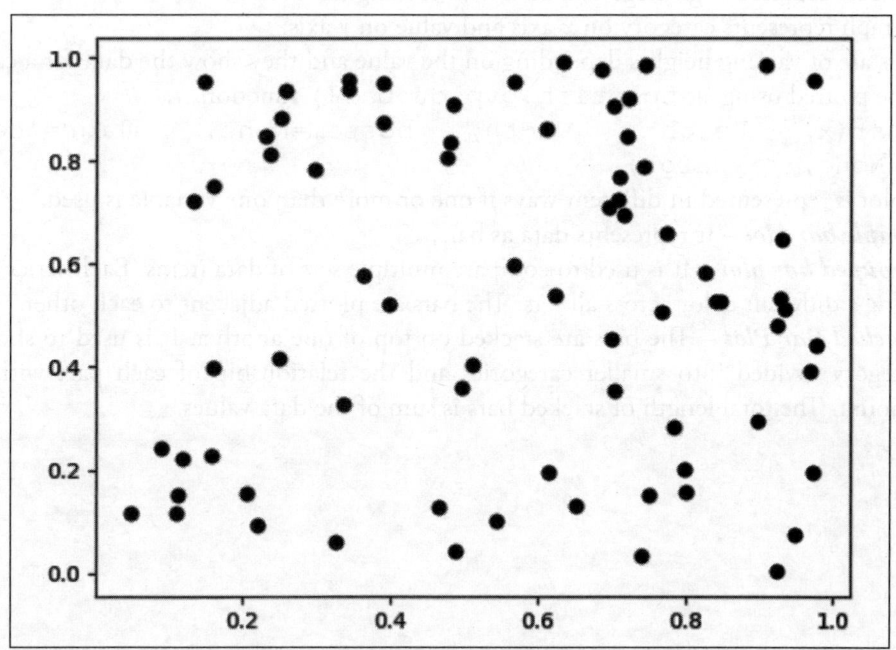

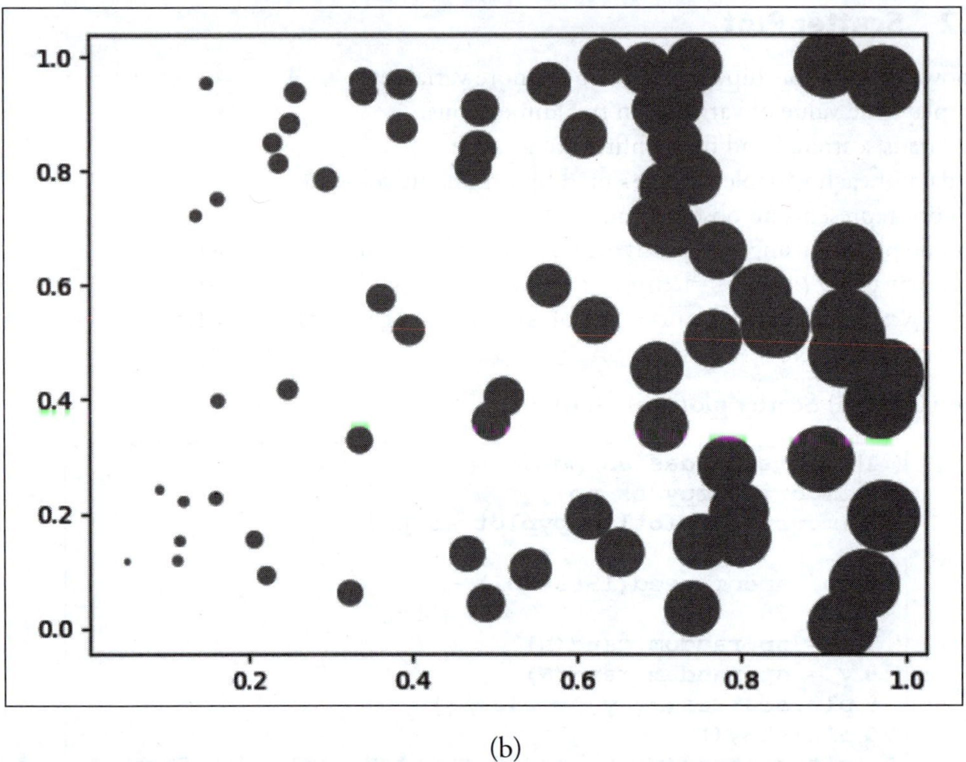

(b)

16.12.3 Bar Plot

- It is used for representing categorical data with rectangular bars.
- A bar graph represents category on *x*-axis and value on *y*-axis.
- The bars are of varying heights depending on the value and they show the data for a category.
- It can be plotted using `matplotlib.pyplot.bar()` function.
  `plt.bar(x, height, width, bottom=None, align='center', data=None, **kwargs)`
- A bar plot is represented in different ways if one or more than one variable is used.
  - ***Simple bar plot*** – It represents data as bars.
  - ***Grouped bar plot*** – It is used to compare multiple sets of data items. Each series is denoted using a different color across all sets. The bars are plotted adjacent to each other.
  - ***Stacked Bar Plot*** – The bars are stacked on top of one another. It is used to show a larger category divided into smaller categories and the relationship of each part with the total amount. The total length of stacked bars is sum of the data values.

Example 16.15: (a) Bar plot – Simple, grouped and stacked plots (b) Output

```
import pandas as pd
import numpy as np
import matplotlib.pyplot as plt
fig1 = plt.figure()
axs = plt.axes()
Height=[160, 156, 165, 156, 155, 148, 163]
Stud = ["Asha", "Usha", "Isha", "Disha", "Sasha","Risha", "Nisha"]
Weight = [65, 66, 55, 80, 90, 56, 70]
plt.ylabel('Student')
plt.xlabel('Height')
plt.title('Student-Height Plot')
axs.bar(Stud, Height,width=0.5,color='blue',alpha=0.5 )
plt.show()
#=========Grouped Bar Plot=========
data = [[80, 72, 95],[76, 88, 90],[90, 95, 99]]
label=['Test-1','Test-2','Test-3']
X = np.arange(len(label))
Y = [0.25,1.25, 2.25]
fig = plt.figure()
ax = plt.axes()
ax.bar(X + 0.00, data[0], color = 'black',width = 0.2,
       alpha=0.5,label='Asha')
ax.bar(X + 0.25, data[1], color = 'red', width = 0.20,
       alpha=0.5,label='Usha')
ax.bar(X + 0.50, data[2], color = 'orange', width = 0.20,
       alpha=0.5,label='Isha')
plt.title('Subjects-Marks comparison of 3 students')
plt.xlabel('Subjects')
plt.xticks(Y,label)
plt.ylabel('Marks')
plt.legend()
plt.show()
```

```
#==========Stacked Bar Plot===============
# Marks stacked marks of each student
test1 = [80, 72, 95]
test2 = [76, 88, 90]
test3 = [90, 95, 99]
x = np.arange(3)
plt.bar(x, test1, width= 0.20, color='k',label='Test-1')
plt.bar(x, test2, width= 0.20, bottom=test1,
        color='orange',label='Test-2')
plt.bar(x, test3, width= 0.20, bottom=np.add(test1, test2),
        color='r',label='Test-3')
plt.title('Name of Student')
plt.xlabel('Students')
plt.xticks(x, ('Asha', 'Usha', 'Isha'))
plt.ylabel('Marks')
plt.yticks(np.arange(0, 350, 40))
plt.legend()
plt.show()
```

(a)

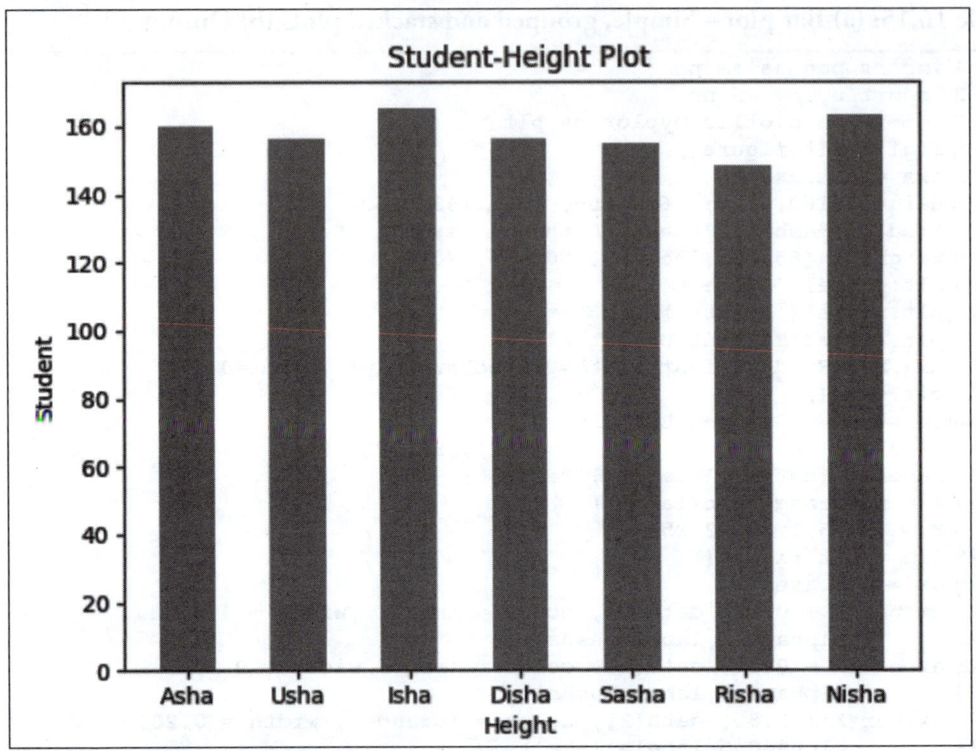
Student-Height Plot
Student
Height
160
140
120
100
80
60
40
20
0
Asha
Usha
Isha
Disha
Sasha
Risha
Nisha

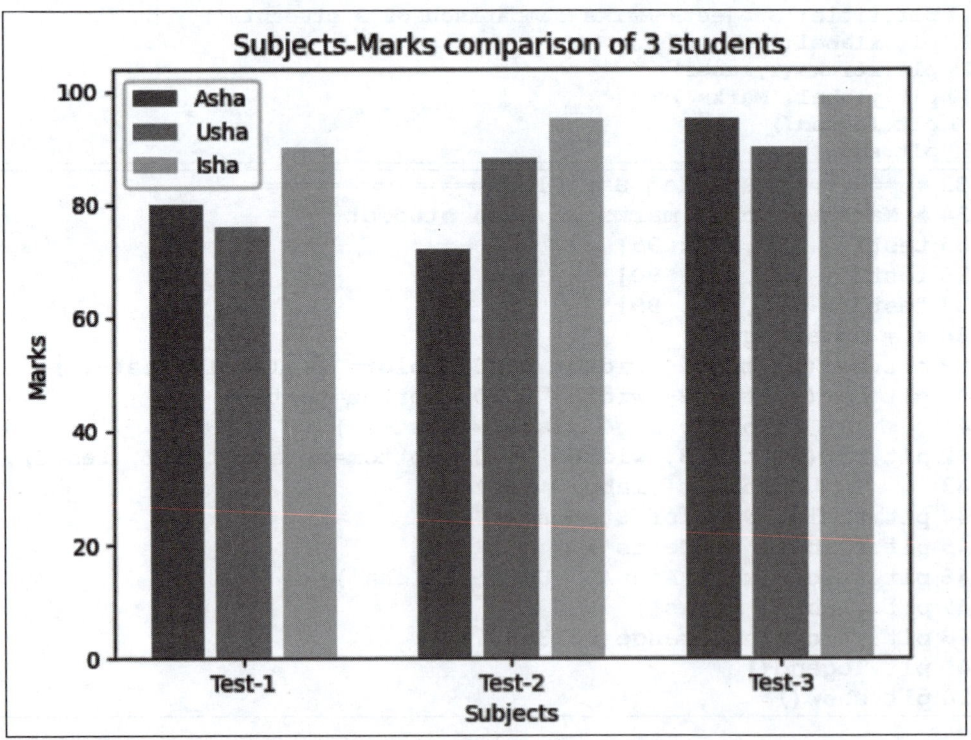
Subjects-Marks comparison of 3 students
Asha
Usha
Isha
Marks
Subjects
100
80
60
40
20
0
Test-1
Test-2
Test-3

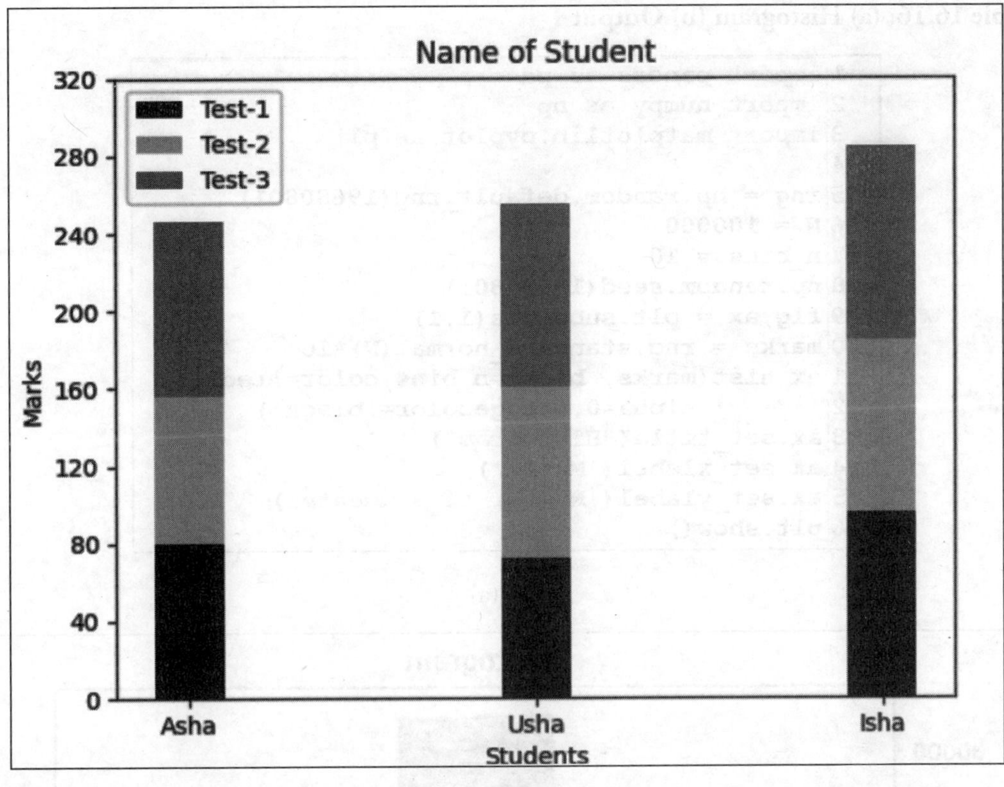

(b)

16.12.4 Histogram

- It is used for representing distribution of numerical data.
- It is an estimate of the probability distribution of a continuous variable.
- Histogram is used to plot data over a range of values.
- It uses bar representation to show the data belonging to each range.
- A histogram represents range on *x*-axis and height of data for a range on *y*-axis.
- It can be plotted using `matplotlib.pyplot.hist()` function.

```
plt.hist(x, bins=None, range=None, density=None, weights=None,
cumulative=False, bottom=None, histtype='bar', align='mid',
orientation='vertical', rwidth=None, log=False, color=None,
label=None, stacked=False, normed=None, data=None,)
```

Example 16.16: (a) Histogram (b) Output

```
import pandas as pd
import numpy as np
import matplotlib.pyplot as plt

rng = np.random.default_rng(19680801)
N = 100000
n_bins = 10
np.random.seed(19680801)
fig,ax = plt.subplots(1,1)
marks = rng.standard_normal(N)*10
ax.hist(marks, bins =n_bins,color='red',
        alpha=0.5,edgecolor='black')
ax.set_title("Histogram")
ax.set_xlabel('Marks')
ax.set_ylabel('Number of Students')
plt.show()
```

(a)

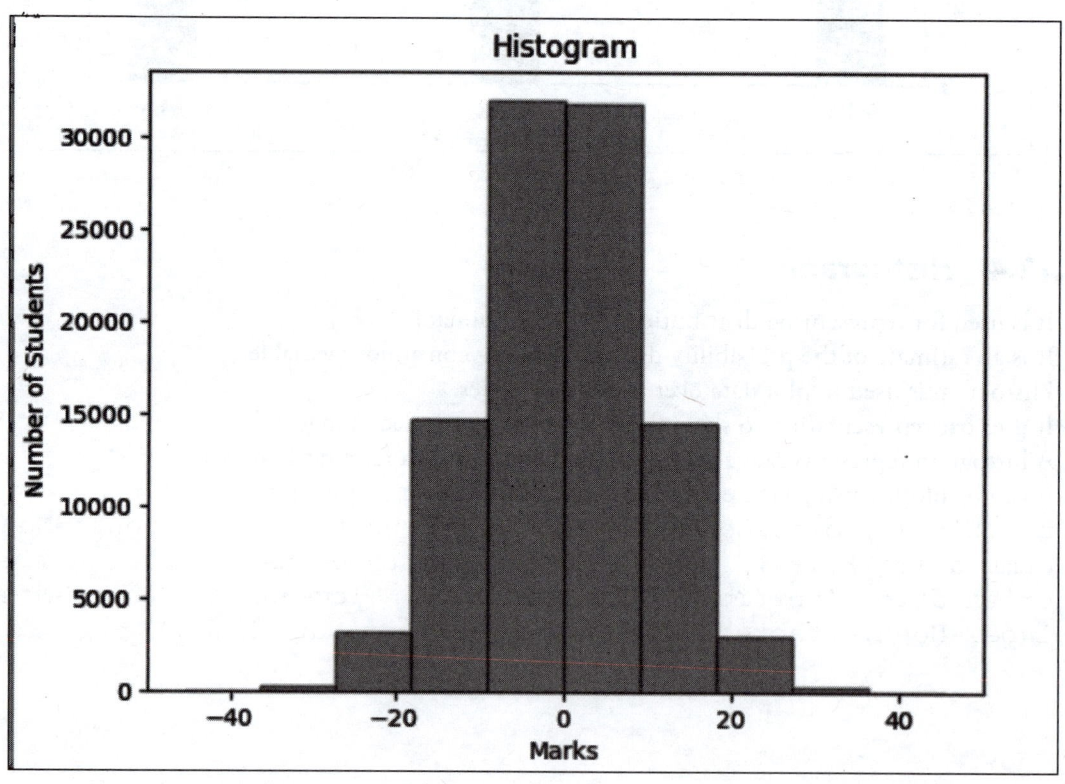

(b)

16.12.5 Pie Plot

- A step-type histogram does not have bars filled with any color.
- It is a circular statistical graphic.
- It is divided into slices to illustrate numerical proportion.
- The arc length of each slice is proportional to the quantity it represents.
- It can be plotted using `matplotlib.pyplot.pie()` function.

```
plt.pie(x, explode=None, labels=None, colors=None, autopct=None,
pctdistance=0.6, shadow=False, labeldistance=1.1, radius=None,
counterclock=True,center=(0, 0), frame=False, rotatelabels=False,
data=None)
```

- A **nested pie plot** is a multi-level pie plot. It displays multiple series in a single pie chart.

Example 16.16: (a) Pie chart (b) Output

```
import pandas as pd
import numpy as np
import matplotlib.pyplot as plt
labels = 'Long Q', 'MCQ', 'True-False','Coding','Find Error'
marks = [20, 40, 25, 50,30]
color={'grey', 'orange','red','c','pink'}
fig1, axs = plt.subplots()
axs.set(title='Marks in different sections of Test paper')
axs.pie(marks, colors=color,labels=labels,autopct='%1.1f%%',
        shadow=False, startangle=90,radius=1)
axs.axis('equal')  # pie drawn as a circle.
plt.show()
```

(a)

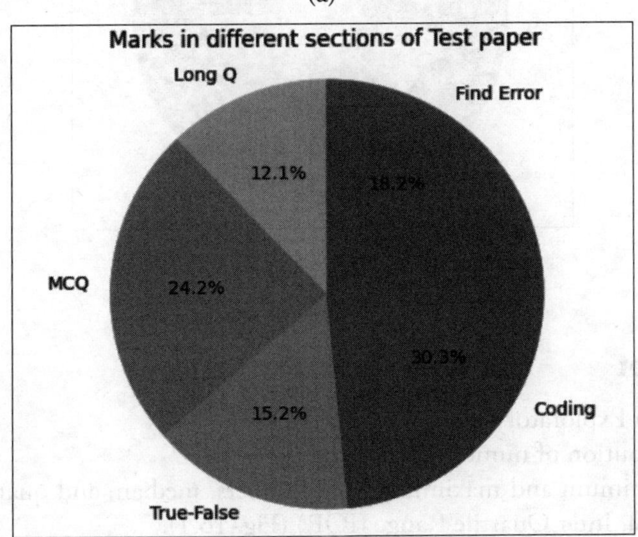

(b)

Example 16.17: (a) Nested Pie chart (b) Output

```
import pandas as pd
import numpy as np
import matplotlib.pyplot as plt

fig, axs = plt.subplots()
size = 0.4
data = np.array([[50., 44.], [29., 30.], [69., 20.]])
lbl = 'A', 'B', 'C'
cmap = plt.get_cmap("tab20c")
color_out = cmap(np.arange(3)*4)
color_in = cmap(np.array([1, 2, 5, 7, 9, 10]))
axs.pie(data.sum(axis=1), radius=1,labels=lbl,colors=color_out,
        wedgeprops=dict(width=size, edgecolor='w'))
axs.pie(data.flatten(), radius=1-size, autopct='%1.1f%%',colors=color_in,
        wedgeprops=dict(width=size, edgecolor='w'))
axs.set(aspect="equal", title='Nested Pie')
plt.show()
```

(a)

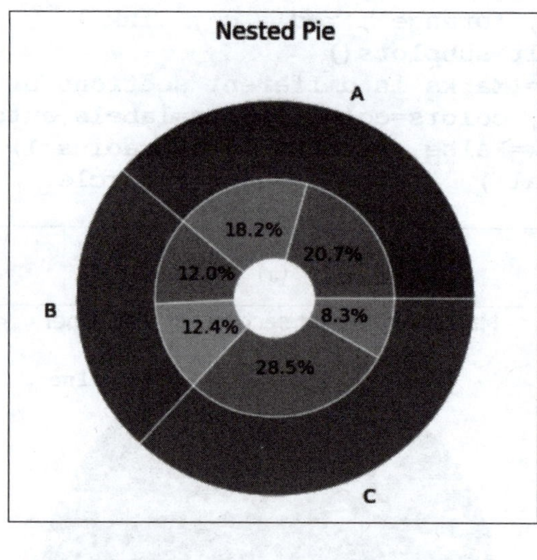

(b)

16.12.6 Box Plot

- Box plot is used in Exploratory Data Analysis (EDA).
- It shows the distribution of numerical data and skewness.
- It displays the minimum and maximum score, outliers, median, and quartiles – lower quartile, upper quartile, and, Inter Quartile Range (IQR) (Fig. 16.1).

- It can be plotted using `matplotlib.pyplot.boxplot()` function.
  `plt.boxplot(x,patch_artist=False,notch=False)`
- A box plot is represented in different ways:
  - o Single box plot or Multiple box plots
  - o Box plots filled with same color or different colors

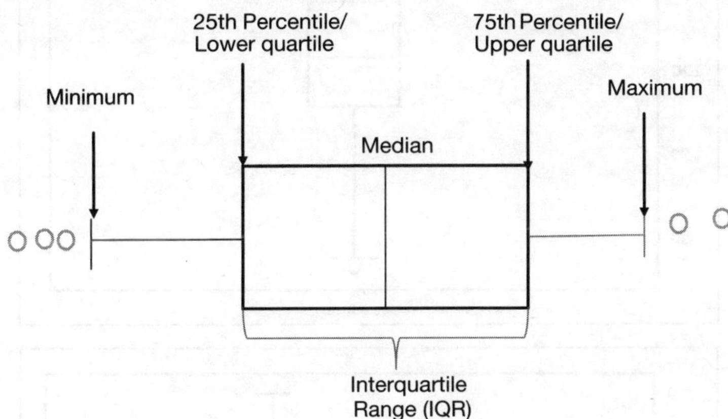

Figure 16.1 Box plot markings

Example 16.18: (a) Box plot – Simple and Multiple with color (b) Output

```
import pandas as pd
import numpy as np
import matplotlib.pyplot as plt
#======Simple box plot===========
box_plot_data=[np.random.normal(100, 10, 200)]
plt.boxplot(box_plot_data,patch_artist=False)
plt.show()
#===Multiple box plot with color==========
data1 =np.linspace(-10,100,num=1000)
data2 =np.linspace(-5,200,num=1000)
data3 =np.linspace(-10,300,num=1000)
data4 =np.linspace(-10,250,num=1500)
box_plot_data=[data1,data2,data3,data4]
box = plt.boxplot(box_plot_data, patch_artist=True,
                labels=['N1','N2','N3','N4'], )
colors = ['orange', 'c', 'cyan', 'pink']
for patch, color in zip(box['boxes'], colors):
    patch.set_facecolor(color)
plt.show()
```

(a)

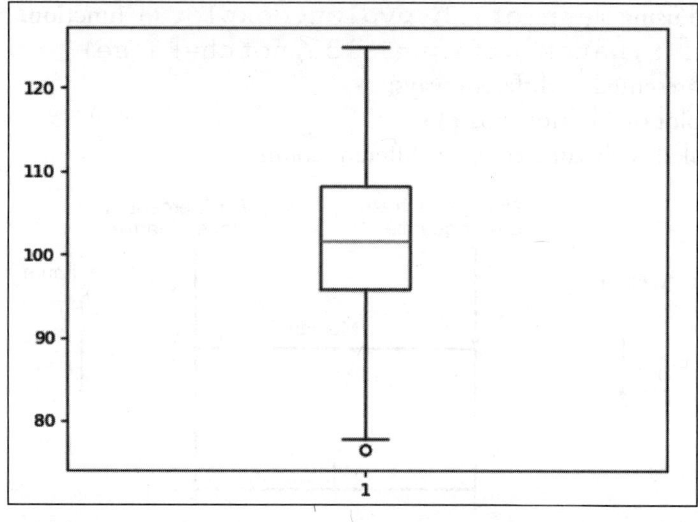

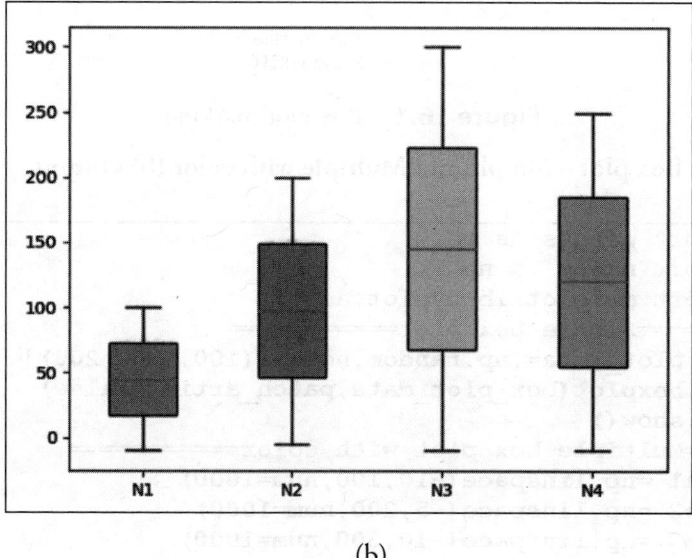

(b)

16.12.7 Stem Plot

- Stem plot is also known as the Stem-and-Leaf plot.
- It is used to display quantitative data, generally from small datasets (50 or fewer observations).
- It shows absolute frequency in different classes similar to the frequency distribution table or a histogram.
- It can be plotted using `matplotlib.pyplot.stem()` function.
  `plt.stem(x, y, linefmt=None, markerfmt=None, basefmt=None, bottom=0, label=None, use_line_collection=False, data=None)`

Example 16.19: (a) Stem plot (b) Output

```
import pandas as pd
import numpy as np
import matplotlib.pyplot as plt

marks = [80, 76, 90, 72, 88, 95, 95, 90, 99, 78, 88, 89]
stud = [1, 1, 1, 2, 2, 2, 3, 3, 3, 4, 4, 4]
plt.ylabel('marks')
plt.xlabel('stud')
plt.xlim(0, 5)
plt.stem(stud, marks,use_line_collection=True,markerfmt='C3o',
        linefmt='C7-',basefmt='C7-')
plt.show()
```

(a)

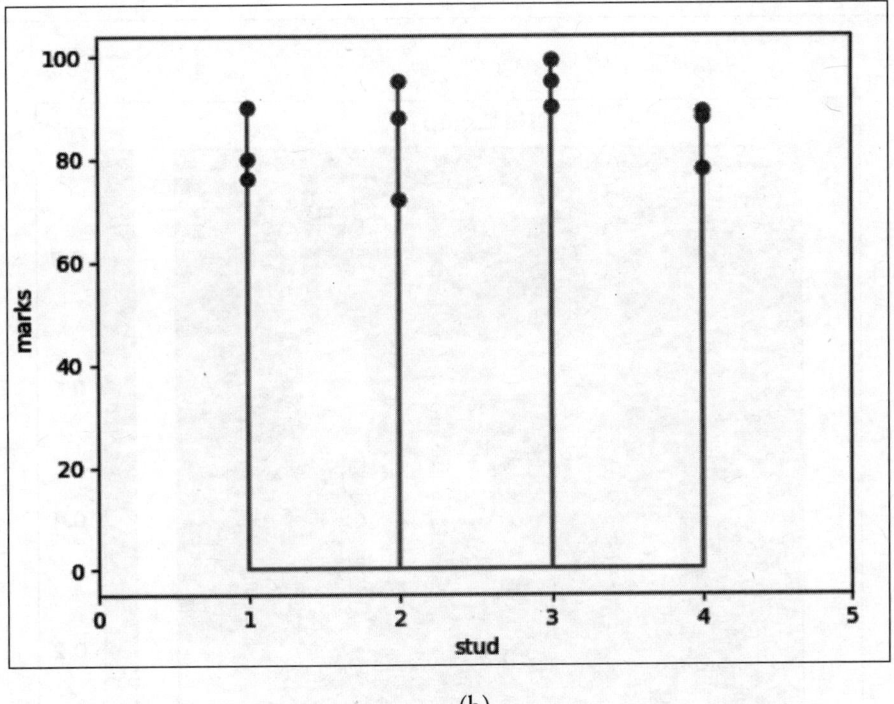

(b)

16.12.8 Heatmap

- Heatmap is used to see changes in behavior or gradual changes in data.
- It uses different colors to represent different values.
- Based on how the colors range in hues, intensity, etc., it tells us how the phenomenon varies.

- It is a 2-D visualization technique in which numerical data (where individual data points contained in the matrix) are represented using different colors.
- It is a very useful technique for multivariate data analysis.
- It displays variance across multiple variables and the correlation between them.
- It can be plotted using `matplotlib.pyplot.imshow()` function.

Example 16.20: (a) Heatmap (b) Output

```
import pandas as pd
import numpy as np
import matplotlib.pyplot as plt

data = np.random.random(( 10 , 10 ))
plt.title( "Heatmap" )
plt.imshow(data, cmap='Reds', interpolation='nearest')
plt.colorbar()
plt.show()
```

(a)

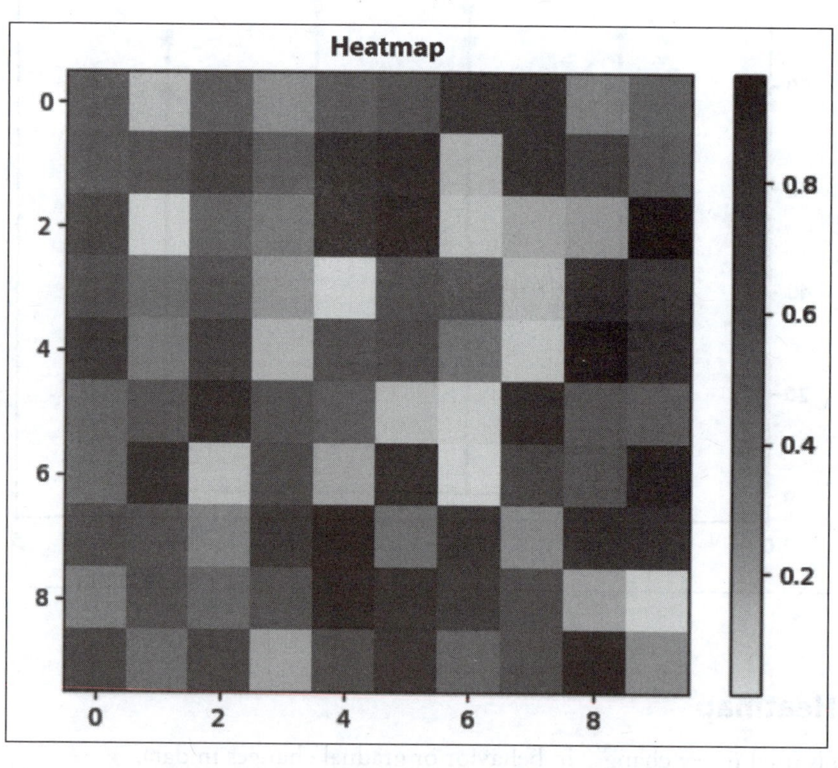

(b)

16.13 Solved Examples

1. Find the output.

```
import numpy as np
a = np.array([[1, 2, 3, 4, 5]])
print(a[1])
```

Output

```
IndexError: index 1 is out of bounds for axis 0 with size 1
```

2. Find the output.

```
a = np.array([[1, 2, 3, 4, 5]])
print(a[0])
print(a[:, 1])
```

Output

```
[1 2 3 4 5]
[2]
```

3. Find the output

```
a = np.array([1, 2, 3], dtype = complex)
print(a)
```

Output

```
[1.+0.j 2.+0.j 3.+0.j]
```

4. Find the output.

```
import numpy as np
a = np.array([[1, 2], [3, 4]])
b = np.array([[5, 6], [7, 8]])
c = np.dot(a, b)
print(c)
```

Output

```
[[19 22]
 [43 50]]
```

5. Find the output.

```
import numpy as np
a = np.array([3, 5, 7])
b = np.array([2, 4, 6])
c = np.outer(a, b)
print(c)
```

Output

```
[[ 6 12 18]
 [10 20 30]
 [14 28 42]]
```

6. Find the output.

```
my_dict = {1: ['12', '13'], 2: ['11', '21'], 3: ['22', '44']}
print(pd.DataFrame(my_dict))
```

Output

```
    1   2   3
0  12  11  22
1  13  21  44
```

7. Find the output.

```
a = np.arange(2, 12).reshape(5, 2)
print(a.ndim)
print(a.shape)
s1 = pd.Series(a)
print(s1)
```

Output

```
2
(5, 2)
```

```
ValueError: Data must be 1-dimensional, got ndarray of shape
(5, 2) instead
```

16.14 Programming Examples

Program 16.1: Write a NumPy program to compute the cross product of two given vectors.
x = [2, 4]
y = [6, 6]
result = np.cross(x, y) = 2 * 6 – 4 * 6=12-24 = -12

```
import numpy as np
# Cross product of 1D arrays
x = [2, 4]
y = [6, 6]
result = np.cross(x, y)
print(result)

# Cross product of 2D arrays
import numpy as np
x = [[2, 4],
     [5, 6]]
y = [[4, 5],
     [6, 7]]
result = np.cross(x, y)
print(result)

#Cross product of 2D arrays using @ operator.
import numpy as np
X = np.array([[1,2,3],
              [2,5,6],
              [1,2,1]])
Y = np.array([[-5, 5,-10],
              [ 1, 2, 8],
              [ 5, 4, 1]])
Z = X @ Y
print(Z)
```

Output

```
-12
[-6 -1]
[[12 21  9]
 [25 44 26]
 [ 2 13  7]]
```

Program 16.2: Write a NumPy program to calculate the QR decomposition of a given matrix.
The QR decomposition of a matrix A is:
A = Q R
where, Q is orthogonal, and
R is an upper-triangular matrix.
In NumPy, QR decomposition is calculated with `numpy.linalg.qr()`.

```
import numpy as np

mat1 = np.array([[1, 2, 3], [2, 3, 4]])
print("Matrix \n",mat1)
q, r = np.linalg.qr(mat1)
print('Q:\n', q)
print('R:\n', r)
print("*" * 20)
mat2 = np.array([[1, 1], [2, 2]])
print("Matrix \n",mat2)
q, r = np.linalg.qr(mat2)
print('Q:\n', q)
print('R:\n', r)
print("*" * 20)
mat3 = np.array([[5, 10, -10], [12, 24, -30],
                 [-20, -40, 76]], dtype=np.int32)
print("Matrix \n",mat3)
q, r = np.linalg.qr(mat3)
print('Q:\n', q)
print('R:\n', r)
```

Output

```
Matrix
 [[1 2 3]
 [2 3 4]]
Q:
 [[-0.4472136  -0.89442719]
 [-0.89442719  0.4472136 ]]
R:
 [[-2.23606798 -3.57770876 -4.91934955]
 [ 0.         -0.4472136  -0.89442719]]
********************
Matrix
 [[1 1]
 [2 2]]
Q:
 [[-0.4472136  -0.89442719]
 [-0.89442719  0.4472136 ]]
R:
 [[-2.23606798e+00 -2.23606798e+00]
 [ 0.00000000e+00  2.22044605e-16]]
********************
Matrix
 [[  5  10 -10]
 [ 12  24 -30]
 [-20 -40  76]]
Q:
 [[-0.2096109   0.9749048  -0.07499268]
 [-0.50306617 -0.04175956  0.86323842]
 [ 0.83844362  0.21867046  0.49919488]]
R:
 [[-2.38537209e+01 -4.77074418e+01  8.09098090e+01]
 [ 0.00000000e+00  7.94410929e-15  8.12269407e+00]
 [ 0.00000000e+00  0.00000000e+00  1.27915852e+01]]
```

Program 16.3: WAP to find Eigenvalues and Eigenvectors of a 2 × 2 and 3 × 3 matrix.

```
import numpy as np
import pandas as pd

m1 = np.array([[1, 2], [2, 3]])
print("Array:\n", m1)
eg_val1, eg_vec1 = np.linalg.eig(m1)
print("Eigen values of array:\n", eg_val1)
print("Eigenvectors of array:\n", eg_vec1)
print("*" * 20)
m2 = np.array([[1, 2, 3],
               [2, 3, 4],
               [4, 5, 6]])
print("Array:\n",m2)
eg_val2, eg_vec2 = np.linalg.eig(m2)
print("Eigen values of array:\n", eg_val2)
print("Eigenvectors of array:\n",eg_vec2)
```

Output

```
Array:
 [[1 2]
 [2 3]]
Eigen values of array:
 [-0.23606798  4.23606798]
Eigenvectors of array:
 [[-0.85065081 -0.52573111]
 [ 0.52573111 -0.85065081]]
********************
Array:
 [[1 2 3]
 [2 3 4]
 [4 5 6]]
Eigen values of array:
 [ 1.08309519e+01 -8.30951895e-01  1.01486082e-16]
Eigenvectors of array:
 [[ 0.34416959  0.72770285  0.40824829]
 [ 0.49532111  0.27580256 -0.81649658]
 [ 0.79762415 -0.62799801  0.40824829]]
```

Program 16.4: Write a Pandas program to convert a NumPy array to a Pandas series.

```
import numpy as np
import pandas as pd

arr = np.array([11, 34, 23, 56, 44, 77, 67, 87, 96, 99])
print("Numpy array\n", arr)
ser1 = pd.Series(arr)
print("Array to Series\n", ser1)

array = np.random.rand(7)
print("Numpy array \n", array)
series = pd.Series(array)
print("Pandas Series\n", series)
```

Output

```
Numpy array
 [11 34 23 56 44 77 67 87 96 99]
Array to Series
 0    11
1    34
2    23
3    56
4    44
5    77
6    67
7    87
8    96
9    99
dtype: int32
Numpy array
 [0.55648092 0.37390981 0.80484373 0.58615253 0.41530951 0.35
178071
 0.77276301]
Pandas Series
 0    0.556481
1    0.373910
2    0.804844
3    0.586153
4    0.415310
5    0.351781
6    0.772763
dtype: float64
```

Program 16.5: Write a Pandas program to convert a Pandas module series to Python lists and its type.

```
import numpy as np
import pandas as pd

num_df = pd.Series([2, 4, 6, 8, 10])
print("Series\n",num_df, "\tType =", type(num_df))
num_lst = num_df.tolist()
print("\nSeries to Python list")
print(num_lst,type(num_lst), '\n')
print("*" * 20)

d1 = np.array(['Apple','Banana','Orange','Pineapple'])
d1_ser = pd.Series(d1,index=[1, 2, 3,4])
print("Series\n",d1_ser, "\tType =", type(d1_ser))
print("\nSeries to Python list")
d1_lst = d1_ser.tolist()
print(d1_lst, type(d1_lst))
print("*" * 20)

item_qty = {'Pen':100., 'Pencil':80., 'Eraser': 95.}
item_qty_s = pd.Series(item_qty)
print("Series\n",item_qty_s,"\tType =",type(item_qty_s))
item_qty_lst = item_qty_s.tolist()
print("\nSeries to Python list")
print(item_qty_lst, type(item_qty_lst))
```

Output

```
Series
 0     2
1     4
2     6
3     8
4    10
dtype: int64     Type = <class 'pandas.core.series.Series'>

Series to Python list
[2, 4, 6, 8, 10] <class 'list'>
********************
Series
 1        Apple
2        Banana
3        Orange
4    Pineapple
dtype: object    Type = <class 'pandas.core.series.Series'>

Series to Python list
['Apple', 'Banana', 'Orange', 'Pineapple'] <class 'list'>
********************
Series
 Pen       100.0
Pencil     80.0
Eraser     95.0
dtype: float64   Type = <class 'pandas.core.series.Series'>

Series to Python list
[100.0, 80.0, 95.0] <class 'list'>
```

SUMMARY

- Python Standard Library consists of more than two hundred core modules.
- Python open-source libraries play a critical role in machine learning and data science for data preprocessing, data modeling and data visualization.
- NumPy, Pandas, Matplotlib, SciPy, and Scikit learn are some popular open-source libraries.
- Data cleaning, data transformation, and data selection are three common steps in data preprocessing.
- Handling duplicates, missing data and outliers, normalizing data, encoding categorical data, feature selection, and handling data errors are some tasks in data cleaning.
- Scaling, normalization, aggregation, discretization, encoding, and feature engineering are techniques for data transformation.
- Random sampling, stratified sampling, feature selection, and instance selection are techniques for data selection.
- Data modeling focuses on transformation of raw data into structural data to derive insights from the data.
- Data visualization deals with visual representation of data.
- NumPy is a popular scientific library for working with arrays in Python.
- Add, slice, multiply, flatten, reshape, and index are some basic array operations in NumPy.
- Python NumPy arrays are faster than Python list.
- The important attributes of ndarray, a *N*-dimensional array object in Python are – ndim, size, shape, dtype, itemsize, and data.
- A NumPy array can be created using – `array()`, `zeros()`, `ones()`, `empty()`, and `arrange()`.
- A vector is a single-dimension array.
- Several operations can be performed to update an array – sort, concatenate, reshape and flatten.
- Indexing and slicing are used to access the elements of NumPy arrays.
- Arithmetic operations and linear algebra operations can be performed on the NumPy arrays.
- Pandas is a popular open-source machine learning library for working with datasets.
- Pandas has two main data structures for storing and manipulating large datasets – Series and DataFrame.
- Pandas can vectorize the code.
- Data cleaning, data transformation, and data wrangling features are provided by Pandas
- Data cleaning provides tools to handle missing data, remove duplicates, and replace values.
- Data transformation provides several methods for transforming data.
- Data wrangling allows merge or join of two or more datasets on a common column or key.
- A series can be created using one-dimension ndarray, list, dictionary and scalar value.
- DataFrame is a two-dimension data structure composed of rows and columns.
- DataFrame can be created using two-dimension ndarray, dictionary of dictionaries, dictionary list, dictionary of series, and file or table.
- Matplotlib is a popular plotting library for numerical data.
- In Matplotlib, the figure object is the top-level container and holds the graphs or plots.
- Line plot displays information as a series of data points connected by a straight line.
- Scatter plot shows the relationship between two or more variables.

- Bar plot is used for representing categorical data with rectangular bars.
- Histogram is used for representing distribution of numerical data.
- Pie plot is used to divide data into slices to illustrate numerical proportion.
- Box plot shows the distribution of numerical data and skewness.
- Stem plot is used to display quantitative data, generally from small datasets.
- Heatmap is used to see changes in behavior or gradual changes in data.

Keywords

Open-source library
Standard library
Data preprocessing
Data modeling
Data visualization
NumPy
Pandas
Matplotlib
Modules
Array
Vector
Matrix
Rank
Data accuracy
Data suitability
Feature scaling
Encoding categorical data
Data cleaning
Data transformation
Data selection
Normalizing data
Feature selection
Scaling
Normalization
Aggregation
Discretization
Feature engineering
Random sampling
Stratified sampling
Instance selection
Row vector
Column vector
Indexing arrays
Slicing arrays
Boolean array indexing
Universal function ufunc
Linear algebra
Eigenvalues
Eigenvector
Series
DataFrame
Data wrangling
Series data
Series index
Axes
Label
Ticks
Legend
Grid lines
Markers
Line chart
Scatter plot
Bar plot
Histogram
Pie chart
Box plot
Stem plot
Heatmap
Area plot
Grouped bar plot
Stacked bar plot
Nested pie plot
Inter Quartile Range (IQR)

Programming Language Keywords

```
import
ndarray
numpy.array
ndarray.ndim
ndarray.shape
ndarray.size
ndarray.dtype
ndarray.itemsize
ndarray.data
np.array()
np.add()
np.subtract()
np.multiply()
np.divide()
plt.axes()
matplotlib pyplot
figure
numpy.linalg
sort()
concatenate()
reshape()
flatten()
transpose()
dot()
vdot()
cross()
inner()
outer()
df.head(n)
df.tail(n)
```

```
df.index                  df.concat()          pd.series()
df.shape()                det()                pd.dataframe()
df.dtypes                 solve()              plt.plot()
df.columns                trace()              plt.stem()
df.values                 matmul()             plt.boxplot()
df.describe()             linalg.inv()         plt.scatter()
df.loc                    linalg.qr()          plt.bar()
df.iloc                   linalg.svd()         plt.hist()
df.drop()                 linalg.eig()         plt.pie()
df.isnull()               linalg.eigvals()     plt.grid()
df.dropna()               dtype                plt.xlabel()
df.fillna()               zeros()              plt.ylabel()
df.sort_values()          ones()               plt.xticks()
df.rename()               empty()              plt.legend()
df.replace()              arange()             plt.savefig()
df.drop_duplicates()      identity()           plt.title()
df.groupby()              full()               plt.annotate()
df.merge()                np.linspace()        plt.show()
df.join()                 np.random.randn()
```

Assessment

A.1 Bloom Level: Knowledge/Remember

Review Questions

1. Define – Data preprocessing, Data modeling, Data visualization, Data cleaning, Data transformation, Data selection, Axis, Rank.
2. What is open-source library?
3. Name five open-source libraries in Python.
4. What is the full-form for – GPL, NumPy.
5. What is Python Standard Library?
6. Name three tasks of data preprocessing.
7. Name three techniques used for data preprocessing.
8. Name three tasks used for data cleaning.
9. Name three techniques for data transformation.
10. Name three techniques for data selection.
11. What is the purpose of data modeling?
12. Name a library for data modeling.
13. Name two libraries for data preprocessing.
14. Name two libraries for data visualization.
15. Why is data visualization used?
16. Name three important attributes of NumPy array object.
17. List four ways for the creation of NumPy arrays.
18. What is a row vector?
19. What is a column vector?
20. List three operations to update an array.

21. What is Boolean array indexing?

22. What are eigenvalues and eigenvectors?

23. List three ways to create Pandas Series.

24. List three ways to create Pandas DataFrame.

25. List the statistical summary provided by – `df.describe()`.

26. List the purpose in context of `Figure` – Axes, Label, Ticks, legend, Grid Lines, Markers.

27. Match the following:

(a) `ndarray.ndim`	(i) Create array in a range of integer elements
(b) `ndarray.shape`	(ii) Create array with floating-point values, in a specified interval
(c) `ndarray.size`	(iii) Calculate sum of diagonal elements
(d) `np.arange()`	(iv) Number of axes
(e) `np.linspace()`	(v) Size of each dimension
(f) `trace()`	(vi) Total number of elements of the array

28. Match the following:

(a) Line plot	(i) Divided into slices to illustrate numerical proportion
(b) Scatter plot	(ii) Represents categorical data with rectangular bars
(c) Bar plot	(iii) Shows relationship between two or more variables
(d) Histogram	(iv) Display quantitative data, generally from small data sets
(e) Pie plot	(v) Display information as a series of data points connected by a straight line
(f) Box plot	(vi) To see changes in behavior or gradual changes in data
(g) Stem plot	(vii) Represents distribution of numerical data
(h) Heatmap	(viii) Shows distribution of numerical data and skewness

Fill in the blanks

1. __________ ensures all features have the same scale.

2. ________ is a collection of homogeneous elements.

3. ________ is an array of one-dimension.

4. ________ is an array of two-dimension.

5. ____________ is the *N*-dimensional array object of NumPy.

6. ________ creates a square array with 1 on main diagonal and 0 elsewhere.

7. ________ creates array filled with 0's.

8. In Pandas, ________ is a 1-dimension data structure.

9. In Pandas, ________ is a 2-dimension data structure.

10. The plotted points in a plot are called ________.

State True/False

1. The numpy.array handles only one-dimensional arrays.
2. `concat()` concatenates multiple DataFrames on a column key.
3. `loc[]` is used to select rows and columns by label.
4. Series are mutable.
5. Label is used to assign names to x-axis and y-axis or title of the plot.
6. Aggregation converts continuous data into categorical data.
7. Feature selection is used for selecting subset of instance from dataset by relevance to task.
8. Scaling rescales the data to a common scale, such as between 0 and 1.
9. The results get skewed due to outliers.
10. DataFrame is both value-mutable and size-mutable.

Multiple Choice Questions (MCQ)

1. Identify the operation that is NOT used for updating an array.
   (i) concatenate (ii) reshape
   (iii) flatten (iv) `np.add()`
2. Identify the method for data cleaning.
   (i) `loc[]`
   (ii) `iloc[]`
   (iii) `dropna()`
   (iv) `sort_values()`
3. `fillna()`, `drop_duplicates()` and `replace()` are methods for:
   (i) Data cleaning
   (ii) Data visualization
   (iii Data transformation
   (iv) Data wrangling
4. `merge()` and `join()` are methods for:
   (i) Data cleaning
   (ii) Data visualization
   (iii) Data transformation
   (iv) Data wrangling
5. `sort_values()` and `groupby()` are methods for:
   (i) Data cleaning
   (ii) Data visualization
   (iii) Data transformation
   (iv) Data wrangling
6. Identify the statement that is NOT true about Python open-source libraries.
   (i) Each library has its own code.
   (ii) The libraries consist of several modules, each having a specific purpose.
   (iii) The libraries provide a comprehensive set of tools for working with the data.
   (iv) The libraries get installed with the installation of Python; so, its modules can be used without having to download them.

A.2 Bloom Level: Comprehend/Understand

Review Questions

1. Explain the purpose of open-source libraries for the following:
   (1) Data preprocessing
   (2) Data modeling
   (3) Data visualization
   (4) Data cleaning
   (5) Data transformation
   (6) Data selection
2. Describe the meaning of the following methods:
   `ndarray.ndim, ndarray.shape, ndarray.size, ndarray.dtype, ndarray.itemsize, ndarray.data, np.array(), np.add(), np.subtract(), np.multiply(), np.divide(), plt.axes(), numpy.linalg, sort(), concatenate(), reshape(), flatten(), transpose(), dot(), vdot(), cross(), inner(), outer(), df.head(n), df.tail(n), df.index, df.shape(), df.dtypes, df.columns, df.values, df.describe(), df.loc, df.iloc, df.drop(), df.isnull(), df.dropna(), df.fillna(), df.sort_values(), df.rename(), df.replace(), df.drop_duplicates(), df.groupby(), df.merge() , df.join(), df.concat(), det(), solve(), trace(), matmul(), linalg.inv(), linalg.qr(), linalg.svd(), linalg.eig(), linalg.eigvals(), dtype, zeros(), ones(), empty(), arange(), identity(),full(), np.linspace(), np.random.randn(), pd.series(), pd.dataframe(), plt.plot(), plt.stem(), plt.boxplot(), plt.scatter(), plt.bar(), plt.hist(), plt.pie(), plt.grid(), plt.xlabel(),plt.xticks(), plt.legend(), plt.savefig(), plt.title(), plt.annotate(), plt.show()`
3. Describe the syntax for the following:
   (i) Importing Python library
   (ii) Importing NumPy
   (iii) Importing Pandas
   (iv) Importing Pyplot
   (v) Creation of series
   (vi) Creation of DataFrame
4. What is the purpose of using 'import' when using a open-source library?
5. Explain the difference between NumPy arrays and Python lists.
6. What are the key benefits of importing NumPy in a program?
7. What are the key benefits of importing Pandas in a program?
8. What is the purpose of using Matplotlib?
9. What are the key benefits of importing `matplotlib.pyplot`.
10. What is the purpose of using `Figure` in Matplotlib?

A.3 Bloom Level: Application/Apply

1. Write a Python statement that, when applied on the array a1, will give the output, as shown.

```
a1 = np.array
([[1,3,2],[10,1,4]])
```

(i)
```
[[ 1  3]
 [ 2 10]
 [ 1  4]]
```

(ii)
```
[[ 1  2  3]
 [ 1  4 10]]
```

(iii)
```
[ 1  3  2 10  1  4]
```

(iv)
```
[[ 1 10]
 [ 3  1]
 [ 2  4]]
```

(v) `[[1 3 2]]` (Slicing)

2. Perform the following operations on the table.

Index	Fruits	Color
0	Apple	Red
1	Banana	Yellow
2	Guava	Green
3	Oranges	Orange
4	Strawberries	Red

(i) Create a DataFrame.
(ii) Print the column names of your DataFrame.
(iii) Print the number of rows and columns of DataFrame.
(iv) Add a new row to the existing DataFrame.
(v) Add a new column indicating the quantity in the existing Dataframe.
(vi) Sort the DataFrame.
(vii) Print all fruits of red color from the DataFrame.

3. Multiple Choice Questions (MCQ)

A. The output of the following code is:

```
arr = np.array([1,2,3,5,8])
arr = arr + 1
print(arr[1])
```

(i) 1 (ii) 3 (iii) 2 (iv) 4

B. Find the output of

```
arr = np.array
([[1,2,3],[0,1,4]])
print(arr.size, arr.ndim)
```

(i) 2, 3 (ii) 6, 2
(iii) 2, 6 (iv) 1, 6

C. Find the output of

```
arr = np.array([1,2,3])
print(arr)
```

(i) `([1,2,3])` (ii) [1, 2, 3]
(iii) [[1, 2, 3]] (iv) 1, 2, 3

D. Find the output of

```
a = np.array([10, 20, 30])
b = np.array([50, 60, 70])
c = np.concatenate((a, b))
print©
```

(i) `[10 20 30 50 60 70]`
(ii) `[[10, 20, 30] [50, 60, 70]]`
(iii) `[[10, 50, 20, 60, 30, 70]]`
(iv) `[[10, 50], [20, 60], [30, 70]]`

4. Find the errors and correct the code:

(i)
```
arr1 = np.arange(30)
arr1_r1 = arr1.reshape(3, 10)
arr1_r2 = arr1.reshape(4, 10)
print(arr1_r2)
```

(ii)
```
arr1 = np.array([[2, 4, 6, 8], [1, 2, 3, 4, 5, 6, 7, 8]])
print(arr1)
```

(iii)
```
a1 = [11, 22, 33, 44, 55]
print(a1/11)
```

(iv)
```
a1 = [11, 22, 33, 44, 55]
print(a1/11)
```

(v)
```
arr1 = np.arange(36)
a1 = arr1[(arr1 % 3 ==0) | (arr1 % 5 ==0)]
print(a1)
a2 = arr1[(arr1 % 3 ==0) or (arr1 % 5 ==0)]
print(a2)
```

(vi)
```
s =pd.Series([1,2,3,4],index= ['a','b','c','d'])
print(s['e'])
```

(vii)
```
a = np.arange(1, 12).reshape(5, 2)
print(a)
print("Axes = ", a.ndim)
print("Shape = ",a.shape)
```

5. Write a Python statements to create the given plots:

(i) Import the required modules.
Create a new figure of size (10, 6) (use `figure()`).
Add four plots to the figure. (use `add_subplot()`).
The first plot lies on 1st row 1st column, second plot on 1st row 2nd column, third plot on 2nd row 1st column, fourth plot on 2nd row 2nd column.
Add a common title to figure (use `suptitle()`).
Show the figure (use `show()`).

(ii) Import the required modules.
Create a new figure of size (10, 6), face color – orange and dpi as 100.
On x-axis plot 1000 floating-point numbers from –10 to 10.
On y-axis, the equation is x**2 + 2*x + 5.
Plot on a grid, with the title 'An Orange Figure'; of font size 15.
Add labels on x-axis and y-axis of font size 15.
Plot and show the figure.

6. Create a line plot that plots the sales data for six months. Use appropriate labels, etc.
Changing the figure size.
Changing resolution of the plot.

Add subplots to a figure.
Show multiple scatter plot on the same figure.
Change the face color and edge color of the figure.

7. Define an array a having the elements as – [[1, 2, 3, 4], [5, 6, 7, 8], [9, 10, 11, 12]]
Write the statements to do the following:
(a) Dimension of array
(b) Size of each dimension
(c) Total number of elements of array
(d) Datatype of elements of array.
(e) Size of each element of array, in bytes

A.4 Bloom Level: Analyze

1. Explain the difference between the following:
   (i) Python standard library and Open-source libraries
   (ii) Row vector and column vector
   (iii) `np.zeros()` and `np.ones()`
   (iv) `np.empty()` and `np.random.randn()`
   (v) `np.arange()` and `np.linspace()`
   (vi) `concatenate()` and `append()`
   (vii) `reshape()` and `flatten()`
   (viii) `reshape()` and `transpose()`
   (ix) `dot()` and `vdor()`
   (x) `vdot()` and `cross()`
   (xi) `inner()` and `outer()`

2. Analyze the following code. What is the output? Is the output for the two codes same? If not, explain the difference in the output and the reasons for the same.
(i)

```
a = np.array([[1, 3],[5, 7]])
b = np.array([[2, 4],[6, 8]])
print("Array a \n", a, "shape=", a.shape)
print("Array b \n", b, "shape=", b.shape)
c = np.concatenate((a, b))
print("Concat a and b \n", c, "shape=",c.shape)
```

(ii)

```
print("Array a \n", a, "shape=", a.shape)
print("Array b \n", b, "shape=", b.shape)
a = np.array([[1, 3],[5, 7]])
b = np.array([[2, 4],[6, 8]])
d = np.append(a, b)
print("Append a and b \n", d, "shape=",d.shape)
```

3. Analyze the difference in (a) and (b). What is the output and the reasons for difference in the output?
a)

```
df = pd.DataFrame(data=np.array([[1, 2, 3], [4, 5, 6], [7, 8, 9]]),
                  index= [2, 4, 6], columns=['A', 'B', 'C'])
print(df.loc[2])
```

b)

```
df = pd.DataFrame(data=np.array([[1, 2, 3], [4, 5, 6], [7, 8, 9]]),
                  index= [2, 4, 6], columns=['A', 'B', 'C'])
print(df.iloc[2])
```

4. print(df.iloc[[0, 2]]) will print the rows from 0 to 2. Is it True or False?
5. The task performed by `df['A'].idxmax()` is______.
6. The resolution of a plot figure can be changed by changing the value of dpi in a `figure()` `function.` Is it True or False?
7. Analyze the following code. What is the task performed? What is the output?
   (a)

```
arr = np.ones(3, dtype=([('x', int), ('y', float)]))
print(arr['x'])
print(arr['y'])
print(arr)
print(arr.ndim)
```

   (b)

```
a = np.array([1, 2, 3], dtype = complex)
print(a)
```

8. Analyze the difference between (a) and (b). What is the output? Justify.
   (a)

```
a = np.array([1, 2, 3])
b = np.array([4, 5, 6])
print("outer product=\n", np.outer(a, b))
```

   (b)

```
a = np.array([1, 2, 3])
b = np.array([4, 5, 6])
print("inner product=", np.inner(a, b))
```

9. Differentiate and analyze the output with justification.

```
a = np.array([[5, 5],[0, 4]])
b = np.array([[3, 0],[6, 7]])
print("a * b=\n", a * b)   #----(1)
print("a.dot(b)\n=", a.dot(b)) #----(2)
```

10. Evaluate the code. (i) What is the type of graph plotted by each code? (ii) How many points are plotted? ((iii) What are the points that are plotted for each code? What is the output?

```
import matplotlib.pyplot as plt
x = [1, 2, 3]
y = [2, 4, 6]
plt.stem(x, y)
plt.title('Plots')
plt.show()
plt.plot(x, y)
plt.show()
plt.bar(x, y, color='red', width=0.5, align='center')
plt.show()
```

(a)

```
import matplotlib.pyplot as plt
fig = plt.figure(figsize=(10,6))
fig1= fig.add_subplot(2,2,1)
fig1.plot(x,y)
fig2= fig.add_subplot(2,2,2)
fig2.stem(x, y)
fig3= fig.add_subplot(2,2,3)
fig3.bar(x, y, color='red', width=0.5, align='center')
fig4= fig.add_subplot(2,2,4)
fig4.pie(x)
fig.suptitle('Multiple Subplots')
plt.show()
```

(b)

A.5 Bloom Level: Evaluate

1. The desired output from the code is given. Evaluate the output and complete the code, so that the desired output is displayed.

```
a1 = np.array([[3, 5, 7], [4, 6, 8], [10, 11, 12]])
print("Array= \n", a1)
print("Array element < 8 = ", a1[a1 < 8])
```

:

:

Output

```
Array=
 [[ 3  5  7]
 [ 4  6  8]
 [10 11 12]]
Array element < 8 =  [3 5 7 4 6]
Array elemnt >= 8 =  [ 8 10 11 12]
Array elements divisible by 2 =  [ 4  6  8 10 12]
Array in range 6 and 12 =  [ 7  8 10 11]
Array >= 3 and divisible by 3 =  [ 3  6 12]
```

2. The desired output from the code is given. Evaluate the code and to perform the operations on the matrix to achieve the displayed output.

```
a1 = np.array([[6, 1],
               [4, -2]])

print("Rank of a1:", np.linalg.matrix_rank(a1))  #Rank of matrix
print("\nTrace of a1:", np.trace(a1))            #Trace of matrix
print("\nDeterminant of a1:", np.linalg.det(a1)) #Determinant of matrix
print("\nInverse of a1:\n", np.linalg.inv(a1))   #Inverse of matrix A
print("\nMatrix a1 to power 2:\n", np.linalg.matrix_power(a1, 2))
```

Output

```
Rank of a1: 2

Trace of a1: 4

Determinant of a1: -15.999999999999998

Inverse of a1:
 [[ 0.125   0.0625]
 [ 0.25   -0.375 ]]

Matrix a1 to power 2:
 [[40  4]
 [16  8]]
```

3. Evaluate the code. (i) What is the task performed at each code row? (ii) What is the output?

```
import pandas as pd

data={'Name': ['Asha', 'Usha', 'Risha', 'Disha'],
      'Age': [20, 19, 15, 18],
      'Stream': ['Science', 'Commerce','Humanities','Engineering'],
      'Percentage': [90, 95, 97, 79]}
df = pd.DataFrame(data, columns=['Name', 'Age','Stream', 'Percentage'])
print("Dataframe :\n", df)
for index, row in df.iterrows():
    print(row["Name"], row["Age"])
```

4. Evaluate the code, (i) What is the type of graph plotted by each code. (ii) How many points are plotted. ((iii) What are the points that are plotted for each code. What is the output.

```
import matplotlib.pyplot as plt
x = [1, 2, 3]
y = [2, 4, 6]
plt.stem(x, y)
plt.title('Plots')
plt.show()
plt.plot(x, y)
plt.show()
plt.bar(x, y, color='red', width=0.5, align='center')
plt.show()
```

(a)

```
import matplotlib.pyplot as plt
fig = plt.figure(figsize=(10,6))
fig1= fig.add_subplot(2,2,1)
fig1.plot(x,y)
fig2= fig.add_subplot(2,2,2)
fig2.stem(x, y)
fig3= fig.add_subplot(2,2,3)
fig3.bar(x, y, color='red', width=0.5, align='center')
fig4= fig.add_subplot(2,2,4)
fig4.pie(x)
fig.suptitle('Multiple Subplots')
plt.show()
```

(b)

5. Utilize the marks of the 20 students to generate various visual representations of the data using Matplotlib libraries with proper legends and labels. Evaluate results from representation of the plots.
   math_marks = [88, 92, 80, 89, 100, 80, 60, 100, 80, 34, 90, 94, 82, 91, 100, 88, 65, 100, 89, 39]
   science_marks = [35, 79, 79, 48, 100, 88, 32, 45, 20, 30, 38, 80, 80, 58, 100, 88, 36, 49, 28 35]
   marks_range = [10, 20, 30, 40, 50, 60, 70, 80, 90, 100]
   a) Create a scatter plot to visualize the relationship between math marks and science marks of the students.
   b) Generate a histogram to display the data distribution for each subject mark.
   c) Construct a pie chart to illustrate the frequency count of each subject.

A.6 Bloom Level: Create/Synthesize

Programming Assignment

1. Write a program using the NumPy library to perform the following tasks:
   - o Define a 4 × 3 array of integers and name it as arr1. The array has values ranging from 30 to 60, randomly. Reshape arr1 to a size of 2 × 6.
2. Create a 2-D array using `arange()` having 10 rows and 3 columns with start value = –1, having step size 0.5.
   - o Find the sum of all elements.
   - o Find the sum of all elements, row-wise.
   - o Find the sum of all elements, column-wise.
   - o Find the max of all elements.
   - o Find the min of all elements in each row.
   - o Find the mean of all elements in each row.
   - o Find the standard deviation, column-wise
3. Create a Series using NumPy array of marks. The index is the names of students who scored the marks.
4. Create a Series using a NumPy array of ages, but customize the indices to be the names that correspond to each age
5. Create a NumPy 2-D array using `arange()`, having 3 rows and 5 columns with start value = 4, step size 4 and dtype as float. Use the array to write NumPy commands for the following:

- Find dimensions, shape, size, datatype of items and item size of the array.
- Reshape the array to have all the 15 elements in a single row.
- Display the 2nd and 3rd element of the array.
- Display all elements in row 2 and row 3 of the array.
- Display elements in column 1 and column 2 of the array.
- Display elements in column 1 and rows 2, 3 of the array.
- Reverse the array.
- Find the square root of all elements of array and divide the resulting array by 2. The result should be rounded to two places of decimals.
- Find the transpose of the array.

6. Write a program using NumPy library to perform the following tasks:
- Define a 4 × 3 array of integers and name it as arr1. The array has values ranging from 30 to 60, randomly. Reshape arr1 to a size of 2 × 6.
- Create a 1-dimension array having float random values between 1 to 50. Perform the statistical operations on the array – mean, median, standard deviation, number of unique values, and count of unique values.
- Create a 3 × 3 identity matrix where all the diagonal elements are set to the value 5.

7. Consider a dataset containing the heights (in centimeters) and weights (in kilograms) of 20 persons.
- Create a NumPy array called "heights".
- Create a NumPy array called "weights".
- Draw a bar chart for the data.
- Create a new NumPy array called "H-W" by stacking the heights and weights arrays such that the shape of the resulting array is 20 × 2.
- Print the mean height and weight of the persons.
- Sort the array based on height of the persons.
- Swap the positions of the two columns in the array.
- Retrieve records of persons having weight more than 55 kg.

8. Consider the data shown in the table. Write Python code for the following operations.

Order_no	Region	Rep_Name	Item_Name	Units_sold	Unit_cost
1	UP	Ashu	Pencil	100	10
2	Delhi	Vishu	Eraser	300	5
3	Haryana	Dishu	Gel pen	345	20
4	Punjab	Mishu	Ink pen	335	50
5	Uttarakhand	Sishu	Ball point	250	30
6	Kerala	Pishu	Notebooks	200	50
7	Rajasthan	Lishu	Files	150	60
8	Assam	Zishu	Pencil	300	25
9	Gujarat	Kishu	Ink pen	350	75
10	Tamil Nadu	Nishu	Gel pen	250	80

a) Create a DataFrame from the table.
b) Print the number of records and number of attributes in the DataFrame.
c) Display names of the attributes, row indexes, and datatypes of each attribute in the DataFrame.
d) Display the first 5 and last 5 records of the DataFrame.
e) Retrieve the values of the second column for the third and fifth records.
f) Display a summary of the data distribution for all attributes in DataFrame.
g) Add a column "Total_cost" that is the product of Units_sold and Unit_cost

9. On the DataFrame created in the previous question, write Python code to perform the following:
   a) Print (`df.iloc[1:6]`).
   b) Print (`df.iloc[3,:]`).
   c) Print (`df.loc[6]`).
   d) Drop the column 'Rep_Name'.
   e) Find the value counts of each 'Item_Name'.
   f) Add two new rows with null values for Units_sold.
   g) Fill the null values with 100.

Answers

A.1 Bloom Level: Knowledge/Remember

Review Questions

27. (a)– (iv), (b) – (v), (c) – (vi), (d) – (i) (e) – (ii), (f) – (iii)

28. (a)– (v), (b) – (iii), (c) – (ii), (d) – (vii) (e) – (i), (f) – v(iii), (g) – (iv), (h) – (vi)

Fill in the Blanks

1. Feature scaling	2. Array	3. Vector	4. Matrix
5. ndarray	6. Identity	7. `zeros()`	8. Series
9. DataFrame	10. Markers		

True/False

1. False	2. False	3. True	4. True	5. True	6. False	7. False	8. True
9. True	10. True						

Multiple Choice Questions (MCQ)

1. (iv) 2. (iii) 3. (i) 4. (iv) 5. (iii) 6. (iv)

A.3 Bloom Level: Application/Apply

1.

```
(i) a2 = a1.reshape(3, 2)
    print("Reshape = \n", a2)
(ii) print("Sorted Array = \n", np.sort(a1))
```

```
(iii)a2 = a1.flatten()
    print("Array after Flatten = \n", a2)
(iv) a2 = np.transpose(a1)
    print("Transposed Matrix: \n",a2)
 (v) print("a1[0:2]=\n ",a1[0:1])
```

3. A - (ii), B - (ii), C - (ii), D - (i)

4. (i)

```
ValueError: cannot reshape array of size 30 into shape (4,10)
```

(ii)

```
ValueError: setting an array element with a sequence.
The requested array has an inhomogeneous shape after 1 dimensions
The detected shape was (2,) + inhomogeneous part.
```

(iii)

```
TypeError: array() takes from 1 to 2 positional arguments but 4 were given
```

(iv)

```
TypeError: unsupported operand type(s) for /: 'list' and 'int'
```

(v)

```
ValueError: The truth value of an array with more than one element is ambiguous.
Use a.any() or a.all()
```

(vi)

```
KeyError: 'e'
```

(vii)

```
ValueError: cannot reshape array of size 11 into shape (5,2)
```

A.4 Bloom Level: Analyze

2.

```
Array a
 [[1 3]
 [5 7]] shape= (2, 2)
Array b
 [[2 4]
 [6 8]] shape= (2, 2)
Concat a and b
 [[1 3]
 [5 7]
 [2 4]
 [6 8]] shape= (4, 2)
```

```
Array a
 [[1 3]
 [5 7]] shape= (2, 2)
Array b
 [[2 4]
 [6 8]] shape= (2, 2)
Append a and b
 [1 3 5 7 2 4 6 8] shape= (8,)
```

3.

```
A    1
B    2
C    3
Name: 2, dtype: int32
```

```
A    7
B    8
C    9
Name: 6, dtype: int32
```

4. False
5. Return index of maximum value for 'A'
6. True
7. Analyze the following code. What is the task performed? What is the output.

(a)

```
[1 1 1]
[1. 1. 1.]
[(1, 1.) (1, 1.) (1, 1.)]
1
```

(b)

```
[1.+0.j 2.+0.j 3.+0.j]
```

8.

```
outer product=
 [[ 4  5  6]
 [ 8 10 12]
 [12 15 18]]
inner product= 32
```

9.

```
a * b=
 [[15  0]
 [ 0 28]]
a.dot(b)
= [[45 35]
 [24 28]]
```

A.5. Bloom Level: Evaluate

3. Define a dictionary containing students data.
   Convert the dictionary into DataFrame.
   Iterate through each row and select 'Name' and 'Age' columns respectively.

```
Dataframe :
     Name  Age       Stream  Percentage
0    Asha   20      Science          90
1    Usha   19     Commerce          95
2   Risha   15   Humanities          97
3   Disha   18  Engineering          79
Asha 20
Usha 19
Risha 15
Disha 18
```

CHAPTER 17

Using Python to Access Web Data

Contents

17.1 Introduction

A website is accessed by using a web browser. However, sometimes there is a need to get the content from the website in a program. Python has several third-party libraries that support the accessing of website via the code. At the program level, Python provides support for retrieving the web pages and then parsing the retrieved content. In contrast to rendering content visually when using a browser, here via the code, the content is rendered as text. To get the desired information from the web content, regular expression is one of the powerful tools. A regular expression matches string patterns to extract sub-strings from text data, find a pattern or replace a matched pattern.

Sockets connect the server and the requesting client, and they are the underlying concept for transmitting messages over the network. During communication, the delivery of content may or may not be assured. For connection and delivery, certain protocols must be followed, both by the client and the server.

There are several libraries in Python to support the extraction and parsing of web content. In this chapter, we discuss in detail, the libraries, regular expression, sockets, client–server communication, and, retrieval and parsing of web pages.

Learning Outcomes of this chapter

After completion of the chapter, the learner will be able to:

- Understand the use of regular expressions in Python
- Formulate regular expressions for extracting data
- Understand the accessing of web data in Python
- Use socket module in Python for communication
- Understand the retrieval and parsing of web pages
- Understand the use of third-party libraries for accessing web data.

17.2 Regular Expression

Regular Expression, also referred to as *regex or regexp,* is used for searching and manipulating text strings, generally, in a text file. Text can be – emails, HTTP address, phone numbers, special text pattern, and id. Regular expression is supported in all scripting languages, like Perl, Python, PHP, and JavaScript. Regex is extensively used in data cleaning and preprocessing.

According to Ken Thompson, "*A regular expression is a pattern which specifies a set of strings of characters; it is said to match certain strings.*"

- Regular expression is a text string, defined specifically for describing a search pattern. It is a set of rules that is defined to find patterns in strings.
- *Pattern* is a sequence of characters that is matched inside a string. To define the pattern, the regular expression has combinations of special character operators.
- The special character operators are defined using – Metacharacters, Unicode characters, Sets, and Regex functions.

- Regex works as follows:
  1) Specify – (i) pattern, (ii) string in which pattern is to be matched, and (iii) what to do if the pattern is matched in the string.
  2) Execute pattern – Pattern match engine executes it and matches the pattern with the string.
  3) Action – Perform the specified action.
- Regular expression is used for (i) Matching patterns in a string, (ii) Extracting sub-strings from text data, and (iii) Finding a pattern or replacing matched pattern.
- In Python, regular expression is pre-built. Python has a built-in package called `re`, that handles regular expressions. The `re` must be imported in the program, using the command:

```
import re
```

- Regular expressions are used for pattern matching because:
  1) Regular expressions are faster than the usual python code. It saves a lot of time.
  2) Code becomes compact; one line of regex replaces several lines of code.

We discuss regular expression in the following sections.

17.3 Metacharacters

- Metacharacters are characters that have special meaning in a pattern.
- The characters of metacharacters do not match themselves in a string. They are useful for matching multiple character patterns at once.
- The metacharacters used are –

```
. ^ $ * + ? { } [ ] \ | ()
```

- Table 17.1 shows the metacharacters and their description. It also shows an example for each.

Table 17.1 Metacharacters and their description

S. No.	Character	Description	Example	Matches
1	[]	Indicates a set of characters. Matches anything in braces	[and] [b-z]	a, n or d bc, coin, xyz
2	[^...]	Matches anything not in bracket	[^abc]	pqr, 12a, 2bo
3	\	Escapes character after backslash or creates escape sequence	"b\sc"	b c
4	.	Matches any character except new line	"ha.y"	hacy, hazy, ha1y
5	^	Matches start of string	"^happy"	happyworld, happyyou,happy1
6	$	Matches end of string just before new line	"world$"	123world, oneworld, theworld

(*Continued*)

Table 17.1 (Continued)

S. No.	Character	Description	Example	Matches
7	*	Matches 0 or more repetition of preceding character	"he*o"	ho, heo, heeo
8	+	Matches 1 or more repetition of preceding character	"he+o"	heo, heeo, heeeo
9	?	Matches 0 or 1 repetition of preceding regex	"he?o"	ho, heo
10	{m}	Matches *m* times or more of previous regex	"h{2}o"	hho, hhho, hhhho
11	{m, n}	Matches *m* to *n* times of previous regex	"h{2,4}o"	hho, hhho
12	()	Matches whatever expression is inside the parentheses	(a)b(c)	matches a and c
13	|	Matches either A or B	"they|you"	they and you

17.4 Unicode Characters

- Unicode characters are special sets of characters used for defining the whole set of matching attributes.
- They are a combination of the symbol \ and one character.
- A Unicode character is defined as –

```
[\character]
```

- The Unicode characters used are – \A\b \B \d \D \s \S \w \W\Z.
- One Unicode character matches only one occurrence inside the string.
- To match all occurrences in the string, combine Unicode characters with metacharacters.
- The Unicode characters and their description are shown in Table 17.2

Table 17.2 Unicode characters and their description

Character	Description
`\A`	Matches if specified characters are at the beginning of a string
`\b`	Matches if specified characters are at the beginning or the end of a word ("r" in beginning means that the string is a "raw string")
`\B`	Matches if specified characters are NOT at the beginning or the end of a word ("r" in beginning means that the string is treated as "raw string")

(*Continued*)

Table 17.2 (Continued)

Character	Description
`\d`	Matches if a string contains digits (numbers from 0–9)
`\D`	Matches if a string has any non-digit characters
`\s`	Matches if a string contains any whitespace characters [\n\t\f]
`\S`	Matches if a string contains non-whitespace characters
`\w`	Matches if a string contains alphanumeric (a–Z, 0–9, underscore _) characters
`\W`	Matches if a string DOES NOT contain alphanumeric characters
`\Z`	Matches if specified characters are at the end of the string

17.5 Sets

- A set is a combination of characters inside square brackets [] with a special meaning.
- They are used to match the pattern among them inside the string.
- A set may contain single or a combination of Unicode characters and metacharacters.
- A set is defined as:

```
[string combination]
```

- The string combination is shown in Table 17.3.

Table 17.3 Sets and their description

Set	Description
`[ajy]`	Matches one of specified characters (`a`, `j`, or `y`) is present
`[a-z]`	Matches any lower-case alphabet from a to z
`[A-Z]`	Matches any upper-case alphabet from A to Z
`[^arn]`	Matches any character that is NOT `a`, `r`, and `n`
`[0123]`	Returns a match where any of the digits (`0`, `1`, `2`, or `3`) are present
`[0-9]`	Matches any digit between `0` and `9`
`[0-5][0-9]`	Returns any two-digit number from `00` and `59`
`[a-zA-Z]` or `[a-Z]`	Matches any character between `a` and `Z`, lower case or upper case
`[+]`	Returns an exact match for + character

17.6 REGEX FUNCTIONS AND EXTRACTING DATA

- The `re` module of Python provides a set of functions that allow us to search for a pattern inside a string, replace it with some value or split from the point of pattern, and many more.
- The functions that are popular and useful are – `match()`, `search()`, `findall()`, `split()` and `sub()`.
- For all the functions, Python allows option "flags" as one of the arguments. Flags are regular expression options. The flags can be used for various purposes. Table 17.4 shows the flags and their shortform with their description. The flags shall be used in the functions discussed in the following subsections.

Table 17.4 Flags and their description

Flags or Flag shortform	Description
`re.IGNORECASE` or `re.I`	Ignores a case
`re.DOTALL` or `re.S`	Allows "." metacharacter to match a newline
`re.MULTILINE` or `re.M`	Allows "^" and "$" metacharacters to match each line
`re.VERBOSE` or `re.X`	Allows whitespaces and comments in pattern compilation
`re.ASCII` or `re.A`	Makes \w, \W, \b, \B, \s, \S match only ASCII characters

17.6.1 `match()` Function

- `re.match()` function checks for a pattern in the string and returns the first occurrence of the pattern match in the string. It checks for a match at the beginning of a string.
- If a match is found, it returns the match object; if there is no match, the value `None` is returned.
- The syntax of using the function is –

```
re.match(pattern, string, flags=0)
```

where, `pattern` is regular expression, `string` is the string to be checked for match, and `flags` are regular expression options.

- The match object has methods that retrieve information about the search.
  - `.span()` returns a tuple containing start and end positions of match
  - `.string` returns the string passed into the function
  - `.group()` returns the part of the string where there was a match.

Example 17.1: WAP using regular expression to –

(i) Match words that start with "b".

(ii) Match words that start with "b" or "B".

(i)

```
import re
str = ['beautiful baby', 'beautiful Blessing','Beautiful Bat']
pat = "(b\w+)\W(b\w+)"
for s in str:                    # extract each string group
    res = re.match(pat,s)
    if res:
        print("Span= ", res.span()) #start-end position of match
        print("Separate String= ", res.groups()) # separate strings
        print("Single String= ", res.group()) # single string
        print("***************")
```

Output

```
Span=  (0, 14)
Separate String=  ('beautiful', 'baby')
Single String=  beautiful baby
***************
```

(ii)

```
import re
str = ['beautiful baby', 'beautiful Blessing','Beautiful Bat']
pat = "(b\w+)\W(b\w+)"
for s in str:                    # extract each string group
    res = re.match(pat,s, re.I) # re.I - ignore case
    if res:
        print("Span= ", res.span()) #start-end position of match
        print("Separate String= ", res.groups()) # separate strings
        print("Single String= ", res.group()) # single string
        print("***************")
```

Output

```
Span=  (0, 14)
Separate String=  ('beautiful', 'baby')
Single String=  beautiful baby
***************
Span=  (0, 18)
Separate String=  ('beautiful', 'Blessing')
Single String=  beautiful Blessing
***************
Span=  (0, 13)
Separate String=  ('Beautiful', 'Bat')
Single String=  Beautiful Bat
***************
```

In regex "(b\w+)\W(b\w+)"

- (b\w+) matches words starting with letter "b" followed by one or more repetition of alphanumeric characters.
- \W matches a non-alphanumeric character (for e.g. Blank).

re.I ignores the case.

17.6.2 search() Function

- `re.search()` searches for a regular expression pattern inside a string and returns the first occurrence of the pattern match in the string. It searches for a match anywhere in the string.
- If a pattern is found, it returns a match object; if no match is found, `None` is returned.
- The syntax of using the function is –

```
re.search(pattern, string, flags=0)
```

where, `pattern` is regular expression, `string` is the string to be checked for match, and `flags` are regular expression options.

- Data can be further retrieved from a match object by applying functions, such as
  `span()` : Returns start and end index of matched element
  `group()` : Returns subgroup(s) of match by indices or names.

Example 17.2: WAP using regular expression to –

(i) Search for the first whitespace character in the string.
(ii) Search for the word "human" in the string.
(iii) Search for the "earth" in the string.

```
import re
txt = "Everything is placed on earth by the God perfectly."

print("The string is\n", txt)
print("Search first whitespace\n",re.search("\s", txt))
print("Search- human\n", re.search("human", txt))
print("Search- earth\n", re.search("earth", txt))
```

Output

```
The string is
 Everything is placed on earth by the God perfectly.
Search first whitespace
 <re.Match object; span=(10, 11), match=' '>
Search- human
 None
Search- earth
 <re.Match object; span=(24, 29), match='earth'>
```

Example 17.3: WAP using regular expression to –

(i) Find the first character.
(ii) Find the first dot.

```
import re
s="""Save our earth. Save our beautiful nature
The soothing winds in the woods. The lovely sky.
And beautiful mountains. Lakes and ponds and oceans"""

print("Match any first character\n", re.search(r'.', s) )
print("Match first dot\n", re.search(r'\.', s) )
```

Output

```
Match any first character
 <re.Match object; span=(0, 1), match='S'>
Match first dot
 <re.Match object; span=(14, 15), match='.'>
```

Please note that to find a dot, we precede it with the special character '\'.

17.6.3 `findall()` Function

- It matches all the instances of pattern inside the string and returns them in a list.
- The syntax of using the function is –

```
re.findall(pattern, string, flags=0)
```

where, `pattern` is regular expression, `string` is the string to be checked for match, and `flags` are regular expression options.

- `findall()` returns a list containing all matches.
- The list contains the matches in the order they are found.
- If no matches are found, an empty list is returned.

Example 17.4: WAP using regular expression to –

(i) List all matches for "in" in string.
(ii) List all matches for "ful" in string.

```
import re
txt = "The soothing winds in the woods, the lovely sky."

print("String=", txt)
print("List of all match for -in\n", re.findall("in", txt))
print("List of all match for -ful\n", re.findall("ful", txt))
```

Output

```
String= The soothing winds in the woods, the lovely sky.
List of all match for -in
 ['in', 'in', 'in']
List of all match for -ful
 []
```

17.6.4 split() Function

- The syntax of using the function is –

```
re.split(pattern, string, maxsplit=0, flags=0)
```

where, `pattern` is regular expression, `string` is the string to be matched for split, and `flags` are regular expression options.

If `maxsplit` is nonzero, at most `maxsplit` splits occur, and the remainder of the string is returned as the final element of the list.

- Split the `string` into a list using the delimiter `pattern` to be matched inside the string.
- The `split()` function returns a list where the string has been split at each match.

Example 17.5: WAP using regular expression to –

(i) Split the string at each white-space character.
(ii) Split the string at only the first occurrence of white-space character.

```
import re
txt = "God created this world flawlessly"
print("Split at whitespace\n",  re.split("\s", txt))
print("Split at first whitespace only\n", re.split("\s", txt, 1))
```

Output

```
Split at whitespace
 ['God', 'created', 'this', 'world', 'flawlessly']
Split at first whitespace only
 ['God', 'created this world flawlessly']
```

Example 17.6: WAP using regular expression to –

(i) Split the string at each digit character.
(ii) Split the string at each non-digit character.
(iii) Split the string at a particular character.

```
import re
txt = "12/04/2024 10:30:AM Check IN"
pat = '\d'
print("***\d***\n", re.split(pat, txt))
pat = '\D'
print("***\D***\n",re.split(pat, txt))
pat = ':'
print("***:***\n",re.split(pat, txt))
```

Output

```
***\d***
 ['', '', '/', '', '/', '', '', '', ' ', '', ':', '', ':AM Check IN']
***\D***
 ['12', '04', '2024', '10', '30', '', '', '', '', '', '', '', '', '', '', '', '']
***:***
 ['12/04/2024 10', '30', 'AM Check IN']
```

17.6.5 sub() Function

- The syntax of using the function is –

    `re.sub(pattern, repl, string, count=0, flags=0)`

  where, `pattern` is regular expression, `repl` is text to be replaced, `string` is the string to be matched, `flags` are regular expression options, `count` is the maximum number of pattern occurrences to be replaced

- `sub()` replaces the `pattern` matches with the `repl` in the `string`.
- You can control the number of replacements by specifying the count parameter.

Example 17.7: WAP using regular expression to –

(i) Substitute whitespace with "-".
(ii) Substitute first three whitespace with "-".

```
import re
txt = "Save our earth, save our beautiful nature."
print("Sub whitespace with -\n", re.sub("\s", "-", txt))
print("Sub first three whitespace with -\n",  re.sub("\s","-",txt,3))
```

Output

```
Sub whitespace with -
 Save-our-earth,-save-our-beautiful-nature.
Sub first three whitespace with -
 Save-our-earth,-save our beautiful nature.
```

Example 17.8: WAP using regular expression to –

(i) Substitute "and" with "&" with ignorecase.
(ii) Substitute without ignorecase.

```
import re
str = "Fruits and Veggies AND less Sugar and more water are good"
print("String: ", str)
print("AND with & ignorecase****",re.sub(r'\sAND\s', ' & ',
      str, flags=re.I))
print("No ignorecase****", re.sub(r'\sAND\s', ' & ', str))
```

Output

```
String:  Fruits and Veggies AND less Sugar and more water are good
AND with & ignorecase**** Fruits & Veggies & less Sugar & more water are good
No ignorecase**** Fruits and Veggies & less Sugar and more water are good
```

17.7 BASICS OF NETWORKING

- Networking connects two or more devices for communication and exchange of information.
- Network is a collection of such interconnected devices.
- Internet is a network that connects a myriad of devices.
- Internet contains many networks:
  - **(i)** Local Area Network (LAN) – connects computers located close to one another,
  - **(ii)** Personal Area Network (PAN) – connects devices like smartphone and laptop via Bluetooth,
  - **(iii)** Metropolitan Area Network (MAN) – connects devices in a city, and
  - **(iv)** Wide Area Network (WAN) – interconnects devices across countries and continents.
- Communication protocol facilitates interaction among the connected devices in a network.
- Communication protocols specify rules and format in which the information should be sent and received among the communicating devices. It determines who is to go first, what they are to do, and what the responses are to the message, and who sends next, and so on.
- WiFi, Internet Protocol (IP), Transmission Control Protocol (TCP), User Datagram Protocol (UDP), and HyperText Transfer Protocol (HTTP) are some popular communication protocols.
  - **(i)** WiFi is for sending data, wirelessly, from one device to other.
  - **(ii)** IP is responsible for routing packets over Internet and IP addressing.
  - **(iii)** TCP is a reliable, connection-oriented protocol. It ensures data integrity and delivery.
  - **(iv)** UDP is a fast, unreliable, connectionless protocol. It does not perform any checks during delivery.
  - **(v)** HTTP is a commonly used protocol for communication on the web from browser to server. It is used for connecting to websites. HTTP is built on top of TCP.
- Some of the key concepts and terms in networking are –
  - **(i)** *Packet*: a standard unit of data transmission in a network.
  - **(ii)** *Endpoint*: a destination where packets arrive.
  - **(iii)** *IP address*: uniquely identifies a device on the network, via a numerical identifier. For example, 192.168.0.0

(iv) *Port*: uniquely identifies a process or an application, running on a device. Different ports are used for different services and processes. To identify a port to a service, a numerical identifier, i.e., a port number is used. Services are assigned to port numbers. For example, Port 80 is used by server applications to manage HTTP traffic; the file transfer protocol uses port number 21.

- The communication protocols use *sockets* for network communications in modern devices.

17.8 Sockets

- Socket is an interface (gate) for inter-process communication. Two processes that run on the same computer or on two different computers can communicate via a socket.
- Several software, like web browsers, file sharing software, and WhatsApp application that depends on instant messaging, use sockets.
- Socket provides a two-way connection between programs. You can both read from and write to the same socket.
  (i) If you write to a socket, the data is sent to the application at another end of the socket.
  (ii) If you read from a socket, you get the data which the other application has sent.

- A socket is made up of –
  (i) IP address of a system that identifies the host machine and device, and
  (ii) Port number of a program within the system that identifies the process.

A socket looks like - 192.168.242.127:8080, where 192.168.242.127 is the IP address and 8080 is the port number.

- A key difference between port and socket is that –
  (i) A port does not identify a computer uniquely because a program running on different computers can use the same port number.
  (ii) A socket identifies a computer and program within the computer uniquely because it is a combination of IP address and port number.
- Socket programming is a means of communication between nodes (clients and servers) over a network. Socket is an identifier for uniquely identifying connection on a port. It is where a connection starts or begins.
  (i) Client is a requester of service. A client requests resources from the server.
  (ii) Server responds to the request. It is a software program that waits for client requests and serves the incoming processes.
- Every client uses the same ip:port (server) to request data. On receiving a connection request, the server assigns a unique identifier to a connection, i.e., socket. This facilitates the server to identify each connection uniquely.
- Socket is used to establish connection between a client and a server. The sequence is –
  (i) Create a socket in each program
  (ii) Connect both sockets together
  (iii) Once socket connection is established, the nodes can exchange data.

17.9 Socket Module in Python

- Python has a built-in `socket` module for socket programming.
- The `socket` module provides a way to connect with the socket.
- The `socket` module provides an interface to the Berkeley sockets API, a low-level socket interface implemented by modern operating systems. It is easy to make network connections and retrieve data over sockets. The module allows network connections over both TCP and UDP protocols.
- In Python, for socket programming, the built-in Python socket module is used. It consists of functions, constants, and classes that are used to create, manage, and work with sockets.
- Firstly, import the `socket` module in the code.
- To create a socket object, use the socket function `socket.socket()`. It creates a new socket object with system resource allocation.

The syntax of `socket()` is:

```
socket.socket(socket.address_family, socket.socket_type)
```

where,

`socket_type` can either be –

- SOCK_DGRAM for message-oriented datagram transport with UDP. It provides unreliable delivery of messages. It is used when the order of messages is not important, like, sending same data to multiple clients.
- SOCK_STREAM for stream-oriented transport with TCP. It provides a reliable and ordered delivery between two hosts. It is used for transfer of large amounts of data.

`Address_family` can be either of –

- AF_INET – uses IPv4 for network addressing
- AF_INET6 – uses IPv6 for network addressing
- AF_UNIX – for Unix Domain Sockets (UDS), a protocol for POSIX-compliant systems. The data exchange is on an operating system without going through the network.
- The socket object has methods. Some of the key methods that work on socket object are –
    1. `bind()` – binds the socket object to a network address (IP address and port number).
    2. `listen()` – allows the server to listen for incoming connection.
    3. `accept()` – accepts incoming connections on a server socket. It returns a tuple `(conn, address)` where `conn` is a new socket object that shares a connection with client and `address` is a tuple of client IP address and port.
    4. `close()` – closes and terminates the connection. It releases the associated resources.
    5. `connect()` – connects the client socket to a server.
    6. `send()` – sends data to the connected endpoints. It is used both by the client and the server.
    7. `sendall()` – similar to `send()`. It continues to send data from bytes until all data has been sent or an error occurs. None is returned on success.

8. `recv()` – to receive data from each other. It is used both by the client and the server.
9. `sendto()` – same as `send()`. Used for UDP protocol only.
10. `recvfrom()` – same as `recv()`. Used for UDP protocol.

In the following sections, we learn to create socket-based, server and client application in Python.

17.10 TCP Client–Server Communication

For communication over TCP, the sockets can be configured to act as a server or as a client. It uses the SOCK_STREAM family.

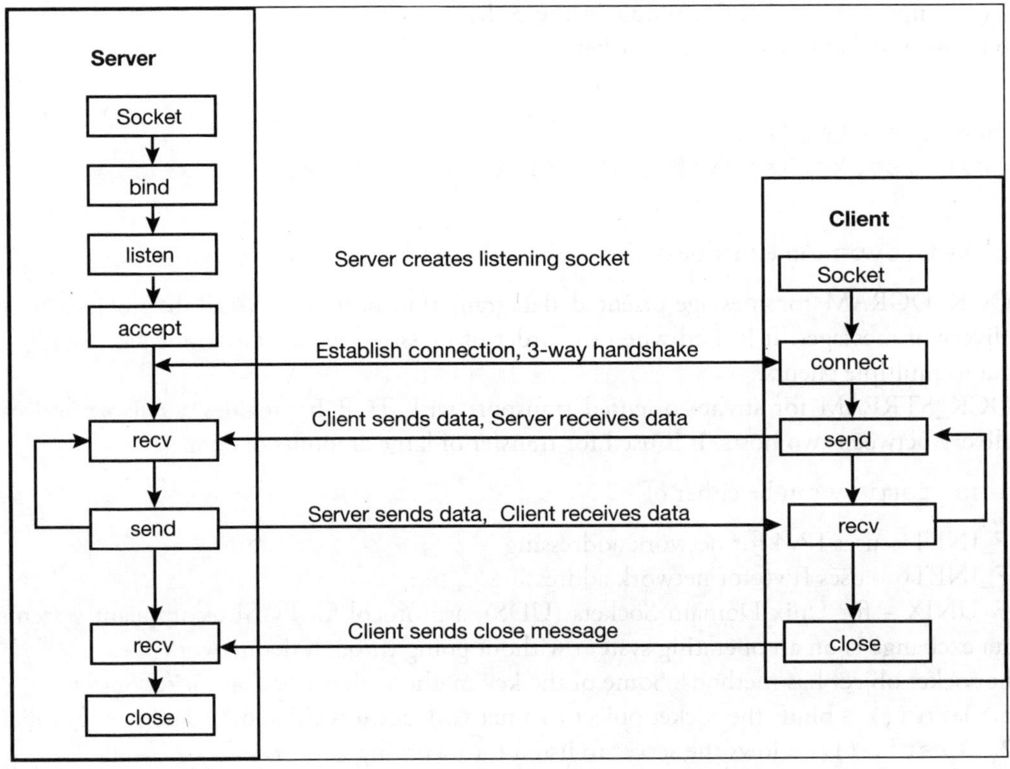

Figure 17.1 TCP socket flow

Figure 17.1 shows the communication between the client and the server in a TCP connection. We see that the socket server executes first and waits for request from the clients. The sequence of socket API calls and data flow are as follows:

- The left side of the diagram represents the server, the right-side is the client.
- On the server side, first set up a listening socket to listen for connections from clients. Use the APIs – `socket()`, `.bind()`, `.listen()`, and `.accept()`.

- The client calls `.connect()` API to establish a connection to the server. When a client connects, the server calls `.accept()` to accept or complete the connection.
- This initiates a three-way handshake or TCP handshake or SYN-SYN-ACK. Both client and server exchange SYN (synchronization) and ACK (acknowledgment) packets before data communication.
- Data is exchanged between the client and server using calls to `.send()` and `.recv()`.
- Both client and server use `.close()` to close their respective sockets.

In the following sub-sections, we see how to code both the server and the client so that they can easily communicate with each other.

17.10.1 Python Socket Server–Socket Client

The steps for creating a Python **socket server** are shown in Table 17.5.

Table 17.5 Steps for Socket Server

Steps	Code
1. Import socket module	`import socket`
2. Instantiate socket object	`sok=socket.socket(socket.AF_INET, socket.SOCK_STREAM)`
3. Bind server socket to IP address and port	`srv_addr = ('localhost', 8080)` `sok.bind(srv_addr)` *See(*4)*
4*. Listen for incoming connections	`sok.listen(1)` *See(*5)*
5#. Accept incoming connections	`conn, clnt_addr = sok.accept()`
6. Create communication loop	`while True loop: do the task`
7. Send response back to client	`data = conn.recv()` `conn.sendall(data)`
8. Free resources	`conn.close()`

* We bind IP address of localhost on the same machine. If empty string is passed, then server listens to requests coming from other computers on the network.

The argument is backlog, the maximum number of queued unaccepted connections.

Example 17.9: Implement the server socket for an echo application that receives all incoming data and sends them back in chunks of 24 to the sender. The local loopback address 127.0.0.1 or localhost at port 8080 is used for the connection.

```
import socket
sok = socket.socket(socket.AF_INET, socket.SOCK_STREAM)
srv_addr = ('localhost', 8080)
sok.bind(srv_addr)
print('Bind Server Socket to {} at port {}'.format(*srv_addr))
sok.listen(1)
while True:
    print('***Keep Listening***')
    conn, clnt_addr = sok.accept()
    try:
        print('***Accept from Client***', clnt_addr)
        while True:
            data = conn.recv(24) # in chunks
            print('Data Received: {!r}'.format(data))
            if data:
                print('Data retransmit to Client')
                conn.sendall(data)
            else:
                print('End of Data from', clnt_addr)
                break
    finally:
        print("Close Connection")
        conn.close()
```

The steps for creating a Python **socket client** are shown in Table 17.6.

Table 17.6 Steps for Socket Client

Steps		Code
1.	Import socket module	`import socket`
2.	Instantiate socket object	`sok=socket.socket(socket.AF_INET, socket.SOCK_STREAM)`
3.	Connect to server socket	`srv_addr = ('localhost', 8080)` `sok.connect(srv_addr)`
4.	Create communication loop	`sok.sendall(msg)`
5.	Handle server response	`data = sok.recv()`
6.	Free resources	`sok.close()`

Example 17.10: Implement the client socket for an echo application that sends data to the server and receives the incoming data in chunks of 24 from the server. The socket client starts the interaction with the server. In the client program, `connect()` connects the client to the server.

```
import socket
sok = socket.socket(socket.AF_INET, socket.SOCK_STREAM)
srv_addr = ('localhost', 8080)
print('Connecting to Server: {} port {}'.format(*srv_addr))
sok.connect(srv_addr)
try:
    msg = b'This data is being sent to server for transmission'
    print('Send Data: {!r}'.format(msg))
    sok.sendall(msg)

    data_rcvd = 0
    data_expcted = len(msg)
    while data_rcvd < data_expcted:
        data = sok.recv(24)
        data_rcvd += len(data)
        print('Received {!r}'.format(data))
finally:
    print('Close Client socket')
    sok.close()
```

17.10.2 Testing Client and Server

Having written the code for the server and the client, there is a need to test it. For testing, perform the following steps:

- We name the server program as Socket.py and the client program as Socket–Client.py.
- The two programs need to be working simultaneously.
- First, we execute the server program. For this,
  - **(i)** Open the IDLE shell.
  - **(ii)** Open the server program "Socket.py" here.
  - **(iii)** Run the program.
  - **(iv)** We get:

```
Bind Server Socket to localhost at port 8080
***Keep Listening***
```

- Next, we execute the client program. For this,
  - **(i)** Open the IDLE shell.
  - **(ii)** Open the client program "Socket–Client.py" here.
  - **(iii)** Run the program.
  - **(iv)** We get:

```
Connecting to Server: localhost port 8080
Send Data: b'This data is being sent to server for transmission'
Received b'This data is being sent '
Received b'to server for transmissi'
Received b'on'
Close Client socket
>>>
```

- Now, the server window shows –

```
Bind Server Socket to localhost at port 8080
***Keep Listening***
***Accept from Client*** ('127.0.0.1', 61272)
Data Received: b'This data is being sent '
Data retransmit to Client
Data Received: b'to server for transmissi'
Data retransmit to Client
Data Received: b'on'
Data retransmit to Client
Data Received: b''
End of Data from ('127.0.0.1', 61272)
Close Connection
***Keep Listening***
```

17.11 UDP Client–Server Communication

UDP is message-oriented. It does not require a long-lived connection. A message fits within a single datagram. The delivery is not assured.

On the server side, `socket()` and `bind()` sequences are executed because there is not really a connection to listen. We bind the socket to an address and wait for incoming messages. `recvfrom()` reads incoming messages, and `sendto()` sends them back.

- `recvfrom()` receives data from a socket. It returns a tuple (bytes, address) where, "bytes" is a bytes object having the received data and "address" is the address of sender.
- `sendto(bytes,address)` sends data (in bytes) to a socket bound to the address.

The sequence of socket API calls and data flow are as follows:

- Create a socket object using

    `socket.socket(socket.AF_INET,socket.SOCK_DGRAM).`

- Bind the socket to the ('localhost', 8000) and wait for incoming messages.
- When a message arrives, read it and unpack the return value into data and address.
- If data is received, send it back to the sender.
- This client is like the server, but it does not bind the socket to any address. It sends messages to the server address.

Example 17.11: For UDP, implement the server socket for an echo application that receives all incoming data and sends them back in chunks of 2048 to the sender. The local loopback address 127.0.0.1 or localhost at port 8080 is used for the connection. The client socket sends data to the server and receives the incoming data in chunks of 2048 from the server.

Server Program

```
import socket
sok = socket.socket(socket.AF_INET, socket.SOCK_DGRAM)
srv_addr = ('localhost', 8000)
print('Start on {} at port {}'.format(*srv_addr))
sok.bind(srv_addr)
while True:
    print('\nWaiting')
    data, addr = sok.recvfrom(2048)
    print('Received', len(data), 'bytes from:',addr)
    print('Data Received:', data)
    if data:
        sent = sok.sendto(data, addr)
        print('Sent', sent, 'bytes back to:', addr)
```

Client Program

```
import socket
sok = socket.socket(socket.AF_INET, socket.SOCK_DGRAM)
srv_addr = ('localhost', 8000)
msg = b'Our complete message'
try:
    print('Sending Data:', msg)
    snt = sok.sendto(msg, srv_addr)
    print('Waiting to receive')
    data, srv = sok.recvfrom(2048)
    print('Received:', data)
finally:
    print('Close Socket')
    sok.close()
```

Output: Server

```
Start on localhost at port 8000

Waiting
Received 20 bytes from: ('127.0.0.1', 51658)
Data Received: b'Our complete message'
Sent 20 bytes back to: ('127.0.0.1', 51658)

Waiting
```

Output: Client

```
Sending Data: b'Our complete message'
Waiting to receive
Received: b'Our complete message'
Close Socket
>>>
```

17.12 Using Developer Console to Explore HTTP

When writing Python programs for the Internet, sometimes there is a need for debugging the page we are working on. The Developer Console provides information about the interaction between the browser and the server. It allows us to find out various things about the request–response cycle. Here, we see how to use the developer console in the browser.

- To open the developer console, perform the following steps:
  - **(i)** In the browser, open the menu in upper-right hand corner of the browser window.
  - **(ii)** Select <More Tools><Developer Tools>
  - **(iii)** Also, a shortcut on Windows/Linux to open developer console is <shift + ctrl + J>
- Next, we open a page on the browser, *http://people.du.ac.in/~agoel/books.html*
- Click on the <Network> tab and refresh the page. It shows each of the request–response cycle.
  - **(i)** We see the names associated with the html page. The total number of requests are 29. We can see the type and status of each request.

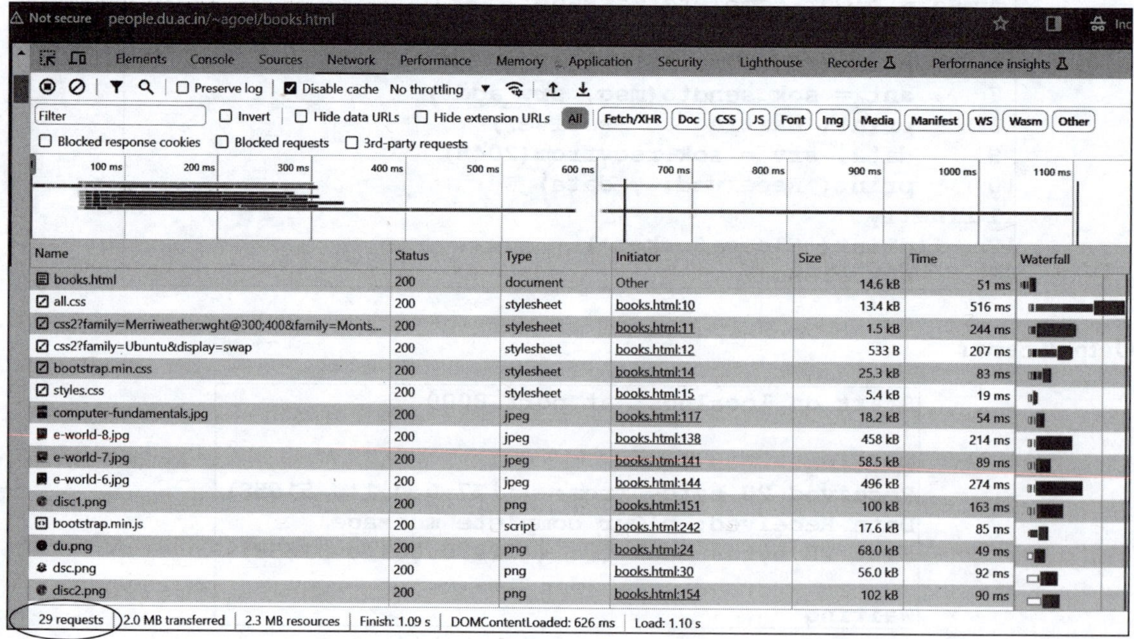

- Click on the <books.html> name. It shows five tabs – Headers, Preview, Response, Initiator and Timing.
- Click <Headers> to see all the requests.
  (i) We see it is a GET request. Status code 200, everything is fine (OK).
  (ii) Remote Address shows the IP address where the request is going.
  (iii) In Response Headers, we see content-type is text/html, and date of last modification.
  (iv) In Request-Header, we see the language is English, and the host web address.

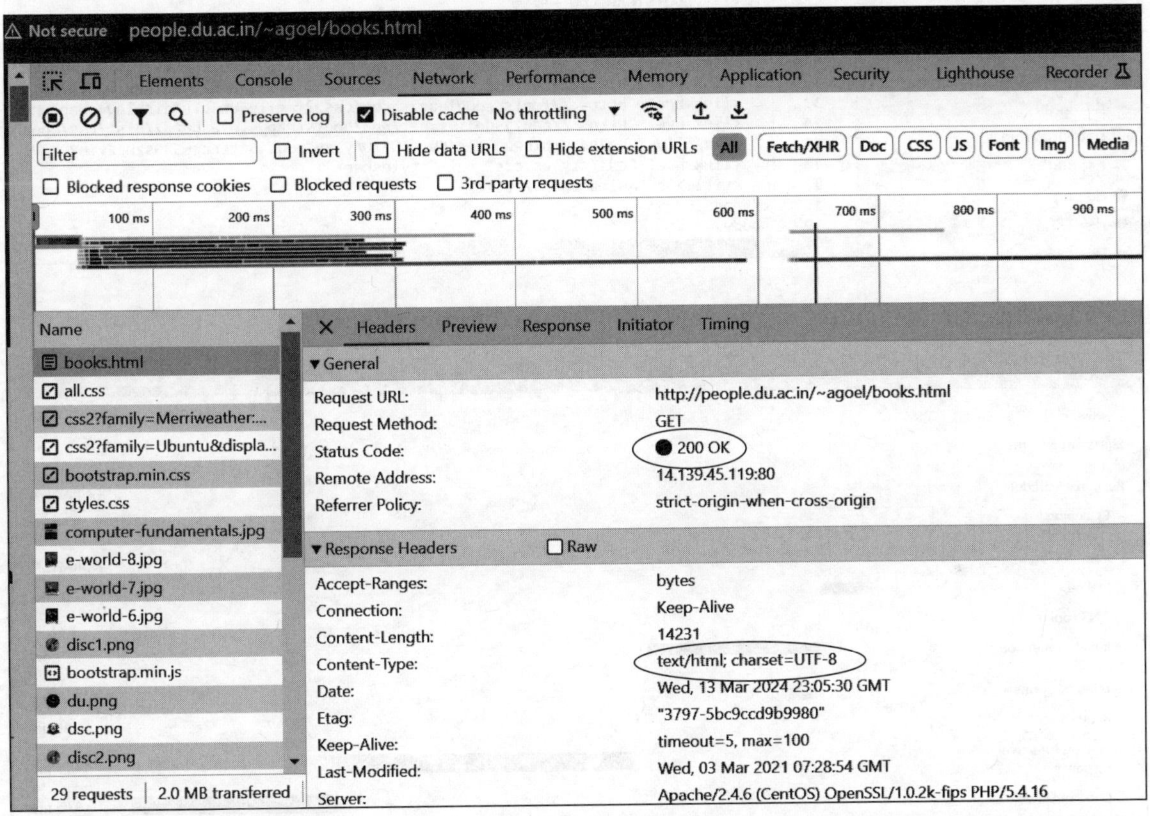

Not secure people.du.ac.in/~agoel/books.html

Elements Console Sources Network Performance Memory Application Security Lighthouse Recorder

Preserve log | Disable cache | No throttling

Filter | Invert | Hide data URLs | Hide extension URLs | All | Fetch/XHR | Doc | CSS | JS | Font | Img | Media

Blocked response cookies | Blocked requests | 3rd-party requests

100 ms 200 ms 300 ms 400 ms 500 ms 600 ms 700 ms 800 ms 900 ms

Name: books.html, all.css, css2?family=Merriweather:..., css2?family=Ubuntu&displa..., bootstrap.min.css, styles.css, computer-fundamentals.jpg, e-world-8.jpg, e-world-7.jpg, e-world-6.jpg, disc1.png, bootstrap.min.js, du.png, dsc.png, disc2.png

29 requests | 2.0 MB transferred

Headers | Preview | Response | Initiator | Timing

▼ General

Request URL:	http://people.du.ac.in/~agoel/books.html
Request Method:	GET
Status Code:	200 OK
Remote Address:	14.139.45.119:80
Referrer Policy:	strict-origin-when-cross-origin

▼ Response Headers Raw

Accept-Ranges:	bytes
Connection:	Keep-Alive
Content-Length:	14231
Content-Type:	text/html; charset=UTF-8
Date:	Wed, 13 Mar 2024 23:05:30 GMT
Etag:	"3797-5bc9ccd9b9980"
Keep-Alive:	timeout=5, max=100
Last-Modified:	Wed, 03 Mar 2021 07:28:54 GMT
Server:	Apache/2.4.6 (CentOS) OpenSSL/1.0.2k-fips PHP/5.4.16

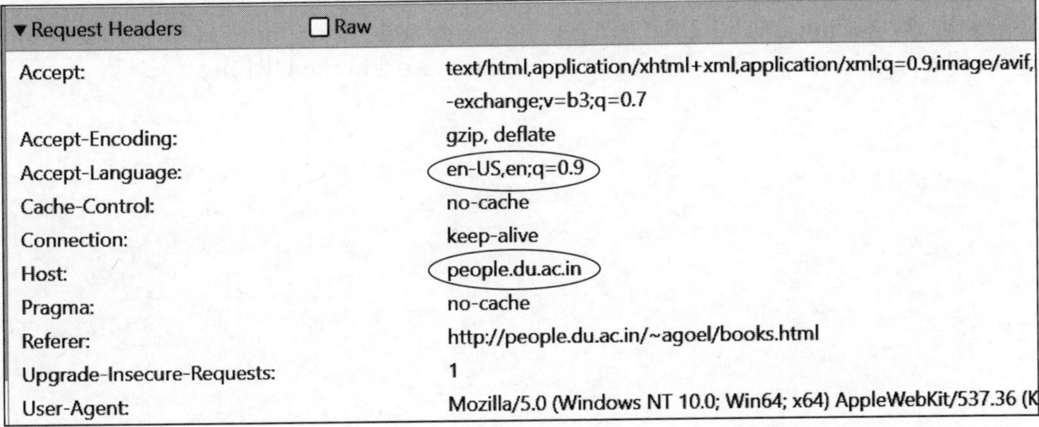
▼ Request Headers Raw

Accept:	text/html,application/xhtml+xml,application/xml;q=0.9,image/avif, -exchange;v=b3;q=0.7
Accept-Encoding:	gzip, deflate
Accept-Language:	en-US,en;q=0.9
Cache-Control:	no-cache
Connection:	keep-alive
Host:	people.du.ac.in
Pragma:	no-cache
Referer:	http://people.du.ac.in/~agoel/books.html
Upgrade-Insecure-Requests:	1
User-Agent:	Mozilla/5.0 (Windows NT 10.0; Win64; x64) AppleWebKit/537.36 (K

- Click on <Response> to see the Response.

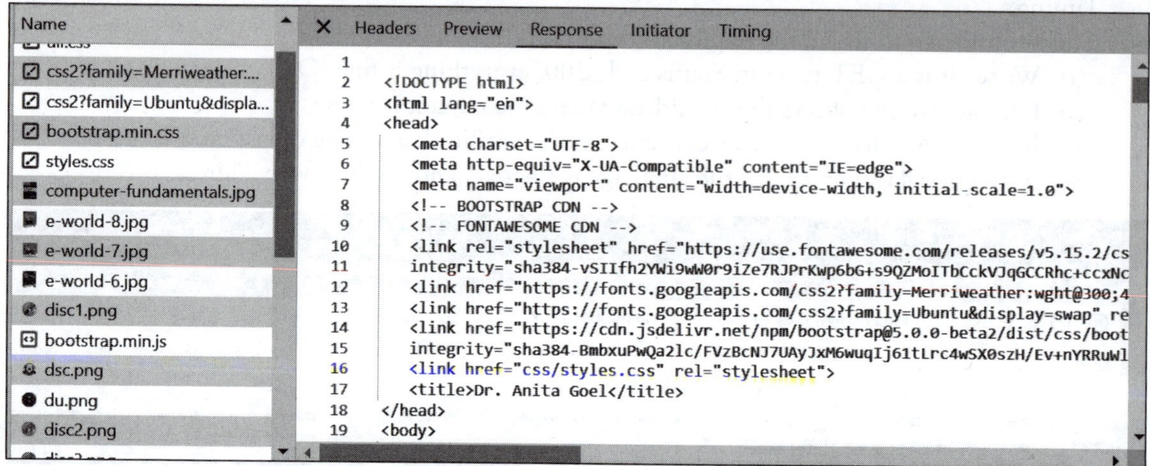

- Click on <Timing>. It shows the time taken for the different events.

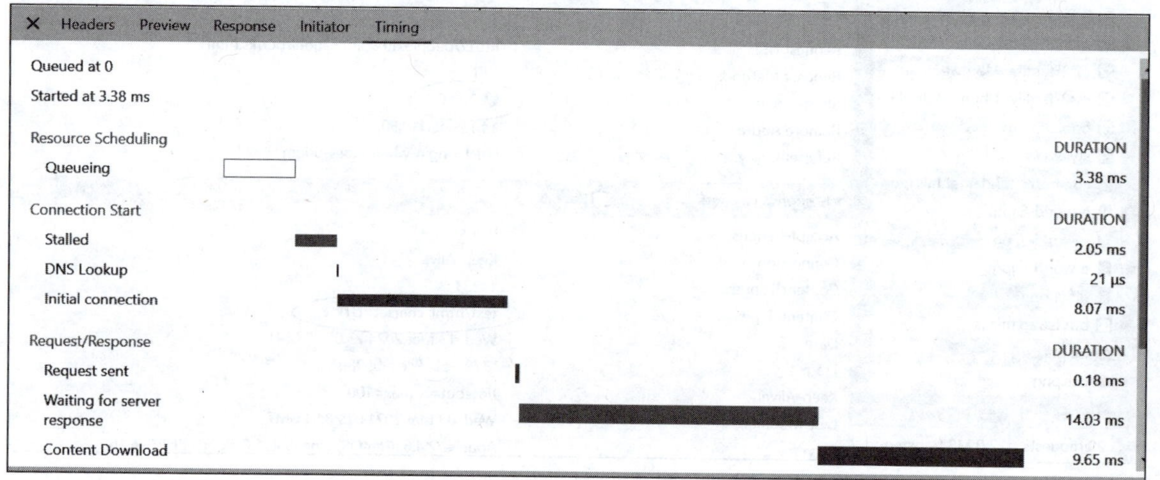

- When we do not put a valid URL, we get the Status code in response as 404 (Not Found). It means the page is not present. (Here, we have added `.aed` in the URL.)

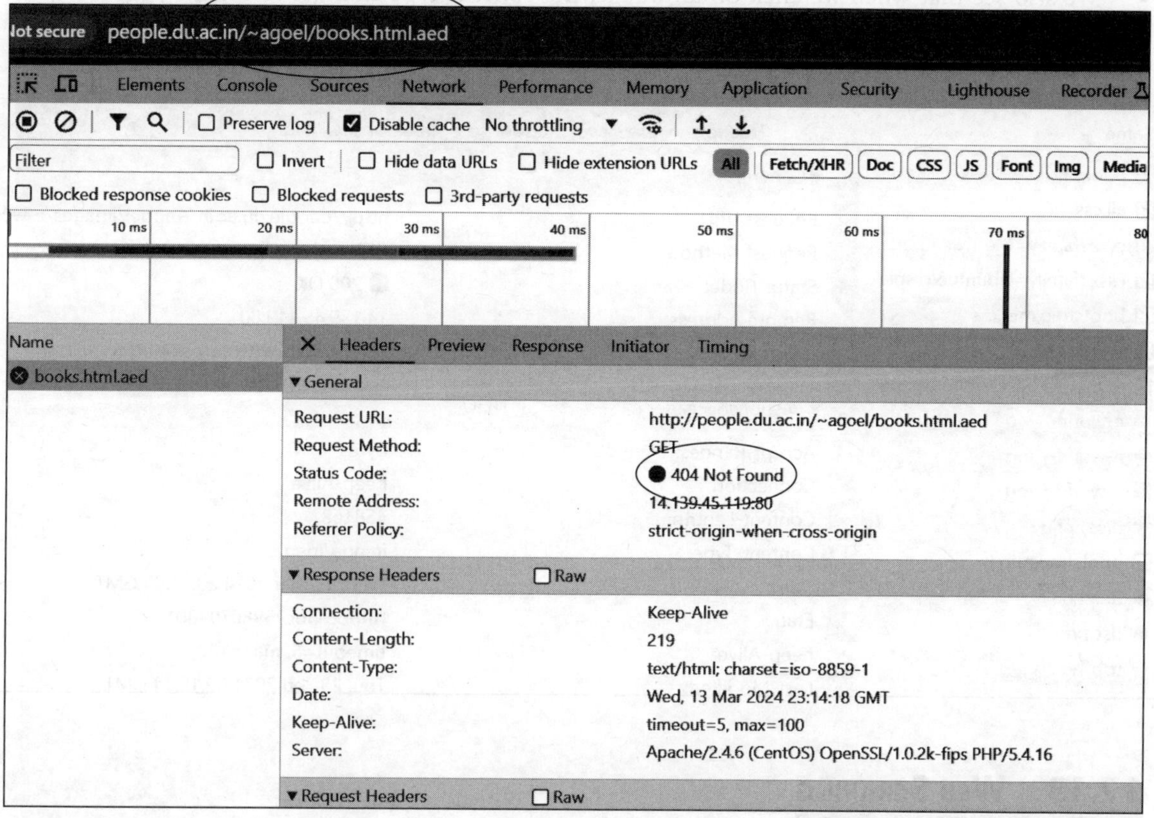

Not secure people.du.ac.in/~agoel/books.html.aed

Elements Console Sources Network Performance Memory Application Security Lighthouse Recorder

Preserve log Disable cache No throttling

Filter Invert Hide data URLs Hide extension URLs All Fetch/XHR Doc CSS JS Font Img Media

Blocked response cookies Blocked requests 3rd-party requests

10 ms 20 ms 30 ms 40 ms 50 ms 60 ms 70 ms 80

Name

books.html.aed

Headers Preview Response Initiator Timing

▼General

Request URL: http://people.du.ac.in/~agoel/books.html.aed
Request Method: GET
Status Code: 404 Not Found
Remote Address: 14.139.45.119:80
Referrer Policy: strict-origin-when-cross-origin

▼Response Headers Raw

Connection: Keep-Alive
Content-Length: 219
Content-Type: text/html; charset=iso-8859-1
Date: Wed, 13 Mar 2024 23:14:18 GMT
Keep-Alive: timeout=5, max=100
Server: Apache/2.4.6 (CentOS) OpenSSL/1.0.2k-fips PHP/5.4.16

▼Request Headers Raw

- We also see that if the cache is not disabled, then after the first access, the next time we when we access the same page, we get the code 304, which means the page has not been modified.

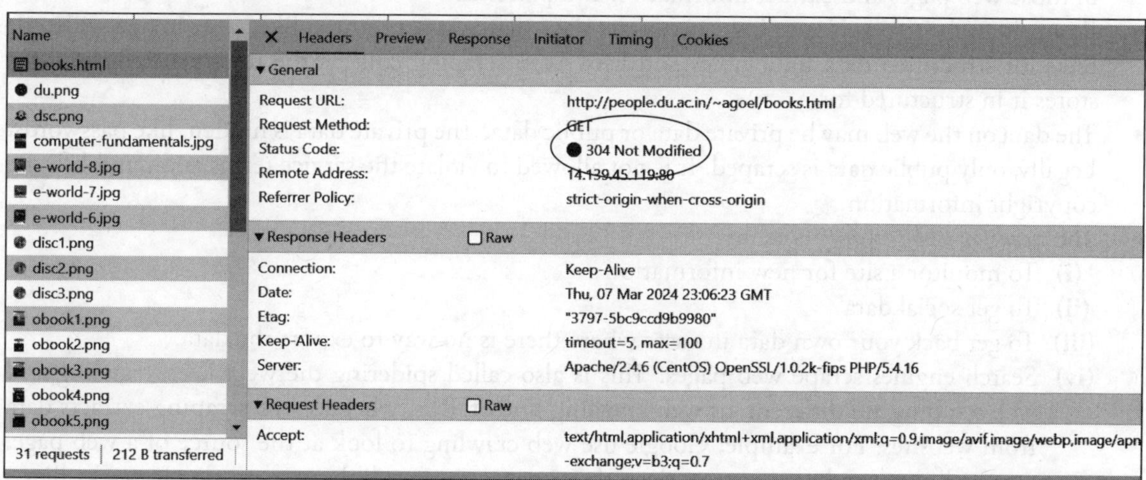

- We also see that when we click on an image, the content-type changes to image/jpeg. We get a GET request. That means whatever was reqeusted has been provided. We see the content-type changes. Now it is image/jpeg.

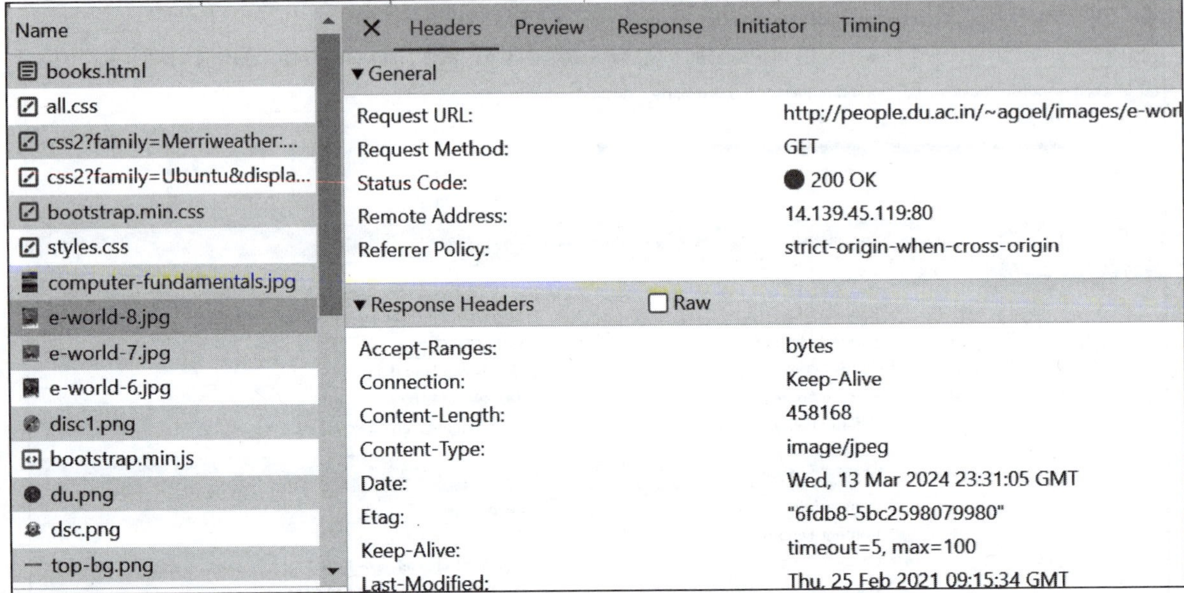

17.13 Web Scraping

- Web scraping is the process to extract data from the websites. It is an automated method. Web scraping is when a program pretends to be a web browser and retrieves web pages, to examine data in those web pages and extract information and patterns.
- From the websites, web scraping can extract data that is unstructured like, text, image, video or links; or structured data like, tables and lists. Web scraping collects the unstructured data and stores it in structured form.
- The data on the web may be private data or public data. The private data is hidden, like passwords. Legally, only public data is scraped. It is not allowed to violate the service terms and republish the copyright information.
- The *need for web scraping* is many:
  - **(i)** To monitor a site for new information
  - **(ii)** To get social data
  - **(iii)** To get back your own data in cases where there is no way to export the data.
  - **(iv)** Search engines scrape web pages. This is also called spidering the web. Web crawling and web scraping are different, as web crawling finds URLs, whereas web scraping extracts data from websites. For example, Google use web crawling to look at the source of a web page, extract links to other pages, retrieve those pages, extract links, and so on. It works like a

spider and goes through nearly all pages on the web. It uses the frequency of links to a particular page as a measure of importance of a page and decides the position (high, low) of the web page in its search results.

- The process of web scraping can be classified into three steps, broadly:
  (i) Send a request to a website
  (ii) Parse HTML code to extract relevant data.
  (iii) Clean the data and structure it into a format that can be easily analyzed.
- **Python is popular for web scraping.** It has several third-party libraries to scrape HTML structures, parse text, and interact with HTML form.
- Some popular libraries and tools in Python for web scraping are:
  (i) **Urllib and Urllib3** – HTTP client library for Python, making it easy to programmatically perform HTTP requests.
    - `urllib` is part of Python Standard Library. There is no need to install it separately. urllib package is a collection of several modules, such as urllib.requests, urllib.error , and urllib.parse.
    - `urllib3` is not included in Python Standard Library. It is a third-party HTTP client for Python; so, it must be installed. It provides much more functionality than urllib. It handles HTTP headers, retries, redirects, and other low-level details. It supports SSL verification, connection pooling, and proxying.

  (ii) **Requests** – It is a third-party Python library for making HTTP requests. It must be installed. It is easy to use and is simple with a consistent API. It is used for sending GET and POST requests, handle cookies, authentication, and other HTTP features.
  (iii) **BeautifulSoup** – It is third-party Python library for parsing HTML and XML documents. The APIs allow easy navigation through the HTML document tree and extract tags, meta titles, attributes, text, and other content. It does robust error handling.
  (iv) **MechanicalSoup** – It automates interaction between a web browser and a website efficiently. It provides a high-level API that simulates human behavior. It allows interaction with HTML forms, click buttons, and interacts with elements like a real user. It is used with HTML forms.
  (v) **Selenium** – To automate web browsers, like Chrome, Firefox, and Safari and simulate human interaction with websites.
  (vi) **Pandas** – To store and manipulate data in formats like, CSV, Excel, JSON, and SQL databases. It cleans, transforms, and analyzes data extracted from websites.

- For web scraping, two tools are needed in Python: HTTP Client and HTML Parser.
  (i) HTTP API Client retrieves web pages. For example, Requests, urllib3, pycurl.
  (ii) HTML Parser parses and extracts data from the fetched pages. e.g. BeautifulSoup, lxml, pyquery.

17.13.1 Steps for Scraping Data

Let us look at the step-by-step process of using Python to scrape website data.

1) Get URL of website to be scraped.

2) Inspect the website or webpage to find the data to be extracted. For this, there is a need to understand the website structure, elements and their attributes that are of interest. On right-click of the website, a pop-up window appears. Select <Inspect>. It opens the HTML code of the website. Note down the names of elements, their class names, and ids, for use in the Python scraping code to be written.
3) Write the code to extract information, provide relevant information and run the code.
   a) Install the important libraries.
      - Requests or urllib3 – to make HTTP requests to the website to get HTML content.
      - BeautifulSoup – to parse HTML code to extract data from rendered content to scrape the HTML page.
      - Pandas – to store scraped data in a data frame
   b) Write the Python code.
      - Using Requests to send an HTTP GET request.
      - Using BeautifulSoup to parse HTML code.
      - Extract the required data from HTML code.
      - Store the information in a Pandas dataframe.
   c) On running a web scraping code, the following actions happen:
      - The code sends a request to the mentioned URL (website).
      - The website responds to the request by sending data and allows the code to read XML/HTML page.
      - The code extracts the required data from the XML/HTML page.
4) Store the data in the file in required csv, xml, JSON file format.

Here, we shall discuss the retrieving of web pages and parsing the web pages.

17.14 Retrieving Web Pages

Python has two popular libraries – `Requests` and `urllib3` for sending HTTP requests and handling responses. The following points may help the user to choose among the libraries:

- `Requests` is a higher-level library with a Python-like interface for sending HTTP requests; `urllib3` is a lower-level library with API for handling HTTP requests and responses.
- `Requests` is built on top of `urllib3`. It includes `urllib3` functionality and additional features.
- `Requests` has built-in support for features, like authentication, cookie handling, and session management, unlike `urllib3`.
- `urllib3` is a standalone library; `Requests` has some dependencies, such as on `urllib3`.

It is suggested that if you need simplicity and ease of use, then use `Requests`.

If more fine-grained control over low-level HTTP features is required, then use `urllib3`.

17.14.1 Need for Encoding and Decoding

- The computers do not understand letters; they understand numbers. To represent a character, a mapping between letters and numbers was formed. The most common mapping of the 1980s is called ASCII (American Standard Code for Information Interchange). It tells the number that equals the letter. As we see, the capital "A' is denoted by 65, the lowercase 'e' by 101 and the newline character by 10. Each character is represented by a number between 0 and 256, and stored in 8-bit (byte) memory. The numbers could be represented in hexadecimal, octal or binary forms. The `ord()` function tells the numeric value of an ASCII character.

```
>>> print(ord('H'))
72
```

The lowercase letters are all greater than the uppercase letters, because they are ordinal for ASCII. So, 'Hi' < 'aaa'.

- When the Japanese, Arabic, Chinese and many more character sets came up, each had their own way of representing letters, but the Japanese, Arabic and other computers could not interact with one another. Then the Unicode came.
- Unicode is universal code for hundreds of millions of different characters and hundreds of different character sets. Unicode can be represented in a computer as – UTF-8, UTF-16, and UTF-32. The UTF-8 is the best practice for encoding data moving between systems. UTF overlaps with ASCII. So, if the characters are original ASCII, then UTF-8 and ASCII are the same thing.
- In Python 3, the regular string and Unicode string are same and are strings. All the strings internally are Unicode. But byte string and regular string are different. Bytes are raw and unencoded. In a network, we note that files and strings are inside the computer; but network connections and databases are not inside the computer. So, we must manage the different strings when we deal with data from outside.
- In a network, one of the requirements for using the HTTP protocol is the need to send and receive data as bytes objects, instead of strings. For this, `encode()` and `decode()` methods are used. The data is moved between the systems via the sockets.
  - **(i)** `data.decode` is used to go from bytes to Unicode. Decode is a method in the bytes class. When we receive data, it converts byte objects into strings.
  - **(ii)** Encode takes the string and makes it into bytes. So, when we send out data, it converts strings into bytes objects.

17.14.2 Using Requests

- `Requests` is a simple python web scraping library.
- It is an HTTP library used for accessing web pages.
- Using `Requests`, we get raw HTML of web pages. This can be parsed for retrieving the data.
- For using `requests`-
  - **(i)** Install the library using the pip command.

```
pip install requests
```

  - **(ii)** Import the modules in your program.

```
import requests
```

- Using `requests` –
  (i) We access a webpage using GET HTTP request. For example,

```
data = requests.get('https://google.com/')
```

  (ii) One of the ways is to retrieve content using the.text property. For example,

```
data.text[:200]
```

Example 17.12: (a) Using requests to extract HTML code (b) Snapshot of Output.

```
import requests

req = requests.get("https://en.wikipedia.org/wiki/Python")
print("Object type:",type(req))
print(req.text[:200])
```

(a)

```
Object type: <class 'requests.models.Response'>
<!DOCTYPE html>
<html class="client-nojs vector-feature-language-in-header-enabled ve
ctor-feature-language-in-main-page-header-disabled vector-feature-sti
cky-header-disabled vector-feature-page-tools-
```

(b)

17.14.3 Using `urllib3`

- `Urllib3` wraps the socket.
- `Urllib3` is a Python library that is used for getting the raw data (HTML) from a web page.
- Using `urllib3` –
  (i) We access a website in the same way as using a browser.
  (ii) The content is not rendered visually as with a browser, but we get the source code as text.
  (iii) From the HTML received as text, extract the desired information.

- For using `urllib3`, import the library. For using `urllib`, there is no need to import.
- Use `urllib.request.urlopen`. It opens the library and returns a file handle.
- It does not read the data. Use a for-loop in this handle to iterate through all the lines of this URL. The line iteration is a byte array, not a string. Decode it to get a string.
- It shows only the data and not the headers.
- When we read a web page in Python, it gets data of the web page and treats it as a file.
- We use Python to get web data, we can read HTML files. We also note that though the headers are there, they do not come out in the for-loop.

Example 17.13: (a) Using `urllib` to extract HTML code (b) Snapshot of Output.

We write the code to extract data from the wepage http://people.du.ac.in/~agoel/research.html. We see that we get the HTML code.

```
import urllib.request

data = urllib.request.urlopen('http://people.du.ac.in/~agoel/research.html')
for aline in data:
    print(aline.decode().strip())
```

(a)

```
<!DOCTYPE html>
<html lang="en">
<head>
<meta charset="UTF-8">
<meta http-equiv="X-UA-Compatible" content="IE=edge">
<meta name="viewport" content="width=device-width, initial-scale=1.0">
<!-- BOOTSTRAP CDN -->
<link href="https://cdn.jsdelivr.net/npm/bootstrap@5.0.0-beta2/dist/css/bootstra
p.min.css" rel="stylesheet"
integrity="sha384-BmbxuPwQa2lc/FVzBcNJ7UAyJxM6wuqIj61tLrc4wSX0szH/Ev+nYRRuWlolfl
fl" crossorigin="anonymous">
<!-- FONTAWESOME CDN -->
<link rel="stylesheet" href="https://use.fontawesome.com/releases/v5.15.2/css/al
l.css"
integrity="sha384-vSIIfh2YWi9wW0r9iZe7RJPrKwp6bG+s9QZMoITbCckVJqGCCRhc+ccxNcdpHu
Yu" crossorigin="anonymous">
<link href="https://fonts.googleapis.com/css2?family=Merriweather:wght@300;400&f
amily=Montserrat:wght@300;400;500&family=Noto+Sans&family=Quattrocento:wght@700&
family=Quicksand&family=Raleway&family=Roboto:wght@300;400&display=swap" rel="st
ylesheet">
<link href="https://fonts.googleapis.com/css2?family=Ubuntu&display=swap" rel="s
```

(b)

Example 17.14: (a) Use `urllib` to extract HTML code and count the number of tags (b) Snapshot of Output.

```
import urllib.request, urllib.parse, urllib.error

data = urllib.request.urlopen('http://people.du.ac.in/~agoel/research.html')
ct = dict()
for line in data:
    wds = line.decode().split()
    for w in wds:
        ct[w] = ct.get(w, 0) + 1
print(ct)
```

(a)

```
{'<!DOCTYPE': 1, 'html>': 1, '<html': 1, 'lang="en">': 1, '<head>': 1, '<meta':
3, 'charset="UTF-8">': 1, 'http-equiv="X-UA-Compatible"': 1, 'content="IE=edge">
': 1, 'name="viewport"': 1, 'content="width=device-width,': 1, 'initial-scale=1.
0">': 1, '<!--': 3, 'BOOTSTRAP': 1, 'CDN': 2, '-->': 3, '<link': 5, 'href="https
://cdn.jsdelivr.net/npm/bootstrap@5.0.0-beta2/dist/css/bootstrap.min.css"': 1, '
rel="stylesheet"': 2, 'integrity="sha384-BmbxuPwQa2lc/FVzBcNJ7UAyJxM6wuqIj61tLrc
4wSX0szH/Ev+nYRRuWlolflfl"': 1, 'crossorigin="anonymous">': 2, 'FONTAWESOME': 1,
 'href="https://use.fontawesome.com/releases/v5.15.2/css/all.css"': 1, 'integrit
y="sha384-vSIIfh2YWi9wW0r9iZe7RJPrKwp6bG+s9QZMoITbCckVJqGCCRhc+ccxNcdpHuYu"': 1,
 'href="https://fonts.googleapis.com/css2?family=Merriweather:wght@300;400&famil
y=Montserrat:wght@300;400;500&family=Noto+Sans&family=Quattrocento:wght@700&fami
ly=Quicksand&family=Raleway&family=Roboto:wght@300;400&display=swap"': 1, 'rel="
stylesheet">': 3, 'href="https://fonts.googleapis.com/css2?family=Ubuntu&display
=swap"': 1, 'href="css/styles.css"': 1, '<title>Dr.': 1, 'Anita': 3, 'Goel</titl
```

(b)

Example 17.15: (a) Use `urllib3` to extract HTML code and find all <a> tags. (b) Snapshot of Output.

```
import urllib3
import bs4
http = urllib3.PoolManager()
r = http.request('GET','http://people.du.ac.in/~agoel/research.html')
soup = bs4.BeautifulSoup(r.data, 'html.parser')
# find all <a> tags
links = soup.find_all('a')
for link in links:
    print(link.get('href'))
```

(a)

```
index.html
about.html
teaching.html
research.html
publications.html
books.html
other.html
gallery.html
#top
#interests
#phd
#mphil
#projects
#mtech
#doctoral
```

(b)

17.15 Parsing Web Pages

The data retrieved from the web page needs to be parsed to get the desired information. Here, we discuss two ways to get the content:

- Extraction using regular Expression, and
- Using a HTML parser, BeautifulSoup.

17.15.1 Extract Text from HTML with Regular Expressions

The retrieved HTML content needs to be parsed to get relevant data from the code. Regular expression is a way for extracting data from the HTML content. We have discussed regular expressions in the earlier sections. The `re.findall()` method is used for the same.

Example 17.16: (a) Use regular expression to extract from HTML code to find data in <p> and <li> tags. (b) Snapshot of Output.

```
import re
import urllib.request, urllib.parse, urllib.error
data = urllib.request.urlopen('http://people.du.ac.in/~agoel/teaching.html')
data_bytes = data.read()
txt = data_bytes.decode('utf-8')
print(re.findall("<p>(.*?)</p>", txt), '\n')
x1= (re.findall("<li>(.*?)</li>", txt))
for w in x1:
    print(w)
```

(a)

```
['All Rights Reserved <i class="far fa-copyright"></i>  by : Dr. Anit
a Goel']

RCS-001 Research Methodology-Module 5:Scientific Writing (2019)
RCS-001 Research Methodology-Module 5:Scientific Writing (2018)
RCS-001 Research Methodology-Module 5:Scientific Writing (2017)
RCS01a Advance Data Structure (2012)
Foundations of Software Testing (2009)
Testing of Web Applications (2009)
```

(b)

In the code, we look at the regular expression in the pattern string by breaking it down into three parts:

- <p> and <li> matches the opening <p> and <li> tag in html.
- (.*?) non-greedily matches all text after the opening <p> and <li>, stopping at the first match for </p> and </li>, respectively.
- </p> and </li> matches the closing </p> and </li> tag, respectively in html.

- `findall()` finds all the matches.

17.15.2 Using HTML Parser – BeautifulSoup

Regular expressions are good for pattern matching. It is generally easy to use an HTML parser designed for parsing the HTML pages. BeautifulSoup is a library for parsing HTML code.

For using the BeautifulSoup library in the code, do the following:

- Install the BeautifulSoup library using the pip command.
  `pip install beautifulsoup4`
- Import the modules in your program.
  `From bs4 import BeautifulSoup`
- Use the library to parse the HTML content, like,
  `soup = BeautifulSoup(response.text, 'html.parser')`
- Extract the data from HTML, for example, get text content of webpage using text attribute.
  ```
  text = soup.get_text()
  print(text)
  ```

Example 17.17: (a) Use BeautifulSoup to extract all headings by class name from wikipedia page. (b) Snapshot of Output.

```
import bs4
import requests

r = requests.get("https://en.wikipedia.org/wiki/Python")
data = bs4.BeautifulSoup(r.text,'html.parser')
print("Object type:",type(data), '\n')
print("Headlines from-https://en.wikipedia.org/wiki/Python")
print("----" * 15)
for x in data.select('.mw-headline'):
    print(x.text,end = ',')
```

(a)

```
Object type: <class 'bs4.BeautifulSoup'>

Headlines from-https://en.wikipedia.org/wiki/Python
------------------------------------------------------------
Snakes,Computing,People,Roller coasters,Vehicles,Weaponry,Other uses,
See also,
```

(b)

This program does the following:

- Requests gets the data from the wiki page in variable `r`.
- BeautifulSoup object is created with two arguments:

(i) The first argument is HTML to be parsed (r.text),
(ii) The second argument is string "html.parser" that tells the parser to be used ("html. parser" is Python's built-in HTML parser).

- The parsed HTML page is stored in data.
- Select the headlines using select() method (data.select).

17.16 Solved Examples

1. Find the output:

```
import re
str = 'abcdabcpqr'
print("String=", str)
pat = input('Enter pattern to check: ')
a = re.match(pat, str)
if a != None:
 print("Match-","pat=",a.group(), "string=",a.string)
else:
 print("*No Match*", pat, "not in beginning")
```

Output

```
String= abcdabcpqr
Enter pattern to check: abc
Match- pat= abc string= abcdabcpqr
```

```
String= abcdabcpqr
Enter pattern to check: pqr
*No Match* pqr not in beginning
```

Explanation: Match matches the pattern at the start of the string. The pattern "pqr" is in the string but not at the start, so it is not matched,

2. Find the output:

```
import re
txt = "The pain in Belpain"
print("Search ai : ", re.search("ai", txt))
print("Findall ai: ", re.findall("ai", txt))
```

Output

```
Search ai :  <re.Match object; span=(5, 7), match='ai'>
Findall ai:  ['ai', 'ai']
```

3. Find the output:

```
import re
txt = "The pain in Spain"
x = re.search(r"\bS\w+", txt)
print("The span is  : ", x.span())
print("The string is: ", x.string)
print("The match is : ", x.group())
```

Output

```
The span is  :  (12, 17)
The string is:  The pain in Spain
The match is :  Spain
```

Explanation: It searches a word that starts with an upper case "S".

4. Find the output:

```
import re
strng = "The quick brown fox jumps over the lazy dog"
pat = "[a-g]"
print(re.findall(pat, strng) )
```

Output

```
['e', 'c', 'b', 'f', 'e', 'e', 'a', 'd', 'g']
```

Explanation: It prints all characters in the string from a to g.

5. Use the command to view the state of the socket.
For this, use `netstat` command
`>netstat -an`
where `an` is active network.

```
TCP    192.168.29.239:55221   162.125.40.1:443       ESTABLISHED
TCP    192.168.29.239:55222   204.79.197.254:443     ESTABLISHED
TCP    192.168.29.239:55223   204.79.197.200:443     ESTABLISHED
TCP    192.168.29.239:55224   20.185.212.106:443     TIME_WAIT
TCP    192.168.29.239:55225   10.115.18.208:7680     SYN_SENT
TCP    192.168.29.239:55226   10.40.132.54:7680      SYN_SENT
TCP    192.168.29.239:55227   20.50.201.200:443      ESTABLISHED
TCP    [::]:135               [::]:0                 LISTENING
TCP    [::]:445               [::]:0                 LISTENING
TCP    [::]:808               [::]:0                 LISTENING
TCP    [::]:5357              [::]:0                 LISTENING
TCP    [::]:7680              [::]:0                 LISTENING
TCP    [::]:9001              [::]:0                 LISTENING
TCP    [::]:17500             [::]:0                 LISTENING
TCP    [::]:49664             [::]:0                 LISTENING
TCP    [::]:49665             [::]:0                 LISTENING
TCP    [::]:49666             [::]:0                 LISTENING
TCP    [::]:49668             [::]:0                 LISTENING
TCP    [::]:49669             [::]:0                 LISTENING
TCP    [::]:49671             [::]:0                 LISTENING
TCP    [::1]:49670            [::]:0                 LISTENING
TCP    [2405:201:4003:8924:ed87:6d85:23b6:990e]:53789  [2404:6800:4003:c03::bc]:5228  ESTABLISHED
TCP    [2405:201:4003:8924:ed87:6d85:23b6:990e]:55151  [2404:6800:4002:82e::2005]:443  TIME_WAIT
TCP    [2405:201:4003:8924:ed87:6d85:23b6:990e]:55153  [2600:140f:5::17d9:6e93]:443  ESTABLISHED
```

```
UDP    127.0.0.1:49668        127.0.0.1:49668
UDP    127.0.0.1:58174        *:*
UDP    127.0.0.1:64060        *:*
UDP    192.168.29.239:137     *:*
UDP    192.168.29.239:138     *:*
UDP    192.168.29.239:1900    *:*
UDP    192.168.29.239:2177    *:*
UDP    192.168.29.239:58173   *:*
UDP    [::]:123               *:*
UDP    [::]:500               *:*
UDP    [::]:3702              *:*
UDP    [::]:3702              *:*
UDP    [::]:3702              *:*
UDP    [::]:3702              *:*
UDP    [::]:4500              *:*
UDP    [::]:5353              *:*
UDP    [::]:5353              *:*
UDP    [::]:5353              *:*
UDP    [::]:5353              *:*
UDP    [::]:5355              *:*
UDP    [::]:50339             [2404:6800:4002:80a::2003]:443
UDP    [::]:51309             *:*
UDP    [::]:51992             *:*
UDP    [::]:53166             [2404:6800:4002:821::200a]:443
UDP    [::]:55145             *:*
UDP    [::]:56347             [2404:6800:4002:822::200a]:443
UDP    [::]:62696             [2404:6800:4002:825::200e]:443
UDP    [::1]:1900             *:*
```

17.17 Programming Examples

Program 17.1: WAP to search for a particular pattern inside a string.

```
import re
text = 'Nature Nurtures us #PK:222 #DS:22 #ab:22 @abcdef22'
#TASK: Extract #Log:314
print(re.findall(r'(#[A-Z]+:\d{1,3})+',text))
```

Output

```
['#PK:222', '#DS:22']
```

Explanation

In (#[A-Z]+:\d{1,3})+

#[A-Z]+: matches for a hash followed by one or more capital letters, followed by colon.

\d{1,3} looks for any digit with 1 to 3 times repetition.

+ The last plus sign looks for 1 or n repetitions of the RegEx.

Program 17.2: WAP to extract the email address of specific providers. (i) Print all email addresses (ii) Print all.com email addresses, and (iii) Print all (gmail/yahoo).com email addresses.

```
import re
data = 'abcd22@gmail.com pqrs121@wp.com xyz123@yahoo.com\
          aabbaa@hotmail.com XX.in YY.ac.in'
print("All data:\n", '\t',data)
print(".com email:\n", '\t',re.findall(r'\w+@[A-z]+.com',data))
sel_email = re.findall(r'(\w+@(gmail|yahoo).com)', data)
s_email = [x[0] for x in sel_email]
print("(gmail|yahoo).com email\n",'\t', s_email)
```

Output

```
All data:
        abcd22@gmail.com pqrs121@wp.com xyz123@yahoo.com
        aabbaa@hotmail.com XX.in YY.ac.in
.com email:
        ['abcd22@gmail.com', 'pqrs121@wp.com', 'xyz123@yahoo
.com', 'aabbaa@hotmail.com']
(gmail|yahoo).com email
        ['abcd22@gmail.com', 'xyz123@yahoo.com']
```

Explanation

In \w+@\w+.com

\w+ matches alphanumeric character (a–z, A–Z, 0–9) with 1 or n repetitions.

@ , .com matches exactly for the pattern inside the string.

[A–z]+ matches alphabet between A–z with 1 or n repetitions.

In \w+@(gmail|yahoo).com

(gmail|yahoo) looks for either Gmail or Yahoo.

Program 17.3: WAP to match and extract the link values from the text.

```
import re
data = '\
<h1>The First Page</h1>\
<p>\
If you like, you can access the \
<a href="http://people.du.ac.in/~agoel/books.html">\
webpage</a>.\
</p>'
print(re.findall(r'(href="http[s]?://.+?")', data))
```

Output

```
['href="http://people.du.ac.in/~agoel/books.html"']
```

Program 17.4: WAP to extract the date from a string.

```
import re
data = "The Happiness quotient of my country on 15/06/2023 is 7.2"
print(re.findall('[0-9]{1,2}\/[0-9]{1,2}\/[0-9]{4}', data))
```

Output

```
['15/06/2023']
```

Program 17.5: WAP to parse text from a website using BeautifulSoup.

```
import requests
from bs4 import BeautifulSoup
response = requests.get("https://www.google.com")
souup = BeautifulSoup(response.content, "html.parser")
print("Parsed Text from: https://www.google.com:\n\n", souup.get_text())
```

Output

```
Parsed Text from: https://www.google.com:

 GoogleSearch Images Maps Play YouTube News Gmail Drive More
»Web History | Settings | Sign in Advanced searchGoogle offer
ed in:  हिन्दी বাংলা తెలుగు मराठी தமிழ் ગુજરાતી ಕನ್ನಡ മലയാളം
ਪੰਜਾਬੀ AdvertisingBusiness SolutionsAbout GoogleGoogle.co.in© 2
024 - Privacy - Terms
```

Program 17.6: Create a Python project to get the citation from Google scholar using title and year of publication, volume and pages of journal.

Let us now write a program for this. The requirements are listed below:

- Google Scholar does not provide an official API to retrieve citation information.
- We use web scraping techniques.

Solution

- Import libraries - `requests` and `BeautifulSoup`
- Define `get_citation()` function.
- Define the parameters.
- Use BeautifulSoup to parse the HTML content of the response.
- Print and return the citation information.

The solution code is shown below:

```
import requests
from bs4 import BeautifulSoup

#return citation number
def get_citation(base_url: str, params: dict) -> str:
    soup = BeautifulSoup(requests.get(base_url, params=params).
    content, "html.parser")
    div = soup.find("div", attrs={"class": "gs_ri"})
    anchors = div.find("div", attrs={"class": "gs_fl"}).find_
    all("a")
    return anchors[2].get_text()

if __name__ == "__main__":
    params = {
        "title": (
            "A systematic literature review on online assessment
            security: "
            "Current challenges and integrity strategies "),
        "journal": "Computers and Security",
        "volume": 113,
        "pages": "1-13",
        "year": 2022,
        "hl": "en",
    }
print(get_citation("http://scholar.google.com/scholar_lookup",
    params=params))
```

Summary

- Regular expression is used for matching patterns, searching, and manipulating text strings.
- Pattern is a sequence of characters matched inside a string.
- Metacharacters, Unicode characters, sets, and regex functions are special characters used by Python.
- Regular expressions are used for pattern matching as they are fast and the code is compact.
- Metacharacters are useful for matching multiple character patterns at once.
- Unicode characters are a combination of the symbol \ and one character.
- Sets are used to match the pattern inside the string.
- `match()`, `search()`, `findall()`, `split()` and `sub()` are functions in re module of Python for pattern matching.
- Internet is a network that connects a myriad of devices.
- Internet contains many networks – LAN, MAN, PAN, and WAN.
- WiFi, Internet Protocol (IP), Transmission Control Protocol (TCP), User Datagram Protocol (UDP), and HyperText Transfer Protocol (HTTP) are communication protocols.

- Packet is a unit of data transmission in a network.
- IP address uniquely identifies a device on the network.
- Port uniquely identifies a process running on a device.
- Socket provides a two-way connection for inter-process communication.
- A socket is made up of IP address and port number.
- Socket programming is a means of communication between clients and servers over a network. Python has built-in socket module for socket programming.
- `bind()`, `listen()`, `accept()`, `close()`, `connect()`, `send`, `sendall()`, `recv()`, `sendto()`, and `recvfrom()` are key methods that work on socket object.
- Developer console provides information about the interaction between browser and server.
- Web scraping is an automated method to extract data from the websites.
- Web crawling is used by search engines to scrape web pages for finding URLs.
- Python is popular for web scraping.
- Python provides support for retrieving of web pages and parsing the retrieved content.
- Urllib, Urllib3, Requests, Beautifulsoup, Mechanicalsoup, Selenium, and Pandas are third-party libraries for web scraping in Python.
- ASCII code is used to represent a character. It is a mapping between the letters and the numbers.
- Unicode is the universal code for millions of characters and different character sets, represented as – UTF-8, UTF-16, and UTF-32.
- Encoding and decoding are needed to send and receive data as bytes objects in a network, for using the HTTP protocol.

Keywords

Regular expression
Regex or regexp
Pattern
Metacharacters
Unicode characters
Sets
Regex functions
Flags
Networking
Local Area Network (LAN)
Personal Area Network (PAN)
Metropolitan Area Network (MAN)
Wide area network (WAN)
Communication protocol
WiFi
Internet Protocol (IP)
Transmission Control Protocol (TCP)
User Datagram Protocol (UDP)
HyperText Transfer Protocol (HTTP)
Packet
Endpoint
IP address
Port
Socket
Client
Server
Socket programming
Socket server
Socket client
Developer console
urllib
urllib3
Get request
Remote address
Response header
Request-header
Web scraping
Web crawler
Search engine
Parsing
Requests
BeautifulSoup
MechanicalSoup
Selenium
Pandas
Encoding
Decoding
American Standard Code for Information Interchange (ASCII)
Unicode

Programming Language Keywords

`import re`	`re.split()`	`.connect()`
`re.IGNORECASE or re.I`	`re.sub()`	`.send()`
`re.DOTALL or re.S`	`socket.socket()`	`.sendall()`
`re.MULTILINE or re.M`	`SOCK_DGRAM`	`.recv()`
`re.VERBOSE or re.X`	`SOCK_STREAM`	`.sendto()`
`re.ASCII or re.A`	`AF_INET`	`.recvfrom()`
`re.match()`	`AF_INET6`	`ord()`
`.span()`	`AF_UNIX`	`UTF-8`
`.string`	`.bind()`	`UTF-16`
`.group()`	`.listen()`	`UTF-32`
`re.search()`	`.accept()`	`.encode()`
`re.findall()`	`.close()`	`.decode()`

Assessment

A.1 Bloom Level: Knowledge/Remember

Review Questions

1. Define regular expression.
2. Name three scripting languages that support regular expression.
3. List any five metacharacters.
4. List the purpose of using these metacharacters:
   `. ^ $ * + ? {} [] \ | ()`
5. List any five Unicode characters.
6. List the purpose of using these Unicode characters:
   \A\b \B \d \D \s \S \w \W\Z
7. What is the task of `match()` function in regular expression?
8. What is the task of `search()` function in regular expression?
9. What is the task of `sub()` function in regular expression?
10. What is the task of `split()` function in regular expression?
11. What is the task of `findall()` function in regular expression?
12. Give the full form of:
    LAN, MAN, WAN, PAN, regex, IP, TCP, UDP, HTTP, SYN. ACK.
13. Name four communication protocols.
14. Name a connectionless protocol.
15. Name a protocol for communication on the web from browser to server.
16. What is a packet?
17. What is a port?
18. What is the significance of port number?
19. What is a socket?
20. List the steps for establishing connection between a client and a server using a socket.

21. What does it mean when the status code is (a) 304, (b) 404 in the developer console?
22. What is web scraping?
23. What is web crawling?
24. Name three popular libraries and tools in Python for web scraping.
25. Name a third-party library for parsing of HTML content.
26. Name a third-party Python library for making HTTP requests.

Fill in the Blanks

1. Regular expression is a __________ string.
2. __________ is a sequence of characters that are matched inside a string.
3. The special character operations are defined using _______, __________, __________ and __________.
4. Unicode characters are a combination of the symbol _____and ______ character.
5. To match all occurrences in the string, combine Unicode characters with __________.
6. A set is a combination of characters inside __________ brackets.
7. __________ connects computers located close to one another,
8. __________ is a destination where packets arrive.
9. Port number _______ is used by server applications to manage HTTP traffic.
10. The file transfer protocol uses port number __________.
11. The address_family in `socket.socket()` can be __________, ________ and ________.
12. __________ function is used to accept incoming connections on a server socket.
13. The local loopback address is __________.
14. The localhost is at port _______.
15. The request is a GET request, the status code is 200. This information can be seen on ____________ in the developer console.

State True/False

1. In Python, regular expression is not pre-built.
2. The characters of metacharacters match themselves in a string.
3. One Unicode character matches only one occurrence inside the string.
4. PAN connects devices in a city.
5. IP is responsible for routing packets over the Internet and IP addressing.
6. IP address uniquely identifies a device on the network, via a numerical identifier.
7. Socket provides one-way connection between programs.
8. AF_INET uses IPv6 for network addressing.
9. `sendto()` function is same as `send()` and is used for UDP protocol only.

10. `listen()` allows client to listen for incoming connection.

11. In Request-Header, we see the language is English and the host web address.

Multiple Choice Questions (MCQ)

1. Identify the network in which the devices are connected across countries and continents.
   (i) LAN (ii) MAN
   (iii) PAN (iv) WAN

2. Identify the symbol to match the start of a string.
   (i) * (ii) +
   (iii) ^ (iv) #

3. The flag that allows "." metacharacter to match a newline is ______.
   (i) `re.S` (ii) `re.I`
   (iii) `re.M` (iv) `re.A`

4. If the set is defined as: [0–5][0–9]. The valid number is ________.
   (i) 36 (ii) 95
   (iii) 99 (iv) 69

5. If we want to match words starting with letter "b" followed by one or more repetition of alphanumeric characters, the correct expression is ________.
   (i) W\b+ (ii) W\b-
   (iii) (b\w+) (iv) (b\W+)

A.2 Bloom Level: Comprehend/Understand

Review Questions

1. Explain the purpose of open-source libraries for the following:
   (1) HTML parser (2) Web page retrieval (3) Web scraping
2. Describe the meaning of following methods:
   `re.match()`, `re.search()`, `re.findall()`, `re.split()`, `re.sub()`, `re.IGNORECASE`, `re.DOTALL`, `re.MULTILINE`, `re.VERBOSE`, `re.ASCII`,. `span()`,.`string` ,.`group()`, `bind()`, `listen()`, `accept()`, `close()`, `connect()`, `send()`, `sendall()`, `recv()`, `sendto()`, `recvfrom()`
3. Describe the syntax for the following:
   (i) Importing regular expression
   (ii) Match function regular expression
   (iii) Search function in regular expression
   (iv) `socket.socket()`
4. Explain the working of regular expression.
5. What is the purpose of using a regular expression?
6. Explain the need for using regular expression for pattern matching.
7. What is the purpose of communication protocols?
8. Explain the purpose of using sockets.
9. How does the socket identify a device uniquely in a network?
10. Explain the socket flow for communication between client and server in a TCP connection.
11. Write the steps for socket server.
12. Write the steps for socket client.
13. Write the sequence of socket API calls and data flow for UDP protocol.

14. What is the purpose of developer console?
15. Explain the need for web scraping.
16. Explain the steps for web scraping with third-party libraries.
17. In a network, what is the need for encoding and decoding the data?
18. List the steps to use the HTML parser – BeautifulSoup.

A.3 Bloom Level: Application/Apply

1. Identify whether the following are used for retrieving web pages or for parsing.
   (i) Requests
   (ii) urllib3
   (iii) pycurl
   (iv) BeautifulSoup
   (v) urllib
   (vi) lxml
   (vii) pyquery

2. Find output for the code and the meaning of the regular expressions in the following codes:
   (i)

```
import re
s = 'GeeksforGeeks: A computer science portal for geeks'
match = re.search(r'portal', s)
print('Start Index:', match.start())
print('End Index:', match.end())
```

   (ii)

```
import re
string = "From manya.mit@act.ac.in Thur Jan 20"
print(re.findall("^From .*@([^ ]*)", string))
print(re.search("^From .*@([^ ]*)", string))
```

   (iii)

```
import re
s1 = "Hello World!"
s2 = "Hello World! I am here"
pattern = r"World!$"
print(re.search(pattern, s1))
print(re.search(pattern, s2))
```

   (iv)

```
import re
print(re.split(r'(\W+)', 'Sweets, sweets, sweets.'))
print(re.split(r'\W+', 'Sweets, sweets, sweets.', 1))
```

(v)

```
import re
print((re.split(r'\s','we are searching the lakes')))
print((re.split(r's','search the lakes')))
print((re.split(r's','we are searching the lakes')))
```

3. Fill in the regular expression so that the output shown is displayed.

(i) import re
s = 'Python is a programming language'
pat = '________'
print(re.findall(pat, s))
Output

```
['ython', 'is', 'a', 'programming', 'language']
```

(ii) import re
s = 'Python is a programming language'
pat = '________'
print(re.findall(pat, s))
Output

```
['Python', 'is', 'a', 'programming', 'language']
```

(iii) import re
txt = "My email-id: AbC@gmail.com created on 10th Mar 2000."
print(re.findall(________, txt))
Output

```
['My', 'email', 'id', 'AbC', 'gmail', 'com', 'created', 'on', '10th', 'Mar', '20
00']
```

(iv) import re
x1 = re.findall(________,'abcdab789cnmh0122jjh')
print(x1)
Output

```
['7', '8', '9', '0', '1', '2', '2']
```

(v) import re
x2 = re.sub(________,'abcdab789cnmh0122jjh')
print(x2)

Output

```
abcdab###cnmh####jjh
```

(vi) import re
x3 = re.split(_______,'192.168.1.289')
print(x3)
Output

```
['192', '168', '1', '289']
```

4. Write a code to extract a username from a string.
5. Write a code to extract multiple usernames from a string.
6. Define regular expression that can do the following:
   (a) Find all characters in a string from range a to m.
   (b) Check whether an email id is valid or not.
   (c) Find all vowels in a string.
   (d) Find all consonants in a string.

A.4 Bloom Level: Analyze

1. Explain the difference between the following:
   (i) Socket and Port
   (ii) SOCK_DGRAM and SOCK_STREAM
   (iii) `Urllib and urllib3`
   (iv) ASCII and Unicode
   (v) `re.search()` and `re.findall()`
   (vi) Extraction and Parsing.
2. What is the difference between the two codes (i) and (ii)? What does the number in curly braces mean? What is the output?

```
import re
string = "India Indiaaa Indiaa "
print(re.findall('India{3}', string))
```

(i)

```
import re
string = "India Indiaaa Indiaa "
print(re.findall('India{2}', string))
```

(ii)

3. Analyze the following code. What is the output? Is the output for the two codes same? If not, explain the difference in the output and the reasons for the same.
   (i)

```
import re
target_string = "Prakash is a basketball player born on May 15."
result = re.search(r"(\w{10}).+(\d{2})", target_string)
print(result.group(1))
```

   (ii)

```
import re
target_string = "Prakash is a basketball player born on May 15."
result = re.search(r"(\w{10}).+(\d{2})", target_string)
print(result.group(2))
```

4. Analyze the difference between (i) and (ii). What is the output and the reasons for difference in the output?

   a)

```
import re
print(re.split('[a-f]+', '0a3K9', flags=re.I))
```

   b)

```
import re
print(re.split('[a-f]+', '0a3C9', flags=re.I))
```

5. The code prints all user names.
   a) What is the output in the two cases?
   b) Which of the following codes displays the correct answer?
   c) Give reasons for the difference in outputs.

```
import re
text = 'Beautiful #ABC:777. @abcdpqrs33 @hijk225 @Cloudfirst'
print(re.findall('@[A-z]+\d*',text))
```

(i)

```
import re
text = 'Beautiful #ABC:777. @abcdpqrs33 @hijk225 @Cloudfirst'
print(re.findall(r'@[A-z]+\d{1,5}',text))
```

(ii)

A.5 Bloom Level: Evaluate

1. Evaluate the following code.
   (a) What is the purpose of pipe (|) operator?
   (b) What is the purpose of \b?
   (c) What output does the print statement display?

```
import re
s1 = "Asha is a basketball player who was born in the year 1990."
print(re.findall(r"\bAsha\b|\bplayer\b|\bborn\b", s1))
```

2. Evaluate the following code.
   (a) What does (g\w+)\W(g\w+) match?
   (b) What does `groups()` do?
   (c) What output does the print statement display?

```
import re
lst = ["good gold", "good game", "good mane"]
for elmt in lst:
    x = re.match("(g\w+)\W(g\w+)", elmt)
    if x:
        print("groups:", x.groups())
```

3. Evaluate the following code. What is the task performed? What is the output?

```
import re
amt = ['$110', '₦500', '$3000', '$990', '€500']
pat = r'[$ ₦ €]'
amt_new = []
for i in amt:
    j = re.sub(pat, " ", i)
    amt_new.append(j.strip())
print (amt_new)
```

4. Evaluate the following regular expressions. Explain what they do.
   (a) @[a-z]+\d+
   (b) [A-z]+
   (c) \d{1,5}
   (d) re.search(r"\w{8}", s1)
   (e) re.findall("\S", s)
   (f) re.findall("(s$)", s))
   (g) re.findall("oo*",s))
   (h) re.findall("oo?",s))
   (i) re.findall("Good|Fair",s))

5. Evaluate the given code. The output is shown. What is the purpose of line number 7 and line number 10. If line 10 was replaced by `print(title)`, what difference would it make to the output? Justify your answer.

```
import re
from urllib.request import urlopen

url = 'http://google.com'
pg = urlopen(url)
html = pg.read().decode("utf-8")
pat = "<title.*?>.*?</title.*?>"
match_pat = re.search(pat, html)
title = match_pat.group()
print(re.sub("<.*?>", "", title) )
```

Output

```
Google
```

A.6 Bloom Level: Create/Synthesize

Programming Assignment

1. WAP to implement the following tasks using regular expression:
   a) To check that a string contains only a–z, A–Z and 0–9.
   b) To match a string that has an *a* followed by one or more *g*'s.
   c) To find lowercase letters joined by an underscore.
   d) To match a word at the beginning of a string.
   e) To match a word at the end of a string.
   f) To remove leading zeros from an IP address.
   g) To find the occurrence and position of substrings within a string.
   h) To convert a date of mm-dd-yyyy format to dd-mm-yyyy format.
   i) To separate and print the numbers and their position in a given string.
   j) To replace all occurrences of a comma, or dot with a '*'.
   k) To find all six-character words in a string.
   l) To remove all whitespaces from a string.
   m) To remove words from a string of length between 1 and 6.
2. Implement the server socket for an application that receives all incoming data, prints it and sends random ASCII letters as a response to the sender. Implement the client socket for an application that sends data to the server and receives the incoming response from the server.
3. WAP to transfer a file with socket module.
4. Parse the HTML content using:
   a) Tag – get all <h1> elements on the page.
   b) Id – get the element with id="main-title".
   c) Text – find all the centered elements on the page.
   d) Attribute – find the email input element through its "name" attribute.
   e) Class – get all "li" elements # in the ".navbar" element.
5. Use urllib3 to extract HTML code and do the following:

a) Count the <img> tags.
b) Find <ol> <ul> tags.
c) Find <input> <h1> <h2> tags.
d) Find <div> tags.

6. WAP to scrape the top-rated movies from IMDb.

7. WAP to scrape the job posting from an employer site and show it.

8. WAP to scrape a website and present the list of topics discussed there.

9. WAP to display the topics discussed in github page.

ANSWERS

A.1 Bloom Level: Knowledge/Remember

Review Questions

20. (a) – (v), (b) – (iv), (c) – (vi), (d) – (ii), (e) – (i), (f) – (iii)

Fill in the Blanks

1. text **2.** Pattern **3.** Metacharacters, Unicode characters, Sets, and Regex functions
4. \, one **5.** metacharacters **6.** square **7.** LAN **8.** Endpoint
9. 80 **10.** 21 **11.** AF_INET, AF_INET6, AF_UNIX **12.** accept()
13. 127.0.0.1 **14.** 8080 **15.** Headers

True/False

1. False **2.** False **3.** True **4.** False **5.** True **6.** True **7.** False **8.** False
9. True **10.** False **11.** true

Multiple Choice Questions (MCQ)

1. (iv) **2.** (iii) **3.** (i) **4.** (i) **5.** (iii)

A.3. Bloom Level: Application/Apply

2.

(i)

```
Start Index: 34
End Index: 40
```

Print the matching start index and end index

(ii)

```
['act.ac.in']
<re.Match object; span=(0, 24), match='From manya.mit@act.ac.in'>
```

It matches the string that starts with 'From' and after that matches any character any number of times until '@' and then matches any character except space(' ') according to RE written inside parentheses.

(iii)

```
<re.Match object; span=(6, 12), match='World!'>
None
```

$matches characters at the end of the string.

(iv)

```
['Sweets', ', ', 'sweets', ', ', 'sweets', '.', '']
['Sweets', 'sweets, sweets.']
```

(v)

```
['we', 'are', 'searching', 'the', 'lakes']
['', 'earch the lake', '']
['we are ', 'earching the lake', '']
```

We have split each word using the "re.split" function and at the same time we have used expression \s that allows each word in the string to be parsed separately. If you remove "\" from s, there is no 's' alphabet in the output; this is because we have removed '\' from the string, and it evaluates "s" as a regular character and thus splits the words wherever it finds "s" in the string.

3.

(i) pat = '[a-z]+'
(ii) pat = '[A-z]+'
(iii) '\w+
(iv) '[0-9]'
(v) '[0-9]','#'
(vi) '\.'

A.4 Bloom Level: Analyze

2. ['Indiaaa']
['Indiaa', 'Indiaa']
It specifies exactly 3 copies and 2 copies of the previous re (a)should be matched

3.

```
basketball
15
```

The two groups are enclosed in separate (and) brackets.
The first will print the ten-letter word.
The second will print the two-digit number.

4. ['0', '3G9']
['0', '3', '9']
The flag is Ignorecase in both cases. G does fall in between a and f whereas C falls in between.

5. @[A-z]+,\d* looks for 0 to n digits repetition.
['@abcdpqrs33', '@hijk225', '@Cloudfirst']
['@abcdpqrs33', '@hijk225']
.

A.5 Bloom Level: Evaluate

1.
```
['Asha', 'player', 'born']
```

2.
```
groups: ('good', 'gold')
groups: ('good', 'game')
```

3.
```
['110', '500', '3000', '990', '500']
```
remove currency symbol

4.
(a) Matches @ inside the string.
(b) Matches any alphabet from a–z with 1 or n repetition.
(c) Matches any digit character with 1 to 5 times repetition.
(d) Searches for eight-letter word in s1
(e) Escapes metacharacter sequence.
(f) Matches end of string just before a new line.
(g) Matches 0 or n repetitions of o.
(h) Matches 0 or 1 repetition of o.
(i) Matches either Good or Fair.

CHAPTER 18 Using Databases with Python

CONTENTS

18.1 Introduction

Databases are a crucial part of our life. We interact with non-computerized databases frequently. For example, we search for address in an address book and search for the meaning of a word in a dictionary. Computerized databases use computer to store, manipulate and manage the database. We interact with these databases when we reserve air tickets and movie tickets, check bank account balance and, much more. Databases are also used to store pictures, video, audio, and photos.

This chapter discusses the using of databases with Python. It describes components of the database system and the design and representation of data models. The chapter discusses performing different operations on the databases. It describes the creation of databases in Python, using different database interfaces for Python.

Learning Outcomes of this chapter

After completion of the chapter, the learner will be able to:

- Understand the terminologies related to databases
- Understand the databases in Python
- Use Python databases
- Formulate CRUD operations on a single table and multiple tables
- Understand the many-to-many relationships
- Understand design and representation of data model.

18.2 Database

Database is a collection of logically related and similar data. The data stored in a database is in an organized form to facilitate modification, addition, retrieval, updates and much more. In real-life situations we already use databases such as dictionary, telephone directory, air flights time table, and customer accounts in a bank.

A ***database*** is defined as a collection of data having an organized structure, and for a specific purpose. The data stored in a database is useful to an organization. The database contains data based on the kind of application for which it is required. For example, a train database may contain data about the train schedules, train booking and reservation; a university database may contain data about the faculty, departments, students, staff, and courses; a database for a production environment may contain data about the raw materials, inventory, employee duties, and orders.

The main **characteristics of database approach** are defined as follows:

- **Data redundancy is minimized** as the data is stored centrally that can be accessed by different applications.
- **Data inconsistency gets reduced** because of minimizing of data redundancy. Since data is centrally stored, update of data values does not lead to disagreement in the stored values.
- **Data is shared**, so the users have access to same data for their use. The users are provided with views of the data to facilitate its use.
- **Data independence** is the separation of data description from the application programs that use it. As a result, the data can evolve without changing the application programs that process the data. *Data dictionary* stores the description of data.

- **Data integrity is maintained** via constraints on values that data items can have. Data dictionary stores the constraint definitions.
- **Data security is improved** as access to database is controlled by providing passwords to authorized personnel.
- **Backup and recovery support** helps in recovering state of the database in case of system failure. For this, database logs are maintained.
- **Standards are enforced** for naming conventions, update, access, and protection of data. It is easy to enforce standards on the database as the data is stored centrally.
- **Application development time is reduced** as the programmer can focus on the task to be done without having to worry about design or low-level implementation details.

Additionally, databases provide several other advantages like multiple user interfaces, representation of complex relationships, and concurrent data access.

18.3 Data Models, Schema, and Instances

The information stored inside a database is represented using data modeling. **Data model** describes the structure of the database. It consists of components for describing data, relationships among them, semantics of data and constraints on data. The data model is commonly divided into three categories based on the way they describe structure of the database, as follows:

- High-level or conceptual data model,
- Representation or implementation data model, and
- Low-level or physical data model

Schema is the logical structure of a database. It contains information about description of the database like, names of record type, data items within a record type and constraints. Schema does not show the data in the database. The database schema does not change frequently.

Instances are actual data contained in the database at a particular point in time. The content of the database may change from time to time.

18.3.1 Conceptual Data Model

The conceptual data model specifies, conceptually, all the functional requirements and data requirements of the users. It is not concerned with the implementation details. The conceptual model uses concepts like, entity, attribute, and relationships. The Entity–Relationship model (E–R model) is a high-level conceptual data model.

- An **entity** is the basic unit for modeling. An entity may exist physically, or may be conceptual. An entity may be a real-world object that is tangible and exist physically, like, student, employee, part, and supplier; or, a conceptual, non-tangible object, such as project, event, and job title. For example, student information system may consist of entities, like *student_profile, marks* and *course*. A set of entities of the same type having same properties or attributes is defined as an **entity set**. For example, a set of all parts is an entity set *Part*. An entity and entity set are usually referred to by the same name. For example, *Part* is an entity set of *all part entities* in the database.

- An **attribute** describes characteristics or a property of an entity. For example, *part number, part name, part category* are attributes of the entity *Part.* For an entity in entity set, similar information is stored for each attribute in the database, though each attribute of an entity may have its own value. The set of values permitted for an attribute is called **domain** of the attribute. For example, the domain of attribute *part name* is text string, and domain of *part number* is alphanumeric.
- A **relationship** is an association between two entities. For example, "*Part* sold to *Buyer*" is a relationship between entities *Part* and *Buyer.* A set of relationships of the same type form a **relationship set. Cardinality ratio** is the number of entities associated to another entity in a relationship set. The cardinality ratio is of four kinds. For any two entity sets A and B, the different kinds of cardinality ratio imply the following:
  - ***One-to-One***: An entity in A is associated with at most one entity in B and vice-versa.
  - ***One-to-Many***: An entity in A is associated with any number of entities in B; an entity in B is associated with at most one entity in A.
  - ***Many-to-One***: An entity in A is associated with at most one entity in B; an entity in B is associated with any number of entities in A.
  - ***Many-to-Many***: An entity in A is associated with any number of entities in B and vice-versa.
- **Entity–Relationship model** (E–R model) is a model of the real world. It represents the entities contained in the database, their attributes and relationship between the entities. It also shows cardinality constraints to be adhered to by the database. The E–R model is represented diagrammatically using an E–R diagram. In an E–R diagram,
  - Entity is represented using a *rectangle*;
  - Attribute is represented as an *ellipse* connected to the entity with a line; and,
  - Relationship is represented using a *diamond* connected to the entity by a line.

Figure 18.1 shows an E–R diagram with two entities *Part* and *Buyer*. The *Part_No* and *Part_Name* are attributes of the entity Part. The *Buyer_Id* and *Buyer_Name* are attributes of the entity Buyer. The *Sold_to* relationship associates the part and buyer. The design in E–R model is converted to design in the representation model for storage and processing.

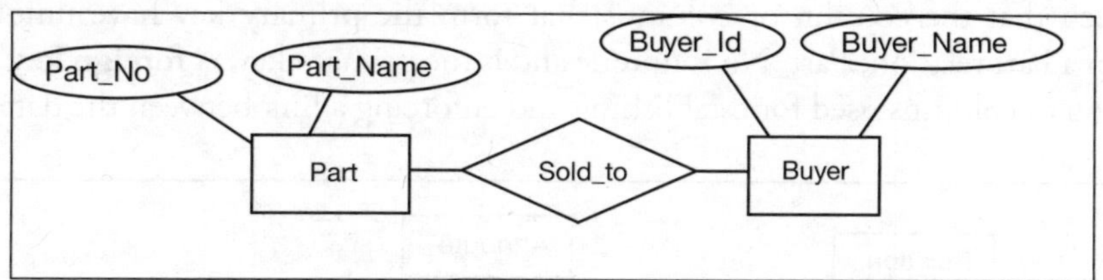

Figure 18.1 E–R diagram

18.3.2 Representation Data Model

The conceptual data model is transformed into the representation data model. Representation data model uses concepts that are understood by the end-user and are also close to the way the data is organized in the computer. This model hides the details of data storage. Representation data model is used in traditional database management systems, such as (1) hierarchical, (2) relational, and (3) network data models.

The *hierarchical database model* is the oldest and was developed by IBM. Its schema is represented using a tree-structure diagram, based on the parent–child relationship. The Information Management System (IMS) from IBM and the System 2000 from MRI systems are some hierarchical database implementations. The *relational database model* is the most common type of database model. The *network database model* was formalized by DataBase Task Group (DBTG) group of Conference on Data Systems Languages (CODASYL) in the late 1960s. Its schema is represented using a data-structure diagram, based on the owner–member relationship. IDMS, DMS 1100 and IMAGE are some network database implementations.

The hierarchical and network models are also called legacy models as most current systems support the relational model. Here, we discuss the relational database model in detail.

18.3.3 Relational Database Model

In 1970, E F Codd proposed the relational database model. The relational database model uses concepts such as table, record, field, key, and data values (Fig. 18.2). The data elements are stored in tables made up of rows and columns, and different tables are related via common data attributes. In a relational database model, the terms are defined as follows:

- **Data Values** are raw data represented in numeric, character, alphanumeric, or alphabetic form. Examples of data values are 'Abhinav Bindra', '26', 'shooting', 'Chandigarh', etc.
- **Attribute or Column** stores the data values. For example, attributes of entity Part can be Part_No, Part_Name, Part_Category.
- **Tuple or Row** is a group of data for related field. For example, for entity Part, the related attributes are (Part_No, Part_Name, Part_Category). The data about Part #1, ('101', 'Nut', 'A', for example) is one tuple.
- **Relation or Table** is a collection of logically related tuples. A relation has a set of columns and any number of rows. For example, a relation Part has three columns and rows for 100 parts.
- **Key** is an identifier in a table that uniquely identifies a tuple in a relation. The key can be the attribute of a single column or multiple columns. A **primary key** is a unique identifier for the relation such that the column or columns that form the primary key have unique values. For example, in a Part relation, Part_No is unique and is the primary key. A **foreign key** is a column or combination of columns used for establishing and enforcing a link between the data in two tables.

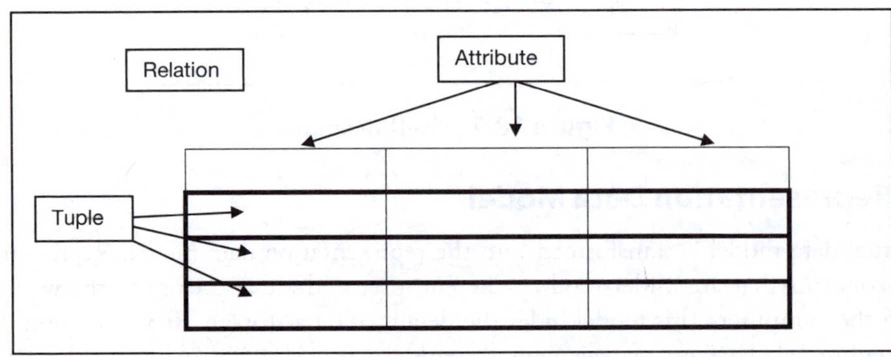

Figure 18.2 Relational database model

A database may contain a single table stored as a file, or, a collection of related tables stored together. For example, a student database may contain a table for student_profile, student result, and student courses.

18.3.4 Physical Data Model

The physical model describes how a record is stored, internally. It describes the internal storage structure, access mechanism, and organization of files in the database. Sequential files, direct files, and indexed sequential files are the different types of file organizations at the physical level.

18.4 Database System

A **database system** is an integration of collection, storage, and dissemination of data for operations of an organization. It is a computerized record-keeping system. The database system maintains the data and makes the information available on demand. A database system has four main components: (1) Users, (2) Hardware, (3) Software, and (4) Data.

- **Users** are people who interact with the database system.
    - *Application programmers* develop application programs that manipulate the database. The application programs operate on data for insertion, deletion, and retrieval.
    - *End users* interact with the database to get information for business purposes. They interact with the system through menus, forms, or query languages. The managers, executives, and clerical staff are some end users.
    - *Data administrator* is the manager who defines policies for maintenance and handling of stored data. *Database Administrator (DBA)* is a technical person who is responsible for creation of the database and implementation of policies. It may be noted that Data Administrator is a managerial role and DBA is technical in nature.
- **Software** lies between stored data and users. Software is classified into three types:
    - *DBMS* handles requests from the users to access the database for addition, deletion, or retrieval of data.
    - *Application software* uses DBMS facilities to manipulate the database for a specific business function.
    - *User interface* has the menus and screens used by the user to interact with application programs and DBMS.
- **Hardware** is the physical device on which the database system resides.
- **Data** is raw numbers, characters or facts represented by values. The data in a database system is integrated and shared.
    - *Integrated data* means several distinct data files are unified in a manner that redundancy is wholly or partially eliminated.
    - *Shared data* is that data stored in the database can be shared among multiple users.

The architecture of a database system provides a general framework for database systems. Different database systems may not support all aspects, but it can be matched to the framework. The **ANSI/SPARC architecture** for database systems is proposed by ANSI/SPARC study group. It provides a general framework for database systems. Schema contains information about description of the database. The ANSI/SPARC architecture is divided into three levels –

1) **Physical Level** has an internal schema that describes physical storage structure of the database, how data is stored physically.
2) **Conceptual Level** has a conceptual schema that describes the structure of the *whole* database for the users; entities, their relationships, and constraints.
3) **External Level or View Level** provides user and application view of the data.

18.5 Database Management System

Database Management System (DBMS) is a software system for creating, organizing, and managing the database. It provides a convenient environment to the user to perform operations on the database for creation, insertion, deletion, updating and retrieval of data. DBMS defines the scope of use of the database to prevent unauthorized access. DBMS implements the three-schema architecture.

Mapping is used for transforming requests and results between different levels of the DBMS architecture – external, physical and conceptual level. Oracle Database, IBM's DB2, Microsoft's SQL Server and Microsoft Access are some commercial DBMS. MySQL is a popular open-source DBMS.

Data independence is defined as the ability to change a schema at one level without affecting the schema at another level. DBMS provides ***logical data independence*** that allows users to modify the conceptual schema without changing the external schema. ***Physical data independence*** is the ability to modify physical schema without changing the conceptual schema.

Data dictionary stores metadata, i.e., data about the data stored in database. Metadata includes data definitions, data structure, rules, constraints, data item, type and length, and a brief description of each data item. Data dictionary keeps track of the following: definitions of data items, relationships between data structures, indexes for accessing data quickly, and screen or report format definitions used by application programs.

Database Administrator (DBA) is a person who coordinates all activities of the database system. DBA is responsible for creating, modifying, and maintaining three levels of the DBMS architecture. DBA defines the schema, storage structure and access method, modifies schema and physical organization, grants user authority to access the database, and acts as liaison with users.

A **set of languages** – Data Definition Language (DDL) and Data Manipulation Language (DML) are provided by the DBMS. DDL is used for defining the database schema. DML is used for manipulation of the data. **Structured Query Language (SQL)** is a relational database language that is a combination of both DDL and DML.

DDL is a specification notation for defining the database schema. For example, a DDL command in SQL is as follows:

```
create table part (
     part_no integer(3),
     part_name char(20),
     part_category char(1)
```

It creates a table named part having three fields – *part_no* of type integer and size 3, *part_name* of type character and size 20, and *part_category* of type char of size 1.

DML is a query language for accessing and manipulating data stored in the database. For example, the SQL query to find name of the part having part_no 101, in the table *part* is:

```
select part.part_name
    from part
    where part_no = '101'
```

There are three common ways of designing the **architecture of database system**:

- **Centralized databases** are traditional, where all database functionality, data, application program and user interface processing are located on one machine. Access to the database from remote locations is via communication links.
- **Client–server systems** involve client machine and server machine. Clients are PCs or workstations having user interface capability and functionality for local processing. Servers are powerful computers that can manage files, printer, or, e-mails. The client is connected to the server via a communication link. The client–server architecture has three components: user interface programs, application programs that contain application logic and DBMS that stores data. DBMS architecture on client–server systems are two-tier client–server architecture and three-tier client–server architecture. In two-tier client–server architecture, user interface programs and application programs run on client side, and DBMS at server side. The three-tier client–server architecture is commonly used for web applications. In addition to client and database server, it has an intermediate layer called application or web server that stores the business logic part of the application.
- **Distributed database** has complete functionality of the DBMS distributed among a number of computers. The computers may be physically placed at different geographical locations, but they are logically related. Access to distributed databases from remote locations is via communication links.

18.6 Python Databases

Relational database is the most popular database system. MySQL, Oracle DB, Sybase, Informix, IBM DB2, PostgreSQL, Microsoft SQL Server, SQLite, and NO SQL are some relational databases. MySQL is an open-source relational database management system and is an easy database to work with. Structured Query Language (SQL) is a standard language for relational databases that allow users to perform operations on data like, create, read, update, and delete data.

In Python, the most common databases that are used are: SQLite, MySQL and PostgresSQL.

- **SQLite** is a file-based light-weight transactional relational database, already built into Python.
- **MySQL** is a commonly used open-source database to store data for Python applications. It has less features than PostgreSQL, but learning to use MySQL is much easier.
- **PostgreSQL** is an open-source database for working with Python web applications. Because of its rich feature set, active development and stability, several web applications use PostgreSQL.

We shall discuss working with SQLite and MySQL databases.

18.6.1 SQLite

Python Enhancement Proposal (PEP) defines the Python Database Application Program Interface (DB-API) specification. The purpose of the specification is to facilitate similarity and consistency in Python modules that are used for accessing the database. The modules are easily understood, and the code is portable across databases. Currently, the PEP 249 – Python Database API Specification v2.0 is available. An SQL interface compliant with DB-API 2.0 specification is sqlite3. It was written by Gerhard Häring.

- SQLite is a light-weight disk-based database that works in syntax, like the SQL. It is self-contained, highly reliable, embedded, full-featured, public-domain SQL database engine.
- SQLite does not require a separate server process. It allows accessing the database using a nonstandard variant of the SQL query language.
- It is the most-used database engine on the world wide web. It is suited to data manipulation problems like Twitter spider application.
- It does not require separate installation and login credentials (username, password) from the user to provide access to the database, since it is built into Python,
- It is stored in a single file on disk and is accessed by a single connection at a time.
- It is designed to be embedded into applications to provide database support within the application. For example, Firefox browser uses SQLite database, internally.
- It is not used to run a production web application.
- sqlite3 is a library in Python to access SQLite databases.
    - By default, Python installation contains sqlite3.
    - SQLite database read and write data to a file because it is serverless and self-contained. Therefore, there is no need to install and run an SQLite server to perform database operations, unlike MySQL.
    - It is a straightforward database to connect to a Python application.

18.6.2 MySQL Database

- Python MySQL Connector is an interface for connecting to MySQL database server from Python.
- It is built on top of MySQL.
- The Connector implements Python Database API and does not require any third-party library.
- Python MySQL library allows the conversion between Python and MySQL data types.

- MySQL is a server-based DBMS. One MySQL server can have multiple databases. This is in contrast to SQLite, where creating a connection creates a single database.

18.7 Using Databases: Connect to SQLite

Let us learn how to use sqlite3 for database access with Python.

- **Import the sqlite3** library in the program
  `import sqlite3.`
- **Create a connection object.** For this, connect to the database using the `connect()` method. The connect method returns a connection object.
  `var1= sqlite3.connect('`*database_name*`')`
  where,
  database_name is the path of the database file to be accessed.
  `var1` is a connection object that refers to the database.
  If *database_name* database does not exist, it will be created.
  The connection class has methods to define custom functions and aggregates to be used in SQL queries.
- **Get cursor object from connection object.** For this, use `cursor()` method on connection object.
  `var2 = var1.cursor()`
  where,
  `var1` is a connection object that refers to the database.
  `var2` is the cursor object.
  The `cursor()` method on connection object returns the cursor object. The cursor object is a handle to the database when performing CRUD (Create, Read, Update, Delete) operations on database.
- `Execute()` method is used on cursor object to execute queries once the connection is made. The query is written in the form of a string, and then executed by calling the `execute()` method.
- `fetchall()` method is used on cursor object to fetch the result from the server.

Example 18.1: Write a function to connect to SQLite database.

```
import sqlite3
from sqlite3 import Error
def create_connect(path):
    cnnect = None
    try:
        cnnect = sqlite3.connect(path)
        print("Database connected")
    except Error as e:
        print(f"Error '{e}'")
    return cnnect
create_connect('sq1.db')
```

Output

```
Database connected
```

- *Lines 1 and 2*: Imports sqlite3 and the module Error class.
- *Line 6*: `connect()` from sqlite3 module takes SQLite database path as a parameter.
- *Line 8*: Catches exception if `connect()` fails.

Example 18.2: WAP to connect to SQLite database and run a simple query to find the version of the SQLite being used.

```
1 import sqlite3
2 try:
3     sqlte_conn = sqlite3.connect('sql.db')
4     crsr = sqlte_conn.cursor()
5     print('Initialize database')
6     query = 'select sqlite_version();'
7     crsr.execute(query)
8     res = crsr.fetchall()
9     print('Version of SQLite {}'.format(res))
10    crsr.close()
11
12 except sqlite3.Error as error:
13     print('An error: ', error)
14 finally:
15     if sqlte_conn:
16         sqlte_conn.close()
17         print('Connection closed')
```

Output

```
Initialize database
Version of SQLite [('3.35.5',)]
Connection closed
```

- *Lines 1 and 2*: Imports sqlite3 and the module Error class.
- *Line 3*: `connect()` from sqlite3 module takes SQLite database path as a parameter.
- *Lines 4, 7, 8*: Creates cursor object; uses `execute()` to run query; uses `fetchall()` to get result.
- *Line 16*: `close()` the connection.

18.8 Designing Data Model

To design the data model for a scenario, there is a need to understand the scenario in detail. Then we proceed with identifying the entities, attributes, relationships and then model the system.

Let us consider a simple Employee-pay scenario. We have employees who work in different departments. For each employee, detail of the pay is stored, like, basic salary, deductions, bonus and date of joining. Also, the date on which the pay is to be given to an employee is also stored to know the start of the payroll for the employee.

Let us design and model for the above example. We identify the entities, their attributes, and relation between the entities to model the system.

- Four entities are identified – Employee, Department, PayDetails, Payroll.

- Attributes for each entity are defined. We define employee and department attributes. Then, we define the attribute of PayDetails. Here, we see that each employee belongs to a particular department and its pay details must be stored. So, in PayDetails we include the emp_id from Employee and dept_id from Department in addition to basic, deductions and bonus to calculate the net salary, and date of joining, DOJ. Also, for each employee there is a pay date that is kept in Payroll entity, the payroll_id, and the emp_id from Employee. The attributes of the entities are as follows:
  - o Employee (emp_id:integer, emp_name:string, emp_gender:string)
  - o Department (dept_id:integer, dept_name:string)
  - o PayDetails (emp_id:integer, dept_id:integer, basic:integer, deductions:integer, bonus:integer, DOJ:date)
  - o Payroll (payroll_id:integer, emp_id: integer, pay_date: date)
- Next, the keys and relationships are identified. Each Employee has a unique id that is its primary key. Each Department has a unique id which is its primary key. The PayDetails are for an employee belonging to a department. To connect the PayDetails with the Employee and Department, we include the emp_id and dept_id in the PayDetails, and make their combination as a primary key. Also, each Employee has a date for its pay So, emp_id is also included in Payroll. The payroll_id is the primary key.
- We define cardinality of the relationship. An employee belongs to one department. A department can have many employees. Each employee has one PayDetails and one Payroll. A Payroll is for multiple employees. The PayDetails is for different employees belonging to different departments.

We have designed the data model for the Employee–Payroll scenario. Figure 18.3 depicts the data model design.

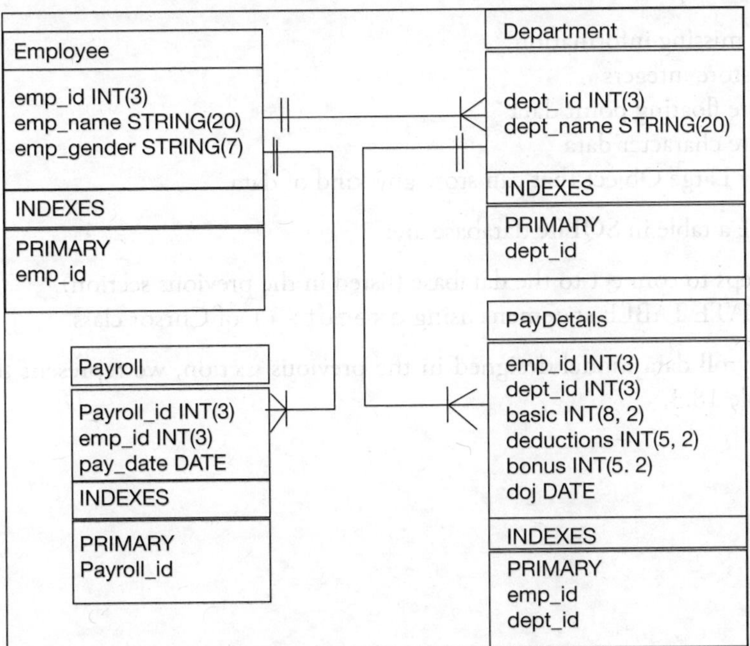

Figure 18.3 Design of Employee–Payroll data model

18.9 Representing Data Model

For a given scenario, once the logical model has been designed, there is a need to represent the model in the database. We use the relational database for representing the model in Python.

- The entities are represented as tables.
- The attributes are the columns.
- For each table, the keys are specified.

For this, we create a table for each entity.

The syntax to create a table in SQLite database is:

```
CREATE TABLE dbname.table_name(
   col1 datatype PRIMARY KEY(one/more columns),
   col2 datatype,
   col3 datatype,
   .....
   colN datatype);
```

where, table_name is the name of table.
dbname is the name of the database.
col1, col2,...colN are names of columns.
datatype is the type of data for the columns.

Specify one column as a primary key, at least

The datatypes in sqlite3 are:

- NULL – For missing information
- Integer – To store integers
- Real – To store floating point data
- Text – To store character data
- Blob – Binary Large Object that can store any kind of data.

The steps to create a table in SQLite database are:

- Follow the steps to connect to the database (listed in the previous section).
- Execute CREATE TABLE statement using `execute()` of Cursor class.

For employee–payroll data model designed in the previous section, we represent the data model in Python in Example 18.3.

Example 18.3: WAP to create tables for Employee, Department, PayDetails and Payroll, with the schema discussed in earlier sections.

```
1 import sqlite3
2 conn = sqlite3.connect(r'C:\Anita Goel\Python\Empexample.db')
3 crsr = conn.cursor()
4 try:
5     crsr.executescript('''
6     CREATE TABLE employee (
7       emp_id INTEGER PRIMARY KEY,
8       emp_name TEXT(20),
9       emp_gender TEXT(7));
10
11    CREATE TABLE department(
12      dept_id INTEGER PRIMARY KEY,
13      dept_name TEXT(20));
14
15    CREATE TABLE paydetails(
16      emp_id INTEGER,
17      dept_id INTEGER,
18      basic REAL,
19      deductions REAL,
20      bonus REAL,
21      doj DATE,
22      foreign KEY(emp_id) references employee(emp_id),
23      foreign KEY(dept_id) references department(dept_id));
24
25    CREATE TABLE payroll(
26      payroll_id INTEGER,
27      emp_id INTEGER,
28      pay_date DATE,
29      foreign KEY(emp_id)references employee(emp_id));    ''' )
30    print ('Table created')
31 except:
32    print ('Error in Table Creation')
33 conn.commit()
34 conn.close()
```

Output

```
Table created
```

- *Line 5*: Uses `executescript()` to execute multiple SQL statements.
- *Line 6-29*: Creates four tables.
- *Line 33*: `commit()` on connection object commits the transaction.

Example 18.4: WAP to create an Employee table having fields – (EmpID, FIRST_NAME, LAST_NAME, AGE, SEX and INCOME). EmpID is the primary key.

```
import sqlite3
conn=sqlite3.connect('sample.sqlite3')
crsr=conn.cursor()
qrey='''
CREATE TABLE Employee (
EmpID INTEGER PRIMARY KEY AUTOINCREMENT,
FIRST_NAME TEXT (20),
LAST_NAME TEXT(20),
AGE INTEGER,
SEX TEXT(1),
INCOME FLOAT
);
'''
try:
    crsr.execute(qrey)
    print ('Table created')
except:
    print ('Error in Table Creation')
conn.close()
```

Output

```
Table created
```

After having represented the data model in relational database, we learn to perform operations on the database.

18.10 Single Table CRUD

CRUD refers to Create, Read, Update and Delete operations that may be performed on databases. Using CRUD, the data can be stored in the databases and accessed successfully. For the four operations of CRUD, there is a corresponding command in SQL – INSERT for creating, SELECT for reading, UPDATE for updating and DELETE for deleting.

- INSERT allows the user to add new records to a table.
- SELECT retrieves specific information from data – single value, set of records, or complex relationships between data.
- UPDATE allows modification of data, i.e., it allows the user to edit or change an existing item.
- DELETE allows the user to permanently remove an item from the database.

18.10.1 Insert Operation

The INSERT operation is required for the addition of records into a database table. The INSERT command can be written in two ways in SQLite database. The syntax are as follows:

Syntax 1

```
INSERT INTO table_name (col1, col2, col3,…) VALUES (val1, val2, val3,…);
```

where, table_name is the name of the table.
col1, col2, col3, … are names of columns.
val1, val2, … are valued for col1, col2, respectively.

Syntax 2

```
INSERT INTO table_name VALUES (val1, val2, val3,…);
```

where, table_name is the name of the table.
val1, val2, … are valued for col1, col2, respectively.

We show the use of the INSERT statement with examples.

Example 18.5: WAP to insert data into the four tables – Employee, Department, PayDetails and Payroll.

```
import sqlite3
conn = sqlite3.connect(r'C:\Anita Goel\Python\Empexample.db')
crsr = conn.cursor()
try:crsr.executescript('''
    INSERT INTO employee(emp_id, emp_name, emp_gender) VALUES
    (101, 'Ram', 'M'),
    (102, 'Maxi', 'F'),
    (103, 'Olive', 'M'),
    (104, 'Steven', 'M'),
    (105, 'Suman', 'F');

    INSERT INTO department(dept_id, dept_name) VALUES
    (111, 'Sales'),
    (222, 'Publicity'),
    (333, 'Taxes'),
    (444, 'HR'),
    (555, 'Product');

    INSERT INTO paydetails(emp_id,dept_id,basic,deductions,bonus,doj)VALUES
    (101,111,20000,500,1000,'2024-01-11'),
    (102,222,21000,1500,2000,'2024-01-12'),
    (103,333,25450,2500,3000,'2024-01-13'),
    (104,444,30000,750,1500,'2024-01-14'),
    (105,555,35000,350,2880,'2024-01-15');

    INSERT INTO payroll(payroll_id, emp_id, pay_date) VALUES
    (900, 101,'2024-01-20'),
    (901, 102,'2024-01-21'),
    (902, 103,'2024-01-22'),
    (903, 104,'2024-01-23'),
    (904, 105,'2024-01-25');    ''' )
    print("Insertion successful")
except:
    print ('Error in Table Insertion')
conn.commit()
conn.close()
```

Output

```
Insertion successful
>>>
```

Example 18.6: WAP to insert records in Employee table – (i) with column names, and (ii) only with values.

```
1 import sqlite3
2 conn=sqlite3.connect('sample.sqlite3')
3 crsr=conn.cursor()
4 qrey='''
5     INSERT INTO Employee(FIRST_NAME,
6     LAST_NAME, AGE, SEX, INCOME)
7     VALUES ('Ashi', 'Gupta', 30, 'F', 900000)'''
8 try:
9     crsr.execute(qrey)
10    conn.commit()
11    data=crsr.execute('''SELECT * FROM EMPLOYEE''')
12    for row in data:
13        print(row)
14 except:
15    conn.rollback()
16    print ('INSERT error')
17 conn.close()
```

(i)

Output

```
Table created
(1, 'Ashi', 'Gupta', 30, 'F', 900000.0)
```

Lines 4, 5, 6, 7: The INSERT is defined with column names and values.
Lines 11, 12, 13: To print the content of the table.
Line 15: The ROLLBACK command is used to roll back a transaction state. It is like an undo function. In case of error, the transaction state is rolled back.

```
import sqlite3
conn = sqlite3.connect('sample.sqlite3')
crsr = conn.cursor()
qrey='''
    INSERT INTO Employee(FIRST_NAME,
    LAST_NAME, AGE, SEX, INCOME)
    VALUES (?,?,?,?,?)'''
try:
    crsr.execute(qrey, ('Akshat', 'Placid', 21, 'M', 55000))
    crsr.execute(qrey, ('Ananya', 'Mohan', 31, 'F', 85000))
    crsr.execute(qrey, ('Aviral', 'Mac', 41, 'M', 75000))
    conn.commit()
    print("All Data after Insertion: ")
    data=crsr.execute('''SELECT * FROM EMPLOYEE''')
    for row in data:
        print(row)
except Exception as e:
   conn.rollback()
   print ('error in INSERT operation')
conn.close()
```

(ii)

Output

```
All Data after Insertion:
(1, 'Ashi', 'Gupta', 30, 'F', 900000.0)
(2, 'Akshat', 'Placid', 21, 'M', 55000.0)
(3, 'Ananya', 'Mohan', 31, 'F', 85000.0)
(4, 'Aviral', 'Mac', 41, 'M', 75000.0)
```

Line 7: In INSERT, the values are denoted by a question mark.
Lines 9, 10, 11: The column values for three records are given.

18.10.2 Select Operation

The SELECT operation is required for retrieving records from a database table. The syntax of SELECT statement in SQLite is as follows:

Syntax-1

```
SELECT * FROM table_name;
```

where, * means all columns from the table.

A complete SELECT statement is as follows:

Syntax-2

```
SELECT DISTINCT col_list
FROM table_name
JOIN table ON join_condition
WHERE row_filter
ORDER BY column
LIMIT count OFFSET offset
GROUP BY column
HAVING group_filter
```

The different parts of the SELECT statement are used for the following purposes-

- ORDER BY – to sort the result set.
- DISTINCT – to query unique rows in a table.
- WHERE – to filter rows in the result set.
- LIMIT – to constrain the number of rows returned.
- JOIN – to query data from multiple tables using join.
- GROUP BY – to group rows into groups.
- HAVING – to filter groups.

In Example 18.6 (i), statement 11; and Example 18.6 (ii), statement 14; we have used the SELECT statement to get the records from the table.

In Example 18.6 (ii), statement 14, if we replace the SELECT statement with the statement as follows:

```
data=crsr.execute('''SELECT * FROM EMPLOYEE ORDER BY AGE ''')
```

We see that the output records are ordered by AGE:

Output

```
(2, 'Akshat', 'Placid', 21, 'M', 55000.0)
(1, 'Ashi', 'Gupta', 30, 'F', 900000.0)
(3, 'Ananya', 'Mohan', 31, 'F', 85000.0)
(4, 'Aviral', 'Mac', 41, 'M', 75000.0)
```

SQLite also provides `fetch` method to fetch the data. The sqlite3.Cursor class provides three methods:

- `fetchall()` retrieves all rows in the result. It returns a list of tuples.
- `fetchone()` fetches the next row in the result. It returns the row as a tuple.
- `fetchmany()` retrieves the next set of rows in the result. It returns the set of rows as a tuple.

In Example 18.6(ii) if we replace statements 14, 15, 16, with the following code,

```
crsr.execute('''SELECT * FROM EMPLOYEE''')
res = crsr.fetchall()
print("Fetchall: ",res)
```

The result is:

```
All Data after Insertion:
Fetchall:  [(1, 'Ashi', 'Gupta', 30, 'F', 900000.0), (2,
'Akshat', 'Placid', 21, 'M', 55000.0), (3, 'Ananya', 'Moh
an', 31, 'F', 85000.0), (4, 'Aviral', 'Mac', 41, 'M', 750
00.0)]
```

Example 18.7: WAP to print (i) all records in employee table, and (ii) employee_id and date of joining of employee from paydetails table.

```
import sqlite3
conn = sqlite3.connect(r'C:\Anita Goel\Python\Empexample.db')
crsr = conn.cursor()

sqlqry = '''
SELECT *
FROM EMPLOYEE;
'''
crsr.execute(sqlqry)
res = crsr.fetchall()
for row in res:
    print(row)

sqlqry = '''
SELECT emp_id, doj
FROM paydetails;
'''
crsr.execute(sqlqry)
res = crsr.fetchall()
for row in res:
    print(row)
conn.close()
```

Output

```
(101, 'Ram', 'M')
(102, 'Maxi', 'F')
(103, 'Olive', 'M')
(104, 'Steven', 'M')
(105, 'Suman', 'F')
(101, '2024-01-11')
(102, '2024-01-12')
(103, '2024-01-13')
(104, '2024-01-14')
(105, '2024-01-15')
>>>
```

18.10.3 Update Operation

The UPDATE statement is required for modifying the values of one or more records that are already present in the table. A single column or multiple columns can be updated.

The syntax of UPDATE statement in SQLite is:

```
UPDATE table_name SET col1 = val1, col2 = val2,…
WHERE condition;
```

where, SET is used to set new values val1, val2, … to col1, col2, …, respectively.
WHERE is used to select the rows for which the columns are to be updated.

In Example 18.4 (ii), we add the following statements after statement 16, where we update the income if AGE is less than or equal to 30.

```
crsr.execute('''UPDATE EMPLOYEE SET INCOME = 80000 WHERE Age<=30;''')
print('\nAfter Update...\n')
data=crsr.execute('''SELECT * FROM EMPLOYEE''')
for row in data:
    print(row)
```

The output is:

Output

```
After Update...

(1, 'Ashi', 'Gupta', 30, 'F', 80000.0)
(2, 'Akshat', 'Placid', 21, 'M', 80000.0)
(3, 'Ananya', 'Mohan', 31, 'F', 85000.0)
(4, 'Aviral', 'Mac', 41, 'M', 75000.0)
```

Here, we see that in the two records having age less than equal to 30, the salary is updated to 80000.

Example 18.8: WAP to update the bonus to 5000 for all employees who have basic greater than equal to 25,000, with reference to paydetails table.

```
import sqlite3
conn = sqlite3.connect(r'C:\Anita Goel\Python\Empexample.db')
crsr = conn.cursor()

sqlqry = '''
UPDATE paydetails
SET bonus = 5000
WHERE basic >=25000;
'''
crsr.execute(sqlqry)
res = crsr.fetchall()
for row in res:
    print(row)

sqlqry = '''
SELECT *
FROM paydetails;
'''
crsr.execute(sqlqry)
res = crsr.fetchall()
for row in res:
    print(row)

conn.close()
```

Output

```
(101, 111, 20000.0, 500.0, 1000.0, '2024-01-11')
(102, 222, 21000.0, 1500.0, 2000.0, '2024-01-12')
(103, 333, 25450.0, 2500.0, 5000.0, '2024-01-13')
(104, 444, 30000.0, 750.0, 5000.0, '2024-01-14')
(105, 555, 35000.0, 350.0, 5000.0, '2024-01-15')
>>>
```

18.10.4 Delete Operation

The DELETE statement is required for deleting data from the table. It allows to delete specific rows from the table.

The syntax of DELETE statement in SQLite is-

```
DELETE FROM table_name [WHERE Clause]
```

where, WHERE is to filter the rows for deletion.

In Example 18.6(ii), we delete the records having AGE less than 30, by including the following statements after statement 16.

```
crsr.execute('''DELETE FROM EMPLOYEE WHERE AGE <30''')
print('\nAfter Deletion...\n')
data=crsr.execute('''SELECT * FROM EMPLOYEE''')
for row in data:
    print(row)
```

Output

```
Table created
(1, 'Ashi', 'Gupta', 30, 'F', 900000.0)
All Data after Insertion:
(1, 'Ashi', 'Gupta', 30, 'F', 900000.0)
(2, 'Akshat', 'Placid', 21, 'M', 55000.0)
(3, 'Ananya', 'Mohan', 31, 'F', 85000.0)
(4, 'Aviral', 'Mac', 41, 'M', 75000.0)

After Deletion...

(1, 'Ashi', 'Gupta', 30, 'F', 900000.0)
(3, 'Ananya', 'Mohan', 31, 'F', 85000.0)
(4, 'Aviral', 'Mac', 41, 'M', 75000.0)
```

Here, we see that one record having age less than 30 is deleted.

The CRUD statements allow basic operations to be performed on the table to create and maintain the data. The CRUD operations were applied on single tables.

18.11 Reconstructing Data with JOIN

- The JOIN operation links across several tables as part of Select operation.
- Join operation combines the records from two tables based on their common attributes.
- You must tell the Join how to use the keys that make the connection between the tables using an ON clause.
- Join is also called the inner join.
- Joining two tables without ON clause gives all possible combinations of rows.

Example 18.9: WAP to print (i) emp_id, emp_name and their basic salary where the employee date of joining is after 2024-01-12, and (ii)) emp_id, emp_name and their basic salary for all employees.

(i) For solving the query, there is a need to join two tables, employee and paydetails. The emp_name and emp_id are in employee table and basic pay is in paydetails. From the paydetails table, the emp_ids satisfying the condition are identified. And from the employee table, their names are identified.

(ii) Similar to (i).

(iii) There is no condition for Join. So, all the combinations are printed.

```
import sqlite3
conn = sqlite3.connect(r'C:\Anita Goel\Python\Empexample.db')
crsr = conn.cursor()

sqlqry = '''
SELECT employee.emp_id, emp_name, basic
FROM employee
JOIN paydetails
ON employee.emp_id = paydetails.emp_id
WHERE paydetails.doj>'2024-01-12' ;  '''
crsr.execute(sqlqry)
res = crsr.fetchall()
for row in res:
    print(row)
print("=========")
sqlqry = '''
SELECT employee.emp_id, emp_name, department.dept_id, department.dept_name, basic
FROM employee, department
JOIN paydetails
ON employee.emp_id = paydetails.emp_id and department.dept_id = paydetails.dept_id;  '''
crsr.execute(sqlqry)
res = crsr.fetchall()
for row in res:
    print(row)
print("=========")
sqlqry = '''
SELECT employee.emp_id, emp_name, basic
FROM employee
JOIN paydetails;  '''
crsr.execute(sqlqry)
res = crsr.fetchall()
for row in res:
    print(row)
conn.close()
```

Output

```
(103, 'Olive', 25450.0)
(104, 'Steven', 30000.0)
(105, 'Suman', 35000.0)
=========
(101, 'Ram', 111, 'Sales', 20000.0)
(102, 'Maxi', 222, 'Publicity', 21000.0)
(103, 'Olive', 333, 'Taxes', 25450.0)
(104, 'Steven', 444, 'HR', 30000.0)
(105, 'Suman', 555, 'Product', 35000.0)
=========
(101, 'Ram', 20000.0)
(101, 'Ram', 21000.0)
(101, 'Ram', 25450.0)
(101, 'Ram', 30000.0)
(101, 'Ram', 35000.0)
(102, 'Maxi', 20000.0)
(102, 'Maxi', 21000.0)
(102, 'Maxi', 25450.0)
(102, 'Maxi', 30000.0)
(102, 'Maxi', 35000.0)
(103, 'Olive', 20000.0)
(103, 'Olive', 21000.0)
(103, 'Olive', 25450.0)
```

```
(103, 'Olive', 30000.0)
(103, 'Olive', 35000.0)
(104, 'Steven', 20000.0)
(104, 'Steven', 21000.0)
(104, 'Steven', 25450.0)
(104, 'Steven', 30000.0)
(104, 'Steven', 35000.0)
(105, 'Suman', 20000.0)
(105, 'Suman', 21000.0)
(105, 'Suman', 25450.0)
(105, 'Suman', 30000.0)
(105, 'Suman', 35000.0)
>>>
```

Lines 6–10: Query (i)
Lines 17–20: Query (ii)
Lines 27–29: Query (iii)

18.12 Many-to-Many Relationships

- A many-to-many relationship is multivalued in both directions. For example, an employee works on more than one project, and a project can have more than one employee assigned.
- There is a need to model many-to-many relationships. For this, we decompose the many-to-many relationship into two, many-to-one relationships.
- Then we model the two many-to-one tables as we have done in earlier sections.
- We need to add a connection table with two foreign keys.
- To illustrate the many-to-many relationship, we do the following:

(i) In our employee–payroll scenario, we create a table with fields –
  - `projct(proj_id, proj_name, proj_date)`

(ii) The project–employee relationship is a many-to-many relationship.

(iii) To handle this, we create another table – projemp
  - `projemp(proj_id, emp_id, role)`

(iv) Projemp consists of keys of both the tables, employee and projct, and a field role. The role can be 0 or 1, where, 0 signifies Manager, and 1 signifies Member. The table projemp has foreign keys (emp_id, proj_id).

(v) The primary key for projemp is a composite key of emp_no and proj_no.

(vi) Each connection in projemp has one row for each employee and a project.

(vii) By introducing projemp table, we have decomposed many-to-many relationship between employee and projct to two one-to-many relationships – employee and projemp, and, projct and projemp.

Let us use the code in an example.

Example 18.10: WAP to –

(i) Create a table projct(proj_id, proj_name, proj_date).
(ii) Create a table projemp(proj_id, emp_id, role).
(iii) Insert data in the two tables.
(iv) Write a query to print the data of the tables.
(v) Write a query to print the id of employee, id of project and name of projects on which the employees are working.

```
import sqlite3
conn = sqlite3.connect(r'C:\Anita Goel\Python\Empexample.db')
crsr = conn.cursor()

sqlqry = ''' SELECT * FROM employee;   '''
crsr.execute(sqlqry)
res = crsr.fetchall()
print("======Employee Data======")
for row in res:
    print(row)

sqlqry = ''' SELECT * FROM projct;  '''
crsr.execute(sqlqry)
res = crsr.fetchall()
print("======Project Data======")
for row in res:
    print(row)

sqlqry = ''' SELECT * FROM projemp;  '''
crsr.execute(sqlqry)
res = crsr.fetchall()
print("======Project-Emp Data======")
for row in res:
    print(row)

sqlqry = '''
SELECT employee.emp_id, projct.proj_id, projct.proj_name
FROM employee JOIN projemp JOIN projct
ON employee.emp_id = projemp.e_id and projct.proj_id = projemp.p_id;  '''
crsr.execute(sqlqry)
res = crsr.fetchall()
print("======Join Data======")
for row in res:
    print(row)
conn.close()
```

Output

```
======Employee Data======
(101, 'Ram', 'M')
(102, 'Maxi', 'F')
(103, 'Olive', 'M')
(104, 'Steven', 'M')
(105, 'Suman', 'F')
======Project Data======
(1111, 'proj1', '2024-01-11')
(1112, 'proj2', '2024-05-14')
(1113, 'proj3', '2024-04-16')
(1114, 'proj4', '2024-03-14')
(1115, 'proj5', '2024-01-19')
======Project-Emp Data======
(1111, 101, 0)
(1112, 102, 1)
(1112, 103, 0)
(1113, 104, 1)
(1114, 104, 1)
(1115, 105, 1)
======Join Data======
(101, 1111, 'proj1')
(102, 1112, 'proj2')
(103, 1112, 'proj2')
(104, 1113, 'proj3')
(104, 1114, 'proj4')
(105, 1115, 'proj5')
>>>
```

18.13 Using DB Browser for SQLite

- DB Browser for SQLite is an open-source tool to design, create, and edit database files.
- The users can create databases, search, and edit data.
- DB Browser uses a general spreadsheet-like interface. There is no need to learn complicated SQL commands.
- It is a tool that can be used by both developers and end-users.
- To start, install the DB Browser.
- The interface to use the DB Browser is simple. We do not discuss it here. Figure 18.4 shows some interface snapshots with different tasks.

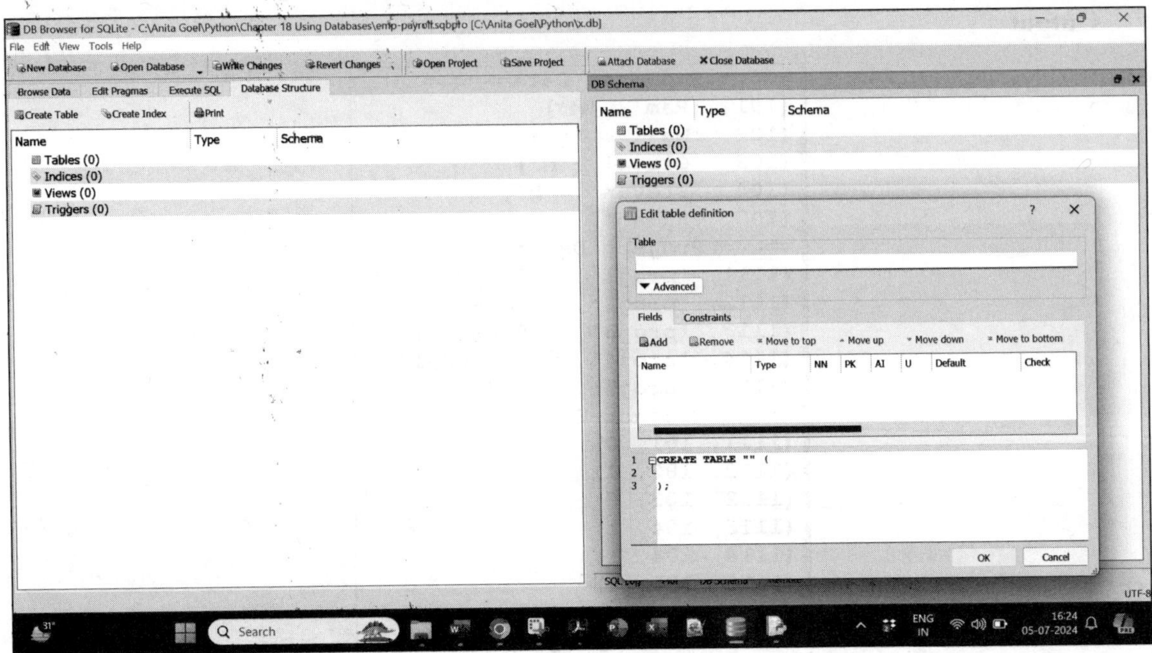

Figure 18.4 (i): Interface

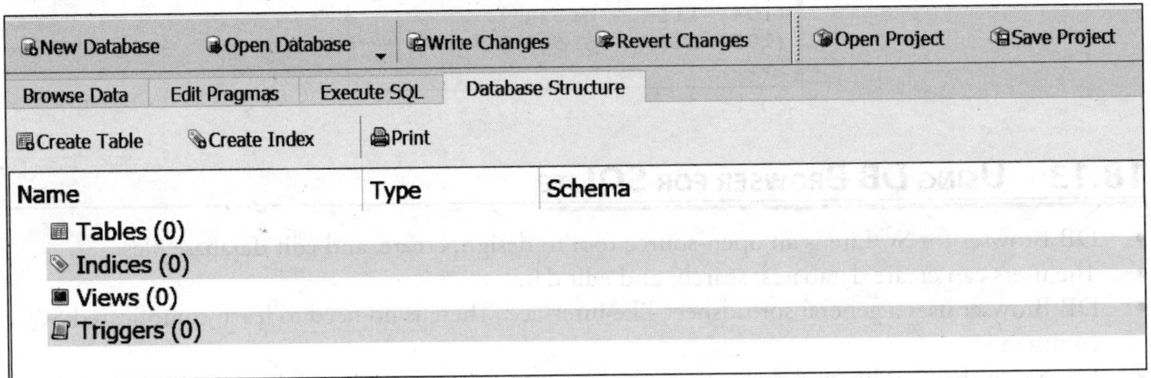

Figure 18.4 (ii): Tabs (New database, Browse data, …)

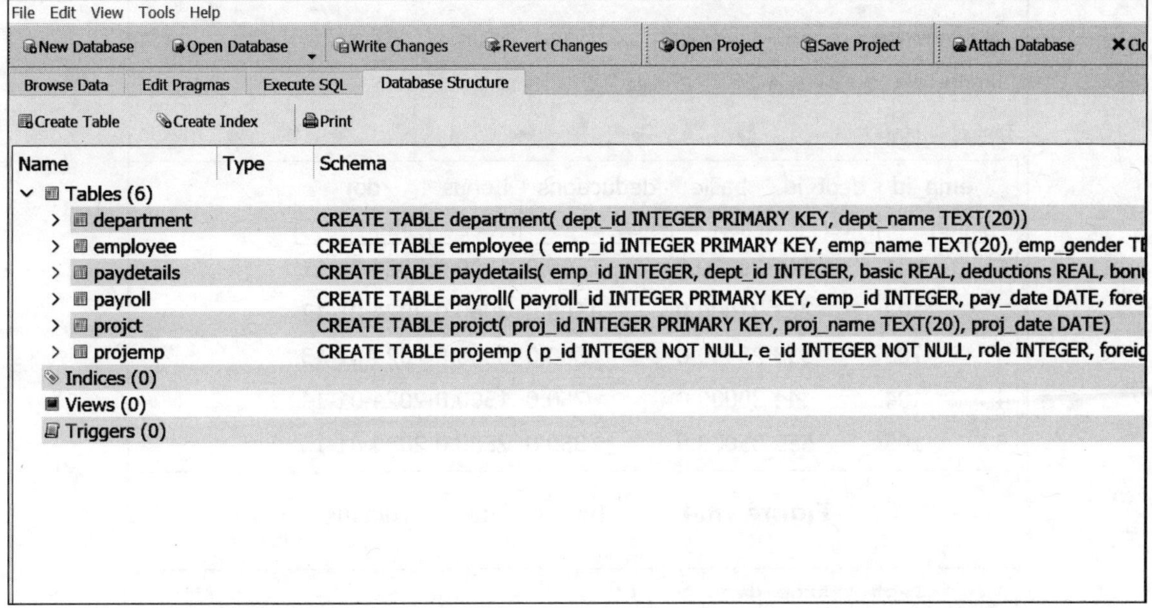

Figure 18.4 (iii): Database structure of employee–payroll scenario

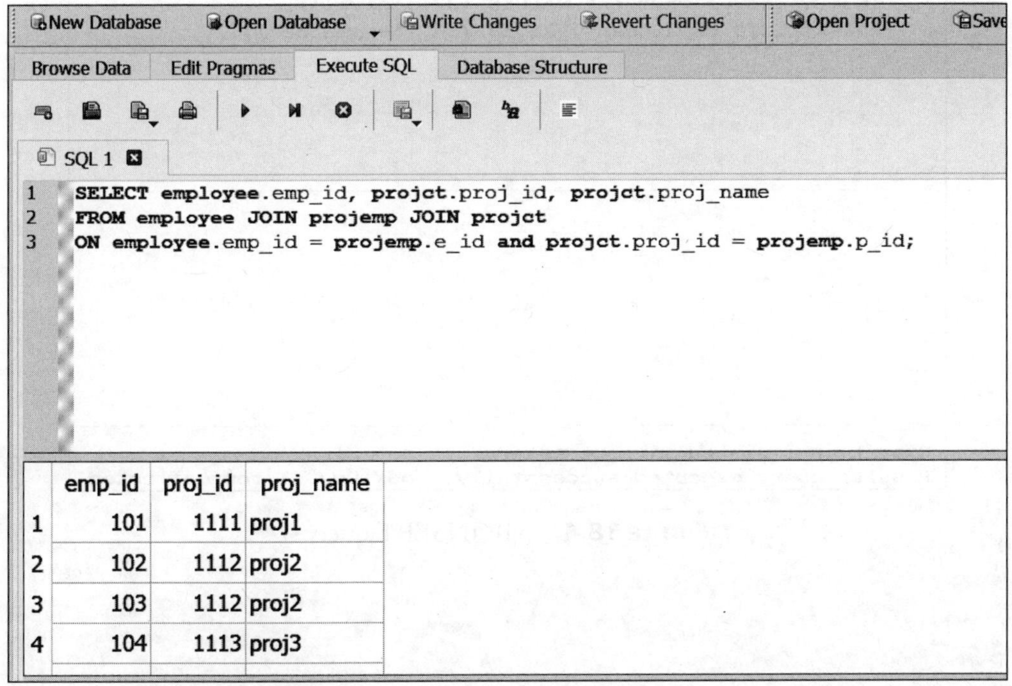

Figure 18.4 (iv): Execute SQL – A query executed

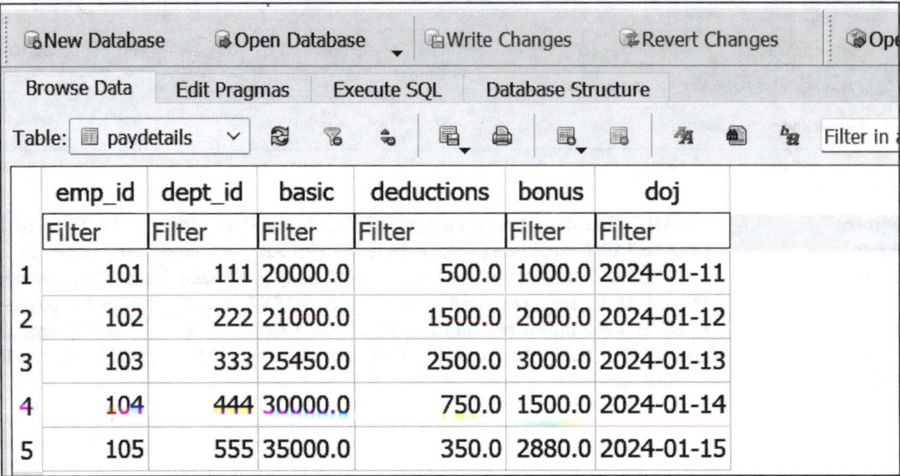

	emp_id	dept_id	basic	deductions	bonus	doj
1	101	111	20000.0	500.0	1000.0	2024-01-11
2	102	222	21000.0	1500.0	2000.0	2024-01-12
3	103	333	25450.0	2500.0	3000.0	2024-01-13
4	104	444	30000.0	750.0	1500.0	2024-01-14
5	105	555	35000.0	350.0	2880.0	2024-01-15

Figure 18.4 (v): Browse data – paydetails

```
select * from department;
INSERT INTO department VALUES (30, 'manage');
INSERT INTO department VALUES (31, 'science');
INSERT INTO department VALUES (32, 'arts');
INSERT INTO department VALUES (33, 'civil');
INSERT INTO department VALUES (34, 'commerce');
```

```
Execution finished without errors.
Result: query executed successfully. Took 0ms, 1 rows affected
```

Figure 18.4 (vi): INSERT query

18.14 Using MySQL with Python

To establish a connection to MySQL via Python, use the following steps.

1) Install MySQL Driver
   - o Establish connection with MySQL using Python.
   - o To download and install "MySQL Connector", use PIP command.
   - o The syntax to download the connector is –

     ```
     python -m pip install mysql-connector-python
     ```
   - o Once installed, use the following import statement in your program.

     ```
     import mysql.connector
     ```
2) Create a connection object
   - o Establish a connection using the `connect()` constructor.
   - o It accepts username, password, host and, name of database to connect.
     - Username is given by user. Default username is *root.*
     - Password is given by user. For example, 'password123.'
     - Host is server name or IP address on which your MySQL is running. For 'localhost', the IP address is 127.0.0.0.
     - Name of database is provided by the user.
   - o It returns an object of MySQLConnection class. The syntax is –

     ```
     db_obj = mysql.connector.connect()
     ```
   - o For example,

     ```
     sqldb = mysql.connector.connect(
     host="localhost",
             user="root",
             password="12345",
             database="db2")
     ```
3) Create a cursor Object:
   - o Use connection.cursor()
   - o For example –

     ```
     crsr = sqldb.cursor()
     ```
4) Execute the Query:
   - o Use Cursor.execute()
   - o The syntax of the queries is same as we have discussed earlier.
   - o For example –

```
crsr.execute("CREATE   TABLE   cust(name   TEXT(20),   address
TEXT(30))")
```

Example 18.11: WAP to – (i) create a database in MySQL, (ii) insert four records, (iii) delete one record, and (iv) print the result.

```
import mysql.connector
sqldb = mysql.connector.connect(         # CONNECT to MySQL
  host="localhost",
  user="root",
  password="12345"      )
print(sqldb)

crsr = sqldb.cursor()                   #CREATE DATABASE and create cursor
crsr.execute("CREATE DATABASE db2")


sqldb = mysql.connector.connect(   #Connect to database db2 CREATE TABLE
  host="localhost",
  user="root",
  password="12345",
  database="db2"  )
crsr = sqldb.cursor()
crsr.execute("CREATE TABLE cust (name TEXT(20), address TEXT(30))")

sql = "INSERT INTO cust (name, address) VALUES (%s, %s)"        #INSERT DATA
val = [("Ajay", "India"), ("Ashi", "USA"), ("Mahesh", "UK"), ("Suchi", "India")]
crsr.executemany(sql, val)
sqldb.commit()

crsr.execute("SELECT * FROM cust")      #SELECT
res = crsr.fetchall()
for row in res:
  print(row)

sql = "DELETE FROM cust WHERE name = 'Mahesh'"      #DELETE DATA
crsr.execute(sql)
sqldb.commit()
crsr.execute("SELECT * FROM cust")
res = crsr.fetchall()
print("===========")
for row in res:
  print(row)
```

Output

```
<mysql.connector.connection_cext.CMySQLConnection object at 0x
000001CDE74886A0>
('Ajay', 'India')
('Ashi', 'USA')
('Mahesh', 'UK')
('Suchi', 'India')
===========
('Ajay', 'India')
('Ashi', 'USA')
('Suchi', 'India')
>>>
```

18.15 Solved Examples

1. Consider two tables, EMP and PROJECT. The two tables are created with the given fields:

   Create table EMP (
   e_no number (5) not null, e_name varchar2 (35) not null,
   e_jb varchar2 (15), e_mgr number (5), e_hiredate date,
   e_sal number (6,2), e_dno number (3));

   Create table PROJECT (
   Proj_no number (5), proj_name varchar2 (50) unique,
   Proj_mgr number (5), proj_person number (5),
   proj_budget number (10, 2), proj_start date, proj_end date);

   Create table DEPT (
   deptno number (5) not null,dept_name varchar2 (35) not null,
   job varchar2 (15), loc number varchar(5),);

Find the meaning of the SQL queries applied on the two tables.

(i) Delete from project where proj_pend < sysdate.
   - o delete all projects that have finished before the actual date (sysdate).

(ii) Select e.e_name, e.e_dno from emp e, dept d and e.e_dno=d.deptno and job='salesman'.
   - o for each salesman, his name, number and name of department where he is working.

(iii) Select e1.e_name, e2.e_name from emp e1, emp e2 where e1.e_mgr = e2.e_no.
   - o names of all employees with the names of their managers.

(iv) Select *from emp where e_dno in (select e_dno from emp where loc = 'Boston');
   - o list all employees who are working in a department located in Boston.

(v) Select * from emp where e_sal >= (select e_sal from emp where e_dno = 30) e_dno= 30) and e_dno = 10;
   - o Retrieve all employees working in department 10 and earn at least as much as any employee working in department 30.

2. Using the two tables, EMP and PROJECT in Question 1, write the queries.

(i) List all departments that have no employee.
   - o select * from dept where not exits (select * from emp where deptno = dept.deptno).

(ii) For each project, retrieve its name, the name of the manager, and name of the department where the manager is working.
   - o Select ename, dname, pname from emp e, dept d, project p where e.empno = e.deptno

(iii) List all employees who are not working in department 30 and who earn more than all employees working in department 30.
   - o select * from emp where sal > all (select sal from emp where deptno = 30) and dept ≠ 30

(iv) List names and salary of employees of department 20, who are leading a project that started before December 31, 1990.
   - o select ename, sal from emp where empno in (select pmgr from project where pstart < '31-DEC-90) and deptno = 20;

(v) List of all employees' maximum and minimum salaries of each department.
- select deptno, min(sal), max (sal) from emp group by deptno

(vi) List of all employees' maximum and minimum salaries of clerks in each department having more than three clerks.
- select deptno, min(sal), max (sal) from emp where job = 'clerk' having count (*) > 3

(vii) Find all those employees who are working in the same department as their manager.
- select * from emp e1 where deptno in (select deptno from emp where empno = e1.mgr)

18.16 Programming Examples

Program 18.1: WAP to create a Player-game database. Create the table, insert data and perform queries on it.

```
import sqlite3
conn = sqlite3.connect(r'C:\Anita Goel\Python\ex4.db')
cursor = conn.cursor()
cursor.executescript('''
    CREATE TABLE IF NOT EXISTS players (
        player_id INT PRIMARY KEY,
        name VARCHAR(50),
        age INT,
        gender CHAR(1),
        team VARCHAR(50) );
    CREATE TABLE IF NOT EXISTS games (
        game_id INT PRIMARY KEY,
        game_name VARCHAR(50),
        game_date DATE``);
    CREATE TABLE IF NOT EXISTS player_games (
        player_id INT,
        game_id INT,
        FOREIGN KEY (player_id) REFERENCES players(player_id),
        FOREIGN KEY (game_id) REFERENCES games(game_id),
        PRIMARY KEY (player_id, game_id)    );''')
cursor.executescript('''
    INSERT INTO players (player_id, name, age, gender, team) VALUES
    (1, 'Alice', 24, 'F', 'Team A'),
    (2, 'Bob', 27, 'M', 'Team B'),
    (3, 'Charlie', 22, 'M', 'Team A'),
    (4, 'David', 29, 'M', 'Team C'),
    (5, 'Eve', 23, 'F', 'Team B');
    INSERT INTO games (game_id, game_name, game_date) VALUES
    (1, 'Soccer', '2024-07-01'),
    (2, 'Basketball', '2024-07-02'),
    (3, 'Tennis', '2024-07-03');
    INSERT INTO player_games (player_id, game_id) VALUES
    (1, 1),    (2, 1),  (3, 2),    (4, 3),
    (5, 2),    (1, 2),  (2, 3);    ''')
conn.commit()
```

```
cursor.execute("SELECT p.name AS player_name, g.game_name
               FROM players p JOIN player_games pg
               ON p.player_id = pg.player_id JOIN games g
               ON pg.game_id = g.game_id");
rows = cursor.fetchall()
for row in rows:
    print(row)

cursor.execute("SELECT g.game_name, COUNT(pg.player_id)
               AS player_count FROM games g JOIN player_games pg
               ON g.game_id = pg.game_id GROUP BY g.game_name;");
rows = cursor.fetchall()
for row in rows:
    print(row)
```

Output

```
('Alice', 'Soccer')
('Bob', 'Soccer')
('Charlie', 'Basketball')
('David', 'Tennis')
('Eve', 'Basketball')
('Alice', 'Basketball')
('Bob', 'Tennis')
```

```
('Basketball', 3)
('Soccer', 2)
('Tennis', 2)
```

Program 18.2: Create a Python project to get total Covid-19 cases, total deaths due to Covid-19 and total Covid-19 patients who recovered, in the world.

Let us now write a program for this. The requirements are listed below:

- From a suitable website we get the data about Covid cases.

Output

- Import libraries - `requests` and `BeautifulSoup`.
- Define `get_info()` function that provides data about a country.
- Define the parameters.
- Use BeautifulSoup to parse the HTML content of the response.
- Find the total, recovered and death cases for a country.
- Print the information.

  The solution code is shown below. It shows data for two countries.

  Likewise, data for other countries can be taken to write the respective codes.

```
from bs4 import BeautifulSoup as BS
import requests
def get_info(cntry):
   url = "https://www.worldometers.info/coronavirus/country/"
   + cntry + "/"
   data = requests.get(url)
   soup = BS(data.text, 'html.parser')
   cases = soup.find_all("div", class_ = "maincounter-number")
   tot_cases = cases[0].text
   tot_cases = tot_cases[1: len(tot_cases) - 2]
   recov_cases = cases[2].text
   recov_cases = recov_cases[1: len(recov_cases) - 1]
   deaths = cases[1].text
   deaths = deaths[1: len(deaths) - 1]
   ans ={'Total': tot_cases, 'Recovered': recov_cases,
   'Deaths': deaths}
   return ans
cntry = "us"
us = get_info(cntry)
print("Covid Cases Data for US")
for i, j in us.items():
   print(i + ": " + j)
print("---------------------------")
cntry = "india"
india = get_info(cntry)
print("Covid Cases Data for India")
for i, j in india.items():
   print(i + ": " + j)
```

SUMMARY

- A database is a collection of data, having an organized structure, and for a specific purpose.
- The characteristics of database approach are – minimizing data redundancy and data inconsistency, data sharing, data independence, maintaining data integrity, improved data security, support for backup and recovery, enforcing standards, and reduction of application development time.
- Data model is divided into three categories – conceptual data model, representation data model, and physical data model.
- Schema is a logical structure of database. Instances are actual data in the database.
- The conceptual model uses concepts like, entity, attribute, and relationships.
- Entity–Relationship model is a high-level conceptual data model. It represents entities, their attributes and relationship between the entities.
- Cardinality ratio is number of entities associated to another entity in a relationship set.
- Representation data model is used in hierarchical, relational, and network data models.

- The relational database model uses concepts such as table, record, field, key, and data values.
- The physical model describes how a record is stored, internally.
- A database system has four main components – Users, Hardware, Software, and Data.
- ANSI/SPARC architecture is divided into three levels – Physical level, Conceptual level and External level.
- DBMS is a software system for creating, organizing, and managing the database.
- DBMS provides logical data independence, and physical data independence.
- Database Administrator is a person who coordinates all activities of the database system.
- DDL and DML are languages provided by the DBMS. DDL is used for defining database schema, and DML for manipulation of the data.
- SQL is a relational database language that is a combination of both DDL and DML.
- Centralized databases, client–server systems, and distributed database are three common ways of designing architecture of database system.
- SQLite is a light-weight disk-based database that works like SQL.
- sqlite3 is a library in Python to access SQLite databases.
- Python MySQL Connector is for connecting to MySQL database server.
- MySQL is a server-based DBMS.
- INSERT operation is required for addition of records into a database table.
- SELECT operation is required for retrieving records from a database table.
- UPDATE statement modifies values of records that are already present in the table.
- DELETE statement is required for deleting data from the table.
- JOIN operation links across several tables in select operation.
- A many-to-many relationship is multivalued in both directions.
- DB Browser for SQLite is an open-source tool to design, create, and edit database files.

KEYWORDS

Database
Data redundancy
Data inconsistency
Data sharing
Data independence
Data integrity
Data security
Data Model
Schema
Instance
Conceptual data model
Representation data model
Physical data model
Entity
Attribute
Relationships
Entity–Relationship model
E–R diagram
Entity set
Domain
Relationship set
Cardinality ratio
One-to-On
One-to-Many
Many-to-One
Hierarchical database model
Relational database model
Network database model
Data values
Attribute
Column
Tuple
Row
Relation
Table
Key
Primary key
Foreign key
Database system
Users
Application programmers
End users
Data administrator
Data base administrator
Software
DBMS
Application software
User interface
Hardware
Integrated data
Shared data

ANSI/SPARC architecture
Physical Level
Conceptual Level
External level
View level
Mapping
Logical data independence
Physical data independence
Data dictionary
Metadata
Data definition language (DDL)
Data manipulation language (DML)
Structured query language (SQL)
Centralized databases
Client-server systems
Two-tier architecture
Three-tier architecture
Distributed database
SQLite
MySQL
PostgreSQL
Python MySQL Connector
Data model design
CRUD
DB Browser

Programming Language Keywords

```
sqlite3
connect()
cursor()
execute()
fetchall()
CREATE TABLE
INSERT
SELECT
UPDATE
DELETE
ORDER BY
DISTINCT
WHERE
LIMIT
JOIN
GROUP BY
HAVING
fetchall()
fetchone()
fetchmany()
```

Assessment

A.1 Bloom Level: Knowledge/Remember

Review Questions

1. Define – database, data model, schema, instances, entity, entity set, attribute, domain, relationship, relationship set, data values, tuple, row, attribute, table, key.
2. Give some examples of databases in real-life applications.
3. What is data independence?
4. What does the data dictionary store?
5. List the three categories of data model.
6. What is an E–R model?
7. Give three examples of tangible entities and non-tangible entities.
8. Give an example of entity set.
9. Give examples of three attributes of any entity and their domains.
10. What is cardinality ratio?
11. List the four kinds of cardinality ratio.
12. Give two examples each of – (i) one-to-one, (ii) one-to-many, (iii) many-to-many, and (iv) many-to-many relationships.
13. Name the three kinds of representational model.
14. List any two hierarchical database models.
15. List any two network database models.
16. List any two relational database models.
17. For a student-record table, give the entities, attributes and five tuples.
18. What is a foreign key?
19. Give an example of primary key in a table.

20. Give an example of foreign key in a table.
21. List the four components of database system.
22. Name a type of file organization at the physical level
23. List the three kinds of users of a database.
24. What is logical data independence?
25. What is physical data independence?
26. What is metadata?
27. Give the full form of – DBA, E–R diagram, DDL, DML, SQL, DBMS, CODASYL, DBTG, PEP, DB-API, CRUD
28. List the three common ways of designing the architecture of a database system.
29. What is a centralized database?
30. What is a distributed database?
31. Name the three components of client–server database.
32. List three common databases in Python.
33. Name the SQL commands for CRUD operations.
34. Name an open-source tool to design, create, and edit database files for SQLite database.
35. List the main step in modeling the many-to-many relationship.

Fill in the Blanks

1. The update of data values does not lead to disagreement in stored values, this ________ data inconsistency.
2. ________ stores the description of data.
3. Data ________ describes structure of the database.
4. ________ contains information about description of database like, names of record type, and constraints.
5. The three main concepts in conceptual model are ________, ________ and ________.
6. An ________ is a basic unit for the modeling.
7. The set of values permitted for an attribute is called ________ of the attribute.
8. An entity in A is associated with any number of entities in B; an entity in B is associated with at most one entity in A. This is ________ relationship.
9. The E–R model is represented diagrammatically using an ________.
10. In E–R diagram, attribute is represented as an ________.
11. In E–R diagram, relationship is represented using a ________.
12. ________ proposed the relational database model.
13. A relation has a set of ________ and any number of ________.
14. ________ interact with the database to get information for business purposes.
15. The ANSI/SPARC architecture is divided into ________ levels.
16. ________ stores metadata.
17. Structured Query Language (SQL) is a relational database language that is a combination of ________ and ________ languages.
18. ________ is a file-based lightweight transactional relational database in Python.

19. `sqlite3` was written by ________.

20. `sqlite3` is a ________ in Python to access SQLite databases.

21. ________ method is used on cursor object to execute queries once the connection is made in `sq3lite` database.

22. ________ SQL command is used for reading data from the database.

23. The data is stored centrally in databases, thus reducing data ____________.

State True/False

1. Data is shared, so the users have access to the same data for their use.
2. Schema shows the data in the database.
3. The Entity–Relationship model (E–R model) is a high-level conceptual data model.
4. In E–R diagram, entity is represented using an ellipse.
5. Table is a collection of logically related tuples.
6. Application software are menus and screens used by the user to interact with application programs and DBMS.
7. Physical level schema describes the structure of the whole database for the users.
8. Physical data independence allows modifying the conceptual schema without changing the external schema.
9. DDL is used for defining the database schema.
10. MySQL is an open-source relational database management system.
11. MySQL is an in-built database in Python.
12. Joining two tables without ON clause gives a few key combinations of rows.

Multiple Choice Questions (MCQ)

1. A data model is a collection of conceptual tools for describing
   (i) data and data relationships.
   (ii) data semantics and consistence constraints.
   (iii) data, data relationship, data semantics and consistency constraints.
   (iv) None.

2. Choose the INCORRECT statements.
   (i) In network model, data is represented by a collection of records, and relationship among data are represented by links.
   (ii) In hierarchical model, the records are organized as a collection of arbitrary graphs.
   (iii) In network model, the records are organized as collection of trees.
   (iv) (ii) and (iii).

3. Which of the following is NOT a relational database?
   (i) Oracle DB
   (ii) IBM DB2
   (iii) Microsoft SQL Server
   (iv) Reflex

4. Which of the following is not characteristic of a relational database model?
   (i) Tables
   (ii) Tree-like structure
   (iii) Complex logical relationship
   (iv) Records

5. One column in a table is equivalent to
   (i) a record. (ii) a field.
   (iii) a database. (iv) a cell.
6. Choose the most appropriate choice with respect to conceptual design.
   (i) Conceptual design is a documentation technique.
   (ii) Conceptual design is done to determine the size of database.
   (iii) E–R diagram is an output for any conceptual design.
   (iv) Conceptual design involves modeling data requirements independent of the DBMS, operating system, and hardware.

A.2 Bloom Level: Comprehend/Understand

Review Questions

1. Describe the meaning of following methods: `connect()`, `cursor()`, `execute()`, `fetchall()`, `fetchone()`, `fetchmany()`, `CREATE`, `SELECT`, `INSERT`, `UPDATE`, `DELETE`, `JOIN`
2. Describe the syntax for the following:
   (i) Import sqlite3
   (ii) Create a connection object in sqlite3
   (iii) Get cursor object from connection object
   (iv) Install MySQL Driver
   (v) Create a connection object in Python MySQL
   (vi) SELECT statement
   (vii) CREATE statement
   (viii) INSERT statement
   (ix) UPDATE statement
   (x) DELETE statement
   (xi) JOIN statement
3. Describe the main characteristics of database approach.
4. What is the advantage of data independence?
5. What is data sharing in databases?
6. How does data redundancy and data inconsistency get minimized in databases?
7. Describe the E–R relationship.
8. What is a conceptual model?
9. What is a representational model?
10. What is a relational database model?
11. What is the purpose of primary key?
12. What is a physical data model?
13. What is a database system?
14. What is meant by: "Data in a database is integrated and shared."
15. In ANSI/SPARC architecture, describe the purpose of the three levels.
16. What is a Database Management System?
17. Write a short note on data independence in databases.
18. What is the purpose of data dictionary?
19. Describe the task of a database administrator.
20. What is the purpose of DDL and DML languages?
21. Write short note of client–server database.
22. What is the purpose of DB-API specification?
23. List the key features of sq3lite database in Python.
24. What is the purpose of using the JOIN operation in SQL?

A.3 Bloom Level: Application/Apply

1. Identify whether the following relationships are one-to-one, one-to-many, or many-to-many.
   (i) Person–Passport
   (ii) Teacher–Student
   (iii) Surgeries–Doctor
   (iv) Engineer–Project
   (v) Student–Course
   (vi) Order–Customer
   (vii) Author–Book
   (viii) Film–Actor
   (ix) Publisher–Title
   (x) Customer–Account

2. Design a relational database corresponding to the E–R diagram.

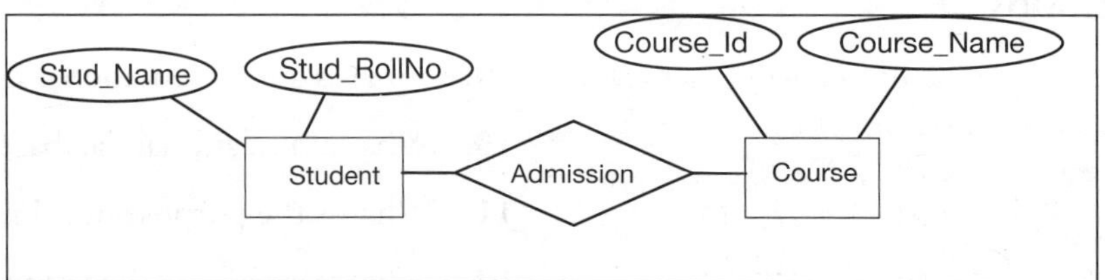

3. Study the code shown below:

```
import sqlite3
conn = sqlite3.connect(r'C:\Anita Goel\Python\ex.db')
crsr = conn.cursor()
crsr.execute('''
CREATE TABLE IF NOT EXISTS table1(
    id INTEGER PRIMARY KEY,
    name TEXT,
    age INTEGER,
    salary REAL )   ''')
crsr.executemany('''
INSERT INTO table1(name, age, salary) VALUES (?, ?, ?)''', [
     ('Asha', 30, 70000),          ('Babli', 25, 50000),
     ('Charlie', 35, 60000),      ('Deva', 40, 80000),
     ('Evelyn', 30, 900000),      ('Abha', 32, 1000000),
     ('Babloo', 35, 320000),      ('Charu', 45, 990000),
     ('Devyani', 41, 880000),      ('Ester', 37, 700000)        ])
conn.commit()
crsr.execute('SELECT COUNT(*) FROM table1')
print('Total rows:', crsr.fetchone()[0])
crsr.execute('SELECT DISTINCT name FROM table1')
print('Unique names:', crsr.fetchall())
crsr.execute('SELECT AVG(age) FROM table1')
print('Average age:', crsr.fetchone()[0])
crsr.execute('SELECT MAX(salary), MIN(salary) FROM table1')
print('Max and Min salary:', crsr.fetchone())
crsr.execute('SELECT COUNT(DISTINCT age) FROM table1')
print('Distinct ages:', crsr.fetchone()[0])
conn.close()
```

a) Find the output of the print statements at:
   (i) Line 19
   (ii) Line 21
   (iii) Line 23
   (iv) Line 25
   (v) Line 27

b) Write the SQL queries to answer the following questions:
   (i) What are the top three most frequent values in age column?
   (ii) What is the total sum of salary in the table?
   (iii) How many rows are there with age more than 30?
   (iv) What is the most frequent value in age column?
   (v) How many rows are there per age group?

4. Multiple Choice Questions (MCQ)

A. In an airline reservation system, the entities are date, flight number, departure source, destination, plane type and seats available. The primary key is _________.
   (i) flight number
   (ii) flight number + departure source
   (iii) flight number + date
   (iv) flight number + destination

B. The student and courses enrolled is an example of_________.
   (i) one-to-many
   (ii) many-to-many
   (iii) one-to-one
   (iv) many-to-many

C. The employee information in a company is stored in the relation employee (emp_name, gender, salary, dept_name)
   Consider the following SQL query:
   Select dept_name from employee where gender = 'M' group by dept_name having avg (salary) > (select avg salary from employee)
   It returns the names of departments in which
   (i) the average salary is more than two average salaries in the company.
   (ii) the average salary of all employees is more than average salary of all male employees in the company.
   (iii) the average salary of male employees is more than the average salary of employees in the same department.
   (iv) the average salary of male employees is more than the average salary in the company.

5. Define a database schema in SQL for Part inventory. Apply any two queries on it.

6. Write the command to create a connection object in sq3lite database.

7. Write the command to get cursor object from connection object in sq3lite database.

A.4 Bloom Level: Analyze

1. Explain difference between the following:
   (i) Two-tier client–server architecture and three-tier client architecture
   (ii) sqlite in Python and MySQL for Python
   (iii) Conceptual data model and Representation data model
   (iv) Schema and Instance
   (v) Centralized databases and Distributed databases.

2. Given the code in (a). What is the difference in the statements in codes (i), (ii) and (iii)? What are the statements doing? What is the output?

```
import sqlite3
conn = sqlite3.connect(r'C:\Anita Goel\Python\ex2.db')
cursor = conn.cursor()
cursor.execute('''
    CREATE TABLE IF NOT EXISTS employees (
        employee_id INTEGER PRIMARY KEY,
        first_name TEXT,
        last_name TEXT,
        department_id INTEGER,
        salary INTEGER    )''')
cursor.execute('''
    INSERT INTO employees (first_name, last_name, department_id, salary)
    VALUES
    ('Joen', 'Doe', 101, 60000),
    ('Jade', 'Sally', 102, 90000),
    ('Amily', 'John', 101, 65000),
    ('Bobby', 'Bain', 103, 70000)  ''')
conn.commit()

cursor.execute('SELECT * FROM employees')
rows = cursor.fetchall()
for row in rows:
    print(row)


cursor.execute('SELECT * FROM employees')
row = cursor.fetchone()
print(row)

while row is not None:
    print(row)
    row = cursor.fetchone()
```

(a)

```
cursor.execute('SELECT * FROM employees')
rows = cursor.fetchall()
for row in rows:
    print(row)
```

(i)

```
cursor.execute('SELECT * FROM employees')
row = cursor.fetchone()
print(row)
```

(ii)

```
while row is not None:
    print(row)
    row = cursor.fetchone()
```

(iii)

3. Given the code (a). Analyze the difference between (i) and (ii). What is the output? Give the reasons for difference in the output.

```
import sqlite3
conn = sqlite3.connect(r'C:\Anita Goel\Python\ex3.db')
cursor = conn.cursor()
cursor.execute('''
    CREATE TABLE IF NOT EXISTS employees (
        emp_id INTEGER PRIMARY KEY,
        name TEXT,
        age INTEGER,
        dept_id INTEGER,
        dept_name TEXT,
        salary INTEGER    )''')
cursor.execute('''
    INSERT INTO employees (name, age, dept_id, dept_name, salary)
    VALUES
    ('Joen', 25, 101, 'Sales', 60000),
    ('Jade', 33, 102, 'Prod', 90000),
    ('Amily', 29, 101, 'Sales', 65000),
    ('Bobby', 37, 103, 'Sales', 70000),
    ('Shane', 35, 104, 'HR', 88000)  ''')
conn.commit()
```

(a)

```
cursor.execute("SELECT * FROM employees WHERE age >= 30 AND dept_name= 'Sales'")
rows = cursor.fetchall()
for row in rows:
    print(row)
```

(i)

```
cursor.execute("SELECT * FROM employees WHERE age >= 30 OR dept_name= 'Sales'");
rows = cursor.fetchall()
for row in rows:
    print(row)
```

(ii)

4. Given the following relations.

Employee(emp_id, name, age, dept)

Projects(proj_id, proj_name, dept)

Employee_projects(emp_id, proj_id)

Answer the following:

a) What is the output for the three queries shown below?

b) What task do the three queries do?

SELECT e.name, p.proj_name
FROM employees e
JOIN employee_projects ep ON e.emp_id = ep.emp_id
JOIN projects p ON ep.proj_id = p.proj_id
WHERE e.age > 30 AND p.dept = 'Sales';

(i)

SELECT e.name, p.proj_name
FROM employees e
JOIN employee_projects ep ON e.emp_id = ep.emp_id
JOIN projects p ON ep.proj_id = p.proj_id
WHERE p.dept = 'Sales' OR p.dept = 'IT';

(ii)

SELECT e.name, p.proj_name
FROM employees e
JOIN employee_projects ep ON e.emp_id = ep.emp_id
JOIN projects p ON ep.proj_id = p.proj_id
WHERE e.dept = p.dept;

(iii)

A.5 Bloom Level: Evaluate

1. Evaluate the following requirement and develop the code.
   CREATE TABLE staff (id INT PRIMARY KEY,
   name VARCHAR(50), dept VARCHAR(50), gender CHAR(1), experience INT);
   INSERT INTO staff (id, name, dept, gender, experience) VALUES
   (1, 'Alice', 'HR', 'F', 5),
   (2, 'Bob', 'Sales', 'M', 8),
   (3, 'Charlie', 'Sales', 'M', 3),
   (4, 'David', 'IT', 'M', 10),
   (5, 'Eve', 'HR', 'F', 7),
   (6, 'Frank', 'IT', 'M', 2),
   (7, 'Grace', 'Finance', 'F', 6),
   (8, 'Hank', 'Marketing', 'M', 4),
   (9, 'Ivy', 'IT', 'F', 9),
   (10, 'Jack', 'Sales', 'M', 1);
   Verify the data inserted:
   SELECT * FROM staff;

2. Evaluate the following codes. Write the output. What is the task performed?
   (a)
   ```
   cursor.execute('SELECT * FROM employees')
   row = cursor.fetchone()
   print(row)
   ```
   (b)
   ```
   cursor.execute('SELECT * FROM employees WHERE salary > 55000')
   rows = cursor.fetchall()
   for row in rows:
   print(row)
   ```
   (c)
   ```
   cursor.execute('''
   SELECT e.first_name, e.last_name, d.department_name
   FROM employees e
   JOIN departments d ON e.department_id = d.department_id
   ''')
     rows = cursor.fetchall()
     for row in rows:
         print(row)
   ```
   (d)
   ```
   cursor.execute('SELECT * FROM employees WHERE department_id = 101')
     row = cursor.fetchone()
     while row is not None:
       print(row)
       row=cursor.fetchone()
   ```

3. Evaluate the code. What is the task performed? What is the output?
   (i) Assume a table "patient". Write commands in SQL for the following:
      (a) Select name from patient where age>23 order by name desc;
      (b) select avg(payment) from patient group by age;
      (c) Select * from patient table where payment is between 300 and 3000;

```
(d) Select  sum(payment)
    from  patient  where
    city= "Delhi";
(e) Select name, city from
    patient group by age
    having count(age)>2;
```

(ii) Assume the employee, department table. Write commands in SQL for the following:
   (a) Get the total salary of all employees.
   (b) Find the average salary of employees in each department.
   (c) Find employees with salary greater than 90,000 and order the results by last_name.
   (d) Find the highest-paid employee in each department.
   (e) Get a list of departments and the number of employees in each department, including departments with no employees.
   (f) Find the names of employees who do not belong to any department.

4. Convert the following to many-to-many relationships, by creating new tables.
   (a) Real estate can be owned by one/many people. A person can own several houses or ownership share of many houses.
   Person(PersonId, …..)
   RealEstate(real_estate_id, ….)
   (b) Table Employee, Company, Position, Project, Skill
   Company and employee have a many-to-many relationship since an employee could work for different companies, and the companies can have many employees. Position and employee have many-to-many relationship because many employees can work in one position in one company and in different companies. Project and skill relate as many-to-many.

A.6 Bloom Level: Create/Synthesize

Programming Assignment

1. Define a schema based on the following statements. Write queries to perform the following tasks.
   a) List the employee details department-wise.
   b) List the names of all employees who joined after a particular date.
   c) List the details of employees whose basic salary is between 10,000 and 20,000.
   d) Give a count of the number of employees working in each department.
   e) Give a name of the employees whose net salary is greater than 10,000.
   f) List the details for an employee_id=9.

2. WAP to create tables, insert data. Create DDL and DML commands. Show the results.
   Customerdetail (custid, custname, phone, city, pincode)
   Shipment (shipid, from_port, from_country, departure, to_port, to_country, arrive, schedulename, custid)
   Container (contid, cont_type, status, shipid, custid)
   Session (sessionid, sessionname, sessioncharge, shipid)
   Payment (invoiceid, cost, custid, shipid, contid)

3. Define a schema based on the following statements. Write queries to perform the following tasks. Create tables for the following. Define the primary key, the characteristics of the primary key, the data type and size of each attribute.
   a) Retrieve a list of employees ordered by department ID.
   b) Retrieve a list of employees ordered in descending order by department ID and within each department, ordered alphabetically in descending order by last name.
   c) Use department name instead of department ID. Retrieve a list of employees ordered by department name, and within each department, ordered alphabetically in descending order by last name.
   d) For each department ID, retrieve the number of employees in the department.
   e) For each department, retrieve the number of employees in the department, and the average employee salary in the department.
   f) Label the computed columns in the result set of SQL as NUM_EMPLOYEES and AVG_SALARY.
   g) In SQL, order the result set by Average Salary.
   h) In SQL, limit the result to departments with fewer than 4 employees.
4. Write SQL commands for the following. Make assumptions wherever required. The queries may be unrelated to each other.
   a) Delete all rows where the "name" is "Akshay" in the Student Table.
   b) Select all data from the Breed column in the Dog table.
   c) Add a row to Dog table with name "Sally" and breed "Bulldog."
   d) CREATE TABLE for grades with student_id of type integer, test_name of type text, English score of type integer and math score of type integer.
   e) INSERT statement to add a new entry to grades table. Set student_id to 12, English score to 97 and math score to 93.
   f) UPDATE to change entry with student_id 11 and set English score to 90.
   g) SELECT statement to retrieve student_id, test_name, and English for all entries whose English value is less than 80 and math value is more than 80.
   h) SELECT statement with JOIN to select math from grades table and name from students table, where student_id in grades table is equal to id in students table.
   i) SELECT statement with JOIN to: select date and name from test table and student_id from grades table, where test_name in grades table is same as name in test table.
5. The database schema is provided as follows:
   Student(stud_no, stud_name)
   Membership(mem_no, stud_no)
   Book(book_no, book_name, author)
   Iss_rec(iss_no, iss_datem mem_no)
   Membership table references Student.
   Iss_rec table references membership table and book table.
   Write the program to create tables, insert data. Write queries for the following.
   a) List student names and their membership number.
   b) List all issues for date "09-07-2024" with student and book names.
   c) List details for students who borrowed books of author "auth1".
   d) Provide a count of books issued to each student.
   e) Provide a list of books taken by student No. 3.

6. For the database shown in Example discussed in Section 18.8, the following queries are applied. Find the output.

a)

```
select employee.*,department.dept_
name from department
join paydetails on department.dept_
id=paydetails.dept_id
join employee on paydetails.emp_
id=employee.emp_id
group by dept_name;
```

b)

```
select employee.emp_name
from employee
join paydetails
on employee.emp_id=paydetails.
emp_id
where paydetails.doj>'2021-11-12';
```

c)

```
select employee.* from employee
join paydetails
on employee.emp_id=paydetails.
emp_id
where paydetails.basic BETWEEN
10000 and 20000;
```

d)

```
select department.dept_
name,count(employee.emp_id)
from employee
join paydetails on employee.emp_
id=paydetails.emp_id
join department on paydetails.
dept_id=department.dept_id group
by dept_name;
```

e)

```
select employee.*
from employee
where employee.emp_id=(select emp_
id from paydetails where basic+addi-
tion-deductions>10000);
```

f)

```
select emp_name,paydetails.*
from employee
join paydetails on employee.emp_
id=paydetails.emp_id
where employee.emp_id=5;
```

Answers

A.1 Bloom Level: Knowledge/Remember

Review Questions

20. (a)– (v), (b) – (iv), (c) – (vi), (d) – (ii) (e) – (i), (f) – (iii)

Fill in the Blanks

1. reduces
2. Dictionary
3. Model
4. Schema
5. entity, attribute, relationships
6. entity
7. domain
8. One-to-many
9. E–R diagram
10. ellipse
11. diamond
12. E F Codd
13. columns, rows
14. End users
15. three
16. Data dictionary
17. DDL, DML
18. SQLite
19. Gerhard Häring
20. Library
21. `execute()`
22. SELECT
23. redundancy

True/False

1. True
2. False
3. True
4. False
5. True
6. False
7. False
8. False
9. True
10. True
11. False
12. False

Multiple Choice Questions (MCQ)

1. (iii) **2.** (iv) **3.** (iv) **4.** (ii) **5.** (ii) **6.** (iv)

A.3. Bloom Level: Application/Apply

3. (a)

(i) Total rows: 10

(ii) Unique names: [('Asha',), ('Babli',), ('Charlie',), ('Deva',), ('Evelyn',), ('Abha',), ('Babloo',), ('Charu',), ('Devyani',), ('Ester',)]

(iii) Average age: 35.0

(iv) Max and Min salary: (1000000.0, 50000.0)

(v) Distinct ages: 8

(b)

(i)
```
SELECT age, COUNT(age) as count
FROM table1
GROUP BY age
ORDER BY count DESC
LIMIT 3
```

(ii)
```
SELECT SUM(salary) FROM table1
```

(iii)
```
SELECT COUNT(*) FROM table1 WHERE age > 30
```

(iv)
```
SELECT age
FROM table1
GROUP BY age
ORDER BY COUNT(age) DESC
LIMIT 1
```

(v)
```
SELECT age, COUNT(*)
FROM table1
GROUP BY age
```

4. Multiple Choice Questions (MCQ)

1. (iii) **2.** (iv) **3.** (iv)

A.4 Bloom Level: Analyze

2.

```
(1, 'Joen', 'Doe', 101, 60000)
(2, 'Jade', 'Sally', 102, 90000)
(3, 'Amily', 'John', 101, 65000)
(4, 'Bobby', 'Bain', 103, 70000)
```

(i)

```
(1, 'Joen', 'Doe', 101, 60000)
```

(ii)

```
(1, 'Joen', 'Doe', 101, 60000)
(2, 'Jade', 'Sally', 102, 90000)
(3, 'Amily', 'John', 101, 65000)
(4, 'Bobby', 'Bain', 103, 70000)
```

(iii)

3.

```
(4, 'Bobby', 37, 103, 'Sales', 70000)
```

```
(1, 'Joen', 25, 101, 'Sales', 60000)
(2, 'Jade', 33, 102, 'Prod', 90000)
(3, 'Amily', 29, 101, 'Sales', 65000)
(4, 'Bobby', 37, 103, 'Sales', 70000)
(5, 'Shane', 35, 104, 'HR', 88000)
```

4. (i) Employees with age more than 30 and working on Sales Projects
(ii) Employees working on Sales or IT Projects
(iii) Employees working in their own departments.

A.5 Bloom Level: Evaluate

2.

(i) Retrieve and display first row from the employees table.
(ii) Retrieve and display all rows where the salary is greater than 55000.
(iii) Retrieve names of all employees and their departments using a join with departments table.
(iv) Fetch rows one by one where department_id is 101.

3. (i)

a) Display name in descending order whose age is more than 23.
b) Find average fee grouped by age from customer table.
c) From coaching table where fee is between 30000 and 40000.

(ii)

a) SELECT SUM(salary) AS total_salary FROM employees;
b) SELECT department_id, AVG(salary) AS avg_salary
FROM employees
GROUP BY department_id;
c) SELECT * FROM employees
WHERE salary > 50000
ORDER BY last_name;
d) SELECT e.*
FROM employees e
JOIN (
SELECT department_id, MAX(salary) AS max_salary
FROM employees
GROUP BY department_id
) d ON e.department_id = d.department_id AND e.salary = d.max_salary;

e)
```
SELECT d.department_name, COUNT(e.employee_id) AS employee_count
FROM departments d
LEFT JOIN employees e ON d.department_id = e.department_id
GROUP BY d.department_name;
```
f)
```
SELECT first_name, last_name
FROM employees
WHERE department_id IS NULL;
```

4.

[Person_RealEstate]
[JobHistory] [project_skill]

CHAPTER 19 Case Studies

Contents

19.1 INTRODUCTION

Development of projects helps the students to understand the process of design, get the nuances of programming and create something useful for the society. In this chapter, some case studies are presented. The case studies may be divided into beginner, intermediate and advanced levels. We present seven solved case studies with output:

Beginner Level – CS-1, CS-2

Intermediate Level – CS-3, CS-4

Advanced Level – CS-5, CS-6, CS-7

Learning Outcomes of this chapter

After completion of the chapter, the learner will be able to:

- Recognize the nuances of creating long projects
- Develop expertise in the development of long projects
- Grasp the thought process while designing long and complex projects
- Understand the approach to handle complex projects.

19.2 CS-1. DEVELOP A UNIT CONVERTER

A Unit Converter convert units of measurement (e.g., meters to feet, Celsius to Fahrenheit). Let us now write a program for the following requirements:

- Length Converter
  - Meter to Feet
  - Feet to Meter
  - Kilometer to Mile
  - Mile to Kilometer
- Weight Converter
  - Kilogram to Pound
  - Pound to Kilogram
- Temperature Converter
  - Celsius to Fahrenheit
  - Fahrenheit to Celsius
- Make a menu-driven program, as follows:

```
Unit Converter
================
1. Length Converter
2. Weight Converstern
3. Temperature Converter
4. Exit
Choose an option:
```

On choosing an option, further menu opens as:

```
Length Converter
1. Meter -> Feet
2. Feet -> Meter
3. KM -> Mile
4. Mile -> KM
Choose an option:
```

The solution code is shown below.

```
def length_conversion():
    print("\nLength Converter")
    print("1. Meter -> Feet")
    print("2. Feet -> Meter")
    print("3. KM -> Mile")
    print("4. Mile -> KM")
    ch = input("Choose an option: ").strip()
    if ch == '1':
        meter = float(input("Enter value in meters: "))
        feet = meter * 3.28084
        print(f"\n{meter} meter is {feet:.2f} feet")
    elif ch == '2':
        feet = float(input("Enter value in feet: "))
        meter = feet / 3.28084
        print(f"\n{feet} feet is {meter:.2f} meters")
    elif ch == '3':
        km = float(input("Enter value in kilometer: "))
        miles = km * 0.621371
        print(f"\n{km} kilometer is {miles:.2f} miles")
    elif ch == '4':
        miles = float(input("Enter value in miles: "))
        km = miles / 0.621371
        print(f"\n{miles} miles is {km:.2f} kilometer")
    else:
        print("Invalid choice.")
def weight_conversion():
    print("\nWeight Converter")
    print("1. Kilogram -> Pound")
    print("2. Pound -> Kilogram")
    ch = input("Choose an option: ").strip()
    if ch == '1':
        kg = float(input("Enter value in kilograms: "))
        pound = kg * 2.20462
        print(f"\n{kg} kilogram is {pound:.2f} pounds")
```

```
    elif ch == '2':
        pound = float(input("Enter value in pounds: "))
        kg = pound / 2.20462
        print(f"\n{pound} pounds is {kg:.2f} kilogram")
    else:
        print("Invalid choice.")
def temperature_conversion():
    print("\nTemperature Converter")
    print("1. Celsius -> Fahrenheit")
    print("2. Fahrenheit -> Celsius")
    choice = input("Choose an option: ").strip()
    if choice == '1':
        cel = float(input("Enter value in Celsius: "))
        fah = (cel * 9/5) + 32
        print(f"\n{cel}°C is {fah:.2f}°F")
    elif choice == '2':
        fah = float(input("Enter value in Fahrenheit: "))
        cel = (fah - 32) * 5/9
        print(f"\n{fah}°F is {cel:.2f}°C")
    else:
        print("Invalid choice.")
def main():
    while True:
        print("\nUnit Converter")
        print("================")
        print("1. Length Converter")
        print("2. Weight Converter")
        print("3. Temperature Converter")
        print("4. Exit")
        ch = input("Choose an option: ").strip()
        if ch == '1':
            length_conversion()
        elif ch == '2':
            weight_conversion()
        elif ch == '3':
            temperature_conversion()
        elif ch == '4':
            print("Exit.")
            break
        else:
           print("Invalid choice. Please choose a valid option.")
if __name__ == "__main__":
    main(
```

Output

```
Unit Converter
================
1. Length Converter
2. Weight Converstern
3. Temperature Converter
4. Exit
Choose an option: 1

Length Converter
1. Meter -> Feet
2. Feet -> Meter
3. KM -> Mile
4. Mile -> KM
Choose an option: 1
Enter value in meters: 10

10.0 meter is 32.81 feet

Unit Converter
================
1. Length Converter
2. Weight Converstern
3. Temperature Converter
4. Exit
Choose an option: 2

Weight Converter
1. Kilogram -> Pound
2. Pound -> Kilogram
Choose an option: 1
Enter value in kilograms: 10

10.0 kilogram is 22.05 pounds
```

```
Unit Converter
=================
1. Length Converter
2. Weight Converstern
3. Temperature Converter
4. Exit
Choose an option: 3

Temperature Converter
1. Celsius -> Fahrenheit
2. Fahrenheit -> Celsius
Choose an option: 2
Enter value in Fahrenheit: 99.4

99.4°F is 37.44°C

Unit Converter
=================
1. Length Converter
2. Weight Converstern
3. Temperature Converter
4. Exit
Choose an option: 4
Exit.
>>>
```

19.3 CS-2. Develop a To-do List

A To-do list is where users can add, remove, and view tasks. Make a command-line or GUI-based application. Let us now write a program to create a simple To-do list. The user should be allowed to (i) add a task to an existing task, (ii) delete an existing task, and (iii) view the tasks in the To-do list. Here, we show the To-do list to the user, by default.

The requirements are listed below:

- Six functions –
  - add_task() – Append task to list.
  - delete_task() – Delete task from list. Accept the task number to delete from user.
  - list_task() – List all the tasks with task number.
  - display_menu() – Display Todo list and take options from the user for the operations.
  - clear screen() – Clears the screen on start.
  - main()

The solution code is shown below:

```
import os
def list_tsks(tsk):
    if not tsk:
        print("No Pending Task")
    else:
        print("\nTo do Tasks")
        for i, t1 in enumerate(tsk, 1):
            print(f"{i}. {t1}")
def add_tsk(tsk):
    t1 = input("Enter a new task: ").strip()
    if t1:
        tsk.append(t1)
        print(f"Task '{t1}' added.")
    else:
        print("Please write the task")
def delete_tsk(tsk):
    if not tsk:
        print("No tasks")
        return
    try:
        num = int(input("Enter Task number to remove: "))
        if 1 <= num <= len(tsk):
            rem_task = tsk.pop(num - 1)
            print(f"Task '{rem_task}' removed.")
        else:
            print("Task Number is invalid")
    except ValueError:
        print("Please enter a valid number.")
def display_menu(tsk):
    while True:
        clear_screen()
        print("To do List")
        print("=================")
        list_tsks(tsk)
        print("\nOperations on Task")
        print("=================")
        print("1. Add task")
        print("2. Remove task")
        print("3. Exit")
        choice = input("Choose an option: ").strip()
       if choice == '1':
            add_tsk(tsk)
        elif choice == '2':
            delete_tsk(tsk)
```

```
        elif choice == '3':
            print("Exiting...")
            break
        else:
            print("Please choose a valid option.")
        input("\nTo Continue: Press <enter>")

def clear_screen():
    os.system('cls' if os.name == 'nt' else 'clear')
def main():
    tsk = []
    display_menu(tsk)
if __name__ == "__main__":
    main()
```

Output

```
To do List
=================

To do Tasks
1. draw

Operations on Task
=================
1. Add task
2. Remove task
3. Exit
Choose an option: 1
Enter a new task: login
Task 'login' added.

To Continue: Press <enter>
To do List
=================

To do Tasks
1. draw
2. login

Operations on Task
=================
1. Add task
2. Remove task
3. Exit
Choose an option: 2
Enter Task number to remove: 2
Task 'login' removed.

To Continue: Press <enter>
```

19.4 CS-3. Develop a Password Generator

Password generator is a program that generates random, strong passwords based on a criterion.

- Create password based on the following criteria:
  - o Include uppercase letters
  - o Include lowercase letters
  - o Include digits
  - o Include special characters.
- Ask the user to select the criteria from the menu.

  The solution code is shown below:

```
import random
import string
def generate_pwd(length, upper, lower, digits, sp_char):
    char = ''
    if upper:
        char += string.ascii_uppercase
    if lower:
        char += string.ascii_lowercase
    if digits:
        char += string.digits
    if sp_char:
        char += string.punctuation
    if not char:
        print("Error: No character types selected.")
        return None
    pwd = ''.join(random.choice(char) for _ in range(length))
    return pwd
def main():
    print("Password Generator")
    print("==================")
    length = int(input("Enter Length of password: "))
    upper = input("Include uppercase letters? (y/n): ").strip().
lower() == 'y'
    lower = input("Include lowercase letters? (y/n): ").strip().
lower() == 'y'
    digits = input("Include digits? (y/n): ").strip().lower() ==
'y'
    sp_char = input("Include special characters? (y/n): ").strip().
lower() == 'y'
    pwd = generate_pwd(length, upper, lower, digits, sp_char)
```

```
    if pwd:
        print("\nPassword: ", pwd)
    else:
        print("Failed to generate password.")
if __name__ == "__main__":
    main()
```

Output

```
Password Generator
==================
Enter Length of password: 8
Include uppercase letters? (y/n): y
Include lowercase letters? (y/n): n
Include digits? (y/n): y
Include special characters? (y/n): n

Password:  B8NOKOCI
>>>
```

```
Password Generator
==================
Enter Length of password: 8
Include uppercase letters? (y/n): n
Include lowercase letters? (y/n): y
Include digits? (y/n): y
Include special characters? (y/n): y

Password:  j89?56*u
>>>
```

19.5 CS-4. Develop a Calculator using Tkinter

Let us now write a program to create a simple calculator. The interface should look like a simple calculator. On clicking buttons 0–9 or their combination, the expression should display on the top row of the calculator. It should allow for four basic operations – add, subtract, multiply and divide. There should be a button to clear contents. There should be a button for "=" to get the result. The requirements are listed below:

- Total 16 buttons (4 × 4)
  - 10 buttons for digit 0–9
  - Four buttons for operations – add, subtract, multiply and divide.

  - o One button to Clear content
  - o One button for "="
- Text Area on top of the first row of buttons.
  - o On clicking the buttons, the clicked values should appear in the text area.
- On press of "=", it should display
  - o Result, if expression is correct.
  - o Error, if expression is incorrect.
- On press of "C", it should clear the clicked expression from text area.

Organize the calculator as shown below:

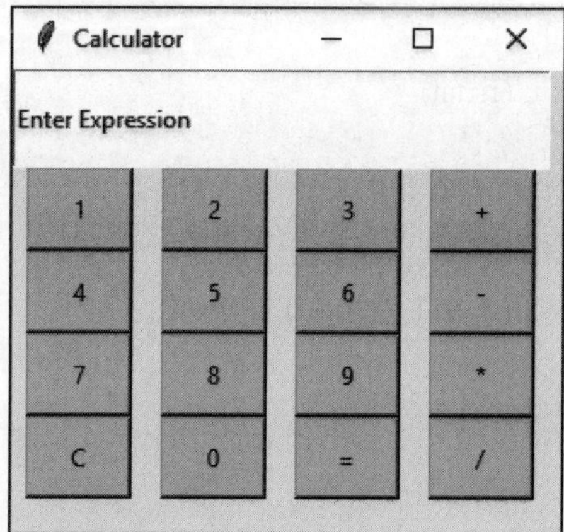

Solution

Creating a GUI application consists of two parts:

(1) Creating user interface
(2) Adding functionality to the interface.

Let us start:

(1) Creating User Interface

- Create a window (**Hint**: use `geometry()`).
- Disallow resizing the window. (**Hint**: use `window.resizable(0, 0)`.
- Create Entry area for expression in the first row spanning four columns.
- Select the background color of grid as "yellow".
- Create buttons in a grid of 4 × 4 with background color "cyan" and foreground color "black".
- Create the calculator interface as shown in the figure.

(2) Add functionality to the interface.

- Use `StringVar` to get entry from user. (Get instance of input field.)
- Create the action to be taken when a button is pressed

- **Clear** – It will clear the expression Entry area. (**Hint**: Use.`set("")` option.)
- **Result** – It will evaluate the expression and display it, on press of "=". (**Hint**: Use `str(eval(expression))`. The `eval` function evaluates string expression.
- **Click** – It will create an expression from the values of the pressed buttons. It keeps on updating the expression when a button is clicked. (**Hint**: To accept values, define a global variable)

The solution code is shown below:

```
from tkinter import *

expr = ""
def clk(num):
    global expr
    expr = expr + str(num)
    eqton.set(expr)
def reslt():
    try:
        global expr
        eqton.set(str(eval(expr)))
        expr = ""
    except:
        eqton.set("Sorry! Incorrect Input..")
        expr = ""
def clr():
    global expr
    expr = ""
    eqton.set("")

if __name__ == "__main__":
    top = Tk()
    top.configure(bg="yellow")
    top.title("Calculator")
    top.geometry("270x230")

    eqton = StringVar()
    expr_data = Entry(top, textvar=eqton)
    expr_data.grid(columnspan=4, ipadx=70, ipady=15)
    eqton.set('Enter Expression')

        bt20  =  Button(top,  text='1',  fg='black',  bg='cyan',
command=lambda: clk(1), height=2, width=6)
    bt20.grid(row=2, column=0)
```

```
    bt21 = Button(top, text='2', fg='black', bg='cyan',
command=lambda: clk(2), height=2, width=6)
  bt21.grid(row=2, column=1)
    bt22 = Button(top, text='3', fg='black', bg='cyan',
command=lambda: clk(3), height=2, width=6)
  bt22.grid(row=2, column=2)
    bt23add = Button(top, text='+', fg='black', bg='cyan',
command=lambda: clk("+"), height=2, width=6)
  bt23add.grid(row=2, column=3)
    bt30 = Button(top, text='4', fg='black', bg='cyan',
command=lambda: clk(4), height=2, width=6)
  bt30.grid(row=3, column=0)
    bt31 = Button(top, text='5', fg='black', bg='cyan',
command=lambda: clk(5), height=2, width=6)
  bt31.grid(row=3, column=1)
    bt32 = Button(top, text='6', fg='black', bg='cyan',
command=lambda: clk(6), height=2, width=6)
  bt32.grid(row=3, column=2)
    bt33sub = Button(top, text='-', fg='black', bg='cyan',
command=lambda: clk("-"), height=2, width=6)
  bt33sub.grid(row=3, column=3)
    bt40 = Button(top, text='7', fg='black', bg='cyan',
command=lambda: clk(7), height=2, width=6)
  bt40.grid(row=4, column=0)
    bt41 = Button(top, text='8', fg='black', bg='cyan',
command=lambda: clk(8), height=2, width=6)
  bt41.grid(row=4, column=1)
    bt42 = Button(top, text='9', fg='black', bg='cyan',
command=lambda: clk(9), height=2, width=6)
  bt42.grid(row=4, column=2)
    bt43mul = Button(top, text='*', fg='black', bg='cyan',
command=lambda: clk("*"), height=2, width=6)
  bt43mul.grid(row=4, column=3)

    bt50clr = Button(top, text='C', fg='black', bg='cyan',
command=clr, height=2, width=6)
  bt50clr.grid(row=5, column=0)
    bt51 = Button(top, text='0', fg='black', bg='cyan',
command=lambda: clk(0), height=2, width=6)
  bt51.grid(row=5, column=1)
    bt52res = Button(top, text='=', fg='black', bg='cyan',
command=reslt, height=2, width=6)
  bt52res.grid(row=5, column=2)
```

```
    bt53div = Button(top, text='/', fg='black', bg='cyan',
command=lambda: clk("/"), height=2, width=6)
    bt53div.grid(row=5, column=3)

    top.mainloop()
```

19.6 CS-5. Automate Tasks for Computer Directory

Let us now write a program that can scan through your computer and perform operations on the directory and files. The requirements are listed below:

- Search for a file or folder.
- Delete a particular file or folder.
- Search for a particular type of file, like files with extension,.txt
- Print the size of each file.
- Print the content of the directory in the form of sub-directories and files within it and content of the sub-directories too.
- Find files having size more than a specified size.
- Take input from the user for the options as follows:

```
Enter your choice:
1. Search for a file or folder.
2. Search for a pru1icular type of file, like all files with extension, .txt.
3. Search files having size more than a specified size.
4. Print size of each file.
5. Print content of directory: all sub-directories and files and content of sub-directories too.

Enter your choice: 5
```

Solution

Creating a GUI application consists of two parts:

(1) Creating user interface.
(2) Add functionality to the interface.

Let us start:

(1) Create User Interface

- Create an interface for the user to select an option.

(2) Add functionality to the interface.

- Use `os.walk` to walk through all the directories and files in a tree.
  The solution code is shown below:

```
import os
import sys
from os.path import expanduser, join, isdir
from pathlib import Path
def user_input():
    return(input("Enter the directory path "))
def user_filetype():
    return(input("Enter the file type to search "))
def user_filesize():
    return(int(input("Enter the minimum size of file to search
")))
#==1. Search File ==============================
def search_file(dir):
    ctr=0
    for pack in os.walk(dir):
        for f in pack[2]:
                fullpath = pack[0] + "\\" + f
                print(fullpath)
                ctr += 1
    if ctr > 0:
        print('-' * 60, "\n", "Number of files in " + dir + "`:
" + str(ctr) + " files\n", '-' * 60)
#==2. Search File Type==============================
def search_filetype(dir, filetype):
    ctr=0
    for pack in os.walk(dir):
        for f in pack[2]:
            if f.endswith(filetype):
                fullpath = pack[0] + "\\" + f
                print(fullpath)
                ctr += 1
    if ctr > 0:
        print('-' * 60, "\n", "Number of files in " + dir + "`:
" + str(ctr) + " files\n", '-' * 60)
 #==3. Search File Size==============================
def search_filesize(dir, filesize):
    ctr=0
    for pack in os.walk(dir):
        for f in pack[2]:
            fullpath = pack[0] + "\\" + f
            if os.path.getsize(fullpath) > filesize:
               print(os.path.getsize(fullpath), "\t", fullpath)
                ctr += 1
```

```
    if ctr > 0:
        print('-' * 60, "\n", "Number of files in " + dir + "`:
" + str(ctr) + " files\n", '-' * 60)
#==4. Print File Size==================================
def print_filesize(dir):
    ctr=0
    for pack in os.walk(dir):
        for f in pack[2]:
            fullpath = pack[0] + "\\" + f
            print(os.path.getsize(fullpath), "\t", fullpath)
            ctr += 1
    if ctr > 0:
        print('-' * 60, "\n", "Number of files in " + dir + "`:
" + str(ctr) + " files\n", '-' * 60)
#==5. Print content of directory==============================
def print_all(dir):
    for (root, dirs, files) in os.walk(os.getcwd(), topdown=True):
        print('-' * 10,"The root is: ", "\t", root,  '-' * 10)
        print('-' * 10, "The directories are: ", '-' * 10)
        for name in dirs:
            print(os.path.join(root, name))
        print('-' * 10,"The files are: ", '-' * 10)
        for name in files:
            print(os.path.join(root, name))
#=============================================================
def choose_func(choice):
    if choice == 1:
        search_file(user_input())
    elif choice == 2:
        search_filetype(user_input(), user_filetype())
    elif choice == 3:
        search_filesize(user_input(), user_filesize())
    elif choice == 4:
        print_filesize(user_input())
    elif choice == 5:
        print_all(user_input())
    else: print("You have entered wrong choice")
#=============================================================
```

```
def menu():
    print("Enter your choice")
    print("1. Search for a file or folder")
     print("2. Search for a particular type of file, like all
files with extension-.txt")
     print("3. Search files having size more than a specified
size")
    print("4. Print size of each file")
   print("5. Print content of directory- all sub-directories and
files and content of sub-directories too")
    return(int(input("Enter your choice ")))
#============================================
def main():
    c = 1
    while c:
        choose_func(menu())
        c = input("Do you want to continue(N/n/no) ")
        if c == "N" or c == "n" or c == "no":
            c = 0
if __name__ == '__main__':
    main()
```

19.7 CS-6. Shuffle a Deck of Cards

A deck has 52 cards of four suits – Hearts, Spades, Club, Diamonds. Each suit has 13 cards of ranks – 2 to 10, Jack, Queen, King and Ace. To shuffle and display the Hearts cards in the shuffled deck, the following is to be done:

- Define Suits and Ranks
- Create Deck
- Shuffle Deck. Use random.shuffle method to shuffle the deck.
- Display Deck
- From shuffled deck, display only the cards that belong to "Hearts" suit.

The code is as follows:

```
import random
suits = ['Hearts', 'Diamonds', 'Clubs', 'Spades']
ranks = ['2', '3', '4', '5', '6', '7', '8', '9', '10', 'Jack',
'Queen', 'King', 'Ace']
dek = [f'{rank} of {suit}' for suit in suits for rank in ranks]
```

```
def shuffle_dek(dek):
    random.shuffle(dek)
    return dek
def print_heart_cards(dek):
    heart_cards = [card for card in dek if 'Hearts' in card]
    print("SHUFFLED HEART CARD")
    for card in heart_cards:
        print(card)
def main():
    print("Shuffling the deck...\n")
    shuff_dek = shuffle_dek(dek)
    print("Shuffled Deck:")
    for card in shuff_dek:
        print(card)
    print("================")
    print_heart_cards(shuff_dek)
if __name__ == "__main__":
    main()
```

Output

```
Shuffling the deck...

Shuffled Deck:
Ace of Clubs
7 of Clubs
4 of Diamonds
Queen of Clubs
7 of Diamonds
8 of Spades
8 of Diamonds
3 of Clubs
Queen of Spades
5 of Diamonds
5 of Clubs
9 of Diamonds
5 of Spades
9 of Hearts
King of Spades
3 of Diamonds
Jack of Diamonds
2 of Clubs
Ace of Spades
6 of Diamonds
8 of Hearts
8 of Clubs
2 of Spades
```

```
Queen of Hearts
Jack of Clubs
Ace of Diamonds
4 of Spades
9 of Clubs
7 of Spades
King of Diamonds
Jack of Hearts
Jack of Spades
```

```
4 of Hearts
6 of Spades
4 of Clubs
Ace of Hearts
King of Hearts
2 of Diamonds
9 of Spades
King of Clubs
10 of Clubs
10 of Diamonds
3 of Hearts
10 of Spades
Queen of Diamonds
7 of Hearts
5 of Hearts
2 of Hearts
6 of Clubs
6 of Hearts
3 of Spades
10 of Hearts
================
SHUFFLED HEART CARD
9 of Hearts
8 of Hearts
Queen of Hearts
Jack of Hearts
4 of Hearts
Ace of Hearts
King of Hearts
3 of Hearts
7 of Hearts
5 of Hearts
2 of Hearts
6 of Hearts
10 of Hearts
```

19.8 CS-7. Develop a Simple File-sharing App

We shall make a **simple** file-sharing **app.** The file sharing can happen via an IP address or a QR code. The modules that will be required in the project are:

- HTTPServer – creates and listens at HTTP socket.
- socketserver – for writing network servers.

- webbrowser – allows and displays Web-based documents.
- pyqrcode – to generate QR Code.
- OS module – for interacting with OS.
- PyPNG – for PNG image files to be read and written.

For writing the software, there is a need to import a few modules:
pip install pyqrcode
pip install pypng
Assign port and name of user.
Find IP address of PC. Convert it to QR code.
Create HTTP request. Display QR code in browser.
The code is as follows:

```
import http.server
import socket
import socketserver
import webbrowser
import pyqrcode
from pyqrcode import QRCode
import png
import os

PORT = 8010                                   # assign port
os.environ['USERPROFILE']                  # find name of computer user
# change directory to access files
desktop = os.path.join(os.path.join(os.environ['USERPROFILE']),
                       'OneDrive')
os.chdir(desktop)
# create HTTP request
Handler = http.server.SimpleHTTPRequestHandler
hostname = socket.gethostname()          #return host name of system
# find IP address of PC
s = socket.socket(socket.AF_INET, socket.SOCK_DGRAM)
s.connect(("8.8.8.8", 80))
IP = "http://" + s.getsockname()[0] + ":" + str(PORT)
link = IP
url = pyqrcode.create(link)    # convert IP address to QRcode
url.svg("myqr.svg", scale=8)   # save Qrcode information of svg
webbrowser.open('myqr.svg')   # open Qrcode image in web browser

with socketserver.TCPServer(("", PORT), Handler) as httpd:
    print("At port", PORT)
    print("Type IP address in Browser", IP)
    print("OR Use QR Code")
    httpd.serve_forever()
```

Output

```
At port 8010
Type IP address in Browser http://192.168.29.239:8010
OR Use QR Code
```

19.9 EXERCISES AND PROJECTS

1. Extend CS-1 by using Tkinter to display the interface.
2. Extend CS-2 by using Tkinter to develop GUI interfaces.
3. Extend CS-3 to generate password that (i) contains at least one character from each selected type, and (ii) options for password strength (e.g., weak, medium, strong).
4. Ask students to create a simple calculator without Tkinter. Next, extend it to use Tkinter as in CS-4.
5. Extend CS-5 to include more tasks to be automated.
6. Extend CS-6 to display a menu and allow user to select the type of shuffled cards to display. For e.g., Hearts, Spades, Diamonds, and Clubs.
7. Develop a GUI-based application that fetches weather data from an API and displays it to the user.
8. Develop a diary application that allows users to write, save, and manage journal entries.
9. Develop a multiple-choice quiz game that can pull questions from a database or API.
10. Develop a basic web application using Flask or Django where users can create, edit, and delete blog posts.
11. Develop a game where the computer randomly selects a number, and the player guesses it within a range.
12. Develop a tool to analyze datasets (e.g., CSV files) and provide insights through visualizations.
13. Develop a system to control home devices like lights using IoT devices and Python.

14. Develop a RESTful API using Flask or Django Rest Framework for managing and serving data.
15. Develop a tool that can analyze and process text data, such as a sentiment analysis tool or a chatbot.
16. Develop a real-time chat application using web sockets.
17. Develop a personal portfolio website with a backend for managing content.

ANNEXURE 1 The Python Standard Library*

While The Python Language Reference describes the exact syntax and semantics of the Python language, this library reference manual describes the standard library that is distributed with Python. It also describes some of the optional components that are commonly included in Python distributions.

Python's standard library is very extensive, offering a wide range of facilities as indicated by the long table of contents listed below. The library contains built-in modules (written in C) that provide access to system functionality such as file I/O that would otherwise be inaccessible to Python programmers, as well as modules written in Python that provide standardized solutions for many problems that occur in everyday programming. Some of these modules are explicitly designed to encourage and enhance the portability of Python programs by abstracting away platform-specifics into platform-neutral APIs.

The Python installers for the Windows platform usually include the entire standard library and often also include many additional components. For Unix-like operating systems Python is normally provided as a collection of packages, so it may be necessary to use the packaging tools provided with the operating system to obtain some or all of the optional components.

In addition to the standard library, there is a growing collection of several thousand components (from individual programs and modules to packages and entire application development frameworks), available from the Python Package Index.

- Introduction
  - o Notes on availability
- Built-in Functions
- Built-in Constants
  - o Constants added by the site module
- Built-in Types
  - o Truth Value Testing
  - o Boolean Operations — `and`, `or`, `not`
  - o Comparisons
  - o Numeric Types — `int`, `float`, `complex`
  - o Iterator Types
  - o Sequence Types — `list`, `tuple`, `range`
  - o Text Sequence Type — `str`
  - o Binary Sequence Types — `bytes`, `bytearray`, `memoryview`

* **Source:** https://docs.python.org/3.9/library/

- Set Types — `set, frozenset`
- Mapping Types — `dict`
- Context Manager Types
- Generic Alias Type Other
- Built-in Types
- Special Attributes

• Built-in Exceptions
- Base classes
- Concrete exceptions
- Warnings
- Exception hierarchy

• Text Processing Services
- `string` — Common string operations
- `re` — Regular expression operations
- `difflib` — Helpers for computing deltas
- `textwrap` — Text wrapping and filling
- `unicodedata` — Unicode Database
- `stringprep` — Internet String Preparation
- `readline` — GNU readline interface
- `rlcompleter` — Completion function for GNU readline

• Binary Data Services
- `struct` — Interpret bytes as packed binary data
- `codecs` — Codec registry and base classes

• Data Types
- `datetime` — Basic date and time types
- `zoneinfo` — IANA time zone support
- `calendar` — General calendar-related functions
- `collections` — Container datatypes
- `collections.abc` — Abstract Base Classes for Containers
- `heapq` — Heap queue algorithm
- `bisect` — Array bisection algorithm
- `array` — Efficient arrays of numeric values
- `weakref` — Weak references
- `types` — Dynamic type creation and names for built-in types
- `copy` — Shallow and deep copy operations
- `pprint` — Data pretty printer
- `reprlib` — Alternate `repr()` implementation
- `enum` — Support for enumerations
- `graphlib` — Functionality to operate with graph-like structures

• Numeric and Mathematical Modules
- `numbers` — Numeric abstract base classes
- `math` — Mathematical functions
- `cmath` — Mathematical functions for complex numbers

- o `decimal` — Decimal fixed point and floating-point arithmetic
- o `fractions` — Rational numbers
- o `random` — Generates pseudo-random numbers
- o `statistics` — Mathematical statistics functions

- Functional Programming Modules
  - o `itertools` — Functions creating iterators for efficient looping
  - o `functools` — Higher-order functions and operations on callable objects
  - o `operator` — Standard operators as functions
- File and Directory Access
  - o `pathlib` — Object-oriented filesystem paths
  - o `os.path` — Common pathname manipulations
  - o `fileinput` — Iterate over lines from multiple input streams
  - o `stat` — Interpreting stat() results
  - o `filecmp` — File and Directory Comparisons
  - o `tempfile` — Generate temporary files and directories
  - o `glob` — Unix style pathname pattern expansion
  - o `fnmatch` — Unix filename pattern matching
  - o `linecache` — Random access to text lines
  - o `shutil` — High-level file operations
- Data Persistence
  - o `pickle` — Python object serialization
  - o `copyreg` — Register pickle support functions
  - o `shelve` — Python object persistence
  - o `marshal` — Internal Python object serialization
  - o `dbm` — Interfaces to Unix "databases"
  - o `sqlite3` — DB-API 2.0 interface for SQLite databases
- Data Compression and Archiving
  - o `zlib` — Compression compatible with **gzip**
  - o `gzip` — Support for **gzip** files
  - o `bz2` — Support for **bzip2** compression
  - o `lzma` — Compression using the LZMA algorithm
  - o `zipfile` — Work with ZIP archives
  - o `tarfile` — Read and write tar archive files
- File Formats
  - o `csv` — CSV file reading and writing
  - o `configparser` — Configuration file parser
  - o `netrc` — netrc file processing
  - o `xdrlib` — Encode and decode XDR data
  - o `plistlib` — Generate and parse Apple.`plist` files
- Cryptographic Services
  - o `hashlib` — Secure hashes and message digests
  - o `hmac` — Keyed-Hashing for Message Authentication
  - o `secrets` — Generate secure random numbers for managing secrets

- Generic Operating System Services
  - o `os` — Miscellaneous operating system interfaces
  - o `io` — Core tools for working with streams
  - o `time` — Time access and conversions
  - o `argparse` — Parser for command-line options, arguments and sub-commands
  - o `getopt` — C-style parser for command line options
  - o `logging` — Logging facility for Python
  - o `logging.config` — Logging configuration
  - o `logging.handlers` — Logging handlers
  - o `getpass` — Portable password input
  - o `curses` — Terminal handling for character-cell displays
  - o `curses.textpad` — Text input widget for curses programs
  - o `curses.ascii` — Utilities for ASCII characters
  - o `curses.panel` — A panel stack extension for curses
  - o `platform` — Access to underlying platform's identifying data
  - o `errno` — Standard errno system symbols
  - o `ctypes` — A foreign function library for Python
- Concurrent Execution
  - o `threading` — Thread-based parallelism
  - o `multiprocessing` — Process-based parallelism
  - o `multiprocessing.shared_memory` — Provides shared memory for direct access across processes
  - o The `concurrent` package
  - o `concurrent.futures` — Launching parallel tasks
  - o `subprocess` — Subprocess management
  - o `sched` — Event scheduler
  - o `queue` — A synchronized queue class
  - o `contextvars` — Context Variables
  - o `_thread` — Low-level threading API
- Networking and Interprocess Communication
  - o `asyncio` — Asynchronous I/O
  - o `socket` — Low-level networking interface
  - o `ssl` — TLS/SSL wrapper for socket objects
  - o `select` — Waiting for I/O completion
  - o `selectors` — High-level I/O multiplexing
  - o `asyncore` — Asynchronous socket handler
  - o `asynchat` — Asynchronous socket command/response handler
  - o `signal` — Set handlers for asynchronous events
  - o `mmap` — Memory-mapped file support
- Internet Data Handling
  - o `email` — An email and MIME handling package
  - o `json` — JSON encoder and decoder
  - o `mailcap` — Mailcap file handling

- mailbox — Manipulate mailboxes in various formats
- mimetypes — Map filenames to MIME types
- base64 — Base16, Base32, Base64, Base85 Data Encodings
- binhex — Encode and decode binhex4 files
- binascii — Convert between binary and ASCII
- quopri — Encode and decode MIME quoted-printable data
- uu — Encode and decode uuencode files

- Structured Markup Processing Tools
  - html — HyperText Markup Language support
  - html.parser — Simple HTML and XHTML parser
  - html.entities — Definitions of HTML general entities
  - XML Processing Modules
  - xml.etree.ElementTree — The ElementTree XML API
  - xml.dom — The Document Object Model API
  - xml.dom.minidom — Minimal DOM implementation
  - xml.dom.pulldom — Support for building partial DOM trees
  - xml.sax — Support for SAX2 parsers
  - xml.sax.handler — Base classes for SAX handlers
  - xml.sax.saxutils — SAX Utilities
  - xml.sax.xmlreader — Interface for XML parsers
  - xml.parsers.expat — Fast XML parsing using Expat
- Internet Protocols and Support
  - webbrowser — Convenient Web-browser controller
  - cgi — Common Gateway Interface support
  - cgitb — Traceback manager for CGI scripts
  - wsgiref — WSGI Utilities and Reference Implementation
  - urllib — URL handling modules
  - urllib.request — Extensible library for opening URLs
  - urllib.response — Response classes used by urllib
  - urllib.parse — Parse URLs into components
  - urllib.error — Exception classes raised by urllib.request
  - urllib.robotparser — Parser for robots.txt
  - http — HTTP modules
  - http.client — HTTP protocol client
  - ftplib — FTP protocol client
  - poplib — POP3 protocol client
  - imaplib — IMAP4 protocol client
  - nntplib — NNTP protocol client
  - smtplib — SMTP protocol client
  - smtpd — SMTP Server
  - telnetlib — Telnet client
  - uuid — UUID objects according to **RFC 4122**
  - socketserver — A framework for network servers
  - http.server — HTTP servers

- o `http.cookies` — HTTP state management
- o `http.cookiejar` — Cookie handling for HTTP clients
- o `xmlrpc` — XMLRPC server and client modules
- o `xmlrpc.client` — XML-RPC client access
- o `xmlrpc.server` — Basic XML-RPC servers
- o `ipaddress` — IPv4/IPv6 manipulation library

- Multimedia Services
  - o `audioop` — Manipulate raw audio data
  - o `aifc` — Read and write AIFF and AIFC files
  - o `sunau` — Read and write Sun AU files
  - o `wave` — Read and write WAV files
  - o `chunk` — Read IFF chunked data
  - o `colorsys` — Conversions between color systems
  - o `imghdr` — Determine the type of an image
  - o `sndhdr` — Determine type of sound file
  - o `ossaudiodev` — Access to OSS-compatible audio devices
- Internationalization
  - o `gettext` — Multilingual internationalization services
  - o `locale` — Internationalization services
- Program Frameworks
  - o `turtle` — Turtle graphics
  - o `cmd` — Support for line-oriented command interpreters
  - o `shlex` — Simple lexical analysis Graphical User Interfaces with Tk
  - o `tkinter` — Python interface to Tcl/Tk
  - o `tkinter.colorchooser` — Color choosing dialog
  - o `tkinter.font` — Tkinter font wrapper
  - o Tkinter Dialogs
  - o `tkinter.messagebox` — Tkinter message prompts
  - o `tkinter.scrolledtext` — Scrolled text widget
  - o `tkinter.dnd` — Drag and drop support
  - o `tkinter.ttk` — Tk themed widgets
  - o `tkinter.tix` — Extension widgets for Tk IDLE
  - o Other Graphical User Interface Packages
- Development Tools
  - o `typing` — Support for type hints
  - o `pydoc` — Documentation generator and online help system
  - o Python Development Mode
  - o Effects of the Python Development Mode
  - o ResourceWarning Example
  - o Bad file descriptor error example
  - o `doctest` — Test interactive Python examples
  - o `unittest` — Unit testing framework
  - o `unittest.mock` — mock object library
  - o `unittest.mock` — getting started

  - 2to3 — Automated Python 2 to 3 code translation
  - `test` — Regression tests package for Python
  - `test.support` — Utilities for the Python test suite
  - `test.support.socket_helper` — Utilities for socket tests
  - `test.support.script_helper` — Utilities for the Python execution tests
  - `test.support.bytecode_helper` — Support tools for testing correct bytecode generation
- Debugging and Profiling
  - Audit events table
  - `bdb` — Debugger framework
  - `faulthandler` — Dump the Python traceback
  - `pdb` — The Python Debugger
  - The Python Profilers
  - `timeit` — Measure execution time of small code snippets
  - `trace` — Trace or track Python statement execution
  - `tracemalloc` — Trace memory allocations
- Software Packaging and Distribution
  - `distutils` — Building and installing Python modules
  - `ensurepip` — Bootstrapping the pip installer
  - `venv` — Creation of virtual environments
  - `zipapp` — Manage executable Python zip archives
- Python Runtime Services
  - `sys` — System-specific parameters and functions
  - `sysconfig` — Provide access to Python's configuration information
  - `builtins` — Built-in objects
  - `main` — Top-level script environment
  - `warnings` — Warning control
  - `dataclasses` — Data Classes
  - `contextlib` — Utilities for with-statement contexts
  - `abc` — Abstract Base Classes
  - `atexit` — Exit handlers
  - `traceback` — Print or retrieve a stack traceback
  - `future` — Future statement definitions
  - `gc` — Garbage Collector interface
  - `inspect` — Inspect live objects
  - `site` — Site-specific configuration hook
- Custom Python Interpreters
  - `code` — Interpreter base classes
  - `codeop` — Compile Python code
- Importing Modules
  - `zipimport` — Import modules from Zip archives
  - `pkgutil` — Package extension utility
  - `modulefinder` — Find modules used by a script

  - runpy — Locating and executing Python modules
  - importlib — The implementation of import
  - Using importlib.metadata
- Python Language Services
  - parser — Access Python parse trees
  - ast — Abstract Syntax Trees
  - symtable — Access to the compiler's symbol tables
  - symbol — Constants used with Python parse trees
  - token — Constants used with Python parse trees
  - keyword — Testing for Python keywords
  - tokenize — Tokenizer for Python source
  - tabnanny — Detection of ambiguous indentation
  - pyclbr — Python module browser support
  - py_compile — Compile Python source files
  - compileall — Byte-compile Python libraries
  - dis — Disassembler for Python bytecode
  - pickletools — Tools for pickle developers
- Miscellaneous Services
  - formatter — Generic output formatting MS
- Windows Specific Services
  - msilib — Read and write Microsoft Installer files
  - msvcrt — Useful routines from the MS VC++ runtime
  - winreg — Windows registry access
  - winsound — Sound-playing interface for Windows
- Unix Specific Services
  - posix — The most common POSIX system calls
  - pwd — The password database
  - spwd — The shadow password database
  - grp — The group database
  - crypt — Function to check Unix passwords
  - termios — POSIX style tty control
  - tty — Terminal control functions
  - pty — Pseudo-terminal utilities
  - fcntl — The fcntl and ioctl system calls
  - pipes — Interface to shell pipelines
  - resource — Resource usage information
  - nis — Interface to Sun's NIS (Yellow Pages)
  - syslog — Unix syslog library routines
- Superseded Modules
  - optparse — Parser for command line options
  - imp — Access the import internals
- Undocumented Modules
  - Platform specific modules

ANNEXURE 2 os.path – Common Pathname Manipulations

Source code: `Lib/posixpath.py` (for POSIX) and `Lib/ntpath.py` (for Windows NT).

This module implements some useful functions on pathnames. To read or write files see `open()`, and for accessing the filesystem see the `os` module. The path parameters can be passed as either strings, or bytes. Applications are encouraged to represent file names as (Unicode) character strings. Unfortunately, some file names may not be representable as strings on Unix, so applications that need to support arbitrary file names on Unix should use bytes objects to represent path names. Vice versa, using bytes objects cannot represent all file names on Windows (in the standard `mbcs` encoding), hence Windows applications should use string objects to access all files.

Unlike a Unix shell, Python does not do any *automatic* path expansions. Functions such as `expanduser()` and `expandvars()` can be invoked explicitly when an application desires shell- like path expansion. (See also the `glob` module.)

See also: The `pathlib` module offers high-level path objects.

Note: All of these functions accept either only bytes or only string objects as their parameters. The result is an object of the same type, if a path or file name is returned.

Note: Since different operating systems have different path name conventions, there are several versions of this module in the standard library. The `os.path` module is always the path module suitable for the operating system Python is running on, and therefore usable for local paths. However, you can also import and use the individual modules if you want to manipulate a path that is *always* in one of the different formats. They all have the same interface:

- `posixpath` for UNIX-style paths
- `ntpath` for Windows paths

Changed in version 3.8: `exists()`, `lexists()`, `isdir()`, `isfile()`, `islink()`, and `ismount()` now return `False` instead of raising an exception for paths that contain characters or bytes unrepresentable at the OS level.

os.path.*abspath*(path)

Returns a normalized absolutized version of the pathname *path*. On most platforms, this is equivalent to calling the function `normpath()` as follows: `normpath(join(os.getcwd(), path))`.

Changed in version 3.6: Accepts a `path-like object`.

os.path.*basename*(path)

Returns the base name of pathname *path*. This is the second element of the pair returned by passing *path* to the function `split()`. Note that the result of this function is different from the Unix **basename** program; where **basename** for `'/foo/bar/'` returns `'bar'`, the `basename()` function returns an empty string (`''`).

Changed in version 3.6: Accepts a `path-like object`.

os.path.*commonpath*(paths)

Returns the longest common sub-path of each pathname in the sequence *paths*. Raise `ValueError` if *paths* contain both absolute and relative pathnames, the *paths* are on the different drives or if *paths* is empty. Unlike `commonprefix()`, this returns a valid path.

`Availability`: Unix, Windows.
New in version 3.5.
Changed in version 3.6: Accepts a sequence of `path-like objects`.

os.path.*commonprefix*(list)

Returns the longest path prefix (taken character-by-character) that is a prefix of all paths in *list*. If *list* is empty, return the empty string (`''`).

Note: This function may return invalid paths because it works a character at a time. To obtain a valid path, see `commonpath()`.

```
>>> os.path.commonpath(['/usr/lib', '/usr/local/lib'])
'/usr'
>>>
>>> os.path.commonprefix(['/usr/lib', '/usr/local/lib'])
'/usr/l'
```

Changed in version 3.6: Accepts a `path-like object`.

os.path.*dirname*(path)

Returns the directory name of pathname *path*. This is the first element of the pair returned by passing *path* to the function `split()`.

Changed in version 3.6: Accepts a `path-like object`.

os.path.*exists*(path)

Returns `True` if *path* refers to an existing path or an open file descriptor. Returns `False` for broken symbolic links. On some platforms, this function may return `False` if permission is not granted to execute `os.stat()` on the requested file, even if the *path* physically exists.

Changed in version 3.3: path can now be an integer: `True` is returned if it is an open file descriptor, `False` otherwise.

Changed in version 3.6: Accepts a `path-like object`.

`os.path.lexists(path)`

Returns `True` if *path* refers to an existing path. Returns `True` for broken symbolic links. Equivalent to `exists()` on platforms lacking `os.lstat()`.

Changed in version 3.6: Accepts a `path-like object`.

`os.path.expanduser(path)`

On Unix and Windows, returns the argument with an initial component of `~` or `~user` replaced by that *user*'s home directory.

On Unix, an initial `~` is replaced by the environment variable `HOME` if it is set; otherwise, the current user's home directory is looked up in the password directory through the built-in module `pwd`. An initial `~user` is looked up directly in the password directory.

On Windows, `USERPROFILE` will be used if set, otherwise a combination of `HOMEPATH` and `HOMEDRIVE` will be used. An initial `~user` is handled by stripping the last directory component from the created user path derived above.

If the expansion fails or if the path does not begin with a tilde, the path is returned unchanged.

Changed in version 3.6: Accepts a `path-like object`.

Changed in version 3.8: No longer uses `HOME` on Windows.

`os.path.expandvars(path)`

Returns the argument with environment variables expanded. Substrings of the form `$name` or `${name}` are replaced by the value of environment variable *name*. Malformed variable names and references to non-existing variables are left unchanged.

On Windows, `%name%` expansions are supported in addition to `$name` and `${name}`.

Changed in version 3.6: Accepts a `path-like object`.

`os.path.getatime(path)`

Returns the time of last access of *path*. The return value is a floating-point number giving the number of seconds since the epoch (see the `time` module). Raisees `OSError` if the file does not exist or is inaccessible.

`os.path.getmtime(path)`

Returns the time of last modification of *path*. The return value is a floating-point number giving the number of seconds since the epoch (see the `time` module). Raises `OSError` if the file does not exist or is inaccessible.

Changed in version 3.6: Accepts a `path-like object`.

`os.path.`***`getctime`***`(path)`

Returns the system's ctime which, on some systems (like Unix) is the time of the last metadata change, and, on others (like Windows), is the creation time for *path*. The return value is a number giving the number of seconds since the epoch (see the `time` module). Raises `OSError` if the file does not exist or is inaccessible.

Changed in version 3.6: Accepts a `path-like object`.

`os.path.`***`getsize`***`(path)`

Returns the size, in bytes, of *path*. Raises `OSError` if the file does not exist or is inaccessible.

Changed in version 3.6: Accepts a `path-like object`.

`os.path.`***`isabs`***`(path)`

Returns `True` if *path* is an absolute pathname. On Unix, that means it begins with a slash, on Windows that it begins with a (back)slash after chopping off a potential drive letter.

Changed in version 3.6: Accepts a `path-like object`.

`os.path.`***`isfile`***`(path)`

Returns `True` if *path* is an `existing` regular file. This follows symbolic links, so both `islink()` and `isfile()` can be true for the same path.

Changed in version 3.6: Accepts a `path-like object`.

`os.path.`***`isdir`***`(path)`

Returns `True` if *path* is an `existing` directory. This follows symbolic links, so both `islink()` and `isdir()` can be true for the same path.

Changed in version 3.6: Accepts a `path-like object`.

`os.path.`***`islink`***`(path)`

Returns `True` if *path* refers to an `existing` directory entry that is a symbolic link. Always `False` if symbolic links are not supported by the Python runtime.

Changed in version 3.6: Accepts a `path-like object`.

`os.path.`***`ismount`***`(path)`

Returns `True` if pathname *path* is a *mount point*: a point in a file system where a different file system has been mounted. On POSIX, the function checks whether *path*'s parent, *path*`/..`, is on a different device than *path*, or whether *path*`/..` and *path* point to the same i-node on the same device — this should detect mount points for all Unix and POSIX variants. It is not able to reliably detect bind mounts on the same filesystem. On Windows, a drive letter root and a share UNC are always mount points, and for any other path `GetVolumePathName` is called to see if it is different from the input path.

New in version 3.4: Support for detecting non-root mount points on Windows.

Changed in version 3.6: Accepts a `path-like object`.

os.path.*join*(path, *paths)

Joins one or more path components intelligently. The return value is the concatenation of *path* and any members of *paths* with exactly one directory separator following each non-empty part except the last, meaning that the result will only end in a separator if the last part is empty. If a component is an absolute path, all previous components are thrown away and joining continues from the absolute path component.

On Windows, the drive letter is not reset when an absolute path component (e.g., `r'\foo'`) is encountered. If a component contains a drive letter, all previous components are thrown away and the drive letter is reset. Note that since there is a current directory for each drive, `os.path.join("c:", "foo")` represents a path relative to the current directory on drive `C:` (`c:foo`), not `c:\foo`.

Changed in version 3.6: Accepts a `path-like object` for *path* and *paths*.

os.path.*normcase*(path)

Normalizes the case of a pathname. On Windows, it converts all characters in the pathname to lowercase, and also converts forward slashes to backward slashes. On other operating systems, it returns the path unchanged.

Changed in version 3.6: Accepts a `path-like object`.

os.path.*normpath*(path)

Normalizes a pathname by collapsing redundant separators and up-level references so that `A//B`, `A/B/`, `A/./B` and `A/foo/../B` all become `A/B`. This string manipulation may change the meaning of a path that contains symbolic links. On Windows, it converts forward slashes to backward slashes. To normalize case, use `normcase()`.

Note: On POSIX systems, in accordance with `IEEE Std 1003.1 2013 Edition; 4.13 Pathname Resolution`, if a pathname begins with exactly two slashes, the first component following the leading characters may be interpreted in an implementation-defined manner, although more than two leading characters shall be treated as a single character.

Changed in version 3.6: Accepts a `path-like object`.

os.path.*realpath*(path)

Returns the canonical path of the specified filename, eliminating any symbolic links encountered in the path (if they are supported by the operating system).

Note: When symbolic link cycles occur, the returned path will be one member of the cycle, but no guarantee is made about which member that will be.

Changed in version 3.6: Accepts a `path-like object`.

Changed in version 3.8: Symbolic links and junctions are now resolved on Windows.

`os.path.relpath`(path, start=os.curdir)

Returns a relative filepath to *path* either from the current directory or from an optional *start* directory. This is a path computation: the filesystem is not accessed to confirm the existence or nature of *path* or *start*. On Windows, `ValueError` is raised when *path* and *start* are on different drives.

start defaults to `os.curdir`. `Availability`: Unix, Windows.

Changed in version 3.6: Accepts a `path-like object`.

`os.path.samefile`(path1, path2)

Returns `True` if both pathname arguments refer to the same file or directory. This is determined by the device number and i-node number and raises an exception if an `os.stat()` call on either pathname fails.

`Availability`: Unix, Windows.
Changed in version 3.2: Added Windows support.
Changed in version 3.4: Windows now uses the same implementation as all other platforms.
Changed in version 3.6: Accepts a `path-like object`.

`os.path.sameopenfile`(fp1, fp2)

Returns `True` if the file descriptors *fp1* and *fp2* refer to the same file.
`Availability`: Unix, Windows.

Changed in version 3.2: Added Windows support.
Changed in version 3.6: Accepts a `path-like object`.

`os.path.samestat`(stat1, stat2)

Returns `True` if the stat tuples *stat1* and *stat2* refer to the same file. These structures may have been returned by `os.fstat()`, `os.lstat()`, or `os.stat()`. This function implements the underlying comparison used by `samefile()` and `sameopenfile()`.
`Availability`: Unix, Windows.
Changed in version 3.4: Added Windows support.
Changed in version 3.6: Accepts a `path-like object`.

`os.path.split`(path)

Splits the pathname *path* into a pair, `(head, tail)` where *tail* is the last pathname component and *head* is everything leading up to that. The *tail* part will never contain a slash; if *path* ends in a slash, *tail* will be empty. If there is no slash in *path*, *head* will be empty. If *path* is empty, both *head* and *tail* are empty. Trailing slashes are stripped from *head* unless it is the root (one or more slashes only). In all cases, `join(head, tail)` returns a path to the same location as *path* (but the strings may differ). Also see the functions `dirname()` and `basename()`.

Changed in version 3.6: Accepts a `path-like object`.

`os.path.splitdrive(path)`

Splits the pathname *path* into a pair `(drive, tail)` where *drive* is either a mount point or the empty string. On systems which do not use drive specifications, *drive* will always be the empty string. In all cases, `drive + tail` will be the same as *path*.

On Windows, splits a pathname into drive/UNC sharepoint and relative path.

If the path contains a drive letter, drive will contain everything up to and including the colon:

```
>>> splitdrive("c:/dir")
("c:", "/dir")
```

If the path contains a UNC path, drive will contain the host name and share, up to but not including the fourth separator:

```
>>> splitdrive("//host/computer/dir")
("//host/computer", "/dir")
```

Changed in version 3.6: Accepts a `path-like object`.

`os.path.splitext(path)`

Splits the pathname *path* into a pair `(root, ext)` such that `root + ext == path`, and the extension, *ext*, is empty or begins with a period and contains at most one period.

If the path contains no extension, *ext* will be `''`:

```
>>> splitext('bar')
('bar', '')
```

If the path contains an extension, then *ext* will be set to this extension, including the leading period. Note that previous periods will be ignored:

```
>>> splitext('foo.bar.exe')
('foo.bar', '.exe')
```

Leading periods on the basename are ignored:

```
>>> splitext('.cshrc')
('.cshrc', '')
```

Changed in version 3.6: Accepts a `path-like object`.

`os.path.supports_unicode_filenames`

`True` if arbitrary Unicode strings can be used as file names (within limitations imposed by the file system).

ANNEXURE 3 | `pathlib` – Object-Oriented Filesystem Paths

New in version 3.4.

Source code: `Lib/pathlib.py`

This module offers classes representing filesystem paths with semantics appropriate for different operating systems. Path classes are divided between `pure paths`, which provide purely computational operations without I/O, and `concrete paths`, which inherit from pure paths and also provide I/O operations.

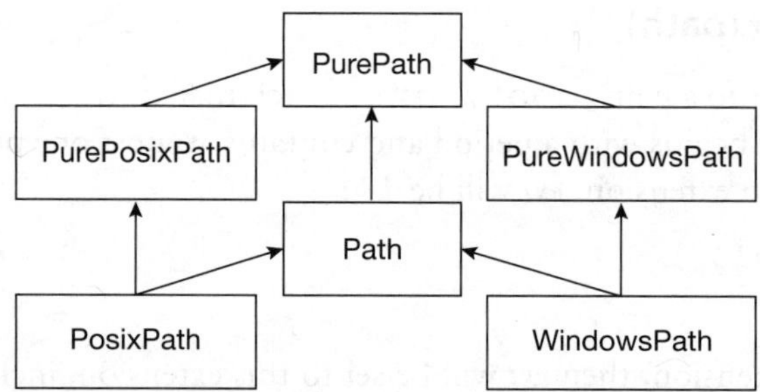

If you've never used this module before or just aren't sure which class is right for your task, `Path` is most likely what you need. It instantiates a `concrete path` for the platform the code is running on.

Pure paths are useful in some special cases; for example:

1. If you want to manipulate Windows paths on a Unix machine (or vice versa). You cannot instantiate a `WindowsPath` when running on Unix, but you can instantiate `PureWindowsPath`.
2. You want to make sure that your code only manipulates paths without actually accessing the OS. In this case, instantiating one of the pure classes may be useful since they simply don't have any OS-accessing operations.

See also: **`PEP 428`**: The pathlib module – object-oriented filesystem paths.

See also: For low-level path manipulation on strings, you can also use the `os.path` module.

Basic Use

Importing the main class:

```
>>> from pathlib import Path
```

Listing subdirectories:

```
>>> p = Path('.')
>>> [x for x in p.iterdir() if x.is_dir()]
[PosixPath('.hg'), PosixPath('docs'), PosixPath('dist'),
 PosixPath('__pycache__'), PosixPath('build')]
```

Listing Python source files in this directory tree:

```
>>> list(p.glob('**/*.py'))
[PosixPath('test_pathlib.py'), PosixPath('setup.py'),
 PosixPath('pathlib.py'), PosixPath('docs/conf.py'),
 PosixPath('build/lib/pathlib.py')]
```

Navigating inside a directory tree:

```
>>> p = Path('/etc')
>>> q = p / 'init.d' / 'reboot'
>>> q
PosixPath('/etc/init.d/reboot')
>>> q.resolve() PosixPath('/etc/rc.d/init.d/halt')
```

Querying path properties:

```
>>> q.exists()
True
>>> q.is_dir()
False
```

Opening a file:

```
>>> with q.open() as f: f.readline()
...
'#!/bin/bash\n'
```

Pure Paths

Pure path objects provide path-handling operations which don't actually access a filesystem. There are three ways to access these classes, which we also call *flavours*:

class `pathlib.PurePath(*pathsegments)`

A generic class that represents the system's path flavour (instantiating it creates either a `PurePosixPath` or a `PureWindowsPath`):

```
>>> PurePath('setup.py')      # Running on a Unix machine
PurePosixPath('setup.py')
```

Each element of *pathsegments* can be either a string representing a path segment, an object implementing the `os.PathLike` interface which returns a string, or another path object:

```
>>> PurePath('foo', 'some/path', 'bar')
PurePosixPath('foo/some/path/bar')
>>> PurePath(Path('foo'), Path('bar'))
PurePosixPath('foo/bar')
```

When *pathsegments* is empty, the current directory is assumed:

```
>>> PurePath()
PurePosixPath('.')
```

When several absolute paths are given, the last is taken as an anchor (mimicking `os.path.join()`'s behaviour):

```
>>> PurePath('/etc', '/usr', 'lib64')
PurePosixPath('/usr/lib64')
>>> PureWindowsPath('c:/Windows', 'd:bar')
PureWindowsPath('d:bar')
```

However, in a Windows path, changing the local root doesn't discard the previous drive setting:

```
>>> PureWindowsPath('c:/Windows', '/Program Files')
PureWindowsPath('c:/Program Files')
```

Spurious slashes and single dots are collapsed, but double dots (`'..'`) are not, since this would change the meaning of a path in the face of symbolic links:

```
>>> PurePath('foo//bar')
PurePosixPath('foo/bar')
>>> PurePath('foo/./bar')
PurePosixPath('foo/bar')
>>> PurePath('foo/../bar')
PurePosixPath('foo/../bar')
```

(a naïve approach would make `PurePosixPath('foo/../bar')` equivalent to `PurePosixPath('bar')`, which is wrong if `foo` is a symbolic link to another directory)
Pure path objects implement the `os.PathLike` interface, allowing them to be used anywhere the interface is accepted.

Changed in version 3.6: Added support for the `os.PathLike` interface.

class pathlib.*PurePosixPath*(*pathsegments)

A subclass of PurePath, this path flavour represents non-Windows filesystem paths:

```
>>> PurePosixPath('/etc')
PurePosixPath('/etc')
```

pathsegments is specified similarly to PurePath.

class pathlib. **PureWindowsPath**(**pathsegments*)

A subclass of PurePath, this path flavour represents Windows filesystem paths:

```
>>> PureWindowsPath('c:/Program Files/')
PureWindowsPath('c:/Program Files')
```

pathsegments is specified similarly to PurePath.

Regardless of the system you're running on, you can instantiate all of these classes, since they don't provide any operation that does system calls.

General Properties

Paths are immutable and hashable. Paths of a same flavour are comparable and orderable. These properties respect the flavour's case-folding semantics:

```
>>> PurePosixPath('foo') == PurePosixPath('FOO')
False
>>> PureWindowsPath('foo') == PureWindowsPath('FOO')
True
>>> PureWindowsPath('FOO') in { PureWindowsPath('foo') }
True
>>> PureWindowsPath('C:') < PureWindowsPath('d:') True
```

Paths of a different flavour compare unequal and cannot be ordered:

```
>>> PureWindowsPath('foo') == PurePosixPath('foo')
False
>>> PureWindowsPath('foo') < PurePosixPath('foo')
Traceback (most recent call last):
  File "<stdin>", line 1, in <module>
TypeError: '<' not supported between instances of 'PureWindowsPath'
and 'PurePos
```

Operators

The slash operator helps create child paths, similarly to `os.path.join()`:

```
>>> p = PurePath('/etc')
>>> p
PurePosixPath('/etc')
>>> p / 'init.d' / 'apache2'
PurePosixPath('/etc/init.d/apache2')
>>> q = PurePath('bin')
>>> '/usr' / q
PurePosixPath('/usr/bin')
```

A path object can be used anywhere an object implementing `os.PathLike` is accepted:

```
>>> import os
>>> p = PurePath('/etc')
>>> os.fspath(p)
'/etc'
```

The string representation of a path is the raw filesystem path itself (in native form, e.g., with backslashes under Windows), which you can pass to any function taking a file path as a string:

```
>>> p = PurePath('/etc')
>>> str(p)
'/etc'
>>> p = PureWindowsPath('c:/Program Files')
>>> str(p)
'c:\\Program Files'
```

Similarly, calling `bytes` on a path gives the raw filesystem path as a bytes object, as encoded by `os.fsencode()`:

```
>>> bytes(p)
b'/etc'
```

Note: Calling `bytes` is only recommended under Unix. Under Windows, the unicode form is the canonical representation of filesystem paths.

Accessing Individual Parts

To access the individual "parts" (components) of a path, use the following property:

`PurePath.` **`parts`**

A tuple giving access to the path's various components:

```
>>> p = PurePath('/usr/bin/python3')
>>> p.parts
('/', 'usr', 'bin', 'python3')
>>> p = PureWindowsPath('c:/Program Files/PSF')
>>> p.parts
('c:\\', 'Program Files', 'PSF')
```

(Note how the drive and local root are regrouped in a single part).

METHODS AND PROPERTIES

Pure paths provide the following methods and properties:

PurePath.*drive*

A string representing the drive letter or name, if any:

```
>>> PureWindowsPath('c:/Program Files/').drive
'c:'
>>> PureWindowsPath('/Program Files/').drive
''
>>> PurePosixPath('/etc').drive
''
```

UNC shares are also considered drives:

```
>>> PureWindowsPath('//host/share/foo.txt').drive
'\\\\host\\share'
```

PurePath.*root*

A string representing the (local or global) root, if any:

```
>>> PureWindowsPath('c:/Program Files/').root
'\\'
>>> PureWindowsPath('c:Program Files/').root
''
>>> PurePosixPath('/etc').root
'/'
```

UNC shares always have a root:

```
>>> PureWindowsPath('//host/share').root
'\\'
```

PurePath.*anchor*

The concatenation of the drive and root:

```
>>> PureWindowsPath('c:/Program Files/').anchor
'c:\\'
>>> PureWindowsPath('c:Program Files/').anchor
'c:'
>>> PurePosixPath('/etc').anchor
'/'
>>> PureWindowsPath('//host/share').anchor
'\\\\host\\share\\'
```

`PurePath.`*`parents`*

An immutable sequence providing access to the logical ancestors of the path:

```
>>> p = PureWindowsPath('c:/foo/bar/setup.py')
>>> p.parents[0]
PureWindowsPath('c:/foo/bar')
>>> p.parents[1]
PureWindowsPath('c:/foo')
>>> p.parents[2]
PureWindowsPath('c:/')
```

`PurePath.`*`parent`*

The logical parent of the path:

```
>>> p = PurePosixPath('/a/b/c/d')
>>> p.parent
PurePosixPath('/a/b/c')
```

You cannot go past an anchor, or empty path:

```
>>> p = PurePosixPath('/')
>>> p.parent
PurePosixPath('/')
>>> p = PurePosixPath('.')
>>> p.parent
PurePosixPath('.')
```

Note: This is a purely lexical operation, hence the following behaviour:

```
>>> p = PurePosixPath('foo/..')
>>> p.parent
PurePosixPath('foo')
```

If you want to walk an arbitrary filesystem path upwards, it is recommended to first call `Path.resolve()` so as to resolve symlinks and eliminate ".." components.

`PurePath.`*`name`*

A string representing the final path component, excluding the drive and root, if any:

```
>>> PurePosixPath('my/library/setup.py').name
'setup.py'
```

UNC drive names are not considered:

```
>>> PureWindowsPath('//some/share/setup.py').name
'setup.py'
>>> PureWindowsPath('//some/share').name
''
```

PurePath.*suffix*

The file extension of the final component, if any:

```
>>> PurePosixPath('my/library/setup.py').suffix
'.py'
>>> PurePosixPath('my/library.tar.gz').suffix
'.gz'
>>> PurePosixPath('my/library').suffix
''
```

PurePath.*suffixes*

A list of the path's file extensions:

```
>>> PurePosixPath('my/library.tar.gar').suffixes
['.tar', '.gar']
>>> PurePosixPath('my/library.tar.gz').suffixes
['.tar', '.gz']
>>> PurePosixPath('my/library').suffixes
[]
```

PurePath.*stem*

The final path component, without its suffix:

```
>>> PurePosixPath('my/library.tar.gz').stem
'library.tar'
>>> PurePosixPath('my/library.tar').stem
'library'
>>> PurePosixPath('my/library').stem
'library'
```

PurePath.*as_posix*()

Returns a string representation of the path with forward slashes (/):

```
>>> p = PureWindowsPath('c:\\windows')
>>> str(p)
'c:\\windows'
>>> p.as_posix()
'c:/windows'
```

PurePath.*as_uri*()

Represents the path as a `file` URI. `ValueError` is raised if the path isn't absolute.

```
>>> p = PurePosixPath('/etc/passwd')
>>> p.as_uri()
'file:///etc/passwd'
>>> p = PureWindowsPath('c:/Windows')
>>> p.as_uri()
'file:///c:/Windows'
```

PurePath.*is_absolute*()

Returns whether the path is absolute or not. A path is considered absolute if it has both a root and (if the flavour allows) a drive:

```
>>> PurePosixPath('/a/b').is_absolute()
True
>>> PurePosixPath('a/b').is_absolute()
False
>>> PureWindowsPath('c:/a/b').is_absolute()
True
>>> PureWindowsPath('/a/b').is_absolute()
False
>>> PureWindowsPath('c:').is_absolute()
False
>>> PureWindowsPath('//some/share').is_absolute()
True
```

PurePath.*is_relative_to*(*other)

Returns whether or not this path is relative to the *other* path.

```
>>> p = PurePath('/etc/passwd')
>>> p.is_relative_to('/etc')
True
>>> p.is_relative_to('/usr')
False
```

New in version 3.9.

PurePath.*is_reserved*()

With `PureWindowsPath`, it returns `True` if the path is considered reserved under Windows, `False` otherwise. With `PurePosixPath`, `False` is always returned.

```
>>> PureWindowsPath('nul').is_reserved()
True
>>> PurePosixPath('nul').is_reserved()
False
```

File system calls on reserved paths can fail mysteriously or have unintended effects.

PurePath.*Joinpath*(*other)

Calling this method is equivalent to combining the path with each of the *other* arguments in turn:

```
>>> PurePosixPath('/etc').joinpath('passwd')
PurePosixPath('/etc/passwd')
>>> PurePosixPath('/etc').joinpath(PurePosixPath('passwd'))
PurePosixPath('/etc/passwd')
>>> PurePosixPath('/etc').joinpath('init.d', 'apache2')
PurePosixPath('/etc/init.d/apache2')
>>> PureWindowsPath('c:').joinpath('/Program Files')
PureWindowsPath('c:/Program Files')
```

PurePath.*Match*(pattern)

Matches this path against the provided glob-style pattern. Returns `True` if matching is successful, `False` otherwise.

If *pattern* is relative, the path can be either relative or absolute, and matching is done from the right:

```
>>> PurePath('a/b.py').match('*.py')
True
>>> PurePath('/a/b/c.py').match('b/*.py')
True
>>> PurePath('/a/b/c.py').match('a/*.py')
False
```

If *pattern* is absolute, the path must be absolute, and the whole path must match:

```
>>> PurePath('/a.py').match('/*.py')
True
>>> PurePath('a/b.py').match('/*.py')
False
```

As with the other methods, case-sensitivity follows platform defaults:

```
>>> PurePosixPath('b.py').match('*.PY')
False
>>> PureWindowsPath('b.py').match('*.PY')
True
```

PurePath.*relative_to*(*other)

Compute a version of this path relative to the path represented by *other*. If it is impossible, ValueError is raised:

```
>>> p = PurePosixPath('/etc/passwd')
>>> p.relative_to('/')
PurePosixPath('etc/passwd')
>>> p.relative_to('/etc')
PurePosixPath('passwd')
>>> p.relative_to('/usr')
Traceback (most recent call last):
  File "<stdin>", line 1, in <module>
  File "pathlib.py", line 694, in relative_to
    .format(str(self), str(formatted)))
ValueError: '/etc/passwd' is not in the subpath of '/usr' OR one
path is relative and the other, absolute.
```

Note: This function is part of `PurePath` and works with strings. It does not check or access the underlying file structure.

`PurePath.`*`with_name`*(name)

Returns a new path with the `name` changed. If the original path doesn't have a name, ValueError is raised:

```
>>> p = PureWindowsPath('c:/Downloads/pathlib.tar.gz')
>>> p.with_name('setup.py')
PureWindowsPath('c:/Downloads/setup.py')
>>> p = PureWindowsPath('c:/')
>>> p.with_name('setup.py')
Traceback (most recent call last):
  File "<stdin>", line 1, in <module>
  File "/home/antoine/cpython/default/Lib/pathlib.py", line 751,
    in with_name
    raise ValueError("%r has an empty name" % (self,))
ValueError: PureWindowsPath('c:/') has an empty name
```

`PurePath.`*`with_stem`*(stem)

Returns a new path with the `stem` changed. If the original path doesn't have a name, ValueError is raised:

```
>>> p = PureWindowsPath('c:/Downloads/draft.txt')
>>> p.with_stem('final')
PureWindowsPath('c:/Downloads/final.txt')
>>> p = PureWindowsPath('c:/Downloads/pathlib.tar.gz')
>>> p.with_stem('lib')
PureWindowsPath('c:/Downloads/lib.gz')
>>> p = PureWindowsPath('c:/')
>>> p.with_stem('')
```

```
Traceback (most recent call last):
  File "<stdin>", line 1, in <module>
  File "/home/antoine/cpython/default/Lib/pathlib.py", line 861,
    in with_stem
    return self.with_name(stem + self.suffix)
  File "/home/antoine/cpython/default/Lib/pathlib.py", line 851,
    in with_name
    raise ValueError("%r has an empty name" % (self,))
ValueError: PureWindowsPath('c:/') has an empty name
```

New in version 3.9.

PurePath.*with_suffix*(suffix)

Returns a new path with the `suffix` changed. If the original path doesn't have a suffix, the new *suffix* is appended instead. If the *suffix* is an empty string, the original suffix is removed:

```
>>> p = PureWindowsPath('c:/Downloads/pathlib.tar.gz')
>>> p.with_suffix('.bz2')
PureWindowsPath('c:/Downloads/pathlib.tar.bz2')
>>> p = PureWindowsPath('README')
>>> p.with_suffix('.txt')
PureWindowsPath('README.txt')
>>> p = PureWindowsPath('README.txt')
>>> p.with_suffix('')
PureWindowsPath('README')
```

Concrete Paths

Concrete paths are subclasses of the pure path classes. In addition to operations provided by the latter, they also provide methods to do system calls on path objects. There are three ways to instantiate concrete paths:

class pathlib.*Path*(*pathsegments)

A subclass of `PurePath`, this class represents concrete paths of the system's path flavour (instantiating it creates either a `PosixPath` or a `WindowsPath`):

```
>>> Path('setup.py')
PosixPath('setup.py')
```

pathsegments is specified similarly to `PurePath`.

class pathlib.*PosixPath*(*pathsegments)

A subclass of `Path` and `PurePosixPath`, this class represents concrete non-Windows filesystem paths:

```
>>> PosixPath('/etc')
PosixPath('/etc')
```

pathsegments is specified similarly to `PurePath`.

class pathlib.*WindowsPath*(*pathsegments)

A subclass of `Path` and `PureWindowsPath`, this class represents concrete Windows filesystem paths:

```
>>> WindowsPath('c:/Program Files/')
WindowsPath('c:/Program Files')
```

pathsegments is specified similarly to `PurePath`.

You can only instantiate the class flavour that corresponds to your system (allowing system calls on non-compatible path flavours could lead to bugs or failures in your application):

```
>>> import os
>>> os.name
'posix'
>>> Path('setup.py')
PosixPath('setup.py')
>>> PosixPath('setup.py')
PosixPath('setup.py')
>>> WindowsPath('setup.py')
Traceback (most recent call last):
  File "<stdin>", line 1, in <module>
  File "pathlib.py", line 798, in __new__
    %(cls.__name__,))
NotImplementedError: cannot instantiate 'WindowsPath' on your system
```

Methods

Concrete paths provide the following methods in addition to pure paths methods. Many of these methods can raise an `OSError` if a system call fails (for example because the path doesn't exist).

Changed in version 3.8: `exists()`, `is_dir()`, `is_file()`, `is_mount()`, `is_symlink()`, `is_block_device()`, `is_char_device()`, `is_fifo()`, `is_socket()` now return `False` instead of raising an exception for paths that contain characters unrepresentable at the OS level.

classmethod Path.*cwd*()

Returns a new path object representing the current directory (as returned by `os.getcwd()`):

```
>>> Path.cwd()
PosixPath('/home/antoine/pathlib')
```

classmethod Path. **home**()

Returns a new path object representing the user's home directory (as returned by `os.path.expanduser()` with ~ construct):

```
>>> Path.home()
PosixPath('/home/antoine')
```

New in version 3.5.

Path.*stat*()

Returns a `os.stat_result` object containing information about this path, like `os.stat()`. The result is looked up at each call to this method.

```
>>> p = Path('setup.py')
>>> p.stat().st_size
956
>>> p.stat().st_mtime
1327883547.852554
```

Path.*chmod*(mode)

Changes the file mode and permissions, like `os.chmod()`:

```
>>> p = Path('setup.py')
>>> p.stat().st_mode
33277
>>> p.chmod(0o444)
>>> p.stat().st_mode
33060
```

Path.*exists*()

Shows whether the path points to an existing file or directory:

```
>>> Path('.').exists()
True
>>> Path('setup.py').exists()
True
>>> Path('/etc').exists()
True
>>> Path('nonexistentfile').exists()
False
```

Note: If the path points to a symlink, `exists()` returns whether the symlink *points to* an existing file or directory.

Path.*expanduser*()

Returns a new path with expanded ~ and ~user constructs, as returned by os.path.expanduser():

```
>>> p = PosixPath('~/films/Monty Python')
>>> p.expanduser()
PosixPath('/home/eric/films/Monty Python')
```

New in version 3.5.

Path.*glob*(pattern)

Glob the given relative *pattern* in the directory represented by this path, yielding all matching files (of any kind):

```
>>> sorted(Path('.').glob('*.py'))
[PosixPath('pathlib.py'), PosixPath('setup.py'), PosixPath('test_
  pathlib.py')
>>> sorted(Path('.').glob('*/*.py'))
[PosixPath('docs/conf.py')]
```

The "**" pattern means "this directory and all subdirectories, recursively". In other words, it enables recursive globbing:

```
>>> sorted(Path('.').glob('**/*.py'))
[PosixPath('build/lib/pathlib.py'),
 PosixPath('docs/conf.py'),
 PosixPath('pathlib.py'),
 PosixPath('setup.py'),
 PosixPath('test_pathlib.py')]
```

Note: Using the "**" pattern in large directory trees may consume an inordinate amount of time.

Raises an auditing event pathlib.Path.glob with arguments self, pattern.

Path.*group*()

Returns the name of the group owning the file. KeyError is raised if the file's gid isn't found in the system database.

Path.*is_dir*()

Returns True if the path points to a directory (or a symbolic link pointing to a directory), False if it points to another kind of file.

False is also returned if the path doesn't exist or is a broken symlink; other errors (such as permission errors) are propagated.

Path.*is_file*()

Returns `True` if the path points to a regular file (or a symbolic link pointing to a regular file), `False` if it points to another kind of file.

`False` is also returned if the path doesn't exist or is a broken symlink; other errors (such as permission errors) are propagated.

Path.*is_mount*()

Returns `True` if the path is a *mount point*: a point in a file system where a different file system has been mounted. On POSIX, the function checks whether the *path*'s parent, `path/..`, is on a different device than *path*, or whether `path/..` and *path* point to the same i-node on the same device — this should detect mount points for all Unix and POSIX variants. However, it is not implemented on Windows.

New in version 3.7.

Path.*is_symlink*()

Returns `True` if the path points to a symbolic link, `False` otherwise.
`False` is also returned if the path doesn't exist; other errors (such as permission errors) are propagated.

Path.*is_socket*()

Returns `True` if the path points to a Unix socket (or a symbolic link pointing to a Unix socket), `False` if it points to another kind of file.
`False` is also returned if the path doesn't exist or is a broken symlink; other errors (such as permission errors) are propagated.

Path.*is_fifo*()

Returns `True` if the path points to a FIFO (or a symbolic link pointing to a FIFO), `False` if it points to another kind of file.

`False` is also returned if the path doesn't exist or is a broken symlink; other errors (such as permission errors) are propagated.

Path.*is_block_device*()

Returns `True` if the path points to a block device (or a symbolic link pointing to a block device), `False` if it points to another kind of file.

`False` is also returned if the path doesn't exist or is a broken symlink; other errors (such as permission errors) are propagated.

Path.*is_char_device*()

Returns `True` if the path points to a character device (or a symbolic link pointing to a character device), `False` if it points to another kind of file.

`False` is also returned if the path doesn't exist or is a broken symlink; other errors (such as permission errors) are propagated.

Path.*iterdir*()

When the path points to a directory, it yields path objects of the directory contents:

```
>>> p = Path('docs')
>>> for child in p.iterdir(): child
...
PosixPath('docs/conf.py')
PosixPath('docs/_templates')
PosixPath('docs/make.bat')
PosixPath('docs/index.rst')
PosixPath('docs/_build')
PosixPath('docs/_static')
PosixPath('docs/Makefile')
```

The children are yielded in arbitrary order, and the special entries `'.'` and `'..'` are not included. If a file is removed from or added to the directory after creating the iterator, it does not specify whether a path object for that file is included.

Path.*lchmod*(mode)

Like `Path.chmod()` but, if the path points to a symbolic link, the symbolic link's mode is changed rather than its target's.

Path.*lstat*()

Like `Path.stat()` but, if the path points to a symbolic link, it returns the symbolic link's information rather than its target's.

Path.*mkdir*(mode=0o777, parents=False, exist_ok=False)

Creates a new directory at this given path. If *mode* is given, it is combined with the process' `umask` value to determine the file mode and access flags. If the path already exists, `FileExistsError` is raised.

If *parents* is true, any missing parents of this path are created as needed; they are created with the default permissions without taking *mode* into account (mimicking the POSIX `mkdir -p` command).

If *parents* is false (the default), a missing parent raises `FileNotFoundError.`

If *exist_ok* is false (the default), `FileExistsError` is raised if the target directory already exists.

If *exist_ok* is true, `FileExistsError` exceptions will be ignored (same behavior as the POSIX `mkdir -p` command), but only if the last path component is not an existing non- directory file.

Changed in version 3.5: The *exist_ok* parameter was added.

Path. **open**(*mode='r', buffering=-1, encoding=None, errors=None, newline=None*)

Opens the file pointed to by the path, like the built-in `open()` function does:

```
>>> p = Path('setup.py')
>>> with p.open() as f:
...     f.readline()
...
'#!/usr/bin/env python3\n'
```

Path.*owner*()

Returns the name of the user owning the file. `KeyError` is raised if the file's uid isn't found in the system database.

Path.*read_bytes*()

Return the binary contents of the pointed-to file as a bytes object:

```
>>> p = Path('my_binary_file')
>>> p.write_bytes(b'Binary file contents')
20
>>> p.read_bytes()
b'Binary file contents'
```

New in version 3.5.

Path.*read_text*(encoding=None, errors=None)

Returns the decoded contents of the pointed-to file as a string:

```
>>> p = Path('my_text_file')
>>> p.write_text('Text file contents')
18
>>> p.read_text()
'Text file contents'
```

The file is opened and then closed. The optional parameters have the same meaning as in `open()`.

New in version 3.5.

Path.*readlink*()

Returns the path to which the symbolic link points (as returned by `os.readlink()`):

```
>>> p = Path('mylink')
>>> p.symlink_to('setup.py')
>>> p.readlink()
PosixPath('setup.py')
```

New in version 3.9.

Path.*rename*(target)

Renames this file or directory to the given *target*, and returns a new Path instance pointing to *target*. On Unix, if *target* exists and is a file, it will be replaced silently if the user has permission. *target* can be either a string or another path object:

```
>>> p = Path('foo')
>>> p.open('w').write('some text')
9
>>> target = Path('bar')
>>> p.rename(target)
PosixPath('bar')
>>> target.open().read()
'some text'
```

The target path may be absolute or relative. Relative paths are interpreted relative to the current working directory, *not* the directory of the Path object.

Changed in version 3.8: Added return value, returns the new Path instance.

Path.*replace*(target)

Renames this file or directory to the given *target*, and returns a new Path instance pointing to *target*. If *target* points to an existing file or directory, it will be unconditionally replaced.

The target path may be absolute or relative. Relative paths are interpreted relative to the current working directory, *not* the directory of the Path object.

Changed in version 3.8: Added return value, returns the new Path instance.

Path.*resolve*(strict=False)

Makes the path absolute, resolving any symlinks. A new path object is returned:

```
>>> p = Path()
>>> p
PosixPath('.')
>>> p.resolve()
PosixPath('/home/antoine/pathlib')
```

"`..`" components are also eliminated (this is the only method to do so):

```
>>> p = Path('docs/../setup.py')
>>> p.resolve()
PosixPath('/home/antoine/pathlib/setup.py')
```

If the path doesn't exist and *strict* is `True`, `FileNotFoundError` is raised. If *strict* is `False`, the path is resolved as far as possible and any remainder is appended without checking whether it exists. If an infinite loop is encountered along the resolution path, `RuntimeError` is raised.

New in version 3.6: The *strict* argument (pre-3.6 behavior is strict).

Path.*rglob*(pattern)

This is like calling `Path.glob()` with "`**/`" added in front of the given relative *pattern*:

```
>>> sorted(Path().rglob("*.py"))
[PosixPath('build/lib/pathlib.py'),
 PosixPath('docs/conf.py'),
 PosixPath('pathlib.py'),
 PosixPath('setup.py'),
 PosixPath('test_pathlib.py')]
```

Raises an `auditing event pathlib.Path.rglob` with arguments `self`, `pattern`.

Path.*rmdir*()

Remove this directory. The directory must be empty.

Path.*samefile*(other_path)

Returns whether this path points to the same file as *other_path*, which can be either a Path object, or a string. The semantics are similar to `os.path.samefile()` and `os.path.samestat()`. An `OSError` can be raised if either file cannot be accessed for some reason.

```
>>> p = Path('spam')
>>> q = Path('eggs')
>>> p.samefile(q)
False
>>> p.samefile('spam')
True
```

New in version 3.5.

Path.*symlink_to*(target, target_is_directory=False)

Make this path a symbolic link to *target*. Under Windows, *target_is_directory* must be true (default `False`) if the link's target is a directory. Under POSIX, *target_is_directory*'s value is ignored.

```
>>> p = Path('mylink')
>>> p.symlink_to('setup.py')
>>> p.resolve()
PosixPath('/home/antoine/pathlib/setup.py')
>>> p.stat().st_size
956
>>> p.lstat().st_size
8
```

Note: The order of arguments (link, target) is the reverse of `os.symlink()`'s.

`Path.`***`link_to`***(target)

Makes *target* a hard link to this path.

Warning: This function does not make this path a hard link to *target*, despite the implication of the function and argument names. The argument order (target, link) is the reverse of `Path.symlink_to()`, but matches that of `os.link()`.

New in version 3.8.

`Path.`***`touch`***(mode=0o666, exist_ok=True)

Creates a file at this given path. If *mode* is given, it is combined with the process' `umask` value to determine the file mode and access flags. If the file already exists, the function succeeds if *exist_ok* is true (and its modification time is updated to the current time), otherwise `FileExistsError` is raised.

`Path.`***`unlink`***(missing_ok=False)

Removes this file or symbolic link. If the path points to a directory, use `Path.rmdir()` instead. If *missing_ok* is false (the default), `FileNotFoundError` is raised if the path does not exist.

If *missing_ok* is true, `FileNotFoundError` exceptions will be ignored (same behavior as the POSIX `rm -f` command).

Changed in version 3.8: The *missing_ok* parameter was added.

`Path.`***`write_bytes`***(data)

Opens the file pointed to in bytes mode, write *data* to it, and closes the file:

```
>>> p = Path('my_binary_file')
>>> p.write_bytes(b'Binary file contents')
20
>>> p.read_bytes()
b'Binary file contents'
```

An existing file of the same name is overwritten.

New in version 3.5.

`Path.`***`write_text`***(data, encoding=None, errors=None)

Opens the file pointed to in text mode, write *data* to it, and closes the file:

```
>>> p = Path('my_text_file')
>>> p.write_text('Text file contents')
18
>>> p.read_text()
'Text file contents'
```

An existing file of the same name is overwritten. The optional parameters have the same meaning as in `open()`.

New in version 3.5.

Correspondence to Tools in the os Module

Table A3.1 maps various `os` functions to their corresponding `PurePath/Path` equivalents.

Note: Although `os.path.relpath()` and `PurePath.relative_to()` have some overlapping use-cases, their semantics differ enough to warrant not considering them as equivalent.

Table A3.1 os functions and their corresponding PurePath/Path equivalents

os and os.path	pathlib
`os.path.abspath()`	`Path.resolve()`
`os.chmod()`	`Path.chmod()`
`os.mkdir()`	`Path.mkdir()`
`os.makedirs()`	`Path.mkdir()`
`os.rename()`	`Path.rename()`
`os.replace()`	`Path.replace()`
`os.rmdir()`	`Path.rmdir()`
`os.remove()`, `os.unlink()`	`Path.unlink()`
`os.getcwd()`	`Path.cwd()`
`os.path.exists()`	`Path.exists()`
`os.path.expanduser()`	`Path.expanduser()` and `Path.home()`
`os.listdir()`	`Path.iterdir()`
`os.path.isdir()`	`Path.is_dir()`
`os.path.isfile()`	`Path.is_file()`
`os.path.islink()`	`Path.is_symlink()`
`os.link()`	`Path.link_to()`
`os.symlink()`	`Path.symlink_to()`
`os.readlink()`	`Path.readlink()`
`os.stat()`	`Path.stat()`, `Path.owner()`, `Path.group()`
`os.path.isabs()`	`PurePath.is_absolute()`
`os.path.join()`	`PurePath.joinpath()`
`os.path.basename()`	`PurePath.name`
`os.path.dirname()`	`PurePath.parent`
`os.path.samefile()`	`Path.samefile()`
`os.path.splitext()`	`PurePath.suffix`

[illegible] The optional parameters have the same meaning as in open().

Correspondence to Tools in the os Module

[illegible]

Index